THE INSCRIPTION OF THINGS

The Inscription of Things

WRITING AND MATERIALITY IN EARLY MODERN CHINA

Thomas Kelly

Columbia University Press
New York

This publication was made possible in part by
an award from the James P. Geiss and Margaret Y. Hsu Foundation.

Columbia University Press
Publishers Since 1893
New York   Chichester, West Sussex
cup.columbia.edu

Copyright © 2023 Columbia University Press
All rights reserved

Library of Congress Cataloging-in-Publication Data
Names: Kelly, Thomas (Thomas Patrick), author.
Title: The inscription of things : writing and materiality in
early modern China / Thomas Kelly.
Other titles: Writing and materiality in early modern China
Description: New York : Columbia University Press, 2023. |
Includes bibliographical references and index.
Identifiers: LCCN 2023009340 | ISBN 9780231209625 (hardback) |
ISBN 9780231209632 (trade paperback) | ISBN 9780231558037 (ebook)
Subjects: LCSH: Inscriptions—China.
Classification: LCC CN1160 .K455 2023 | DDC 495.11/109—dc23/eng/20230422
LC record available at https://lccn.loc.gov/2023009340

Cover image: Rubbing No. 112 from Gao Fenghan's 高鳳翰 (1683–1749)
History of Inkstones 硯史. The design shows three sides of a seal that had
been owned and inscribed by Zhou Lianggong 周亮工 (1612–1672).
From Gao Fenghan, *Yanshi* 硯史, ed. Wang Xiang 王相 (1852), 112. Image courtesy of
Harvard-Yenching Library, Harvard University, Cambridge, MA.

*To my parents,
Anne and Paul*

CONTENTS

ACKNOWLEDGMENTS ix

Introduction
The Matter of Inscription 1

Chapter One
On Remnant Things 37

Chapter Two
Writing with a Knife 78

Chapter Three
The Ink-Maker's Mark 134

Chapter Four
Antiquarian Poetry 188

Epilogue
Broken Stones 233

NOTES 261

BIBLIOGRAPHY 319

INDEX 341

ACKNOWLEDGMENTS

Many teachers, colleagues, friends, and family members have helped me complete this book. I am unable, however, to properly recount here the ways in which such generosity and encouragement has sustained me over the past few years.

My greatest academic debt is to my advisor, Judith Zeitlin. Her teaching and research moved me to think about the literary lives of things. I am especially grateful for the support she has offered me since I left Hyde Park. I would also like to thank my former teachers at the University of Chicago: Haun Saussy, Wu Hung, Yuming He, Tamara Chin, and Reginald Jackson. James Chandler, Robert Kendrick, and the 2016–17 Franke Fellows—a group that exemplified the very best of the University of Chicago's interdisciplinary ethos—helped me start to think beyond my dissertation. I am also indebted to Dorothy Ko for her inspirational advice and incisive feedback on earlier versions of this project.

My work since leaving the University of Chicago has benefited immeasurably from the mentorship of both Xiaofei Tian and Wai-yee Li. I cannot fully express my gratitude to Xiaofei for her intellectual generosity and unstinting encouragement. Wai-yee's sage counsel on matters of literature and life has meanwhile been a constant source of support. Her essays drew me to this topic years before we met. I would also like to thank Stephen Owen and David Der-wei Wang; their books prompted me to first study Chinese literature as an undergraduate. It was Hilde De Weerdt's teaching and tutorials at the University of Oxford, however, that encouraged me to consider graduate school.

ACKNOWLEDGMENTS

I count myself deeply fortunate to have been able to complete this book as a junior faculty member in the Department of East Asian Languages and Civilizations (EALC) at Harvard University. I am indebted to David Howell, Shigehisa Kuriyama, and Melissa McCormick for their generous backing. My brilliant colleagues in EALC set the highest standards in their own research, service, and teaching. I am grateful to each of them for their consideration and advice. Walks with Alex Zahlten, Jie Li, Si Nae Park, and David Atherton helped me navigate life at Harvard. I feel very lucky to be their colleague. I have meanwhile continued to learn a great deal about the study of premodern Chinese society and thought from Peter Bol, Michael Szonyi, James Robson, Michael Puett, Mark Elliott, and Eugene Wang. Robin Kelsey, Nina Zipser, and Kendra H. Barber have offered me invaluable support, especially during the 2021–22 academic year.

I began this book during two rewarding years as a junior fellow at the Michigan Society of Fellows. I am grateful to Donald Lopez, David Rolston, Martin Powers, David Porter, and Christian de Pee for their feedback on my work during my time in Ann Arbor. I would especially like to thank S. E. Kile for his camaraderie over the years. My greatest teachers at Michigan were my talented fellow fellows: Cynthia Gerlein-Safdi, Linda Gosner, Laura Finch, Benjamin Mangrum, Brendan McMahon, and Lynette Shaw.

Colleagues from around the world have been instrumental in helping me write this book. I am especially grateful to Sophie Volpp for her inspiring example and generous advice. Yuhang Li, Jeehee Hong, Suyoung Son, Mei Mei Rado, Paize Keulemans, Ling Hon Lam, and Rivi-Handler Spitz have each helped me learn what it means to be a scholar. For their questions, thoughtful suggestions, and invitations to present work, I thank Bruce Rusk, Shang Wei, Tina Lu, Ariel Fox, Cheng-hua Wang, Giovanni Vitiello, Michele Matteini, Jun Hu, Kaijun Chen, Yan Zinan, Martin Heijdra, Anna Shields, Paula Varsano, Huijun Mai, Chiung-yun Evelyn Liu, Zeb Raft, and Chen Liu. Zhu Wanshu introduced me to the study of Huizhou and Ming-Qing literature during my time in Beijing on an international dissertation research fellowship from the Social Science Research Council. Conversations with Lin Li-chiang and Tsai Mei-fen as a graduate student introduced me to the study of the Chinese decorative arts. Ming Tak Ted Hui generously read the manuscript and helped me identify several areas for improvement. Sarah Schneewind, Qiao Yang, Anne Gerritsen, Dagmar Schäfer, David Robinson, and other members of the "Ability and Authority

ACKNOWLEDGMENTS

in East Asia 1200–1450" working group at the Max Planck Institute for the History of Science offered invaluable feedback on sections of this project and helped me think through the ways it might speak to audiences beyond literary studies.

Christine Dunbar at Columbia University Press has been the best editor a first-time author could hope for. I am also indebted to Christian Winting, Kathryn Jorge, and Ben Kolstad for their support throughout the publication process.

Sections of chapter 1 are based upon the journal article "The Inscription of Remnant Things: Zhang Dai's 'Twenty-Eight Friends,'" *Late Imperial China* 42, no. 1 (2021): 1–43. I am grateful to Steven Miles, the *LIC* editors, and anonymous readers for their input. Generous grants from the Geiss-Hsu Foundation and the Arts and Humanities Division at Harvard helped with the final production of the book.

Ma Xiaohe provided invaluable assistance in obtaining rare materials for this project. I would also like to gratefully acknowledge the assistance I received from librarians and curators at the National Central Library in Taiwan, the Wuxi Museum, the Palace Museum, the National Palace Museum, and the Tianjin Museum. Sun Bo at the National Museum of China generously helped me obtain permissions for images in chapter 2. Canaan Morse selflessly assisted with a last-minute request in Taipei.

I continue to learn from friends and former Chicago classmates, many of whom now teach at institutions around the world. I am especially grateful to Boqun Zhou, Naixi Feng, Max Bohnenkamp, Katherine Alexander, Anne Rebull, Alex Hsu, Daniela Licandro, Yiren Zheng, Alex Murphy, Minna Lee, and Kyle Peters. David Lebovitz and Alia Goehr generously took time out from their own work to offer invaluable comments on earlier drafts. Adhira Mangalagiri has been there every step of the way. More than anyone else she has helped me finish this book.

My parents, Anne and Paul, gave everything to allow me to pursue my dreams. I could never properly repay the faith they have placed in me. Ruth, Mark, and Jesse remind me without trying of what truly matters in life.

Without Anne Feng's unwavering belief and daily companionship (with Nadja), none of this would have been possible. I dedicate this book to her, with all my love.

THE INSCRIPTION OF THINGS

INTRODUCTION

The Matter of Inscription

"Someone asked me about inscription. 'Inscriptions! Inscriptions! They would have us be vigilant!'"
或問『銘』。曰：『銘哉！銘哉！有意於慎也。』[1]

YANG XIONG 揚雄 (53 BCE–18 CE)

In addition to working with a brush and ink, early modern Chinese writers carved their words onto cups and ladles, animal horns and seashells, walking sticks, boxes, fans, daggers, teapots, and an assortment of musical instruments. Calligraphers meanwhile etched and molded messages onto the basic implements—inkstones, brushes, brush pots, wrist-rests, solid ink cakes—with which they ordinarily wrote on paper. When they did so, they turned to a literary form named "inscription" (*ming* 銘), one that typically resembles a short poem or epigram—a terse composition in verse or unrhymed prose, unbound by rules of prosody and meter.[2] Not every *ming* was engraved upon a hard surface (collectors wrote on inkstones and brush racks that they encountered in their dreams), and there were many other sets of marks incised onto artifacts, yet inscription served as a unique interface in premodern China between the domain of literary writing about things and the physical practice of writing upon things. This book's central claim is that the act of inscribing an object became, in the late Ming and early- to mid-Qing dynasties (from roughly 1550 to 1800), a central means through which writers grappled with the material contingencies and technical preconditions of writing in general, a space where they came to reflect upon their investments in, and dependencies on, the permanence of the written word. The most eloquent inscriptions on objects from this period of profound societal upheaval consequently conceive of durability—the capacity to withstand destruction and damage—as a pressing matter of literary concern.

INTRODUCTION

THE "STUDIO FOR CONTEMPLATING LIFE," CA. 1670

Seventeenth-century prose stylists amid the turmoil and temporal aporias of dynastic transition (lasting approximately from 1618 to 1683) reenvisioned the possibilities of inscribed literature, confronting fears of being dominated by or reduced to things, by writing upon the surfaces of objects.[3] In reclusion as a self-professed "recalcitrant rock" at Stone Boat Mountain after the Manchu invasion of Ming (1368–1644) China, the loyalist philosopher Wang Fuzhi 王夫之 (1619–1692) composed a sequence of inscriptions on the material appurtenances of his "Studio for Contemplating Life" (Guansheng ju 觀生居; dated 1670), talking with and through writing implements (brush, inkstone, inkstick, inkstone case, wrist-rest) to assess his own suspended agency, neither dead nor fully alive, unsure whether or how to act.[4] In the wake of the Chongzhen 崇禎 emperor's (1611–1644; r. 1627–1644) suicide, several regional princes vied to reestablish Ming rule in the south.[5] Wang served in the staff of the last major pretender to the Ming throne, Zhu Youlang 朱由榔 ([1623–1662]; the so-called Yongli 永曆 emperor [r. 1646–1662]), before the retreat of Yongli's entourage to Yunnan in 1658 and flight to Burma in 1661 where he was eventually executed by Qing forces the following year.[6] Memories of loss and political failure haunt Wang's meditations on the unassuming tools that lie scattered upon his desk.

His first inscription on a writing brush approaches the implement as a provisional means with which to redraw broken distinctions between heavenly patterns ("starlight") and ghostly phosphorescence ("will-o'-the-wisp"), between providence ("an auspicious unicorn") and evil ("a sinister owl"):

INSCRIPTION ON A BRUSH

Only you can distinguish starlight from will-o'-the-wisp,
Only you can truly portray an omen,
Whether a sinister owl or an auspicious unicorn.
Alas! I fear ghosts and spirits!

筆銘

為星為燐，於爾分畛。
為梟為麟，於爾傳真。
吁嗟乎，吾懼鬼神。[7]

INTRODUCTION

Wang's eulogy to his brush might also be read as the brush's admonishment of Wang, as if the instrument were reminding its handler ("you") of what it means to write—a theme he develops in his subsequent inscription on an inkstone, a partially censored composition that imagines a small turtle-shaped slab speaking to him in the voice of a recently deceased friend.[8]

Wang Fuzhi first notes that this humble implement served as compensation for a prized inkstone from the Duan Brook 端溪 (the site of the Yongli emperor's rump court)—a gift from the son of a prominent military commander that was later stolen by rebel lictors as they harassed Wang's family during the collapse of the Southern Ming resistance at Guilin in 1650.[9] Rather than bring an inanimate thing to life, Wang's inscription casts the stone as a spirit medium, a portal through which he might gather, commune with, and heed the admonitions of the dead. The turtle slab's first word "Alas!" (*zi* 咨) wavers between a withering command (ho!) and lamentation, before summoning cryptic images of Laozi and Buddha as heterodox officiants at China's funeral:

INSCRIPTION ON AN INKSTONE

Alas! Heaven was willing to leave you for dead yet has not put an end to your thoughts. You have [BLANK] understanding, so I offer you this black turtle. May it still your state of mind and take down your words, so that others might find distance from delusion. It was [BLANK, BLANK; censored references to the Qing Manchus] that caused chaos in China, erecting tablets to Laozi and Buddha. Sharpen the tip of your brush. If you don't moisten the remnant seeds on this soil, then you will have no remnant of me. This turtle kowtows, how can one dare not foster the example of your splendor.

硯銘

咨，天憖爾以死，不替爾思。爾有□知，錫爾玄龜。蠲爾心，奠爾辭，以斯人遜於迷疑。維□□亂夏，聃曇為之尸。砥勵爾鋒，無滋遺種於茲土，爾尚不余遺。龜拜稽首，曷敢不式承子之光施。[10]

The inkstone's ghostly admonitions elicit a chorus of voices as other calligraphic tools on Wang's desk proffer their advice: an inscribed inkstick recommends suicide in the name of resistance, just as its own body ought to be ground down for writing; his wrist-rest urges him to fight on even without a dependable weapon; while his inkstone cover, finally, promises its owner temporary safety through concealment as a recluse.¹¹ These terse inscriptions work in concert to present the "remnant subject" (*yimin* 遺民) as an entity constituted and ultimately defined by its attachments to the implements of literary expression—writing upon brush and inkstone initiate Wang's reflections on the very meaning of "contemplating life."

My book asks what motivated an intellectual like Wang Fuzhi in the wake of the Ming cataclysm to evaluate his predicament as a writer by composing short messages dedicated to, and ostensibly "carved" upon, the basic tools and media of writing. Wang's inscribed words at once insinuate a chauvinistic will to affirm the continuity of *wen* 文 (writing, civility, Chinese culture) under foreign occupation and yet divulge a heightened sensitivity toward the fragile supports that sustain this vision. Wang's makeshift inkslab invokes venerable approaches to inscribed literature in premodern China, writing on the hard surface of a stone to record the name and virtues of a deceased person, harnessing the properties of an object to orient and instruct future readers, tearing down alien votive tablets to rectify public rituals of commemoration.¹² And yet, the very implement that enables Wang to write in self-imposed exile—an imperfect, unhewn grinder, one that presents itself as an interim substitute for stolen property—also raises the question of what endurance might entail amid the breakdown of reliable frameworks for understanding permanence and longevity.

This study returns to the upheavals of the Ming-Qing dynastic transition not simply to examine the ways in which literary writings about things responded to historical events, but to investigate the more consequential issue of how materiality becomes meaningful amid the interruption and reconfiguration of habitual interactions with objects. It is when the implements of daily life falter or fail to function as expected—when their purpose no longer seems self-evident—that they might become newly significant for their handlers.¹³ Disruption, Wang Fuzhi's inscriptions on his writing tools imply, creates conditions of possibility for reimagining the relationship between words and things. The destruction of family collections amid inter-dynastic war in this respect revitalized inquiry into the ethics and meaning of ownership. Post-conquest reactions to the perceived insubstantiality of strains in late Ming Neo-Confucian thought meanwhile prompted far-reaching reassessments of material evidence in the study of nature, language, and the past—tendencies that dovetailed with the Jesuit dissemination of European technical knowledge in Chinese intellectual circles.[14] Rampant boom and bust in the mid seventeenth century at the same time provoked widespread concern with the place and boundaries of the market in early modern social life, exacerbating late Ming anxieties around the promiscuous circulation and counterfeiting of South American silver.[15] As a literary form that dwells on the relationship between writing and its material supports, inscription intimately registered, and yet sought to imaginatively redress, the fall-out from these disturbances. To properly parse the significance of mid-seventeenth century literary reflections on durability—the inscribed admonitions of a writer like Wang Fuzhi—I first look back to the crises of the late Ming, before tracing the lasting influence of such developments into the Qing (1636–1912).

THE INSCRIPTION OF THINGS (1550–1800)

Woodblock printing—a medieval invention that came to maturity as a technology for the mass production of books during the Ming dynasty—undermined assumptions that inscriptions on hard surfaces remained a secure means with which to forestall loss or counter fears of oblivion.[16] And yet, the period from 1550 to 1800 witnessed an inscription boom as a growing number of writers from increasingly diverse backgrounds carved their words onto a wide range of solid objects—with some going so far as to study artisanal knifework.[17] While it remains difficult to ascertain whether the abundance of literary inscriptions and extant inscribed objects from the late Ming and early- to mid-Qing—an era of precipitous growth in transregional markets for consumer goods—reflects heightened interest in writing upon things when compared to earlier periods, it is only in the long seventeenth century that we find widespread evidence of calligraphers moving beyond brush-based calligraphy to personally write with a knife. My book considers how we might explain this development. Why did writers work to revivify the practice of writing upon things precisely when it was no longer seen as a reliable strategy with which to ensure longevity or to guard against material decay?

Inscriptions on objects challenge oversimplifying approaches to early modern China as a "print culture" in two respects: first, by decentering views of the woodblock-printed book as a self-contained vehicle of thought, revealing a diverse range of substrates and techniques that continued to shape understandings of the written word. And second, by proving that acts of preservation were not predetermined by the ascendancy of any single publishing apparatus but were at once contingent and open to contestation. Print's duplicative powers—its capacity to generate interchangeable copies—ostensibly made it a more effective means with which to transmit writing than signature manuscripts or stone monuments. And yet, an overabundance of printed material also raised new questions as to what could or should survive—did print, for instance, threaten to preserve too much? Inscriptions at once reflect the far-reaching impact of woodblock printing on early modern understandings of permanence, and yet at the same time unsettle book-based notions of endurance and expendability. These often-neglected artifacts invite their readers to look beyond the boundaries of the paper page to reconsider the material formats through which literature might speak.

Seventeenth-century writers amid far-reaching commercial upheavals and the fallout from inter-dynastic war start to treat the difficulties of inscription as the subject of their inscriptions; that is, they turn to inscribed literature not simply to affirm but to query the meanings of durability. Their carved compositions ask whether a sense of the durable simply specifies the steadfast properties of an object or if it might instead designate a mode of relation, a way of looking at and thinking with materials.[18] Remnant poet Du Jun 杜濬 (1611–1687) poses this question in his six-character inscription on a gravestone for a batch of discarded tea leaves, a slab he claims he polished (*moshi* 磨石) and then engraved (*keming* 刻銘): "Stones might split, yet a bond cannot be severed" 石可泐，交不絕.[19] The very word Du selects to describe stone's perishability, *le* 泐 (to split along veins of stone; to erode; to wear away from exposure), is homophonous with, and might be used interchangeably for, the word *le* 勒 (to engrave).[20] Writing in the wake of the Ming cataclysm, Du inverts the logic whereby a hefty monument secures the survival of memory; here, a constancy borne of obsessive devotion—or what Du terms a "connection of innate disposition" (*xingming zhi jiao* 性命之交)—outlasts stone.[21] The remnant poet suggests that a capacity to endure the vicissitudes of time inheres not in the recalcitrance of things but in contingent structures of attention and care.

By writing inscriptions about the instability of inscription, the writers at the center of this study interrogated, and worked to overcome, rigid dichotomies between solidity and evanescence, immutable essence and metamorphosis. They instead sought resilience and a provisional means of survival not by denying but by naming lived experiences of change.²² A heightened self-consciousness around the difficulties of inscription did not, however, entail an introspective retreat from the material world. On the contrary, it motivated many of these same figures to study knifework to tinker with and imaginatively refabricate their surroundings. In place of a linear progression from carving inscriptions on hard surfaces to drafting "un-inscribed inscriptions" on paper for preservation in print, the late imperial fate of *ming* indicates the converse: that as printed books became more widely available, writers for the first time turned to inscription as a means with which to personally carve their own calligraphy onto solid objects.²³ Certain prose stylists such as Du Jun's close friend, the celebrity author Li Yu 李漁 (1611–1680), even made the question of whether or not an inscription was "carved" a focal point of their material designs.²⁴ An inveterate tinkerer, Li wryly named a "hamper" outwardly fashioned to resemble a stash of calligraphic rubbings his "Stele with No Words" (Meizibei 沒字碑), inscribing the object as "possessing the form of a stele yet lacking the substance of a stele" 有碑之形，無碑之實—the hamper's empty interior could, however, store his ink and brushes so that "[that] which is wordless becomes the progenitor of that which has words" 是沒字為有字之祖.²⁵

My two lines of inquiry—the literary and the material—converge around the central development in Ming and Qing approaches to inscription, namely that writers repurposed this archaic form of literature, one associated with the sages of antiquity, bronze ritual vessels, and imposing stone stelae, to carve their words onto writing implements: inkstones, solid ink tablets, brushes, wrist-rests, and related calligraphic paraphernalia (brush pots, racks, boxes for the storage of letters and seals, paperweights, water dippers).²⁶ Seventeenth-century authors composed *ming* not simply to reflect on the fraught relations between names and objects, but to grapple with writing's technological basis, carving messages on the tools typically used to grind and mix solid ink with water. Collectors had since at least the Five Dynasties and Ten Kingdoms (907–79) period inscribed inkstones with elaborate professions of intimacy, yet the scope and complexity of Ming-Qing literature on calligraphic equipment was unprecedented.²⁷ Technical developments in seal carving—the craft of engraving seal-script calligraphy (*zhuan* 篆) onto small stamping devices (*yin* 印)—prompted calligraphers to improvise with the knife (rather than, as had previously been the case, soliciting the services of intermediary carvers).[28] Inscription consequently became a means through which writers could move beyond their use of the brush—a space where distinctions between thinking and making might be transformed.[29]

Rather than dwell at length on the description of objects in poems, essays, novels, or plays, I consider how inscribed artifacts from the early modern period recondition assumptions of what constitutes a work of literature, demonstrating the extent to which the literary lives of things in the long seventeenth century were shaped by underlying concerns with the materiality of the written word. My study investigates how attempts to animate or invest things with meaning concurrently broach the fraught question of literature's own durability. The late Ming and early to mid-Qing dynasties not only mark, as literary historians have elsewhere demonstrated, a highpoint in fictional or dramatic representations of the object world, but also comprise a moment of extensive interchange and transposition between literature and other practices of art making centered upon things.[30] Many of the most influential prose-stylists and poets from the late sixteenth to the eighteenth century wrote upon studio implements, with some masquerading as inkstone designers, seal carvers, and brush or ink makers. By foregrounding the engagements of prominent early modern writers with artisanal crafts such as inkstone engraving, seal carving, and ink production, my book elucidates the extent to which a renewed attentiveness to the implements, techniques, and labor of writing—borne of wider societal pressures on the parameters and basis of a writer's autonomy—unsettled and enlarged conceptions of literary creativity.

Acts of inscription—together with the many poems, prefaces, colophons, records, and letters that scenes of mark-making inspired—at the same time raised questions that preoccupy, yet remain largely overlooked in current accounts of the late imperial literary imagination: What does it mean to enlist inert materials in the interest of keeping memory alive? Is it even possible to ensure fixity and permanence without running the risk of paralysis and petrifaction? Does the survival of an inscribed message somehow depend on its material metamorphoses, its plasticity? These concerns reverberate within some of the most significant works of Qing literature. Cao Xueqin's 曹雪芹 (1715–1763) *Story of the Stone* (*Shitouji* 石頭記; or *Honglou meng* 紅樓夢), an extended meditation on the transience of things much indebted to the sensibilities of mid seventeenth-century writers like Du Jun opens with a perplexing fictional conceit in which the plot has been inscribed upon the surface of an imposing stele (one nevertheless devoid of any references to a dynasty, date, or location)—a sentient stone that then reappears in transmuted form as the story's protagonist.[31] "Rouge Inkstone" (Zhiyan 脂硯), the mysterious pseudonym of a prominent commentator on the novel as it circulated in manuscript form, likely refers to a late Ming inkstone, a prized slab stored in a coral box, fashioned by the Suzhou artisan Wu Wanyou 吳萬有 (n.d.) and inscribed by the poet Wang Zhideng 王穉登 (1535–1612) as a love token for the celebrity Nanjing-based courtesan Xue Susu 薛素素 (1564–1650).[32]

By adapting a literary form bound to the historical fate of monuments to inscribe studio objects, writers ostensibly entrusted their hopes for the permanence of the Chinese written word to the tools that render writing a possibility. In doing so, however, they confronted and came to reassess this project's increasingly precarious foundations, treating the material contingencies and technical preconditions of writing as the very ground of literary invention.[33] By seeking to discern an ever more elusive sense of durability amid experiences of destruction and loss, the most eloquent early modern inscriptions resonate beyond the historical moment of the Ming cataclysm. They remind us that the resilience of an object is not foreordained but rather rests upon humble labors of maintenance; and that the requisite vigilance to sustain such work might at the same time renovate our sense of what it means to write.

The remainder of this introduction first outlines the affordances and literary history of *ming* in premodern China, before returning to the mid-seventeenth century, demonstrating how the commercial volatility, intellectual upheavals, and political violence surrounding the dynastic transition prompted a resurgence of interest in writing on objects as a means with which to parse crises of continuity while locating latent openings for renewal through refabrication. Broken routine, as Wang Fuzhi's inscriptions on the appurtenances of his "Studio for Contemplating Life" suggest, might at the same time elicit unanticipated ways of apprehending basic tools anew.[34] I conclude by considering early modern inscribed literature's enduring relevance for humanistic reflections on the question of what it means to speak of an object's durability.

INSCRIPTION AND CHINESE LITERATURE

Why write on things? This question is among the oldest topics in Chinese literary thought. "Inscription" later came to designate a genre of Chinese literature, yet the etymology of *ming* broached broader concerns with the origins of writing, rituals for mourning the dead, and the philosophical issue of naming. Qing philologists went so far as to suggest that the definition of "name" (*ming* 名) in early comprehensive dictionaries of Chinese characters—"name is self-designation" 名，自命也—derives from the *locus classicus* for "inscription" in the "Protocols of Sacrifice" (Jitong 祭統): "in the inscription one names oneself" 銘，自名也.³⁵ In early Chinese writing, "inscription" could be written as "name" without a metal (*jin* 金) signific, a transcription that appears on a handful of excavated bronzes from the Eastern Zhou (770–256 BCE).

The earliest definitions of inscription appear in ritual manuals concerned either with the use of bronze vessels in ancestral worship or the placement of funerary banners (*mingjing* 明旌 or *mingjing* 銘旌) in the preparation and posthumous identification of corpses.³⁶ In the former case, "Protocols of Sacrifice" articulates a Rujia 儒家 (School of Confucians) concern with the relationship between *qi* 器 (vessel, insignia, instrument) and *li* 禮 (ritual, rite, propriety), arguing that self-identification through writing on bronze honors one's ancestors and displays virtue through the performance of praise:³⁷ "With regard to cauldrons with inscriptions: in the 'inscription' (*ming* 銘), one 'names' (*ming* 名) oneself. One names oneself in order to cite and extol what is beautiful in one's ancestors, and clearly exhibit it for later generations" 夫鼎有銘，銘者，自名也。自名以稱揚其先祖之美，而明著之後世者也.³⁸ In the latter case, the *Book of Ceremony and Ritual* (*Yili* 儀禮) suggests that "inscribed banners" (pennants that bear the deceased's name and official title) served to establish a posthumous reputation and preserve the "social body" of the dead from the funeral, to the tomb, and into the afterlife.³⁹ Both passages coalesce around a shared preoccupation with the challenge of how to establish and commemorate a reputation, or that for which one should be known.

"Inscription" came to refer to two interrelated modes of writing in premodern Chinese literature, what we might term the *memorial* inscription and the *admonitory* inscription.⁴⁰ The former emerged from the "canonically sanctioned conventions of elite commemoration," a genealogy that extends from Zhou era (1046–256 BCE) inscriptions on bronze vessels and tuned sets of bronze bells to the mortuary stelae that flourished in the last years of the Eastern Han (25–220).[41] For the most part, early Zhou inscriptions on bronze contain only single characters or terse phrases of five words or less, simply naming the donor of the artifact.[42] After bureaucratic reforms under King Mu 周穆王 (r. 956–918 BCE)—precipitated in part by his predecessor's military failures in the south—Zhou bronze inscriptions assume a longer and relatively fixed tripartite structure: (1) a record of speeches from an appointment ceremony addressing the appointee's accomplishments, his ancestors' virtue, and royal approval of these accounts; (2) the donor's dedication, a statement that describes the casting and use of the bronze artifact; (3) a formulaic prayer in rhyme in which the donor appeals to his ancestors for future blessings in response to ritual sacrifices.[43] Western Zhou bronze inscriptions from the mid-tenth century BCE onward closely resemble royal speeches and ritual hymns preserved in the *Classic of Documents* (*Shujing* 書經) and *Classic of Poetry* (*Shijing* 詩經), effectively forming the "fountainhead of Chinese literature."[44]

Bronze ritual vessels and bells appear in early literary thought as models for the later inscription of stone monuments.[45] Cai Yong's 蔡邕 (ca. 133–192) "Disquisition on Inscription" ("Ming lun" 銘論), the earliest treatise on *ming* as a genre, for instance, concludes by charting an epochal transition from bronze to stone:

> Bells and cauldrons are implements of ritual and music, when inscribed they can illuminate virtue and record merit, displaying this for sons and grandsons. Of things that do not decay, nothing is more durable than bronze and stone. Therefore, stelae are located between the two staircases of the lineage temple. In recent generations, everyone inscribes virtue and merit upon stelae.
>
> 鐘鼎禮樂之器，昭德紀功以示子孫。物不朽者，莫不朽於金石。故碑在宗廟兩陛之間。近世以來咸銘之于碑。[46]

For early medieval thinkers like Cai, this substantive conversion from bronze in the Zhou to stone in the Han (202 BCE–220 CE) implicitly registers a spatial shift in ancestral worship from lineage-based temples (where ancestors could be collectively worshipped) to the gravesite (where individuals might receive personal sacrifices).⁴⁷ As Mark Lewis suggests, an inscription in either setting serves to link *present* action to *past* virtue in order to instruct *future* people.⁴⁸

While Cai Yong's disquisition primarily dwells on the commemorative function of writing on metal and stone, he identifies an alternative lineage for the inscription of objects by listing examples of sagely exhortations placed on everyday implements, beginning with the Yellow Emperor's (Huangdi 黃帝; the legendary founder of Chinese civilization) "Kerchief Table Methods" ("Jinji fa" 巾機法), a set of short mottoes for correct deportment allegedly carved upon a type of clothing rack.⁴⁹ Cai's distinction between inscribed memorials on monuments and terse admonitions on household belongings anticipates the emergence of a generic distinction between "stele" (*bei* 碑) for the former and "inscription" (*ming*) for the latter in strains of medieval literary thought.⁵⁰

Memorial Inscription

Memorial inscriptions in stone, beginning with the First Qin Emperor's (Qin Shi Huang 秦始皇; 259–210 BCE) seven commemorative stelae, proclaim power over space: "[their] very meaning and efficacy," Martin Kern notes, "rests on their physical adhesion to [these] places . . . and these sites, geographically real and cosmologically meaningful, are literally inscribed within the texts."⁵¹ These memorials adopt the tetra-syllabic meter of lengthy "eulogies" (*song* 頌) to early Zhou rulers in the *Classic of Poetry*, as pseudo-hymns celebrating the constancy of imperial order. The First Qin Emperor's stelae as prototypical stone monuments sought to realize a "petrification of history," absorbing individual historical sites "into the common suprahistorical frame of the new empire, designed for eternity."⁵² Ritual acts of inscribing stone markers on mountaintops anticipate later Han practices of erecting stelae or *moya* 摩崖 (inscriptions carved onto cliffs or unquarried boulders) to proclaim the violent subjugation of non-Han nomadic communities.⁵³ Ban Gu's 班固 (32–92) canonical "Inscription on the Ceremonial Mounding of Mount Yanran" ("Feng Yanran shan ming" 封燕然山銘), carved by the general Dou Xian 竇憲 (d. 92) onto a cliff face in the Delgerkhangai Mountains to celebrate the bloody extermination of Xiongnu 匈奴 fighters, became the most celebrated literary example of this strategy.⁵⁴

The subsequent ascendancy of the stele as an independent genre and tool for the management of public memory can be dated, however, to the waning years of the Eastern Han dynasty, a moment when intense political factionalism and institutional decline prompted families to inscribe monuments with values they feared might be lost.[55] Professions of faith in "metal and stone" first proliferate, as Mark Asselin has shown, in the wake of new apprehensions over the transient nature of the imperial mandate, the arbitrary length of an individual's "life-mandate," and the "entropy of memory."[56] The concurrent spread of Buddhist movements throughout North China gave rise to other modes of calligraphic carving on monumental substrates, practices that exceed or were deemed extraneous to literary histories of *ming* such as the copying of colossal sutra transcriptions onto the sides of mountains to generate karmic merit for donors and suggest the illimitability of Buddhist teachings amid fears of imminent persecution.[57]

The early medieval period finally witnessed the development of a related mode of memorial inscription, one that flourished in late imperial China: the *muzhiming* 墓誌銘 (the entombed account with inscription). As Timothy Davis has noted, the *muzhiming* embodies the convergence of Eastern Han stelae inscriptions and "common" forms of entombed epigraphy with apotropaic or talismanic functions: "burial-plot purchase contracts" (*maidiquan* 買地券), "tomb-stabilizing writs" (*zhenmuwen* 鎮墓文), and "tomb inventories" (*qiance* 遣策).[58] Six Dynasties (220–589) epitaphs start to question Han notions of physical transcendence or "immortality" (*xian* 僊) in the afterlife to instead predict the eventual ruination of tombs, articulating as Jie Shi has shown, a new distinction between the perishability of the deceased's body or tomb structure and the "deathlessness of words"—a distinction that dovetails with the claims of contemporaneous thinkers like Cao Pi 曹丕 (187–226) that "writing is a great method to administer a state and a noble business to attain imperishability" 蓋文章，經國之大業，不朽之盛事.[59] Epitaphic faith in the deathlessness of words nevertheless rests, as Shi notes, on a "troubling paradox": on the one hand, early medieval epitaphs praise the endurance of writing over perishable materials like stone; on the other, they recognize the need for durable substrates upon which to transmit words, a search that led back to stone as the least perishable of perishable materials.[60]

Admonitory Inscription

In contrast to memorials cast onto bronze vessels and bells or carved upon stone monuments, admonitory inscriptions claimed descent from legendary tales of cultural paragons who allegedly wrote short mottoes on furniture, clothing, daily utensils, and weapons to correct human behavior—proto-poems that Bruce Rusk has compared to "motivational posters and bumper stickers."[61] In what became a principal model for *ming* as a genre of belles lettres, King Wu 武王 (ca. 1076–1043 BCE), the founder of the Zhou dynasty, supposedly engraved maxims onto household objects, precepts that harness ordinary implements to encode trite instructions. Boqun Zhou suggests that the banality of King Wu's inscriptive program is part of its point: what matters is embodying "boring truth" through its mundane repetition in real life, that "by establishing a relationship between the moral lessons and the function of objects, [King Wu's sequence] carves [. . .] moral ideology deeply into the full range of the king's quotidian experience"[62]:

The staff inscription reads: How does danger arise? From becoming angry. How does one lose the way? Through lust and desire. How might one forget the other? Through riches and nobility.

杖之銘曰：「惡乎危？於忿疐。惡乎失道？於嗜慾。惡乎相忘？於富貴」。[63]

Later commentators note that this aphorism makes a point about cultivating oneself to pursue the Way (Dao 道) by invoking the reliable use of a staff for walking along a path (*dao* 道): the medium again determines the message.[64] While King Wu's inscriptions were apocryphal or pseudo-epigraphic texts preserved on bamboo, his admonitions resemble inscribed messages on excavated artifacts from the Warring States (475—221 BCE) period.[65] A "Fish Cauldron Ladle" (Yuding bi 魚鼎匕), now held in the Liaoning Museum, urges its handler to cautiously copy the example of a spoon as it enters a cauldron of boiling fish soup: "Be careful! When you set out to swim with watery beasts! Ordinary people don't understand; take heed of the fate of [tyrant-rebel] Chiyou [蚩尤]! If you're assigned to the thick soup, leaping in and out, who knows where you will meet your end"

欽哉，出游水蟲，下民無智（知），參蚩（尤）命，帛（薄）命入糞，忽入忽出，毋处其所。[66] The fish cauldron ladle makes its point by invoking tales concerning the Yellow Emperor rather than by claiming to be a relic or his possession. How, later Han dynasty writers start to ask, might an inscription discern wisdom within everyday things in the absence of a secure connection to a sage.[67] When is a spoon simply a spoon?

In addition to inscriptions on a sage's property, Han sources record admonitory inscriptions on images or "statue doubles" of sages—examples that begin to suggest how an inscribed object might deliver an imperative form of "first-person testimony."[68] Confucius allegedly encountered one of these statues while inspecting a Zhou ancestral temple, discovering a "Metal Man" (*jinren* 金人) with a "thrice-bound mouth" and an inscription on his back. This detail again proves to be critical to the admonition the inscribed object imparts: "This is a man of olden times who was careful of his speech. Take heed! Take heed! Do not speak much; much speech results in much defeat" 古之慎言人也，戒之哉！戒之哉！無多言，多口多敗。[69] The thing is no longer the prosthetic extension of a sage, but an anthropomorphic image that demands his submission. An inscribed admonition—encapsulated in the image of a "thrice-bound mouth" or the metal statue's injunction to be "cautious in speaking"—subjugates its reader, forcing a human (in this instance Confucius) to surrender his or her mastery of speech to the command of an inanimate object.[70] The "Metal Man" suggests how the act of writing upon a thing at once dislocates and provides an occasion to rethink the purpose of speech, indulging forms of ventriloquism and testing the proper "uses" of a human voice.[71] Whereas memorial inscriptions on metal and stone call out to spirits of the deceased, admonitory inscriptions in the wake of the "Metal Man" imagine the possibility that an inanimate object might speak through its reader. "Writing," as Jesper Svenbro observes, "makes it possible for inscribed objects to refer to themselves in the first person despite their being just objects, not living, thinking beings endowed with the power of speech."[72]

By the medieval period, memorial inscriptions tend to be found *in situ*, on mountains, bridges, buildings, or static stone monuments such as stelae and epitaphs.[73] Inscriptions on portable objects such as brushes and inkstones, by contrast, tend to assume a terse monitory disposition, harnessing the properties of an implement to instruct or reprove its handler.[74] And yet, writers frequently draw upon and combine elements of these divergent genealogies. An inkstone inscription, for instance, might simultaneously invoke sagely admonitions on household tools or the direct address of the "Metal Man" while alluding to the calligraphic format of a stele or the somber ambience of an epitaph. Han Yu 韓愈 (768–824), a leader of the Ancient Prose Movement and a formative influence on many of the writers included in this book, adopted an idiom of friendship with things in his "Inscription for a Buried Inkstone" ("Yi yan ming" 瘞硯銘), a piece that mimics the form of an epitaph, personifying the stone as though its death warranted the funerary rituals usually reserved for humans: "[His/its] case returned to be buried in the ward where he lived" 乃匣歸埋於京師里中—conflating the inkstone's "case" with a human coffin.[75] As Xiaofei Tian notes, Han Yu's inscription wavers between celebrating his own friendship with the inkstone's devoted owner and friendship with the inkstone itself. When Han prefaces the inscription by saying "I, Changli Han Yu, was [his/its] friend" 昌黎韓愈，其友人也, it is unclear which of the two he is referring to.[76]

Transposition between different forms of inscribed literature becomes a key theme in the following chapters as I consider how writers explored correspondences between these outwardly incongruous genealogies: What did it mean to compare an inkstone or an ink cake to a stele or an epitaph? Was the act of adopting a literary genre associated with ritual media and legendary sages to engrave desktop objects a sincere expression of reverence for the prestige of writing or a potentially ironic act, one with the power to reconstitute orthodox forms of public commemoration through ventriloquism and formally innovative idioms of care, intimacy, and playfulness? The most evocative early modern inscriptions pose and reflect upon these questions, searching in the absence of consensus on the meaning of monumental permanence for unlikely sources of instruction in relations with quotidian tools.

The Collector's Inscription

The principal literary model for the developments that I examine in this book emerges most clearly, however, in the work of the preeminent Northern Song poet, painter-calligrapher, and art collector, Su Shi 蘇軾 (1037–1101). Su not only composed considerably more inscriptions than previous prose stylists like Han Yu, but he also wrote more inscriptions on the same types of objects: whereas Han's collected writings contain only two *ming*, at least seventy inscriptions were attributed to Su Shi—twenty-eight of which were dedicated to inkstones.⁷⁷ Inscribed "Su Shi inkstones"—some of dubious authenticity—in turn passed through the hands of many leading Ming and Qing dynasty collectors.⁷⁸

Ouyang Xiu's 歐陽修 (1007–1072) *Colophons on Collected Records of the Past* (*Jigulu bawei* 集古錄跋尾), a collection of more than four hundred vignettes on ink-squeeze rubbings of inscribed stone monuments and bronze vessels, presaged a momentous turn in the eleventh century toward the study of epigraphy ("learning from metal and stone"; *jinshixue* 金石學), as historiographers consulted messages preserved on unearthed objects to corroborate or correct transmitted records.⁷⁹ While the literary significance of Ouyang's reflections on the ruination of carved words has been discussed at great length, the question of how Song antiquarianism relates to a surge of interest, especially among members of Su Shi's circle, in the inscription of studio objects has received comparatively little consideration.⁸⁰ How in other words did the antiquarian's encounter with excavated or ruined "traces" condition contemporaneous practices of writing with a knife? The interplay between epigraphy (*jinshixue*) and literary inscription (*ming*) became a critical issue for seventeenth-century writers, some of whom engraved desktop objects to supplement their antiquarian research—acts that again typically center upon the refabrication of inkslabs.⁸¹

In Su Shi's hands, *ming* became a means with which to master and manipulate the connoisseurship of studio objects in a burgeoning market for luxury commodities. His widely cited "Inscription on Kong Yifu's Dragon Tail Inkstone" encapsulates latent tensions between the desire to endorse a regional product—the Dragon Tail inkstone (Longwei yan 龍尾硯) of Wuyuan 婺源 (in present-day Jiangxi)—by promoting authoritative distinctions on the one hand, and a newfound investment in treating writing implements as biographical objects that illuminate the personalities of their custodians on the other:

INSCRIPTION ON KONG YIFU'S DRAGON TAIL INKSTONE

Coarse yet you won't thwart the brush; sleek yet you won't repel the ink cake.
    Clawed skin and crepe-gauze, a metallic chime with the virtue of jade.
    Substantive and firm, watching over the people of the past and the present. Unaffected and weighty, unwilling to follow a man from south to north.

INTRODUCTION

孔毅甫龍尾硯銘

澀不留筆，滑不拒墨。爪膚而縠理，金聲而玉德。厚而堅，足以閱人於古今；朴而重，不能隨人以南北。[82]

Su Shi first adheres to the conventions of this ancient genre by identifying moral values encoded in the inkstone: "virtue of jade" describes the character of a refined gentleman, while "metallic chime" or "golden repute" connotes human fame. References to jade and gold invest the slab with the weighty significance attributed to writing on "metal and stone." As Zhiyi Yang and Zhang Yuanqing note, Su invites the reader of the inscription to copy the inkstone in studying moral exemplars of the past and present, assuming a recessive agency by refusing indiscriminate service.[83]

Su Shi's portrayal of Kong's Dragon Tail as a recluse reflects a calculated strategy to redeem his own standing among fellow connoisseurs after his controversial endorsement of an otherwise obscure rock from Fujian, the so-called Phoenix Beak inkstone (Fengzhou yan 鳳咮硯). In an earlier inscription he had castigated the inkstones of She 歙 County to promote his new favorite rock: "Master Su, upon one single glance, named it 'Phoenix Beak'; it makes the Dragon Tail feel itself inferior to the rear of a bull" 蘇子一見名鳳咮，坐令龍尾羞牛後。[84] Having angered the locals of She County, Su needed to win back their favor both to buttress his standing as a leading judge of inkstones (his Phoenix Beak proved to be a flop) and to acquire a new Dragon Tail for his own collection.[85] He subsequently sought to deflect from the criticisms he had received by imagining the rock's defense of his actions.[86] Su Shi's claim of empathetic identification concurrently works to conceal his efforts to promote a repeatable formula for the judgment not just of Dragon Tails but of all inkstones. He presents the opening line of the inscription—"Coarse yet you won't thwart the brush; sleek yet you won't repel the ink cake"—not as his evaluation of a particular specimen but as a "famous saying" (*mingyan* 名言) that might be used to assess any slab in correspondence with other prominent collectors.[87]

In an influential essay on the "cultural biography of things," Igor Kopytoff reconsiders the production of commodities as a "cultural and cognitive process," arguing that physical objects "must not only be produced materially as things, but also [must be] *culturally marked* as being a certain kind of thing."[88] A technical history of inscription lends granularity to this claim, demonstrating how "concrete mechanisms of sealing, labelling, and marking" inform the social construction of value.[89] Latent tensions in Su's endorsement for Kong between idiosyncratic resistance to and calculated engagement with the market reached a tipping point in the late sixteenth and seventeenth centuries with the emergence of entrepreneurial inkstone and ink manufacturers from the home of the Dragon Tail in She County (or what became Huizhou 徽州 prefecture), the spread of urban pawnshops marketing studio objects, and newfound uncertainties surrounding the issue of who could write with a knife.

Inscribed Objects in the Early Modern Marketplace

My book's central concern with the significance of *ming* in early modern China departs from a prevalent focus in earlier studies on issues of conspicuous consumption, social distinction, and the politics of taste to instead investigate how acts of naming and mark making generate and structure the oppositions that have framed discussions of Chinese literature's engagement with material culture—person and object, real and fake, elegance (*ya* 雅) and vulgarity (*su* 俗), singleton and multiple.[90] Troubled poet and calligrapher Xu Wei's 徐渭 (1521–1593) writings on inkstones in prison speak to this dynamic, foregrounding the power of an inscription to produce and recalibrate distinctions between self and other, "me" and "you."[91]

What determines the durability of a mark when impermanence appears to be a fixed feature of everyday life? Writing on a Dragon Tail inkstone six centuries later, Xu Wei still felt a need to wrestle with Su Shi's pronouncements both to vindicate his own connoisseurial prowess and to flaunt his individuality. Xu's focus on tracking the movements of his inconstant stone might be construed as a wry rejoinder to the "unwillingness" of Su's inkstone to "follow a man from south to north," a sign of the latter's stubborn integrity. While Su Shi eschews any overt references to the market, Xu explicitly foregrounds trade (*shi* 市) from the outset:[92]

INSCRIPTION ON A SHE COUNTY STONE INKSLAB

> Purchased in She County, you returned to Yue and then back to She County, finally you returned to Yue. Are you stone? Can you forget your feelings?
>
> Inscribed in prison to be cut by Wu; how can I guarantee that you eventually end up with me? Are you human? Do you have feelings?[93]

歙石硯銘

市於歙，歸於越，復返於歙，終來歸於越。石耶？ 能忘情耶？
銘於若盧，斫於吳，安保其終於吾。人耶？ 能有情耶？[94]

Xu uses his Dragon Tail to limn experiences of bondage as a private secretary or ghostwriter for the Ming general Hu Zongxian 胡宗憲 (1512–1565). Xu's reflections on service for Hu in turn elicit more uncomfortable memories of incarceration in 1566 for the murder of his wife after his self-castration and several failed suicides due to prolonged bouts of mental instability.[95] In contrast to Su Shi, Xu Wei's inscription offers little by way of description or material analogy: much of his wording—simply tracking movements from place to place—can refer interchangeably to human or rock. The career of the inkstone emplots Xu Wei's own recent past, his sense of alienation as a ghostwriter, his travels back and forth from She County (the home of his patron) to his hometown in Yue [in present-day Zhejiang], and crucially, his incarceration.[96] The details of Xu Wei's biography, meanwhile, reflect the life of the rock—bought and sold, employed by others for writing, by turns hard-edged, stubborn, and unfeeling.

Xu's open question—"Can you forget your feelings?" 能忘情耶？—wryly alludes to mid-Tang poet Bai Juyi's 白居易 (772–846) "Song of Past Feelings" ("Buneng wangqing yin" 不能忘情吟), a poem he intoned to a beloved horse and twenty-year-old concubine as he inventoried his "superfluous possessions" for sale to raise funds in old age and sick health: "Alas! I am no Sage. I could neither forget past feelings nor could I reach the point of being one incapable of feeling! Affairs take hold of my emotions, and when my emotions are stirred, I cannot control them" 噫！予非聖達，不能忘情，又不至於不及情者。事來攪情，情動不可梔。[97] Within his poem, Bai Juyi ventriloquizes his concubine's remonstrance on behalf of both herself and the sorrowful horse, imagining his possessions pleading with their owner to resist being sold: "This person has feelings, this horse has feelings, how can it be that their master alone has no feelings?" 此人之情也，馬之情也。豈主君獨無情哉？[98] The poet eventually yields to the entreaties of his "things," pouring himself a drink and proclaiming: "I will take you with me back to the Land of Drunkenness" 我與爾歸醉鄉去來.[99] Xu Wei's inkstone invokes yet resists offering its owner the closure Bai Juyi found in keeping hold of his sorrowful horse and concubine. The Ming poet's ambivalent address to the rock might be read as a wistful lament for the slab's inconstancy, as if he is unsure whether a possession can reciprocate its owner's devotion.[100] Yet Xu's implicit allusion also invites his readers to entertain a more unsettling proposition: that of an eloquent thing weighing its master's compromised humanity in conditions of deprivation: "Are you human? Do you have feelings?"[101]

Xu's inscription finally pivots upon his own inconclusive act of inscription ("Inscribed in prison to be cut by/[in] Wu" 銘於若廬, 斫於吳). The line dwells on the gap between the occasion of literary composition and a concomitant need to entrust the stone to another so that the inscription can be carved: commentators disagree as to whether "to be cut by/[in] Wu" means that Xu leaves the slab with his friend Wu Chengqi 吳成器 (n.d.) or that he intends for the Huizhou stone to be transported to the workshops of Suzhou (Wu 吳) where his words can be engraved.[102] His ambivalent invocation to the rock, his fear that it might not "end up" with him, in either case, intimates an underlying concern that the inscription he is drafting might not end up carved upon the thing it names. Xu at once evokes his incapacities in prison and yet seeks to transcend his fettered predicament by writing an inscription that foregrounds the impermanence of inscription.[103] These themes assumed heightened significance for Xu Wei's followers—the generation of Zhang Dai 張岱 (1597–?1684), the protagonist of chapter 1—as they lived through the collapse of the Ming dynasty in 1644 and the destruction of inter-dynastic war, voicing sentiments of redundancy or recalcitrance, not by rejecting but by embracing attachments to leftover things. It was during the seventeenth century that Chinese poets and prose stylists came to explicitly reflect upon three interrelated questions in composing inscriptions: (1) What to write upon things? (2) How to write upon things? (3) Who was able to write upon things?

WRITING AND MATERIALITY IN EARLY MODERN CHINA

Like other forms of epigrammatic verse, concrete poetry, or elite graffiti from across the premodern world, the noun *ming* denotes a "two-fold entity," referring at once to a literary composition and to an inscribed surface or artifact.[104] The aim of this book is to take seriously both aspects of *ming*, investigating what literary inscriptions say while attending to the ways they interact with the visual and material properties of the objects upon which they appear. How, in other words, might the presentation of an inscription condition its message? How does the act of reading an inscription, meanwhile, structure a viewer's handling and experience of an object?[105] Early modern writers start to foreground and comment upon these same questions, assessing the interplay between an exhortation or words of praise and the properties of a substrate.

Jonathan Hay has identified the importance of "inscriptional topographies" as resources in the early modern decorative arts, an approach to design that became increasingly prevalent as scholars participated in the production of objects, transforming surface into a "generalized field of potentiality" out of which writing emerged, "and within which it danced."[106] For Hay, the crucial element in what he terms "literati inscriptionality," however, was not the selection of a literary or calligraphic composition, but the "analogization" of the edges of the object to edges of the paper writing surface.[107] Dorothy Ko's research on handwork and skill, meanwhile, has elucidated the extent to which artisanal expertise sustained Qing cultures of learning by excavating a "material craft of *wen*" in the practice of Fujianese scholar-calligraphers—figures involved in the inscription of inkstones.[108] My book builds upon the insights of both Hay and Ko and yet still insists on the value of a literary approach to inscribed objects. I read inscribed literature not in the first instance as decoration or as historical evidence for understanding negotiations between scholars and artisans but as a form of prose-poetry capable of critical reflection upon the contingencies of writing's embodiment and presence. Conflicting approaches to the meaning of *ming* among seventeenth century writers from diverse backgrounds and localities belie claims that early modern inscriptions propagate a coherent account of male public writing's fate. Nor was literary inscription an exclusively masculine practice: various accounts suggest that the courtesan-artist Ma Xianglan 馬湘蘭 (1548–1604) (Ma Shouzhen 馬守真; Ma Ruqian 馬汝謙)—a contemporary of the celebrated female seal carver Han Yuesu 韓約素 (n.d.) that I discuss in chapter 2—took up the knife to "personally inscribe" (*ziming* 自銘) inkstones.[109]

THE LITERARY LIVES OF WRITING TOOLS

Late Ming and early- to mid-Qing writers composed inscriptions to advance a composite art of writing, one that generated innovative forms of inter-medial transposition between otherwise discrete sectors of the Chinese written landscape: literature, calligraphy, seal carving, epigraphy, and artisanal mark making. Concern with the relationship between an inscription and its object, over the course of the long seventeenth century, became ancillary to the issue of how an inscription might manage the interplay between different forms of graphic art. Such negotiations play out in responses to inkstones, inksticks, and seals—three basic devices for written communication in the Ming-Qing period. Inscriptions on calligraphic tools in this respect start to cultivate what after Christina Lupton I term a "consciousness of mediation"—a mode of literary thought uniquely attuned to material factors behind the production and transmission of the written word.[110] I am concerned then not simply with the extent to which writing's substructures condition the creation of meaning but also with literature's enduring capacity to identify and assess this dynamic. My approach here in turn responds to Lisa Gitelman's argument that media histories of writing machines often "fail to explore technology as plural, decentered, indeterminate, as the reciprocal product of textual practices, rather than just a causal agent of change."[111]

To introduce the historical convergence of these themes, I turn to one final case, that of Li Yu and Du Jun's close associate, the eminent early Qing collector and calligrapher, Zhou Lianggong 周亮工 (1612–1672).[112] While I began with Wang Fuzhi's literary meditations on the purpose of writing in self-imposed exile, I conclude by attending to Zhou's contemporaneous engagement with techniques of mark making, modeling a shift in focus that my following four chapters elucidate in more detail, moving from the close reading of *ming* as prose-poetry to the material and technical investigation of inscribed artifacts. The book's structure thus underscores what I take to be a *rematerialization* of inscription in early modern China—the way, that is, a literary form of writing about objects (one that need not necessarily entail engraving) became a *techne* through which individual writers might simultaneously draft and carve their own words upon hard surfaces.

Inkstone

The Tianjin Museum holds a Duan inkstone that bears a short inscription attributed to Zhou in an elegant running script that approximates the appearance of calligraphic brushwork on silk or paper: "This slab may not possess the luster of jade or the hardness of bronze. But as for the essence of bronze and jade, don't sneer at this field of stone" 匪玉斯潤，非金斷（斯）堅。金玉之精，莫誚石田 (figures 0.1 and 0.2).[113] Zhou's terse eulogy to the stone's hidden jade and bronze virtues (the attributes of a gentleman) is, however, less intriguing than the clues the object offers as to how this message might have been written. The side of the inkstone bears a further inscription by the seal carver Zhang Zhen 張貞 (1636–1712) that refers to Zhou's *ming* as "[that which] Master Liyuan [Zhou Lianggong] carved" 櫟園師所刻, introducing the possibility as Hye-shim Yi has noted, that Zhou not only drafted this literary composition but also engraved it himself. This line is perhaps a response to Zhou's own admission in the note alongside his inscription that: "[I] then *carved* (*le* 勒) a couple of lines [in response to the

FIGURE 0.1. A Duan inkstone inscribed by Zhou Lianggong 周亮工 (1612–1672), now held in the Tianjin Museum (19.4 cm × 12.5 cm × 5 cm). The side of the inkstone bears an additional inscription by the seal carver Zhang Zhen 張貞 (1636–1712). *Source*: Tianjin Museum.

FIGURE 0.2. A rubbing of the Duan inkstone inscribed by Zhou Lianggong now held in the Tianjin Museum. Zhou's inscription and an appended note are legible in running script on the bottom of the slab, and Zhang Zhen's inscription runs along the base of the inkstone's walls. *Source*: Tianjin Museum.

request for an inscription]" 即為勒數語應之.[114] Cai Hongru, by contrast, suspects due to differences with surviving models of Zhou's calligraphy that Zhang Zhen likely transcribed and carved his self-professed teacher, Zhou's words. Zhang's inference that Zhou could engrave his own handwriting nevertheless anticipates the widescale application of seal-carving techniques to self-carved calligraphic inscriptions on inkstones in the early- to mid-eighteenth century.[115] Other surviving inkstones bearing Zhou's signature likewise invoke his reputation as an eminent patron of seal carvers and connoisseur of seals (and perhaps an amateur seal carver himself).[116]

The final ink-squeeze rubbing in Gao Fenghan's 高鳳翰 (1683–1749) widely influential *History of Inkstones* (*Yanshi* 硯史; 1727–1739)—a collection of inkstone designs that forms the centerpiece of my book's epilogue—documents a rare oblong seal (an object easily mistaken for an inkslab) bearing what Gao claims to be Zhou's self-carved inscription (figure E.1).[117]

Inkstick

Zhou Lianggong at the same time experimented with making his own brushes and participated in the design of limited-edition inksticks, including an "ox-tongue" (*niushe* 牛舌) shaped tablet bearing two inscriptions: "A Treasured Possession of Zhou Liyuan" 周櫟園珍藏 (molded in relief in regular script [*kaishu* 楷書]); and "Ink for Transcribing Sutras in the Laigu ["Relying on the Ancient"] Studio" 賴古堂寫經墨 (in clerical script [*lishu* 隸書] with gold inlay) (figure 0.3).[118] Eminent twentieth-century ink connoisseur Zhou Shaoliang 周紹良 (1917–2005) claimed that the choice of the characters Zhou Liyuan 周櫟園 rather than Master Liyuan 櫟園先生 on the Palace Museum tablet implies that Zhou Lianggong personally supervised the production of this inkstick for his own use.[119] Whereas Zhou's inkstone inscription was carved (either by himself, Zhang Zhen, or a hired artisan) onto a singular object from a signature calligraphic draft, his inkstick inscription was cut into a wooden mold within which black ink paste, a viscous mixture of carbon lampblack and glue, could be set. His markings were not responses to the properties of the artifact upon which they appear, but titles that precede the object's assembly, features embedded in the inkstick's design and facture. Later collectors prized this specimen (and refrained from testing it with a brush) in part due to Zhou's legendary "ink obsessions" (*mo pi* 墨癖).[120] Early Qing poems note that Zhou organized "sacrificial offerings for inksticks" (*jimo zhi hui* 祭墨之會) on New Year's Eve, making libations with wine, before grinding ink to compose poems dedicated to the sacrifice.[121] The fortuitous survival of Zhou's limited-edition inkstick recalls his fame for the poetic consecration and ceremonial destruction of inksticks at yearly ritual gatherings.[122]

Seal

A prominent participant in both the seventeenth-century revival of antiquarian research on bronze and stone inscriptions and the ascendancy of the "epigraphic style" (bei feng 碑風) in early Qing calligraphy, Zhou

FIGURES 0.3A AND 0.3B. An "ox-tongue" (*niushe* 牛舌) inkstick commissioned by Zhou Lianggong, now held in the Palace Museum (7.9 cm × 2 cm × 0.7 cm). The inkstick bears two inscriptions: the first (*top*) molded in relief in regular script reads "A Treasured Possession of Zhou Liyuan" 周櫟園珍藏; the second (*bottom*) in clerical script with gold inlay reads "Ink for Transcribing Sutras in the Laigu Studio" 賴古堂寫經墨. *Source*: The Palace Museum.

saw seal carving as a conduit for the pursuit and transmission of epigraphic scholarship: "Study of the six ancient scripts has died; only one form remains through the copying of seals" 六書之學亡，賴摹印尚存其一體.[123] Zhou's prose and poetry meanwhile treat this seventeenth-century material turn toward inscribing solid objects as a matter of heightened literary concern, focusing on the tools and technical media of writing in grappling with the repercussions of dynastic transition. His elegiac colophons on sets of seal impressions, vignettes posthumously published by his sons as *Biographies of Seal Carvers* (*Yinren zhuan* 印人傳) in 1673, cast the carver as a literary protagonist, one whose enterprising mobility in wielding the knife at once exploits and works to redress the political ruptures of the 1640s.[124] Many of the vignettes in this unfinished masterpiece of early Qing literature—a work I discuss in more depth in chapter 2—were composed after Zhou Lianggong destroyed the wooden printing blocks for his own collected poetry and prose on the fifth day of the second lunar month of 1671 in a self-inflicted bibliocaust. Zhou's reflections on the affordances of calligraphic carving in *Biographies of Seal Carvers*, in other words, emerge against the backdrop of his own painful rejection of print as a secure means of preservation.[125] His case serves as a stark reminder of the divergent approaches among mid-seventeenth century writers toward both the purpose and perils of woodblock publication.

Zhou Lianggong concurrently started to explore the symbiosis between carving and literary remembrance, using poems and letters to expound the meaning of impressions in his personal collection while treating impressions as stimuli for poems. He claimed to an imprisoned friend, for instance, that "this technique [seal carving] and poetics are the same" 此道與聲詩同, and that "as Ming poetry has been through several upheavals, so seals have followed suit" 明詩數變，而印章從之, before comparing clusters of carvers to the three major literary "schools" of the late Ming.[126] Certain seals in his collection even comment upon mainstream developments in seventeenth-century literary thought, such as: "Don't Read the Poems of Wang [Shizhen] 王世貞 (1526–1590), Li [Panlong] 李攀龍 (1526–1590), Zhong [Xing] 鍾惺 (1574–1624), and Tan [Yuanchun] 譚元春 (1585–1634)" 不讀王李鍾譚之詩 (figure 0.4).

His seal catalogue contains several impressions that became kernels for poetic reminiscences, including "Don't Forget Today" (*Wuwang jinri*

INTRODUCTION

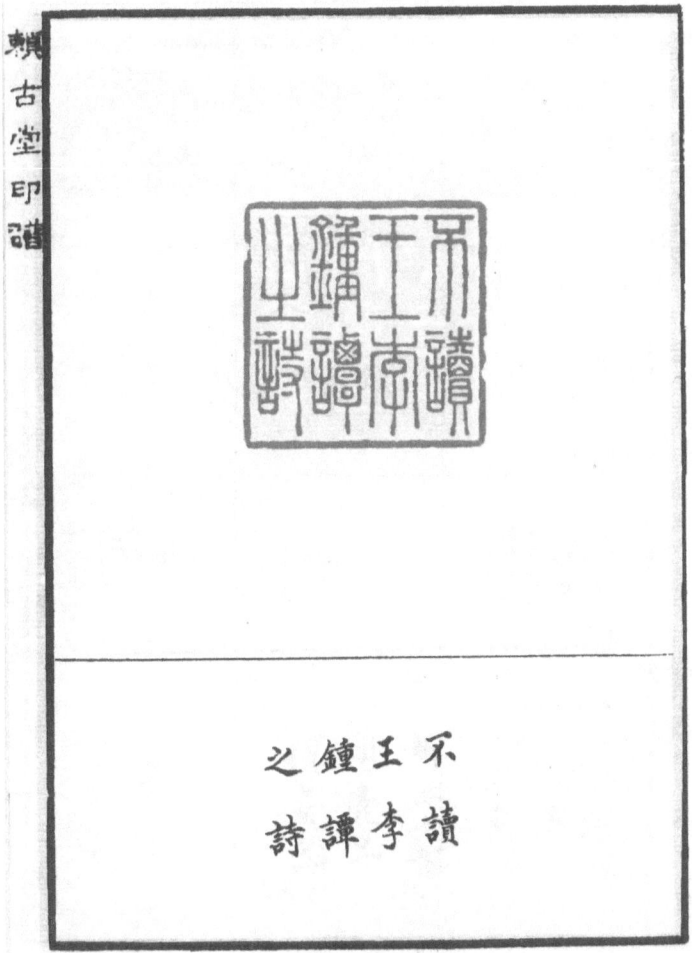

FIGURE 0.4. "Don't Read the Poems of Wang, Li, Zhong, and Tan" 不讀王李鍾譚之詩. *Source*: Zhou Lianggong 周亮工, ed., *Laigutang yinpu: si juan* 賴古堂印譜：四卷, 2. 4a. Image courtesy of Harvard-Yenching Library.

勿忘今日) (figure 0.5)—an evocative phrase that recalls Zhou's own experiences of imprisonment from 1655 to 1661 on false charges of official corruption. The final line of a self-annotated poem by Zhou for his imprisoned friend Huang Jing 黃經 (n.d.) identifies the meaning behind these four characters: "Pack up once more and sculpt Today; in the dusty sands of one hundred *kalpas*, pledge Don't Forget" 裝成更為鐫今日，百劫塵沙愿勿忘.[127]

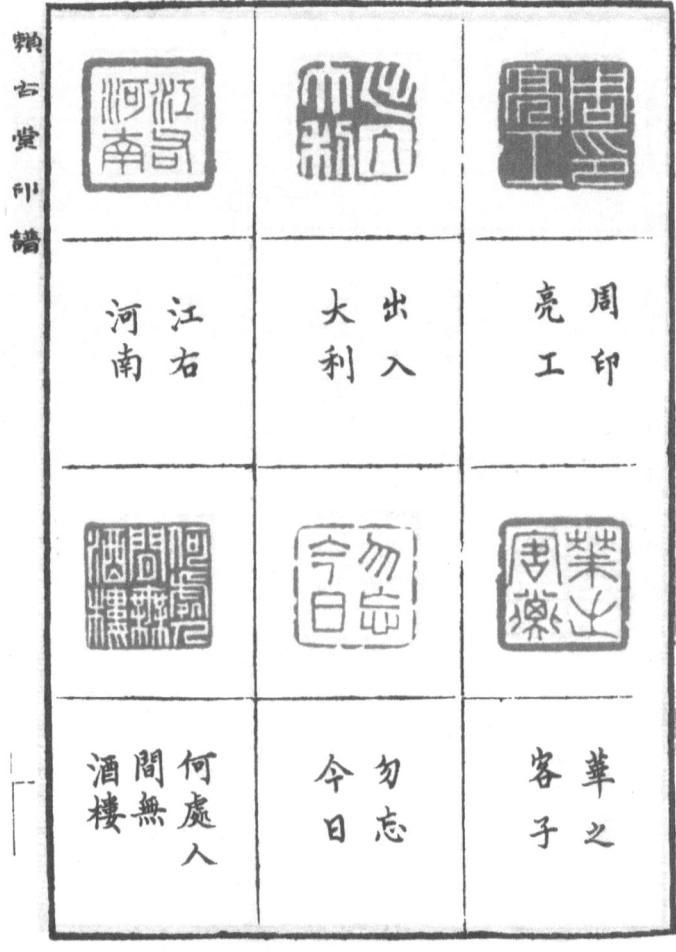

FIGURE 0.5. "Don't Forget Today" 勿忘今日. *Source:* Zhou Lianggong, ed., *Laigutang yinpu: si juan*, 6. 21a. Image courtesy of Harvard-Yenching Library.

At the end of the poem, Zhou makes the following note: "When [Huang] was about to depart [from prison] he carved 'Don't Forget Today' as a gift for me" 濟叔瀕行，鐫「勿忘今日」貽予.[128] After Huang's death many years later, Zhou sought to commemorate his friend by compiling a makeshift folio of their correspondence under the title "Don't Forget Today" (a decision he divulges following an exchange with Du Jun, author of the epitaph for tea leaves). Zhou reads the seal as the memento of a distinct occasion (that day), and yet finds in its capacity to generate fresh imprints a means for coming to terms with evanescence (this day): "Don't Forget Today" locates within memories of past struggles admonishments to exploit the fleeting opportunities of the present. A seal's imprint—as a marker of both physical connection and absence, then and now—thus speaks to the way recollection demands preservation and erasure, the retention of indelible traces and forgetting, or a receptiveness to the new.¹²⁹

Inscriptions upon inkstones, inksticks, and seals—three basic tools for written communication—elucidate competing approaches toward the permanence of the written word: writing on an inkslab searches for longevity in the weighty matter of stone; a molded inscription on an inkstick meanwhile represents an effort to forestall oblivion through the prospect of serial production, making do with cycles of destruction and regeneration. Seals—as devices for the mechanical replication of impressions and as substrates for carved signatures in a range of other calligraphic styles—occupy a middle space between these two poles. Cultivating a renewed attentiveness to ancient inscriptions on bronze vessels and stone stelae, seals stimulated innovative forms of conceptual transfer from imposing monuments to the staple implements on a writer's desk. Zhou argued that seal carving might supplement and help restore inscriptions on stone monuments in the present. He noted, for instance, how an engraver famed for carving local stelae might use stone seals to transmit ancient stone inscriptions: "he in turn transmitted in stone that which he obtained through the transmission of stone" 其得以傳之石者石傳之.¹³⁰

My book proceeds from the example of Zhou Lianggong to investigate the intertwined development of these three methods for making a mark—inkstone engraving, inkstick molding, and seal carving—in the late Ming and early- to mid-Qing, assessing the way these techniques in turn transformed understandings of inscription in general, notably with regard to the antiquarian study of past traces and the uncertain fate of monuments in the present. This material turn toward writing upon writing tools evokes a consequential shift in focus from a sense of the durable as a quality inherent in cumbersome substrates to a sense of endurance as an open-ended process, one cultivated and maintained through diligent labor. As Zhou's case starts to suggest, the seemingly incidental issue of how to inscribe an object in early modern China—by bringing together concerns with the historiography, material transmission, and technical substructures of the Chinese script—became a venue for critical reflection on the question of what it means to write.

CHAPTERS

To elucidate the significance of inscription in late Ming and early- to mid-Qing China, this book surveys four sets of materials: (1) inscriptions carved or molded upon artifacts that are still accessible today; (2) literary inscriptions preserved in manuscripts, printed books, or ink-squeeze rubbings, for which an original object no longer survives; (3) records of an inscribed object where the inscription itself has not been preserved; (4) poems and prose accounts (prefaces, colophons, records, biographies, letters) that discuss the act of carving or viewing inscriptions. Rather than privilege either literary or material evidence, I ask how the former might recondition critical assessments of the latter and vice versa.

The book's four chapters excavate distinct yet interrelated perspectives on how early modern inscriptions query the meanings of permanence. In doing so, I bring together writers and objects that are not typically studied alongside each other, moving from some of the most revered prose stylists in the classical tradition (chapter 1), to itinerant carvers and entrepreneurial manufacturers (chapters 2 and 3), to preeminent Qing antiquarians (chapter 4). I read these seemingly divergent cases as interconnected reactions to the same system of objects. The literary responses of figures like Zhou Lianggong or Zhang Dai to the fates of Ming artifacts (chapter 1) were shaped by a newfound interest in artisanal knifework (chapter 2) and the transmission of carved words in the Ming marketplace (chapter 3). The innovations of late Ming carvers (chapter 2) and ink makers (chapter 3) at the same time informed Qing antiquarian efforts to transform desktop objects into unlikely monuments and in certain cases to pick up the knife to carve their own inkstones (chapter 4 and epilogue). The book's structure eschews a strict chronological narrative to instead investigate the development, tensions, and intersections between these competing perspectives on the question of what it means to speak of an object's durability.

Chapter 1 outlines the affordances of inscription in early modern China by examining the collections of Xu Wei's devotee and Zhou Lianggong's collaborator—the renowned prose stylist Zhang Dai. One of the most celebrated writers of the seventeenth century, Zhang's responses to Ming history and the violence of dynastic transition were shaped by underlying preoccupations with the ethical stakes and material contingencies of writing upon things. Zhang's sixty-eight inscriptions on objects ranging from driftwood fragments, antique zithers, and rain-flower pebbles to censers, hairpins, and damaged inkstones personify family possessions as "friends," asking what lessons things might impart amid the destruction of inter-dynastic war. Following Xu Wei's example, Zhang Dai composes anti-closural inscriptions both to gauge the ruptures of the Ming cataclysm and to overcome his compromised predicament by modeling an ironic capacity to indulge competing perspectives on recent events. He searches for endurance within experiences of transience, composing inscriptions that expound a philosophical acceptance of change.

The next three chapters outline potential responses to the concerns of Zhang Dai's inscriptions, adopting the perspectives of the three main protagonists in early modern object culture—merchant (chapter 2), artisan (chapter 3), and antiquarian (chapter 4)—while suggesting how acts of writing upon things undermined the distinctiveness of these roles. Chapter 2 reconsiders the resurgence of interest in writing with a knife during the late Ming and the Qing dynasties. Calligraphers had for centuries commissioned artisans to carve traces of their handwriting onto hard substrates, yet late-sixteenth-century artists started to challenge this rigid division of labor, fusing brush and knifework. The chapter investigates the motivations behind and far-reaching consequences of this material turn to carving words by foregrounding the emergence of a new knife-wielding protagonist, the so-called Confucian Knight-Errant (*ruxia* 儒俠) of Huizhou prefecture—a martial figure whose practice traversed and ultimately recalibrated lines between the brush-based arts, shopkeeping, and craft. The precarious fate of monumental stone inscriptions amid Ming border conflicts and the fallout from internecine factional strife created new conditions of possibility—openings for those previously involved in the infrastructural management of stelae to make their own mark on everyday objects in urban markets. Huizhou entrepreneurs, as self-styled "swordsmen," subsequently found in carved calligraphy a means with which to master and make sense of commercial upheaval. Their inscriptions turn from concerns with the longevity of writing on stone to the carver's chivalric capacity to improvise in and redress present-day turmoil with the blade.

Chapter 3 investigates the inscription of inksticks, asking what it meant for writers to mold their words upon mass-produced tablets designed to be ground down or finished up through their use. Competition in the East Asian ink market, extending from the ateliers of southern China to stationery stores in Korea and Japan, spawned sophisticated strategies of product labeling, with celebrity manufacturers composing inscriptions to promote ink brands. Working with surviving ink cakes and catalogues of illustrated ink-cake designs from the late Ming and early Qing, the chapter examines the interplay between inscribed literature and innovative practices of advertisement, showing how writers turned their attention from discrete or tangible artifacts to the endorsement of product labels. In doing so, ink makers reconceive of durability in terms of an object's duplication and material transmutations.

In response to these developments, chapter 4 investigates the efforts of leading Qing antiquarians to establish new collective monuments in the wake of violent rupture. The chapter reconsiders the distinctive contributions of writers who lived through inter-dynastic war to the resurgence of antiquarianism in the late seventeenth and early eighteenth centuries. Concerns with the unlikely recovery of Ming remnant things in Qing antiquarian circles divulge the anachronism, artistic creativity, and collective fantasies of restitution that haunt the outwardly austere discipline of "studying metal and stone." Qing responses to the afterlives of Ming inscriptions ultimately disclose a newfound acceptance that continuity with the past demands transition.

The epilogue brings together the themes outlined in chapters 1–4 by reassessing the early- to mid-Qing trend for inscribing inkstones. The inscription of broken, damaged, or ruined stones, a practice that entailed the recarving of discarded bricks, pillars, or roof tiles as new inkslabs, encapsulates a dynamic behind the book as a whole; namely, that even as early modern writers used inscriptions to project chauvinistic hopes for the permanence of Chinese written culture onto writing tools, this very act began to illuminate the contingencies, compromises, and contradictions that lay behind this ideal. The most creative writers of the mid-Qing period make these inconsistencies the subject of their inscriptions.

THE SIGNIFICANCE OF DURABILITY

My aim in this book is to refrain from broad or ahistorical generalizations about "Chinese attitudes" toward permanence to consider instead how writers against the backdrop of protracted societal upheaval posed the question of what durability might mean. I focus on the motivations behind and the terms with which writers pose these questions rather than seeking to distill any straightforward answer. Inscribed literature, at once admitting the physical constraints that writers face while creating a space where the interplay between words and things might be imagined otherwise, possessed a unique power to identify and address such concerns.

Leading sinologists from Pierre Ryckmans (1935–2014; Simon Leys) to Frederick W. Mote (1922–2005) have made strident and widely cited claims for the distinctiveness of premodern Chinese understandings of durability. For Ryckmans, Chinese antiquarianism—a discipline concerned not so much with material traces of the past but with their relationship to writing—ultimately privileged the transmission of names above and beyond the preservation of solid things: "life-after-life was not to be found in a supernature, nor could it rely upon artefacts: man only survives in man—which means, in practical terms, in the memory of posterity, through the medium of the written word."[131] The resilience of the classical Chinese tradition, he concludes, "may well derive from the fact [it] never let itself be trapped into set forms, static objects and things, where it would have run the risk of paralysis and death."[132] Permanence, in other words, does not foreclose but rather implies adaptation and renewal. Continuity "does not inhabit monuments," Ryckmans writes, nor is it "ensured by the immobility of inanimate objects," rather it is "achieved through the fluidity of the successive generations."[133]

Reflecting on the absence of monumental ruins comparable in stature to the Acropolis or Roman Forum, Mote similarly concluded that Chinese civilization did not lodge its history in "authentically ancient" physical objects but rather in their literary associations:

> The physical object is entirely secondary. Anyone planning to achieve immortality in the minds of his fellow men might well give a lower priority to building some great stone monument than to cultivating his human capacities so that he might express himself imperishably in words, or at least be alluded to in some enduring line by a poet or essayist of immortal achievement.[134]

The past, Mote observed in a still popular formulation, "was a past of words not of stones." Various critics have subsequently taken issue with such claims by questioning their implicit opposition between names ("permanence is first and foremost a *permanence of names*") and things (as "static" forms that connote "paralysis and death").[135] For Ryckmans and Mote, literature ("the word") transcends materiality and is thus imperishable ("the only truly enduring embodiments of the eternal human moments are the literary ones"), while mere things are by implication inert, immovable, or deathly.

The inscriptions I have read across the course of this introduction, from Wang Fuzhi's brush and Du Jun's tombstone for tea leaves to Li Yu's makeshift hamper and Zhou Lianggong's "self-made" inkstick, unsettle and exceed the terms of these dichotomies: they refute assumptions that things are fixed or static, divulging instead a mode of literary thought attuned to the mutable or inconstant properties of diverse substrates; they suggest how literary attention to the impermanence of the material world might enlarge the ways we think about notions of endurance and expendability, that survival in large measure rests on care and chance. These inscriptions instead elucidate the ways in which the materials, technical implements, and humble labor involved in making a mark modulate or temper strident claims for literature's imperishability (whether Ryckmans's "permanence of names" or Mote's "eternal moments realized in words"). Literary inscriptions ultimately advance the understanding that durability "inheres in a process of interpretation rather than a positing of the characteristics of the object."[136] The propensities of materials inevitably condition the social values assigned to them. Yet these values remain relational and contingent. They can be interrogated and remade. To the extent that early modern inscriptions embrace metamorphosis and change, they conceive of these processes in material terms, as a means of thinking and working with, rather than seeking to deny, the ineluctable transformation of things.

Chapter One

ON REMNANT THINGS

What does it mean to make a durable mark when transience and loss seem permanent? Historian and renowned prose stylist Zhang Dai returned to this question throughout his life in the many inscriptions and prose vignettes or poems that were based on inscribed objects in his literary collections.¹ His writings suggest that a sense of permanence had, amid the temporal aporias of the Ming-Qing dynastic transition, become inconceivable except in terms of the inevitability of change.² Rather than deny such a predicament, Zhang makes tensions between endurance and evanescence, solidity and ephemerality the very subject of his literary inscriptions: his most prestigious mark, for instance, names a driftwood fragment "Autumn Tides and Summer Clouds" (*qiutao xiayun* 秋濤夏雲), numinous impressions of flux and ethereality. By treating the fraught connection between a purportedly engraved message and its underlying substrate as a matter of literary concern, Zhang at once investigates and seeks to repair larger ruptures between words and things in the mid-seventeenth century. Rather than lament inconstancy or seek refuge in antiquated notions of monumentality, he found resilience and a provisional means of survival through an acceptance of different modes of existence.

Zhang Dai's widely consulted writings on Ming things are based almost exclusively on inscriptions that he or his relatives carved upon them. Vignettes from his masterpiece, *Dream Reminiscences of Tao'an* (*Tao'an mengyi* 陶庵夢憶), including "Shen Meigang" 沈梅岡, "Leftover Stones from the Flower and Rock Flotilla" ("Huashigang yishi" 花石綱遺石), "Pine Fossil" ("Songhuashi" 松花石), "Wood Like a Dragon" ("Mu you long" 木猶龍), "Second Uncle's Antiques" ("Zhongshu gudong" 仲叔古董), and "Celestial Inkstone" ("Tian yan" 天硯), are less biographies of charismatic objects than responses to encounters with, or retrospective prefaces for, inscribed lines of prose and verse. The number of Zhang Dai's own inscriptions in his *Collected Writings of Langhuan* (*Langhuan wenji* 瑯嬛文集), at least sixty-eight, exceeds the quantity of compositions by this preeminent belletrist in any other prose form. At the heart of this collection lies Zhang's "Inscriptions on Twenty-Eight Friends" ("Ershiba you ming" 二十八友銘), an elegiac sequence that looks askance from the biographies of his relatives to address their displaced antiques as faithful interlocutors: "As for my family's old things" 余家舊物, he writes in a short preface, "more than half have been lost, yet I still remember their names. They are just like old friends, so I call them 'friends'" 失去強半，而余尚識其姓氏，如得故友，故曰友也.[3]

Early Qing acts of inscribing Ming "remnant things" (*yiwu* 遺物), amid the coexistence of competing temporal frameworks in the mid-seventeenth century, elucidate struggles to reconcile a professed search for durability with lived experiences of dislocation.[4] Short studies of artisanal brands—"The Best Crafts in Suzhou" ("Wuzhong jueji" 吳中絕技), "Gan Wentai's Censers" ("Gan Wentai lu" 甘文臺爐), "Stoneware Jar, Pewter Carafe" ("Shaguan xizhu" 砂罐錫注), "Select Craftsmen" ("Zhu gong" 諸工)—and popular sketches of carvers such as "Pu Zhongqian's Carving" ("Pu Zhongqian diaoke" 濮仲謙雕刻) in *Dream Reminiscences*, nevertheless, evidence the extent to which Zhang's reflections on the difficulties of literary inscription were conditioned by a keen attentiveness to the material craft of writing with a knife.[5] The hitherto unacknowledged centrality of carved words to the oeuvre of this leading seventeenth-century belletrist invites reconsideration of inscription's place in the late Ming and early Qing literary imagination more broadly. Historians typically make use of Zhang's writings to investigate tensions between conceptions of elegance and vulgarity, authenticity and imitation, the nonpareil souvenir and commodity, person and thing in literary responses to early modern material culture. My concern with the significance of inscription departs from a prevalent focus in such work on issues of taste, connoisseurship, and conspicuous consumption. Zhang, I argue, instead foregrounds the way techniques of mark making generate and structure these polarities—his prose-poetry thus prompts consideration of how such distinctions might at a moment of crisis be rewritten.

Zhang Dai turns to inscribed literature to query the meaning and purpose of carving words. Vignettes on scenes of mark making in *Dream Reminiscences of Tao'an* adapt Zhang's great-grandfather and grandfather's inscriptions on objects as kernels for mournful reflections on the imbrication of familial and dynastic decline, elucidating the development of approaches to writing on things during the Ming and the transformation of such attitudes in the wake of transition. These vignettes divulge two tendencies: the pseudo-epitaphic commemoration of lost lives on the one hand and empathetic understanding or friendship with responsive possessions on the other. Both impulses shape Zhang Dai's own collection of inscriptions on objects, "The Twenty-Eight Friends"—a sequence that treats the difficulties of inscription, or the challenge of how to make a lasting mark when impermanence seems constant, as its central concern. Zhang's attention to strains between words and things—encapsulated in inscriptions that question their own durability—eloquently registers the upheavals of the mid-seventeenth-century moment, adumbrating increasingly unstable configurations of self and other, "me" and "you." And yet, in his ironic distance from the fixity that inscriptions on hard surfaces ought to affirm, Zhang finds a means with which to entertain competing perspectives on recent events—a way of reconciling lingering faith in and searching scrutiny of human devotion to things. He works to transcend his compromised predicament by naming and striving to possess the contradictions of his age.

SCENES OF INSCRIPTION

Across historical memoirs and biographical writings, Zhang Dai introduces himself as a sensitive reader of inscribed objects, one highly attentive to the contingencies and aspirations behind acts of mark making. Several of the most celebrated vignettes in *Dream Reminiscences of Tao'an* are not so much essays as retrospectively composed prefaces for literary inscriptions. These compositions suggest how inscribed objects might inspire further historiographical reflection in related forms of prose and verse. More specifically, they reveal how Zhang's memoirs of the Ming—often read as dream-like ruminations on the vagaries of nostalgia—were conditioned by underlying concerns with the physical formats and substructures of writing. In reminiscences based upon his great-grandfather's inscriptions, Zhang dwells on the durability and collective significance of carved memorials. In remembering his grandfather's inscriptions, by contrast, he considers how engraved professions of intimacy with possessions articulate feelings of redundancy and stubborn recalcitrance, reflecting on whether the darker underside of carving objects to remember people might be the reduction of people to things. Zhang Dai's own inscriptions seek to reconcile these seemingly incongruous tendencies, asking what it means to enlist inert materials in the interest of keeping memory alive.

The Prisoner's Box and Fan

In "Shen Meigang," Zhang creates a portrait of a scholar-craftsman (Shen Shu 沈束 [1515–1581]) and Kuaiji 會稽 resident from the details of his great-grandfather's markings on a box and a fan: the vignette is an extended record of Zhang Dai's reading of Zhang Yuanbian's 張元忭 (1538–1588) engraved words.[6] The entry in *Dream Reminiscences* begins with Shen Meigang's prison sentence for offending the controversial grand secretary Yan Song 嚴嵩 (1480–1567), before following Shen's virtuosic experiments as a craftsman in jail, whittling his own tools and making boxes, cases, and a round eighteen-rib fan from a fragment of olivewood and some palm slats.[7] The real point of interest for Zhang is that Shen's wife later approached his great-grandfather, Zhang Yuanbian, with these hand-carved artifacts as gifts in exchange for an epitaph.[8] Yuanbian accepted the commission, yet Zhang Dai redirects focus from whatever it was the epitaph said to the inscriptions his great-grandfather engraved onto the small curios.[9] For Zhang Dai, a vocal critic of the rhetorical pretensions of Ming entombed epigraphy, the markings on Shen's box and fan constitute a more fitting memorial to the aspects of Shen's life deemed worth remembering.[10] Zhang's abrupt transition from the public history of Yan Song's political corruption to Shen Meigang's creativity in prison dovetails with his turn from an imposing mortuary monument to the comparatively miniature inscriptions that adorn Shen's handmade objects.

ON REMNANT THINGS

Zhang Yuanbian composed two inscriptions, the first for Shen Meigang's case and the second for the body of his handmade fan. Invoking an analogy to the Han dynasty envoy Su Wu 蘇武 (140–60 BCE)—held for nineteen years by the Xiongnu and starved into submission—Zhang celebrates Shen's self-sufficiency, making tools to make things that might earn a true memorial for his name. Zhang Yuanbian, who himself won fame as a protestor against Yan Song's illicit execution of the Confucian moralist Yang Jisheng 楊繼盛 (1516–1555), approaches inscription as an act of remonstrance, using the properties of both objects to celebrate the untrammeled character of a loyal minister, marking a durable surface to restore for posterity the integrity of a once-tainted reputation[11]:

[He] inscribed the case: For nineteen years, the "Gentleman of the Household" carried a tally with yaktail streamers; for eighteen years, the Supervising Secretary held this case.[12] A tally! A case! Both belong to the same track.

銘其匣曰：十九年，中郎節；十八年，給諫匣；節邪匣邪，同一轍。[13]

[He] inscribed the fan: Scraps of a felt rug from beyond the border, sustenance to eat when starved.[14] A fan in jail, unsullied by dirt and dust; before there was Su now there is Shen, their names shine resplendently.

銘其箑曰：塞外氈，饑可飡；獄中箑，塵莫干；前蘇後沈，名班班。[15]

Zhang Yuanbian's comparison of Shen and Su Wu alludes to an anecdote concerning a magpie that made a clamor in Shen's jail cell. In response to the raspy bird, Shen remarked: "can happiness befall a prisoner?" 那有喜到罪囚邪, a saying that when passed to the Jiajing 嘉靖 emperor (r. 1521–1567) as a secret "overseer's memorandum" (*jiantie* 監帖) prompted the Ming ruler to say: "why must this prisoner be unhappy?" 囚何遂無喜, and release him.[16] The anecdote became the basis of a popular saying in the Jiajing reign: "Su Wu returned home due to the goose's letter [Su had strapped a letter to the foot of a wild goose to inform the Han emperor he was not dead]; Shen Shu returned home due to the magpie's memorandum" 蘇武歸以雁書，沈束歸以鵲帖。[17] In claiming Su and Shen "both belong to the same track," Yuanbian's inscriptions draw analogies between their material traces (a tally with yaktail streamers and a palmwood box; scraps of a felt rug and a round fan made of bamboo slats), lending tangible form to the correspondences between their reputations. Zhang Yuanbian effectively establishes miniature memorials to the "magpie memorandum" and the scene of imperial recognition of virtue under duress that it denotes.

After transcribing and hence ensuring the future transmission of the two inscriptions, Zhang Dai attends to the physicality of the engravings, noting that his great-grandfather's *ming* for Shen's objects were first drafted with the brush by Xu Wei (Xu Wenchang *shu* 徐文長書; it was Yuanbian who helped secure Xu's release from prison for the murder of his wife in 1573), then engraved by a carver named Zhang Yingyao 張應堯 (Zhang Yinggyao *juan* 張應堯鐫). Republican-era antiquarian Deng Zhicheng 鄧之誠 (1887–1960) claimed to have owned a wooden wrist-rest with an inscription and a painting of a hibiscus by Xu Wei both engraved by Zhang Yingyao, attesting, he notes, to the name-brand quality of a "Xu and Zhang" collaboration in late Ming China.[18] Xu elsewhere named Yingyao as a talented carver within inscriptions on a bamboo wrist-rest, treating the artisan's signature as the subject of his own carved message: "Such virtuosic handiwork is by whom? Old Yingyao Zhang" 妙手為誰，應堯張叟.[19]

The pair of inscriptions can, Zhang Dai suggests, be seen to constitute a collection, a gathering of "four perfections"—literature (Zhang Yuanbian), calligraphy (Xu Wei), engraving (Zhang Yingyao), and craft (Shen Meigang)—a palimpsest formed from the traces of different hands.[20] Yuanbian's inscription was not a solipsistic act, but a collective effort to establish a memorial rooted in Shaoxing, one that his great-grandson worked to restore almost a century later. Zhang Dai not only uses the two *ming* as a kernel for his vignette "Shen Meigang" in *Dream Reminiscences* but also recycles these same words as the basis for a further "appraisal" of Shen's woodcut visage in the "Loyal Remonstrators" ("Zhongjian" 忠諫) chapter of his 1680 book, *Encomia on Portraits of the Ming Dynasty Imperishable Worthies of Yue* (*Ming yu Yue sanbuxiu mingxian tuzan* 明於越三不朽名賢圖贊)—a compendium of portraits depicting local celebrities.[21] Peeling back sedimented layers of significance to Yingyao's knifework or Xu Wei's brushwork, Zhang recovers a pseudo-epitaph for the deceased prisoner. The material history of the two inscriptions, in Zhang's eyes, comes to embody the collaborative and local character of this shared protest against political corruption.

"Shen Meigang" attests to the centrality of object inscription in Zhang Dai's broader engagement with the project of historical judgment. Nevertheless, in his own inscriptions, writings that invoke the destruction and loss of the transition, Zhang begins to question both the durability of engraved markings and the correspondences between human virtue and thing that his great-grandfather's inscribed slogans presume. Whereas Zhang Dai carefully attends to the quiddity of his great-grandfather's *ming*, physical traces that warrant veneration in and of themselves, his own inscriptions possess a less stable objecthood, assuming an increasingly mutable and provisional character.[22] If Zhang Yuanbian commemorates the integrity of a person by praising the properties of an object, Zhang Dai considers how possessions might stand apart from their owners, assuming independent personae, even judging those who failed them.

Pine Fossil

While Zhang Dai found in his great-grandfather's miniature monuments resources for an alternative late Ming history of local resistance to corruption, he looked to his grandfather, Zhang Rulin 張汝霖 (?1558–1625), to recover a private model of friendship between human and thing. He faithfully records, for instance, Rulin's inscription on a rock found while traveling in the Yandang 雁宕 mountains that his grandfather subsequently repurposed as an inkstone:

> I made your acquaintance at the side of a mountain stream.
> If someone else calls upon you, it's Cold Mountain [or the monk Hanshan].
> If I call upon you, it's Pick-me Up [or the monk Shide].

> 與女識，谿之側。
> 人喚女，是寒山。
> 我喚女，是拾得。[23]

Rulin's inscription puns on the "cold stream" (Hanxi 寒谿) where he "picked up" (*shide* 拾得) the stone by invoking the names of two legendary Chan eccentrics: Hanshan 寒山 (fl. 9th century) and Shide 拾得 (fl. 9th century)—the latter obtained his name when a monk found him crying at the bottom of a rocky ridge, "picked him up," and took him to a temple where he was raised.

Zhang Rulin's empathetic identification with otherwise neglected rocks finds more sophisticated expression in his inscription on a petrified chunk of pinewood (*songhuashi* 松化石), likely opal or chalcedony, from Qingjiang 清江, an object that later became the kernel of Zhang Dai's vignette "Pine Fossil" in *Dream Reminiscences*.[24] Fossilized remains of terrestrial vegetation, often described as five-hundred-year-old pieces of pinewood suddenly struck by lightning at night, waver in late imperial pharmacological accounts between sentience and insentience.[25] Zhang Dai appears drawn to the fossil for the way it embodies the prospect of endurance through ruination. Beyond his discussion of *songhuashi* in a chapter on "spring rocks" from his encyclopedia, *Night Ferry* (*Yehang chuan* 夜航船), Zhang elsewhere alludes to "pine-turned-stone" in his inscription on a prized "pine knot" inkstone ("wind and lightning in one's sleeve, old pine turns to stone" 肘後風雷，老松化石) and in an inscription for a bamboo wrist-rest adorned with a carved illustration of *songhuashi* by his friend, the eminent painter Chen Hongshou 陳洪綬 (1598–1652).[26]

Zhang Rulin's rugged engraving on "Pine Fossil" (compared to a *moya* carving on an unquarried boulder) evokes both an assertion of conquest and a search for an unadorned "naturalness," yet its austere demeanor is mitigated by the conversational intimacy and shape-shifting perspectives of his message:

> You used to be hairy, shaking it! You were pine.
> But now you've shed it all, petrified. You're a stone.
> While you can swap forms,
> Your integrity remains constant.
> You gaze at me, and I smile,
> With you I have complete concord.

> 爾昔鬣而鼓兮，松也；
> 爾今脫而骨兮，石也。
> 爾形可使代兮，貞勿易也；
> 爾視余笑兮，莫余逆也。[27]

Zhang Dai revives the storyline in his grandfather's inscription for his own dream reminiscence: beginning with an account of sacrifices at a riverside shrine, where locals sprinkled the blood and hair of butchered animals onto the rock, before turning to the object's "gnarled corpulence" as it stands at the "foot of the stairs," holding a planter, unfit for other uses: "it cannot be called functional" 不稱使.²⁸ The domestication of the found object resembles a kind of enslavement, with Zhang Rulin taming the totemic aura of this blood-spattered, hairy monstrosity, cutting its mane and restricting its movements within the local *yamen*. These acts culminate in Rulin naming the object "Elder Stone" (*shizhang* 石丈), a reference to legendary petromaniac Mi Fu's 米芾 (1051–1107) obeisance before a rock dressed in scholar's garb and a paradigmatic example of friendship between the self and inorganic others in late imperial literature.

Zhang Rulin repeatedly calls upon the object, each line addressing "you," as if beseeching the fossil to talk back. The first two lines mix a selection of body parts (manes and bones) with direct references to the materials of pine and stone, and yet, by the final line, Rulin has removed any stable indicators to person or thing, with the positions of "I" and "you" becoming almost interchangeable: Are you looking at me or am I smiling at you? The inscription proceeds from the metamorphoses of the object—its oscillations between wood and rock—to refract the direction of address, so that these engraved declarations of affinity might be read from the perspective of either human or thing. Rulin's final lines pivot on an allusion to a repeated passage in "The Great Source as Teacher" ("Dazong shi" 大宗師) from *Zhuangzi* 莊子: "[they] looked at one another and burst out laughing, feeling complete concord, and thus did they become friends" […] 相視而笑，莫逆於心，遂相與為友.²⁹ Any sense that Rulin finds in his stone's smile a generative source of vitality cannot, however, be extricated from darker traces of mortality and death. In *Zhuangzi*, after bursting out laughing and "feeling complete concord," one of the friends, after a short silence, without warning falls down dead.³⁰ The inscription queries straightforward conceptions of liveliness and inanimacy to sustain a space of "fresh surmise," finding evidence of the former in the latter and vice versa, reminding readers that they cannot know in advance what kinds of life or death carved words might bestow.³¹

Zhang Dai's retrospective account of Rulin's mark, opening a gap between inscribed ideal and its inferred context, frames his grandfather's devotion to the rock in terms of its initial subjugation and subsequent neglect. He remains ambivalent as to whether Rulin's claim of empathetic understanding redeems or is vitiated by the thing's experience of displacement. Zhang at once bemoans the gnarled fragment's loss of "pine-like" vigor in *Dream Reminiscences*, comparing it unfavorably to a local family's two intertwined pine branches, and yet elsewhere celebrates the pride of place "Pine Fossil" eventually assumed as a souvenir of his grandfather's official service at his own study, Cloudy Grove's Secret Belvedere (Yunlin bige 雲林閟閣).[32] This vignette's ironic distance from the inscription upon which it is based evokes a shift in attention from treating an object as a friend to assessing the hopes and anxieties that elicit human longing for the faithful companionship of a rock, or the fiction of its eloquence. In "Pine Fossil" the certainties of "Shen Meigang" start to unravel. The inscribed object no longer serves as uncomplicated evidence of human virtue but instead registers the idiosyncratic whims and deficiencies of its custodians. Can the search for human traces within non-human forms, Zhang asks, be construed not simply as narcissistic self-projection but as a means of attending to the appropriation and extractive violence that haunt the construction of collections.

FRIENDSHIP WITH REMNANT THINGS

If "Elder Stone" in its allusion to Mi Fu adheres to established conceptions of friendship with things, Zhang Dai's own inscriptions, engaging the dislocation of feeling "left behind," envision comparatively unstable configurations of self and object. *Collected Writings of Langhuan* reveals that Zhang Dai authored a considerable number of inscriptions for the possessions of friends and family throughout his literary career. Across this larger collection of inscriptions, remnant possessions come to embody memories of deceased family members.

An inscription on a "Broken Bronze Water Dipper" ("Cantong shuizhong cheng ming" 殘銅水中丞銘)—"bequeathed" or left behind by Zhang's grandfather, Zhang Rulin—concludes with an invocation not to "forget the hand's moisture" 毋忘手澤, or the perspiration from the hands of the deceased that clings to objects they once held:

INSCRIPTION ON A BROKEN BRONZE WATER DIPPER
(LEFT BEHIND BY MY GRANDFATHER)

Despite your hurt mouth, you brook no shame.
Despite your broken legs, you won't "spill the food."

Drip by drip, drop by drop.
Do not forget the hand's moisture.

殘銅水中丞銘（大父所遺）

雖戕口，不起羞。
雖折足，不覆餗。
點點滴滴，毋忘手澤。³³

Zhang Dai praises the use of this leftover tool by slyly misreading two classical admonitions, finding hidden evidence of virtue in the implement's flaws or physical deficiencies. The *Classic of Documents* warns that "only the mouth brooks shame" 惟口起羞.³⁴ The *Classic of Changes* (*Yijing* 易經) presents an image of a bronze cauldron with "broken legs" (*zhezu* 折足), one that falls over and thus "spills the duke's food" 覆公餗, as a menacing omen.³⁵ Despite its "damaged" (*can* 殘) form, this old dipper still fulfills its basic task (providing "drip by drip, drop by drop" to moisten a brush), offering its custodian a fragile means of staying in touch with the physical presence of the past.³⁶

The author's attentiveness to the character for "mouth" (*kou* 口) reflects late Ming conventions in inscriptive poetics. Zhong Xing and Tan Yuanchun's seminal anthology, *Poetry Return* (*Shigui* 詩歸), treats Zhang's source for the phrase "hurt/mutilated mouth" (*qiangkou* 戕口), King Wu's "Inscription on an Armrest" ("Jiming" 几銘), not only as an exemplary inscription but also as an early model of Chinese poetry: "Be alert in diligence. The mouth produces revilement. The mouth hurts the mouth" 皇皇惟敬口，口生垢，口戕口.³⁷ For Zhong and Tan, major influences on Zhang Dai's writing, the four repetitions of the word *kou* 口 underscore the extent to which an effective inscription should impel its reader to reflect on the proper uses of a human voice: "reading 'mouth hurts the mouth,' awestruck, I'm startled to the bone" 讀『口戕口』，竦然骨驚 (Zhong Xing); "The four 'mouth' characters pile up to elicit a marvelous expression, one does not criticize it for being overly clever" 四口字疊出妙語，不以為纖 (Tan Yuanchun).³⁸ Zhang Dai deploys this same allusion in a further inscription on a "Treasure Vase Inkstone," warning writers to be vigilant in working with ink and brush:

ON REMNANT THINGS

INSCRIPTION ON A TREASURE VASE INKSTONE

The mouth might hurt the mouth in the City of Brushes.
Ancient gentlemen kept their mouths sealed like bottles.

寶瓶研銘

口戕口，在管城。古君子，守如瓶。³⁹

Zhang's contemporary Zhou Lianggong, anticipating an increased attentiveness to early epigraphic sources in the late seventeenth century, mocked Zhong and Tan (and their late Ming adherents) for misreading King Wu's "Inscription on an Armrest." What late Ming critics took to be the character *kou* 口 in 'mouth hurts the mouth' 口戕口 was, Zhou claimed, more likely the square marker for an illegible or missing character □.⁴⁰

The Twenty-Eight Friends

The central tenets of Zhang's engagement with literary inscription are distilled in a mini-collection entitled "Inscriptions on Twenty-Eight Friends," a sequence that in its treatment of remnant objects wavers between the pseudo-epitaphic commemoration of "Shen Meigang" and empathetic identification with the thing as an interlocutor in "Pine Fossil." This ensemble comprises artifacts belonging to the author's grandfather Zhang Rulin (two objects), second paternal uncle Zhang Lianfang 張聯芳 (?1575–1644) (five objects), fourth uncle Zhang Yefang 張燁芳 (?1585–1615) (four objects), cousin Zhang E 張萼 (?d. 1646) or Yanke 燕客 (four objects), his mysterious fifth younger brother Daozi 道子 (four objects), and youngest brother Zhang Min 張岷 (?1605–?1673) or Shanmin 山民 (six objects)—in addition to three of Zhang Dai's own things (table 1.1).⁴¹ While the collection begins with Rulin ("Elder Stone's" companion), it is bookended by the Zhang family's two preeminent antiquaries: Lianfang, "one of the five greatest collectors south of the Yangzi River," and Zhang Dai's beloved younger brother Min, the "last" of the family's true collectors, an heir to Lianfang, and an avid author of his own inscriptions.⁴² Zhang's epitaph for Min, for instance, dwells on the central place of object inscription in a consummate collector's devotion to his possessions:

When an object entered his hands, he had to caress it day and night, until it emanated a strange sheen; he would wrap it up in unusual brocades and store it in a camphor chest, seeking out "famous hands" for his inscriptions.

一物入手，必旦晚撫摩，光怪畢露，襲以異錦，藏以檀匣，必求名手為之作銘。[43]

TABLE 1.1
Zhang Dai's "Inscriptions on Twenty-Eight Friends"

Title	Owner of Object
Inscription on Rain Flower Stones 雨花石銘	Dafu 大父 Zhang Rulin 張汝霖 (?1558–1625) (Zhang Dai's grandfather)
Inscription on an Inkstone Mountain 研山銘	Eryou 二酉 Zhang Lianfang 張聯芳 (?1575–1644) (Zhang Dai's second uncle)
Inscription on a Small Orchid Pyxis from the Imperial Workshop 蘭花小廠盒銘	Dafu
Inscription on a White Ding Ware Censer 白定爐銘	Eryou
Inscription on a Small Beauty Chalice 小美人觚銘	Eryou
Inscription on a Ge Ware Flagon 哥窯卮銘	Eryou
Inscription on a Ge Ware Topknot Tuft Vase 哥窯丱髻瓶銘	Eryou
Inscription on a Cyan Jade Hairpin 碧玉簪銘	Eryun 爾蘊 Zhang Yefang 張燁芳 (?1585–1615) (Zhang Dai's fourth uncle)
Inscription on a Xuan Bronze Elephant Censer 宣銅象格爐銘	Eryun
Inscription on a Ge Ware Seal Paste Pool 哥窯印池銘	Eryun
Inscription on Jin Tang Smaller Regular Script 晉唐小楷銘	Eryun
Inscription on a Maplewood Staff 茶條杖銘	Tao'an 陶庵 (Zhang Dai)

(continued)

TABLE 1.1
(*continued*)

Title	Owner of Object
Inscription on a Burst Pattern Antique Zither 斷紋古琴銘	Tao'an
Inscription on a Xuande Filled-In Lacquer Pyxis 宣德填漆盒銘	Tao'an
Inscription on a Small Chest with Mutton Fat Jade Images of the Kun Fish and Peng Bird 羊脂玉鯤鵬圖書匣銘	Yanke 燕客 Zhang E 張萼 (?d. 1646) (Zhang Dai's cousin; Zhang Lianfang's son)
Inscription on Lü Wenan's Gaozhuo Inkstone 呂文安糕拙研銘	Yanke
Inscription on Lü Jishi's Han Dynasty Jade Ferule Paperweight 呂吉士漢玉昭文帶戒尺銘	Yanke
Inscription on Yang Yao's Sanxian 楊繇之三絃子銘	Yanke
Inscription on Master Qian's Ancient Mirror 錢子方古鏡銘	Daozi 道子 (Zhang Dai's fifth brother)
Inscription on Li Jincheng's Gong Chun Stand 李錦城龔春臺銘	Daozi
Inscription on a Ding Ware Water Dipper 定窯水中丞銘	Daozi
Inscription on a Xuan Bronze Stacked Lotus Flower Slop Bowl 宣銅反覆蓮花水盂銘	Daozi
Inscription on a Stone of White Translucent Jade 白瑛石銘	Shanmin 山民 Zhang Min 張岷 (?1605–?1673) (Zhang Dai's youngest brother)
Inscription on a Bronze Censer in the Shape of a Partitioned-Crotch Cauldron with Corded Ears 大繩耳分襠銅爐銘	Shanmin
Inscription on a White Ding Ware Inkstone Vase 白定研頭瓶銘	Shanmin
Inscription on a Stoneskin Inkslab 石皮研銘	Shanmin
Inscription on a Guan Ware Bronze Censer in the Shape of a Partitioned-Crotch Cauldron 官窯分襠銅爐銘	Shanmin
Inscription on Wang Ergong's Xu Family–Owned Teapot 王二公徐氏家藏壺銘	Shanmin

Prominent Zhang family members, notably Zhang's great-grandfather Yuanbian (author of inscriptions for Shen Meigang and a paragon of frugality), his father Zhang Yaofang 張耀芳 (1574–1632), and all his female relatives, are excluded from this fellowship of exemplary connoisseurs.[44]

The collection of friends encompasses the major categories of inscribed objects in late imperial China: rocks, bronze vessels and censers, mirrors, bodily accoutrements (staff and hairpin), lacquerware, porcelain, teapots ("purple sand" stoneware), musical instruments (a zither and a three-stringed lute), and writing tools (inkstones and related calligraphic paraphernalia)—perhaps the only exception being the absence of a weapon. Zhang's friends, however, are not generic or exemplary types of artifact, but singular or nonpareil things: a cousin's "purple sandalwood case" (*zitan xia* 紫檀匣), to take one example, with carved pictures of the mythical *kun* 鯤 fish transforming into the *peng* 鵬 bird in snow-white "mutton fat jade" (*yangzhi yu* 羊脂玉)—a stubbornly particular memento, one that ostensibly resists substitution, abstraction, or exchange. With the exception of a strange bronze chalice from the Han dynasty, the majority of objects are of specifically Ming provenance, bear Ming reign marks, or passed through the hands of eminent Ming dynasty collectors like Wang Shimao 王世懋 (1536–1588) and Xiang Yuanbian 項元忭 (1525–1590).[45] At least one artifact—Zhang Rulin's orchid pyxis—claims to be a product of Beijing's "Orchard Factory" (Guoyuanchang 果園廠) a lacquer workshop for the imperial court until 1436, affirming the status of Zhang's friends as remnant things with ties to Ming royalty.[46]

For each "friend," Zhang Dai composes a brief preface, no more than two or three lines, inventorying the collector, measurements, and surface patina of the thing, before writing a pithy *ming*—the longest runs to nineteen characters, while the shortest is only six.[47] Many of the inscriptions exploit the rhetoric of "friendship" (*you* 友) to assess the meaning of "possession" (*you* 有) in the wake of cataclysmic loss. Zhang's eight-character inscription on his "burst-pattern" antique zither, for instance, implicitly casts the object as a "knower of tones" (*zhiyin* 知音), a term for an intimate companion with a shared understanding of music, or the harmony between two "heart-minds" (*xin* 心).[48] He treats the instrument that once sustained shared pleasures with now-deceased friends—*Dream Reminiscences* records Zhang's youthful collaboration in a local quartet—as his surviving friend.[49] A true "knower of tones" ought to destroy his zither in the wake of a dear companion's death; Zhang's reluctance to do so implies an incapacity to properly mourn the memories his zither embodies and his own compromised condition as a leftover thing:

INSCRIPTION ON A BURST PATTERN ANTIQUE ZITHER

Tao'an's possession. Exquisite burst patterning: sharp, severe, like the blade of a sword; not a single hair out of place.
I speak with you; you respond to me.

斷紋古琴銘

陶庵收藏。斷紋之妙，棱棱如劍鋒，毫髮不毯。
吾與爾言，爾亦予諾。⁵⁰

The first four characters of the inscription—"I speak with you" 吾與爾言—allude to a scene at the beginning of chapter 17 in the *Analects* where amid the decline of feudal order, a steward attempts to force a meeting with Confucius by offering him a gift: "I have something to tell you . . . " 予與爾言.⁵¹ The steward pushes Confucius to accept public office: "Can a man be called virtuous if he clutches a cherished possession in his bosom while his country is going astray? 懷其寶而迷其邦，可謂仁乎 . . . Can a man be called wise if he is eager to act, yet misses every opportunity to do so? 好從事而亟失時，可謂知乎 . . . The days and months go by, time is not with us" 日月逝矣，歲不我與.⁵² Confucius eventually assents to the steward's brash request, yet the terms of his final agreement remain ambiguous: "All right, I shall accept an office" 諾。吾將仕矣.⁵³ Read in this light, Zhang Dai's address to the zither insinuates his own ambivalent attitudes toward his cherished possessions or the choice of retirement in times of disorder, and yet also wryly suggests his long-suffering instrument's begrudging service for its stubborn custodian. The inscription's call and response, that a future "you" might one day hear "me," nevertheless finds pathos in irony, invoking the power of a sound-producing object to communicate on its own terms with a faithful interlocutor, bringing the lingering tones of the past into the present.⁵⁴

Although individual inscriptions dwell on the peculiar details of the twenty-eight objects, Zhang Dai asks his readers to approach the ensemble as a single composition. Adhering to classical prescriptions, Zhang's sequence begins with the topic of naming. Invoking his own cognomen, Tao'an 陶庵, the preface reflects on the relationship between a personal "name" (*hao* 號 or *ming*) and famous collections of objects, suggesting that the motivation for his twenty-eight inscriptions was the recognition, and a concomitant desire to preserve the "surname" (*xingshi* 姓氏) of his family's things. While his notional objective is to restore "Zhang" family property, the appeal to horizontal relations of friendship suspends hierarchical chains of patrimony among grandfather, uncles, and cousins. By removing his father and his father's things from this collective of "friends," he sidesteps the thorny topic of reclaiming his own inheritance[55]:

INSCRIPTIONS ON TWENTY-EIGHT FRIENDS (WITH PREFACE)

Tao'an remarked: Luling [Ouyang Xiu] had a taste for the uncommon and took "Six Ones" as his sobriquet. "Old Iron" [Yang Weizhen 楊維楨 (1296–1370)] was fond of antiquities and was renowned for his "Seven Guests." As for my family's old things, more than half have been lost, yet I still remember their names. They are just like old friends, so I call them "friends."

二十八友銘并序

陶庵曰：廬陵嗜奇，六一為號；老鐵好古，七客著名。余家舊物，失去強半，而余尚識其姓氏，如得故友，故曰友也。[56]

The author's short preface identifies a model for his collection in Ouyang Xiu's group of "Six Ones" (Liuyi 六一). Forced out of office, Ouyang coined a new literary epithet, "Retired Scholar of Six Ones" (Liuyi jushi 六一居士), placing himself as one more object alongside his five possessions: books, his collection of rubbings, a zither, a chess set, and a wine jug.[57] Ouyang Xiu did not inscribe his fellow "ones," and Zhang Dai did not place himself within his group of friends or adopt the title of his collection as a cognomen; nevertheless, the reference suggests that Zhang, like Ouyang, was concerned with the way a collector's sense of self both emerges from and yet can be hidden or dispersed within his things.[58]

In writing on his "Twenty-Eight Friends," Zhang at once seeks continuity with the legacies of earlier connoisseurs and works to revivify what had become a comparatively tired trope.[59] Zhang's reference to poet-collector and fellow "imperishable worthy" of Yue, Yang Weizhen, resonates with a broader early Qing investment in promoting the Yuan dynasty (1279–1368), despite its Mongolian heritage, as a "legitimate object" of loyalist longing.[60] Following Ouyang Xiu, Yang Weizhen presented himself as the seventh thing in his "Hut of Seven Guests" 七客者之寮, joining "Sir Iron Dragon of Dongting" 洞庭鐵龍君 (an iron cross-flute), "Hulü of the Western Regions' Pearl" 西域斛律珠 (a *huqin* 胡琴 or "spike fiddle"), "Master Guan Tong of Xiangshan" 象山管氏筒 (a bamboo flute with no holes), "Master Autumn Jiao of Chicheng" 赤城焦氏秋 (a zither), "Wenshan's Jade Girdle Stone" 文山玉帶石 (Wen Tianxiang's inkstone), and "Master Tao's Ancient Spring" 陶氏太古春 (a ceramic pot once owned by the First Qin Emperor).[61] "We each forget [distinctions] among the six" 蓋相忘于六者之間, Yang writes, "so it is unknown if the master is a guest, or the guest is a master" 不知主為客, 客為主也 [. . .] "to the extent that the self forgets things, and things forget the self, do the positions of 'master' and 'guest' still pertain?" 至我忘物, 物忘我，主客何有哉.[62]

In contrast to the models offered by Ouyang Xiu or Yang Weizhen, however, the relationship between Tao'an and his twenty-eight friends appears provisional and open ended. Zhang's assembly of partly absent presences—a sprawling collection of miniature collections that registers the unfortunate fates of other deceased collectors—fails to secure a titular cognomen ("Six Ones") or designate a shared residence ("Hut of Seven Guests"). His unruly congregation, in this sense, thwarts a single, straightforward act of ownership through naming. Yang's erasure of the boundary between master and possession assumes for Zhang a temporal dimension as the remembering self dwells within what remains of his family's fragile mementos. The owner's loss of mastery in making friends with things cannot now be extricated from the human deaths these leftover objects call to mind or the pseudo-epitaphic themes of sacrifice and burial that his inscriptions upon them broach.

VIRTUAL INSCRIPTION

How many of Zhang Dai's inscriptions were engraved onto the objects they describe remains unclear (more than half of his "friends," he admits, were lost). Dream reminiscences like "Shen Meigang," "Pine Fossil," "Wood Like a Dragon," and "Celestial Inkstone," in addition to Zhang's comments on his brother Shanmin's proclivities as an antiquarian, nevertheless, suggest that he understood *ming* to be not a merely literary exercise but a material practice of carving words, one that required collaboration with a hired artisan. Efforts to discern whether any or which of his words might have been written with a knife overlook the way Zhang purposefully foregrounds such ambiguity in order to cast the notion of durability as an aesthetic problem and open question.[63] In addressing his "Twenty-Eight Friends," Zhang treats the fraught connection between a purportedly engraved message and its underlying substrate as a critical theme, a means of assessing tensions between a professed search for resilience and lived experiences of dislocation in the mid-seventeenth century.[64]

The first object in the collection is a mini-collection of some thirteen rain-flower pebbles (*yuhua shi* 雨花石), souvenirs of Nanjing, amassed by Zhang Rulin, then passed to an uncle, and finally to Zhang Dai. As the reader begins to survey Zhang's group of friends, any sense of a discrete thing unspools into an array of colors, as the collection discloses a series of smaller collections. Noting their "strange forms and weird shapes," Zhang's six-character inscription, itself a marvel of lapidary concision, addresses the friend as a collective:

INSCRIPTION ON RAIN FLOWER STONES

My grandfather's possession. Rain flower stones passed from my grandfather to my uncle and then to me. Thirteen pebbles amassed over three generations, with strange forms and weird shapes that cannot be fathomed.

Offering of strange stones, are they dissimilar?

雨花石銘

大父收藏。雨花石，自余祖余叔及余，積三世而得十三枚，奇形怪狀，不可思議。
怪石供, 將毋同。[65]

Zhang's *ming* weaves together two allusions: "offering of strange stones" (*guaishi gong* 怪石供) refers to a collection of 298 strange pebbles that Northern Song poet Su Shi bequeathed to the monk Foyin 佛印

(1032–1098).⁶⁶ "Are they dissimilar" 將毋同 invokes Ruan Xiu's 阮修 (ca. 270–312) famous response to Wang Yan's 王衍 (256–311) question as to the similarities between Daoist and Confucian teachings in the early medieval anthology, *A New Account of Tales of the World* (*Shishuo xinyu* 世說新語).⁶⁷ Ruan's answer is a diffident affirmation of affinity ("they are not unalike"), one that earned him the title "Three Word Aide" (*sanyu yuan* 三語掾) and became a euphemism for his intimate friendship with Wei Jie 衛玠 (d. 312). Zhang Dai begins with the three-character allusion to Su Shi's legendary collection, before complementing it with the perfect "three-word aide," one that evokes memories of mutual appreciation between kindred spirits and an overarching synthesis of Buddhist, Daoist, and Confucian perspectives.

Zhang's allusion to Su Shi's "offering of strange stones" finally calls into question the very purpose of carving words in stone. After receiving Su's gift, the monk "Foyin wanted to carve Su's words in stone" 佛印以其言刻諸石, a request that led Su and Foyin's friend, the monk Daoqian 道潛 (1043–?), to note that "carving words is an illusion" 刻其言者，亦幻也, yet that when one grasps the nature of such illusoriness, "as for carving or not carving words, neither is not feasible" 刻與不刻，無不可者.⁶⁸ In asking whether Rulin's pebbles are any different from Su Shi's gift, Zhang implicitly reminds himself and his readers to avoid attachment to the idea of making a mark while avoiding attachment to the idea that "not carving words" somehow transcends this same illusion. Inscription should be a contingent practice or expedient means, one that gestures beyond possessive desire yet invites a measure of lingering intimacy with things to obviate attachment to feelings of detachment.⁶⁹ Making a mark, here, is not a simple expression of ownership or a naïve assertion of faith in the relative permanence of hard materials but a means of disciplining perception to cultivate superior levels of discernment.

Whereas "Rain Flower Stones" questions the relationship between an inscribed message and its underlying substrate, Zhang elsewhere presents inscription as an imaginative attempt to re-mark a surface that already bears engraved script. Historians of material culture have, as Deng Zhicheng's research on Zhang Yingyao attests, frequently used Zhang Dai's writings as evidence for the appraisal of Ming makers' marks and artisanal brands.⁷⁰ Three of the friends are associated with the alluring yet likely spurious Xuande 宣德 (1426–1435) reign mark, a source of fascination for late Ming sojourners to the temple markets of Beijing and a later focus of loyalist lament.[71] Zhang's seven-character "Inscription on a Xuande Filled-In Lacquer Pyxis" hints at the latent political implications of the Xuande reign mark in the early Qing—a label that evokes a halcyon era of peace and cultural splendor—by concealing the characters for "return [to]" 復 and Ming 明:

INSCRIPTION ON A XUANDE FILLED-IN LACQUER PYXIS

Tao'an's possession. A Xuande pyxis, with the air of peeled off lacquer wood. With an orchid cactus above. Red like coral, green like emerald.
   Layer upon layer, so bright and brilliant.

宣德填漆盒銘

陶庵收藏。宣德盒，脫盡漆木之氣，上有曇花，赤如珊瑚，綠如祖母。
   層復層，既鮮且明。[72]

The last four characters ("so bright and brilliant" 既鮮且明) allude to a paragon of loyalty in the *Classic of Poetry*: "Very clear-sighted was he and wise. He assured his own safety" 既明且哲，以保其身.[73] Zhang's inscription seeks continuity with the past in its self-presentation as a supplement to the Xuande mark, even as its indefinite objecthood (whether the *ming* was carved or written for an already lost thing) transpose these attachments to the domains of reminiscence and longing. His inscription's uncertain connection to its time-worn substrate—and the central motif of a night-blooming "orchid cactus" (*tanhua* 曇花), an image of fleeting brilliance—insinuates a belated and comparatively insecure loyalism.

Across his selection of friends, Zhang Dai highlights yet queries the significance of artisanal markings. He flaunts, for instance, the prestige of palace provenance for Zhang Rulin's orchid pyxis and the attribution of a three-stringed lute to Fan Kunbai while boasting that Shanmin's bronze censer was superior to a Gan Wentai 甘文臺 make or that Silversmith Shi could "never dream" of matching such a product.[74] In another inscription, Zhang dwells on his ability to recognize the identity of a maker and hence appreciate the value of an object without needing to rely on the presence of a maker's mark, bragging: "Since antiquity there have been many famous paintings that bear no autographs; as for this pot, I took a look and knew right away it was a Gong Chun make" 古來名畫，多不落款。此壺望而知為龔春也.⁷⁵ Against this backdrop, Zhang Dai presents his inscription on Zhang Yefang's jade hairpin—an object with newfound political significance for the remnant subjects who resisted the Manchu order to shave one's head—as a wistful attempt to write over an artisan's mark⁷⁶:

INSCRIPTION ON A CYAN JADE HAIRPIN

Uncle Eryun owned a hairpin of western cyan jade, around three inches in length, the whole thing covered with ornate wyverns. On its surface are twelve characters in seal script, carved in relief: "Thinking of my lord, he is as temperate as jade, made by Lu Zigang."
 Don't take me as ugly, accompany my head of white hair,
 You are my tightly bound friend.

碧玉簪銘

爾蘊叔收藏。西碧水料簪，長三寸許，遍體文螭。上有「言念君子，溫其如玉，陸子岡制」陽篆文十二字。
 不我醜，伴白首，是我結髮之友。⁷⁷

Lu Zigang's stamp was among the most fashionable jade brands in the late Ming marketplace. Presented as a visual ornament comparable to the patina and textures of other surfaces in the collection, Lu's twelve-character etching is based on a stock allusion to the *Classic of Poetry*, a common analogy between the qualities of jade and the integrity of a gentleman.⁷⁸ Zhang Dai responds to this message on his own terms, offering a nostalgic and comparatively intimate expression of the companionship the hairpin now proffers in old age, punning on "holding up hair" (*jiefa* 結髮) and a "tightly bound" friendship. The phrase "holding up hair" could refer to a wedding ritual, in which bride and groom tie their hair together as a symbol of marriage, or to adolescence: fourteen-year-olds were expected to knot their hair upon reaching adulthood (the "year of bound hair" 束髮之年). From either perspective, the inscription foregrounds the irony that this alluring souvenir of youth might find renewed purpose in its aged owner's stubborn refusal to cut his "white" locks.

Zhang Dai reclaims Lu Zigang's generic label, rewording a trademark slogan: literary inscription as an expression of friendship supplants the artisanal, or merely physical act of engraving script. Disavowal of attachment to makers' marks, nevertheless, fails to conceal the care Zhang invests in determining their details: by foregrounding the dispersal of these old things, he finds a new pretext for the connoisseurship of brands, recasting his calculated performance of discernment as an act of recognizing old acquaintances, as if he might be acquisitive and ascetic at once. His inscribed profession of devotion goes beyond Lu Zigang's praise for the "jade-like" virtues of the hairpin's owner by allowing the thing to occupy the position of an "I" (*wo* 我). Introducing the possibility of a split between the "subject of enunciation" (the "I" to whom the act of speaking is attributed) and the "subject of speech" (the "I" represented within the poem), his message to the hairpin "unmoors" the first-person pronoun from its "contextual and bodily grounding."[79]

INSCRIPTION AND METAMORPHOSIS

A generative tension between the claim of inscriptional permanence and experiences of change and loss is crystallized in Zhang's most illustrious inscriptions, on a fragment named "Wood Like a Dragon." Zhang's two *ming* for this peculiar piece of petrified driftwood were included in *Collected Writings of Langhuan* as the first two of his sixty-eight inscriptions on objects—they also form a kernel for the vignette "Wood Like a Dragon," a piece Philip Kafalas reads as a "suggestive microcosm" for *Dream Reminiscences* as a whole.[80] Emerging from the Liao Sea to find Chang Yuchun 常遇春 (1330–1369), or Prince Chang of Kaiping 常開平王, a pivotal figure in the founding of the Ming dynasty, the object survives the conflagration of the Kaiping residence and journeys to the marketplace where Zhang Dai's father, Zhang Yaofang, offers seventeen rhinoceros horn cups in exchange for the charred "dragon."[81] Yaofang repurposes the fossilized fragment to earn himself a position as an assistant administrator to Zhu Shouyong 朱壽鏞 (d. 1639; the eleventh Prince of Lu 魯王), before being dismissed for a minor indiscretion: the object consequently emblematizes the vicissitudes of the Zhang family's connections to Ming royalty. For Zhang Dai, the "dragon" embodies an underlying tension between his faith in the cyclical progression of time and traumatic experiences of rupture: Does the death and rebirth of the fossil suggest the inevitability of renewal—that destruction entails creation?[82] Or does its uncertain fate in the 1640s evoke a violent rift between two temporal orders—a "before" and "after"—that cannot be overcome? Zhang's own inscriptions name and preserve, rather than work to resolve, this sense of interpretative instability.

The wooden dragon's apparently self-motivated travels throughout China during the course of the Ming dynasty ironically recall legendary tales of dynastic portents like the "nine cauldrons" (*jiuding* 九鼎) cast by the sage-king Yu 禹, animate monuments whose movements and metamorphoses embody the "progression of History," conferring upon their custodians a legitimacy to rule.[83] The Zhang family's own mutable "mandate of sovereignty" subsequently appears to be caught between its owners' professions of political loyalism and bathetic spectacle. When Zhu Yihai 朱以海 (1618–1662), the thirteenth Prince of Lu and an ineffectual Southern Ming regent during the Manchu invasion, left Taizhou to retreat to Shaoxing in the ninth month of 1646, Zhang Dai welcomed the royal entourage into his residence for a lavish feast and operatic performance.[84] Late at night they retired to his Apricot Blossom Bookroom where they discussed opera and drank with the painter Chen Hongshou into the early hours of the morning—the prince, Zhang notes, took this opportunity to sit upon "Wood Like a Dragon" as if it were some kind of makeshift throne.[85] This moment becomes an ironic inversion of the episode where Zhang Dai's father had offered the same piece of driftwood to the former Prince of Lu (Zhu Shouyong) for official advancement before his dismissal for misnaming the thing with a forbidden character (*fanhui* 犯諱).[86]

In contrast to previous accounts of this enigmatic artifact, I read Zhang Dai's engraved verse and retrospective preface as a meditation on the challenge of making a mark, a reprise of his concern across the "Twenty-Eight Friends" sequence with the meaning of inscriptive durability when transience seems permanent: "Wood Like a Dragon" is, in effect, an inscription about the difficulties of inscription. To begin with, this is the sole instance where Zhang Dai inscribes an artifact from his dead father's collection. And yet, the object only enters the Zhang household after Zhang Yaofang's hapless act of misnaming it at court: "So [the Prince of Lu] vigorously refused it and it was left in the chief administrator's office. When my father died, I brought it home to pass it down as a precious heirloom" 峻辭之，遂留長史署中。先君子棄世，余載歸，傳為世寶.[87] Zhang Dai's inscription on a memento of his father oddly recalls not Yaofang's virtue but his errors.

Over half of the piece in *Dream Reminiscences* subsequently focuses on failures to devise a fitting name for this elusive thing: Yaofang violated a taboo in labeling the object "Wooden Dragon" (Mulong 木龍); Zhang's coterie came up with five competing names:

> At a poetry gathering held in 1637 I invited renowned gentlemen to bestow a name upon [the thing] and to eulogize it with pithy expressions. Zhou Monong (n.d.) named it "Wood Like a Dragon," Ni Hongbao [Ni Yuanlu 倪元璐 (1594–1644)] named it "Wood Residing Dragon," Qi Shipei [Qi Biaojia 祁彪佳 (1603–1645)] named it "Sea Raft," Wang Shimei [Wang Yexun 王業洵 (n.d.)] named it "Raft Wave," and Zhang Yiru [Zhang Hong 張弘 (n.d.)] named it "Land Raft." Their poems filled an album.
>
> 丁丑詩社，懇名公人錫之名，并賦小言咏之。周墨農字以木猶龍，倪鴻寶字以木寓龍，祁世培字以海槎，王士美字以槎浪，張毅儒字以陸槎，詩遂盈帙。[88]

Zhang's own names draw attention to their inadequacy, emphasizing either provisionality ("Residing . . .") or vague semblance ("Like . . ."). Poetic descriptions of the log from both Zhang and his coterie copy the rhyme scheme and imagery of Su Shi's account of a "Wooden Artificial Mound" (mu jiashan 木假山), an object cherished by two generations of the Su family as a weathered embodiment of their integrity in spite of Song dynasty factional strife. It is as though Zhang concedes that the best way to account for the "wooden dragon's" significance was through strained allusion to earlier poems.[89] His dream reminiscence ends with an incongruous account of the marooned "dragon's fat and clumsy body, weighing over a thousand pounds" 木龍體肥癡，重千餘斤, before calculating the sums spent on the log's transportation: "From beginning to end, costs reached one hundred taels, not to mention the prices of gifts given away in exchange. Ah! The wooden dragon might be said to have met fortune" 前後費至百金，所易價不與焉。嗚呼，木龍可謂遇矣。[90] Zhang's concluding remarks pun on the name he had initially bestowed on the log ("Wood Residing Dragon"), swapping "lodge" (*yu* 寓) with "to encounter fortune" (*yu* 遇), as if wryly begrudging his family's unlikely heirloom the capital invested in its recovery. Read against this "preface," his inscriptions evoke a compromised effort to name a seemingly un-nameable fragment, to inscribe something—whether an "empty vessel" or a "node of interlocking loyalties" to princely pastimes and lost moments of friendship—that cannot be fully inscribed.[91]

This pervasive sense of indeterminacy is compounded by the admission of Zhang Dai's close friend Qi Biaojia, who attended the 1637 gathering, that not only did the name "Wood Like a Dragon" come from another attendee (Zhou Monong), but that it was he, Qi, who inscribed the charred log ("Who inscribed it? The retired scholar of Allegory Mountain" 誰其銘之？寓山居士).[92] At least two of the friends in this potlatch gathering to name the thing (Ni Yuanlu and Qi Biaojia) committed suicide seven years later with the fall of the Ming—their deaths haunt Zhang's post-conquest reminiscences of inscribing his enigmatic possession, inflecting the poet's themes of revival and transcendence, perhaps explaining the reticence he feels toward the prospect of inscriptive closure:

> I rubbed a mound-like protuberance on the dragon's skull and inscribed it:[93]

> In the chasm of night, wind and thunder,
> Soaring raft, transforms to stone[94];
> Seas rise up, mountains quake,
> Mist and clouds are wiped away;
> It is said there is a dragon lodging within,
> Call to it and it will emerge!

> Furthermore:

> He who disturbed the dragon, Master Zhang,
> On a mound-like protuberance, inscribed:
> With what might I compare it?
> Autumn tides and summer clouds.

余磨其龍腦尺木，勒銘志之，曰：

夜壑風雷，騫槎化石；
海立山崩，烟雲滅沒；
謂有龍焉，呼之或出。

又曰:

擾龍張子，尺木書銘。
何以似之？秋濤夏雲。[95]

Zhang's *ming* disclose a struggle between a desire to make an authoritative mark on a hard surface (he underscores this physical gesture: "I rubbed a mound-like protuberance on the dragon's skull and inscribed it") and the substrate's status as an elusive, almost intangible entity. The first line of the second *ming* draws attention to the embodied act of writing, presenting the mark as an intrusion that disturbs or "agitates" (*rao* 擾) the spirit of the thing, while the second line—the closest Zhang comes to his own "fine name" (*meiming* 美名) for the object—is an image of "autumn tides and summer clouds," numinous impressions of flux and ethereality.[96] The materiality of the mark appears similarly inconsistent: Zhang's prefatory vignette claims he "carved" (*le* 勒) the inscription (*ming* 銘), yet the inscription itself states that it was "drafted" (*shu* 書) with brush-based calligraphy on the dragon's "mound-like protuberance" (*chimu* 尺木), a lump in the shape of a mountain-censer on the dragon's skull without which the creature could not ascend to heaven.[97] Zhang's inscription, in other words, wavers between fixity and a sense of elegant improvisation or inky ephemerality, as if reconciling the reader to contingency and evanescence in order to forestall fears of finality.

Zhang Dai aspires for his inscriptions to resist ossification as a set of mute markings, inviting later readers to reactivate his words as a spoken summons to a still-sentient thing: "It is said there is a dragon lodging within, call to it and it will emerge!" Zhang incorporates this same line in his sequence of poems on the (ironically named) Happy Garden (Kuai yuan 快園), a dilapidated estate that he moves into after the fall of the Ming: "Call out and it will emerge, there is supposed to be a dragon residing within" 呼之或出，謂有龍焉.[98] His friend's eyebrow commentary takes this to be a veiled form of self-reference, that Zhang identifies himself as the sleeping dragon lying in the ruined garden.[99] These correspondences suggest the possibility of a degree of self-projection in Zhang's call to the "recumbent dragon" concealed within this driftwood fragment, that he hopes his inscribed apostrophe to the thing becomes the thing's address to its future readers, a friend who might intuit and revivify his dormant intent.

Zhang's preoccupation with the challenge of naming "Wood Like a Dragon," the central theme in his inscription and the accompanying vignette it inspired, suggests the difficulty of accounting for the competing memories that this enigmatic fragment elicits—the ineptitude of current pretenders to the Ming throne, his father's death, the traumatic suicides of his close friends. His fascination with the dragon's shape-shifting body, however, intimates an underlying concern that his inscription will not harm or deny this object's capacity for further transformations—extolling metamorphosis becomes a way of adapting to uncertainty and ineluctable change.[100] The act of making a mark manifests Zhang's fraught search for vitality amid charred ruins, or a promise of rebirth within recalcitrant fragments of the recent past.[101]

THE JUDGMENT OF THINGS

While the burdens of commemoration conditioned the ways in which inscriptions were written and read, late imperial critics conceived of the *ming* genre as an admonitory apparatus, with writers using the properties of household objects to reprove and correct human behavior. A final comment on Zhang Dai's sequence identifies the significance of this genealogy, claiming that the "Twenty-Eight Friends" as a group are no different from "Yao's warnings" (Yao jie 堯誡) and the "inscriptions of monarchs" (*diwang zhu ming* 帝王諸銘), examples of sagely admonitions etched onto tools for moral cultivation.[102]

The monitory resources of inscription offered remnant subjects like Wang Fuzhi in the company of his brush and small turtle-shaped inkstone on Stone Boat Mountain a means with which to orient, instruct, and repair loyalist bodies. Zhang Dai's readers infer similarities between the "Twenty-Eight Friends" sequence and King Wu's engraved maxims on objects ranging from his mat and wrist-rest to walking stick and wash basin.[103] Their comments invite reflection on the extent to which themes of self-correction inform Zhang's treatment of things as friends. Beyond commemoration, what other messages might object inscriptions impart?

Zhang's meditations on inscriptive impermanence for his "Burst Pattern Antique Zither," "Rain Flower Stones," "Xuande Filled-In Lacquer Pyxis," and "Cyan Jade Hairpin" seek to reconcile philosophical detachment with loyalist attachments to the past, themes taken up in "Wood Like a Dragon's" evocation of endurance through metamorphosis. Tensions between words and things elsewhere in the "Twenty-Eight Friends" sequence, however, intimate more unnerving ruptures, drawing attention back to the decadence and depravity that led to the breakup of the Zhang family collections, threatening to undermine any straightforward search for transcendence. Confusion between the positions of "me" and "you," already apparent in "Burst Pattern Antique Zither" and "Cyan Jade Hairpin," elsewhere assumes disquieting undertones as eloquent objects adopt the perspective of an "I" to reprove their owners' loss of dignity.

By following the passage of certain possessions from fathers to sons, Zhang Dai implies that his family's greatest accomplishments as connoisseurs were inextricably entangled with some of their worst excesses. Five of the "friends" come from Zhang's second eldest paternal uncle (Zhongshu), Zhang Lianfang's famed collection: "Inkstone Mountain," "White Ding Ware Censer," "Small Beauty Chalice," "Ge Ware Flagon," and "Ge Ware Topknot Tuft Vase." These objects later passed to his only son, Zhang Dai's sadistic cousin Yanke. Lianfang embodies a family connection to the flourishing artistic milieu of late Ming Jiangnan while personifying the circumstances of its demise. Yanke, meanwhile, represents the dangers of sentimental excess, with a murderous disposition that emerges from tyrannical obsessions with things. In inscribing several of the objects that passed from Lianfang to Yanke as friends, Zhang Dai examines the behavior of these two men from the perspective of their possessions, sympathizing with objects as victims of human folly. After failing the provincial examinations in 1603 and acquiring a "pitch-black ironwood table with a natural aspect" from a local official in Huaian, Zhang Lianfang worked to become one of the five top collectors south of the Yangzi.[104] Lianfang eventually passed away from illness during his service with a local militia in the midst of the dynastic transition: his valiant defense of Wanshui's parapets was defined by an unflagging commitment to the redemptive powers of art, vigorously painting landscapes for friends under candlelight in spite of the danger around him.[105] His only son, Zhang Dai's impulsive cousin Yanke, sold his father's collection immediately and frittered away the money he made:

> Second Uncle [Lianfang] had a single son, E [Yanke], who could not be disciplined and never tried to earn his own living. He instantly depleted several

tens of thousands of *taels* from Second Uncle's official stipend. Second Uncle was fond of antiques and bequeathed his goblets and wine-vases, libation vessels and offering cups, famous paintings and bolts of fine silk to his son, a collection of a thousand myriad things; his son exhausted all of this in a matter of days.

仲叔一子萼，任誕不羈，不事生業，仲叔計數万輒盡，宦囊又數万亦輒盡。仲叔好古玩，其所遺尊罍卣彝，名畫法錦以千萬計，不數日亦輒盡。[106]

Zhang Dai was selective in his identification of "friends" from Lianfang's large reserves of antiques, identifying things that speak both to Lianfang's fame as a collector and the circumstances surrounding the breakup and dispersal of his collection. A short vignette in *Dream Reminiscences* on "Second Uncle's Antiques" begins with Lianfang's acquisition of a "White Ding Ware Censer" (and his "Ge Ware Flagon" and "Ge Ware Topknot Tuft Vase") and concludes with a reference to a "Small Beauty Chalice" obtained when Lianfang finally assumed an official position in 1628 in Henan, the seat of the late Zhou kings.

Zhang Dai presents these two sets of objects as bookends to Lianfang's life: his apprenticeship as a youth with Zhu Shimen 朱石門 (n.d.) and the demise of his collection in the hands of his son, Yanke:

Uncle Lianfang followed Weiyang [Zhu Shimen] in his youth and became a refined connoisseur. He obtained a white Ding ware censer, a Ge ware bottle and a Guan ware wine tureen. Xiang Molin [Xiang Yuanbian] wanted to buy them for five-hundred catties, but Lianfang refused: "I want to keep them to be buried with me."

葆生叔少從渭陽遊，遂精賞鑑。得白定爐、哥窯瓶、官窯酒匜，項墨林以五百金售之，辭曰：留以殉葬。

Henan is a "repository of bronze" and so he [Lianfang] obtained several cartloads of bronze artifacts. The "Small Beauty Chalice" was one of fifteen or sixteen specimens, with a verdant patina penetrating its bones, like jadeite, or "ghostly pupils,"[107] some couldn't look at it properly. It returned to Yanke and was one day lost, or it may have been taken into the Dragon's Lair.

河南為銅藪，所得銅器盈數車，「美人觚」一種，大小十五六枚，青綠徹骨，如翡翠，如鬼眼青，有不可正視之者，歸之燕客，一日失之。或是龍藏收去。[108]

These two memories—Lianfang's refusal to sell his censer to Xiang Yuanbian and the disappearance of the enigmatic "small beauty"—form the basis for his inscriptions on these two members of the collective. The censer evokes Lianfang's fidelity to his things, attachments that transcend the logic of the market and end up being carried to the grave. The chalice, meanwhile, stands as a witness to the breakup and dispersal of Lianfang's collection, critiquing the decadence and impropriety of Zhang's family members. Just as Yanke's recklessness represents the dark underside to his father's fastidious refinement, Zhang suggests that censer and chalice tell two versions of the same story.

Into the Tomb: White Ding Ware Censer

As with each of his friends, Zhang Dai begins with a short description of the object, specifying its dimensions and patina, before composing a terse *ming* that addresses the thing. While in the essay on "Second Uncle's Antiques," the White Ding Ware Censer and the Small Beauty Chalice are mentioned as props in an account of Lianfang's personality, in the "Twenty-Eight Friends" sequence they are cast as independent protagonists, with Zhang Dai talking to them directly:

INSCRIPTION ON A WHITE DING WARE CENSER

Uncle Eryou owned a white ding ware censer, murky like the patterns in pinewood. Xiang Molin of Jiahe wanted to buy it for five-hundred catties, yet Second Uncle declined, and had it buried with him.[109]

    Five hundred strings of coins, was I deceived?
    And so, the offer was declined in order to be buried with him.

白定爐銘

二酉叔收藏。白定爐，松文慘澹。嘉禾項墨林以五百金售之，二叔辭，以殉葬。
　　五百緡，豈余誑？固辭之，以殉葬。[110]

Other early Qing writers use white Ding censers to limn the destruction of the transition and the decadence or greed that prefigured the Ming collapse: the mid-seventeenth-century miscellany, *Speaking of the Past at Flower Village* (*Huacun tan wang* 花村談往), as Wai-yee Li notes, records the convoluted fate of a white Ding censer, an object that also passed through Xiang Yuanbian's hands, to describe "calamities brought about by antiques" 古玩致禍.[111] Jiang Shaoshu's 姜紹書 (ca. 1580–ca. 1650s) *Notes from the Resonant Rock Studio* (*Yunshi zhai bitan* 韻石齋筆談) narrates the biography and eventual destruction of his family's "white Ding cauldron-censer" (Dingyao ding 定窯鼎), a ceramic imitation of a bronze ritual vessel, one that generates counterfeit doubles and thus negates any reliable sense of an authentic original.[112]

In his own take on this multivalent trope, Zhang Dai restages the script of Lianfang declining to sell his possession to Xiang, this time taking up the issue with, or even as, the object itself (it is unclear to whom Zhang's "I" ultimately refers).[113] Lianfang claimed that he would take his porcelain to the tomb, a stubborn display of his devotion as a collector staunchly opposed to the lure of money—now the censer's fate of being "buried alive" becomes an expression of its fidelity. "To accompany [them/him] in death" (*xun* 殉), a recurring motif in the art of remnant subjects, recalls the practice of palace ladies being put to death and buried with their lords: the choice of words, here, subtly invokes themes of martyrdom and sacrifice at the fall of a dynasty.[114] What from Lianfang's perspective looks like an untrammeled relationship with his possessions, from the censer's viewpoint appears as forced suicide on behalf of an uncompromising master.

Out of the Tomb: Small Beauty Chalice

Zhang Dai repeatedly alludes to the links between Yanke's tyrannical impulses in the acquisition of material goods and his violence toward women: impatiently smashing rocks from his estate, earning the title "Unbound First Emperor of Qin" 窮極秦始皇, he abused his slaves, tortured a maid, and almost incited a local revolt after her husband's suicide.[115] In a biography of his cousin, Zhang recalls how Yanke once spent fifty *taels* on a Xuan bronze censer, yet destroyed the object when he hastily threw it into a fire to improve its patina.[116] At a monastery outside Hangzhou, Yanke acquired a Lingbi ink grinder 靈璧硯 named "Verdant Hills, White

Clouds" (Qingshan baiyun 青山白雲), an object he accidentally split in two while chiseling its ridge—in response to this mistake, he smashes the stone's purple sandalwood stand with an iron hammer before throwing the debris into West Lake.[117] The small bronze beauty's experience in Yanke's possession tacitly registers these depredations, hinting at both the despotic whims and sadistic cruelty that subtend this wealthy family's concern for its property—unlike the melted censer or shattered inkstone, however, Zhang's inscription endows the chalice with a recessive agency, asking how the object views and eludes its former owner's caprice.[118]

In addressing the bronze vessel, Zhang Dai notes "her" superlative beauty, while reciting the line "a chalice that isn't a chalice" (*gu bu gu* 觚不觚), a byword in the late Ming for decadence and ritual impropriety, one that invokes the specter of Yanke's profligacy and the subsequent loss of the Zhang family vessels in his hands.[119] As if subverting the Confucian view of inscription as a means of "rectifying names," Zhang dwells upon ruptures between name and thing, using Confucius's words to commemorate a ritual object that has lost its original and therefore proper form:

INSCRIPTION ON A SMALL BEAUTY CHALICE

Uncle Eryou owned a Han dynasty bronze chalice in the shape of a small beauty; it was a foot and three inches in height. Half embellished with patterns, the whole body in halcyon hue.
 A chalice that isn't a chalice, with an elegant halcyon hue.

小美人觚銘

二酉叔收藏。漢銅小美人觚，長尺有三寸，半截花紋，渾身翡翠。觚不觚，翡翠之都。[120]

The chalice, to begin with, is one of the more enigmatic objects in Zhang's collective: as "Second Uncle's Antiques" reveals, Lianfang acquired fifteen or sixteen variously sized "small beauty" vessels, so called due to their "slender waists" (*xiyao* 細腰), suggesting that Zhang's friend stands as the remnant of a larger lost ensemble. Zhang elsewhere notes that the bronze for this particular type of Han dynasty chalice suffered from extensive corrosion due to the brine and salt-blanched soil of Henan, and thus that the "substance" (*zhi* 質) of such damaged metal was "less valuable" than the Zhou dynasty cauldrons (*ding* 鼎) or Shang dynasty libation vessels (*yi* 彝) of Shaanxi.[121] As Lianfang bragged of dragging his white censer to the grave, the small beauty chalice emerges as an object at once out of time and out of place, an interred antique, dormant for millennia, exhumed whether through tomb robbery or happenstance from the earth.[122]

Standing apart from the cartloads of ritual artifacts Lianfang found in the ancestral homes of the Zhou lords, the "small beauty's" seductive "body" (*hunshen feicui* 渾身翡翠) and "flowery patina" (*huawen* 花紋) evoke, in miniature, the role of the femme fatale as emblem of dynastic fall.[123] This alluring, yet improper bronze vessel, one whose ghostly demeanor deflects its custodian's gaze, emerges as a witness to Yanke's recklessness. Zhang Dai's attention to this sensuous object's "feminine" charms infers Lianfang's decadent taste as a bronze connoisseur (a possible portent of his misplaced priorities), while its loss in Yanke's hands echoes the way his concubines were said to have "scattered overnight," as if "they had been an illusion."[124] Yanke's erratic behavior appears to be to blame for the beauty's disappearance, yet Zhang Dai holds out the possibility that the object escaped the manmade destruction of the Ming cataclysm, finding refuge beyond the human domain in a treasure-filled "dragon's palace" at the bottom of the sea.[125] Zhang's terse inscription discloses an ambivalent attitude toward the object, as if he is unsure whether the glamorous vessel was ultimately a symptom or another victim of his family's misfortunes. Were the attachments things elicit to blame for recent tragedies or were they casualties of human misdemeanor? While Lianfang's censer exemplifies a loyalty that transcends death, the chalice invokes an uncomfortable family history of overindulgence and dissipation. Zhang Dai's inscription suggests how a single object might inspire conflicting feelings of nostalgia and remorse, longing and critical reflection. Such ambivalence extends to the fate of the artifact: Was the beauty a casualty of Yanke's failures or did it survive his family's demise? Is Zhang Dai's inscription for his friend another pseudo-epitaph mourning "her" death or—as in the final lines of "Pine Fossil" and "Wood Like a Dragon"—a call to see if this enigmatic thing might yet respond? By posing these questions, this recalcitrant bronze vessel resists service as an inscribed monument to the virtues of Zhang's family name.

ON REMNANT THINGS

CELESTIAL INKSTONE

I have traced Zhang Dai's propensity to compose inscriptions about the difficulties of inscription in the wake of dynastic transition from his elegiac responses to the inscribed possessions of his great-grandfather ("Shen Meigang") and grandfather ("Pine Fossil") in his prose masterpiece *Dream Reminiscences of Tao'an* to his self-conscious reflections on the impermanence of carved words in writing upon his "Twenty-Eight Friends." This sequence dramatizes tensions between nostalgic longing ("Rain Flower Stones," "Xuande Filled-In Lacquer Pyxis," or "Cyan Jade Hairpin") and critical introspection ("White Ding Ware Censer" and "Small Beauty Chalice"), attachment and detachment, asking whether an inability to ensure fixity amounts to a persistent symptom of rupture or a precondition of its transcendence. I wish to conclude by considering how Zhang Dai works to reconcile these competing impulses within a single inscription.

"Celestial Inkstone"—like "Shen Meigang," "Pine Fossil," and "Wood Like a Dragon"—reads as a retrospective preface for a literary inscription, in this case Zhang's *ming* for his cousin Yanke's inkstone. Like those aforementioned vignettes, the piece may have been written before the fall of the Ming, yet Zhang's meditations on naturalness and artifice, creation and destruction—encapsulated in Yanke's violent obsession with the slab—evoke a heightened pathos when read in light of the dynastic cataclysm.

While in *Dream Reminiscences*, Zhang's vignette concludes with his inscription, it makes more sense to read the piece in reverse, beginning with the *ming* and then following Zhang's thoughts on the contingencies, shady misconduct, and ironic compromises behind his ostensibly conclusive act of naming.[126] This is one of the few inscriptions Zhang composed where the rhetoric of friendship seems misplaced—the inkstone's few anthropomorphic features (its "bulging eyeballs," for instance) read not as evidence of virtue or faithful companionship but as signs of a disturbing alterity. Unlike "Wood Like a Dragon," the vignette that precedes "Celestial Inkstone" in *Dream Reminiscences*, Yanke's inkslab does not recall memories of shared pleasures between lost friends; rather, it evokes sly games of one-upmanship and a tangled web of lies. As if to underscore an uneasy preoccupation with theft, Zhang notes that this superlative stone first appeared in the hands of a brigand imprisoned in a local jail. Unlike "Wood Like a Dragon," Zhang did not preserve his inscription for Yanke's inkstone in his *Collected Writings of Langhuan*:

CELESTIAL INKSTONE

In my youth I saw many inkstones yet did not know how to discern their virtues. When Wang "Uncle Inkstone" of Huizhou arrived, he used archaic markings on discarded inkslabs to establish their value, almost exhausting the reserve of stones in Yue. The more inkstones I observed, their inherent principle began to emerge.

Once I entrusted my friend Qin Yisheng to search for stones, yet he couldn't find any throughout the town. A brigand imprisoned in the Shanyin jail brought a stone, an unhewn rock, in search of two pounds of silver. At that time, I was about to depart for Wulin, and Yisheng, given this pressing matter, was unsure how to make a judgment so presented the stone for Yanke. Yanke pointed at the white eyes of the stone and said: "an ugly mouth of yellow teeth, one should only use it to prop up a wobbly table." And so Yisheng returned the stone to the brigand.

That same night, Yanke used thirty *taels* to snatch the slab, before commissioning Uncle Inkstone to carve it into a celestial inkstone, with five small stars and one great star, a specimen listed as: "Five Stars Surrounding the Moon." Yanke still feared Yisheng might recognize the stone and so pared away the largest star and a smaller one, leaving only three stars.

When Yisheng found out, he was enraged and told me. I laughed and said: "My nephews are like sons." And so, we went to inspect the stone together. Yanke brought it out with both hands. It was red like a horse's liver, smooth and shiny like jade. Below, there were white threads like the nerve fibers in agate, the coiled traces of a fingerprint or a fine seal-script. Above, three stars protrude like bulging eyes. Grinding an inkstick, without a sound, the inky liquid pools and gives off vapors. Yisheng was stupefied, his mouth gaping wide open.

Yanke entrusted me to compose an inscription. My inscription read:

Nüwa repaired heaven,
Without distinguishing between jade and stone.
With the blood of a Great Sea Turtle and the ashes of reeds,

She boiled the glowing clouds of twilight and forged the sun.
The Milky Way was plunged into confusion,
"Three Stars" hang across, "The Winnowing Basket" converges.

天硯

少年視硯，不得硯丑。徽州汪硯伯至，以古款廢硯，立得重价，越中藏石俱盡。閱硯多，硯理出。曾托友人秦一生為余覓石，遍城中無有。山陰獄中大盜出一石，璞耳，索銀二斤。余适往武林，一生造次不能辨，持示燕客。燕客指石中白眼曰：「黃牙臭口，堪留支桌。」賺一生還盜。燕客夜以三十金攫去。命硯伯制一天硯，上五小星一大星，譜曰「五星拱月。」燕客恐一生見，鏟去大小二星，止留三小星。一生知之，大懊恨，向余言。余笑曰：「猶子比儿。」亟往索看。燕客捧出，赤比馬肝，酥潤如玉，背隱白絲類瑪瑙，指螺細篆，面三星墳起如弩眼，著墨無聲而墨沉煙起，一生痴癡，口張而不能翕。燕客屬余銘，銘曰：

女媧煉天，不分玉石；
鰲血蘆灰，烹霞鑄日；
星河溷扰，參橫箕翕。[127]

Zhang Dai's inscription for Yanke's inkslab invokes the violent imagery of the Nüwa reparation myth to eulogize the theme of re-fabrication: the goddess uses broken stones and blood to repair the world, or to restore order amid the wreckage caused by arch-rebel Gonggong's 龔工 revolt—her "creation" is wrought from the circumstances and materials of destruction and ruin. The convergence of the Shen 參 [Three Stars] and Ji 箕 [Winnowing Basket] lunar mansions (Shen: the last of seven lunar mansions in the "White Tiger of the West"; and Ji: the last of seven lunar mansions in the "Azure Dragon of the East"), meanwhile, suggests a momentary union of polar opposites within the disorder of the Milky Way. These images become avatars for the act of inscription as a means of establishing order and identifying meaningful patterns through naming and mark making. It is tempting, given Zhang's themes of violence and restitution (and his use of the Nüwa creation myth elsewhere in his responses to devastated landscapes), to read the inscription against the backdrop of the dynastic transition: Did he compose his *ming* after viewing the inkstone with Yanke and Yisheng or years later as he looked back on the episode as a premonition of his current predicament, another dream reminiscence?

Zhang Dai elsewhere records his inscription on Yanke's inkstone in the preface to a poem that "matches" Tao Qian's 陶潛 (365–427) poem "Composed and Presented to My Cousin Jingyuan in the Twelfth Month of the *Guimao* Year [403]" ("Guimao sui shier yue zhong zuo yu congdi Jingyuan" 癸卯歲十二月中作與從弟敬遠).[128] Zhang in one sense remains faithful to Tao Qian's initial conceit, longing for his cousin's "tacit understanding" 茲契: in Zhang's case, however, the secret they share is no longer the hardship of reclusion but conflicting desires to possess an utterly singular thing. Tao's original poem for his cousin depicts a recluse surrounded by snow, accidentally finding "firmness in adversity" 窮節, reading through "the books of a thousand years" 千載書 to learn from the "blazing deeds" 遺烈 of past exemplars.[129] Zhang grafts an account of his cousin's fraught relationship with the celestial inkstone onto the structure and rhyme-scheme of Tao Qian's poem while invoking further allusions to the tale of Mi Fu's encounter with Inspector Yang Jie 楊傑 (fl.1059). Yang visited Mi to admonish him for his rock obsessions and subsequent dereliction of public duties; Mi responded by pulling three stones from his sleeve to show Yang; Yang, awestruck, confesses his own love of rocks, snatches Mi's stones and hastily departs.[130] The ironic distance between Zhang Dai's couplets and the Tao Qian couplets upon which they are based measures the gap between Yanke's possessiveness and Tao's reclusive ideal: "Hiding my traces behind the rustic door, remote and cut off from the world" 寢跡衡門下，邈與世相絕 (Tao Qian's opening couplet) becomes "As when Mi [Fu] brought the stones out of his sleeve, ties with this rock were severed" 米顛袖石來，邈與石相絕 (Zhang Dai's opening couplet).[131] Whereas Tao Qian tries to share his "self-isolation" with his cousin, as the "one who knows him," Zhang Dai invokes the example of Yang Jie to insinuate both Yanke's theft and his own covetousness for the celestial inkstone: "I lodge my intention beyond these words—who could discern the understanding between us" 寄意一言外，茲契誰能別 (Tao Qian's final couplet) becomes "Send word to Yang [Jie], how could you have been willing to take leave casually? [Zhang, that is, implies he understands why Yang snatched the rocks]" 寄語楊次公，等閒肯作別 (Zhang Dai's final couplet).[132] The ambivalent reference to Yang Jie in this respect implicates Zhang Dai in Yanke's theft: Yanke at once resembles Yang Jie in his attempt to snatch the stone, yet

Zhang also resembles Yang Jie in seeking to admonish his cousin's obsessions, all the while coveting his stolen treasure.

Zhang Dai's later description of the inkslab in *Dream Reminiscences* recycles sections of his matching verses for Tao Qian. The vignette builds upon Zhang's poem to offer an ironic reading of his inscription—that his allusion to Nüwa mending heaven is merely an effort to dress up his cousin Yanke's obsessive acts of mutilation, the way he pared away the inkstone's stars to swindle Yisheng. The idiosyncratic beauty of the slab (the aspect that leaves Yisheng stupefied) is premised on Yanke's deceptiveness and destructive whims. His final enigmatic line: "'Three Stars' hang across, 'The Winnowing Basket' converges" 參橫箕翕—his image for a semblance of order amid chaos—strangely echoes, through repetition of the character *xi* 翕 (draw together, converge), Zhang's description of Yisheng's gaping mouth 口張而不能翕 (an image that in turn calls to mind Yanke's initial name for the stone as an "ugly mouth" 臭口).

Perhaps more than any other literary form, inscription aspires for a definitive and unmodifiable sense of closure, working to identify or characterize something both briefly and permanently, seeking to stand, for all time, as the "ultimately appropriate statement thereupon."[133] Zhang Dai, as this chapter has demonstrated, consistently queries and undermines the closural effects of his own inscribed words. The equivocal relation between his inscription on Yanke's Celestial Inkstone and his poem and vignette on this inscription exemplifies such tendencies. He effectively acknowledges that an inscriptive ideal of fixity cannot be extricated from and may be motivated by human greed, artifice, and violence, even as he suggests that mark making remains a venue where attachments to the stubborn recalcitrance of things, to forms of memory and longing that exceed our worst traits, might yet be redeemed. His inscribed vision of order can be read at once as nostalgic recompense for or as an ironic attempt to cover up his cheated friend's expression of disbelief. Zhang's most searching reflections on the challenges of inscription during the Ming-Qing transition center not upon a palmwood fan, a fossilized log, or an antique vase, but a disfigured inkstone—a basic tool that despite the damage it has suffered still possesses a unique capacity to generate fresh ink: "Grinding an inkstick, without a sound, the inky liquid pools and gives off vapors." No other object so eloquently articulates Zhang's open-ended efforts to rewrite recent experiences of trauma.

THE CARVER

Zhang Dai's vignette finally calls attention to another elusive character, one who might be considered the real protagonist of the plot: Wang "Uncle Inkstone" of Huizhou—a figure whose arrival and talents in carving script initiate the development of a local culture of inkstone connoisseurship in Shaoxing; the artisan who first transforms the brigand's slab into a celestial inkstone; a necessary foil for Yanke's idiosyncratic acts of mutilation and Zhang Dai's own privileged understanding of these objects. In *Dream Reminiscences*, "Celestial Inkstone" precedes Zhang's account of the leading craftsmen of Suzhou and his short biography of the carver Pu Cheng 濮澄 (1582–?), a wizened artisan renowned for carving bamboo artifacts, but also rhinoceros horn, ivory, jade, ebony, red sandalwood, and lacquerware—one whose "markings" (*kuan*) had become self-sufficient tokens of celebrity.[134] Pu Cheng's carvings, Zhang notes, might even be placed among Shang and Zhou bronze vessels and Xuan bronze or Han dynasty jade without losing any luster, inverting presumed hierarchies of value.[135] Indeed, the order of *Dream Reminiscences* evokes an almost oneiric cast of associative thinking, where the transcendence of "Wood Like a Dragon" prompts Zhang to reflect on the darker undertones of object inscription in "Celestial Inkstone," where his memory of "Uncle Inkstone" in turn leads to his thoughts on the carvers of Suzhou and Pu Cheng's knifework. These transitions betray a dynamic that shapes Zhang Dai's inscriptions from "Rain Flower Stones" to "Cyan Jade Hairpin"; namely, that the more Zhang reflected on the impermanence of inscribed literature, the more he became preoccupied with writing about the presence of maker's marks and signature traces of the artisan's blade, as if finding temporary relief from ruptures between words and things in the virtuosic handiwork of craftsmen like Pu Cheng.

Together with his references to carvers Zhang Yingyao (in "Shen Meigang") and Lu Zigang (his fourth-uncle's jade hairpin), these vignettes evidence Zhang Dai's attentiveness to the craft of writing with a knife, the repertoire of artisanal skills that, as his epitaph for his younger brother concedes, made the literary inscription of a thing possible. In a preface composed for Zhou Lianggong, Zhang Dai tried to promote the carvers of Kuaiji over more illustrious rivals from Suzhou and Huizhou, praising seal carving, or the "virtuosity of the iron brush" (*tiebi zhi miao* 鐵筆之妙), as a means of studying script (*zixue* 字學) and conducting epigraphic research on bronze and stone.[136] The author's concern with characters like Wang "Uncle Inkstone" intimates the changing role of the entrepreneurial artisan—many emerging, like Wang, from the merchant lineages of Huizhou prefecture—in assigning meaning and value to objects. In what follows, I turn to these elusive figures, investigating how literary practices of writing on things relate to and were transformed in the late Ming and early Qing by artisanal techniques of writing upon things.

Chapter Two

WRITING WITH A KNIFE

During the late sixteenth century, a shadowy figure named Su Xuan 蘇宣 (1553–ca. 1626) heard that a local grandee had attempted to abduct his sister as a concubine. In a fit of rage, Su asked to borrow the sword of an eminent Huizhou scholar, Wang Daokun 汪道昆 (1525–1593), a weapon ostensibly forged by the general Qi Jiguang 戚繼光 (1528–1588) during the Fujianese anti-pirate campaigns.[1] It remains unclear whether Su ended up murdering his target or rescuing his sister, yet his request to borrow Wang's sword marked the beginning of a successful career carving seals—portable devices for stamping an engraved or cast impression in red ink onto paper or silk. After attempting to exact vengeance, Su Xuan fled to the liminal zone of the "rivers and lakes" (*jianghu* 江湖), adopting the guise of an errant mercenary, or *xia* 俠 (knight-errant; bravo; swordsman), making a name and money by cutting phrases onto small stone blocks. He subsequently earned renown in the Ming marketplace for an inimitable ability to adapt unfamiliar characters from pre-Qin inscriptions for new seal designs.[2]

Su's seals became valuable objets d'art.[3] One collector, Gu Lin 顧林 (1557–1595), even took his carved "Su Xuan" stone to the tomb (figure 2.1).[4] This miniature specimen of Qingtian 青田 rock (2.1 cm × 1.9 cm × 4.4 cm), now held in the Wuxi Museum, appears to have been prized not so much for the impression cut into the seal's face ("Gu Lin's seal" 顧林之印), but for Su Xuan's abrasive signature ("Seal Script Drafted by Su Yingzhi"

WRITING WITH A KNIFE

FIGURE 2.1. A seal bearing the impression "Gu Lin's seal" 顧林之印 carved from Qingtian stone by Su Xuan 蘇宣 (1553–ca. 1626) (2.1 cm × 1.9 cm × 4.4 cm). *Source*: Wuxi Museum.

蘇應製篆) engraved onto the topside of the object in a scratchy cursive script (*caoshu* 草書) by use of the so-called single-knife method (*dandao fa* 單刀法), a technique where each stroke is rendered with a single cut (figure 2.2).[5] These sharp marks accentuate the presence of the knife rather than mimicking brush strokes, hinting at how a carver might move beyond the design of a seal impression to model other techniques for inscribing words onto solid objects. Su's small stone encapsulates two broader developments in late Ming China: first, that a carver could sign his or her own wares, formulating an idiosyncratic claim of authorship by flaunting traces of the blade; and second, that "side markings" (*biankuan* 邊款) or the improvisatory inscriptions on a

FIGURE 2.2. The topside of the seal in figure 2.1, inscribed "Name: Su Yingzhi's seal script" 名氏：蘇應製篆. *Source*: Wuxi Museum.

seal's body, might enlarge the possibilities of calligraphic carving, stimulating novel forms of written expression with the knife.

Writing with a Knife in the Ming Marketplace

Poets commemorated the event of Su Xuan borrowing Wang Daokun's sword in verse.[6] The anecdote betrays the emergence of the "seal carver" (*yinren* 印人) as a literary protagonist: Su, together with a handful of close associates from the merchant lineages of Huizhou prefecture, was among the first figures in Chinese history to earn posthumous renown primarily for his talents in carving seals. Poems subsequently celebrate the way Su's violent disposition informed his creative labor, invoking analogies between his guise as an assassin clutching a prized weapon and his skill in wielding another type of blade, the seal-carver's knife:

> Master Su's precious sword shimmers in light,
> Everyone knows how he took vengeance as a youth.
> Now he has hidden his traces, concealed in the markets of Wu [Suzhou],
> His sword broken up to serve as an awl in his sack.
>
> 蘇生寶劍光陸離，少年報仇人所知。
> 即今隱跡埋吳市，劍鋒折作囊中錐。⁷

The poet finds a striking image for Su's act of vengeance in the stained red impression on the face of the seal: "His forceful intent engraved within a square inch, an enemy's blood stains this cinnabar nugget red" 雄心鏤向方寸中，仇人血漸丹砂紅.⁸ While the poem begins with images of Warring States assassins ("Can't you see, Zhuan Zhu's 專諸 [d. 515 BCE] "Fish Intestine" [so called because the dagger was small enough to be concealed within a fish] transformed in autumn waters; a grievous wind strikes up in the trees at the assassin Yao Li's 要離 (fl. 514–496 BCE) grave" 君不見，專諸魚腸化秋水，要離坟樹悲風起), it concludes with the seal carver taking up a numinous weapon, the Kunwu sword, to face down enemies of the Ming state:

> A pitter patter of fluttering raindrops on autumn waters,
> A cold gleam in the wintry daylight.
> See, his will is still that of a tiger,
> How can he grow old as a sojourner among rivers and lakes?
> Below his waist he has a Kunwu sword,
> Why not in the east behead dwarf pirates or in the west strike Hu barbarians!
> Dust down this fragment of Yanran stone, is it not worthy to be made into another Han inscription?
>
> 秋水飛雨聲颯颯，慘淡光芒寒白日。
> 看君意氣尚如虎，那能老作江湖客。

丈夫腰下有昆吾，何不東梟島夷西擊胡！
試拂燕然一片石，可堪邊勒漢銘無？⁹

These lines remind readers that the Ming empire was rocked throughout the sixteenth century by recurring bouts of violence, from pirate raids along the southeastern China coast to Mongolian incursions at the Great Wall. Both conflicts stimulated a renewed interest among Ming writers in the martial protagonist, or *xia*, as an itinerant figure capable of upending staid conventions and modeling a self-sacrificing integrity.¹⁰ The poet presents the carver not as a retiring connoisseur like Zhang Dai but as a roving knight-errant, one who takes advantage of and yet seeks to redress the insecurity of the age. Having traced Su's transformation from assassin to carver, his move from sword to engraver's awl, the poem concludes by reflecting on the associations between monumental stone inscription and the seal. Dusting down a fragment of "Yanran rock" (Yanran yi pian shi 燕然一片石)—a reference to Han dynasty historian Ban Gu's prototypical stone monument, "Inscription on the Ceremonial Mounding of Mount Yanran," a memorial celebrating Han victory over the nomadic Xiongnu—the poet asks whether the seal might yet become the substrate of a new "Han inscription" (Han ming 漢銘). To what extent, the poet muses, might the ostensibly miniature art of carving seals recover and transmit traces once engraved onto ancient stone slabs.

This chapter proceeds from the anecdote of Su Xuan borrowing Wang Daokun's sword and in three sections reevaluates the late Ming resurgence of calligraphic carving. Beginning with the career of the weapon, I first investigate Wang's prominent role in the installation of Ming military monuments, the failures of these projects amid frontier violence and factional strife, and the subsequent efforts of his circle to improvise with innovative strategies of inscription in the Ming marketplace, approaches that dwell on the Huizhou entrepreneur's resourcefulness and chivalric nonconformity in wielding the blade.

Second, I trace a proliferation of carver "biographies"—such as the poem on Su Xuan's attempt at assassination—in late Ming and early Qing literature, considering how these writings at once respond to and retroactively work to restrain the mobility of Huizhou entrepreneurs, martial figures who traversed once rigid boundaries between the fields of classicism, commerce, and craft. What was at stake in the question of what it meant to carve words onto solid objects? Turning to the career of Su's close collaborator (and another of Wang Daokun's Huizhou associates), He Zhen 何震 (1535–1604), I examine motivating factors and underlying tensions behind the emergence of the seal carver as a literary protagonist, demonstrating how critical assessments of carvers' careers sought to manage the power and perils of copying in the Ming graphic landscape. The literary trend of writing about a carver's character ultimately betrays a fraught effort to discern signature values of authenticity and individuality in a market of increasingly interchangeable imprints.

Third, the chapter moves beyond literary writings about carvers to examine the largest corpus of unexpurgated correspondence from Ming China, a cache of paper-based ephemera compiled by Wang Daokun's retainer and Su Xuan's contemporary, peripatetic Huizhou pawnbroker Fang Yongbin 方用彬 (1542–1608). This archive reveals the extent to which writing with a knife became a tactic for navigating and exploiting the pressures of urban economic life. Fang's knifework exceeds the straightforward production of seals, illuminating instead the imbrication of calligraphic carving with the design and retail of bamboo artifacts and ivory hairpins, solid ink cakes and advertising flyers for a line of local tea. Inscription, for Fang, ultimately serves to renovate his customer's experience of quotidian—and at times disposable—things.

Taken together, these three interrelated lines of inquiry elucidate a dynamic at the heart of the poem narrating Su Xuan's transition from a sword-wielding assassin to carver at large in the "rivers and lakes." Violent disorder and social decay prompted inventive attempts to locate and redeem an elusive sense of the monumental within the everyday, an endeavor that treats disruption as a condition of possibility. In this process, retainers and brokers emerge from their service with officials responsible for the installation of stelae to make their own mark with the knife as self-styled swordsmen. These go-betweens, hitherto imbricated in the infrastructural management of stone monuments, started to make names for themselves by writing upon writing tools. The scene of Su Xuan borrowing Wang Daokun's sword—a weapon whose late Ming biography in turn reveals unacknowledged links between the production of inscriptions on boulders or imposing stone memorials and the design of small seals and inksticks—in this respect encapsulates a central argument of my book: namely, that early modern innovations in carving words were conceived as responses to a crisis of collective faith in monumental permanence amid mounting political unrest and commercial volatility.

THE MING INSCRIBED LANDSCAPE

The notion that acts of inscription shape and subtend a public persona can be read as a response to a recurring theme in the prose and poetry of Wang Daokun.[11] More so than any other late-Ming prose stylist or poet, Wang's literary celebrity stemmed primarily from his writings on hard substrates, from imposing stones installed at the territorial boundaries of the empire proclaiming the violent submission of non-Han ethnic groups and nomadic communities, to urban temple dedications and memorials for Buddhist monks, to epitaphs intoning the Huizhou merchant's mobility, to short inscriptions on inkstones and inksticks still preserved in museum collections.[12] He leads us beyond the secluded studio of a figure like Zhang Dai into a more expansive landscape of inscribed surfaces, redirecting focus from the picture of a solitary connoisseur writing upon his signature possessions to networks of collaboration between archaist poets, knife-wielding traders, and enterprising artisans in Ming urban markets.

Wang's inscriptions—upon daggers and inkstones, lutes and flutes—structure and manage these networks, using objects to model and advertise Huizhou entrepreneurial endeavor (see appendix 2.1 at the end of this chapter). His novel approach to inscription provides necessary context for understanding the development of and technical innovations in the two major fields of Ming mark making: seal carving (the topic of this chapter) and inkstick design (the topic of chapter 3). More specifically, Wang's case elucidates the extent to which early modern writings on writing tools intimately register and sought to mitigate concerns with the instability of monumental stone inscriptions. Carved seals and inscribed inksticks from late Ming Huizhou speak to both the renown and political failures of Wang's circle in coordinating the production of stelae. Marginal members of his family and staff meanwhile used these openings to manipulate the substructures and basic implements of literary communication for their own ends.[13]

Appropriately, the former vice minister of war and scion of a salt merchant lineage sketched a pseudo-autobiography in verse by ruminating on the fate of an inscribed object—the sword that seal carver Su Xuan supposedly borrowed to rescue his abducted sister. The career of this weapon sheds light on Wang's wide-ranging contributions to the inscription of both stone memorials (carved calligraphy on cliffs, boulders, stelae, and entombed epitaphs) and writing implements (inkstones, ink cakes, and seals), inviting reflection on the intersections between these outwardly incongruous endeavors. The travels of the sword chart Wang's role in the installation of military monuments for the Ming state, while accounts of the weapon's retirement to Wang's hometown in Huizhou prefecture initiate and inform his subsequent sponsorship of local merchants through inscription and the promotion of seal carving—in collaboration with apprentices like Su Xuan. Wang's reputation in writing on stone justified the efforts of his circle to improvise with the knife, while these same undertakings in turn raised questions as to what determines the durability of an inscription.

The Career of a Sword

Multiple sources suggest that Wang Daokun (posted to serve as surveillance vice commissioner of Fujian) and Qi Jiguang (a leading Ming general) made a blood oath in 1562 to protect the people of Fujian in their fight against the *wokou* 倭寇 or "dwarf pirates," a multinational conglomeration of Japanese, Portuguese, and Chinese crewmen famed in Ming reports for their brutality.[14] To commemorate their pact, a symbolic union of martial and civil virtues, Qi allegedly cast two iron swords for Wang Daokun to inscribe.[15] While Wang did not divulge what he wrote on the pair of swords he shared with Qi Jiguang, he explicitly links the event of their oath and exchange of weapons in 1562 to his "Inscription to Commemorate Accomplishments at the Pingyuan Terrace" ("Pingyuan tai legong ming" 平遠台勒功銘)—a stone monument that converts the events of the Fujianese anti-pirate campaigns into ancient models of punitive conquest[16]:

> I made three libations and took three bows, the junior guardian [Qi Jiguang] brought out the treasure swords and we each took one, making a pledge and pointing to the heavens: "if one violates this oath then they won't be able to receive sacrifices at the shrine." Thereupon we entered the official residence, and I carved our accomplishments onto the Pingyuan Terrace.

> 余三酹而三拜，少保出百金劍，二分佩之，誓而指天：「渝成言者不祀！」既入省會，勒功平遠台。[17]

Wang's symbolic act of inscribing Qi Jiguang's swords is yoked to his inscription *in situ* memorializing the violent eradication of a ten-year "Japanese poison" (Riben du 日本毒) in Fujian.[18] In keeping with the main prototypes of monumental stone inscription—Ban Gu's "Inscription for the Ceremonial Mounding at Mount Yanran" in Inner Mongolia—Wang's "Inscription to Commemorate Accomplishments at the Pingyuan Terrace" sought to realize a "petrification of history," as a lengthy hymn to "barbarian pacification" and the constancy of imperial order.[19] What mattered most for Wang was that his initial performance of inscribing the pair of swords be retrospectively read in light of his role in the historical commemoration and official inscription of stone monuments for Ming military victories.[20]

Wang Daokun's earliest extended account of the sword dates not to its smelting but to the event of his impeachment in 1566 when a soldier under his command attacked a Hanlin academician. The weapon only becomes legible in Wang's poetry as it escapes obliteration, when its presumed function has been called into question.[21] As he was dismissed from office, Wang depicted the incident as a fire that burned down his official residence, destroying all of his possessions except for the sword. Following its rebirth amid the flames, the object became a symbol of the wrongs Wang had suffered and his underlying wish to be used again by the state:

General Qi cast two swords and asked me to inscribe them. He committed the sword to his old friend's care, so I took one. There was a fire in the government offices and almost everything was destroyed, yet a servant in the residence brought out the sword and so it survived. I brought it back to show to my younger brother, we both rejoiced that it possesses a numinous spirit [that saves it from destruction], so I slapped the sword-hilt and sang, composing three poems:

> Word arrives of the men from the Eastern State,
> The journey for the guests toward the Yan Ford is long.
> As the sword left the turf packed with ramparts,
> To enter the stage of youth.
> Beyond the dipper, the hue of a thousand autumns,
> In front of my bed, one-hundred paces of refulgence.
> I don't know if I'm made of martial bones,
> How could I go back to handling military affairs?

戚將軍鑄良劍二，謁予銘之，托以久要，遂分其一。省署火，故物悉亡，獨舍中兒抱劍出火中，賴得脫。歸示家弟，相與幸其有靈，為之彈鋏而歌，作詩三首。

...

東國人言至，延津客路長。
一辟多壘地，更入少年場。
斗外千秋色，牀頭百步光。
自知非俠骨，寧復事戎行。²²

The poetic life of the sword at once preserves the legacy of Wang's stone memorials to Qi Jiguang's military victories and yet redeems the tarnished reputations of those involved in coordinating their installation.²³ The weapon both documents yet registers the limits to what the static stone monument in Fujian says—mediating between accounts of service and retirement, loyalty and remonstrance.

Other Ming literary leaders competed with Wang Daokun to define the meaning of this weapon. The sword traveled in 1568 to a famed meeting with Qi Jiguang and the eminent Suzhou scholar, Wang Daokun's fellow graduate, Wang Shizhen.²⁴ During the trip, Qi presented their host with a third sword, a gift that helped incite a rivalry between Wang Daokun, a hitherto more successful official, and Wang Shizhen, a hitherto more respected literary figure.²⁵ Wang Shizhen rewrote the birth of all three weapons in his own poetic sequence, imagining Qi's preternatural act of smelting by claiming the metal came from an ancient iron anchor that emanated a strange red light from the seabed.²⁶ Wang Shizhen's invention of a third blade transforms the fellowship of swords into a forum within which Ming intellectuals might discuss their divergent views of military affairs, vying to direct the future course of Ming defense policy. Wang Shizhen's acquisition of a sword marked his emergence onto the stage of political action—his murdered father (beheaded for his failure to halt the incursions of the Mongol leader Batur in 1559) had served as a military superintendent for four coastal prefectures in Fujian, and so Shizhen's repossession of a weapon wrought from a smelted Fujianese anchor emblematized the rehabilitation of his father's "military merits" (*gonglao* 功勞).²⁷ Qi Jiguang was heading north to assume control of the very forces that Wang Shizhen's father had previously presided over and used the meeting with Wang Shizhen to discuss military strategy for the border defense. Wang Daokun, meanwhile, banished for a crime he did not commit, may have found a measure of solace in Shizhen's recently obtained "verdict reversal" (*ping fan* 平反) for his father. The swords were, by this juncture, no longer personal souvenirs but proxies for public political commentary.

The weapons reunited in 1572 when Wang Daokun returned to the bureaucracy as right vice minister of war (Bingbu you shilang 兵部右侍郎), an appointment that involved Wang's inspection of frontier garrisons under Qi Jiguang's command at Jimen 薊門.[28] As with his earlier memorial at Pingyuan in Fujian, Wang linked the meeting of the swords to his composition of a second major monumental inscription in praise of Qi Jiguang's military service entitled "Inscription to Commemorate Accomplishments at Yanshan" ("Yanshan legong ming" 燕山勒功銘)—a title that alludes to Ban Gu's canonical "Inscription on the Ceremonial Mounding of Mount Yanran."[29] This pairing of the Pingyuan and Yanshan monuments bridges the two major military struggles of the sixteenth century: the campaign against pirates on the southeastern coastline and the fight against Mongolian forces in the north—the latter memorial picking up where the former left off.[30] Wang's Yanshan inscription was carved onto ten stone tablets, erected in the vicinity of the Great Wall.[31] Much of this once octangular monument was destroyed in the Cultural Revolution, yet ten fragments, a grainy photograph, and an incomplete rubbing (preserving 544 of the 1650 characters) survive.[32] This set of stones was not, in any case, the only inscriptive project Wang oversaw during his inspection of the frontier garrisons: he also directed the production of a giant *moya* rock carving at Mount Wuling 霧靈山, the main peak in the Yan range. Much of the inscription has weathered away, yet the six-character title—"Pure Realm of Mount Wuling" (Wuling shan qingliang jie 霧靈山清涼界)—still looms large in the landscape, each graph measuring roughly 4 m².[33] The carving adheres to and strives to revitalize the classical ideal of a mountain inscription: a claim to power over space and a warning to would-be rebels.

Like his monument at Pingyuan in Fujian, the fate of Wang's Yanshan inscription quickly became embroiled in the fallout from political upheavals at court. The subject of the Yanshan inscription—praise for Qi Jiguang's role in the Jizhou 薊州 (present-day Tianjin) command—was deemed an increasingly controversial issue. The installation of a powerful general so close to the capital was a topic of concern throughout the civil service, a quandary compounded by Qi's close association with the divisive grand secretary Zhang Juzheng 張居正 (1525–1582), a relationship that precipitated Qi's demise.[34] After Zhang's death, Qi was forced to resign—his wife deserted him, and he eventually died in poverty with no funds for medical care.[35] The failure of Qi's plans for the Jizhou command has subsequently been interpreted as a portent of the military weaknesses that led to the mid-seventeenth-century Ming collapse along the same stretch of border.[36] The Pingyuan and Yanshan inscriptions seek permanence amid mounting violence and political volatility. The victories Wang commemorated were not enough, however, to ensure either his own survival or that of Qi Jiguang—let alone to fix the official historical record. By the late sixteenth century, both sets of stones simultaneously stood as markers of Wang and Qi's service and unintentional monuments of their subsequent political failures. Critics have suggested that it was precisely Wang's prominent role in inscribing stones along the northern border defense that led to disparaging assessments of his literary reputation under the Qing.[37]

Despite dedicating numerous poems to his sword, Wang Daokun never divulged what he inscribed upon its surface: whether it was his own name, the name of the weapon, a date, a motto, a pact, or a literary inscription. The poet repeatedly refers to the performance of engraving without once mentioning what the mark might have said:

[1566] "General Qi [Jiguang] cast two swords and asked me to inscribe them."

戚將軍鑄良劍二，謁予銘之。[38]

[1567] "To the left of [my] couch-bed stands a double-edged sword, cast by the General [Qi], that I inscribed."

榻之左樹佩劍一，蓋大將軍所鑄，余為之銘。[39]

[1592] "In former times, there was an inscription that inspired awe in all four directions, now [the sword] accompanies the gentleman from south to north."

疇昔有銘威四極，今來南北與君俱。[40]

As Wang's inscriptions on the surfaces of a wide range of objects proliferated throughout the late sixteenth century, the mark on his sword remained hidden. What was he holding back? The silent mark attests to Wang's faith in inscription as a means of making oneself known while insinuating a need for flexibility and a receptiveness to upheavals that the fixity of a weighty frontier monument precludes. Wang's revision of the sword's life in poetry inadvertently dwells on the compromises, gaps, and failures that haunt his writing in stone—an endeavor that nevertheless remained central to his self-definition as a writer.

From Stelae to Studio Objects

Insofar as the mark on Wang Daokun's sword embodies tensions between a longing for monumental permanence and lived experiences of disruption, it prefigures his improvisatory engagement with a diverse range of inscriptive projects in the Ming marketplace, endeavors that focus on the Huizhou merchant's martial integrity in responding to upheaval. Wang continued to receive requests for memorials that invoke the legacy of his inscriptions for military victories at Pingyuan in Fujian and Yanshan. As late as 1580, Wang composed a lengthy stone inscription named the "Stele on the Pacification of the Man-Barbarians" ("Ping Man bei" 平蠻碑), erected in Guilin, to commemorate the violent suppression of the "Eight Stockades" (Bazhai 八寨) anti-colonial rebellions in Guangxi (figure 2.3).[41] For the most part, however, Wang turned to the inscription of stelae and epitaphs for private donors, whether religious organizations such as the Pu'an Temple 普安寺 in Beijing (figure 2.4) or individuals such as his dedication on a stupa for the Buddhist monk Changrun 常潤 at the Shaolin Temple 少林寺, a memorial that despite its Chan setting praises the monk for his worldly ventures and martial virtue: "[His] intent was to compile the rites and music [of the ancient sage-kings], with gathered weapons, unifying both the civil and military" 志在集成禮樂，干戈文武并用 (figure 2.5).[42] These projects intersect with Wang's entrepreneurial inscription of less weighty substrates. During the 1580s, as he composed his stele inscription for the colonization of Guilin and his memorial for Changrun, Wang also authored short inscriptions to be molded onto mass-produced inksticks, designs that were subsequently printed in illustrated books such as *Master Fang's*

WRITING WITH A KNIFE

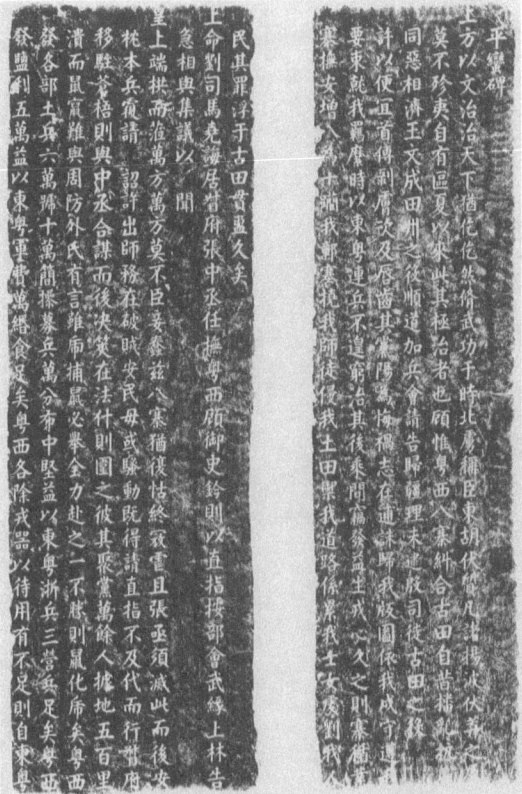

FIGURE 2.3. The first two sections of a six-piece rubbing of Wang Daokun's "Stele Inscription to Pacify the Man-Barbarians" ("Ping Man bei" 平蠻碑). The stele, dated to 1580 and located in Guilin 桂林 in Guangxi Province, measures 258 cm in height and 75 cm in width. The regular-script calligraphy for Wang Daokun's stele inscription was drafted by Zhou Tianqiu 周天球 (1514–1595). Source: Beijing tushuguan 北京圖書館., ed., Beijing tushuguan cang Zhongguo lidai shike taben huibian 北京圖書館藏中國歷代石刻拓本匯編, vol. 57 (Zhengzhou: Zhongzhou guji chubanshe, 1989), 85. Image courtesy of Harvard-Yenching Library.

Ink Catalogue (*Fangshi mopu* 方氏墨譜), a publication that I discuss at length in chapter 3 (figure 2.6).[43]

Wang Daokun's choice of collaborators reveals a striking degree of continuity between such outwardly incongruous inscriptive projects.[44] He worked with Suzhou calligrapher Zhou Tianqiu 周天球 (1514–1595) in each of the aforementioned cases, forming a production line where Wang composed a literary memorial (whether for a Ming colonial project, a Buddhist monk, or the virtues of an ink recipe) that he then entrusted Zhou to draft with

FIGURE 2.4. A rubbing of Wang Daokun's "Stele Inscription for the Pu'an Temple" ("Pu'an si bei" 普安寺碑) dated to 1575. The stele measures 225 cm in height by 119 cm in width. The "stele forehead" measures 45 cm in height by 32 cm in width. *Source:* Beijing tushuguan, ed., *Beijing tushuguan cang Zhongguo lidai shike taben huibian*, vol. 57, 24.

FIGURE 2.5. A rubbing of Wang Daokun's "Record on a Stupa for Chan Master Changrun" ("Changrun chanshi ta ji" 常潤禪師塔記) dated to 1586. The rubbing measures 167 cm by 81 cm. The calligraphy for the inscription was drafted by Zhou Tianqiu and carved by Shen Youwen 沈幼文 (n.d.). *Source:* Harvard-Yenching Library.

the brush.[45] The small, rectangular inkstick from this perspective not only alludes in miniature to the austere format of a stele but also approximates the visual presentation of Wang's writing on stone monuments. At the same time, Wang Daokun worked with his younger brother Wang Daoguan 汪道貫

WRITING WITH A KNIFE

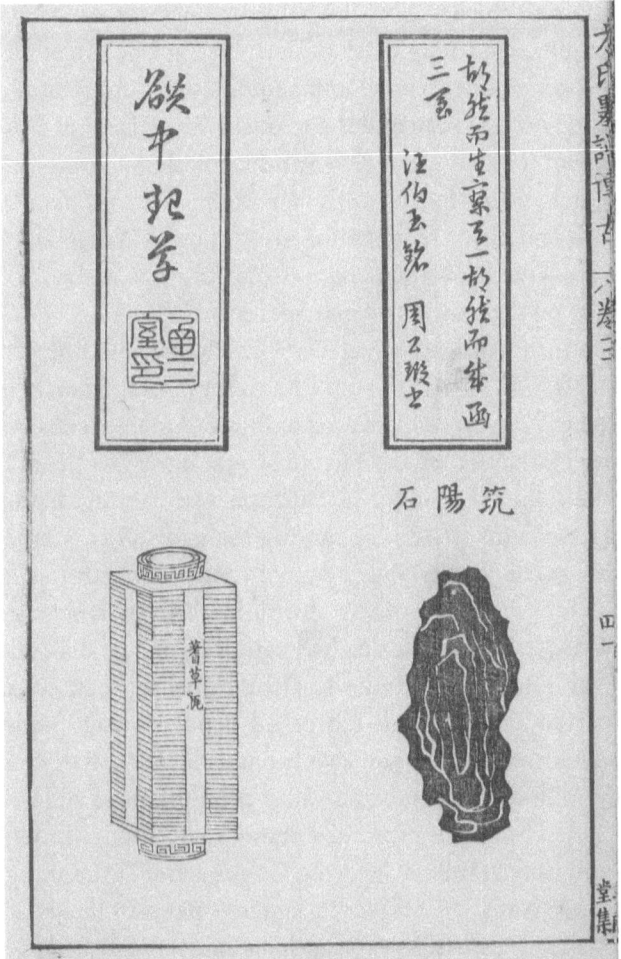

FIGURE 2.6. Fang Yulu's 方于魯 (1541–1608) "Hongzhong qicao" 鴻中起草 inkstick design bears Wang Daokun's seal "Hansan shiyin" 函三室印 and appears to have been commissioned to commemorate Wang's studio. The calligraphy for Wang Daokun's inscription (on the right side of the inkstick) is attributed to Zhou Tianqiu. *Source*: Fang Yulu, *Fangshi mopu* 方氏墨譜 (Shexian: Meiyintang, 1588), 3. 41b. Image courtesy of Harvard-Yenching Library.

(1543–1591) to draft the seal-script calligraphy (*zhuan*) on the "stele forehead" (*bei'e* 碑額) of his stele for Changrun.[46] Wang Daoguan played a role in the promotion of Huizhou seal carving and the early compilation of local seal catalogues (*yinpu* 印譜).[47] He was also a leading editor in the compilation of *Master Fang's Ink Catalogue*, contributing a lengthy technical treatise on ink production for the book.⁴⁸ Ming sources suggest that Daoguan earned money as an inkstone and inkstick dealer.⁴⁹ Wang Daokun admonished his brother for "becoming obsessive in his fondness for antiquities" 道貫好古而癖, yet relied on Daoguan and their cousin Wang Daohui 汪道會 (1544–1613)—Daoguan (or Zhongyan 仲淹) and Daohui (or Zhongjia 仲嘉) were known together as the "Two Zhongs" (Erzhong 二仲)—to manage both his art collections and client requests for inscriptions.⁵⁰ Wang Daohui earned renown as a talented inkstone connoisseur and ink maker, collaborating with Daoguan on their own bespoke ink recipe.⁵¹

As vice minister of war, Wang Daokun claimed he brought "talented Huizhou carvers" 徽人善鐫者 with him to serve in the north, figures that he instructed to help carve his words onto monumental substrates including a military inscription on the Yiwulü Mountain 醫無閭山 in Liaoning.⁵² He Zhen, the nominal founder of Huizhou seal carving, made his name under Wang Daokun's patronage carving seals for officers in Qi Jiguang's military staff at the Great Wall.⁵³ As with Su Xuan's stint as a would-be assassin clutching Wang Daokun's sword, He Zhen's association with the frontier defense informed the aesthetic appreciation of his seals: his preference for the intaglio technique has, for instance, been construed as a response to Han military seals (so-called general's seals [*jiangjun zhang* 將軍章])—engraved rather than cast bronze blanks—often crudely cut in haste before military expeditions or after promotions in the field.⁵⁴ Wang Daokun's circle elsewhere promoted these associations through inkstick design: an ink cake entitled "Supreme Commander" (Yuanrong 元戎; the title with which Wang referred to Qi Jiguang) pairs an image of a military chariot with a Han "general's seal" (*da jiangjun yinzhang* 大將軍印章), the same style of impression that prominent Huizhou carvers like Su Xuan and He Zhen elsewhere sought to replicate (figure 2.7).⁵⁵

Entrepreneurs who pioneered innovative methods in late Ming seal carving and inkstick production began their careers working in Wang Daokun's staff on the installation of stelae. Such connections not only index a redistribution of technical expertise from the domain of stele publishing to the design of seals and inksticks but also create new openings for conceptual transfer between the former and the latter. Huizhou seal carvers and inkstick manufacturers start to present their miniature products—basic implements for written communication—as devices with which to supplement, repair, and reproduce inscriptions on stone monuments. Such

FIGURE 2.7. Fang Yulu's "Yuanrong" 元戎 design. The title alludes to Wang's military service with Qi Jiguang. The ink cake bears a copy of a Han "general's seal" (da jiangjun yinzhang 大將軍印章). Image courtesy of Harvard-Yenching Library. Source: Fang Yulu, Fangshi mopu, 2. 8b.

developments anticipate the mid-seventeenth century comments of Zhou Lianggong that late Ming seal carvers might help build and restore contemporary stelae, "transmitting in stone that which [they] obtained through the transmission of stone."[56] Emerging from frontier service in the infrastructural management of military memorials, Huizhou writers in Wang's circle found in the example of the "knight-errant" at large in the "rivers and lakes" a vocabulary with which to conceptualize their own entrepreneurial mobility in unruly urban markets.

Huizhou Merchants as Collectors

Su Xuan's request to borrow Wang Daokun's sword to rescue his sister siphons this fêted weapon's prestige, yet it also heralds contemporaneous reassessments of the Huizhou merchant's character. As Joseph McDermott has demonstrated, pressure on forested mountain land prompted families in Huizhou prefecture to develop trusts for the sale of timber, aiding the emergence of a local futures market in the late fifteenth century.[57] These lineages, in turn, repurposed the institution of the ancestral hall as a credit association and "protobank," financing members to move into markets throughout the Yangzi delta. With the transition from a grain–salt exchange system to a new policy of "paying silver for salt," instituted in 1491, prosperous Huizhou merchants replaced their counterparts in Shanxi and Shaanxi as the dominant power bloc in the highly lucrative salt business.[58] Huizhou lineages started to strategically alternate between encouraging their sons to pursue careers in the civil service or in trade, so that a single family could earn official renown while developing extensive commercial networks.

During retirement from military service, Wang Daokun emerged as both a prominent advocate for Huizhou merchants and a leading patron of the brush-based arts—the "fashion" for collecting antiques in Huizhou, a seventeenth-century critic notes, "began with Wang Daokun and his brothers" 其風始開於汪司馬兄弟.[59] Erstwhile rivals for Qi Jiguang's spare swords, Wang Daokun and Wang Shizhen became local figureheads for Huizhou and Suzhou in the late Ming art market, competing to promote the collections of their hometowns amid the absence of any single authoritative connoisseur in southern China between the death of Wen Zhengming 文徵明 (1470–1559) and the rise of Dong Qichang 董其昌 (1555–1636) around 1600.[60] This rivalry reached a tipping point in a notorious (yet potentially apocryphal) potlatch-style gathering on the Yellow Mountains where Wang Shizhen brought one hundred specialists from Suzhou—in every art from calligraphy and seal carving to pitch-pot and football—to compete with counterparts recruited by Wang Daokun from Huizhou.[61] The Huizhou collector—and close friend of both Wang Daokun and Wang Shizhen—Zhan Jingfeng 詹景鳳 (1532–1602) exploited such rivalries to brazenly "honor Hui[zhou] and diminish Wu [Suzhou]" 崇徽貶吳, arguing that collectors "equipped with Xin'an [Huizhou] eyes"

新安具眼 could now surpass their contemporaries in Wu.⁶² A popular late Ming anecdote records a witty exchange between Zhan and Wang Shizhen in a curio market at a Nanjing temple: Wang Shizhen remarks that "the wealthy merchants of Xin'an approach the literati of Gusu [Suzhou] like flies around mutton" 新安富賈見姑蘇文人，如蠅之聚一膻, to which Zhan responded: "When the literati of Suzhou approach the wealthy merchants of Xin'an, are they not also like flies around mutton?" 姑蘇文人見新安富賈，亦如蠅之聚一膻，何也—a riposte that Wang Shizhen begrudgingly accepted with a silent smile.⁶³ Zhan elsewhere sought to preserve this symbiotic relationship between Huizhou and Suzhou in material form. After obtaining a rare Song dynasty Duan inkstone, he commissioned a bespoke box for its storage, an object he proudly invited both Wang Daokun and Wang Shizhen to inscribe.⁶⁴

Merchants and Entombed Epigraphy

Wang Daokun's most strident reconsiderations of merchant character surface in another inscriptive genre: the epitaph, or "entombed account with inscription" (*muzhiming*), typically a square-shaped piece of stone (roughly 40 to 160 cm) engraved on one side with the biography of a tomb occupant divided into two sections: a lengthy prose preface (*xu*) recording the deceased's accomplishments and an inscription (*ming*) mourning the tomb occupant's death. Wang Daokun was a leading participant in the burgeoning Ming market for entombed epigraphy, making a name and money by selling mortuary literature to increasingly diverse clients.⁶⁵ By the late sixteenth century, even stone carvers could garner posthumous tomb memorials: Wang Shizhen, for instance, composed a *muzhiming* for the Changzhou stone-cutter Zhang Wen 章文 (1491–1572), an artisan famed for carving Wen Zhengming's calligraphy onto stelae and epitaphic monuments. Wen's letters suggest that he also entrusted Zhang to engrave his inscriptions onto decorative objects including a box for an inkstone, a detail that elucidates the convergence between different modes of calligraphic carving in the late Ming.⁶⁶ Wang Shizhen commemorates Wen's dependencies on Zhang, making the hitherto hidden labor behind the production of a stone monument the subject of a monumental stone inscription: "Whenever [Wen] wrote calligraphy for stone, he was discontent if it wasn't [Zhang] who carved his words in stone" 而所書石，非叟刻石不快.⁶⁷

The numerous epitaphic inscriptions Wang Daokun composed in the 1570s and 1580s query rigid distinctions between Confucian classicist (*ru* 儒) and merchant (*gu* 賈) roles, returning to themes of inversion and transposition in statements that became repeatable formulae:

[For Wu Liangru 吳良儒, a scholar-turned-merchant:]
    In antiquity, the scholar took the right side [of honor], and the merchant was inferior, yet in my prefecture this has been reversed.

古者右儒而左賈，吾郡或右賈而左儒。[68]

[For Jin She 金赦, a merchant's son who gave up scholarship for trade:]
    Xin'an, with one scholar for every three merchants, is a land of great cultural contributions. Just as merchants seek handsome profits, scholars strive for high honor. When one has exhausted all effort on behalf of Confucian learning with no result, he might relinquish study and tighten up with trade. Once he has joined those who enjoy high profits, he prefers his descendants, for the sake of their future, to relinquish trade and tighten up with study. Relinquishing and tightening up thus alternate with each other so that one can enjoy either an income of ten thousand bushels of grain or the prestige of a retinue of one thousand horse carriages. This can be likened to the revolutions of a wheel, with its spokes pointing to the ground in turn.

新都三賈一儒，要之文獻國也。夫賈為厚利，儒為名高。夫人畢事儒不效，則弛儒而張賈。既則身饗其利矣，及為子孫計，寧弛賈而張儒。一弛一張，迭相為用，不萬鍾而千駟，猶之轉轂相巡。[69]

These widely cited claims have been construed as an implicit response to mounting concerns that the circulation of Huizhou sojourners throughout Ming China might threaten the longevity of the local ancestral halls that had provided them with start-up funds.[70] Wang's epitaphs consequently dwell on moments where moneylenders or "mean traders" (*gushuzi* 賈豎子) return to set up spirit tablets, rebuild dilapidated temples, or reclaim ritual lands once attached to ancestral tombs, scenarios that underscore the function of inscribed tombstones as mechanisms with which to restrain or temporarily arrest the flow of Huizhou merchant capital on Huizhou soil, ostensibly rendering short-term acquisitive activity subordinate to the long-term reproduction of patrilineal order from generation to generation.[71] The retail of "Wang Daokun epitaphs" nevertheless put paid to any longed-for diversions from the marketplace among his clientele. Literary historians have noted that many of Wang's "accounts of conduct" (*xingzhuang* 行狀)—the biographical sketches upon which his epitaphs were subsequently based—underscore that the composition is a "true record" (*shilu* 實錄) and warn against "blandishing the tomb" (*yumu* 諛墓) or "extravagant words" (*yici* 溢辭)—claims that betray an anxiety with explicitly proving that a mortuary tribute was not simply bought with money—and thus proof of the extent to which "Wang Daokun epitaphs" were perceived as commodities.[72]

On the one hand, Wang Daokun's entombed epigraphy built upon the fame of his inscriptions on cliffs, boulders, and stelae for Ming military victories: Wang projects himself, for instance, into the last lines of his epitaphs, invoking his own past as a military supervisor (Sima 司馬).[73] On the other hand, the very retainers involved in marketing "Wang Daokun epitaphs" became leading seal carvers, ink makers, and dealers of studio objects in late-sixteenth-century Huizhou.[74] Manuscript letters held in the Harvard-Yenching Library reveal that customers from across the empire traveled to Huizhou to purchase epitaphs for deceased relatives, first contacting Fang Yongbin, a local pawnbroker, seal carver, and secretarial assistant for Wang Daokun, with gifts to win an audience.[75] Fang appears to have used these opportunities to sell brushes and paper from his stationery store to new clients.[76] Beyond whatever a "Wang Daokun epitaph" might say about a particular merchant's behavior, the management of resources involved in and the profits accrued from the production of these inscribed artifacts bolstered the entrepreneurial ventures of his coterie.

Much as Wang's wordless mark on his sword implicitly queries the closure and fixity of stone monuments in responding to lived experiences of upheaval, he and his retainers began to ask how to commemorate Huizhou merchant endeavor without treating the merchant's entombment as a necessary point of departure. Writing on less cumbersome substrates—from daggers to lutes—Wang reconceived of mercantile mobility as the very subject of inscription, on occasion even justifying attempts to make a name outside of lineage institutions.

The Confucian Knight-Errant

A veteran of frontier conflict, Wang Daokun recasts the Huizhou entrepreneur in his own image as a roving martial protagonist, or *xia*, one capable of improvisation in the face of danger along the wharves and waterways of the Grand Canal, stitching together Confucian values of righteousness, classicist learning, and trade. Using the scaffolding of itinerant salt trader Fang Yangeng's 方巖耕 (Jingzhen 景真; n.d.) career, Wang Daokun's "Biography of a Confucian Knight-Errant" ("Ruxia zhuan" 儒俠傳) justifies merchant activity in terms of a synthesis of *ru* (classicist; those learned in ritual; followers of Confucius's teachings) and *xia* (gallant, cavalier, chivalrous) traits: the title transforms chivalric attributes—mobility, a capacity to improvise in the face of danger, and self-sacrificing conduct on behalf of those in need—into a character type.[77] The Confucian Knight-Errant emerges from Sima Qian's 司馬遷 (c.145 BCE–c.86 BCE) description of Zilu 子路 in the "Biographies of Confucius's Disciples" ("Zhongni dizi liezhuan" 仲尼弟子列傳): "Zilu was blunt. He delighted in prowess and strength and was forthright in disposition. Wearing a rooster-hat and carrying a sword ornamented with pigskin, he bullied and humiliated Confucius. . . Later Zilu dressed as a scholar, presented his pledge, and asked to become a student through one of the Master's disciples" 子路性鄙, 好勇力, 志伉直, 冠雄雞, 佩豭豚, 陵暴孔子 . . . 子路後儒服委質, 因門人請為弟子.[78] The Ming Confucian Knight-Errant, as Chi-Yuan Lien has demonstrated, effectively revivifies Zilu's model to take advantage of commercial upheavals: returning stolen dowries to victims of waterway thefts and settling burial disputes; studying with renowned philologists and opening tea shops from charitable donations; managing infrastructural projects and overturning superstitious cults to mountain goblins.[79]

Fang's roving independence vindicates the role of traveling merchants in facilitating the movement of capital throughout the empire, suggesting that such mobility might be salutary rather than detrimental to social cohesion—a theme encapsulated in Wang's image of his Confucian Knight-Errant rebuilding the "White Cloud Bridge" (Baiyun qiao 白雲橋) near Shashi 沙市 in Hubei to sustain trade while selflessly effacing an accompanying stele to commemorate this very achievement. The protagonist claims: "Any benefit lies in the bridge, not in a name, if the bridge is here and my name vanishes then it is still of benefit, but if the bridge vanishes then any benefit goes with it, so what use would a name have" 利在橋，不在名，且橋在名亡，則亦未嘗不利，橋亡則利俱亡矣，焉用名。[80]

The Confucian Knight-Errant's *ru* assets resemble those of Ziyou 子游 (Yan Yan 言偃; 506–443 BCE) and Zixia 子夏 (Bu Shang 卜商; 507–425 BCE)—whose names taken together give "You Xia" 游夏, a pun on "Wandering Knights" (*youxia* 遊俠)—two disciples of Confucius trained in literature and ritual.[81] In both cases, Wang indulges disjunctions between "name" (*ming*) and "conduct" (*xing*). Actions, he argues, reveal more than mere labels. Clear distinctions between *ru* and *xia* start to unravel: the "Confucian Knight-Errant" is simultaneously both and neither, inhabiting the two roles, while exceeding and negating their limits:

> It seems equally acceptable to refer to him as either a "Confucian scholar" or a "Knight-Errant"; or to refer to him as "not a Confucian scholar" or "not a Knight-Errant"; it is even acceptable to refer to him as a "Confucian scholar who isn't a Confucian scholar and a Knight-Errant who isn't a Knight-Errant.

> 謂之儒，謂之俠可也；謂之非儒，謂之非俠，可也；謂之儒非儒俠非俠，亦可也。[82]

In one of his earliest encounters, a wronged party appeals for a "swordsman to assist [me] in [this matter]" 第求劍俠以佐吾事, yet the Confucian Knight-Errant tellingly responds that "[for this] a three-foot sword is no use, just listen to me, a three-inch tongue is sufficient" 即三尺劍無所用之，幸而聽吾，則三寸舌足矣。[83] In line with his protagonist's move from swordsmanship to skills in persuasion, Wang appears invested in transmuting his own chivalric reputation as a veteran of anti-pirate campaigns into literary expertise: in writing narratives that locate and redeem valiant characters in the Ming marketplace, searching for a vision of the heroic within the everyday. Few writings from Fang, the archetypal "Confucian Knight-Errant" survive, except for a set of letters to a fellow Huizhou pawnbroker asking for advice on carving seals. These manuscripts suggest that Fang, renowned for his calligraphic talents and philological training, found a means of reconciling classicism and commerce in the practice of carving words with a knife (figure 2.8).[84]

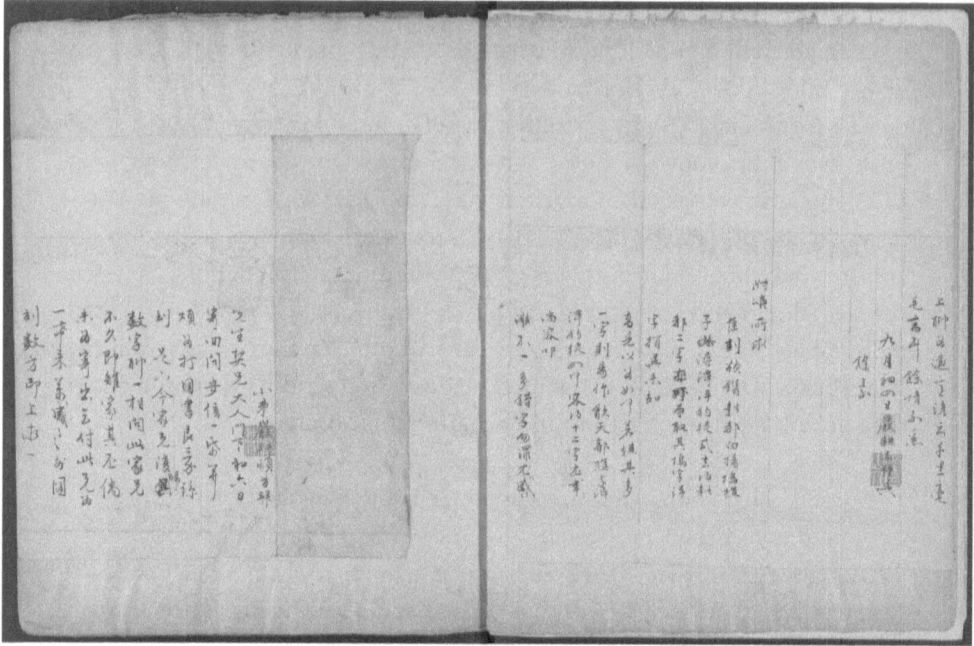

FIGURE 2.8. The final page of a letter from Fang Yangeng 方巖耕 (n.d.; the "Confucian Knight-Errant" 儒俠) to Fang Yongbin 方用彬 (1542-1608) asking for help with carving seals. *Source*: Fang Yuansu 方元素, *Ming zhuming jia chidu, fu renming lüelu* 明諸名家尺牘, 附人名略錄 (1600), jin 金: 2. Image courtesy of Harvard-Yenching Library.

The Merchant's Weapons

Wang Daokun's account of the Confucian Knight-Errant, while initially based on one individual's biography, came to designate a type of martial protagonist, a guise that he invited a range of other Huizhou entrepreneurs to assume. Just as Wang Daokun reflected on his own service through writing on a sword, he used the form and function of other weapons to adumbrate the Confucian Knight-Errant's enterprising mobility. He inscribed, to take one example, a "spoon-head dagger" (*bishou* 匕首) for fellow Huizhou merchant Wang Benhu 汪本湖 (Yuanli 元蠡; n.d.), a weapon that alludes to his own past fighting pirates, while attesting to its new owner's chivalric integrity. In keeping with Benhu's reputation as an itinerant trader, Wang Daokun's inscription treats movement as its central theme, linking memories of military maneuvers to images of animate daggers trying to leap out of scabbards and "roaming dragons" that resist restraint:

WRITING WITH A KNIFE

*AN INSCRIPTION, WITH PREFACE, FOR WANG YUANLI'S
SPOON-HEAD DAGGER*

Yuanli carried a spoon-head dagger as he passed through the Taihang Mountains. He encountered a great gale and his dagger tried to leap out from its scabbard. Yuanli thought this was strange and so tightly fastened it to his girdle. When I was in the army, the troops under my command captured a great number of barbarian weapons. This spoon-head dagger was an inch and a half wide and a little over a foot long. I would say that among so-called "fine weapons," this is the best. I hold Yuanli, a true cavalier, in great esteem so I inscribed it for him. The inscription reads:

Grasping a foot-long box, restraining a roaming dragon.
Thin as Green Duckweed, floating like a white rainbow.
Be sure to hold it at your side,
Giving strength to the martial gallant.

汪元蠡匕首銘有序

元蠡挾匕首過太行山，會大風，匕首自樸中躍出。元蠡以爲異，結佩佩之。余在行間，所部獲夷器何可勝數，匕首廣寸半，長尺有奇，余所謂佳兵此其最也。余多元蠡壯士，遂爲之銘，銘曰：

操尺櫝，擾游龍。
薄青萍，浮白虹。
永言佩之，爲俠者雄。[85]

Benhu made considerable money trading in the Yangzi delta, purchasing a degree and studying with leading philologists while experimenting with ink making, papermaking, and carving his own pinewood artifacts.[86] Connoisseurs praised Benhu's ink cakes, especially those he had inscribed: "Made in the Studio of the Brocade Buddha" (Xiufo zhai zhi 繡佛齋製).[87] The "waterways and wharves of the Yangtze valley" were, as McDermott has noted, sites of real danger and risk in the sixteenth century, plagued by "bandits, pirates, and sharpsters."[88] Renowned for their martial prowess in semiprivate commercial matters and for forming armed bands to escort salt smugglers, Huizhou traders protected themselves by cultivating military ties and studying martial arts.⁸⁹ Wang Daokun's inscription on Benhu's spoon-head dagger invokes lived experience of anti-pirate campaigns to sanction the travails of long-distance entrepreneurs, braving the hazards of river and road.

As Wang's image of a "three-inch tongue" suggests, the Confucian Knight-Errant's shape-shifting character—neither *ru* nor *xia*—at once unsettled and enlarged conceptions of what constitutes a weapon, or an effective medium for the expression of chivalric integrity. Wang Daokun's endorsement of Benhu's dagger was paired, for instance, with an inscription on Zha Bashi's *pipa* ("Zha Bashi pipa ming" 查八十琵琶銘), a four-stringed lute conventionally associated with courtesan performance. Wang's inscription for Zha celebrates the lute's indefinite attributes, praising both the material ("Such fine wood!") and sound of the instrument ("Such a fine melody!") by pairing images from the classics with poetic allusions to the object's exotic provenance:

INSCRIPTION ON ZHA BASHI'S LUTE

Such fine wood! A raccoon-dog's mottled head?
Such a fine melody! Strumming to Wusun?
A thousand autumns of countless blessings!
Suffused with music.

查八十琵琶銘

何哉木，貍首斑。何哉曲，烏孫彈。千秋萬歲，樂以盤。⁹⁰

Wavering between Confucian classicism and frontier romance, these analogies betray both the thing's unstable identity and its player's amorphous persona: Yuan Rang 原壤, an acquaintance of Confucius, extoled the fine grain of his mother's coffin, singing to the wood as a "raccoon-dog's mottled head"; the Han princess Liu Xijun 劉細君 (fl. 110–105 BCE) was sent to be married to the Wusun 烏孫 khan around 108 BCE and was supposedly accompanied by musicians who played the lute to soothe her in her grief—an allusion that again underscores Wang Daokun's preoccupation with itinerancy.⁹¹

Prominent Suzhou poets had praised Zha's musicianship, yet Wang as a fellow Huizhou merchant went further in seeking to authoritatively name and possess the instrument that sustained Zha's talents through inscription. Late Ming anecdotes invoke "Zha Bashi's *pipa*" 查八十琵琶 as the name of a distinctive object—a lute unlike any other lute—and a virtuosic style of strumming, as if the two were mutually constitutive.[92] Wang takes up the relationship between the performer's body and signature tool in a full-length biography of Zha that circulated alongside his inscription, a piece that wavers between using the lute to describe Zha's character and using Zha's charismatic persona to evaluate the malleable attributes of the musical instrument.[93] The biography argues that Zha performed the role of a mercenary like the famous assassin zither player Gao Jianli 高漸離 (n.d.), a co-conspirator to assassinate the First Qin Emperor—remarking: "My hometown has a number of steadfast gallants, surely [Zha] Nai is one?" 吾鄉故多節俠，則鼐其人乎.[94] Much of Wang's account, however, reflects on the meaning of *xia* virtue within a mundane world of markets and brothels, even questioning the knight-errant's masculinity: Zha only learns to play the lute in order to avenge an insult by a courtesan who taunted him for the stigma of his merchant past; he has an extended private affair with a favored concubine of a Ming prince yet refuses to take her as his wife despite her offer of a dowry; he also refuses to have children, thus ending his family line.[95] These details qualify prevalent readings of Wang Daokun as a conservative spokesperson for the hegemony of Confucian lineage institutions in Ming social life, again indicating a measure of incoherence in his approach to inscribed literature as a tool for the management of public memory.[96]

In writing upon Zha Bashi's lute, Wang reimagines the type of thing an inscribed memorial might become. He works to discern a source of longevity not in the weighty matter of stone or a strident proclamation of conquest but in the fleeting pleasures (*le* 樂) that Zha's music (*yue* 樂) sustains, in the musician's transgressive role-playing and improvisation. Wang's inscription intones not a physical object but an evanescent occasion, the way Zha brings this signature instrument to life through his inimitable touch.[97] How much does Wang, as an aspiring dramatist and connoisseur of musical performance, see of himself in Zha's shape-shifting persona?[98] A rare letter that Wang wrote to Zha survives, inviting the musician to visit the former official's estate to perform: Wang addresses Zha as an immortal adept "Old Fuqiu" (Fuqiu weng 浮丘翁), stating his desire to hear Zha's "rare tones" (*xiyin* 希音), a shared means of transport to the

"All-Encompassing Pool" (*xianchi* 咸池), a mythic abode where the sun sets and the name of an ancient musical harmony.[99] This letter, a rare example of a wealthy patron addressing an itinerant performer as an equal in literary prose, evokes a powerful longing for the "suffusion of music" that lay behind Wang Daokun's inscription, suggesting how a musician might find a measure of control in manipulating his audience, slyly eluding Wang's initial pretense of mastery.

I conclude this overview of Wang Daokun's multifaceted engagements with the Ming inscribed landscape by looking at his writing on Zha's lute because it succinctly demonstrates how his concerns with the Huizhou merchant's martial disposition unsettled and enlarged approaches to making a mark. His short inscription on the instrument, straddling exhibition and performance, at once echoes and reconstitutes prior efforts to make a name by inscribing swords and daggers or his intellectual defense of merchant integrity in publishing mortuary literature—indeed, the interplay between Wang's biography of Zha and his inscription on Zha's lute might be read together as an idiosyncratic epitaph. Su Xuan's seemingly incidental request to borrow Wang's sword emerges from and contributes to a broader trend of Ming entrepreneurs inscribing signature objects—whether daggers or lutes—to promote the character of the Confucian Knight-Errant. The guise of the Confucian Knight-Errant, as the embodiment of an almost fugitive capacity to cross and recalibrate lines between classicism, commerce, and craft, provided cover for itinerant entrepreneurs to subsequently trial new approaches to writing with a knife.

THE SEAL CARVER AS A LITERARY PROTAGONIST

Su Xuan's small seal was interred in Gu Lin's tomb in Wuxi with several other stone seals cut by Huizhou carvers, including four attributed to He Zhen—a figure who made his name, with Wang Daokun's assistance, carving seals for members of Qi Jiguang's military staff in garrisons along the Great Wall (figures 2.9 and 2.10).[100] Zhan Lian 詹濂 (?–1609), the carver of five stone seals in Gu's tomb (three of which are signed Zhan Pan 詹泮), also earned fame for his "martial bones" (*xiagu* 俠骨; in addition to his boisterous singing and homosexuality) after he selflessly accepted a prison sentence on behalf of a disgraced friend (the eminent playwright Tu Long 屠隆; 1542–1605), eventually winning his freedom through local public support.[101]

FIGURE 2.9. A seal bearing the impression "Gu Lin's seal" 顧林之印 carved from Qingtian stone by He Zhen 何震 (1535–1604) (1.9 cm × 1.9 cm × 3.8 cm). *Source*: Wuxi Museum.

FIGURE 2.10. He Zhen's signature "Changqing" 長卿, carved on the side of the seal in figure 2.9. *Source*: Wuxi Museum.

He Zhen and Zhan Lian, like Su Xuan, exploited the sides of the seal as a space within which to explore other forms of calligraphic carving, creating both a technical and conceptual foundation for late imperial calligraphers to carve their own inscriptions in regular, running, or cursive scripts.[102] The sides of He Zhen's "Master Gu Yuqing" (Gushi Yuqing 顧氏鬱卿) seal (figure 2.11), for instance, display one version of his signature (Changqing 長卿) carved in cursive script with the single-knife cut method and a top mark *zi* 字 carved in clerical script with the "double-knife" method (*shuangdao fa* 雙刀法) where cuts are made along both sides of a brush stroke. This method was typically associated with stele carving (figures 2.12 and 2.13). Zhan Lian, meanwhile, carved a fourteen-character

FIGURE 2.11. A seal bearing the impression "Master Gu Yuqing" 顧氏鬱卿 carved from Qingtian stone by He Zhen (1.8 cm × 1.7 cm × 4 cm). *Source:* Wuxi Museum.

FIGURE 2.12. Side of He Zhen's "Master Gu Yuqing" seal, signed "Changqing" in cursive script. *Source*: Wuxi Museum.

FIGURE 2.13. The topside of He Zhen's "Master Gu Yuqing" seal bearing the mark *zi* 字 in clerical script. *Source*: Wuxi Museum.

message upon the side of his miniature "Zunsheng" 尊生 seal (measuring only 1.6 cm × 0.9 cm × 3.5 cm) in a fluent small-scale regular script with the single-knife cut method. These markings flaunt his release from the concentrated energy and forcefulness of the "double pushing cut" (*chongdao* 衝刀) used to render his two-character seal-script impression in imitation of a Qin-Han jade seal (figure 2.14): "On the double ninth of the *jichou* year (1589), seal-script drafted for Master 'More Profound' by your younger brother in friendship Zhan Lian" 已丑重九，為又玄先生篆，友弟詹濂.[103] Zhan's dated message for his patron on the double-ninth festival in 1589 reconceives of the seal as the memento of a distinct occasion

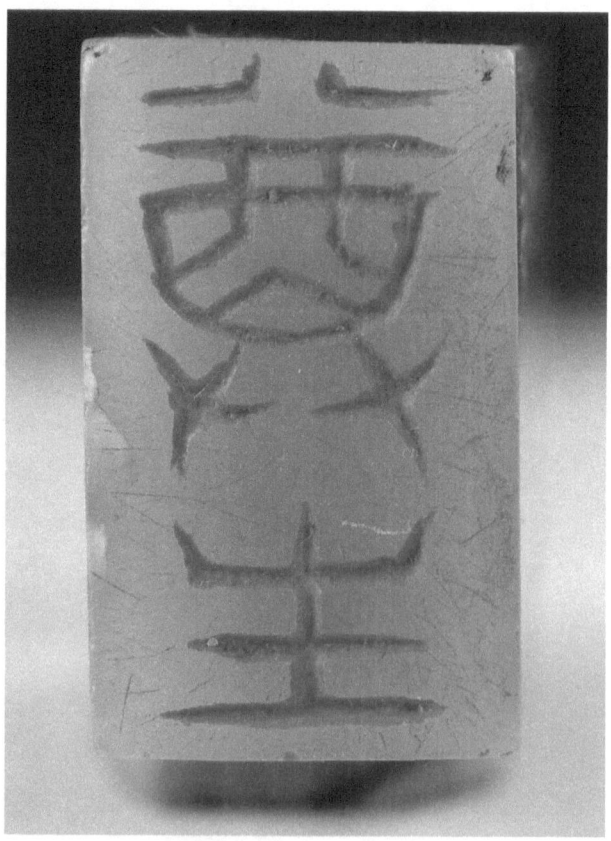

FIGURE 2.14. A seal bearing the impression "Zunsheng" 尊生, carved from Qingtian stone by Zhan Lian 詹濂 (?–1609), now held in the Wuxi Museum (1.6 cm × 0.9 cm × 3.5 cm). *Source:* Wuxi Museum.

(figure 2.15). Su, He, and Zhan—each acclaimed for their chivalric exploits (whether attempted assassinations, frontier service, or prison breaks)—were at the same time among the first figures to be posthumously commemorated as "seal carvers" (*yinren*) rather than as calligraphers who in their leisure dabbled with the knife.

What explains the emergence of the carver as a new literary protagonist in the late sixteenth and the seventeenth centuries? Why did so many late Ming and early Qing writers—as with Zhang Dai's sketches of wizened figures like Pu Cheng or Wang "Uncle Inkstone" discussed in chapter 1—start to write about what it means to carve words? Literary judgments of a carver's character work to liberate the seal's replicatory powers as a tool

FIGURE 2.15. The side of Zhan Lian's "Zunsheng" seal inscribed: "On the double ninth of the *jichou* year (1589), seal-script drafted for Master 'More Profound' by your younger brother in friendship Zhan Lian" 己丑重九，為又玄先生篆，友弟詹濂. *Source*: Wuxi Museum.

for the study and transmission of ancient inscriptions on metal and stone from its imbrication in early modern commercial life—from the spread of pawnshops, the widespread forgery and commodification of calligraphy, and the transgressive mobility of Huizhou traders. Archaeological evidence of Su Xuan and He Zhen's careers, as with the contents of Gu Lin's tomb in Wuxi, conversely suggests the extent to which these developments were coterminous: that the ascendancy of a Qin-Han aesthetic in soft-stone seal carving—a movement that subsequently shaped late imperial approaches to epigraphy—was predicated on the boundary-breaking endeavors of the Confucian Knight-Errant in the Ming marketplace.

A careful reading of writings about He Zhen's career discloses competing motivations and implicit tensions behind the biographical turn in Ming literature on seals. He Zhen came to exemplify two tendencies in the resurgence of sixteenth-century seal carving: first, the discovery of soft stone as a privileged medium and the heightened attention to signature side markings that this entailed; and second, the commercial publication of woodblock-printed "seal catalogues" (*yinpu*) and a concomitant transition from the connoisseurship of "name seals" (authoritative impressions of personal or institutional identity) to "leisure seals" (*xianzhang* 閒章)—impressions based on short mottoes, maxims, or resonant lines of poetry that could be adapted and used by anyone. He Zhen's centrality to both developments intimates the extent to which they were mutually constitutive: that an abundance of mass-produced imprints heightened the value and aura of the real thing, or that a proliferation of mechanical copies stimulated a newfound desire for physical traces of the carver's body.

The excavated contents of Gu Lin's tomb in Wuxi speak to this predicament. Gu's interred seals for the most part display one of two seal-script impressions: "Gu Lin's Seal" or "Master Gu Yuqing."[104] Whereas the square imprints made from these seals (despite slight variations in framing or levels of abrasion) appear outwardly interchangeable, the signature carvings on the sides of the stones in a wider range of calligraphic styles transform these miniature devices into bespoke objets d'art. Even among the four seals He Zhen carved for Gu he switches between different versions of his signature to avoid any duplication.[105] Gu Lin's seals thus embody negotiations between a replicable and widely circulated stamp (his public name) and inimitable "side markings" that lay claim to a sense of intimacy between owner, carver, and object as dimensions concealed from public view—and in this instance eventually buried in a tomb.[106]

WRITING WITH A KNIFE

The woodblock publication of impressions generated an increasingly nuanced vocabulary for discerning the presence of the knife in the production of a seal. In 1572, Gu Congde 顧從德 (1525–?) and Wang Chang 王常 (1535–1607) collaborated on the compilation of *Gushi jigu yinpu* 顧氏集古印譜, a set of twenty folios of impressions from Qin and Han dynasty seals (around 160 jade seals and 1,600 bronze seals) owned by prominent collectors in the Jiangsu and Zhejiang regions.[107] Gu and Wang sought to exploit the subsequent popularity of this project in 1575 by recarving the impressions in *Gushi jigu yinpu* onto woodblocks to facilitate further printing (figure 2.16). The success of this book, retitled *Yinsou* 印藪, stimulated a wave of printed "catalogues collecting ancient seals" (*jigu yinpu* 集古印譜), shaping the late Ming resurgence of a Qin-Han aesthetic in seal carving.[108] At the same time, *Yinsou*'s promiscuity prompted fears among

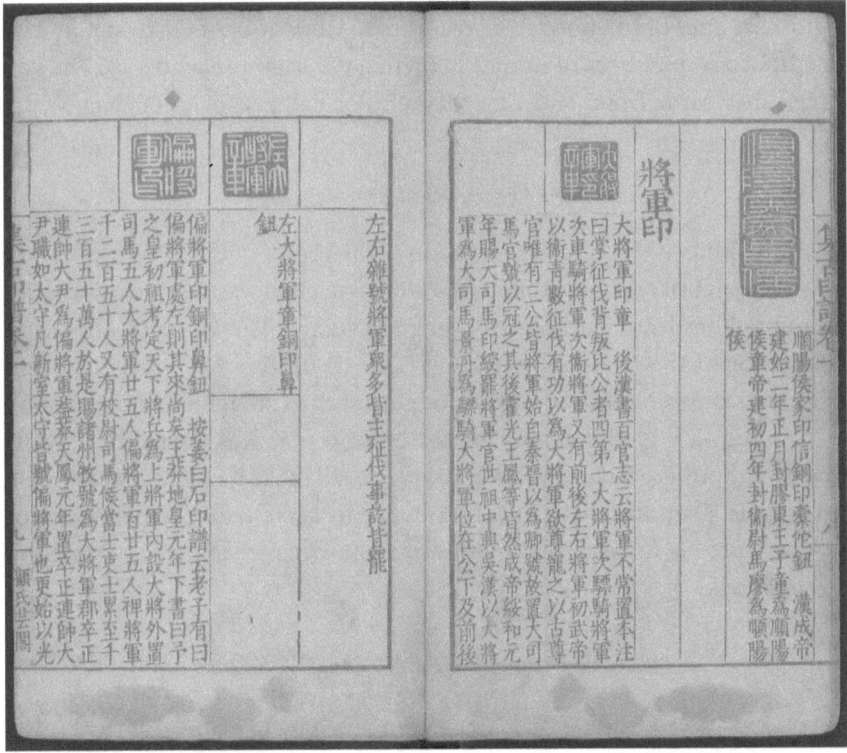

FIGURE 2.16. Han "general's seal" in Wang Chang's 王常 *Jigu yinpu* 集古印譜. *Source*: Wang Chang, ed., *Jigu yinpu* (Wuling: Gushi yunge kan, 1575?), 1. 8b. Image courtesy of Harvard-Yenching Library.

connoisseurs that contemporaneous carvers might study seal scripts not by viewing ancient seals or consulting epigraphic sources in person but by recycling woodcut copies of impressions in printed books. Again, He Zhen's name became a focal point in far-reaching debates over whether *Yinsou* disseminated reliable methods for copying Qin-Han models or whether it precipitated "stagnation" (*zhi* 滯) and a loss of "spirit" (*shenqing* 神情) in carving.[109]

Against this backdrop, the literary device of a carver's biography works to manage fraught relations between signature and replica, manipulating biographical details to discern a sense of individuality in a market filled with increasingly unreliable imprints.[110] Even though seals act as security devices and signatures (or certified emblems of personal and institutional identity), they are also "potentially unstable signifiers," inasmuch as impressions can be easily made from impressions, replicating the original seal and thus facilitating its circumvention as a guarantor of authenticity.[111] Writers of carver biographies attend to the power and perils of copying, extricating legitimate lines of filiation (from teachers to students, fathers to sons) from unauthorized practices of imitation by first ascertaining who a carver was, where they came from, and who they studied calligraphy or carving with.

The Discovery of Soft Stones

The fungibility of He Zhen's reputation as the prototypical Ming seal carver and the celebrity of his stone seals finds succinct expression in a short account of his death, authored by Feng Mengzhen 馮夢禎 (1548–1605), the chancellor of the National Academy (Guozijian 國子監). That the event of a carver's passing in 1604 while lodging at the Cheng'en Temple 承恩寺 in Nanjing (a regional center for the book trade) was deemed noteworthy is again unprecedented. Feng briefly recalls that he had, in years past, invited He Zhen into his official residence to carve seals (some in jade or bronze), yet his focus drifts to popular rumors concerning a specimen of strange rock:

ON A FOLIO OF HE ZHUCHEN'S SEALS

He Zhuchen, a man of She County, name unspecified, style name Xueyu, used his talent for seals to roam throughout the empire. While stationed in Nanjing in years past, I invited him into my offices, entrusting him with jade, stone, and bronze to render several dozen impressions. They all possess an uncommon antique charm. I still treasure them today.

Zhuchen, last year at the age of seventy, passed away while lodging as a guest at the Cheng'en Temple in Nanjing. When they searched his sack, the only thing left was a strange stone. His friends pooled together money to bury him and return his coffin to his hometown. Now there is no one to offer a peal of incense to Zhuchen.

I heard from Ding Nanyu that He Zhuchen, in studying seals, spent all his resources roaming throughout Wu, studying with Wen Xiucheng and Xu Gaoyang for a long time. He effectively combined their strong points and grew more skillful as he matured—he was unrivaled at the time.

Alas! Seal carving is only one art form, yet its virtuosity lies in combining the brush and knife, with intaglio and relief techniques. Without the instruction of a master one cannot attain virtuosity, and without virtuosity one cannot expect transmission to posterity, how much more so for one who goes beyond virtuosity?

Ding Zhenbai's two folios of Zhuchen's seals contain around one thousand impressions. They were obtained from his son and should be truly treasured, in anticipation of their dissemination.

Composed on a rainy summer's day in 1605, while roaming in the Yellow Mountains.

題何主臣符章冊

何主臣，歙人，名某，字雪漁，以善符章奔走天下。昔年在白下，余召之入官署，授之玉，石，銅，成數十面，俱奇古有致，寶用至今。主臣去歲滿七十，客死承恩寺。搜其橐惟奇石一座存焉。友人釀金斂之，歸其柩。今遂無祝瓣香於主臣者。余聞之丁南羽，主臣之學符章也，破產遊吳中，事文休承，許高陽最久，兼得其長，老而益精，遂縱橫一時。嗚呼，符章雖一藝而用筆用刀硃文白文俱有妙解，非得師不能精，不精不能久傳，況其上者乎。丁貞白藏主臣符章二冊，凡千餘面，得之於其子，真可寶也，其俟而廣之。

萬曆乙巳夏日游黃山雨中題。[112]

Feng Mengzhen's attention to the details of He Zhen's career—the carver's travels and training with renowned calligraphers Wen Jia 文嘉 (ca.

1501–1583) and Xu Chu 許初 (n.d.); vectors of legitimate transmission from He Zhen to his followers—stems from efforts to certify a set of impressions and thus publicly broadcast the prestige of seals in his own collection. The vignette centers upon a "strange stone" discovered by monks—a synecdoche for the material with which He Zhen earned renown among late Ming collectors. The recovery of He's last stone underwrites and subsequently raises the value of the carver's remnant traces in the world of the living, whether the early He Zhen seals hidden away in Feng Mengzhen's collection or the two rare folios the connoisseur obtains on his pilgrimage to the Yellow Mountains of Huizhou.[113] The recursive structure of Feng's colophon—the narrator's reminiscences of his early experiences as a collector of seals in Nanjing upon handling a rare folio of impressions on a rainy summer's day many years later—anticipates an early Qing proliferation of elegiac vignettes on Ming carving in response to the ruptures of dynastic transition—a tendency that reaches its apotheosis in Zhou Lianggong's posthumously-published 1673 prose masterpiece, *Biographies of Seal Carvers*.[114]

Who was He Zhen? As Feng Mengzhen's description of the carver's interment suggests, most surviving biographical accounts of He Zhen date from the years after his death. Wang Daokun's poetry, by contrast, constitutes the principal contemporaneous source of information on He Zhen's career. Much of this verse appears to have been composed to "send off" the seal carver on his travels throughout the empire, praising his diligence as a student of epigraphy (studying the "stone drums" [ten granite boulders from the state of Qin bearing the oldest known stone inscriptions] and "nine tripod cauldrons" [a collection of legendary bronze vessels cast by Yu the Great of the Xia dynasty]) and his boisterous persona, drinking and gambling as another Confucian Knight-Errant.[115] Much like his inscription on Zha Bashi's lute, Wang's poems for He Zhen resemble name-brand endorsements, specifying the distinctive traits of a "He [Zhen] ancient seal-script seal" ("He Changqing guzhuan yinzhang" 何長卿古篆印章).[116] Crucially, Wang makes no mention of the materials He Zhen worked with—whether, for instance, he preferred bronze, jade, or stone; instead, his poems underscore how He based his seal designs on his personal inspection of pre-Qin monuments.[117] And yet, He's fieldwork cannot—for Wang—be disentangled from his stubbornly martial disposition as a figure of the "rivers and lakes":

Auspicious vapors from the Palace Walls, a full and favoring sunlit pneuma,
There is a guest who personally copies the script on the Stone Drums.
Don't ask why a drunken reveler should also excel in speaking of swords.
Watch his brushwork limn clouds of valor.

宮牆佳氣日氤氳，有客親摹石鼓文。
莫問酒徒工說劍，看君筆陣摠凌雲。[118]

Writers in Wang's circle similarly allude to He's fame and proclivities as a drinker: one associate remembers how He Zhen came aboard his moored boat in Nanjing for a party at which he drunkenly carved three small seals in an impromptu performance.[119] Just as he lent his sword to Su Xuan, Wang recommended that He serve in Qi Jiguang's military staff stationed in the garrisons along the Great Wall, making money by carving seals for the officers who orchestrated the installation of Wang's monumental stone inscriptions at Yanshan.

Critics started to compose full-length biographies on He Zhen's behalf in the wake of his death. In doing so, commentators sought to reconcile the Confucian Knight-Errant's capacity to traverse boundaries between calligraphy, commerce, and craft with a new narrative justifying scholarly interest in carving soft-stone seals. For Ming critics, calligrapher Wen Peng 文彭 (1497–1573)—scion of Suzhou's most illustrious family of art connoisseurs and brother of the aforementioned Wen Jia—personified a decisive transition from scholars studying *zhuan* (a term that could refer specifically to the standardized scripts of the Qin or more generally to the variant scripts of antiquity) to personally carving their own seals with a knife. The influential Ming treatise on seal aesthetics, *Yinshuo* 印說, for instance, claimed that it was only with Wen's "inspiration passing to carving" 興到或手鐫之, that a crucial connection between early and mid "Ming scholarship on seal script" (Guochao zhuanxue 國朝篆學) and the hitherto minor art of carving seals could be forged.[120]

The same monograph implies that this shift was predicated on a technical transition from "casting" (*zhu* 鑄) bronze and "grinding" (*nian* 碾) jade (the hard materials used for ancient seals) to carving soft stones such as those from Qingtian.¹²¹ Manipulating bronze and jade demanded the intermediary assistance of a professional artisan; these uneducated craftsmen, however, "could not understand seal-script calligraphy" 不識篆, and so "proceeded to lose the calligrapher's intent as ancient methods perished" 往往不得筆意，古法頓亡.¹²² It was only with soft stone, a material that facilitated the "easy entry of the knife" 石，刀易入, that an educated calligrapher could achieve an authentic "unfurling after the self" 展舒隨我, so that "nothing is not as intended, set forth in the manner of the brush" 無不如意，若筆陳然.¹²³ Such statements disclose an underlying irony in late Ming seal criticism: that the recovery and reliable transmission of Qin-Han seal script ostensibly rests upon the recent discovery of soft stones and the subsequent rejection of bronze and jade, the very materials used to make Qin-Han seals.¹²⁴ In elevating Wen Peng as the central figure in the rise of Ming seal carving, *Yinshuo* makes only a passing reference to He Zhen: an enigmatic character referred to as "He of She County" 歙人何, a so-called "professional of the rivers and lakes" 江湖行家, one whom the Suzhou-based author "does not know anything about and so finds it more difficult to account for" 吾所不知，更難備述.¹²⁵

Writing in the wake of the dynastic transition, Zhou Lianggong draws together these two themes—Wen Peng's decision to start carving his own seals and the ascendancy of soft stone—in what became the standard account of "scholarly seal carving's" birth. For Zhou, Wen Peng's decision to take up the knife rests upon his firsthand discovery of a supply of soft stone, or soapstone—a material referred to in contemporary records as "gelid rock" (*dongshi* 凍石), likely pyrophyllite, a hydrous aluminum silicate resembling talc.¹²⁶ Wen had previously commissioned an artisan named Li Shiying 李石英 (ca. 1498–?), a figure renowned for embellishing the sides of ornamental fans, to carve over the inky traces of his calligraphy to produce seals in ivory, yet now he could personally cut his own writing in stone. A seal was no longer a hybrid artifact, but the signature product of a single hand: the true "intent" behind the calligrapher's brush had been liberated from association with the merely mimetic, or uneducated knifework of a paid craftsman.

The fragmentary details of He Zhen's biography invite reassessments of Wen Peng's "discovery" of soft stone in Nanjing as evidence of a calculated effort on the part of later critics to shape a narrative of origins for the soft-stone seal—the material that made "scholarly seal carving" thinkable.[127] In Zhou Lianggong's sketch of Wen Peng, the calligrapher seeks to verify the significance of his initial purchase by displaying the "lamplight glow" (*dengguang* 燈光) of his rocks for none other than Wang Daokun.[128] Inspired by this encounter, Wang procured a large quantity of the same stone (a detail that hints at his power as an official and resourcefulness as a Huizhou merchant), which he divided up between Wen Peng and He Zhen—a gift that contributed to the fame of the material throughout the empire. Wang Daokun's act of splitting the supply of stone reappears as the kernel of He Zhen's biography. For Zhou Lianggong, He Zhen only becomes a seal carver by copying the inky traces of Wen Peng's brushwork. He appears as an imprint of his teacher's model (see box at page bottom).

The details behind this story of discovery are dubious. There is, for instance, no proof that Wen and Wang Daokun ever crossed paths, but there is compelling evidence of calligraphers using soft stones to carve their own seals that predates Wen Peng's fortuitous encounter in Nanjing by centuries.[131] Feng Mengzhen's colophon on the seal carver's burial, as previously noted, claims He Zhen studied with Wen Jia not Wen Peng.[132] The late Ming Huizhou collector Zhan Jingfeng (teller of the "smelly mutton" joke) appears to have been the first to mention Wen Peng and He Zhen together, yet he casts them as rivals rather than as teacher and student, suggesting—perhaps due to local pride and his travels with He

---

Wen Peng's Biography

[Wang Daokun] sought out a hundred [units] of the stone. He gave half to [Wen Peng] and asked [Wen] to draft his handwriting in ink on the other half before getting [He Zhen] to carve these traces. As a result, soft stone's name made an appearance in the world, its beauty spread in the four directions!

徽中乃索其石滿百去。半以屬公,半浼公落墨,而使何主臣鐫之。於是,凍石之名始見於世,艷傳四方矣![129]

He Zhen's Biography

[He Zhen's] fame comes from [Wen Peng] and rose on account of [Wang Daokun]. When [Wang] was residing in Nanjing, he obtained one hundred units of soft stone from [Wen], entrusting half to [Wen] and commissioning [He Zhen] to complete the other half.

主臣之名成於國博,而騰於徽中。司馬徽中在留都,從國博得凍石百,以半屬國博,以半倩主臣成之。[130]

Zhen—that it was He not Wen who "became today's number one seal carver in the empire" 當為今日天下篆刻第一.¹³³ The anachronistic detail of Wang Daokun's gift retroactively secures a vector of transmission from scholar to an itinerant sell-sword at home in the rivers and lakes, from Suzhou to Huizhou, and from calligraphy and epigraphic research on seal scripts to carving. No mention need be made of what Wen Peng might have learned from He Zhen or how the eminent calligrapher mastered knifework. Accounts of He Zhen's apprenticeship present artisanal subordination before a scholar as the necessary condition of the scholar's engagement with craft.

The considerable care that later writers invested in re-creating the details of He's training nevertheless betrays concern with the implicit challenge his mobility presented for once clear-cut distinctions between the brush-based arts, commerce, and artisanal methods of making and knowing. He Zhen supposedly fulfills the promise of his teacher's example, and yet in his exposure to and mastery of Wen's lessons threatens to usurp his teacher's position. Seventeenth-century critics observe that even though Wen Peng "pursued antiquity" (*zhui gu* 追古), he "could not yet shed Song-Yuan traits" 然未脫宋元之習; it was only He Zhen who despite "being unable to eschew a dependency on imitation" 然未免太涉擬議, disseminated an archaic Qin-Han aesthetic throughout the empire.¹³⁴ Zhou Lianggong wryly notes that contemporaries compared the situation to the way Chen She's 陳涉 (d. 208 BCE) failed revolt against the Qin dynasty ultimately provided an impetus for the rebellions that led to the creation of the Han dynasty under Liu Bang 劉邦 (256–195 BCE).¹³⁵ Although archaeological evidence suggests that He Zhen pioneered the Ming fashion for carving soft-stone seals, he could in any case also carve in the hard "artisanal" materials of bronze and jade and so did not depend upon the supple substrates like Qingtian rock that supposedly made it possible for Suzhou calligraphers like Wen Peng to first pick up the knife.¹³⁶

The Seal Catalogue as a Publishing Format

He Zhen's reputation concurrently became entangled with a more controversial development: the commercial publication of seal catalogues and a concomitant proliferation of counterfeit imprints. The challenge of how to identify the genuine "He Zhen" had already become a matter of widespread concern in the late Ming and early Qing dynasties. A book once widely assumed to be the only publication attributable to He Zhen—a two-volume collection of remarks on the history of seal script entitled *A Continuation of Learning from Antiquity* (*Xuxue gubian* 續學古編)—is a later fake.[137] Much as commentators graft He Zhen's biography onto that of his purported teacher, Wen Peng, they present He's followers as derivative copies, none more so than a carver named Liang Zhi 梁褒 (Qianqiu 千秋; d. 1645) from a Huizhou family based in Yangzhou.[138] While residing in Nanjing, Liang reportedly studied with He Zhen and largely imitated He Zhen's seals (much as He Zhen had supposedly studied with and copied Wen Peng), precipitating a situation where "people all thought they had obtained He Zhen's true imprint, but the connoisseur knew Liang Zhi was his top disciple" 人人自以為得何氏心印，識者獨謂梁千秋高第弟子云.[139]

Critics claim that the worst impressions attributed to Liang (some of which, Zhou Lianggong wrote, made "people want to vomit" 令人望而欲嘔耳) were direct copies of He Zhen's work: "Strive to Eat" 努力加餐, "Sipping Wine, Reading Lyrics" 痛飲讀騷, and "Living Amid Verdant Hills" 生涯青山.[140] Confusion between He Zhen and Liang Zhi seals derives from the format and editorial agenda of Liang's catalogue, *Yinjun* 印雋, a 1610 collection of 439 seals that openly mixes the impressions of teacher and student. It is unclear, to take a representative example, whether Liang Zhi's "He Zhen" seal—a design that approximates the calligraphic style of an archaic bronze inscription (*kuanzhi zhuan* 款識篆)—was a He Zhen original, Liang's faithful copy of his teacher's impression, or Liang's own invention—an attempt to siphon something of He's fame (figure 2.17).[141] Contributors to this catalogue go so far as to celebrate slippages between the two carvers' hands, claiming that Liang Zhi's copies essentially resurrect He Zhen: "My old friend Wu Wenzhong brought along some seals made by Liang Qianqiu, mixed with some seals that Zhuchen had made—I could not tell them apart and gasped in surprise. If we have Master Liang, then Master He is not dead!" 舊交吳文仲攜廣陵梁千秋所為印章，雜主臣所為者，余不復能辨，驚嘆不已。有梁生，何生不死矣.[142] The editors of *Yinjun* embrace confusion between original and copy, applauding failures to authenticate individual impressions, approaching duplication as a means with which to forestall fears of oblivion and overcome death.

Although later commentators present Liang Zhi as a derivative copy of He Zhen, he was largely responsible for the collation and transmission in

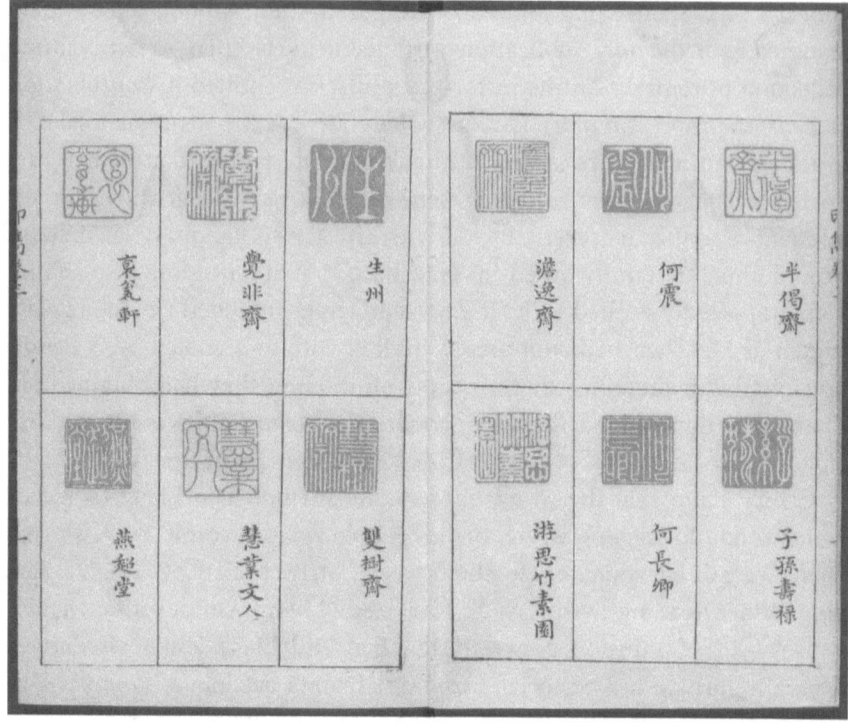

FIGURE 2.17. A page of seal designs from Liang Zhi's 梁裘 (fl. 1610) catalogue *Yinjun* 印雋 displaying seals with the characters He Zhen 何震 and He Changqing 何長卿. *Source*: Liang Zhi, *Yinjun*, ed. Wang Daohui 汪道會 (1544–1613) (1610), 3. 1b. Image courtesy of Harvard-Yenching Library.

print of what came to be seen as the distinctive traits of He Zhen's seal art. His career and the influence of *Yinjun* thus raise the question of how many surviving He Zhen seal impressions were first designed by Liang. Consider, for instance, a soft-stone seal attributed to He Zhen, "Vista of Green Pines and White Clouds" ("Qingsong baiyun chu" 青松白雲處), an object signed and dated to the autumn of 1553—one of He's earliest surviving works (despite ostensibly representing his mature style), carved when he was only nineteen.[143] This seal's impression, however, also appears in the influential 1617 publication *Chengqing guan yinpu* 承清館印譜 where it is attributed to Liang Zhi (and is listed as cut not in stone but in the hard material of agate), raising the question whether Liang's design was a copy of a He Zhen stone or a model for the later production of a fake.[144] Zhou Lianggong also included the "Vista of Green Pines and White Clouds" impression in his personal seal catalogue, preserving a copy of the seal that closely resembles Liang Zhi's carving in the *Chengqing guan* compendium.¹⁴⁵ Zhou does not specify, however, whether this particular seal in his own collection was carved by He Zhen, Liang Zhi, or another later copyist.

The confusion between original and copy precipitated by Liang Zhi's practice concurrently prompted fears of the seal's social and linguistic debasement. Whereas Wen Peng predominantly carved "personal name seals" (*mingzi zhang* 名字章) bearing literary sobriquets or studio names, He Zhen introduced "common sayings" (*shiyu* 世語) into his seals—"[yet] when it came to [Liang Zhi], there was no expression that could not be incorporated" 至千秋則無語不可入矣.¹⁴⁶ For Zhou Lianggong, Liang's promiscuity in his selection of phrases reflects the diverse and unruly makeup of his clientele: Wen Peng only carved for "famous men"—with Liang, anyone (from peddlers and hucksters to petty members of political cliques) could procure a seal.¹⁴⁷ If Wen Peng was an amateur who dabbled with the knife, Liang's whole family attempted to make money by carving seals: his younger brother earned fame for his knifework as did his concubine Han Yuesu, a carver renowned for her small jade seals.¹⁴⁸ Zhou Lianggong lamented how in later life Liang Zhi frittered away his wealth partying with courtesans, working to fulfill client demand by outsourcing his operations to family members: Zhou gauges the integrity of Liang's younger brother as a student of epigraphy by highlighting moments where he stubbornly refused to work as a "ghostwriter" (*zhuodao* 捉刀) for his sibling.¹⁴⁹ Leading Qing connoisseurs meanwhile prided themselves on an ability to spot exemplary "Liang Zhi" seals that had in fact been carved by Han Yuesu.¹⁵⁰ Liang Zhi's household economy builds upon the example, and yet came to emblematize the threat posed by, He Zhen's mobility. Not only could anyone commission a seal (an object that might now bear any phrase), but anyone could also carve a seal.

Seal-carver biographies against this backdrop strive to resolve tensions between good and bad copying—or between He Zhen's apprenticeship with Wen Peng and Liang Zhi's apprenticeship with He Zhen. The biographical turn in Ming seal literature, I have argued, ultimately seeks to discern signature values of authenticity and individuality within an art of mechanical replication, at once embracing the power of copying to overcome loss while reflecting on how the storage and transmission of impressions modulate attachments to a vanishing past. These compositions can be read as creative responses to the challenges seal carving posed for understandings of durability in early modern China; namely, a recognition that the very means by which a seal guarantees longevity—the serial generation of copies—might at the same time undermine its reliability as the authentic trace of either a particular body or a transient moment of material contact.[151] This dilemma precipitated increasingly sophisticated reflections in prose and poetry on the significance of carved words from the late sixteenth century onward, works that focus on the careers of carvers like He Zhen to parse and repair the fraught relationship between writing and its material supports, searching for an authentic presence beyond death.

Liang Zhi, who perhaps more than any other figure mentioned in Zhou Lianggong's *Biographies of Seal Carvers* embodies the worst traits of late Ming seal carving, was killed in 1644 as he "blundered unwittingly, returning south" amid the violence of inter-dynastic war.[152] Despite Zhou's cautious reinterpretation of He Zhen's labor, the Confucian Knight-Errant's persona resurfaces within and haunts his recollections of how certain carvers took up armed resistance against the Qing invasion. Fang Qiyi 方其義 (1620–1649; brother of the renowned philosopher Fang Yizhi 方以智 [1611–1671]), to cite one prominent case, transitioned from his use of the carver's awl back to the "way of the sword" (*jiandao* 劍道) and alcohol.[153] As with Feng Mengzhen's account of He Zhen's burial, the biographer's desire to discern a semblance of presence within inky red imprints appears contingent upon narration of the carver's death. No seal carver from this period wrote a full-length autobiography, raising the question of where we might look to recover the experiences and aspirations of those who made a living by writing with a knife.[154]

THE SHOPKEEPER'S KNIFE

Two archives of notes, invoices, handbills, and manuscript poems compiled by peripatetic Huizhou shopkeeper and pawnbroker Fang Yongbin reveal how calligraphic carving became a strategy for negotiating the demands of quotidian life in the late Ming marketplace.[155] Fang's papers, the largest corpus of handwritten correspondence and ephemera from early modern China, were later divided into two collections: (1) a recently discovered 40-leaf album, first acquired by Robert Van Gulik (1910–1967), containing 104 manuscript poems from 82 poets (alongside receipts and pawnshop bills), now held in the Leiden Institute of Sinology (catalogued as *A Memorial Folio for Fang Yuansu's Glorious Return*)[156]; and (2) a 6-volume archive of letters and ephemera (733 notes, invoices, advertising flyers, and 190 business cards), now held in the Harvard-Yenching Library (catalogued as *Notes from Select Luminaries of the Ming*).[157] Fang's paperware serves as a stark reminder for media historians both of how little is still known about the affordances of handwriting in Ming China and of how many other similar sets of documents may have been lost to the ravages of time. The pawnbroker's carefully curated archive of autographs, receipts, and contact cards appeals to and yet unsettles conceptions of the book as a means of rendering the mobile immobile, of gathering together, or "standing up that which was loose, scattered, or insecure."[158] Fang's scrapbook of ephemera—a sprawling collection of miscellaneous papers tendered by hand, many for payments in escrow—instead contains what Gillian Russell terms a "fissiparous energy," as if its constituent elements might become mobile once more.[159]

Unlike He Zhen or Su Xuan, Fang Yongbin was not posthumously commemorated as a seal carver, yet his correspondence divulges the day-to-day operations of someone who carved words for a living. His work, more significantly, demonstrates how skill in wielding the knife exceeds the production of seals, intersecting with other forms of expertise: from shopkeeping to the publication of literary inscriptions. Born into one of twenty branches of the Fang 方 clan based in Yansi Market Town 巖寺鎮, Yongbin was brought up in a merchant household whose members conducted trade between Huizhou and Yangzhou. He earned a literary education under Wang Daokun's patronage, purchased a licentiate degree from the National Academy in Beijing, and worked closely with the "Two Zhongs" (Wang Daoguan and Wang Daohui) to develop their art collections. Indeed, we have already encountered Fang in various guises throughout this chapter: he personally managed requests for Wang Daokun's epitaphs; offered advice to the first Confucian Knight-Errant on how to carve seals (figure 2.8); and corresponded with He Zhen and the imprisoned carver Zhan Lian.

Like Wang Daokun or He Zhen, Fang Yongbin assumed the role of a martial protagonist, even composing a now-lost chivalric romance on the "Biography of a Worthy Knight Errant" (*Yixia zhuan* 義俠傳), a manuscript that inspired one correspondent to remark that Fang had truly grasped a martial spirit.[160] In the course of his travels—from Guangdong in the deep south to Beijing in the north; from Suzhou in the east to Huguang in the west—Fang obtained business cards and swathes of handwriting from some of the most renowned cultural figures in sixteenth-century China. He received correspondence from Qi Jiguang and Wang Shizhen, shared samples of his handwriting with leading Ming calligraphers, and exchanged verse with celebrated courtesan Ma Xianglan—herself a connoisseur and carver of inkstones and seals.[161] That Fang achieved such levels of celebrity, yet remains largely absent from any surviving Ming imprints, or that he worked to secure a reputation through cataloguing unexpurgated correspondence and manuscript verse cautions media historians against assuming that book publication was necessarily central to Ming economies of prestige.

Fang Yongbin solicited and sustained many of his contacts through his management of a shop and pawnbroking business named the "Treasure Store" (variously transcribed as: Baodian 寶店; Baosi 寶肆; Baopu 寶舖). Invoices preserved in the Harvard cache demonstrate how Fang juggled his work as a pawnbroker (procuring silver for clients and then chasing down debts) with his skills as a connoisseur of art objects (from paintings and calligraphy to books, ceramics, and desktop tools) (figure 2.18).[162] The papers shed light on quotidian economic transactions typically obscured in

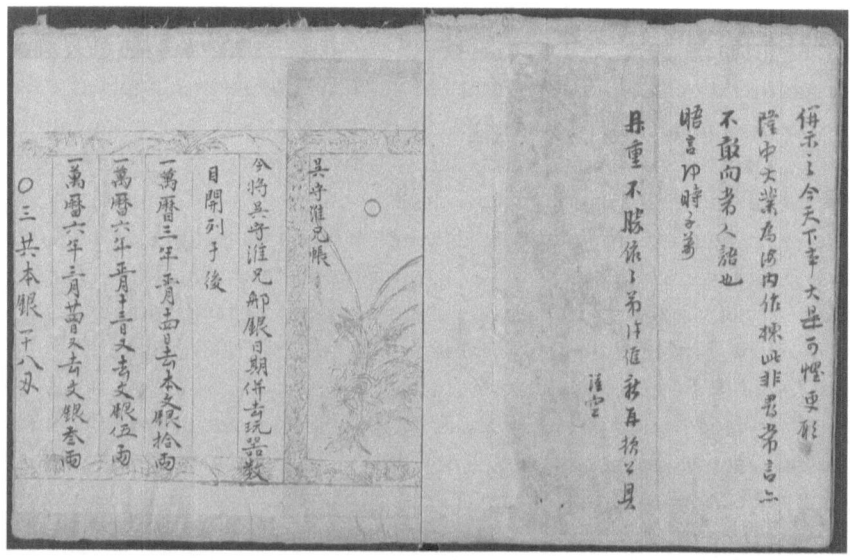

FIGURE 2.18. Invoice for Wu Shouhuai 吳守淮 (n.d.) from Fang Yongbin. *Source: Ming zhuming jia chidu*, huo 火: 114.

printed records, with Fang sending local bullies to forcibly extract payment from a fellow member of Wang Daokun's poetry society, swapping porcelain bowls for a caltrop mirror, or acquiring a selection of peacock feathers for a vase.¹⁶³ Fang Yongbin appears to have garnered modest acclaim among his associates as both a poet and a calligrapher, yet his activities in both fields still speak to his work as a shopkeeper, stationer, and connoisseur of writing tools.¹⁶⁴ Clients, for instance, request Fang's assistance with the authentication and refined judgment of inkstones while alluding to his output as a manufacturer of ink and paper: Wang Daohui, who had collaborated with Fang Yongbin on compiling a "catalogue of [Fang's] hat designs" (*guanpu* 冠譜), sought out Fang's skills as a connoisseur of calligraphic equipment: "I recently obtained an ink-grinder, an exceptional specimen, what day might you come to appraise it?" 近得一研，大是世間希有之物，何日來一鑒賞也.¹⁶⁵ A poetic gathering to celebrate his journey to the National Academy in Beijing was commemorated in his kinsman's design and production of a limited-edition inkstick.¹⁶⁶

Fang Yongbin's practice thwarts the distinctions upon which literary accounts of late Ming soft-stone seal carving were predicated. On the one hand, he curated the production of a manuscript catalogue of seal designs (*yingao* 印稿) and exchanged correspondence with leading Huizhou seal carvers (he refers in one note to He Zhen), even commissioning other artisans to cut seals for his own collection (figure 2.19).¹⁶⁷ A letter from the prominent collector, Zhan Jingfeng, meanwhile, suggests that Fang was a student of epigraphy, one versed in the compilation and connoisseurship of ancient seal scripts.¹⁶⁸ Fang had trained with the acclaimed Cantonese calligrapher Li Minbiao 黎民表 (1515–1581), and his clerical-script writing on fans (referred to as "big script" 大書 in Fang's notes) proved popular with customers: clients consequently praise his deft ability to fuse brushwork with knifework.¹⁶⁹ On the other hand, letters suggest Fang was able to carve seals in the hard "artisanal" media of ivory and bronze in addition to stone.¹⁷⁰

Scrawled addenda to client requests similarly hint at Fang's talent in refabricating scraps of material for new molded knobs, pointing to forms of handiwork that exceed the "scholar seal-carver's" repertoire: "This stone seal is too short. If you could split it in two and then use it to make a knob [for another seal], that would be wonderful" 其石章太倭，倘為分作兩半，以便作鈕，尤妙.¹⁷¹ Fang's skill in engraving script moreover became entangled with his ability to carve other artifacts—including ivory

WRITING WITH A KNIFE

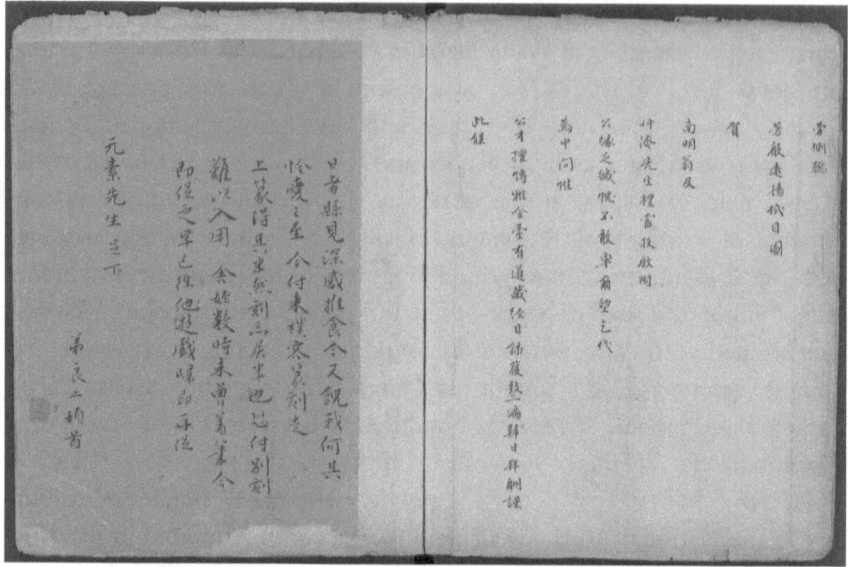

FIGURE 2.19. Letter from the seal carver Wu Liangzhi 吳良止 (n.d.) to Fang Yongbin in response to a request to carve seals. *Source: Ming zhuming jia chidu*, jin: 94.

and bamboo hairpins (*yazan* 牙簪; *zhuzan* 竹簪).[172] A letter from the cache suggests that Fang not only sold bronze and ivory seals, but that his shop also peddled knives for cutting these materials: "[I humbly request] a knife to carve bronze and a knife to carve ivory... I'll express personal thanks" 鐫銅并鐫牙刀各丐一柄 [...] 容面謝.[173] Such comments hint at forms of technical transfer from seal carving to shallow (*qianke* 淺刻) and deep (*shenke* 深刻) carving in bamboo and other hard materials—crafts that both involved the use of a flat, square blade.[174]

Inscription and Ephemera

One of the few surviving documents authored by Fang Yongbin attests to the convergence between his skill as a carver, his career as a shopkeeper, and literary inscription. Two printed handbills or flyers (*fangdan* 仿單) preserved within the cache display Fang's inscription for a brand of local tea: "Fang Yongbin's Inscription for Pine Lichen Splendor" ("Fang Yongbin Songluo lingxiu ming" 方用彬松蘿靈秀銘) (figures 2.20 and 2.21).[175] In both instances, the titular brand name is transcribed in seal script

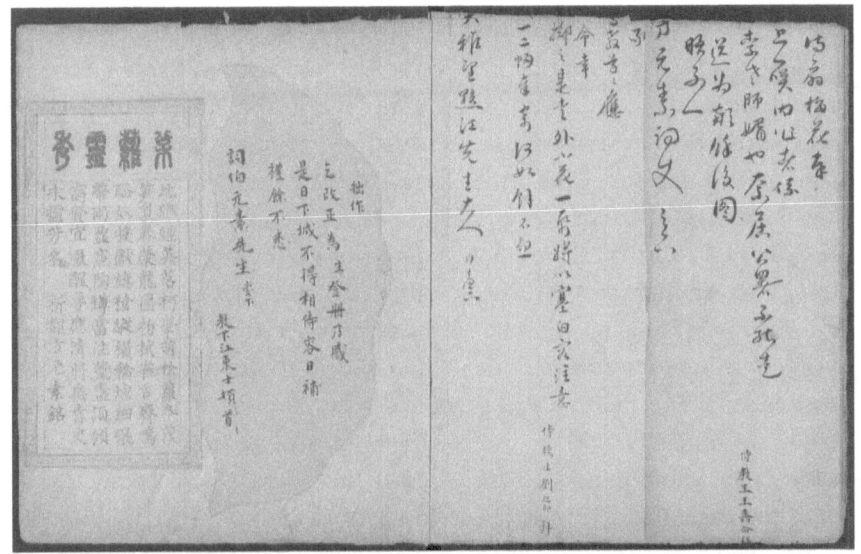

FIGURE 2.20. Handbill with "Fang Yongbin's Fineries of Mount Pine Lichen Inscription" 方用彬松蘿靈秀銘 (a brand of tea) pasted alongside a letter from Jiang Dongshi 江東士 (n.d.) to Fang Yongbin (left). Source: *Ming zhuming jia chidu*, mu 木: 69.

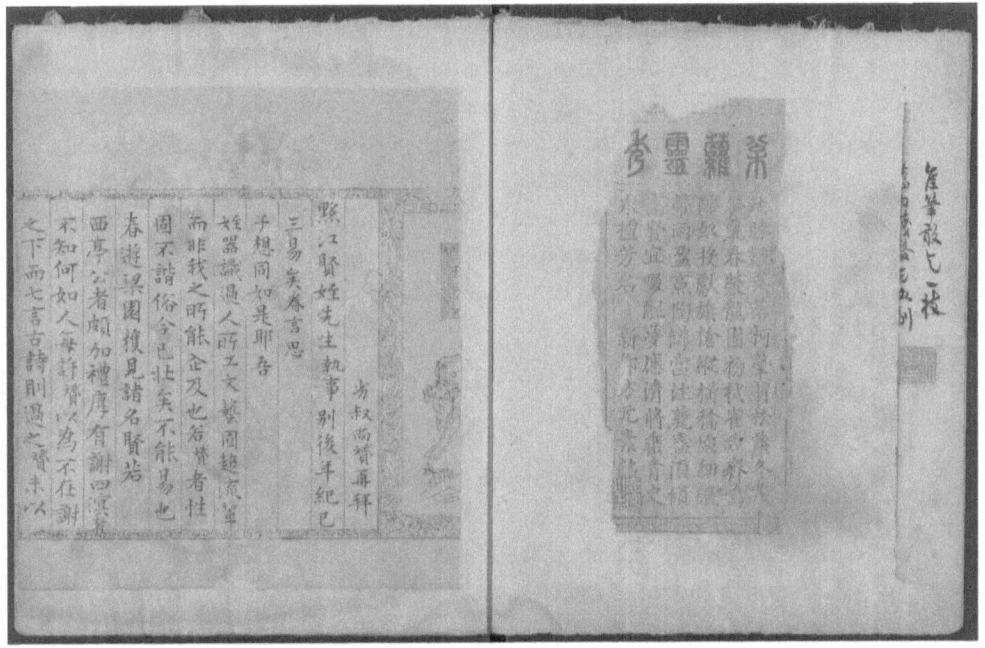

FIGURE 2.21. Handbill with "Fang Yongbin's Fineries of Mount Pine Lichen Inscription" pasted alongside a letter from Qiu Tan 丘坦 (n.d.) to Fang Yongbin (right). Source: *Ming zhuming jia chidu*, shui 水: 44.

(presented in a cartouche as if it were the inscribed seal-script title on the forehead of a stele) and printed in red ink, while Fang's composition and the fret-pattern borders of the advert are printed in blue. One copy of the inscription bears the added detail of Fang Yongbin's personal seal: "Master Sixuan" (Sixuan sheng 思玄生)—a supplement that together with the calligraphy of the title implicitly alludes to the author's reputation as a dealer and carver of seals.[176] Fang's colored ink precedes early examples of its use among Huizhou printers, demonstrating that the design of paper flyers contributed to innovations in woodblock production, enlarging the possibilities for formatting and graphic display in print.[177] Given what we now know of Fang's work as an aspiring poet, seal carver, ink maker, and papermaker, it is tempting to ask whether the product he is promoting is tea or the design and production of the flyer as an innovative multimedia format. The relationship between an inscription and its object now seems secondary to the coordination and interplay between different forms of graphic art.

Amid the upheavals of the late sixteenth century, Wang Daokun and his retainers turned to the Ming marketplace, seeking to recover a vision of the monumental within the everyday, moving from the inscription of boulders and stelae to daggers and lutes, endorsing inksticks and small soft-stone seals. Fang Yongbin emerges from Wang's circle and the inscribed landscape in which they operated, harnessing expertise in ink making and seal carving to design his own miniature mass-produced monument on paper, one that repurposes the visual aesthetics of a stele for an ephemeral advertisement. His first four couplets simply list an array of exemplary tea leaves, punning on the component characters for these titles: "swallow tongues" chirping, etc.:

PINE LICHEN SPLENDOR:

An outstanding scenic spot! The tea has started to bud.
Pine lichen flourishes in winter, while the bamboo shoots bud in spring.
"Dragon balls" are taken first, "swallow tongues" chirp together.
A "maidservant junket" offers up a gift, with "flagpoles" strewn across each other.
With mist, finely ground, bringing rainwater to the boil.
Poured into a ceramic cup, nestled in a saucer.

WRITING WITH A KNIFE

Fit for a great worthy to sip, responding to its freshness as if waking from a dream.

Passed into the annals of history, it will forever possess a fragrant name.

INSCRIPTION BY FANG YUANSU OF XINDU

松蘿靈秀：

地勝鐘英，茗柯肇萌。松蘿冬茂，笋乳春榮。
龍團初拭，雀舌齊鳴。酪奴投獻，旗槍縱橫。
和煙細碾，帶雨盈烹。陶罏當注，甆盞須傾。
高賢宜啜，醒夢應清。將垂青史，永擅芳名。

新都方元素銘。[178]

In the second half of the inscription, Fang recounts step-by-step acts of preparing and drinking tea, tacitly inviting his readers to imagine the experience of testing the product for themselves. The poem concludes with Fang's claims for the prospective longevity of this "fragrant name," by which he means to refer to the brand of tea—and yet his concern with renown betrays an investment in the broader reception of his own identity: "Fang Yuansu of Xindu." Rather than invoke the authority of his name to sanction the significance of an object, he harnesses the nascent celebrity of a local product to promote his signature, yoking his reputation to the fate of an ephemeral commodity.[179] Fang's inscription implicitly reflects upon the way paper-based ephemera disturb preconceived notions of durability and disposability. A flyer might outlast a single stone stele through the prospect of its mass production, and yet the sheer abundance of printed matter in the Ming marketplace that the format of Fang's flyer betrays raises new questions as to what could and should survive. Fang's pseudo-stele advertisements for a package of local tea leaves take pleasure in a recognition that the preservation of writing is not foreordained but is rather contingent and open to contestation.

Fang Yongbin's handbills yield two sets of conclusions. The materiality and layout of the documents reveal that techniques of writing with a knife exceed the production of seals, bringing calligraphic carving into a dynamic relationship with woodblock design to create composite graphic surfaces: part seal, part imprint, part inscription. From a literary perspective, Fang's inscriptions as jingles for a brand inaugurate a shift away from solid artifacts toward the charismatic attributes of a label: his compositions suggest that inscription might enlarge possibilities for naming things in the late Ming, transforming a brand into an aesthetic product, one that draws from, combines, and yet cannot be reduced to the reputations of a person, locality, or object. Both developments were brought together by and find more sophisticated expression in the production of a material that Fang Yongbin also peddled in the Treasure Store, one that sustains writing itself; namely, ink.

The pseudo-stele advertisements for tea in Fang Yongbin's cache tie together the central themes of this chapter. His career as another self-styled Confucian Knight-Errant shows how Wang Daokun's renown as an author of monumental inscriptions—a reputation established through his ill-fated participation in border-defense initiatives for the Ming state—provided cover and necessary funds for younger entrepreneurs in his circle to enlarge the possibilities of seal carving and inkstick production, traversing rigid boundaries between classical scholarship, commerce, and craft. Fang's handbills, in turn, suggest how Huizhou entrepreneurs moved beyond the design of seals and inksticks to improvise with new approaches to inscription, composing *ming* to market ephemeral products such as "Pine Lichen Splendor" in colored ink. Biographies of Huizhou carvers like the martial protagonists Su Xuan and He Zhen—the first figures to be posthumously commemorated for their talents in carving seals—demonstrate the extent to which early modern innovations in writing with a knife were tied in the literary imagination to a perceived crisis of collective faith in the stability of Ming stone monuments. The unexpurgated contents of Fang Yongbin's cache by contrast elucidate how the art of engraving words became a tactic for negotiating volatile markets, forging links between pawnbroking, the retail of epitaphs, the connoisseurship of inkstones, the carving of bamboo and ivory, and the production of seals and inksticks. The shopkeeper's inscriptions treat impermanence not as a threat, but as a condition of possibility.

APPENDIX 2.1
Huizhou Cultural Entrepreneurs in Wang Daokun's Circle

Name	Notes	Wang Daokun's Inscriptions (and Related Endorsements)
Wang Daoguan 汪道貫 (Zhongyan 仲淹; 1543–1591) and Wang Daohui 汪道會 (Zhongjia 仲嘉; 1544–1613), the "Two Zhongs" 二仲	Wang Daokun's younger brother and cousin; collectors and connoisseurs; patrons of Fang Yulu's ink atelier; Daoguan drafted seal-script calligraphy for Wang Daokun's stelae and edited a seal catalogue with Fang Yongbin; Wang Daohui was also an ink maker	
He Zhen 何震 (1535–1604)	The first "seal carver"; founder of Huizhou seal carving; student of Wen Peng; served under Wang Daokun's direction in Qi Jiguang's military staff	"He Changqing guzhuan yinzhang" 何長卿古篆印章
Su Xuan 蘇宣 (1553–ca. 1626)	Associate of He Zhen; became a seal carver by "borrowing" Wang Daokun's sword; possibly also a student of Wen Peng	
Liang Zhi 梁袠 (Qianqiu 千秋)	Seal carver from a Huizhou lineage based in Yangzhou; studied with He Zhen; editor (with Wang Daohui) of *Yinjun* 印雋 (1610); Liang's concubine and younger brother were also seal carvers	
Wang Benhu 汪本湖 (Yuanli 元蠡; n.d.)	Salt merchant; collector; ink maker, papermaker, and carver of pinewood artifacts	"Wang Yuanli bishou ming" 汪元蠡匕首銘
Zha Nai 查鼐 (Bashi 八十; n.d.)	Musician and *pipa* performer	"Zha Bashi pipa ming" 查八十琵琶銘; "Zha Bashi zhuan" 查八十傳; "Zha Bashi" 查八十
Fang Yangeng 方巖耕 (Jingzhen 景真; n.d.)	The "Confucian Knight-Errant" 儒俠; seal carver; affinal relation of Wang Daoguan	"Ruxia zhuan" 儒俠傳
Fang Yongbin 方用彬 (Yuansu 元素); 1542–1608)	Pawnbroker and shopkeeper (owner of the Treasure Store 寶店); seal carver; poet; painter; calligrapher; ink maker and papermaker	"Zeng Fang sheng xu" 贈方生序
Fang Yulu 方于魯 (1541–1608)	Celebrity inkstick manufacturer; poet; papermaker	"Fang Yulu Liaotian yi mo ming" 方于魯寥天一墨銘; "Feiyan mo ming" 非煙墨銘*
Ding Yunpeng 丁雲鵬 (Nanyu 南羽; 1547–1628)	Painter (famous for his paintings on Buddhist and Daoist themes); illustrator for Fang Yulu's *Fangshi mopu* 方氏墨譜 (1588); ink maker; collaborator with He Zhen; Ding's mother was a relative of the Wang 汪 family	"Jieyuan yan ming you xu" 結緣硯銘有序
Wu Tingyu 吳廷羽 (Zuogan 左干; n.d.)	Musician and flutist; painter and student of Ding Yunpeng; ink maker and illustrator for *Fangshi mopu*	"Zuogan xiao ming" 左干簫銘

*Wang also composed a number of inkstick inscriptions for bespoke gifts manufactured by Fang Yulu, see *Taihan ji*, 78. 1613–1615.

Chapter Three

THE INK-MAKER'S MARK

Among the solid tablets of ink held in the collections of the Palace Museum in Beijing, there is a small rectangular stick, weighing 34.7 grams, that bears a short inscription by Wang Daokun (figure 3.1). His words complement an enigmatic label, "One with Clear Heaven" (Liaotian yi 寥天一), and the seal of an elusive manufacturer named Sun Ruiqing 孫瑞卿 (n.d.). The survival of this slender artifact—a piece donated by an eminent twentieth-century chemist, Zhang Zigao 張子高 (1886–1976), and carefully documented as an antique in an ink-squeeze rubbing for the museum—broaches the question of what it was about these markings that warranted protection and storage.[1] Like tea or wine, an inkstick was, after all, supposed to be finished up through its use. The worn base of Sun's tablet hints that it was once lightly ground or tested in the pool of a stone inkslab, yet the preservation of its labels appears to have superseded consumption of the ink itself. Gauging what mattered about these markings demands first assessing how they related to or supplemented one another: How, then, might one parse the interplay between a literary inscription ("Inscribed by Wang Boyu" 汪伯玉銘), an ink-maker's seal ("Made by Sun Ruiqing, Yuquan of Xindu" 新都玉泉, 孫瑞卿制), and the name of a line (Liaotian yi) of ink? What brought these different markings together as components of the same surface?

The Palace Museum inkstick—a supposedly disposable object, yet one that alludes in miniature to the rectangular shape and format of a

THE INK-MAKER'S MARK

FIGURE 3.1. Rubbing of Sun Ruiqing's 孫瑞卿 (n.d.) "One with Clear Heaven" 寰天一 inkstick bearing an inscription attributed to Wang Daokun and the seal "Made by Sun Ruiqing, Yuquan of Xindu" 新都玉泉, 孫瑞卿制. From the collection of Zhang Zigao 張子高 (1886–1976), now in the Palace Museum. *Source:* Ye Gongchuo 葉恭綽, Zhang Jiongbo 張絅伯, Zhang Zigao 張子高, and Yin Runsheng 尹潤生, eds., *Sijia cangmo tulu* 四家藏墨圖錄 (Beijing: Gugong wenwu, 1960?; University of Chicago), 8.

stele—encapsulates transformations in the practice of literary inscription in early modern China (figures 3.2a and 3.2b). Sun Ruiqing did not carve Wang Daokun's endorsement onto this object from a signature calligraphic draft, rather he cut these words intaglio into a six-piece wooden mold within which ink paste, a viscous mixture of carbon lampblack and glue, could be set. At the same time, Wang's inscription reads not as a response to the properties of the artifact upon which it appears but as a promotional message that precedes the object's production, as an endorsement embedded in the inkstick's design and facture.[2] His lines were not, like many

 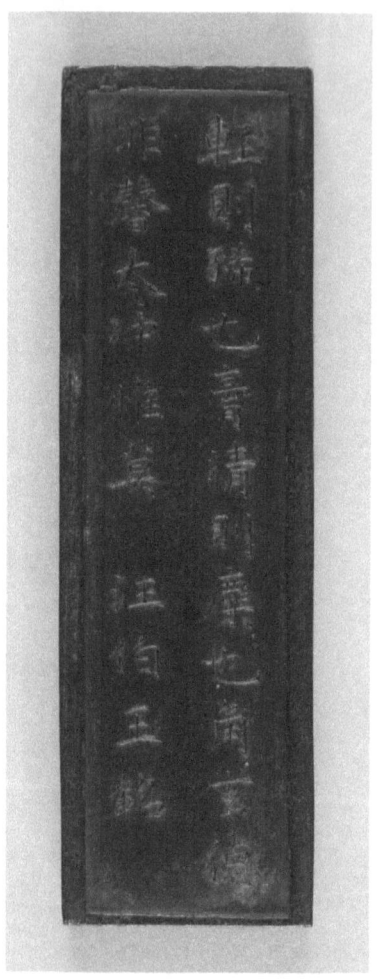

FIGURE 3.2A. Sun Ruiqing's "One with Clear Heaven" inkstick. *Source*: The Palace Museum.

FIGURE 3.2B. Sun Ruiqing's "One with Clear Heaven" inkstick. *Source*: The Palace Museum.

inscriptions on decorative objects from late imperial China, later incisions into the surface of a preformed artifact or an intervention in its circulation and reception but intrinsic components of a reproducible tablet.³

Sun Ruiqing's inkstick concurrently attests to an unprecedented degree of exchange between literary inscription and commodity branding in late Ming China, negotiations that centered upon the fate of labels like "One with Clear Heaven." Wang Daokun's assessment is dedicated not to a singular artifact but to the enigmatic title of an ink recipe. As the state regulation of artisanal markings weakened in the late sixteenth century, private manufacturers improvised with new strategies of product labeling.[4] Solid ink, a basic material that powered early modern cultures of learning, yet one that remained highly susceptible to adulteration, became a vehicle for striking innovations in commercial packaging, as the advertisement of consumer goods spurred unlikely forms of literary invention. The social logic of the brand, as archaeological perspectives on marketing suggest, speaks to an underlying dilemma in the functioning of large-scale economies: a need, amid the circulation of substitutable commodities, to garner trust and ensure exclusivity through practices of labeling.[5] "One with Clear Heaven," a label suspended between a literary endorsement and an artisanal seal, yet one that remains irreducible to either of these templates, embodies a similarly fraught effort to maintain an impression of intimacy or personality while managing ever more impersonal transactions.[6]

WRITING ON AN INK CAKE

The Ming ink cake as a result came to constitute an interface where different approaches to writing—literature, calligraphy, epigraphy, seal carving, and artisanal trademarking—could be brought together and transformed through their contact, enlarging possibilities for the presentation of words on objects. The ink business expanded in the late sixteenth century because of flourishing communication networks, with supply lines stretching from the ateliers of Huizhou and the temple stalls of Beijing to stationery stores in Japanese and Korean cities. Entrepreneurial manufacturers took advantage of these new markets to publish encyclopedic catalogues of designs, orchestrating a heightened level of interchange and transfer between different sectors of the Chinese graphic landscape.[7] Poems, the portentous impressions on dynastic seals, embroidered palindromes, Latin transcriptions of biblical stories, wheels of Sanskrit syllables, and archaic glyphs molded onto ritual bells all surface and vie for attention in Ming inkstick design. The very idea of an ink cake, as a generative source of all words and images, inspired contemporaneous innovations in woodblock illustration, as designers recycled and integrated heterogeneous graphic sources in a bid to outdo competitors.

The design and creation of solid ink thus facilitated extensive collaboration between poets, calligraphers, seal carvers, painters, and woodblock engravers—creating a space where barriers between hitherto discrete fields of graphic art might dissolve. The promiscuous adaptation of words and images for ink-cake design coupled with the ink maker's questionable social provenance, however, elicited anxious commentary from across the Ming world of letters, developments that transformed the infrastructure of Chinese literature—the material contingencies and technical preconditions of writing—into a matter of far-reaching literary concern. Adrian Johns has asked whether ink should be understood as a substance or as a system—a creative industry built upon a symbiosis of "people, places, processes, and papers."[8] Inkstick inscriptions during the late Ming and early Qing worked to manage and mitigate concerns with the inherent instability of these formations—with the fluctuating combinations that ensured ink's permanency.[9]

"One with Clear Heaven" emerged from this volatile ecology of mass-produced designs, with its sponsors striving to delimit the meaning and value consumers might assign to ink. These charismatic brands were initially formed through collaboration between poets and entrepreneurial manufacturers and yet came to exceed the claims to ownership formulated by both parties, transcending the categories of time, place, or human celebrity.[10] The advertisement of such labels was by no means a trivial pursuit in Ming China. Many of the leading literary figures of the late sixteenth and seventeenth centuries composed inscriptions to name and promote lines of ink, short jingles that work to resolve the tensions a brand embodies—between a promise of singularity and the predicament of homogeneity, between longevity and short-term gratification. Poets in this process looked to the mundane properties of lampblack and glue—the consistency, tone, or scent of an ink-maker's ingredients—to renovate an increasingly stale idiom of transcendence, comparing ink's luster to the glow of planets and stars, or its carbon residue to propitious heavenly ethers. They sought unlikely links to writing's material basis in worn-out images of the celestial and the sublime.

After an introduction to the impact of inkstick design on the presentation and display of words on objects, I use the fate of "One with Clear Heaven"—a recipe that was initially attributed to the celebrity Huizhou ink maker Fang Yulu but was later coopted by entrepreneurs like Sun

Ruiqing—to investigate both the motivations for and wide-ranging consequences of Ming ink marketing.[11] While the sponsorship of an ink brand recast inscription as a novel form of commercial publicity, this practice concurrently broached long-standing concerns in writing on things: How to defend the preservation of a useless tool or conversely to advocate for the necessary destruction of a useful implement? An inkstick, perhaps more than any other object, embodies cycles of dissolution and regeneration, as a disposable product yet one that anticipates the prospect of survival through its material metamorphoses. Seemingly superfluous inscriptions for labels like "One with Clear Heaven" eloquently register and at times interrogate shifting conceptions of permanence and obsolescence in the long seventeenth century, searching for an elusive sense of endurance within the ephemeral.

MING INK

More ancient than paper, ink has been an essential component of "self-awareness, learning, culture, and knowledge" across the world for the past two millennia, yet it rarely seems necessary to account for such a claim.[12] This irony: that ink is at once so fundamental to written communication, yet that historians tend to look *through* it, speaks (as Johns has elsewhere observed) to its own inscrutable, shape-shifting materiality.[13] Throughout the preindustrial world, ink making sustained openness and publicity yet became intimately entwined with histories of natural magic, medical secrecy, alchemy, and espionage. With no stable chemical constituent, the precise details of premodern ink recipes still remain shrouded in mystery.[14] Conventionally described as a mixture of lampblack (obtained by burning pinewood, tung oil, petroleum, or possibly lacquer) and glue (from boiled cowhides, deer horn, leather, or fish maw), Chinese ink might also contain quantities of egg white, peony rind, soap-tree pods, pomegranate skins, pearls, carp galls, walnut, copper vitriol, cloves, cinnabar, madder root, yellow reed, tonka beans, camphor, musk, or just garbage—to list only a few of its many pigments, additives, and binding agents.[15]

Mixed with other ingredients like turnip, foxglove juice, bile, and dried ginger, ink from the tenth century onward was used in medicine as a cure for dysentery, nose bleeds, eye irritations, or bleeding after childbirth.[16] Blue ink from indigo and red ink from vermillion or red lead could be used for printing, and evidence from no later than the twelfth century attests to the use of invisible ink (possibly from alum) by magicians.[17] Manufactured and sold in solid forms (as pills, pellets, balls, cakes, tablets, and sticks) from at least the third century BCE, ink became a liquid when ground and mixed with a small amount of water in the cavity of a stone slab. Given its prismatic shape, an inkstick invited poets, calligraphers, and painters from the Tang dynasty onward to experiment with the possibilities of design. Nevertheless, ink's vibrant materiality, blending animal, vegetable, and mineral forms, oscillating between solid and liquid states, exceeds and unsettles conceptions of a discrete, inert artifact.

The enigmatic composition of the substance and the questionable social provenance of the characters who claimed to have manufactured its ingredients meant that ink served as a proxy for broader struggles to determine standards of trust and credit in the seventeenth century. The Ming ink maker emerges in contemporaneous anecdotes as a duplicitous figure of enchantment and public scandal. Sensational gossip spread of murderous affairs between rival manufacturers and their concubines or of greedy entrepreneurs throwing young boys into garden snake pits to refine glue recipes, rumors that conflate suspicions of material and moral integrity.[18] The decorative ink cake encapsulated concerns with slippages between outward appearance and hidden worth, leading to caricatures of the object as an ostentatious celebrity: "Their skin-deep appearance is flashy like dressing up in gaudy brocade. There is a saying that one should not use one's looks to win fame, why then would this be sufficient to value ink?" 即皮相之爛若披錦矣。語云人貌榮名，且胡為其足以重墨也.[19]

The Harvard-Yenching cache of correspondence for shopkeeper and itinerant Huizhou pawnbroker Fang Yongbin—Wang Daokun's enterprising associate from chapter 2—divulges the multifaceted social life of ink in late Ming China. Numerous letters contain requests for supplies of ink with some customers mentioning what appears to be the name of Fang Yongbin's product line: "Homemade Dark Treasure" 家造玄寶.[20] While ink production played a decisive role in the expansion of Fang's Treasure Store, Yongbin never ascended to the ranks of celebrity Huizhou ink manufacturers: entrepreneurial artisans like his kinsman, Fang Yulu—a figure later listed alongside the artist Dong Qichang, the astronomer Xu Guangqi 徐光啓 (1562–1633), Jesuit Matteo Ricci (1552–1610), and seal carver He Zhen as a preeminent cultural luminary of the Wanli 萬曆 reign (1573–1620).[21]

THE INK-MAKER'S MARK

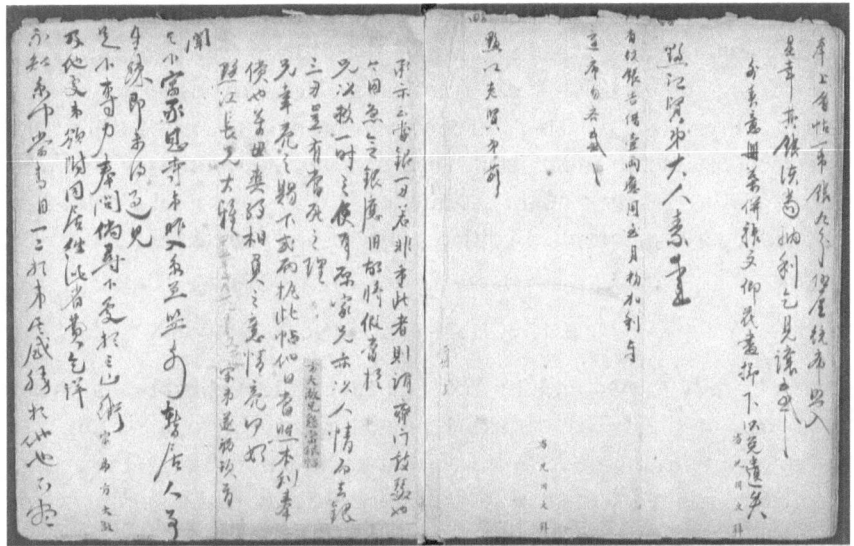

FIGURE 3.3. Letter from Fang Da'ao 方大澂 [Yulu] to Fang Yongbin recording the pawning of an ink cake.
Source: *Ming zhuming jia chidu*, huo: 92.

Fang Yongbin's archive tracks Fang Yulu's precipitous rise to fame. An early letter, datable to 1566, addressed to Fang Yongbin from Fang Yulu (then named Da'ao 大澂) contains a request for silver in a pawn deal (figure 3.3). A later correspondent, by contrast, submits a "family-owned antique Yulu ink cake" as a valuable pledge for a loan. By this point, the ink maker had taken his courtesy name (*zi* 字) Yulu as his proper name (*ming* 名) because the Wanli emperor had praised the "Yulu" marks on his inksticks.[22] In the interval between these two letters, Fang Yulu has transitioned from a young apprentice in need of funds to an acclaimed ink maker whose wares were preserved by collectors as contemporary antiques. His ink was no longer a basic writing material but an imperially endorsed objet d'art.[23]

Fang Yongbin's papers offer a ground-level view of the Ming ink market, showing how a shopkeeper, primarily versed in moneylending and seal carving, might experiment with marketing his own brand of ink alongside retailing his relative's more fashionable products. Customers, for instance, sent in specific requests for Fang Yulu's ink cakes bearing images of the Eighteen Arhats (Shiba zun luohan 十八尊羅漢) and the Bodhidharma (Damo dashi 達磨大士).[24] Fang Yulu's newfound fame in the Wanli era, by contrast, betrays the prestige and economic clout a leading ink maker might attain, earning a place alongside the preeminent celebrities of his age.[25] Yongbin's and Yulu's divergent perspectives nevertheless reveal a shared concern with devising and effectively promoting a name as if it were a valuable product in and of itself. Their back-and-forth limns the multiple guises a Ming inkstick might assume, as a basic commodity, pawnshop pledge, imperial gift, limited-edition souvenir, and vaunted antique.

ENCYCLOPEDIC THINGS

That a "family-owned antique Yulu ink cake" might constitute a pledge for a loan of silver invites further reflection on what made Fang Yulu so famous. Working under Wang Daokun's direction, Fang—the artisan who later invented "One with Clear Heaven"—garnered an empire-wide clientele, using his profits and relations with other Huizhou artists to pioneer an inventive approach to design that brought words, images, and objects into new perceptual configurations. Just as Fang Yulu's products forged connections between hitherto segregated fields of graphic art, so too, Fang himself improvised with different creative roles: he allegedly dabbled in papermaking, and versions of his biography note that he decided to give up on a budding career as a poet for ink production.[26] Fang Yulu's posthumous reputation rests on his ink-cake compendium, *Master Fang's Ink Catalogue*, the first of four major "ink books" (*moshu* 墨書) from the late sixteenth and early seventeenth centuries, an encyclopedic publication that as Li-chiang Lin and Ts'ai Mei-fen have shown spearheaded fêted innovations in woodblock illustration, creating a new space in Chinese visual culture for the subsequent adaptation of European prints.[27]

Ming ink books, from Cheng Junfang's 程君房 (1541–1610+) *Master Cheng's Ink Garden* (*Chengshi moyuan* 程氏墨園; ca. 1606) to Fang Ruisheng's方瑞生 (n.d.) *Sea of Ink* (*Mohai* 墨海; ca. 1620), were among the first Chinese publications to reproduce illustrations, obtained through Jesuit intermediaries based in Portuguese Macao, of *Christ Appearing to Simon Peter and the Miraculous Draught of Fishes*, *The Journey to Emmaus*, *The Sodomites Blinded Before Lot's House*, and *Madonna and Child*.[28] Matteo Ricci submitted Latin transcriptions of biblical stories in Chinese translation to accompany the prints in *Master Cheng's Ink Garden*. These widely discussed attempts to publish European engravings through the unlikely medium of ink-cake design are, however, only one iteration of a more pervasive concern among contemporary ink makers with gathering all the words and images that were believed to exist in the Ming world. Fang Yulu, for instance, had already looked beyond the boundaries of the Chinese language by recycling eighteen "akṣaracakra diagrams" (wheels of Sanskrit syllables) in the Rañjana script for Buddhist tantric meditations from Tangut Tibetan scriptures (figures 3.4a and 3.4b).[29]

FIGURE 3.4A. Round ink cake (yellow), attributed to Fang Yulu, Ming dynasty (1368-1644). *Source*: National Palace Museum; Open Data.

FIGURE 3.4B. Detail of side-marking: "Ink for Transcribing Sutras from the Tripitaka" 大藏寫經之墨. From a round ink cake (yellow), attributed to Fang Yulu. *Source*: National Palace Museum; Open Data.

First published in 1588 and 1589, then reprinted in 1596, 1608, 1620, and 1629, *Master Fang's Ink Catalogue* contains 380 designs in five shapes—"circular disc" (*gui* 規), "square" (*ju* 矩), "cylindrical tablet" (*ting* 珽), "scepter" (*gui* 圭), and "miscellaneous pendants" (*zapei* 雜珮), all categories based on ancient jade ornaments—anthologized in six volumes entitled: "State Treasure" (Guobao 國寶), "State Splendor" (Guohua 國華), "Investigating Antiquity" (Bogu 博古), "Investigating Things" (Bowu 博物), "Dharma Treasure" (Fabao 法寶), and "Vast Treasure" (Hongbao 鴻寶).[30] The relationship between Fang's published designs and his range of ink products remains unclear. Extant Ming ink cakes and inksticks match images within the catalogue, yet it is difficult to ascertain whether such artifacts preceded or copied his popular prints (compare figures 3.4a and 3.4b with figure 3.5). Was his catalogue intended to advertise available merchandise or to envision new conceptual possibilities for ink-cake design through the medium of woodblock illustration? There are, moreover, significant differences between the technologies of ink-cake production and woodblock carving. A standard rectangular inkstick possesses six surfaces for decoration and inscription, yet Fang Yulu's catalogue only displays two: the front and back of the object. When documenting prized inksticks through the creation of ink-squeeze rubbings, however, collectors typically record the markings on the sides of these artifacts—dates, maker's marks, studio names, or the titles of recipes and production techniques—suggesting their critical significance for judgments of value and authenticity. While pictures of inksticks in print superficially resemble solid inksticks, the act of carving an inkstick mold demanded a different repertoire of skills: woodblock carvers cut lines on a planar surface, but a three-dimensional inkstick mold required a comparatively difficult bas-relief effect.[31] The names of woodblock carvers appear in Ming ink books; the identities and innovations of Ming inkstick mold carvers were altogether ignored.[32]

The organizational layout of *Master Fang's Ink Catalogue* promotes late Ming philosophical syncretism, the ideal of "three teachings coalescing as one" (*sanjiao heyi* 三教合一), a vision that reflects the ecumenical commitments of Fang Yulu's leading sponsors and collaborators.[33] "Dharma Treasure" collects Buddhist designs, some of which are labeled as limited-edition commissions for transcribing Buddhist sutras in Wang Daokun's *chan* 禪 meditation group, the Zhaolin Society (Zhaolin she 肇林社).[34] "Vast Treasure" collects Daoist designs bearing talismans and "pacing the

THE INK-MAKER'S MARK

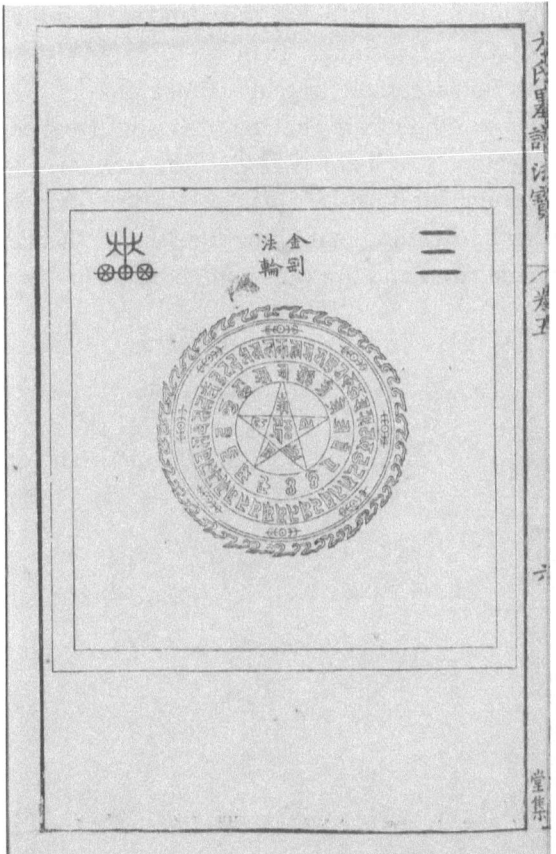

FIGURE 3.5. Fang Yulu's "The Diamond Dharma Wheel" 金剛法輪, design, recto. *Source*: Fang Yulu, *Fangshi mopu*, 5.6b.

void" poems (*buxu ci* 步虛詞) for use in esoteric rituals. "State Treasure" and "State Splendor" collect designs that celebrate imperial statecraft, whether through omens and astrographic portents of dynastic legitimacy in the former volume or auspicious images of good governance, official insignia, and social cohesion in the latter. "Investigating Antiquity" and "Investigating Things," finally, compile designs that reflect trends in Ming Confucian learning: classical scholarship and "broad learning" (*boxue* 博學), or the empirical investigation of the natural world.[35]

Fang Yulu includes a visual emblem of this intellectual synthesis in a circular ink cake entitled "Enveloping the Three as One" (Hansan wei yi

函三為一) with images of Confucius, Laozi, and the Buddha adapted from the "Painting of Three Teachings" (Sanjiao tu 三教圖)—a design reverently marked as "unacceptable to grind" (buke mo 不可磨) (figure 3.6). The title alludes to a line from the Han dynasty "Treatise on Harmonics and the Calendar" (Lü li zhi 律曆志): "the supreme ultimate primal pneuma, enveloping the three as one" 太極元氣，函三為一, a phrase typically understood to designate how the "three" (heaven, earth, and humans) emanate from and are thus contained within the "one," yet in

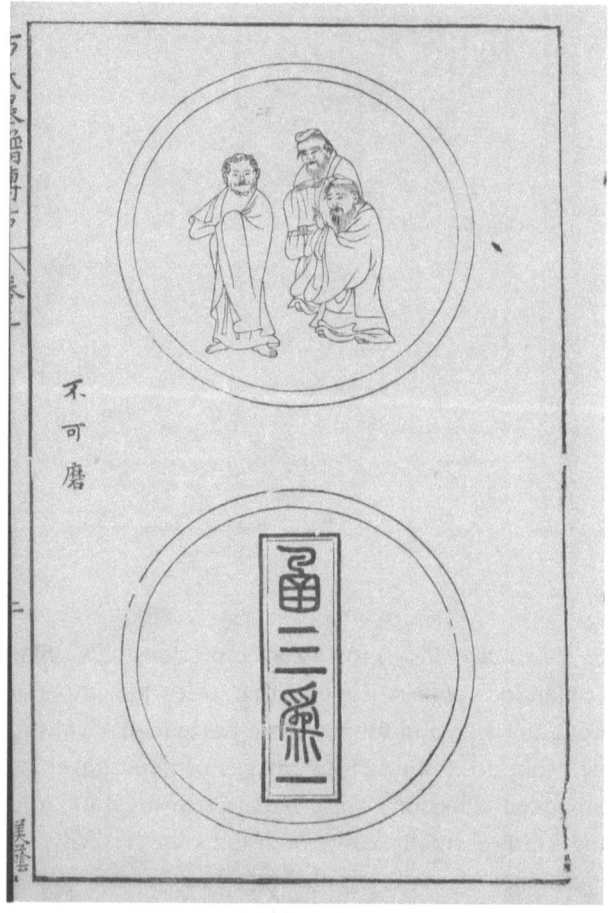

FIGURE 3.6. Fang Yulu's "Enveloping the Three as One" 函三為一 design bearing images of Confucius, Laozi, and the Buddha adapted from the "Painting of Three Teachings" (Sanjiao tu 三教圖). The design is marked as "unacceptable to grind" (buke mo 不可磨). Source: Fang Yulu, Fangshi mopu, 3.2a.

this instance also a punning reference to Wang Daokun's studio name "Studio of the Enveloped Three" (Hansan shi 函三室), a clue to his central role in shaping the intellectual agenda behind Fang's project.[36] Ink, as the huddled congregation in "Enveloping the Three as One" implies, not only constitutes the shared material basis of these three teachings but also serves as a medium through which to grasp the fundamental "unity" or "oneness" (yi 一) that underlies and connects all phenomena. The concept of "oneness" remained key to the Ming Neo-Confucian experience of self and sage-hood, and yet prominent contributors to Fang's catalogue had started to explore other intellectual possibilities in a "post-Neo Confucian world," anticipating an early Qing turn to evidential learning by affirming the value of the factual and the particular in "scholarship about things."[37]

As "Investigating Antiquity" insinuates (and the contents of all six volumes attest), the ink catalogue masquerades as a pseudo-antiquarian project, locating and publishing an encyclopedic array of epigraphic sources. Fang Yulu's focus repeatedly returns to Song dynasty catalogues of ritual vessels, namely the *Illustrated Investigations of Antiquity* (*Kaogu tu* 考古圖) and the *Illustrated Antiquities of Xuanhe Hall* (*Xuanhe bogu tu* 宣和博古圖). Carvers involved in the production of *Master Fang's Ink Catalogue* concurrently worked on reprints of these two Song dynasty books for the same publishing house, so they were able to easily recycle images and glyphs from ritual objects for new ink designs.[38] These acts of cross-media transfer, from venerable bronze and stone monuments to the surfaces of small ink cakes, were not motivated simply by slipshod cost-cutting, but rather betray an "archaist" (*fugu* 復古) mentality that pervades *Master Fang's Ink Catalogue*.[39] Fang Yulu's leading sponsors, Wang Daokun and Wang Shizhen, led the literary movement of "returning to the ancients" under the umbrella of the "later seven masters" (*houqizi* 後七子) in the late sixteenth century: a wide-ranging intellectual program concerned with the recovery of the "essence" of antiquity from classical forms, language, and style.[40] As literary archaists sought to revivify ancient models in contemporary writing, so Fang Yulu and his powerful backers worked to reproduce models of ancient script preserved in catalogues of ritual paraphernalia through new batches of ink. This project dovetails with Wang Daokun and Fang's acquaintance, He Zhen's contemporaneous promotion of a Qin-Han aesthetic in soft-stone seal carving.

THE INK-MAKER'S MARK

Fang Yulu's promiscuous cut-and-paste aesthetic generated unconventional combinations of antique sources, enlarging conceptual possibilities for the presentation of words on an object. Take, for instance, the very first design in the catalogue, a round ink cake entitled "Four Character Seal" (sizi xi 四字璽) that bears two sets of markings drawn from the inscribed surfaces of ancient artifacts (figure 3.7). The first four characters "receiving a mandate for prosperity" (*shouming yongchang* 壽命永昌) are adapted from reprints of the legendary "Qin seal," or "Seal of Dynastic Succession" (*chuanguo xi* 傳國璽), an omen of imperial legitimacy that had been rediscovered and delivered to the Ming court in the summer of 1500.[41] The second set of eight characters on the "Four Character Seal" design resemble the final two lines of an inscribed bronze "Zhou Bell with Jiao-dragon Seal-Script" (Zhou jiaozhuan zhong 周蛟篆鍾) in the *Illustrated*

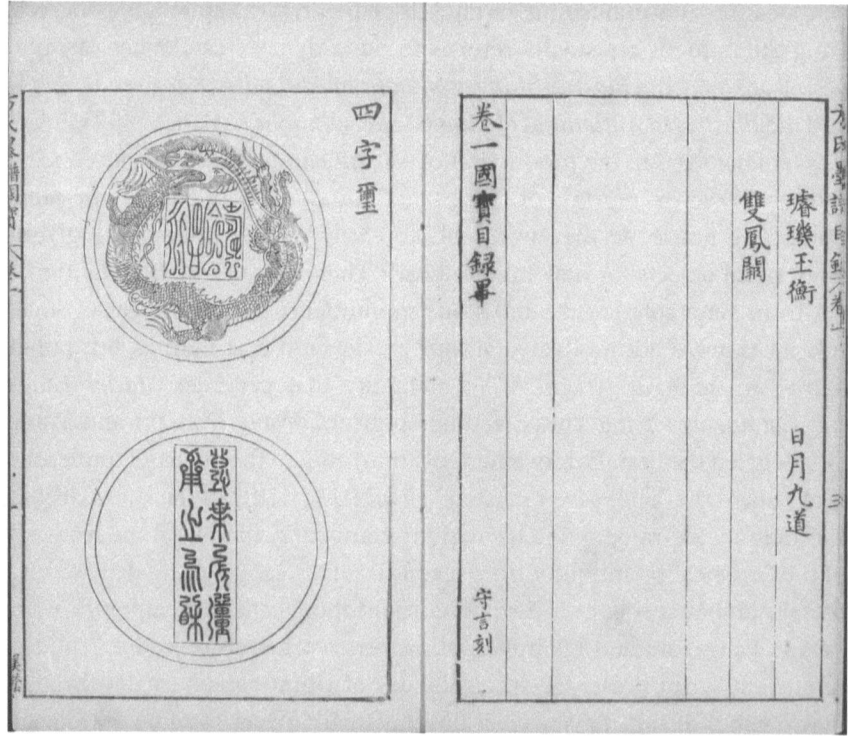

FIGURE 3.7. Fang Yulu's "Four Character Seal" 四字璽 design. This is the first design within the catalogue.
Source: Fang Yulu, *Fangshi mopu*, 1.1a.

Antiquities of Xuanhe Hall: "For a myriad generations, without limit, use it for assistance" 萬葉無彊，用之協相.⁴² The "coiled dragon" (*panlong* 蟠龍) motif, meanwhile, approximates the design of a Tang mirror also preserved in *Xuanhe Hall*.⁴³ As his opening image for the catalogue, Fang's small ink cake invokes the prestige of the Qin seal as a portent of good governance, the significance of a Zhou dynasty bell as an enduring symbol of ritual propriety, and the iconography of an antique iron mirror with its "aura of auspiciousness."⁴⁴ Fang's table of contents adopts the typographical device of *taitou* 抬頭 to present the title of this design on its own line and thus hints that it might be intended for the emperor as a possible viewer of the catalogue.

Enlarging the idea of an ink cake to assimilate and absorb the attributes of illustrious antiques, Fang's title frames his first design as if it were a seal—a symbol of imperial favor and a dynastic omen—a matrix that might generate limitless imprints.⁴⁵ Implicit comparisons between ink cake and seal in turn allude to the function of sealing techniques in the production of solid ink—the shape and appearance of an inkstick was, after all, determined by the intaglio engravings on the mold into which ink paste was pressed.⁴⁶ A cross-media or "skeuomorphic" production, Fang's design evokes a "*substantive* transfer" from the supposedly imperishable materials of jade and bronze to ink, raising the possibility that despite its less weighty or resilient objecthood, an ink cake might now more effectively ensure longevity through the prospect of its mass production and physical transformations.⁴⁷ Ink-cake design was not a marginal pursuit in Ming culture but a practice, propagated by leading intellectuals, that impinged upon how histories of writing might be organized and understood.

INK POETICS

Rather than approach *Master Fang's Ink Catalogue* as a compendium of "ink cake" pictures, I examine the often-overlooked messages inscribed on Fang's tablets to reconsider the book as a self-conscious investigation into the relationship between words and objects in early modern China. This project does not simply adapt calligraphic sources for ink-cake design but uses the idea of an ink cake to weigh the significance of writing upon things more broadly. Fang Yulu's ink book from this perspective can also be read as a literary anthology, one that encompasses a composition about ink in every major genre of poetry and prose yet coalesces around a sizeable collection of inscriptions dedicated to labels like "One with Clear Heaven."[48] Writing on ink cakes concurrently unsettled and enlarged approaches to literary inscription, inviting prominent writers like Wang Daokun to reconsider the rhetoric and medium specificity of the form. What was the "object" of an ink inscription: a single solid cake or a line of mass-produced sticks, the secret ingredients of an ink-maker's recipe or the poetic associations of a product label? What ought to be the proper relationship between a name and a thing when the thing in question was intended to be ground down and used up? Inscribed inksticks, despite evidence of their planned obsolescence, pose and at times comment upon these very questions.

A proliferation of literary inscriptions on both the surfaces of ink cakes and in the pages of ink catalogues reveals the increasingly central role of *ming* in managing claims of ownership amid fraught commercial rivalries and widespread counterfeiting. Reading the endorsements in Ming ink books in turn explains the fate of this publishing format during the late imperial period. Despite the fame of Fang Yulu and Cheng Junfang's pictures, few seventeenth-century ink makers (with the notable exception of Fang Ruisheng) chose to follow their example in printing illustrated catalogues of ink-cake designs: Pan Yingzhi's 潘膺祉 (n.d.) *Evaluation of Ink* (*Moping* 墨評), the third of the four major Ming ink books, contains twelve full-page calligraphic inscriptions (*ming*) and encomia (*zan*) dedicated to the ink-maker's brand but no illustrations of his wares. Leading Kangxi 康熙 (1661–1722) era ink maker, Cao Sugong's 曹素功 (1615–1689) catalogue, *Master Cao's Ink Forest* (*Caoshi molin* 曹氏墨林), the most acclaimed early Qing ink book, similarly included no illustrations, only words.[49]

Master Fang's Ink Catalogue, as a project that took shape over the course of at least two decades, registers transformations in the design and marketing of ink cakes during the late sixteenth century, charting a transition from the display of limited-edition souvenirs or tailor-made gifts to the advertisement of labels for an ink-maker's batch of ink.[50] Such a divergence presages a broader turn in late Ming connoisseurship toward the evaluation of the name of an ink-maker's line of ink ("One with Clear Heaven"), rather than the ink-maker's individual ink-cake designs ("Four Character Seal"). This shift dovetails with Fang's changing relationship to his patron, prominent Huizhou scholar-poet, former vice minister of war, literary archaist, and collector, Wang Daokun. Assessing the ink maker Fang Yulu's relationship to Wang and the members of his coterie, the White Elm Society (Baiyu she 白榆社), not only elucidates the provenance of literary endorsements, calligraphic samples, and pictorial sources within *Master Fang's Ink Catalogue* but also suggests how Wang's innovative approach to writing on ink cakes emerged from and was shaped by his reputation as an author of engraved memorials in stone, his sponsorship of Huizhou merchants through the commemoration of their signature tools, and his promotion of seal carving.[51] Indeed, Wang's role in the compilation of *Master Fang's Ink Catalogue* during the 1580s might be construed as the apotheosis of his career-long engagements with the Ming inscribed landscape—the conclusion to ventures that began with his mark on Qi Jiguang's sword in the 1560s.

Wang Daokun's curatorial role in recycling images for Fang Yulu's ink cakes and the function of Fang's ink cakes in memorializing the activities of the White Elm fellowship assume visual form in various designs within the catalogue. Illustrations of military commanders in chariots allude to Wang's own service fighting Japanese pirates with the general Qi Jiguang in Fujian (figure 2.7), while seemingly innocuous motifs like the two entwined black mushrooms on a "Double Ganoderma" ink cake actually refer to the names of Wang's friends: a black mushroom, auspicious sustenance for a Daoist immortal, was also called a "dragon mushroom" (*longzhi* 龍芝) invoking the surname of local magistrate and White Elm cofounder Long Ying 龍膺 (1560–1622).[52] Several images of ink cakes in the book were intended as birthday presents or bespoke gifts for leading members of the White Elm.[53]

Approaches to the ink cake as a souvenir find sophisticated expression in a pair of illustrations featuring figures from the "Images of the Twenty-Eight Lunar Mansions" (Ershiba xiu tu 二十八宿圖) in the first volume of Fang's catalogue. What initially appear to be a pair of separate designs are actually two sides—recto and verso—of the same ink cake, for a model entitled "The Five Planets Gathering Between the Legs and Wall Mansions" (Wuxing ju kui bi 五星聚奎壁). The two-sided ink-cake design matches anthropomorphized figures for the Legs Lunar Mansion (kuixiu 奎宿) (figure 3.8) and the Wall Lunar Mansion (bixiu 壁宿) (figure 3.9)—figures that appear adjacent to each other on surviving copies of the "Twenty-Eight Lunar Mansions" scroll—to represent the auspicious event of the "Five

FIGURE 3.8. Fang Yulu's "Five Planets Lodging Between the Legs and Wall Mansions" 五星聚奎壁 design, recto (Wall). Wang Daokun's inscription is presented beneath the design. *Source*: Fang Yulu, *Fangshi mopu*, 1.31a.

Major Planets" (Gold 金 [Venus], Wood 木 [Jupiter], Water 水 [Mercury], Fire 火 [Mars], and Earth 土 [Saturn]) "gathering" (*ju* 聚) between these two zodiacal constellations.

Wang Daokun facilitated Fang Yulu's access to these images and hints at his custodianship of the design by composing a literary inscription on its theme.[54] Celebrating how this auspicious heavenly formation registers the

THE INK-MAKER'S MARK

FIGURE 3.9. Fang Yulu's "Five Planets Lodging Between the Legs and Wall Mansions" design, verso. Wang Daokun's inscription is presented beneath the design (Legs). *Source*: Fang Yulu, *Fangshi mopu*, 1.31b.

emperor's munificence and the cultural splendor of the age, Wang uses the conceit of a radiant light emanating from the blackness of the night sky—a trope that would recur in the countless designs of other ink cakes bearing astronomical and astral motifs from the Wanli era—to hint at the dark luster of the ink.[55] Wang's inscription and related poems illuminate the hidden meaning behind the choice of motifs:

INSCRIPTION ON A "FIVE PLANETS GATHERING BETWEEN THE LEGS AND WALL MANSIONS" INK CAKE

A Heavenly Rooster crows, but dawn is yet to arrive.
Between the Wolf and Porcupine, the Five Planets shine resplendently.[56]
Extending North to the Palace Gates, rising at the Eastern Pavilion.
When the Emperor's virtue flourishes, cultural endeavors shimmer radiantly.

五星聚奎壁墨銘

天鷄號，夜未旦。
狼貐墟，五星爛。
亙北閣，起東觀。
帝德隆，人文煥。[57]

The date printed alongside the design featuring the Wall Lodge notifies viewers that this gathering of the planets occurred in the third month of 1584. This was also the date of a major meeting of Wang Daokun's White Elm Society to celebrate local magistrate Long Ying's success in the examinations and the occasion of his twenty-fifth birthday.[58] Amid the factionalism and precariousness of court politics in the sixteenth century, scholars turned to literary societies to foster visions of communal leadership, fashioning a world of their own around principles of worthiness and talent: one that might, in turn, be projected as a heavenly-sanctioned model for the age in which they lived. At once a memento for a one-off event and a prototype for future reproduction, the apparently superfluous form of the ink cake aspires to instantiate this ideal, touting artistic custodianship and entrepreneurial vision while weaving together the lives and official careers of the members of the White Elm Society with auspicious portents in cosmic time. Astrographic patterns attest to the literary endowments of Wang's coterie, and the luminous darkness of the "celestial dome" finds a correlate in a round black ink cake.

During two extended periods of forced retirement from court—from 1566 to 1570 and from 1575 until his death in 1593—Wang Daokun's residence became a hub for artistic and literary activity in Huizhou. In his first spell back in She County, Wang established a small coterie, the Fenggan Society

(Fenggan she 豐干社), to foster the literary education of his brothers: this close-knit organization provided a launchpad for the careers of the pawnbroker Fang Yongbin and his kinsman, Fang Yulu.[59] After his second expulsion from court in 1575, Wang Daokun replaced his earlier Fenggan group with the White Elm, a society that only enlisted "distinguished presented scholars" from across the Yangzi delta or aristocrats like the military commander and Ming princeling Zhu Duozheng 朱多炡 (1541–1589).[60] Fang Yulu was not included as a participant in the White Elm Society, yet every contributor of a literary endorsement for *Master Fang's Ink Catalogue* was either a member of this association or closely affiliated with the eminent Suzhou scholar Wang Shizhen—a connection brokered through Wang Daokun. In effect, Fang Yulu was deemed unworthy of joining the coterie of scholars that wrote about his ink.[61] While segments of Fang Yulu's verse adorn various designs, the literary inscriptions on Fang's ink cakes were composed exclusively by Wang Daokun or members of the White Elm. From this perspective, "Five Planets Gathering Between the Legs and Wall Mansions" conceals an intriguing paradox: the ink cake is intended to promote a product called "Fang Yulu's ink," yet this endeavor is predicated upon a disavowal of the artisan's voice by Wang Daokun and his literary associates. Readers are left with an impression of the Huizhou ink maker as a mute puppet manipulated by the powerful members of a trans-regional poetry society.

"Five Planets" suggests the triumph of literary endorsement over artisanal production, yet developments elsewhere in the Ming marketplace undermined the self-assurance that Wang's eulogy to the White Elm projects. Yulu's bitter rival and erstwhile collaborator Cheng Junfang had started to present "Five Planets" as his own design, one he claimed to have personally submitted to the emperor.[62] The recycling and reproduction of these personified constellations consequently presaged a demand for more sophisticated assertions of proprietorship. Wang Daokun, again affirming the authorship of the White Elm Society (rather than Fang Yulu), remarked on this dilemma by claiming "my party began making ink cake designs yet they were stolen" 吾黨為之製矣，並其製而盜之, "so [we] turned to inscription" 為之銘矣, and "the regulation of names" 亦既系之姓名矣, to forestall counterfeiting.[63] Thieves, Wang admits, subsequently stole these product labels, yet his comments indicate how the White Elm poets started to conceive of inscription as an instrument with which to conceptualize and defend an inchoate notion of intellectual property.

INSCRIPTIONAL DESIGNS

"Five Planets" illustrates how Wang Daokun's collective co-opted Fang Yulu's products as a platform to commemorate their ventures, yet most literary endorsements attributed to White Elm poets in Fang's catalogue are displayed in another distinctive graphic format: a composition I will refer to as the *inscriptional design*. These designs are listed as inscriptions in Fang Yulu's table of contents (that is, the suffix "inscription" [*ming*] appears in their titles) and yet are not included in the ink maker's comprehensive table of merchandise (*mobiao* 墨表), raising the question whether they are images of actual products or limited-edition advertisements for the catalogue. Inscriptional designs share the same features: a pair of plain rectangular frames devoid of any decorative patterns or pictorial themes. The right-hand box of the design contains a literary endorsement from a prominent sponsor affiliated with the White Elm, while the left-hand box displays one of Fang Yulu's trademarks: "Made by Fang Yulu" (Fang Yulu zhi 方于魯製), "Made by Yulu" (Yulu zhi 于魯製), "Jianyuan's Ink" (Jianyuan mo 建元墨), or his studio mark: "Pavilion of Halcyon Days" (Jiari lou 佳日樓).[64] A souvenir ink cake, like the "Five Planets" design, makes use of the folded page as what Anne Burkus-Chasson terms a "semiotic unit," creating meaning through the act of "turning the leaf"—the inscriptional design, by contrast, presents its two rectangular frames within the same field on the same page, as if demanding that the scholar's words and the craftsman's labels now be viewed in tandem as components of the same product.[65] This unique graphic format established a template for inksticks like Sun Ruiqing's "One with Clear Heaven" in the Palace Museum.

Fang Yulu's inscriptional designs elicit new interpretative possibilities, changing how the words of his sponsors, or the White Elm poets, might be read. In certain cases, through the designers' appropriation of enigmatic scripts, the characters of Fang's maker's mark emerge as a focal point of the design. A composition entitled "Old Han's Inscription" ("Hanweng ming" 函翁銘) (figure 3.10) bearing a eulogy contributed by Wang Daokun or "Old Han" (Hanweng 函翁) displays the characters "Halcyon Days" (jiari 佳日), Fang Yulu's studio mark, yet the label is rendered with graphs for *jia* 佳 and *ri* 日 taken from an epitaph on a coffin lid (*guo* 槨) supposedly for Xiaohou Ying 夏侯嬰, Duke of Teng 滕公 (d. 172 BCE) ("Tenggong muming" 滕公墓銘).[66] This epitaph, probably a later forgery or hoax, reflects a

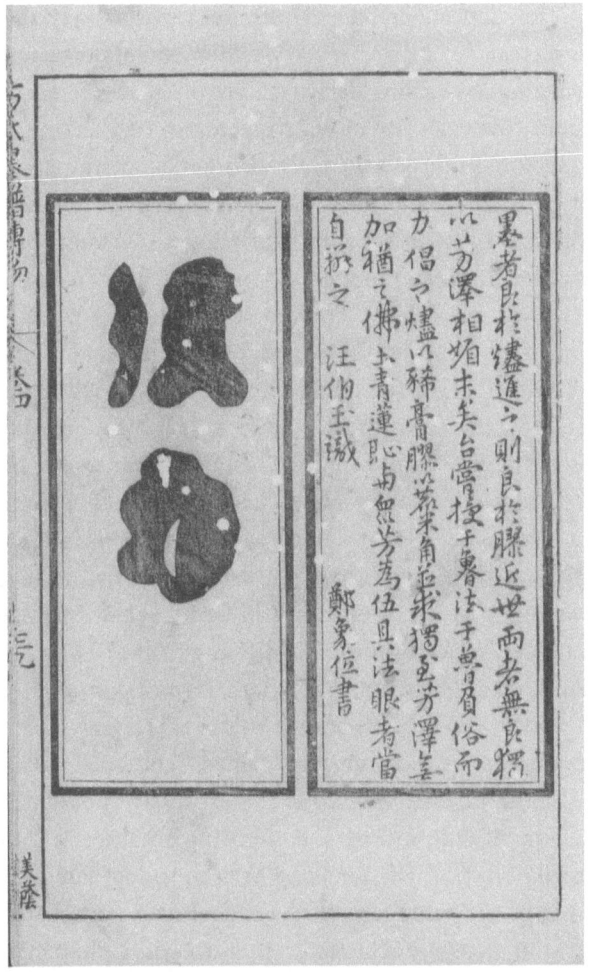

FIGURE 3.10. Fang Yulu's "Old Han's Inscription" 函翁銘 design. The right-hand side of the inkstick bears Wang Daokun's inscription. *Source*: Fang Yulu, *Fangshi mopu*, 4.39a.

contemporary fascination with "primitivist" calligraphy.[67] In this game of visual citation, one that shuttles between Fang Yulu's studio name, reprints of the almost illegible Xiaohou Ying epitaph, and the transcription of its contents in the medieval anthology, *Miscellaneous Records of the Western Capital* (*Xijing zaji* 西京雜記), "Halcyon Days" assumes an eccentric presence, at once legible and opaque, familiar and elusive. The inscriptional design presents Fang Yulu's maker's mark as an interactive graphic spectacle.

In addition to adapting archaic glyphs, inscriptional designs also incorporated leisure seals as supplementary endorsements of a maker's mark. Fang Yulu's catalogue is a singularly rich yet often neglected repository of seal impressions, the majority of which were not markers of ownership—Fang Yulu's personal and studio seals also appear within the book—but were composed of short mottoes that the reader was invited to parse in relation to the main label on the design. Wang Shizhen's younger brother, Wang Shimao, for instance, composed a piece for Fang Yulu that appeared as a preface for the catalogue, "An Evaluation of Fang Yulu's Ink" ("Fang Yulu mo ping" 方于魯墨評), yet was recycled in a design entitled "Wang Cigong's inscription" ("Wang Cigong ming" 王次公銘) alongside the label "Made by Fang Yulu" (Fang Yulu zhi 方于魯製) and a seal composed of the phrase "I will set up your first son" (*jian er yuan zi* 建爾元子) (figure 3.11). These four characters are drawn from a line in the *Classic of Poetry*: "The King said: "Uncle, set up your eldest son, make him lord in Lu"" 王曰叔父，建爾元子，俾侯于魯.[68] Viewers of the seal are left to infer the remainder of the couplet while being asked to misread "make him lord in Lu" as "make him the Lord [Fang] Yulu." The components of the ink-maker's alias (Jianyuan 建元), here, form a puzzle, the solution to which offers up the ink-maker's name (Yulu 于魯).

As if to complement these graphic games, renowned calligrapher and Ming prince Zhu Duozheng explored the expressive possibilities of character rearrangement within poetry, composing an acrostic "Add and Subtract" poem (*lihe shi* 離合詩) for Fang Yulu's product label. In this piece, Zhu invites his participants to subtract a character from each line of the first couplet to make a new character, then to add a character from each line in the second couplet to form another new character, and so on with the third couplet (subtracting 離), and fourth couplet (adding 合), to reveal a new four-character word or phrase. The solution is "Fang Yulu's Ink" (Fang Yulu mo 方于魯墨):

> The dark chamber is deeply secluded. One faces a pillar as one comes out of the door.
>
> The method is as clear as the figure "one," the old man returns to youthful vigor.
>
> What can be taken from humble me? The crescent moon emits radiant light.

THE INK-MAKER'S MARK

FIGURE 3.11. Fang Yulu's "Wang Cigong's Inscription" 王次公銘 design. The seal impression on the left reads: "I will set up your first son" 建爾元子. *Source*: Fang Yulu, *Fangshi mopu*, 4.26b.

Be silent and avoid using one's mouth. The outlying lands submit to the court.⁶⁹

玄房窈窕，　出戶當楹。
法顆畫一，　華顛復丁。
鰍生奚取，　朏月生明。
嘿毋尚口，　率土來庭。⁷⁰

> Solution:
> 玄房窈窕，出戶當楹。[Answer: 房 — 戶 ＝ 方]
> 法顙畫一，華顛復丁。[Answer: 一 ＋ 丁 ＝ 于]
> 鮁生奚取，朒月生明。[Answer: (鮁 — 取 ＝ 魚) ＋ (明 — 月 ＝ 日) ＝ 魯]
> 嘿毋尚口，率土來庭。[Answer: (嘿 — 口 ＝ 黑) ＋ 土 ＝ 墨]
> Full Answer: Fang Yulu's Ink 方于魯墨

Zhu's hermetic imagery appears freighted with significance yet is rendered superfluous as the poem is dismembered. To solve the puzzle, one has to see how the forms of the characters can be visually recombined as opposed to actually reading them. The more superficial a viewer's response to the poem's allusions, the better. Certain motifs in the poem elicit impressions of ink's blackness and light, yet Zhu's focus shifts toward the graphic surface of Fang's mark as its own source of aesthetic captivation.[71] Zhu's anagram in this sense anticipates a movement from writing about ink to writing about the proper name of a product as an elaborate literary conceit.

THE MATTER OF A BRAND

"Reign marks" at the outset of the Ming dynasty, along with the signature stamps of artisans and workshops, served as instruments for the state regulation of material production. With the spread of merchant capital in the late sixteenth century, private manufacturers undermined this imperial apparatus of quality control, improvising with new strategies for advertising ownership through labels. The Xuande emperor's reign mark "Made in the Year of the Xuande Reign of the Great Ming" (Da Ming Xuande nianzhi 大明宣德年製), commonly transcribed in regular script, had by the late Ming become a marketable symbol, one stamped, etched, or cast onto porcelain, enamel, bronze, and lacquer surfaces.[72] Artisanal signatures—the personal, style, and studio names of craftsmen—concurrently came to mimic the "forms of authorship of the literati," raising the possibility that a decorative object could in Jonathan Hay's terms "express its maker's personality," a tendency encapsulated in jade carver Lu Zigang's twelve-character seal-script engraving on Zhang Dai's fourth uncle's hairpin: "Thinking of my lord, he is as temperate as jade, made by Lu Zigang."[73]

As Craig Clunas has observed, the names of certain craftsmen—Zhao Liangbi 趙良璧 (fl. 1522–1566)—for instance, shed ties to particular professions or media, marketing items from combs to pewter-ware.[74] Ming inksticks reflect both developments: surviving tablets from the sixteenth century evidence the recycling of the Xuande reign mark; the "Pavilion of Halcyon Days" label on Fang Yulu's designs, meanwhile, refines earlier conventions for advertising an ink atelier as if it were a scholar's studio.[75]

Within *Master Fang's Ink Catalogue*, Wang Daokun starts to reflect on how an ink-maker's mark relates to this broader ecology of product labels:

> Of those in the present day who are worthy to face the ancients, there are only potters and ink makers. Chai ware and Li Tinggui's ink were the most exceptional products of the past and now they are rarely seen.[76] As for the finest ceramics of our Ming dynasty, nothing can compare to Xuande ware. As far as ink is concerned, it is only "Yulu" that might be sufficient to match them.
>
> 今之足以古者，惟陶氏，墨氏。蓋柴之陶，李之墨，千古稱良，吾見罕矣。我明陶氏之良，莫如宣德，其在于墨，則于魯足以當之。[77]

Wang effectively reduces his acquaintance's personal name to a thing that can be weighed or sold alongside imperial reign marks on ceramic wares. Yulu and Xuande assume a conceptual equivalence as generic symbols of luxury.

A late Ming account of Beijing's "Markets of the City God Temple" (Chenghuangmiao shi 城隍廟市) included in *A Sketch of Sites and Objects in the Imperial Capital* (*Dijing jingwu lüe* 帝京景物略) offers a bird's-eye view of this unruly graphic landscape, illustrating a semiology of branding. This guide for sojourners begins by evaluating the stamps on Xuande bronze censers, providing advice on how to authenticate the calligraphy and material format of this mark (it should be cast in relief not etched, and match the patina of the vessel), before evaluating kiln labels on porcelain, reign titles on lacquerware (here a Xuan mark usually denotes a Yongle artifact), and the leading paper brands ("Chen Qing's Xuan Paper Mark is the best").[78] The survey suggests that skill in evaluating object markings had become a prerequisite for navigating the marketplace, even as the need for publishing fixed guidelines insinuates (and ironically abets) the prevalence of counterfeiting. Zhang Dai, a devoted reader of *A Sketch of*

Sites and Objects in the Imperial Capital, displays a keen awareness of these same guidelines in examining his family's possessions, carefully documenting prestige markings on lacquer, bronze, and porcelain wares, while renouncing attachment to these labels as an objective source of value. Toward the end of "Markets of the City God Temple," discussion turns to ink brands, arcane labels like Cheng Junfang's "Dark Origin of Numinous Vitality" (Xuanyuan lingqi 玄元靈氣).[79] Unlike the other labels on sale in Beijing's temple-market stalls, these abstruse titles exceed and unsettle the categories of material description, time, place, or human celebrity. In addressing his "Twenty-Eight Friends," Zhang Dai downplayed his investments in makers' marks to present literary inscription as a more faithful expression of intimacy with things. Many leading late Ming poets and prose-stylists had, however, composed inscriptions to sponsor and promote these ink brands.

Ink manufacturers started to market their products under distinct "grades," the titles of which were typically stamped onto the sides or backs of inksticks and were intended to mark differences in either the recipe or production process.[80] Later evidence suggests that these grades may have facilitated distinctions in pricing.[81] During the course of the Wanli, Tianqi 天啟 (1620–1628), and Chongzhen periods, grade titles became increasingly visible in both manuals of taste and the jottings of connoisseurs as guidelines for the authentication and judgment of ink. When Xie Zhaozhi 謝肇淛 (1567–1624) remarked on the bitter rivalry between Fang Yulu and Cheng Junfang, for instance, he presented their duel as a contest between competing labels, "Nine Mysteries and Three Absolutes" (Jiuxuan sanji 九玄三極) and "Dark Origin of Numinous Vitality" (figure 3.12):

> In our dynasty Fang Zheng, Luo Xiaohua, and Shao Gezhi all had their fame for a period. In recent times, Fang Yulu began to reach a marvelous level in ink making. The "Nine Mysteries and Three Absolutes" that he made thirty years ago was unprecedented. In the end, Cheng Junfang became his rival and made "Dark Origin of Numinous Vitality" to surpass Fang. They both competed in price and the dispute is unresolved.

> 國朝方正，羅小華，邵格之皆擅名一時，近代方于魯始臻其妙。其三十年前所作九玄三極，前無古人。最後，程君房與為仇敵，製玄元靈氣以壓之。二家各爭其價，紛拿不定。[82]

FIGURE 3.12. "Dark Origin of Numinous Vitality" 玄元靈氣 inkstick, attributed to Cheng Junfang. *Source:* National Palace Museum; Open Data.

Whereas the famous ink makers of the early Ming are listed by name, Xie suggests that by the Wanli era, judgments of quality were determined not on the basis of an ink maker's personal reputation but on the reception of the title bestowed upon the ink maker's top grade. An ink-maker's name was no longer a definitive mark of value or a guarantor of trust: consumers like Xie turned their attention instead to the associations of alluring yet enigmatic titles like "Nine Mysteries and Three Absolutes."

When *Master Fang's Ink Catalogue* was first published, Fang Yulu's name was associated with five grades of ink.[83] In a preface to the table of inksticks at the beginning of the anthology, Wang Daokun offers a brief introduction to the emergence of these titles across the course of Fang's career.[84] Fang's earliest grade was named "Jasper Reed" (Yaocao 瑤草) and was followed by "Fragrance of the Great Kingdom" (Daguo xiang 大國香), then "Great Purple Double Darkness" (Dazi chongxuan 大紫重玄), with "Not Soot" (Feiyan 非煙) and "Nine Mysteries and Three Absolutes" (Jiuxuan sanji 九玄三極) as his latest and top lines.[85] Only one contributor to *Master Fang's Ink Catalogue* reflects on how these titles identify qualitative differences in the substance of the ink. A "Letter on Ink" ("Moshu" 墨書) notes that "Great Purple Double Darkness," "Nine Mysteries and Three Absolutes," and "Not Soot" denote variations in the consistency of the soot or grade of lampblack.[86] In the process of burning a pre-marinated wick in a lamp, the carbon residue that was withdrawn when the flame was at its strongest would be coarsest and provided the material for the lowest grade, "Great Purple Double Darkness." As the flames settled down, a softer and more finely textured soot could be extracted, which became the "top grade," "Nine Mysteries and Three Absolutes." As the flames finally died out, a softer, lighter soot remained, which became Fang's middle grade "Not Soot."[87]

While contemporary sources suggest these titles correspond to distinct concoctions, they gradually shed specific associations to acquire a phantasmatic life as brands. The ink grade became first and foremost a "semiotic assemblage," or what John Frow terms a "connotationally rich and referentially poor proper name . . . structured to designate a rich singularity, coherent, simple, and integral, [one that] evokes a world of beauty, harmony, energy, clarity, desire."[88] Many titles combine Daoist allusions to the celestial and the sublime with an evocation of the sensory qualities of ink: its luster, its fragrance, its tonality, or its texture. Such impulses resonate with what Roland Barthes calls "advertising language," where statements of use-value and invitations for purchase are coupled with broader evocations of harmony and perfection (the "great oneiric themes of humanity"): ice-cream that "makes you melt with pleasure" describes a substance that melts while invoking the "grand theme" of "annihilation by pleasure" or a "perfusion of being"; "golden chips" designates a crisp surface *and* "inestimable worth."[89] For Barthes, the more duplicitous the slogan, the more effective it might be.

"Darkness" (*xuan* 玄) (and its cognates: mystery, abstruseness, obscurity, profundity), a keyword in ink branding, suggests at once the color black (with a deep dark reddish hint) and the creative aspect of the Dao, or the undifferentiated stage from which myriad phenomena emerge. Use of the term invokes the concept of "dark virtue" (*xuande* 玄德), an attribute of the sage who finds communion through inner cultivation with the profound mysteries of the

Dao.⁹⁰ Related formulations include the "three pneumas"—Dark, Original, and Inaugural (*xuanqi* 玄氣, *yuanqi* 元氣, and *shiqi* 始氣)—that are issued sequentially by the Dao and generate the cosmos. Many of these titles resonate with the rhetoric of Daoist cosmography and "Great Clarity" (*Taiqing* 太清) alchemy where the "elixir" is seen to symbolize both the "original state of being that underlies multiplicity and change" and the attainment of that state by the adept.⁹¹ "Dark" might loosely serve as a descriptor yet was worked into almost nonsensical compounds that while laden with associations lack a definite referent: "Nine Mysteries and Three Absolutes" (Jiuxuan sanji 九玄三極), "Dark Origin of Numinous Vitality" (Xuanyuan lingqi 玄元靈氣), "Dark Numen of Primordial Unity" (Taiyi xuanling 太乙玄靈).⁹² The brand, through this process of assembly, assumed a degree of semantic autonomy, becoming a self-signifying proper name (table 3.1).

TABLE 3.1
The Four Major Ming Ink Makers and Their Ink Brands

Ink Maker	Ink Catalogue	Ink Brands
Fang Yulu 方于魯 (1541–1608) (original name: Da'ao 大激; *zi* Jianyuan 建元)	*Fangshi mopu* 方氏墨譜 (*Master Fang's Ink Catalogue*), 1588	Yaocao 瑤草 (Jasper Reed) Daguo xiang 大國香 (Fragrance of the Great State) Dazi chongxuan 大紫重玄 (Great Purple Double Dark) Feiyan 非煙 (Not Soot) Jiuxuan sanji 九玄三極 (Nine Mysteries and Three Absolutes) Alternative Titles: Liaotian yi 寥天一 (One with Clear Heaven) Qinglin sui 青麟髓 (Black Unicorn Marrow)¹ Huayi mo 畫一墨 (Paint the One Ink)²
Cheng Junfang 程君房 (1541–1610+) (*ming* 大約; *zi* Youbo 幼博)	*Chengshi moyuan* 程氏墨園 (*Master Cheng's Ink Garden*), ca. 1606	Xuanyuan lingqi 玄元靈氣 (Dark Origin of Numinous Vitality) Alternative Title: Liaotian yi 寥天一 (One with Clear Heaven)
Pan Yingzhi 潘膺祉 (n.d.) (*zi* Fangkai 方凱)	*Pan Yingzhi moping* 潘膺祉墨評 (*Pan Yingzhi's Evaluation of Ink*), 1610–1612	Kaitian rong mo 開天容墨 (Open Appearance of Heaven Ink)
Fang Ruisheng 方瑞生 (n.d.) (*zi* Danxuan 澹玄)	*Mohai* 墨海 (*Sea of Ink*), 1620	Jiguang 寂光 (Silent Light) Tianjing 天鏡 (Heavenly Mirror) Zixiao feng 紫霄峰 (Purple Mountain Peaks of the Sky)

¹Also attributed to Wang Daohui.
²Released in 1596.

Ink makers also manipulated literary sources to create new titles. Fang Yulu's brand "Not Soot," for instance, alludes to an auspicious vapor, "not mist" (*feiyan* 非煙), from the "Astronomer's Treatise" ("Tianguan shu" 天官書) in Sima Qian's *Records of the Grand Historian*:

> Like mist, but not mist; like clouds, but not clouds; darkly billowing, chilly and swirling: these are called "felicitous clouds."

> 若煙非煙，若雲非雲，郁郁紛紛，蕭索輪囷，是謂卿雲。[93]

A protean poetic image, "not mist" limns the elusive movements and insubstantiality of mist while retaining a symbolic association with cloud portents and other propitious ethers. The motif might loosely allude to the role of clouds and fog as metaphors for the art of calligraphy, yet Fang Yulu redefines the associations of the phrase with the substance of ink through a pun on the character *yan* 煙 as "soot," approximating comparatively literal designations like "pure soot" (*qingyan* 清煙).[94] "Not Soot" consequently appears "twice made," a motif gleaned from the "images and shadows of earlier poems," preserved only so long as it is necessary to see that they have been canceled.[95]

To promote Fang Yulu's "Not Soot" label, Wang Daokun composed a short jingle that rewrites the passage from the "Astronomer's Treatise" in which "not mist" first appeared (figure 3.13). Two versions of the inscription survive: a copy that appears in a design alongside the label "Not Soot" in *Master Fang's Ink Catalogue*, and a copy preserved in Wang's collected poetry and prose. The former visually extends the pun "Not Soot" by switching between three forms of the character *yan* (炟, 烟, 煙), while the latter draws out the lulling iterability of the jingle, repeating the title once more. As Wang's jingle progresses, "Not Soot" fluctuates between the properties of ink and propitious heavenly ethers, as both a description in the "disguise of a proper name" and a proper name in the disguise of a description: "you never know whether he names or describes, nor whether the thing he describes-names is the thing or the name."[96]

INSCRIPTION ON NOT SOOT

Not Soot, yet soot, resplendent polychrome clouds![97]
Soot, yet Not Soot, black dragons shimmer!

THE INK-MAKER'S MARK

Such resplendence is a heavenly pattern!
This shimmering luster is the efflorescence of the state!
The utmost double darkness [variant: "the utmost Not Soot" 非煙之極]⁹⁸:
There is nothing that can be added to it!

非煙銘

非炮而烟，卿雲爛矣。煙而非炮，玄龍煥矣。爛則天章，煥則國華。玄玄之極，其蔑以加。⁹⁹

FIGURE 3.13. Fang Yulu's "Not Soot Inscription" 非煙銘 design. The right-hand side of the inkstick bears Wang Daokun's inscription. *Source*: Fang Yulu, *Fangshi mopu*, 4.33a.

The first half of the inscription pairs an auspicious image of "felicitous clouds" from the same source passage in the *Records of the Grand Historian* with a reference to "shimmering black dragons." Clouds and dragons "follow each other" (*yun cong long* 雲從龍) and, here, resonate with poetic images of calligraphic ink play, as in Su Shi's line: "Spurting clouds and foggy mist emerge, dragons and snakes coil together entwined" 噓噓雲霧出, 奕奕龍蛇綰.[100] As if to visualize this principle of dragons accompanying mist, the editors of *Master Fang's Ink Catalogue* displayed a small image of a jade object fashioned in the shape of a footed winged dragon with a serpent's tail beneath Wang Daokun's "Not Soot" inscription, an antique that according to the Song catalogue *Record of Clouds and Mist Passing Before My Eyes* (*Yunyan guoyan lu* 雲煙過眼錄) once belonged to Yuan dynasty artist Zhao Mengfu 趙孟頫 (1254–1322) and was later acquired by the painter Ding Yunpeng—one of the leading illustrators for Fang's ink book.[101] This visual juxtaposition implicitly weighs the evanescent motif of "Not Soot" against the imperishable properties of a black jade wyvern, as if suggesting the brand deserves the company of a venerable antique. Both "Not Soot" and "black dragon" concurrently recall poetic visions of feminine beauty: Li Shan's 李善 (d. 689) gloss of the poet Lu Yun's 陸雲 (262–303) line: "Forsake that Northern polestar! Solicit these Black Dragons' glories" 棄置北辰星, 問此玄龍煥, notes that "black dragons" refer to the "beautiful girls" 美女 of the capital.[102]

Wang Daokun's inscription is no longer about ink but the duplicity of "Not Soot" and its connotations: auspicious vapors, a dark sheen, a vague sense of feminine seduction. Impressions of Fang Yulu's product emerge as if they were effects of its name's repetition. "Not Soot" thus exemplifies the poetics of a late Ming ink brand, recommending the sensuousness of a product while revivifying tired motifs of beauty and sublimity. As a pun, "Not Soot" at once invokes and ironically negates the materiality of ink, suggesting that this shimmering title supersedes its basic ingredient: the carbon residue of lampblack. "Not Soot" celebrates the very shift from a solid thing to a phantasmal name that a brand might be said to inaugurate. Wang's "Not Soot" jingle in this sense reimagines the meaning of inscriptive permanence, not in terms of weighty resilience but as an expression of what, to borrow a formulation from Wendy Hui Kyong Chun, we might call an "enduring ephemeral," caught between the "passing and the repetitive," anticipating both its own obsolescence and future regeneration.[103] Intoning dark mists, ethers, and shimmering clouds, Wang's endorsement of "Not Soot" seeks longevity within evanescence, intimating the way molded inkstick inscriptions at once entail destruction and yet endure through reduplication and material metamorphoses.

"Not Soot" became Fang Yulu's most popular label during the 1580s. Comments in *Master Fang's Ink Catalogue* reveal a shift from the generic appraisal of Fang Yulu's ink to a focus on this single title. Critics wrote of fears that consumers would hoard "Not Soot" and refrain from testing it with a brush:

> In the past, Master Kong Zhou (103–163) had three swords, the third was called "Tempered by Night," you could see its shadow but not its glitter, yet it was stored away and never put to use. Yulu's ink named "Not Soot" is close to this. I'm only worried that those who get hold of it will store it away and not use it and then the ink will grind them down.
>
> 昔孔周氏三劍，下者宵練，猶見影而不見光，匣而無施於事也。于魯之墨曰非烟，近於是矣。余恐得者匣而不試，墨將磨子。[104]

The impact of Wang Daokun's inscription for "Not Soot" extended beyond *Master Fang's Ink Catalogue*, as the label became a focal point in the infamous and well-documented rivalry between Fang Yulu and Cheng Junfang. Reasons for the fraught relationship between these two men, their so-called "war of ink" (*mobing* 墨兵), became a topic of wild speculation and rumor during the seventeenth century.[105] Writing in the wake of the dynastic transition, Jiang Shaoshu suggested that Fang coveted Cheng's concubine and attempted to marry her while Cheng was in Beijing; when Cheng found out, he allegedly tried to indict Fang, while Fang framed Cheng for murder and had him imprisoned.[106] Cheng and Fang collaborated early on in their careers with Cheng going so far as to claim he had taught Fang ink making. Fang Yulu's publication preceded *Master Cheng's Ink Garden* by more than a decade, yet Cheng still tried to claim many of the visual designs in *Master Fang's Ink Catalogue* as his own. Given the success of Fang's anthology in the 1580s, however, it remains difficult to distinguish between cases where Cheng was identifying designs that emerged from his apprenticeship with Fang and cases where he was simply stealing Fang's work.

Cheng Junfang advertised his proprietorship of "Not Soot" by composing a literary inscription for the brand. Given the dominance of the White Elm, Fang Yulu had yet to endorse any of his personal labels; Cheng, however, took it upon himself to draft his own appraisal of the title. The piece copies the structure and theme of Wang Daokun's inscription, imitating his imagery yet avoiding direct duplication:

> Like fog but not fog, like soot but Not Soot, a gloomy murkiness, before the First Heavenly Emperor. Recognize the white while preserving blackness, dark mystery of dark mystery: its merit preserved on bamboo and paper, and it will last for all of time!

> 似霧非霧，似烟非烟，混混沌沌，象彼帝先。知白守黑，玄之又玄，功存竹素，億萬斯年。[107]

Rewriting Wang Daokun's jingle in his own words, Cheng, the ink maker, simultaneously tried to approximate and challenge the literary authority of a former official. Although Fang Yulu's supporters had written extensively of "Not Soot" as Fang's invention, even detailing its recipe, Cheng goes one step further by presenting himself as author of the label.

To some extent, he succeeded in this endeavor. Cheng's "Record of The Studio of Ink Treasure" ("Baomo zhai ji" 寶墨齋記), a collection of appraisals contributed to his shop by satisfied customers, contains several reviews that take up the poetic connotations of "Not Soot" as a topic and theme. These short consumer ratings in verse riff on Wang and Cheng's jingles:

> Like soot but "Not Soot," material, yet immaterial, redolent without fragrance, a non-sensual sensuousness. Mired in mist, a dim silence, then confusion and flux. Primordial ether seeps out as misty drizzle, as if it had stolen trickling drops of nocturnal vapor.

> 若烟非烟，若質無質，似香非香，似色非色，漠漠嘿嘿，變幻恍惚。漏元氣而涳濛，盜沉瀣之流液。[108]

Although few connoisseurs from the late Ming listed "Not Soot" as Cheng's product and most continued to celebrate it as one of Fang's leading brands, multiple inksticks attributed to Cheng bearing the "Not Soot" mark survive in public and private collections.[109]

Cheng Junfang's appropriation of "Not Soot" was, however, only one thread in the label's checkered career. Other ink makers also tried to stake their claims to the brand. The catalogue *Snow Hall Ink* (*Xuetang Mopin* 雪堂墨品), edited by Zhang Renxi 張仁熙 (fl. 1647) in the early Qing, for instance, records an inkstick bearing the "Not Soot" mark dated to 1612, this time attributed to Fang Ruisheng.[110] Cao Sugong also advertised the "Not Soot" mark as his own merchandise without any attribution to either Fang Yulu or Cheng Junfang.[111] The leading ink maker of the Kangxi reign, Cao published an influential anthology of appraisals for his eighteen ink grades, *Master Cao's Ink Forest*. As part of this project, he solicited a new encomium (*zan*) for "Not Soot," one that like Cheng Junfang simply tweaks Wang Daokun's now infamous advertising slogan: "Like soot but 'Not Soot,' this can be called 'auspicious clouds,' darkly billowing, its luster congeals" 若烟非烟，是謂卿雲。 郁郁芬芬，其光則凝.[112] Cao, who had studied with the prominent Tianqi- and Chongzhen-era ink maker Wu Shuda 吳叔大 (n.d.) as a youth, before later presenting a recipe to Kangxi on the emperor's Southern Tour, found in the act of poetic plagiarism a means to recover a sense of continuity with the material heritage of the late Ming.[113] As "Not Soot" took on a life independent of either Fang or Wang Daokun, the first "Not Soot" inscription also traveled across time and space, resurfacing in 1743 in Matsui Gentai's 松井元泰 (1689–1742) *Kobaien Bokufu* 古梅園墨譜 in Nara, Japan.[114] Eighteenth-century customers perusing stationery stores in East Asian urban centers could choose between multiple versions of "Not Soot," judging the quality of this enigmatic product against the literary endorsements that they deemed most trustworthy.

ORIGINAL FAKE

The career of "Not Soot" broaches the thorny relationship between a brand and practices of counterfeiting. Was the transregional appropriation and reuse of Fang Yulu's label regarded as theft? Was the "Not Soot" brand, when advertised by Cheng Junfang or Cao Sugong, even perceived to be a copy? In the late sixteenth century, these concerns coalesced around "One with Clear Heaven," the label on Sun Ruiqing's inkstick in the Palace Museum— the small artifact with which this chapter began. Fang's enigmatic title was drawn from the "Great Source as Teacher" chapter in *Zhuangzi*: "but when you rest securely in displacement, constantly dropping away each transformation as it goes, then you enter into the oneness of the clear sky, of empty Heaven" 安排而去化，乃入於寥天一.¹¹⁵ The phrase appeals to the ideal of "oneness" encapsulated in the "enveloping three as one" label and the celestial imagery of designs like "Five Planets," evoking the deep dark blackness of the empty space beyond the stars.

As with "Not Soot," Wang Daokun composed an inscription to endorse the brand (figure 3.14). Wang's promotional advertisement lacks the lulling simplicity of his "Not Soot" jingle yet evokes a similar concern with fusing

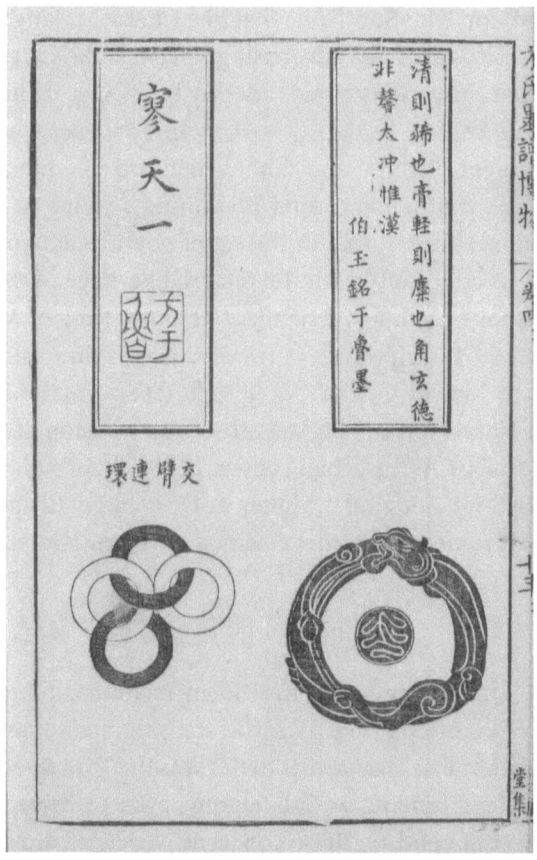

FIGURE 3.14. Fang Yulu's "One with Clear Heaven Inscription" 寥天一銘 design. The right-hand side of the inkstick bears Wang Daokun's inscription. *Source*: Fang Yulu, *Fangshi mopu*, 4.13b.

arcane allusions to cosmic harmony and the sublime, with references to the basic matter of ink:

INSCRIPTION ON FANG YULU'S "ONE WITH CLEAR HEAVEN" INK

> How is it that One with Clear Heaven appears!
> How is it that the Studio of Han is accomplished!
> Clarity from pig's fat, as light as an elaphure horn,
> Dark virtue has no piercing fragrance,
> Ultimate harmony can be nothing but the silent space beyond the stars!

方于魯寥天一墨銘

> 胡然而生寥天一，胡然而成函之室。
> 清則豨也膏，輕則麋也角。
> 玄德非馨，太冲惟漠。[116]

The inscription opens by alluding to the closing lines of "Companion of Her Lord till Death" (Junzi xielao 君子偕老) from the *Classic of Poetry*—"How can she seem to be from heaven? How can she seem to be from the gods?" 胡然而天也、胡然而帝也—pairing praise for the release of Fang Yulu's brand with the name of his own studio: as if he himself were an "overlord" (*di* 帝) to match the "heavenly" (*tian* 天) nature of this ink.[117] Wang then celebrates the "purity" of the lampblack and "lightness" of the glue with awkward recommendations of the materials used: pig's grease and deer horn.

The inscription ends with Wang expounding on the material and ethical merits of ink by manipulating a line from the *Classic of Documents*:

> "It is not the millet and grain which have the piercing fragrance; it is bright virtue"

> 黍稷非馨，明德惟馨爾。[118]

> "Dark virtue has no piercing fragrance,
>   Ultimate harmony can be nothing but the silent space beyond the stars!"

> 玄德非馨，太冲惟漠。

The original line implies that the moral integrity ("bright virtue") behind the presentation of an offering supersedes the materiality of the offering itself ("millet and grain"). Wang tweaks this oft-quoted saying to articulate his own ideal principle for ink: here—changing *wei* 惟 to *fei* 非—it is not the "fragrance" of "dark virtue" that matters; or, perhaps more plainly, it is not important whether ink has a desirable scent from the addition of musk or perfume—common additives intended to mask the natural odor of burnt pine and fish guts.[119] Wang then deploys a further allusion to *Zhuangzi*: "Huzi said: 'just now I showed him the vast gushing surge in which nothing wins out'" 壺子曰：吾鄉示之以太沖莫勝.[120] This abstruse Daoist metaphor invokes the harmony of nothingness and the dark "desolate emptiness," the "silent space beyond the stars" (*mo* 漠) that ensues, hinting at both the profundity of the Dao and the penumbral darkness of ink.[121]

Wang's convoluted wordplay suggests that the lure of an inkstick's scent and any other sensual gimmicks should be superseded by its black tone while at the same time appealing to sage-like self-realization through true communion with the Dao. Just as "Not Soot" invokes and denies the substance of lampblack, "One with Clear Heaven" claims to transcend the smell of the ingredients packed into vulgar inksticks: both brands strive for a poetic negation of ink's crude materiality. Wang's supporters were delighted with this new maxim—"Dark virtue has no piercing fragrance, / Ultimate harmony can be nothing but the silent space beyond the stars!"—and publicized it extensively as a reproducible marketing slogan, claiming that the ink-maker's use of this motto (rather than his actual recipe) led to his dominance in the ink market.[122]

Wang Daokun's literary inscription for "One with Clear Heaven," an austere endorsement that sets out to promote his own studio name, shows how the formal conventions of this ancient genre—concision, praise for the virtues of materials, and admonition—might lend themselves to the contemporary invention of short and memorable jingles. And yet, the advertisement of an ink brand also unsettled and enlarged the possibilities of inscription, challenging staid notions of permanence and fixity, exploiting ink's basic properties to revivify stale images of transcendence.

Fang Yulu's catalogue splits Wang Daokun's inscription between two designs: the first features a copy of the opening couplet transcribed by Suzhou calligrapher (and Wang's frequent collaborator on the production of stelae inscriptions) Zhou Tianqiu with Wang's seal for his studio, "Han's Third Studio Seal" (Hansan shi yin 函三室印), and the title "Draft from the Valley" (Hongzhong qicao 谼中起草) (figure 2.6). The second pairs the line on pig grease and the "fragrance" slogan with the seal "Fang Yulu" and the label "One with Clear Heaven."[123] Just as Wang's inscription begins by matching his praise for the brand with his own studio name, these separate designs make two promotional appeals: one on behalf of Wang, the other for Fang—the brand, however, hovers between, and remains irreducible to the claims of either party.[124]

Shortly after its emergence onto the market, the label elicited a series of complaints from commentators. Xing Tong 邢侗 (1551–1612), a prominent calligrapher, and Peng Haogu 彭好古 (b. 1551) who was appointed as the new magistrate in She County in 1588, voiced particularly forceful criticisms:

> Fang Yulu's ink was renowned in the prefecture of She, and his product prevails in color, luster and design. However, when you grind it, it is like paste with perfume, lacking the scent of ink. "Not Soot" and "One with Clear Heaven" were completely unlike [what they should have been]. The Military Supervisor of the Left [Wang Daokun] should be ashamed as the Dong Hu [Chronicler] of the "Great Black."

> 方于魯墨擅名歙州，當以色澤規橅取勝。磨之若糨，有香氣，無墨氣。所署「非煙」，「寥天一」，殊謬不然。左司馬公差愧太玄氏董狐。[125]

> Xin'an has long been famous for its ink. When I was an official in She County, Master Fang Yulu was widely promoted and among Yulu's inks, his "One with Clear Heaven" was celebrated as a peerless product. I took this top product and sent it as a gift to scholars from the four corners of the state. They all ridiculed it, derisively, saying, "It's bogus." When you grind it and test it, then you see that its glue is actually cheap paste, and its color is like coal. You cannot use it with a brush.

> The county officer Gu Gong bought ink at a high price and Yulu had also given him a fake. Gu Gong was furious and went to check with Wang Daokun, to catch Fang Yulu and have him beaten.

新安以墨名舊矣。方余令歙時推方氏于魯，而于魯墨推「寥天一」為絕勝。余嘗取其絕勝者贈四方修文之士，姍姍胥薄之曰： 是胡屑也。因磨而試之，則見其膏如糊，其色如煤，不可以筆。

郡守古公重價購墨，于魯亦以贗應。古公怒，請驗於汪司馬，逮而笞之。[126]

Both Peng and Xing draw attention to slippages between the reputation of the "One with Clear Heaven" label and the quality of inksticks bearing this mark. There is, for both authors, a disjunction between the reputation of the brand and the substance of the ink. Peng goes so far as to label the products counterfeit, yet despite his talk of "cheap paste and coal" it is unclear what he actually considers "fake": How, for instance, could Fang Yulu forge copies of his own products? The question then becomes whether Peng felt the source of the problem was the spurious reputation of the brand or the sham materiality of the ink.

Wang Daokun, more so than anyone else, bore the brunt of these criticisms. Xing wrote of how he should be "ashamed," while Peng went further in trying to personally confront Wang for duping consumers. Leading art collector and connoisseur Zhan Jingfeng would later pick up on the impact of these allegations on Wang's reputation, comparing the former vice minister of war to a knock-off inkstick: when the "insides of these inksticks were exposed, it led the gentry to doubt the personal character of the military supervisor [Wang Daokun]" 則中藏悉露矣，縉紳至疑司馬為人.[127] Cheng Junfang's *Ink Garden* reprinted both Peng and Xing's complaints, presenting both authors as supporters of a rival atelier. They both, however, gloss over Fang Yulu's responsibility as a craftsman to create products that embody his own integrity, to instead attack Wang Daokun as the author of the endorsements for the two brand names. The reception of "One with Clear Heaven" not only manifests transformations in ink poetry and artisanal practices of product labeling but also reveals how one of the leading literary celebrities of the late sixteenth century might be judged as a faulty commodity on the basis of his role in writing advertising copy.

Given these criticisms, "One with Clear Heaven" might have fallen into disrepute, yet this was not to be the case. Peng and Xing's complaints were included in *Master Cheng's Ink Garden* alongside Cheng Junfang's own attempt to lay claim to the title.[128] The terms of their negative assessments continued to haunt the writings of later connoisseurs: Zhang Renxi, for

THE INK-MAKER'S MARK

instance, celebrated a version of "One with Clear Heaven" attributed to Cheng that had survived the destruction of his family's collections during the Ming-Qing transition by praising its "lack of fragrance" 無香氣 and its "scent of ink" 墨氣, commemorating the inkstick as a superior version of Fang Yulu's recipe.[129] As with "Not Soot," other iterations of the brand proliferated: the National Palace Museum holds a Cheng Junfang ink cake depicting a rabbit in the moon, dated to 1601 bearing a molded "One with Clear Heaven" mark along its side (figures 3.15a, 3.15b, and 3.15c).[130] The Palace Museum in Beijing holds another example of Cheng Junfang's "One with Clear Heaven" mark, in this instance on a rectangular inkstick dated to 1594 bearing two illustrations of peonies carved in relief (figures 3.16a and 3.16b). Pan Yingzhi, the third of the four major late Ming ink makers, also

FIGURE 3.15A. "One with Clear Heaven" inkstick (front), attributed to Cheng Junfang (1604). *Source*: National Palace Museum; Open Data.

FIGURE 3.15B. "One with Clear Heaven" inkstick (back), attributed to Cheng Junfang (1604). *Source*: National Palace Museum; Open Data.

FIGURE 3.15C. "One with Clear Heaven" inkstick (side), attributed to Cheng Junfang (1604). *Source*: National Palace Museum; Open Data.

FIGURE 3.16A. "One with Clear Heaven" inkstick, attributed to Cheng Junfang (1594). Bearing two peonies carved in relief. *Source*: The Palace Museum.

FIGURE 3.16B. "One with Clear Heaven" inkstick, attributed to Cheng Junfang (1594). Bearing two peonies carved in relief. *Source*: The Palace Museum.

repurposed the inscriptional design of "One with Clear Heaven" from *Master Fang's Ink Catalogue* to advertise his own name (figures 3.17a and 3.17b).

The Palace Museum in Beijing, meanwhile, holds copies of inksticks bearing the "One with Clear Heaven" label that are attributed to the Tianqi- and Chongzhen-era ink makers Jin Xuanfu 金玄甫 (n.d.) (figures 3.18, 3.19a, and 3.19b) and Wu Shuda (figures 3.20, 3.21a, and 3.21b).[131] In these instances, the "One with Clear Heaven" mark appears

FIGURE 3.17A. Pan Fangkai's 潘方凱 "One with Clear Heaven" inkstick. *Source:* The Palace Museum.

FIGURE 3.17B. Pan Fangkai's 潘方凱 "One with Clear Heaven" inkstick. *Source*: The Palace Museum.

FIGURE 3.18. Rubbing of Jin Xuanfu's 金玄甫 (n.d.) "One with Clear Heaven" inkstick. *Source*: Ye Gongchuo et al., eds., *Sijia cangmo tulu*, 75.

FIGURE 3.19A. Jin Xuanfu's "One with Clear Heaven" inkstick. *Source*: The Palace Museum.

FIGURE 3.19B. Jin Xuanfu's "One with Clear Heaven" inkstick. *Source*: The Palace Museum.

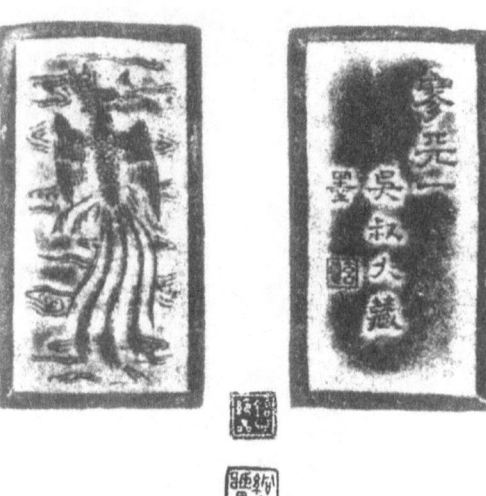

FIGURE 3.20. Rubbing of Wu Shuda's 吳叔大 (n.d.) "One with Clear Heaven" inkstick. *Source:* Ye Gong-chuo et al., eds., *Sijia cangmo tulu*, 110.

FIGURE 3.21A. Wu Shuda's "One with Clear Heaven" inkstick. *Source:* The Palace Museum.

FIGURE 3.21B. Wu Shuda's "One with Clear Heaven" inkstick. *Source:* The Palace Museum.

THE INK-MAKER'S MARK

FIGURE 3.22. Inkstick inscribed "Black Unicorn Marrow," attributed to Fang Yulu and dated 1604. *Source*: National Palace Museum; Open Data.

to have been the primary source of interest for connoisseurs rather than the personal names of craftsmen.[132] Amid a confusing proliferation of "One with Clear Heaven" copies, ink brands with no clear owner started to emerge: "Black Unicorn Marrow" (Qinglin sui 青麟髓), for instance, was initially attributed to both Fang Yulu's atelier (the National Palace Museum holds a stick dated to 1604) and Wang Daokun's cousin, Wang Daohui (figure 3.22).[133] Collector Yin Runsheng, however, owned three ink cakes with the "Black Unicorn Marrow" label from separate, otherwise unknown late Ming artisans. The brand, in such cases, effectively authors the value of the objects upon which it appears.[134]

THE ENDURING EPHEMERAL

How then to interpret Sun Ruiqing's adaptation of Wang Daokun's inscription for "One with Clear Heaven" on the Palace Museum inkstick with which this chapter began (figure 3.1)? Like Jin Xuanfu and Wu Shuda, Sun looked to make the "One with Clear Heaven" label his own, repossessing the title through its juxtaposition with his seal: "Made by Sun Ruiqing, Yuquan of Xindu." As with Jin and Wu's ink cakes, Sun's tablet is a counterfeit, an attempt to impersonate another ink-maker's claim to a recipe. And yet, Sun makes no effort to disguise his act of imitation, proudly displaying his own maker's mark, as if implicitly presenting the object as an improvement on an earlier template. Jin and Wu looked to redeem the "One with Clear Heaven" mark, incorporating the label into new visual programs; Sun, however, openly intervened in the controversial biography of the brand by recycling Wang Daokun's inscription for Fang Yulu, imitating the presentation of Wang's words in the "One with Clear Heaven" inscriptional design from *Master Fang's Ink Catalogue* (figure 3.14). Despite the fallout from Wang's initial endorsement of the title and the backlash his claims for Fang's product provoked, Sun nevertheless returned to the inscription, looking to validate or give new meaning to its slogans.

At first glance, it might seem plausible to read Sun Ruiqing's citation of Wang's pronouncements as a simple attempt to siphon some of the ex-minister's prestige: "In a talismanic economy," Dorothy Ko suggests, "the rigors of connoisseurship and its goal of authentication mattered less than the contagious desire of owning a piece of the legend."[135] This line of interpretation, however, leaves little room for an assessment of the ink-maker's creativity in coordinating the reproduction of words on things, presenting a picture of a craftsman in thrall to the enduring power of literary inscription. Sun Ruiqing did not duplicate Wang Daokun's endorsement, he rewrote it. A comparison of the Palace Museum inkstick with *Master Fang's Ink Catalogue* shows that Sun actually changed the order of two homophonous characters: swapping the words "clarity" (*qing* 清) and "lightness" (*qing* 輕). As Cai Xinquan has observed, this transcription was not necessarily a mistake, but an attempt to correct an error Sun detected in Wang Daokun's initial inscription.[136] Wang pairs words of praise for soot and glue, yet Sun implicitly queries his choice of lead descriptors, suggesting that "clarity" makes more sense for an account of ink's binding agent—an amendment that dovetails with the vocabulary of contemporaneous Ming technical treatises.[137]

The ink maker tests his reader: Were you aware that Wang Daokun's inscription for Fang Yulu's "One with Clear Heaven" was misguided? Did you realize that the terms of his ill-fated endorsement might have been mistaken to begin with? Rather than simply cite Wang Daokun, Sun Ruiqing emends his words, justifying his recourse to this contentious source by insinuating that an improved version of Wang's inscription more accurately endorses his improved version of "One with Clear Heaven" as a recipe. Sun Ruiqing's copy of the inscription presents itself as a more genuine statement than Wang Daokun's original fake. This act of insertion might nevertheless be said to exploit the increasingly elastic relationship between name and thing, singular and multiple, that the first inscription for "Not Soot" envisaged.

"One with Clear Heaven" embodies a transformation in conceptions of inscriptive permanence. The label's fate registers a transition from writing on unique, hard substrates to writing on disposable tablets—copies that anticipate their own destruction and future regeneration. By perturbing notions of authentic original and duplicate, however, "One with Clear Heaven" invited makers to discern new openings for variation within repetition, intervening in the mass production of things to question what could and should survive. The two sides of Sun Ruiqing's inkstick thus reflect two sides of ink branding in early modern material culture. Wang Daokun's inscription emerges from the efforts of the White Elm poets to manipulate Fang Yulu for their own gain, to publicize and protect product labels through inscriptional designs, and to shape the reception of "Not Soot" and "One with Clear Heaven" through inventive puns. This was a high-stakes gamble as the public criticism Wang received from contemporary magistrates and calligraphers attests. By participating in the development of new strategies for naming things, the archaist poet triggered anxieties about the proper bases of a reputation and the insubstantiality of fame, concerns that rebounded on this former vice minister of war's own public standing. And yet, the fate of "One with Clear Heaven" cannot be reduced to controversies surrounding a literary celebrity. The brand, as with "Not Soot," took on a life of its own, traveling throughout East Asia and reappearing on different surfaces into the twentieth century.[138] This second side to Sun Ruiqing's inkstick discloses the inventive efforts of entrepreneurial artisans to recover the promise they saw in "One with Clear Heaven." Figures such as Sun Ruiqing and Jin Xuanfu did not possess established reputations and so looked to reproductions of this now notorious label to win renown for themselves. Inkstick inscriptions, for an artisan like Sun, came to constitute a tactic for exploiting the evanescent opportunities of the present.

"One with Clear Heaven" unsettled understandings of both name and thing. For local magistrates, government ministers, and eminent calligraphers this was a disconcerting development, one that needed to be policed or prohibited. For upstarts like Sun Ruiqing, by contrast, these upheavals in the market for fame prefigured new possibilities for making one's mark. The lightly worn base of the inkstick now preserved in the Palace Museum suggests that subsequent collectors found merit in Sun's sly reproduction of "One with Clear Heaven," refraining from grinding it down, treating the counterfeit as an authentic antique. Again, Sun's appropriation of Wang's "One with Clear Heaven" inscription was not a singular occurrence, but one instance in a more extensive process of inventive duplication: the eighteenth-century ink maker Wang Jinsheng 汪近聖 (n.d.), as one example, adapted the first lines of Wang Daokun's endorsement for "One with Clear Heaven" on a limited-edition set of inksticks now held in the Anhui Provincial Museum.[139]

BLACK MIST

Writing amid the chaos of the mid-seventeenth century, Ma Sanheng 麻三衡 (d. 1645) used his *Treatise on Ink* (*Mozhi* 墨志) to map what he knew of the late Ming ink market, recording the names of more than 120 ink makers and their ink-grade titles. This number dwarfs the recorded names of artisans for any other contemporaneous field of craft. In many cases, it is far from clear which of the two names—the personal name of the ink maker or the impersonal name of his brand—would have been more recognizable to a mid-seventeenth-century consumer.[140] Ma's list attests to an ongoing struggle for producers to devise new names for their ink through kennings and circumlocutions, trying for the most part to simply fit the character *xuan* into more refined combinations. Ma's inventory poses the question whether the challenge for these individuals was to manufacture a new type of ink or simply to coin a name that was discrete yet faintly reminiscent of more prestigious brands: "Ultimate Black" (Taixuan 太玄),

"Black Spirit" (Xuanshen 玄神), "Black Clouds" (Xuanyun 玄雲), "Black Frost" (Xuanshuang 玄霜), "Ultimate Black Mist" (Taixuan yan 太玄烟).[141] Zhou Lianggong's bespoke inkstick and inkstick sacrifices with friends in the years after the dynastic transition might be construed as both a symbolic rejection of this disorderly market and a tacit tribute to the vitality of ink making in late Ming social life. The project of promoting an ink brand emerges, in Ma's list, as a fraught search for durability in the face of homogeneity and impermanence. These impulses, seeking to forestall the inevitability of destruction, found a fitting analogue in repetitive attempts to write lasting words on perhaps the most transient of substrates.

Ma Sanheng led armed resistance to the Manchu invasion and likely completed his treatise on ink in the second or third year of the rump Southern Ming regime—he was eventually killed by Qing forces. Ma's erstwhile compatriot in Nanjing and fellow anti-Qing resistance fighter, Wan Shouqi 萬壽祺 (1603–1652)—a close friend of Zhou Lianggong—concurrently composed an incomplete *Table of Ink* (*Mobiao* 墨表) carefully documenting the dimensions and labels on inksticks he had viewed with his own eyes before the fall of the dynasty.[142] Jiang Shaoshu's reflections on the fallout from Fang Yulu and Cheng Junfang's rivalry appear in his "Study of Ink" ("Mokao" 墨考), the conclusion to his elegiac overview of Ming objects' fates in *Notes from the Resonant Rock Studio*.[143] Not unlike Zhang Dai surrounded by his "Twenty-Eight Friends," Ma Sanheng and Wan Shouqi worked under conditions of violent upheaval to limn the contours of Ming culture by inventorying the fragile tools that sustained it.[144] Neither foresaw the swift resurgence and expansion of the Huizhou ink market under the patronage of early Qing emperors, the unlikely survival of Ming inksticks and ink catalogues in Japan, or the extensive recycling of Ming labels like "One with Clear Heaven" on new ink cakes and tablets throughout the remainder of the late imperial period.

Chapter Four

ANTIQUARIAN POETRY

In 1577, the Wanli court became embroiled in a far-reaching political controversy because of the decision of the grand secretary, Zhang Juzheng, to refrain from observing mourning rites for his deceased father. An already divisive figure due to contentious reformist policies, Zhang invoked *duoqing* 奪情, "cutting short the emotions," a principle conventionally reserved for military personnel in times of national emergency, to remain in the capital. Critics claimed that in doing so he had renounced the demands of Confucian ritual in order to maintain his tight grip on power.[1] After sending a eunuch to stand in as chief mourner for his father, Zhang continued to brazenly flout ritual proscriptions by attending the wedding of the emperor in 1578, a supposedly auspicious event from which anyone in filial grief should have been banned. According to the *History of the Ming*, Zhang Juzheng's actions met with both public and cosmic disapproval: protestors posted placards in the streets as a comet rose in the southeast and slowly made its way across the night sky.[2] The events of the so-called *duoqing* controversy created factions that would continue to fight until the collapse of the Ming in 1644.

The Wanli emperor's acceptance of Zhang's *duoqing* plea prompted vociferous protests at court from nine officials who submitted a string of memorials to impeach the controversial grand secretary. Reports of the severity of Zhang Juzheng's response quickly spread throughout the empire, eliciting condemnation from renowned scholars.[3] Gossip circulated that

Wu Zhongxing 吳中行 (1540 ca.–1598) stopped breathing at one point during the beating, as "[they] sliced off several lumps of flesh, as much as a fistful and an inch deep, so that his limbs were hollowed out" 封去腐肉數十臠，大者盈掌，深至寸，一肢遂空.[4] Zhao Yongxian 趙用賢 (1535–1596), in the course of his punishment, lost a "fistful" of lacerated flesh from his buttocks.[5] Zou Yuanbiao 鄒元標 (1551–1624) received the maximum penalty of a hundred blows of the heavy bamboo before being sent to serve as a soldier in Guizhou.[6] The protests against Zhang Juzheng's dereliction of filial sentiments prefigure the ascendancy of *zhongxiao* 忠孝 (a compound of loyalty and filial piety) as a dominant discourse in late imperial political history. The challenge of how to simultaneously embody the values of *zhong* 忠 and *xiao* 孝 subsequently shaped what Ying Zhang terms "Confucian image politics" and constructions of "masculine morality" throughout the seventeenth century, from the didactic moralism of Donglin 東林 partisans, to the self-righteous suicides of Ming loyalists, to the subsequent efforts of early Qing emperors to justify their legitimacy as Confucian rulers.[7]

As Wu Zhongxing and Zhao Yongxian left the capital, they received small cups—one made of jade, the other made from a rhinoceros horn—both bearing inscriptions attributed to prominent Huizhou scholar and junior censor Xu Guo 許國 (1527–1596).[8] These gifts invite reflection on why the community of officials who supported the punished protestors sought to redress shared grievances by writing upon things. What forms of longing and historical judgment might terse lines of engraved-verse voice? Object inscription, amid the fallout from internecine strife at the Wanli court, became a means through which to participate in protest, affirm resistance to corruption, and propagate an ethics of loyalism. The unlikely travels, loss, and eventual recovery of Zhao's rhinoceros horn cup across the course of the next two centuries, however, raised doubts as to the type of thing a collective monument could be, who could claim to own it, and the uncertain constitution of the public it might address. The inscribed horn helped four generations of Confucian scholars construct a narrative of cultural continuity, and yet the cup's material history reveals the extent to which this narrative was predicated upon a fraught acceptance of transition.

Almost every major antiquarian-poet of the mid-Qing period wrote about this small rhinoceros horn cup. They variously read Xu Guo's inscription as a remonstration against Wanli-era decline, a relic of Ming martyrdom, a token with which to lament or accept service under the new Qing regime, a focal point for reflection on the competing claims of loyalty and filial piety, and finally an epigraphic document for annotation and research in eighteenth-century antiquarian circles. The cup's itinerary against a backdrop of protracted political upheaval at once registers a powerful longing for a shared monument and yet illuminates the inconsistencies, fabrications, and fictions that lay behind this notion. These reinterpretations were contingent on the remediation of the inscription as it traveled across diverse substrates and surfaces, from rhinoceros horn to wood, to stone, to ink-squeeze rubbings (figure 4.1). The fate of Xu's carved

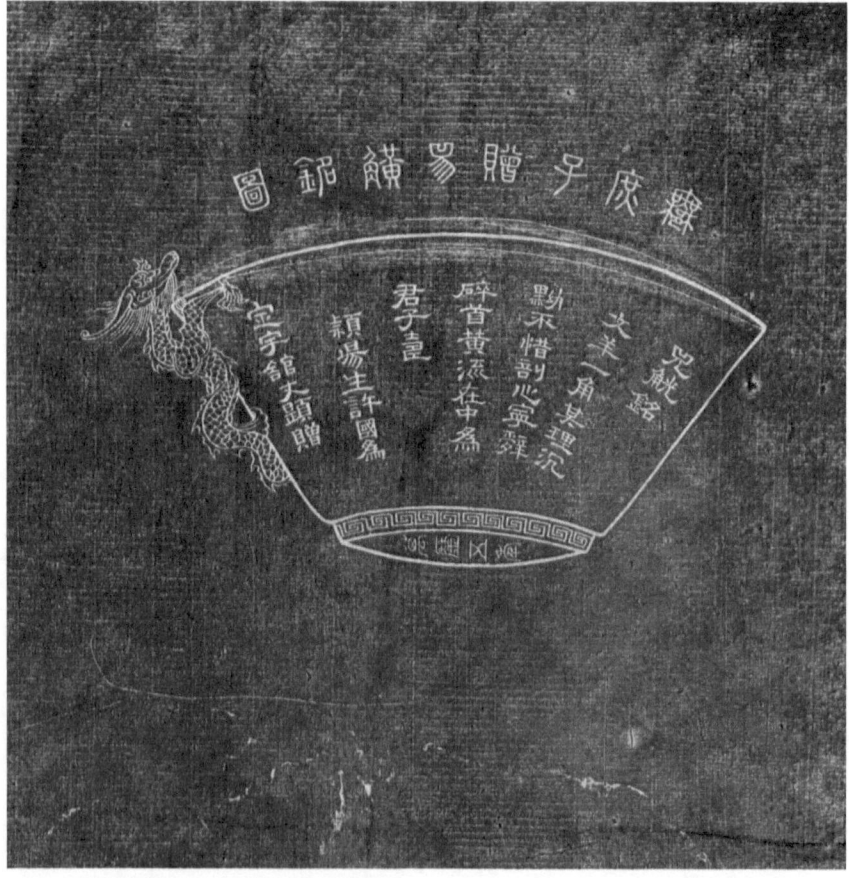

FIGURE 4.1. Detail of Xu Guo's inscription on a rhinoceros horn cup for Zhao Yongxian (rubbing of stone carving). *Source: Sigong gui Zhao shice* 兕觥歸趙詩冊, 20. Image courtesy of National Central Library, Taiwan.

words in late imperial China adumbrates an open-ended process of transposition and material transformation—rather than a coherent search for fixity and closure.

Whereas chapter 1 outlined a heightened self-consciousness around the challenges of inscription during the Ming-Qing transition, and chapters 2 and 3 reconsidered the technical innovations that lay behind seventeenth-century writing upon things, examining both the ascendancy of entrepreneurial artisans and the dynamic forms of cross-media transfer they pioneered, this chapter focuses on the literary interpretation and transmission of early modern inscriptions. The travels of Xu Guo's inscribed message illuminate the competing and at times incoherent commitments to objective knowledge and sentiment that shape the work of late imperial China's leading antiquaries. The central yet largely unacknowledged place of "objects of the former dynasty" (*qianchao yiwu* 前朝遺物) in the resurgence of Qing antiquarianism challenges an oversimplifying picture of eighteenth-century scholarship on artifacts as a strictly empirical project devoted to the reconstruction of inscriptions on ancient bronze and stone monuments. Ming remnant things instead elucidate the extent to which early- to mid-Qing conceptions of the antique, or "metal and stone," were neither preordained nor immutable.

More specifically, the fate of Zhao Yongxian's rhinoceros horn cup reveals the critical place of the poetic imagination in Qing antiquarian responses to past traces. Why, my chapter asks, did so many epigraphers write of their encounters with inscribed objects in verse? Antiquarian poetry at once registers the far-reaching impact of an ascendant mode of critical objectivity on the perception and experience of things during the late seventeenth and eighteenth centuries. At the same time, such poems recall and record feelings—the jolt of an unanticipated discovery, the palpable joy of a perfect match, or the fragile reassurance gleaned from a staged spectacle of restitution—that lurk beneath, inform, and yet cannot be reduced to the empirical investigation of hard evidence. Qing antiquarian poetry enlarged approaches to materiality in Chinese literature, redirecting attention from the ways in which poets invest things with emotional significance to the question of how recalcitrant artifacts—or the stubbornly particular properties of recently rediscovered objects—arrest and affect their viewers. Poetic encounters with carved words at the same time broach the fraught issue of poetry's own durability.

THE POLITICS OF INSCRIPTION

Xu Guo's inscriptions turn the two respective vessels—a jade cup for Wu Zhongxing and a rhinoceros horn cup for Zhao Yongxian—into material metaphors for the virtues of worthy officials. While not an unconventional strategy, Xu's words assume a new illocutionary force when read against the events of Wu and Zhao's punishment on December 1, 1577. The inscription on the jade cup for Wu Zhongxing adapts long-standing analogies between the material and the qualities of a gentleman:

INSCRIPTION ON A JADE CUP

Refined and elegant, is this what made Bian shed tears?
Bright splendor, is this what made Lin so angry?
Pursued, chiseled, ever a vessel for use.

玉杯銘

斑斑者，何卞生淚。
英英者，何藺生氣。
追之琢之，永成器。[9]

"Refined and elegant" (*banban zhe* 斑斑者) and "bright splendor" (*yingying zhe* 英英者) describe, at once, the surface of the cup and the "resplendence" of Wu's reputation. References to the legend of the "Jade Disc of He" (Heshi bi 和氏璧) suggest how jade can both elicit and emblematize moral rectitude. Bian He 卞和 (ca. eighth century BCE) cried for three days and three nights when a piece of priceless jade he had discovered was dismissed by his king as an ordinary stone. Lin Xiangru 藺相如 (d. 260 BCE) angrily threatened to destroy He's jade disc before the King of Qin, a ruse that eventually allowed him to smuggle the artifact back to its home in the state of Zhao upon realizing that the King of Qin had reneged on an initial promise to return fifteen walled cities in exchange for this priceless treasure. Xu Guo's final line invokes a metaphor from the *Record of Rites* of a "vessel carved from jade" for the man who "masters the Way"—"if man does not study, he will not know the way" 人不學，不知道.[10] The inscription not only works to preserve Wu Zhongxing's fame in the supposedly imperishable medium of jade but also harnesses the form and function of the vessel as material proof of its owner's character.

Xu Guo's inscription for the rhinoceros horn cup opens with a reference to the single horn of a "guardian" ram (*shenyang* 神羊) and its deep "black" grain summoning the form of a mythical one-horned animal, the *xiezhi* 獬豸, that was supposedly able to identify and charge at corrupt courtiers:

INSCRIPTION ON A RHINOCEROS HORN CUP

> The single patterned horn of a mystic ram, a deep black grain.[11]
> Having no regret for one's heart being "carved out," how can he balk at "cracking one's skull."[12]
> With yellow wine sparkling inside, this will bring you long life!

犀杯銘

文羊一角，其理沈黝。
不惜剖心，寧辭碎首。
黃流在中，為君子壽。[13]

Implicit allusions to the archaic *xiezhi* index the protocols and insignia of the court. The animal was the identifying "badge of rank"—an embroidered chest-piece—for members of the censorial-supervising branch of the government. Xu moves from celebrating Zhao's remonstrance to a call for the cup to be filled with wine when the rhinoceros horn reveals its putative "poison-detecting" powers. Conventional wishes for long life assume greater symbolic weight as the cup becomes a talisman for Zhao's safety in exile. The apotropaic power of the horn now constitutes a politically charged metaphor for Zhao Yongxian's resistance to Zhang Juzheng's corruption. By presenting the cup as a disinterested gift and performing a toast that extols the actions of a political protestor, Xu Guo—a close associate of Wang Daokun and client of Fang Yongbin—calls for a renewed seriousness of purpose in the act of carving words, seeking to return to the pointed monitions of a classical inscription.

Praising material virtues, as Zhang Dai's great-grandfather's inscriptions on the box and fan for Shen Meigang suggest, offered supporters of prisoners and protestors an indirect means of voicing their solidarity while circumventing repression and further punishment. The gnomic brevity of *ming* lent itself to the invention of memorable slogans, short mottoes, or sententious maxims for dissemination among allies and onlookers.[14] Zhang Dai transcribed Xu Guo's two inscriptions on the jade and rhinoceros horn cups in his manuscript collection of anecdotes on Ming history, *Kuaiyuan daogu* 快園道古, attesting to the public fame of these memorials in the seventeenth century.[15]

Zhang Juzheng died suddenly in 1582 at the age of fifty-seven, and many of those who had protested during the *duoqing* controversy returned to court to ensure that he and his family were posthumously disgraced.[16] Xu Guo subsequently earned the office of junior grand-secretary and publicly set himself apart from the legacy of the previous administration by seeking to defer his promotion in order to honor the memory of his parents and wife. Wu Zhongxing's jade cup faded from view during the late Ming, yet Zhao Yongxian's rhinoceros horn cup resurfaced in the dynastic transition to assume new levels of fame under the Qing. The cup passed from the Zhao household to Yongxian's follower, Huang Duanbo 黃端伯 (1585–1645), a Buddhist layman who was executed for defiantly confronting the Manchu prince Dodo (1614–1649) during the fall of Nanjing.[17] Huang left the cup to his follower Chen Qianfu 陳潛夫 (fl. 1636), a resistance fighter from Zhejiang who committed suicide after being caught with a militia behind Qing lines.[18]

With the deaths of both Huang and Chen during the Manchu conquest and their posthumous enshrinement as martyrs, the journey of the cup became entangled with the history of Ming loyalist resistance, recasting protests against corruption under Wanli as omens of dynastic cataclysm. The cup survived the violence of the 1640s and reappeared in the early Qing, passing between leading antiquarians, from Zhu Yizun 朱彝尊 (1629–1709) to Weng Fanggang 翁方綱 (1733–1818). By the High Qing, a community of scholars managed to return the cup to the Zhao family, an event that was widely commemorated in poetry, stone carving, and ink-squeeze rubbings. The loss and rediscovery of this small cup, its journey from the 1570s to the 1800s, provided leading literary figures with an unlikely means of working through the repercussions of Ming collapse. If Xu Guo's initial inscription secured a collective protest in support of Wu and Zhao, his engraved words were read and remade in other material formats to sustain a community of loyal custodians from the late Ming to the High Qing.

ANTIQUARIAN POETRY

STRANGE ANTIQUES

The efforts of early modern antiquarians to celebrate Xu Guo's gift as an antique led them to embrace anachronism and imaginative projection. No cups challenged existing frameworks for thinking about vessels quite like those wrought from recently imported fragments of dead African and Southeast Asian rhinoceroses in the late Ming and early Qing.[19] Visual and literary sources from the period celebrate the erotic associations of the material, its medicinal or quasi-magical efficacy (illuminating ghosts, dividing water, nullifying toxins), while classicists debated the relationship between this mysterious animal (extinct in the Ming empire) and references to horn-shaped drinking vessels in catalogues of ritual paraphernalia. Artisans exploited such confusion to carve libation cups from foreign rhinoceros horns that imitate the properties of ancient bronze implements. Before attending to the unlikely fate of Zhao Yongxian's rhinoceros horn cup in the wake of inter-dynastic war, I examine the contested properties of the material Xu Guo chose to inscribe and the pressure it exerted on established conceptions of the antique. Such details elucidate how late Ming inscriptions drew from and yet unsettled the study of ritual artifacts, divulging literary investments in writing upon vessels that exceed the purview and detached objectivity of antiquarian scholarship.

An inscription for a vessel fashioned as a mallow (*kui* 葵) (or common hibiscus) composed by Xu Guo's close associate and a fellow Huizhou official, Wang Daokun, illuminates the competing attributes of these objects in the Ming imaginary.[20] This inscription simultaneously attests to novel forms of inter-medial design in Fujianese coastal ateliers, the expansion of global trade networks between Europe, Africa, and Asia, and the extent to which sixteenth-century rhinoceros horn cups started to unsettle typologies of ritual vessels:

INSCRIPTION ON A RHINOCEROS HORN MALLOW CUP

I have a *sigong*, for your splendid banquet.
My heart will always be faithful,
You are like the radiant sun.[21]

犀葵杯銘

我有兕觥，薦君瑤席；
我心靡他，君如皎日。[22]

Wang's inscription encodes a short toast: the handler is invited to inhabit the "I" and, through lending his voice to the words of the vessel, wish a guest long life.[23] Contemporary *materia medica* assumed that the material of the horn could expel poison, and so Wang's stock pronouncements of auspicious blessings, like the final wishes in Xu Guo's *ming*, call forth a sense of the sustenance afforded through ingestion, or oral contact with the surface of the cup.

Ming rhinoceros horn cups, particularly those adorned with floral motifs, can be traced to the prefecture of Zhangzhou 漳州 in Fujian.[24] Located on the Jiulong River 九龍江 estuary, customs-controlled Haicheng 海澄 was a major international trading center with the Spanish Philippines and was one of the chief ports through which foreign goods and exotica like Sumatran, Javan, and African rhinoceros horns passed into Ming China. According to Derek Gillman, cups fashioned from this imported material were likely manufactured in workshops in the Haicheng area where they were produced alongside and appear to have influenced the design of Dehua 德化 white porcelain ware.[25] The label for the vessel inscribed by Wang Daokun alludes to forms of cross-media transfer between decorative art-practices in sixteenth-century Fujian. One such vessel with a ring-stand base, carved in the form of a five-petal hibiscus flower (or mallow) and thus akin to the cup inscribed by Wang Daokun, was as Soame Jenyns has shown, acquired by the Tradescants (John the Elder [~1638] and John the Younger [1608–1662]) and exhibited in their "Ark" in Lambeth, the earliest English cabinet of curiosities and the first public museum in the country.[26]

Wang Daokun's reference to the so-called *sigong* 兕觥 alludes to banquet celebrations from the *Classic of Poetry*. Commentators glossed this enigmatic object as a drinking vessel made from the horn of a *si* 兕—a mythical animal that was, in turn, commonly defined as an ancient ox (*niu* 牛) with a single horn (translated by some scholars as a *gaur*).[27] Han commentator Zheng Xuan 鄭玄 (127–200) classified the *gong* made from a *si* horn (or from wooden imitations) as a "punishment goblet" (*fajue* 罰爵) intended for use in archaic drinking games. Given these associations in commentaries to the *Classic of Poetry*, the *sigong* label served as a useful epithet for a rhinoceros horn cup, hinting at a vessel made from the horn of an enigmatic bovine animal (the character *xi* 犀 was also etymologically linked to the character for an ox 牛) while invoking the sanction and prestige of a classical genealogy. François Louis has uncovered a longer history of associating the *sigong* label with unconventional horn-shaped vessels. *Illustrations to the Three Classics on Ritual* (*San li tu* 三禮圖), a book that did much to set the terms of the antiquarian discourse on ritual vessels in late imperial China, conflated the name of the *sigong* with an image of what appears to be a Hellenistic rhyton.[28] Editors of the influential *Xuanhe*-era *Illustrated Catalogue of Antiquities* also defined a ritual bronze vessel that again approximates the form of a foreign rhyton, the "Sacrificial-Animal-Head Cup of the Han" (Han xishou bei 漢犧首杯), in terms of its resemblance to the *sigong* of the *Classic of Poetry*.[29]

These creative misattributions prefigure the emergence of a generative tension in antiquarian scholarship. On the one hand, the *sigong* label placed exotic horn cups within a classical lineage, enlarging typologies of ancient Chinese material culture; on the other hand, the appearances and visual representations of these horn cups undermined the stability of the *sigong* as the name of an antique vessel, raising concerns as to what material the *sigong* was actually made from (*si*-horn, wood, bronze), what it looked like (a Hellenistic rhyton), and whether or not it was intended for ritual performances.[30] The popular use of the *sigong* label for seventeenth-century rhinoceros horn cups exacerbated such tensions in the Ming and Qing dynasties, a trend that frustrated classicists from the period. Commentator Zhang Cizhong 張次仲 (1589–1676) stressed that the *si* was "not what is nowadays called a rhinoceros" and emphasized that the *sigong* was only made from the horn of the *si*.[31] Yao Bing 姚炳 (fl. 1700–1710) went further by noting that while "nowadays horn vessels are all called 'rhinoceros horn cups,'" even if a *sigong* could be made from wood in imitation of the *si* horn, it was emphatically *not* made from rhinoceros horn.[32] Seemingly trivial questions as to whether the *sigong* possessed a protome or was intended for archaic drinking games attest to deep-seated concerns with how the prestige of a classical name might remain intact in an unruly marketplace of novel things.

Xu Guo's gift for Zhao Yongxian, perhaps the most famous rhinoceros horn cup from late imperial China, became a *sigong* during its travels. Qing poets in their responses to Zhao's cup meanwhile exploit the semantic ambiguity of the *sigong* name, variously invoking scenes of banqueting, punishment, and drunken release while elsewhere appealing to its fungibility with ritual vessels for the performance of ceremonial sacrifices to ancestors. The competing associations of the *sigong*, in other words, partly facilitated the vessel's later role in antiquarian poetry as a means with which to tentatively reconcile the expression of shared grievance through wine and a commitment to filial propriety in mourning rites.

Other authors of inscriptions on late Ming rhinoceros horn cups considered the multivalent associations of the object, or how the exotic and preternatural properties of the horn relate to and exceed the name and prescribed function of a *sigong*. Dong Qichang in an "appended letter" to an inscription on a horn for the official Wang Shiqi 王士琦 (1550–1619), reflects on its "essence within that shines like a mirror to illuminate ghosts" 其中有精若照鬼之鏡, recalling the testimony of an acquaintance at a customs post in Hainan who had recently viewed a cup offered to him by a merchant that changed color with the light of the moon.[33]

Li Weizhen 李維楨 (1547–1626), in a lengthy inscription (918 words) on a picture of the same object, eulogized the horn as an exotic marvel that resembles yet surpasses a drinking vessel, a "miniature mountain," and a curved "as you wish" scepter.[34] Li's literary account of the horn was so eccentric that it won inclusion in Yao Zhiyin's 姚之駰 (n.d.) list of "miscellaneous treasures" (*zabao* 雜寶) in his landmark 1721 compilation *Arranged Anecdotes of the Yuan and the Ming* (*Yuan Ming shilei chao* 元明事類鈔), grouped with other wonders such as a five-foot coral stand for a seventy-two-stringed *pipa* found in a palace built from sandalwood in an eastern city of Kashmir, and the portentous "Cup That 'Reflects Events of the World'" (*zhaoshi bei* 照世杯), discovered to the west of Samarkand.[35] Placed in a "miscellaneous" appendix to a chapter on "precious treasures" (*zhenbao men* 珍寶門), the cup comes as close as possible—in a work that tries to systematically organize trivia on the natural history of the Ming (with lists of anecdotes on everything from stars to ants)—to eluding classification.[36] These examples reveal the novelty, hybridity, and excess with which attempts to present a rhinoceros horn cup as an antique *sigong* were forced to contend. From an alternative perspective, such cases attest to the inventiveness that characterized literary inscription in late Ming China—the power of writing upon objects to create a wonder, or to become the marvelous thing it names.

THE RECOVERY OF LOST THINGS

Inter-dynastic war, as Zhang Dai's dream reminiscences recall, precipitated the wholesale breakup, destruction, and dispersal of family collections. Early Qing writers, as Wai-yee Li has demonstrated, subsequently reflected at length on the rediscovery and repossession of ostensibly lost things.[37] Zhao Yongxian's rhinoceros horn cup diverges from many of these examples in that it evokes not the imperial splendor and prosperity of an earlier age but the protests and punishments that were seen to have prefigured the fall of the dynasty. The object elicits not so much royalist nostalgia for a romantic past (as with Zhang Dai's inscriptions on his "Twenty-Eight Friends" or his reminiscences of "Wood Like a Dragon") but critical reflection on late Ming political corruption, on the fate of *zhongxiao* ethics, and on the seeds of imperial decline.

The cup not only attracted the attention of poets who had lived through the chaos of dynastic transition but also remained a focal point for literary responses to these events during the eighteenth century. Its biography, perhaps more than that of any other thing in this period, registers changing approaches to the meaning of the Ming cataclysm in Qing intellectual circles. Unlike other "objects of the former dynasty" that spurred private reflection on historical upheaval, Zhao's rhinoceros horn cup stimulated discussion around the contested role of things in collective life. More specifically, it raised the issue of how to reconcile a family's claim to private property with the possibility of public attachments to a shared monument. How to resolve tensions between the demands of filial piety and loyalism when a supposedly lost family possession has, through its displacement and travels, facilitated the revival of an open loyalist community? These concerns center upon the material format of Xu Guo's inscription and its subsequent remediations in ink-squeeze rubbings and stone.

"Song for the Sigong," 1677

Having survived the upheavals of the dynastic transition, Xu Guo's cup for Zhao Yongxian resurfaced in the hands of an official named He Yuanying 何元英 (1631–1679) from Xiushui 秀水 in Zhejiang. Yuanying invited acclaimed lyricist and fellow townsman Zhu Yizun to compose a song in praise of the cup's biography. Zhu had been active in the anti-Qing resistance as a youth and was a fugitive until the 1650s. In later life, he broke his loyalist ties to take the 1679 examination as an "Outstanding Scholar of Vast Learning," entering official service and earning rebuke from critics for a "failure to preserve [his] integrity in old age" (*wanjie bubao* 晚節不保).[38] During his time at court, he worked as an editor on the official history of the Ming dynasty yet was dismissed in 1684 for making illegal copies of palace documents for private use. Zhu was not only a leading poet but a dominant figure in the reemergence of antiquarianism as an intellectual movement in the early Qing: his collection of rubbings, *Colophons to Bronze and Stone Artifacts from the Pushu Pavilion* (*Pushuting jinshi bawei* 曝書亭金石跋尾), became an influential model for later epigraphic research.[39] Zhu's "Song for the *Sigong*" ("Sigong ge" 兕觥歌), the first poetic dedication to the cup after the fall of the Ming and a piece composed one hundred years after Xu Guo's initial inscription, uses the history of the object to evaluate the character and integrity of a loyal remonstrator. The cup's new owner, He Yuanying, served the first two Qing emperors, Shunzhi 順治 (1638–1661; r. 1644–1661) and Kangxi. Composed shortly before He's death and Zhu's decision to work for Manchu rulers, the poet uses this fêted vessel to justify the proposition of political service in the late seventeenth century.

Zhu Yizun's song begins by distinguishing the rhinoceros horn from other exotic trinkets that might adorn the tables of a wealthy patron's banquet (jade, fragrant conches, silver, gold). This "dust-expelling" horn—an early epithet for the material that, here, carries Buddhist connotations of purging sensory delusion and defilements—brought from Huangzhi 黃支, the ancient name of an Indian kingdom that presented a rhinoceros as tribute to the Han emperor Pingdi 漢平帝 (r. 1 BCE–5 CE), demands that all other "treasures" (*bao* 寶) be cleared away. Zhu then reads the cup's inscription, an act that leads to his lyrical reconstruction of its history in a sequence organized around Xu Guo's engraved words (the poem builds upon the terms of Xu's inscription: *ningci* 寧辭; *shenyang yijiao* 神羊一角; *manyin huangliu* 滿飲黃流). Having noticed the cup's markings, Zhu makes no further reference to the horn's materiality. The main body of the poem consequently reads as an extended exegesis and reflection on the meaning of Xu's carved slogans. In the course of his song, Zhu renames what had hitherto been called a "rhinoceros horn cup" (*xibei* 犀杯) a *sigong*.

ANTIQUARIAN POETRY

The "Song" was the last of several poems Zhu Yizun composed for He Yuanying in the 1670s.[40] Much of this verse commemorates social gatherings for birthday celebrations or group garden visits. While Zhu's "Song" does not name any other attendees, the banquet setting of his poem suggests that the vessel, in He's hands, sustained collective reflection on events of the recent past:

SONG FOR THE SIGONG

Turn over the jade bowls and discard the fragrant conches,[41]
Remove the engraved silver cups and the archaic golden beakers.
This rhinoceros horn of Huangzhi expels all dust.
Our host brought in the vessel to present it before his guests.
I requested to see the inscription it bore, to display, for all, the events of the past:
[Wanli],[42] in his early years, greatly favored his ministers,
Yet his senior official "cut short the emotions," to the fury and rebuke of the people.
One "Phoenix of the Eastern Slope" descended at the Wu Gate,[43]
Breaking the balustrade,[44] he does not avoid touching the inverted scale![45]
When it came time for him to go into exile, well-wishers filled the inns of the capital,
An offer of protection from Xu Guo as they parted at the fork in the road,
The single horn of a mystic ram, could it have had an equal?
Passed down and then it returned to Loujiang.
Master Zhang bequeathed it to his followers,
In daring to remonstrate, my master copies Zhao Yongxian.
Fond of inviting guests, with no sign of weariness.
As if for Pingyuan's ten-day drinking session, they came to see him.
Court clothes have been pawned, with no regret,
Writing, carefree, suffused with the "Mallard Flower,"
I've drained this beaker a few times,
Before this vessel, why would I reserve passionate lyrics for another occasion?
My master last year moved to the chamberlain temple,

Who on those south-facing couches[46] in the west of the palace has the sharp glance of an osprey?
Now in the Han Palace there is no White Tiger goblet,[47]
Drinking from a cup full of this golden wine, do not put it aside lightly.

兕觥歌

覆玉碗，屏香螺；徹銀甖落金叵羅。
黃支之犀塵盡辟，主人持觥客前席。
請看觥上銘，為君陳夙昔：
定陵沖年資相臣，元老奪情眾怒嗔。
朝陽一鳳午門伏，折檻寧辭逆鱗觸。
歸時餞者滿都亭，珍重臨岐許文穆。
神羊一角詎有雙，流傳既久歸婁江。
張公以之遺弟子，敢諫吾公趙公似。
更兼愛客無倦容，平原十日恆過從。
朝衣典盡且不顧，快意但寫毚花濃。
我浮此觥亦已數，尊前豈惜狂歌重。
吾公週年徙卿寺，西掖南床誰鶚視。
漢殿今無白獸尊，滿飲黃流莫輕寘。[48]

After Zhu's brief introduction to the rhinoceros horn cup, the following ten lines of the poem can be divided into two halves: the historical narrative embedded in Xu's inscription (from the *duoqing* controversy to Zhao Yongxian's dismissal) and its resonance a century later at He's banquet in 1677. This bipartite structure pivots on Zhu's analogy between Zhao Yongxian and He Yuanying ("In daring to remonstrate, my master resembles Zhao Yongxian"). The worthy early Qing official, in his acquisition of this talisman of righteous protest, upholds the historical example established by a Wanli-era memorialist.

Zhu Yizun makes no mention of the anti-Qing martyrs Huang Duanbo and Chen Qianfu within the main body of the poem, suggesting a degree of reticence in grappling with the issue of how to read He Yuanying's service for Shunzhi and Kangxi in relation to the fates of those who sacrificed themselves fighting Manchu armies. The poem similarly contains no explicit references to the events of the dynastic transition. Zhu writes of how an enigmatic "Master Zhang" (Zhang gong 張公) bequeathed (*yi* 遺)

the cup to his followers (*dizi* 弟子). It is unclear, however, whether Zhu purposefully elides the object's fate during the inter-dynastic war or whether he remains unsure of what really happened to the vessel between Zhao's death and He's possession. Did the acquisition of the cup by a servant of the first two Qing emperors necessitate the erasure of its connection to anti-Manchu resistance fighters? In either event, the poem's evocative silence on this matter becomes a key theme in the critical commentary the cup subsequently generated.

The song's conclusion wavers between a celebration and rejection of retirement. Use of the libation cup sustains a mood of momentary release from political pressures and the trauma of the recent past (pawning court clothes; draining wine in an unfettered state). And yet, the vessel's very presence at He's banquet concurrently elicits reflection on its absence at court. Compared in the final couplet to the "white tiger goblet" (*baishou zun* 白獸尊), a medieval lidded-chalice placed in a royal hall to allow ministers who drank from it to directly remonstrate with the ruler, the rhinoceros horn cup's removal from the provocatively named "Han palaces" (Han dian 漢殿) creates a vacuum in the capital that now needs to be filled. The banquet in classical poetry constitutes a space where a "problematic surplus of feeling," one that shifts from despair, to joy, or to "some flurry of action," might be managed and controlled.[49] The final line of Zhu's poem riffs on the concluding words of Xu Guo's inscription, performing a toast that assuages grievance through wine while channeling feelings of uninhibitedness back into the future work of remonstrance. Zhu's song, taking stock of He's career and anticipating momentous changes in his own life, repurposes this token of Ming loyalism as a prop with which to justify the prospect of service for the Qing.

A Double? Zhang Zaogong's Box

Zhu Yizun's song was not the only account of the cup to appear in the late seventeenth century. A Hangzhou-based collector named Zhang Zaogong 章藻功 (n.d.) also composed a lengthy tribute to the vessel, "A Record of Censor Zhao's *Sigong*" ("Cang jiantao Zhao gong sigong ji" 藏檢討趙公兕觥記). This account bears no date and so elicited concerns that two copies of the cup were simultaneously circulating in the early Qing marketplace or that Zhu Yizun and He Yuanying were looking at one version of the vessel at their banquet in 1677 and that Zhang Zaogong was looking at another. The challenge for subsequent commentators became how to decide which one was the fake. These two accounts differ in their respective approaches to the history of the vessel, diverging most clearly in their treatment of the object's experience in the hands of Ming martyrs. Zhu Yizun remains silent on the issue, yet Zhang Zaogong makes these associations the central focus of his reflections on the cup. Zhang's preface reveals that he was a relative of the anti-Manchu resistance fighter Chen Qianfu:

> Later, Zhao [Yongxian] transmitted the cup to his retainer Huang Duanbo, and Huang transmitted it to his retainer Chen Qianfu. Both of these worthies perished in the troubles. I am Chen's son-in-law, so with vigilance I received and stored this possession, making a record of it.

> 後趙傳之門人黃端伯，黃傳之門人陳潛夫，兩賢皆殉國難。余，陳壻也，謹受而藏之，為之記。[50]

The author consequently dwells on the theme of filial piety, reminding his readers that Zhang Juzheng's initial crime and the protestors' intent concerned a failure to properly mourn a deceased parent. Zhang Zaogong shifts focus from Zhao Yongxian's biography to the transmission of the cup in the hands of Huang Duanbo (with an "aura lofty as mountains and broad as rivers" 氣壯山河) and Chen Qianfu (whose "radiance vies with the sun and moon" 光爭日月): what matters is not the cup's relation to a single individual but to a lineage of martyrs, or the way the vessel still bears the fresh "moisture of the mouth" (*kouze*) from these "masters and students."[51] Zhang's account effectively redirects attention from the cup's inscription to the meaning of the four-character seal-script motto he etched on a box he commissioned for the object, "With the Breath from the Mouths of Three Loyal Remonstrators" (*sanzhong kouze* 三忠口澤). For Zhang Zaogong, the cup becomes a medium through which one might offer libations to and thus commune with the assembled spirits of Zhao, Huang, and Chen: a point he makes in his final line: "a cup suffused with clear wine, the loyal spirits of three generations come close" 一杯清酒淋漓，三世之忠魂彷彿。[52] If Zhu Yizun's banquet song seeks lyrical release from a history of violence, Zhang's account of this "deep cup of countless punishments" (*baifa shenbei* 百罰深盃)—"a thrice-passed down treasure, a remnant of rent innards and broken necks" 三傳至寶出自屠腸裂頸之餘—dwells squarely on the drinker's obligations to the martyred dead.⁵³

Zhu Yizun and Zhang Zaogong offer competing interpretations of the cup's meaning in the early Qing. The former uses the object's history to look to the present and future; the latter effaces his own position to gaze backwards, mourning the spirits of his father-in-law and his father-in-law's teacher. Zhu omits mention of the violence of the Ming cataclysm to dwell on the contemporary resonance of Zhao Yongxian's remonstrance; Zhang meanwhile argues that this momentous event is no longer the primary source of the object's historical significance but one facet of the vessel's identity as it passed between three generations of loyalists. These two accounts offer conflicting approaches to the issue of ownership: Zhu celebrates the power of the object to seek out and sustain an open community of worthy custodians, bringing together men who did not know each other or who were otherwise unrelated through their shared use of the vessel. Zhang Zaogong, by contrast, affirms the critical significance of a master-disciple lineage and family ownership, emphasizing that he acquired the cup only through the intercession of his wife's relatives. Zhu's song and Zhang's essay use the vessel to articulate divergent approaches to the dynastic transition: Zhu Yizun, a guest at his friend's banquet, finds in this inscribed rhinoceros horn a pretext for acceptance and accommodation of the new order, one predicated on silence around the matter of loyalist suicide; Zhang, mourning his wife's family's losses, sees a blood-stained relic of martyrdom and historical trauma. The doubling of this small cup (and the related anxiety that one version might be a counterfeit) abets the negotiation between conflicting responses to the fall of the Ming; and yet, the multivalent idea of the vessel offers a means through which such sentiments might be managed and tentatively resolved.

THE RETURN OF THE GIFT

The rhinoceros horn cup eventually returned to the market, finding a new home with the Yan 顏 family—the descendants of Confucius's disciple Yan Hui 顏回 (521–481 BCE)—of Qufu around 1748.⁵⁴ It is at this juncture that prominent antiquarian Weng Fanggang, a Hanlin academician, renowned calligrapher, and compiler of the *Complete Library in Four Sections* (*Siku quanshu* 四庫全書), encountered and decisively rewrote the vessel's biography. As antiquarianism reemerged in eighteenth-century scholarly culture as a dominant intellectual program, Weng coordinated the excavation and reconstruction of monuments like the Wu Liang Shrine. While he promoted innovative methods of empirical research, Weng also pioneered new practices of artmaking, using poetry, painting, and calligraphy to document and disseminate scholarship on antiquities.[55] With his close links to the court, the dealers of Liulichang 琉璃廠, and the temple stalls of the Western Mountains, Weng's Beijing residence became an international center for the discussion and appreciation of art objects: his elaborate birthday ceremonies for Su Shi, as Michele Matteini has shown, inspired similar collective rituals across East Asia.[56] In his encounter with Zhao's rhinoceros horn cup, Weng draws from the antiquarian's toolkit to manipulate the reception of the vessel and its inscription.[57] The case suggests that behind the austere edifice of the study of "metal and stone" lay deep-seated concerns with constructing and controlling narratives of the recent past.

Weng Fanggang's relationship with the cup can be traced back to the summer of 1778 when the Yan family of Qufu sent an ink-squeeze rubbing to Beijing.[58] The Yans invited Weng, a renowned calligrapher, to transcribe Zhu Yizun's "Song for the *Sigong*," so that it might be mounted alongside this document on the same scroll.[59] Weng repeatedly refers to having received from Yan Hengzhai 顏衡齋 (n.d.) a "rubbing of its words" 拓其文, suggesting that the rubbing was made and presented as a copy of Xu Guo's inscription—it remains unclear from Weng's writings, however, whether this was a rubbing taken from the engraved surface of the actual cup or from a transcribed copy of the inscription on wooden board or stone.[60] In a poem written in 1778 to commemorate the rubbing, Weng dwells on the experience of transcribing Zhu Yizun's poem for the scroll:

WRITTEN AFTER A RUBBING OF THE SIGONG INSCRIPTION
FOR ZHAO WENYI BY XU GUO OF THE MING (1778)

Censor Zhu Yizun wrote his "Song for the *Sigong*"
Zhang Zaogong the Worthy has his "Record of the Sigong,"
Recorded on top of the box in large script it says: "Three Loyal Ministers,"
Above and below there are reflections on its one-hundred-year history.

ANTIQUARIAN POETRY

The "Three Loyal Ministers" are Zhao Yongxian, Huang Duanbo, and Chen Qianfu,
Drinking from this vessel will protect your body.
Zhang said he was Chen's son-in-law,
Loujiang and Zhu Yizun had both passed away.
Zhu's poem had still not been carved onto the box,
They wanted me to transcribe it to make a scroll.
First there was He Yuanying and Zhang Zaogong later, why is there any doubt?
Master Gui Fu and Master Yan Hengzhai continued to pass it between them,
Master Gui was drinking in Yan's Studio
Inebriated, he called out to Xu Guo and Zhao Yongxian that "we are united,"
At that time, the lamps at the window dimmed, as moonlight illuminated the room,
A somber mood of the ages suddenly filled their hearts.
There was a forceful aura to the split-stroke clerical-script characters,
The Master of Yingyang, Xu Guo, made it for Zhao Yongxian.
That day, he hurriedly headed out of the gates of the capital,
There is this engraving, which emits a marvelous resonance.
My brush limns this piece, shining light from the sun and stars
[Weng inserts a comment on the manuscript: "Fanggang was editing the "Outlines and Details of the Ming History" and added this inscription under the section for the Fifth Year of the Wanli Reign"],
I will read this directly as history but not as an inscription.
Only a jade cup could be used to toast with this,
Why did well-wishers fill the inns of the capital?
The official's copy has already been a source of envy,
More still, its transmission is truly not fake.
Stored in Qufu for many years,
On encountering a charming guest, only then will it serve in a spirited banquet.
I have yet to see the vessel, but first read the text,
I am not a drinker but can discern the real thing.
It is easy to come across an embellished flashy artifact,
It is more difficult to encounter the towering spirits of great men.

書明許文穆贈趙文毅兕觥銘拓本後

朱檢討作兕觥歌,章吉士有兕觥記。
記端大書曰三忠,上下低回百年事。
三忠趙公黃曁陳,能飲此觥能致身。
章也自言陳氏甥,婁江秀水皆前塵。
秀水之詩未鐫櫝,要我重書合成軸。
何前章後奚必疑,桂生顏生遞相屬。
桂生昨飲顏氏齋,醉呼許趙云吾儕。
其時窗燈暈屋月,萬古鬱勃傾胸懷。
八分小書氣莽莽,潁陽生為定宇丈。
爾日匆匆出國門,有此雕鐫發奇響。
我筆此條光日星,[方綱纂修明綱目謹增此二銘於萬曆五年分注下]
直作史讀弗作銘。
秖有玉杯可交酢,何須送者滿都亭。
政使重摹已堪羨,何況流傳真不贋。
曲阜藏來又幾年,必逢佳客方酣醼。
我未見觥初讀文,我不善飲頗識真。
易逢蹉琢光晶器,難遇嶔崎磊落人。[61]

While Zhu Yizun, at his friend's banquet, alluded to the material of rhinoceros horn, Weng ignores the shape and substance of the cup, adopting an epigrapher's perspective to direct focus to the split-stroke clerical-script characters of the carved inscription. Weng attends to Xu Guo's *ming*—the way "this carving" indexes the event of "hurriedly leaving the capital"—as a self-sufficient source of historical knowledge. At the same time, his poem excises Zhu's violent imagery of Wanli-era protest and Zhang's bloodstained account of loyalist suicide. In an added note from a manuscript edition of the poem, Weng claims that while producing this new copy, he also included the date of Xu Guo's inscription (1577) in the "Outlines and Details of the Ming History," a project for which he served as an editor. In the next half of this broken line, Weng asserts that he is invested in "reading" rather than "making" an inscription: the poem consequently stages a pivot toward treating Xu Guo's *ming* as evidence for annotation, collation, and historical study. This note marks the moment when the 1577 protest is brought back into a state-sanctioned narrative of Ming history.

Weng Fanggang's experience handling the rubbing of Xu Guo's inscription inspired a full-length critical study of the cup, "A Disquisition on the *Sigong*" ("Sigong bian" 兕觥辨), a piece that harnesses the apparatus of philological scholarship to assess this sixteenth-century trinket. The stated aim of this essay is to clear up confusion surrounding Zhu Yizun and Zhang Zaogong's competing accounts by arguing that they may in fact have been describing the same object. Weng asserts that Zhang Zaogong's reference to being a "son-in-law" of Chen refers not to the martyr Chen Qianfu but to his descendant; this time lag then allows Weng to claim that the cup passed from the Chen family to He Yuanying (where Zhu Yizun saw it in 1677) and then returned to the Chen family (where Zhang Zaogong acquired it around 1700). He succinctly restates this conclusion in his poem on the rubbing: "First it belonged to He [Yuanying] and then later to Zhang [Zaogong], why should there be any doubt?" Weng's convoluted argument imaginatively exploits gaps and ambiguities in the fragmentary evidence available to him, seeking to reject the dangerous possibility of a fake. Nevertheless, Weng's supposedly authoritative version of the cup's history hinges on the small and ultimately unprovable detail of what precisely Zhang Zaogong meant when he referred to himself as a "son-in-law of Chen." Weng's painstaking effort to prove his point betrays a keenly felt need to reconcile Zhu Yizun and Zhang Zaogong's contrasting accounts of the vessel—a point he makes in the first couplet of his poem on the rubbing. At stake is the more consequential challenge of how to reconcile the competing sentiments of accommodation and mourning that animated early Qing visions of the cup.

Weng Fanggang's critical study of the vessel participates in a broader intellectual reevaluation of the dynastic transition during the late 1770s. The Qianlong 乾隆 emperor (1711–1799; r. 1735–1796), spurred by a will to promote "absolute loyalty in society" or to "foster the cardinal principles and constant virtues" (*fuzhi gangchang* 扶植綱常), initiated an official biographical project to recognize the sacrifices of Southern Ming loyalists entitled *Records of All Subjects Who Died Out of Loyalty to the Fallen Dynasty, Authorized by the Emperor* (*Qinding shengchao xunjie zhuchen lu* 欽定勝朝殉節諸臣錄).[62] Qianlong's imperial edict proposed that an official posthumous title be granted to commended martyrs and recorded on memorial tablets to be enshrined in county memorial temples for loyalists.[63] This project officially restored the reputations of the two Ming martyrs involved in the passage of the cup: Huang Duanbo, for his service with the Prince of Fu, was one of 599 martyrs given the honorable title *liemin* 烈愍 (bravery and commiseration), and Chen Qianfu, for his service with the Prince of Lu (the ineffectual pretender who visited Zhang Dai's bookroom to sit on Wood Like a Dragon), was one of 120 martyrs given the honorable title *zhongjie* 忠節 (loyalty and integrity). Paradoxically, the *Zhuchen lu* 諸臣錄 project emerged against a backdrop of repressive book bans, literary inquisitions, and the government censorship of Ming loyalist writings.[64] Weng's work on the career of the rhinoceros horn cup at once exploits this opportunity to praise Huang and Chen by proving the authenticity of Zhang Zaogong's tribute to the "three loyalists." And yet, as the Qing state sought to claim hegemonic control over the meanings of Ming loyalism, the cup offered literary leaders like Weng an unlikely means with which to reaffirm their custodianship of the loyalist legacy, or to author their own conclusions to political narratives of the past two centuries.[65]

REUNION

Weng Fanggang carried a copy of the Yan family's mounted rubbing with him when he was reassigned from the capital to Jiangxi in the autumn of 1786.[66] Shortly after arriving at his new post, Weng met with a man traveling to Hunan named Zhao Wanghuai 趙王槐 (Zheting 者庭; fl. 1741) from Changshu 常熟, who revealed that he was the fifth-generation grandson of Zhao Yongxian. Weng brought out the rubbing and showed it to Zhao, recounting their shared experience of viewing the inscription in a colophon dated to the twentieth day of the twelfth month of 1786. Returning to this highly evocative scene in his later writings as if compulsively repeating it, Weng foregrounds the emotional jolt the Zhao descendant felt at this unexpected reunion in the face of presumed loss[67]:

A COLOPHON FOR THE SIGONG

This vessel is presently stored in the Yan household in Qufu. Previously, a rubbing was sent to me and I wrote out a long song and evaluated references in Censor Zhu's collected writings and Zhang Qiji's appended text to ensure there were no mistakes. Today, I met Mr. Jiating who talked of his family background and there was a pure and fragrant air to the words he spoke.

ANTIQUARIAN POETRY

I brought out the rubbing and we viewed it together. His sincerity was deeply moving and this was truly a fortuitous encounter. I wrote out this inscription, with a will to preserve this fated moment in ink.

20TH DAY OF THE 12TH MONTH OF *BINGWU* [1786]

跋兕觥。

是觥今藏曲阜顏氏家，嘗以拓本遺予，為作長歌並為辨朱檢討集與章豈續跋之文，并非歧誤。今得唔嘉庭先生，語及家世，清芬口澤，出此拓本共觀，精誠感召，良非偶然。因為書此銘，以志墨緣。

丙午十二月廿日。[68]

Weng also used the experience of viewing the rubbing as a framing device for a poem he wrote in 1787 that served as both a bargaining chip in recovering the cup from the Yan family and as a memorial to the eventual return of the vessel to the Zhao family temple in Changshu. Opening with the story of Zhao viewing the rubbing, Weng narrates the events of the exchange:

A SONG FOR THE RETURN OF THE SIGONG TO ZHAO (1787)

The *sigong* has been passed down for two hundred years,
From Huang Duanbo, Chen Qianfu, and Zhang Zaogong, it came into the possession of Yan.
Zhu Yizun's poem had yet to be inscribed on the box,
I once more transcribed the poem and an evaluative essay.
This studio and this vessel had a profound destiny.
A copy was made to form an image that was then mounted on a scroll.
The vessel lodging in the East of Lu left me feeling assured,
The album came with me to the West of the Jiang, and I gladly viewed it with a guest.
And who was the guest I happened to speak to?
Zhao Yongxian's fifth-generation grandson.
That night, we prodded the lamp and two streams of tears fell,
The winds rose up and the river surged with force.
Zhao's two eyes flared like lightning,
He looked at it for twenty days without sleeping or eating.
In the third month, a missive from Hunan arrived,

Not thinking a thousand *li* too far, he laid out his intentions.
In response I wrote a letter on his behalf to explain his intent,
A hundred bushels of bright pearls are no recompense.
Just because, through the alleys, I treasured his lofty ideal,
And as a friend, I explained his state of mind, until the autumn.
He visited me, then, at the foot of Mount Lu,
We looked at each other, and I saw his true countenance.
Then from Jiangxi, I passed instructions to Shandong,
Heaven decreed the return of this remnant thing to Changshu.
I alone understood Yan's state of mind,
In his habits, he cherished the extraordinary.
There was nothing in the world to match this horn vessel,
The only thing he wanted from the sack was Weng's poetry.
Zhao proceeded to knock at the door and prostrated, stating his case,
A plain interaction worthy of the superior men of the ages, with a pact as pure as ice and snow.
The light from a lunar halo, still gleams in the traces of wine,
With full-blooded sincerity, an aura that breaks mountains.
Master Yan presented the horn vessel to his guest with a beaming smile,
Old Zhao made a heartfelt pledge of recompense.
The joy of this vessel, after so many years, at finally meeting its old friend,
In tears, the old man returned home, making a proclamation at the family temple.
All along, the tale of the storage of the vessel has been fortuitous,
Yet today, the story can be extended further.
As the compilation is released, a new ballad for the *sigong*!
Overwhelming Mi's boat with rays from a moonlit rainbow.

兕觥歸趙歌

兕觥傳來二百年，黃陳章後今歸顏。
朱檢討詩未銘欵，而我一再詩文編。
此齋此觥緣不淺，摹册成圖褾成卷。
觥居東魯定我懷，卷到西江欣客展。
客爲誰乎可共論，文毅五世之賢孫。
是夕挑燈墮雙淚，天風激盪江怒奔。

趙叟雙瞳爛如電，見此兼旬廢眠飯。
湖湘三月寄書來，不辭千里陳初願。
報書我爲析其由，百斛明珠那惜酬。
只緣陋巷珍高義，代友論心直到秋。
秋來訪我廬山麓，青眼相看眞面目。
地從江介指齊魯，天教舊物歸常熟。
顏公心事惟我知，顏公嗜好乃獨奇。
世間無物此觥配，壓囊只要覃溪詩。
君往叩門再拜說，淡交千古盟冰雪。
月暈光仍舊酒痕，血誠氣可穿山裂。
顏公奉觥向君笑，趙叟傾心誓相報。
觥喜多年逢故人，叟泣還鄉告家廟。
向來藏觥事偶然，今日還觥事更傳。
譜出咒觥新樂府，壓倒米家虹月船。[69]

Weng's poem directs attention to the power of his poetry in bringing about the reunion: through his 1778 poem on the rubbing, he rectified the history of the cup (a point he reiterates in the opening couplet of this new song); his poetry from 1786–1787 then serves to mediate the swap with Yan (he boasts that the only "thing" Yan wanted in exchange for the vessel was a "Weng Fanggang poem"). The poet finally concludes by celebrating his authorship of this new "ballad for the *sigong*," a lyrical account (not so much of the cup, but of the mounted rubbing Weng had earlier praised in verse) that helped broker the restitution it describes. A final allusion to a moonlit rainbow overturning Mi Fu's "Calligraphy and Painting Boat" (*shuhua chuan* 書畫船), and the tales of obsessive acquisition that this craft came to epitomize, argues that the moral dimensions of the cup ultimately override any aesthetic attributes—the conclusion, given Weng's well-documented obsessions with Mi Fu, constitutes a striking moment of poetic askesis. Weng Fanggang, the leading antiquarian-poet of the High Qing, outdoes Zhu Yizun, the leading antiquarian-poet of the previous generation: instead of narrating, as in Zhu's "Song for the *Sigong*," the momentous history of this late Ming object, Weng's "A Song for the Return of the *Sigong* to Zhao" becomes its own event, creating a new poetic topic that countless Qing poets would eulogize over the course of the following century.

While Weng Fanggang's poetry instigated and mediated the return of the cup to Changshu, he also inscribed gifts to compensate the Yan family for letting go of their possession, as if having matched Zhu Yizun's song he wanted to rival Xu Guo's role as an author of vessel inscriptions. The Zhao descendant procured a small jade cup (recalling the original paired gift for Wu Zhongxing) that he asked Weng to inscribe, an artifact now held in the Xintai Museum in Shandong.[70] The counter-gift ostensibly settles outstanding feelings of obligation or debt, generating a sense of empire-wide solidarity between the collectors of Qufu in the north and Changshu in the south. The "Return of the *Sigong* to Zhao" works to affirm the significance of gift-giving as an ideal mode of object relation in the High Qing. Through this exchange of cups, the Yans emerge as selfless collectors concerned not with the protection of private property but with the ethics of historical transmission; the Zhaos emerge as devout filial descendants, embodying the lesson of their ancestor's protest at Zhang Juzheng's failure to mourn his parent; and Weng emerges as an antiquarian poet capable of shaping historical events through the force of his words. The story of one family's rediscovery of a lost possession became an allegory for recuperation in the wake of the dynastic transition. In this celebration of "reunion," the cultural work of mourning—grappling with the trauma of the fall of the Ming by remembering the fates of martyrs like Huang and Chen—was gradually laid to rest. Through a coincidental pun, the story could be grafted onto the template of the "Return of the Jade Disc to Zhao" (wanbi gui Zhao 完璧歸趙), a stock expression for "returning a possession to its rightful owner"—a cliché propitiously alluded to in Xu Guo's inscription on the jade cup for the late Ming protestor Wu Zhongxing.

THE MONUMENTAL VESSEL

The Zhaos subsequently installed the *sigong* in their family temple as if it were a ritual bronze for commemorating ancestors through ceremonial performances. At this point, with the cup hidden in the ancestral temple in Changshu, its biography comes to an end. There are no further reports of encounters with the object and no evidence that it subsequently exchanged hands. Instead, the fame of the cup was eventually superseded by a stone monument completed in 1798, commissioned by the Zhaos on the inner wall of the temple and dedicated to the allegory of "return" (figure 4.2).[71] The centerpiece in this set of carvings was an

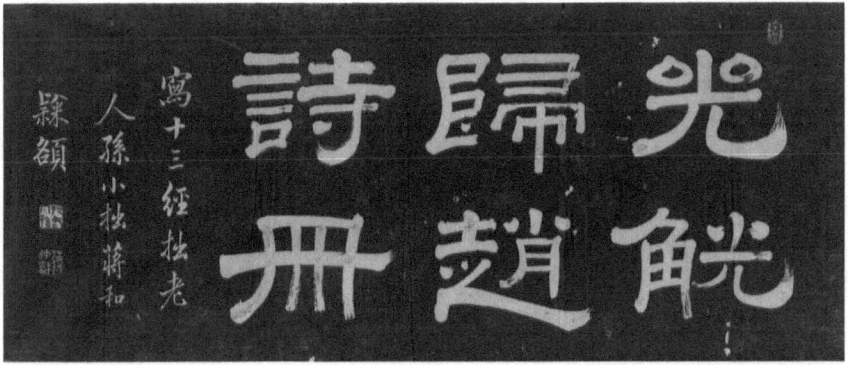

FIGURE 4.2. Frontispiece for "Folio of Poems on the Return of the *Sigong* to Zhao" (rubbing of stone carving). *Source: Sigong gui Zhao shice*, 2. Image courtesy of National Central Library, Taiwan.

annotated copy of Weng Fanggang's "Song for the Return of the *Sigong* to Zhao," which was accompanied by new poems and prefaces contributed by leading scholars and antiquarians from the period, including the calligraphers Wang Wenzhi 王文治 (1730–1802) and Liang Tongshu 梁同書 (1723–1815) (figures 4.3, 4.4, and 4.5). The stone engravings were rendered by the renowned carver Mu Dazhan 穆大展 (n.d.) (table 4.1; see also table 4.2). The temple was demolished in the 1970s to make way for a new hospital, yet six stone panels from the set of carvings have been preserved

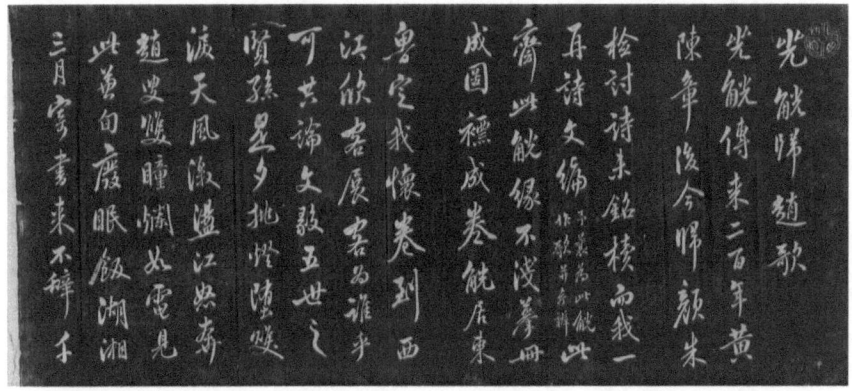

FIGURE 4.3. Weng Fanggang's "Song for the Return of the *Sigong* to Zhao" (rubbing of stone carving). *Source: Sigong gui Zhao shice*, 6. Image courtesy of National Central Library, Taiwan.

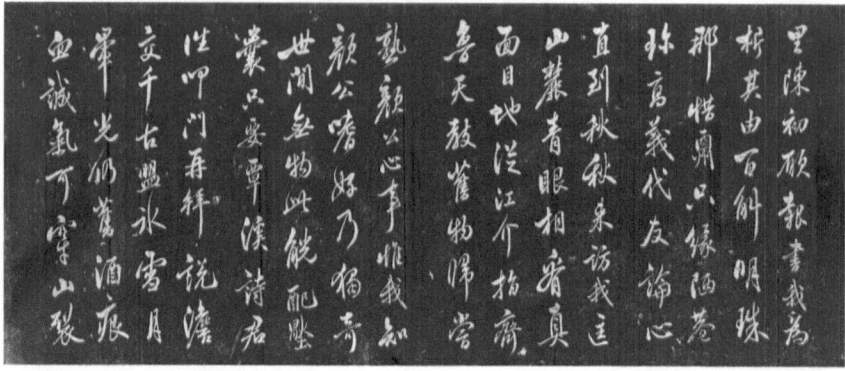

FIGURE 4.4. Weng Fanggang's "Song for the Return of the *Sigong* to Zhao" (rubbing of stone carving). Source: *Sigong gui Zhao shice*, 7. Image courtesy of National Central Library, Taiwan.

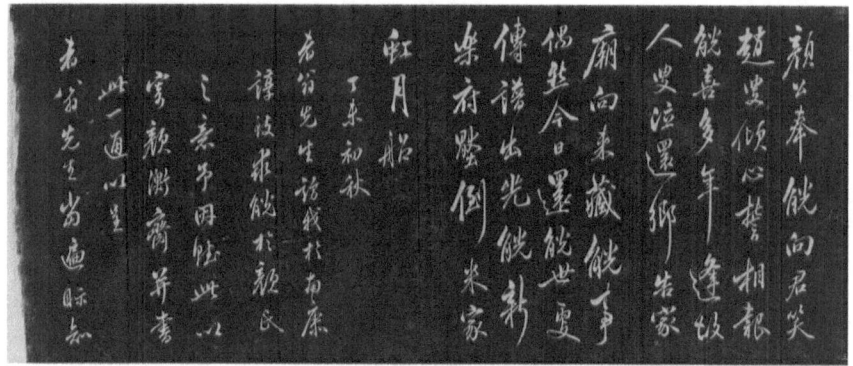

FIGURE 4.5. Weng Fanggang's "Song for the Return of the *Sigong* to Zhao" (rubbing of stone carving). Source: *Sigong gui Zhao shice*, 8. Image courtesy of National Central Library, Taiwan.

in the Changshu City Museum of Stelae Carvings (Changshu shi beike bowuguan 常熟市碑刻博物館). These six panels include Jiang He's 蔣和 (n.d.) carved frontispiece in clerical script, "A Folio of Poems on the Return of the *Sigong* to Zhao" (*Sigong* gui Zhao shice 兕觥歸趙詩冊), and two sections of Weng's "Song for the Return of the *Sigong* to Zhao." The temple memorial was, however, used as a source for rubbings throughout the late eighteenth and early nineteenth centuries, and a folio taken from the Changshu carvings, dated to the Qianlong era, is still preserved in Taiwan's National Central Library.

TABLE 4.1

Poems in Praise of Pictures of the *Sigong's* Return to Zhao 《兇觥歸趙圖》詠 (Set of Stone Carvings in Changshu; 1788–1798)

Carved Text	Author
"A Folio of Poems on the Return of the *Sigong* to Zhao" 兇觥歸趙詩冊	Jiang He 蔣和
"Picture of Inscription on the *Sigong* Presented as a Gift by Official Xu" 許庶子贈兇觥銘圖	Xu Guo 許國 (1527–1596)
"Pictorial Record of the Wooden Box in Which Zhang Dashi Obtained the *Gong* Vessel" 章大史得觥櫝圖記	Zhang Zaogong 章藻功 (*jinshi* 1703)
"Colophon on the Left-Hand Side of the Wooden Box in Which Yan Hongbo Stored the *Gong* Vessel" 顏鴻博藏觥櫝左跋	Yan Maolun 顏懋倫 (b. 1704)
"Record of Fifth-Generation Grandson Wanghuai's Search for the *Gong* Vessel" 五世孫王槐求觥記	Wanghuai 王槐
"Picture of Inscription on a Jade *Jia* Vessel [. . .] for the *Gong* [. . .]" □觥□□玉斝銘圖	Weng Fanggang 翁方綱
"Picture of Inscription on a Silver Boat in Imitation of an Ancient *Jia* Vessel" 仿古安斝銀船銘圖	Weng Fanggang
"Record of the Return of the *Sigong* to Zhao" 兇觥歸趙記	Unsigned
"Song for the Return of the *Sigong* to Zhao" 兇觥歸趙歌	Weng Fanggang; with appended colophons by Liang Tongshu 梁同書 (1723–1815), Su Quji 蘇去疾 (1728–1805), and Zhu Gui 朱珪 (1731–1807)
"Appended to the Heroic Achievement of the Return of the *Sigong* to Zhao, with Preface" 題兇觥歸趙事蹟後有序	Wang Wenzhi 王文治 (1730–1802); with appended colophons by Jiang He, Weng Fanggang, Weng Shupei 翁樹培 (1765–1811), Fei Fu 費浮, and Qian Daxin 錢大昕 (1728–1804)

TABLE 4.2
Poems on the "Return of the *Sigong* to Zhao"

Author	Title	Collection
Chen Tingqing 陳廷慶 (1754–1813)	"Song for the Return of the *Sigong* to Zhao with Preface" 兕觥歸趙歌有序	*Qianshou tang quanji* 謙受堂全集
Fa Shishan 法式善 (1753–1813)	"Song for the Return of the *Sigong* to Zhao, Matching Master Weng Tanxi, Fanggang, with Preface" 兕觥趙歌和翁覃溪方綱先生有序	*Cunsu tang shi chuji lucun* 存素堂詩初集錄存
Fan Henian 范鶴年 (1753–1805)	"Song for the Return of the *Sigong* to Zhao, for Zhao Sima Weixuan, with Preface" 兕觥歸趙歌爲趙司馬韡軒作有叙	*Miaoxue shanfang quanji* 藐雪山房全集
	"Transcribed After a Folio of Poems on the Return of the *Sigong* to Zhao" 書兕觥歸趙詩冊後	*Miaoxue shanfang quanji* 藐雪山房全集
Feng Hao 馮浩 (1719–1801)	"Sixteen Rhymes for the Return of the *Sigong* to Zhao" 兕觥歸趙一十六韻	*Mengting jushi wengao* 孟亭居士文稿
Gu Guangxu 顧光旭 (1731–1797)	"Song for the Return of the *Sigong* to Zhao, Sent to Zhao Zheting, with Preface" 兕觥歸趙歌寄呈趙者庭有序	*Xiangquan ji* 響泉集
	"I Passed Through Qinchuan and Paid a Visit to Zhao Zheting to Drink and View the Scroll of Poems on the Return of the *Sigong* to Zhao. The Next Day, I Visited Yushan to Pay My Respects Before Master Wenyi's Tomb. I Composed Four Poems Matching Tanxi's Rhyme." 過琴川訪趙者庭留飲觀兕觥歸趙詩卷明日遂遊虞山拜文毅公墓下用覃溪韻四首	*Xiangquan ji* 響泉集
Guan Shenglai 管繩萊	"Song for the Return of the *Sigong* to Zhao with Preface" 兕觥歸趙歌有序	*Wanyuan caotang shiji* 萬緣草堂詩集
Hong Liangji 洪亮吉 (1746–1809)	"Song for the Return of the *Sigong* for the Zhao Prefectural Head's Esteemed Inspection" 兕觥還趙歌爲趙大令貴覽賦	*Gengsheng zhai ji* 更生齋集
Jiang Tingen 蔣廷恩 (1751–1822)	"Song for the Return of the *Sigong* to Zhao" 兕觥歸趙歌	*Wanqing xuan shichao* 晚晴軒詩鈔
Jin Zhaoyan 金兆燕 (1719–1791)	"Poem for the Return of the *Sigong* to Zhao" 兕觥歸趙詩	*Guozi xiansheng quanji* 國子先生全集
Li Shuye 李樹穀	"A Song for Master Zhao Wenyi's *Sigong*" 趙文毅公兕觥歌	*Doumen ji* 都門集
Liang Yunchang 梁運昌 (1771–1827)	"Song for the Return of the *Sigong* to Zhao for Magistrate Zhao Binting" 兕觥歸趙歌為趙邠亭明府作	*Qiuzhu zhai shicun* 秋竹齋詩存
Liu Quanzhi 劉權之 (1739–1818)	"Appended to an Image of the Return of the *Sigong* to Zhao, a Long Song Borne of Inexhaustible Intent" 題兕觥歸趙圖後意有未盡因成長歌	*Changsha Liu Wenke gong shiji* 長沙劉文恪公詩集

Author	Title	Source
Liu Siwan 劉嗣綰 (1762–1821)	"Song for the Return of the *Sigong* to Zhao for Magistrate Zhao Zheting" 兕觥歸趙歌爲趙者庭明府作	*Shangjiong tang shiji* 尚絅堂詩集
Pan Yijuan 潘奕雋 (1740–1830)	"Song for the Return of the *Sigong* to Zhao for Magistrate Zhao Zheting of Changshu" 兕觥歸趙歌為常熟趙者庭明府作	*Sansong tang ji* 三松堂集
Qian Daxin 錢大昕 (1728–1804)	"Two Verse Compositions for the Poems on Zhao Wenyi's *Sigong* for Magistrate Zheting" 趙文毅兕觥詩爲者庭明府賦二首	*Qianyan tang ji* 潛研堂集
Qian Feng 錢灃 (1740–1795)	"Preface for the Zhao Family of Changshu's Retrieval of the *Sigong*" 常熟趙氏復兕觥序	*Qian Nanyuan xiansheng yiji* 錢南園先生遺集
Qian Lin 錢林 (1762–1828)	"Song for Master Zhao Wenyi's *Sigong*" 趙文毅公兕觥歌	*Yushan caotang ji* 玉山草堂集
Qian Qi 錢琦 (1709–1790)	"Song for the Return of the *Sigong* to Zhao" 兕觥歸趙歌	*Chengbi zhai shichao* 澄碧齋詩鈔
Qin Ying 秦瀛 (1743–1821)	"Song for the Return of the *Sigong* to Zhao" 兕觥歸趙歌	*Xiaoxian shanren shiwen ji* 小峴山人詩文集
Shen Shuyan 沈叔埏 (1736–1803)	"A Rhapsody on the Return of the *Sigong* to Zhao with Preface" 兕觥歸趙賦有序	*Yicai tang wenji* 頤綵堂文集
Shi Yunyu 石韞玉 (1755–1837)	"Song for the Return of the *Sigong* to Zhao" 兕觥歸趙歌	*Duxue lu chugao* 獨學廬初稿
Sun Yuanxiang 孫原湘 (1760–1829)	"Poem for the Return of the *Sigong* to Zhao" 兕觥歸趙詩	*Tianzhen ge ji* 天真閣集
Tang Xiuye 湯修業 (d. 1863)	"The Zhao Family of Changshu's *Sigong*, Given by Xu Wenmu of Yingyang After Master Wenyi's Beating, Traveled for Two-Hundred Years, Changing Hands Among Multiple Owners, Has Now Returned to Zheting, the Fifth-Generation Grandson, Who Has Now Invited Me to Compose Five Old-Style Poems." 常熟趙氏兕觥文毅公廷杖後潁陽許文穆所贈也流傳二百年屢易數主今復歸趙其五世孫者庭徵詩得五古五首	*Laigu zhai wenji* 賴古齋文集
Wang Dajing 汪大經 (1741–1809)	"Song for the Return of the *Sigong* to Zhao" 兕觥歸趙歌	*Jie Qiushan ju shichao* 借秋山居詩鈔
Wang Jiaxiang 王家相 (1762–1838)	Untitled [Matching "Song for the Return of the *Sigong* to Zhao"]	*Mingxiang tang shiji* 茗香堂詩集
Wang Wenzhi 王文治 (1730–1802)	"Appended to the Heroic Achievement of the Return of the *Sigong* to Zhao, with Preface" 題兕觥歸趙事蹟後有序	*Menglou shiji* 夢樓詩集
Wu Songliang 吳嵩梁 (1766–1834)	"Song for the *Sigong*, Presented to Zhao Wenyi of Changshu's Fifth-Generation Grandson Regional Inspector Zheting" 兕觥歌爲常熟趙文毅公五世孫者庭刺史賦	*Xiangsu shanguan shiji* 香蘇山館詩集

(continued)

TABLE 4.2 *(continued)*

Author	Title	Collection
Wu Tingfeng 吳翌鳳 (1742–1819)	"Song for the Return of the *Sigong* to Zhao, Composed for Zhao Sima Weixuan, with Preface" 兕觥歸趙歌爲趙轄軒司馬賦有序	*Yuji zhai conggao* 與稽齋叢稿
Wu Tingxuan 武廷選 (b. 1749)	"Poem for the Return of the *Sigong* to Zhao" 兕觥歸趙詩	*Lanpu shichao* 蘭圃詩鈔
Xie Qikun 謝啓昆 (1737–1802)	"Four-Verse Compositions for the Poems on the Return of the *Sigong* to Zhao" 兕觥歸趙詩四首	*Shujing tang shi chuji* 樹經堂詩初集
Xu Xiongfei 徐熊飛 (1762–1835)	"Song for the Return of the *Sigong* to Zhao with Preface" 兕觥歸趙歌有序	*Baihe shanfang shichao* 白鵠山房詩鈔
Ye Shaoben 葉紹本 (d. 1861)	"Song for the Return of the *Sigong* to Zhao, for Magistrate Binting, Tongqi, to Display for his Elder Brother Xiangting, Tongxiang" 兕觥歸趙歌爲邠亭明府同岐作即示其兄向亭同湘	*Baihe shanfang shichao* 白鶴山房詩鈔
Yi Bingshou 伊秉綬 (1754–1815)	"Poem for the Return of the *Sigong* to Zhao" 兕觥歸趙詩	*Liuchun caotang shichao* 留春草堂詩鈔
Yu Hongjian 俞鴻漸 (1781–1846)	"Song for the Return of the *Sigong* to Zhao, for Master Wenyi's Seventh-Generation Grandson, Magistrate Huailai, Zhao Xinru, Tongxiang" 兕觥歸趙歌爲文毅公七世孫懷來明府趙心如同湘賦	*Yinxue xuan shichao* 印雪軒詩鈔
Zhang Dunpei 张敦培	"On the Matter of the Return of Master Zhao Wenyi's *Sigong*" 題趙文毅公兕觥復歸事	*Weixiu xuan shicun* 蔚秀軒詩存
Zhang Jiuyue 張九鉞 (1721–1803)	"In Response to County Magistrate Zhao Xuexuan's Request for a Poem to Match Master Weng Tanxi's Song for the Return of the *Sigong* to Zhao" 和翁覃溪學士兕觥歸趙歌應趙轄軒邑候索	*Zixian shanren quan ji* 紫峴山人全集
Zhang Shu 張澍 (1781–1847)	"A Record of the Return of the *Sigong* to Zhao, On Behalf of Lu Xinlan, Fangbo" 兕觥歸趙記代陸心蘭方伯	*Yangsu tang wenji* 養素堂文集
Zhang Yun'ao 張雲璈 (1747–1829)	"Song for the Return of the *Sigong* to Zhao and Preface" 兕觥歸趙歌并序	*Jiansong caotang wenji* 簡松草堂文集
Zhao Huaiyu 趙懷玉 (1747–1823)	"A Song for the Return of the *Sigong* to Zhao Using Supervisor of the Household Weng Fanggang's Rhyme for the Prefectural Head Wanghuai" 兕觥歸趙歌用翁詹事方網韻爲趙家大令王槐	*Yiyou sheng zhai ji* 亦有生齋集
Zhao Yi 趙翼 (1727–1814)	"Song for the Return of the *Sigong* to Zhao" 兕觥歸趙歌	*Oubei ji* 甌北集
Zhu Gui 朱珪 (1731–1806)	"A Song for the Return of the *Sigong* to Zhao, for Zhao Wanghuai" 兕觥歸趙歌爲趙王槐作	*Zhizu zhai shiji* 知足齋詩集

ANTIQUARIAN POETRY

In addition to carved poems, the Taiwan folio shows that Zhao commissioned a scale illustration of the vessel to be cut in stone (figure 4.6). The image reveals a modest wine cup—only 11.5 cm in length and 5.75 cm in height and bearing almost no outward resemblance to a rhinoceros horn—with a slender decorative *chi*-dragon handle (*chi'er* 螭耳) and a simple *leiwen* 雷紋 pattern running around the thin rim of its base-stand. These antique details evoke the use of *chi* handles and *leiwen* on early Qing dynasty archaistic jade carving from the Suzhou area. Archaic trends in rhinoceros horn carving have been securely dated to the late seventeenth

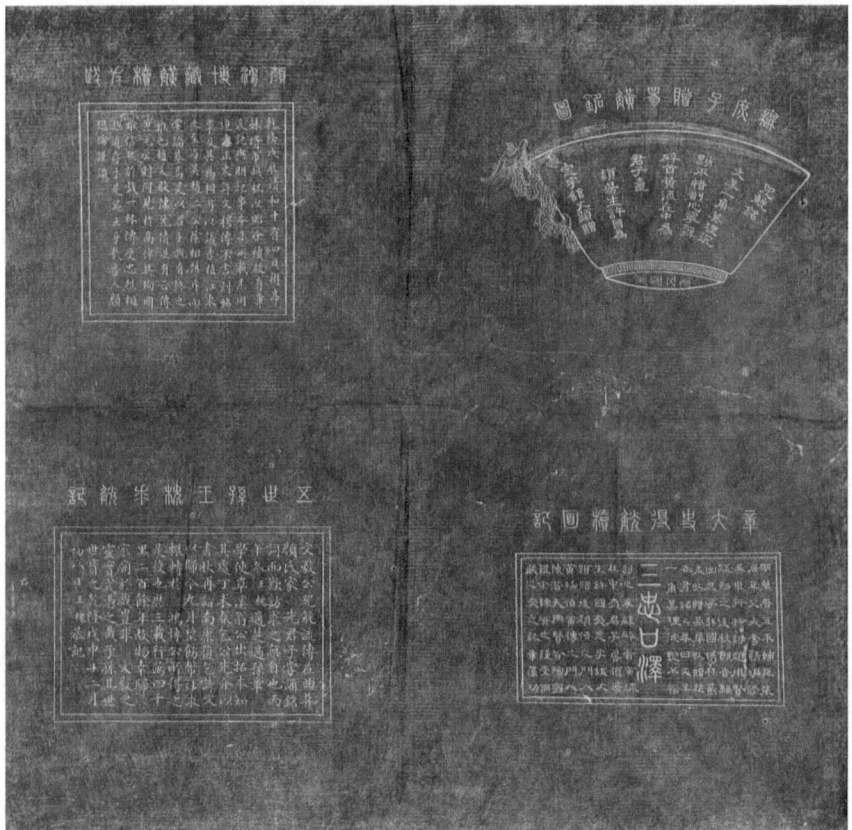

FIGURE 4.6. Image of Zhao family rhinoceros horn cup inscribed by Xu Guo (*top right*) and box inscribed by Zhang Zaogong (*bottom right*) (rubbing of stone carving). Source: *Sigong gui Zhao shice*, 20. Image courtesy of National Central Library, Taiwan.

and eighteenth centuries.[72] There are likewise discrepancies between this carved image and details of the cup in Ming sources. Unlike the copies of Xu Guo's *ming* preserved in the Tianqi-era edition of his collected writings or in other Ming dynasty compendia, which all refer to an inscription for a "rhinoceros horn cup," this version of the text is entitled "Inscription for a *Sigong*" (*sigong ming* 兕觥銘)—a label first used by Zhu Yizun in the early Qing. There are likewise no references prior to Weng Fanggang's account of the copy of the inscription he received from Qufu to the marking of the momentous date "Fifth Year of Wanli" (Wanli wunian 萬曆五年) etched in lesser seal script and now visible on the base of the cup or to Xu Guo's formal sign-off, "an offering from Xu Guo, Master of Yingyang, to the Official Dingyu" 潁陽生許國為定宇館丈題贈. This deliberately archaistic illustration is less a depiction of the cup than a visual frame or cartouche for the calligraphy of Xu Guo's inscription, a short slogan now engraved in the supposedly imperishable medium of stone. The picture of the cup is framed by a scale drawing of its box bearing Zhang Zaogong's preface to his "Record of the *Sigong*," a colophon carved onto the left-hand side of the box attributed to Yan Maolun 顏懋倫 (b. 1704), and a further essay attributed to Wanghuai presumably carved onto the box after he obtained the vessel (figure 4.6). In addition to the box, Zhao commissioned illustrations of the two other vessels—a jade cup and a silver boat-shaped cup bearing Weng's inscriptions—involved in the swap with the Yan family (figure 4.7). As such, the rhinoceros horn cup—occupying just one-sixth of this particular panel—appears circumscribed by a larger memorial to the means and history of the vessel's storage.

If the rhinoceros horn cup had become an *unintentional* monument through the contingencies of its historical transmission and the slow sedimentation of various associations—to anti-corruption at the Wanli court, Ming martyrdom in the trauma of the dynastic transition, and Ming loyalism in the early Qing—this stone carving was an *intentional* monument, one that spatialized the inscription from the cup with the very medium of stone evoking fixity and finality, physically asserting an ending and hence establishing a definitive narrative of the "return" for posterity.[73] The conclusive monument retrospectively constructs an uncontested history of the cup, making its past *past*. A paradox remains, however, in the replacement of an unintentional monument with an intentional monument in that the very qualities that made the inscribed cup so legendary—its movement

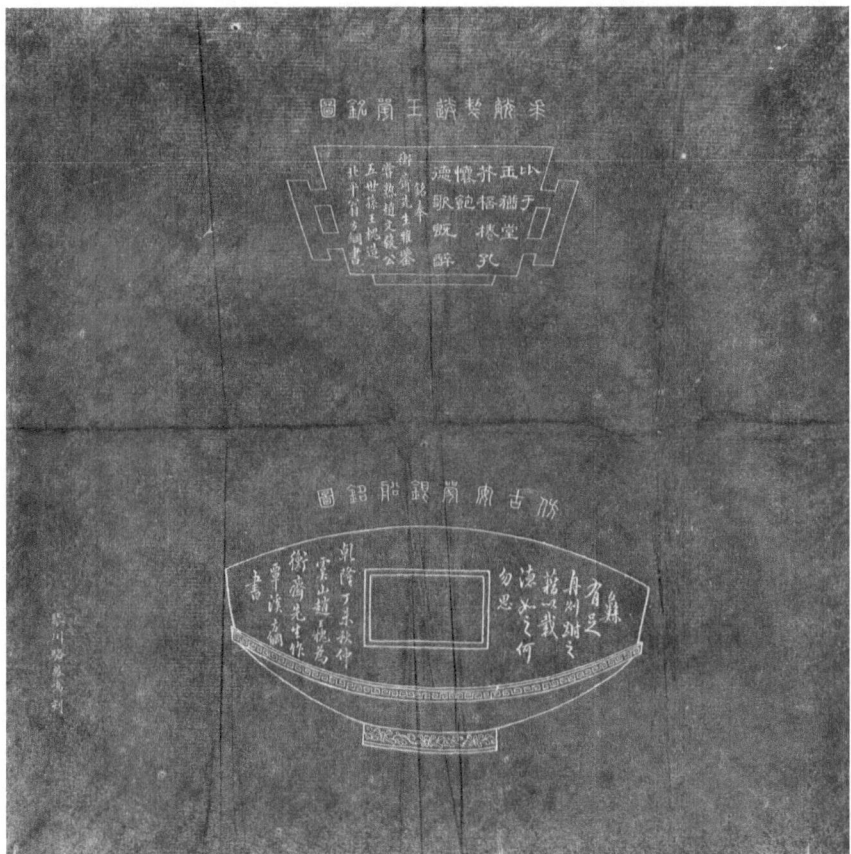

FIGURE 4.7. Images of two vessels inscribed by Weng Fanggang (rubbing of stone carving). *Source: Sigong gui Zhao shice*, 21. Image courtesy of National Central Library, Taiwan.

across the empire from dynasty to dynasty; the way its various owners relinquished personal possession, seeking to form a community that transcended the constrictions of time and space—are denied as the Zhao family arrests its travels and hides it in the family's temple, supplanting the rhinoceros horn with the family's own endorsed set of stone carvings. Xu Guo's inscription for Zhao Yongxian, engraved on the wall of the temple, subsequently assumes an epitaphic ambience.[74] The death of the vessel marks the final victory of a family's claims to property over a community of custodians who had renounced self-interested claims to ownership: the model of the family reunion may represent a shared allegory for reconciliation with the past and full restitution from loss, yet it is predicated on the suspension and eventual demise of the collective commitments instantiated through Xu Guo's initial gift.

Countless Qing poets commemorated the Zhao family's requisition of its cup in verse: one claimed that "at this time, across the state, eulogies [to it] proliferated like clouds" 當時海內題詠如雲.⁷⁵ The event of the "return" even inspired the playwright Zhou Ang 周昂 (n.d.), an affinal relative of the Zhao family, to compose a no-longer-extant *chuanqi* drama in honor of the cup entitled *Tale of the Sigong* (*Sigong ji* 兕觥記).⁷⁶ It would not be an overstatement to claim that every major antiquarian poet of the High Qing had something to say about the fate of this small sixteenth-century cup. Unlike Xu Guo, Zhu Yizun, or Weng Fanggang, however, these poets played no part in the transmission of the vessel or the narration of its history: they instead assume the role of spectator in thrall to the legacy of an object that few of them ever held.

POETRY ON "METAL AND STONE"

The Qianlong and Jiaqing 嘉慶 (1796–1820) reigns have been treated as a high point in philological scholarship on ancient artifacts and a low point in histories of Chinese poetry. And yet, so many leading antiquarians composed poems to record or reflect upon their responses to encounters with inscribed things. Weng Fanggang became the figurehead of this trend as contemporaneous commentators observed how "Tanxi [Weng Fanggang] made poetry from scholarship" 覃溪以學為詩; or how "his corrections to commentaries on the classics and histories, and his combing over ancient inscriptions on metal and stone all thoroughly suffused his verse" 而覃溪自諸經傳疏，以及史傳之攷訂，金石文字之爬梳，皆貫徹洋溢於其詩.⁷⁷ Later critics have suggested that the central concept of "musculature" (*jili* 肌理) in Weng's poetics, a reaction to the perceived insubstantiality of Wang Shizhen's 王士禛 (1634–1711) poetics of "spirit resonance" (*shenyun* 神韻) and Shen Deqian's 沈德潛 (1673–1769) poetics of "form and tone" (*gediao* 格調), may have derived in part from his contemplation of the "grain" or texture of inscriptions on metal and stone.⁷⁸ Yuan Mei 袁枚 (1716–1797), anticipating the disparaging assessments of Weng's poetry in twentieth-century literary historiography, castigated his bitter rival for writing verse as if he were the owner of an antique store.⁷⁹ Weng himself declared that "matters of philological evaluation and exegesis and poetic composition cannot yet be judged to belong to two separate paths" 而考訂訓詁之事，與詞章之事未可判為二途.[80] His verse on ancient objects in turn elicited innovative forms of exchange between epigraphy and literature whereby as Weng's closest Korean interlocutor, Kim Chŏnghŭi 金正喜 (1786–1856), noted, "his classical scholarship and literary writings, his epigraphy, calligraphy, and painting all came together to form a cluster, in a manner that is not easy for shallow people to grasp" 經藝文章，金石書畫，打成一團，非淺人所得易解.[81]

Weng Fanggang and his coterie pioneered a distinctive style of poetry—"poetry on metal and stone" (*jinshi shi* 金石詩) or "philological poetry" (*kaoding shi* 考訂詩), an approach that diverges from standard poetic methods for the representation of objects.[82] As Yip Cheuk-wai notes, such poems clearly depart from the allegorical conventions of *yongwu* 詠物 verse to focus instead on the thing as such, foregrounding its material properties, its stubborn particularities as a solid, silent source of knowledge about the past.[83] "Poems on things" typically treat the object—often a category or class of thing such as a cicada, a fan, a mirror, or a willow—as a screen for the projection of a poet's feelings or mind state: "depicting things to limn one's intent" 體物寫志, "borrowing things to express one's emotion" 借物抒情, "entrusting the expression of one's intent to things" 托物言志.[84] Poems in the *yongwu* mode are less concerned with examining objects as hard evidence than they are with how things figuratively refer to aspects of a poet's inner life.[85]

Even when Weng Fanggang writes *yongwu*-style poems, his approach reveals the unmistakable imprint of his epigraphic scholarship. A painted fan, for instance, constituted a conventional topic in *yongwu* poetry. Weng's "On a Painted Fan Showing Little West Lake Sent to Me from Putian by Yusan's Nephew" 題雨三侄自蒲田見寄小西湖畫扇, conversely, treats the painted fan as a map that allows him to survey the topography of his tenth-generation ancestor's residence in Fujian, using interlinear commentary to verify the location of major stone carvings in the area and the history of a local temple.[86] The features of this particular fan poem betray two recurring themes in Qing critiques of Weng's antiquarian verse: first, that he privileged the "direct presentation" (*fu* 賦) of a thing over established "metaphorical and allegorical" (*bixing* 比興) techniques for indirect emotional expression in *yongwu* poetry; and second, that his copious interlinear annotations create a disjointed reading experience, fracturing the poem's unity.[87]

Qing antiquarian poems depart from venerable models for intoning "metal and stone" in verse, a lineage that can be traced back to Han Yu's "The Song of the Stone Drums" ("Shigu ge" 石鼓歌) and "Goulou Mountain" ("Goulou shan" 岣嶁山).[88] Weng and his associates in their matter-of-fact approach to epigraphy, however, eschew Han's hyperbolic celebration of the numinous, illegible, and strange qualities of ancient inscriptions.[89] A more proximate source of inspiration for Weng's coterie can be found in the poetry of early Qing antiquarians like Zhu Yizun (in his original "Song for the *Sigong*"), Wu Weiye 吳偉業 (1609–1672), or Mao Xiang 冒襄 (1611–1693) with his widely discussed "Song of the Xuande Bronze Censer."[90] Weng's plainspoken verse lacks the subtle allusiveness that allowed these earlier lyricists to evoke personal experiences of lost love or to encode hidden political messages: Weng, for instance, seems uneasy with the evocative silences in Zhu Yizun's 1677 song for the rhinoceros horn cup.[91] Whereas Mao Xiang composed an accompanying set of "Notes on 'The Song of the Xuande Bronze Censer'" to document the technical vocabulary needed to judge a censer, Weng incorporates such information into his poems on antiques, treating annotation and argument as constitutive elements of his poetic diction: even the carving of his "Song for the Return of the *Sigong* to Zhao" includes a line-break note midway through the poem to remind viewers that he also composed an evaluative essay to corroborate his research on the object (figure 4.3).

Weng elsewhere tries to make poetry out of his pedantic corrections to earlier scholarship, taking particular issue with Zhu Yizun's mistakes, notably Zhu's erroneous assessment of an artifact inscribed "second year of the Wufeng reign" (Wufeng ernian 五鳳二年) as a brick rather than a stone: "Old Zhu mistakenly took this stone for a brick" 老朱誤以石作磚; "Old Zhu of Xiushui's colophon transmitted a mistake, he thought clerical script was seal script and thought a stone was a brick" 秀水朱老跋誤傳，以隸為篆石為磚; "If you still want to defend Zhu the Tenth [Yizun] from mockery, look at the fact he thought the Wufeng carving was really a brick (self-note: Zhucha classified a stone inscribed "second year of the Wufeng reign" from Qufu as a brick)" 欲為朱十解嘲否？五鳳此刻方真磚（自注：竹垞以曲阜五鳳二年石目為磚）.[92] Weng's matter-of-fact approach to verse, as these lines suggest, lacks the tragic pathos and darker undertones of destruction that haunt the poetry of earlier antiquarians like

Zhu, Wu Weiye, or Mao Xiang—poets who lived through the turmoil of inter-dynastic war. By refusing to treat the poetic thing as a romantic allegory, however, Weng and his close associates went further than any other late imperial poets in writing what we might call a materialist poetry, advancing an approach to verse that tries to treat its object first and foremost as an object.

Historians of Qing literature have suggested that the analytical style of antiquarian poetry ultimately derives from contemporaneous "examination poems" (*shitie shi* 試帖詩), a subgenre that flourished after the reinstatement of poetic composition as an examination subject in 1757.[93] This assessment, however, overlooks the extent to which embodied acts of handling antiques, visiting stelae or monumental stone carvings, and the labor of making ink-squeeze rubbings might have shaped approaches to writing poetry. As Weng's antiquarian verse (and its subsequent transmission) suggests, attentiveness to the materiality of carved traces broached concerns with the durability of a poem. Weng's associates note how eighteenth-century epigraphic scholarship on metal and stone conditioned formulations of poetry's longevity:

> Silk lasts a hundred years and then it expires. Paper lasts five hundred years and then it expires. Might metal and stone surpass this? Stone, with time, cracks; metal, with time, melts. Only when these materials have been entrusted with writing are they rendered everlasting. When these words have been entrusted to poetry they might be more easily transmitted. The writing of the ancients found longevity in metal and stone, metal and stone then finds longevity in poetry, such is longevity attained from an intermingling of humans and things.
>
> 絹之壽百年，止矣。紙之壽五百年，止矣。過此者其金石乎？石有時而泐，金有時而液，惟託於文字者無窮，詩歌於文字又其易傳者也，古人之文字，以金石壽之，金石也，又以詩歌壽之，是物與人交相引爲壽者也。[94]

The passage continues by noting that "in reading a poem [about "metal and stone"] it is as if you can still see the artifact" 讀其詩如見器焉, and that this "artifact preserves the people [who held it]" 器存斯人.[95] These claims at once affirm poetry's freedom from the material constraints of metal and stone and yet conceive of a poem's power in terms of its capacity to transmit writing on metal and stone—experiences of viewing inscriptions ought, Mei insinuates, to inform understandings of a poem's purpose.

Weng Fanggang developed his distinctive approach to antiquarian verse, as Yip Cheuk-wai has demonstrated, during his tenure as commissioner of education in Guangdong from 1764 to 1771, notably in a set of twenty-one poetic studies on the Jiuyao 九曜 stone monuments appended to his first major work of epigraphic scholarship, *Yuedong jinshi lüe* 粵東金石略, a collection that centers upon his search for enigmatic carvings attributed to Song calligrapher Mi Fu at Yaozhou 藥洲 (so named because the Southern Han (917–971) ruler Liu Yan 劉龑 (889–942) after opening up an artificial lake had assembled a group of alchemists at the site to make elixirs [*yao* 藥]).[96] Weng's printed monograph betrays an attempt not simply to transmit Mi Fu's carved traces but to render it impossible for later scholars to understand Mi's presence at Jiuyao without first reckoning with evidence of his own presence at Jiuyao, inviting his readers to compare Mi's famed carving of the two characters for Yaozhou with his own new carving of the two characters for Yaozhou.[97] These poems divulge three central features of Qing antiquarian poetry, anticipating Weng's approach to the Zhao *sigong*: First, poems yoke scholarly discoveries to the embodied experience of viewing carvings, treating verse as a category of proof or firsthand testimony.[98] Second, the affordances of rhyme allowed antiquarians to create and share matching responses both with earlier antiquarians and with their contemporaries.[99] Third, by carving his poetic studies of stone carvings in stone, Weng sought to establish an independent literary monument to his authoritative research on monuments.

Weng continued to reflect on the fortuitous relocation of lost or forgotten things throughout his life, as if restaging in private the restitution he orchestrated on an empire-wide level with the return of the *sigong* to Zhao. He celebrated his eightieth birthday in 1812, for instance, by commemorating an "imitation copy of a bronze ruler from the Jianchu 建初 (76–84) reign of the Han dynasty" made from Japanese molten copper, a gift that matched the precise dimensions of a wooden replica of a Jianchu ruler he had located in Qufu forty years earlier. The ruler bore the inscribed date "fifteenth day of the eighth month" 八月十五日; Weng Fanggang's birthday was on the "sixteenth day of the eighth month" 八月十六日.[100] The calligraphy of the ruler's inscription reflects, as Yip notes, the transition of *zhuan* seal-script to *li* clerical-script, a central topic in Qing research on Han dynasty epigraphy and reliable evidence with which to verify further research on Han institutional reforms and measurements.[101] And yet, the significance of the inscribed ruler for Weng cannot be reduced to its evidentiary value, as the poet qualifies his own initial stance of detached objectivity with an introspective focus on forty years of reminiscence and fate—it is as though he seeks to belatedly reinvest an epigraphic artifact with the whims and vagaries of a personality that such hard evidence ought to rescind.[102] Weng's poems on the Jiuyao carvings and Jianchu ruler effectively bookend his career as the preeminent antiquarian-poet of the Qianlong-Jiaqing period, yet it was his verse on the Zhao family *sigong* that secured this reputation throughout the empire in the 1780s.

Whereas stone carvings and ancient bronze artifacts constitute conventional topics for epigraphic research, the central place of a late Ming rhinoceros horn cup in mid-Qing antiquarian writings betrays the contingent and contested status of "metal and stone" as a category. The fate of the *sigong* dramatizes a dynamic that shapes mid-Qing antiquarian poetry writ large: that even as empirical research transformed the ways poets saw things in verse, poetry elucidates how subjective experiences of an object—the way a particular thing matters to a particular person at a particular moment—might exceed and qualify scholarship on antiques. This is not to say that the poetic thing as in much *yongwu* verse reappears as a legible figure for the poet's emotions or inner life, but rather that antiquarian poems register feelings at once aroused and supposedly displaced by the exacting scrutiny of material evidence. Weng's poems, in other words, shift from looking at how the poet animates objects through the force of his own "intent" to the way in which the recalcitrant properties of things—and the fragmentary histories of endurance and absence that they conceal—arrest and move the poet as an observer.

The poem becomes a site of productive negotiation between an ascendant mode of critical objectivity and the affective attachments to objects that empirical observation ostensibly sought to renounce, a back-and-forth that precludes any sense of harmony. The antiquarian-poet's mind-set as such appears increasingly at odds with itself, riven between a professed commitment to facts and a lingering sense of their insufficiency in fully apprehending the affective power of past traces—a dynamic encapsulated in the way Weng's pedantic annotations to his own lines of verse strive to supervise, and yet ultimately undermine, the reader's appreciation of his poetry's coherence. A proliferation of antiquarian poems in the eighteenth century at once charts the far-reaching impact and yet betrays the limitations of scholarly inquiry in thinking about things. Qing antiquarians composed so much verse in part because it absorbed sentiments that research alone could not accommodate, whether the jolt of an unanticipated discovery, the palpable joy of a perfect match, or the fragile reassurance gleaned from a staged spectacle of restitution. Inscription, in this process, becomes an artifact worthy of poetic veneration rather than a political intervention that might change the course of history itself.

In facilitating the return of the *sigong* to the Zhao family and building an empire-wide network of matching poetic responses, Weng's verse represents the apotheosis of Qing antiquarian poetry, harnessing the unlikely fate of this small object to affirm a poem's power to counteract loss and secure continuity between past, present, and future. And yet, the poetic afterlife of the Zhao family's *sigong*—a makeshift ritual vessel wrought from a sixteenth-century import—also encapsulates underlying tensions between knowledge and sentiment in eighteenth-century antiquarian practice, illuminating the anachronism, artistic creativity, and collective fantasies of repossession that haunt the outwardly austere discipline of "studying metal and stone." At the heart of the Qing antiquarian enterprise, the rhinoceros horn cup suggests, lay efforts to make sense of ruptures between feelings for and thoughts about things—rifts that can in this case be traced back to the fallout from the Ming cataclysm. Far from achieving any stable sense of closure, however, Weng and his followers in assessing the meaning and material format of Xu Guo's carved words came to accept that longevity might in fact demand transition. The survival of an inscribed message, here, depends upon its metamorphoses, its plasticity. Which is not to say, as Ryckmans or Mote might suggest, that the name of the cup (the "word") supersedes its materiality (or the paralysis of static forms), but rather that this open-ended process of transmission was shaped and sustained by contingent acts of refabrication.

Timeline

Date	Event	Texts
1577	The *duoqing* 奪情 controversy: Zhang Juzheng 張居正 (1525–1582) refuses to leave the capital to mourn his deceased father.	Xu Guo, "Inscription on a Rhinoceros Horn Cup" 犀杯銘
	Xu Guo inscribes a rhinoceros horn cup for Zhao Yongxian and a jade cup for Wu Zhongxing.	Xu Guo, "Inscription on a Jade Cup" 玉杯銘
ca. 1645	The rhinoceros horn cup passes from Zhao Yongxian to Buddhist layman Huang Duanbo 黃端伯 (1585–1645). Huang is executed during the fall of Nanjing.	
	The cup then passes to Huang's follower Chen Qianfu 陳潛夫 (*juren*, 1636), a resistance fighter from Zhejiang who committed suicide after being caught with a militia behind Qing lines.	
1677	The cup has been acquired by an early Qing official named He Yuanying 何元英 (1631–1679). He invites his friend, the eminent lyricist Zhu Yizun 朱彝尊 (1629–1709), to compose a poem celebrating the cup.	Zhu Yizun, "Song for the *Sigong*" 兕觥歌
ca. 1700	Hangzhou-based collector Zhang Zaogong 章藻功 composes an essay on the history of the cup. Zhang claims to be a son-in-law of the Chen family. Zhang concurrently inscribes a box for the cup with the four-character motto "With the Breath from the Mouths of Three Loyal Remonstrators" 三忠口澤.	Zhang Zaogong, "A Record of Censor Zhao's *Sigong*" 藏檢討趙公兕觥記
	At a later point, Zhang reportedly gave the cup to the Sichuan official Fu Zuoji 傅作楫 (1656–1721).	
1748	The Yan 顏 family of Qufu acquires the cup.	
1778	Weng Fanggang 翁方綱 (1733–1818) produces a definitive study of the cup.	Weng Fanggang, "Written After a Rubbing of the *Sigong* Inscription by Xu Guo of the Ming" 書明許文穆贈趙文毅兕觥銘拓本後
		Weng Fanggang, "A Disquisition on the *Sigong*" 兕觥辨
1786	Weng meets Zhao Wanghuai, the fifth-generation grandson of Zhao Yongxian.	Weng Fanggang, "A Colophon for the *Sigong*" 跋兕觥
1787	Weng orchestrates the return of the cup to the Zhao family of Changshu.	Weng Fanggang, "A Preface for Master Zhao of Changshu Seeking the Return of the *Sigong* from Yan Hengzhai of Qufu" 為常熟趙氏乞曲阜顏衡齋歸兕觥序
		Weng Fanggang, "A Song for the Return of the *Sigong* to Zhao" 兕觥歸趙歌
1788	The swap is completed in the ninth month, and the Zhao family commissions stone carvings to commemorate the installation of the cup in the family's temple in Changshu.	

EPILOGUE
Broken Stones

The preceding chapters have traced the development of writing upon objects in early modern China, examining how acts of inscription worked to redress deep-seated concerns with the material contingencies and technical preconditions of writing in general. From the literary treatment of remnant things as loyal friends amid the collapse of the Ming dynasty in 1644, to innovations in seal carving and inkstick design as symbiotic responses to upheavals in the marketplace, to the fraught search for new monuments in the wake of inter-dynastic war, writers looked to inscription to chronicle larger ruptures between words and objects while seeking to repair frayed connections between them. Under these conditions, inscription came to constitute a form of literary thought uniquely attuned to material factors behind the creation, display, and survival of the written word. The most eloquent lines of inscribed prose or verse nevertheless resonate beyond the historical moment of the Ming-Qing transition, asking their readers to reflect on what durability might mean amid the interruption and subsequent reconfiguration of once dependable frameworks for understanding permanence.

Chapter 1 began with Zhang Dai's inscribed reflections on the difficulties of inscription following the break-up and dispersal of his family collections in the mid seventeenth century. Zhang found a pretext for endurance by thinking with, rather than seeking to deny, inconstancy and change. His extended meditations on the fate of inscribed literature from the late Ming to early Qing introduce a central argument of my study: namely, that early modern inscriptions were less concerned with ensuring fixity or closure than with celebrating improvisation, mutability, and the affordances of refabrication. These themes converge in Zhang's inscription on his depraved cousin's mutilated slab, the so-called "Celestial Inkstone."

Chapters 2 and 3 tracked transformations in early modern conceptions of inscriptive permanence by reconsidering technical innovations in the two major fields of Ming mark making—seal carving and inkstick production. Chapter 2 examined the extent to which concern with the impermanence of monumental stone inscription amid frontier violence, factional strife, and volatility in the late Ming marketplace prompted Huizhou carvers to enlarge the possibilities of writing with a knife as self-styled "swordsmen." The challenge of how to extricate legitimate practices of copying from potentially aberrant alternatives refined attempts to discern openings for variation within replication, to recover an ever more elusive sense of individuality—or the authentic traces of He Zhen's blade—among outwardly indistinguishable copies. Chapter 3 turned to ink makers—many of whom worked closely alongside seal carvers—to investigate how inkstick designs recalibrated the interplay between literature and commodity branding. Inscriptions on solid tablets of ink—products designed to be destroyed through their use—reconceive of durability in terms of an object's duplication and metamorphoses. Sun Ruiqing's counterfeit "One with Clear Heaven," a fake that was eventually preserved as an authentic antique in the Palace Museum, reveals how early modern ink makers questioned expectations of endurance and expendability derived from woodblock books. The inkstick elucidates the extent to which acts of preservation are not predetermined by the ascendancy of any single publishing format but instead remain both contingent and open to contestation.

Chapter 4 examined the emergence of Qing antiquarianism by attending to the unlikely fates of Ming remnant things under the new dynasty—objects that unsettle staid approaches to "metal and stone" as a coherent discipline. I asked how, in the face of developments outlined in chapters 1–3, leading antiquarians sought to reestablish their control over the interpretation of inscriptions through techniques of reproduction in stone and ink-squeeze rubbings. By foregrounding the place of "objects of the former dynasty" in Qing intellectual circles, the chapter uncovered the anachronism, artistic creativity, and collective fantasies of restitution that lurk beneath the austere edifice of epigraphic scholarship, demonstrating how these themes were in turn taken up and explored in antiquarian poetry from the late seventeenth and eighteenth centuries.

The ruptures of the Ming-Qing transition fostered a heightened sensitivity toward the tools and media that sustain *wen* (writing, civility, Chinese culture), a dynamic that found succinct expression—as Zhang Dai's "Celestial Inkstone" suggests—in literary inscriptions on calligraphic implements such as inkslabs. By the early eighteenth century, writers uncovered in the inscription of inkstones a means with which to survey and synthesize divergent genealogies of *ming*. Bringing together concerns with the historiography, transmission, and technical substructures of the Chinese script, inscribed inkstones created a venue for critical reflection on the question of what it means to write.

My concern, in this epilogue, is with probing underlying motivations behind the seventeenth-century material turn toward writing on inkslabs, particularly as it intersects with and was shaped by the remnant subject's political predicament, emergent methods of empirical scholarship on stones, and research into the histories of ruined monuments. Dorothy Ko has written extensively on the artisanal episteme of inkstone production in early Qing China. As a literary historian, I am especially interested in why so many of the leading writers of the early- to mid-Qing period, figures at the very center of Chinese written culture, inscribed such large quantities of inkstones and in the related issue of how they came to treat an inkstone's surface as a threshold for reconceptualizing relations between literature and other forms of graphic art. In what follows, I consider these trends not as practices pertaining exclusively to inkstone connoisseurship but as means of enlarging the composite art of inscription, the result of developments—particularly late Ming innovations in seal carving and inkstick design—that I have traced across the four preceding chapters in writings upon a diverse range of objects.

REMNANT INKSLABS

Duan inkstones assumed newfound significance in the wake of the Qing invasion as synecdoches for the loyalist cause. As Wang Fuzhi's inscription on his small turtle-shaped slab concedes, the Yongli emperor set up his rump Southern Ming court in Zhaoqing 肇慶, a short distance from the Duan quarries, while his commanders vied for control of the pits. Contemporaneous remnant poets found within their commitments to the allegorical significance of Duan inkstones an impetus to study the physical properties of rocks, visiting quarries to conduct firsthand petrological research, composing inscriptions that participate in the emergence of early Qing empirical scholarship. Cantonese poet Qu Dajun 屈大均 (1630–1696), renowned for his highly sophisticated use of material symbolism in commenting on themes of loyalty, seclusion, and rebirth, approached the Duan inkstone as a supple means with which to both evoke and potentially overcome the remnant subject's experiences of the Ming cataclysm.[1] The Duan Brook became a multivalent *topos* in Qu Dajun's poetry and prose, a space of haunting absence and material plenitude. As Qu revisited the cliffs and crags of the area to survey its rocks, he simultaneously composed mournful elegies reflecting on the Yongli emperor's makeshift "palace" in the prefectural yamen and the tomb of Yongli's father, the so-called Duan Emperor (Duan Huangdi 端皇帝).[2] Qu's self-professed concern for broken or decayed stones insinuates sentiments of injury and recalcitrance: he finds an unlikely pretext for fulfilment by identifying with a half-broken inkstone in the shape of the character for wind, a damaged tool that stubbornly resists service as a tribute to court:[3]

INSCRIPTION ON A HALF INKSTONE IN THE SHAPE OF THE CHARACTER "WIND" WITH PREFACE

I have a fine inkstone, a rock from the eastern cave of the Duan Brook. The stone has been fashioned in the shape of the character for "wind," and yet is broken in half so that it is shorter on the right-hand side and longer on the left. I polished it slightly and named it "half-inkstone" then inscribed it.

Don't say you're complete, and yet you're fully stone.
Don't say I have a halved state, I'm still half jade.
Alas! A half can still be useful yet can't be recommended as tribute to court.
A gentleman should thus find worth in flaws.

EPILOGUE

風字半硯銘有序

予有佳硯，蓋端溪東洞石也。形如風字，而斷其半，右短而左長，稍磨之，名曰半硯，為之銘。

毋曰爾全，爾全石而。
毋曰予半，予半玉而。
嗚呼，半可用也，而不可貢也。
故君子以玷缺為重也。⁴

Qu's writings on Duan inkstones from the 1680s at the same time reveal how he inscribed local gifts to express his solidarity with a network of friends in the broader loyalist community—including the sons of the martyr Qi Biaojia in "Allegory Mountain," author of an inscription on Zhang Dai's Wood Like a Dragon.⁵ A Duan inkstone was at once a material memento of Zhaoqing and a token for the collective affirmation of ties between remnant subjects.

During his time in Duanzhou, Qu Dajun conducted extensive research on the quarries and various seams of rock in the area. He composed two detailed studies on "Duan Rock" (Duan shi 端石) and "Duan Brook Inkstones" (Duanxi yanshi 端溪硯石) for the "Words on Stone" ("Shiyu" 石語) chapter in his compendium *New Words from Guangdong* (*Guangdong xinyu* 廣東新語), a monumental work of early Qing empirical learning.⁶ Passages from Qu Dajun's two entries on Duan stones were subsequently repackaged as a stand-alone monograph, "An Investigation of Duan Stone" ("Duanshi kao" 端石考).⁷ This treatise became an influential guide to inkstone connoisseurship throughout the remainder of the Qing yet circulated anonymously because of the imperial censorship of Qu's work.⁸ Qu incorporated inkstone inscriptions into his petrological inquiries. In his chapter on "Duan Rock," for instance, Qu verifies his judgment of the best stratum of stone from the Underwater Lode or the Old Pit (Lao Keng 老坑) by citing his writings on a specimen he had procured at the quarry. He presents his *ming* on a so-called "Water Fat Inkstone" ("Shuifang yan" 水肪硯) as proof of the stone's peculiarly "aqueous" substance, the fact that his general assessment of the Lode is based on samples of hard evidence, and that he has held and handled the rock he discusses: "This [inkstone] has an aqueous substance. As the essence of water congeals, if ethereal it becomes clouds, if solid it becomes stone. People see this inkstone and assume it's stone, I saw it and knew [its substance] was water. It can thus be called 'watery fat'" 此水之質也。水之精華所結，虛而為雲，實而為石，人見以為石，吾見以為水，故以水肪稱之。[9] Qu's inscription looks beyond matters of biography to instead study Duan rock's indefinite essence, its capacity to exceed, unsettle, and potentially recalibrate the terms with which observers typically assess stones. Zhu Yizun like his close associate Qu Dajun also personally visited the Duan quarries to inspect inkstones during his service as a tutor in the Zhaoqing area (first in the summer of 1656 and then again in the 1690s), composing song lyrics to commemorate his experiences at the pits.[10] Zhu similarly compiled an influential monograph on the basis of his firsthand judgments of Duan slabs.[11]

Remnant inkslabs continued to haunt the imaginations of prominent eighteenth-century collectors. A comparative study of Jin Nong's 金農 (1687–1763) folio of calligraphic inkstone inscriptions now held in the Guangdong Provincial Museum and published versions of the same compositions suggests that Jin likely refused to transmit two of his inkstone inscriptions in print because of repressive censorship campaigns under the Yongzheng 雍正 (b. 1678; r. 1722–1735) emperor. Jin's "Inscription on a Fitting Inkstone" ("Heyan ming" 合硯銘) contains the phrase "I wash in the light of the sun and bathe in the light of the moon" 沐日浴月 (sun and moon combine to form the character Ming), while his "Inscription on an Inkstone for Copying *Materia Medica*" ("Chao *Bencao* yan ming" 抄本草硯銘) begins: "Elder Stone where do you come from? From the crags of the Antelope Gorge, under those bright vermillion skies [Zhu or "vermillion" was the surname of the Ming royal house]" 石丈何來？來自羚羊之峽，朱明之天.[12] Both inscriptions treat the attributes of inkstones as what Ko terms "qualisigns," material details that in this instance covertly invoke the name of the Ming imperial family.[13]

Jin's self-censored *ming* resonate with the writings of seventeenth century loyalist collectors, and yet start to move beyond the concerns of early Qing connoisseurship both by reflecting at length on the relationship between inkstone inscription and epigraphic scholarship, and by adapting techniques from seal carving to personally inscribe bespoke slabs. The early-nineteenth-century commentator on Yangzhou urban life, Liang Shaoren 梁紹壬 (1793–1834), remarked in an overview of *ming* as a unique form of expression beyond "poetry," that Jin Nong—a prominent member of Weng Fanggang's circle of collaborators—eventually became one of three exemplary Qing masters (alongside his contemporary Zheng Xie 鄭燮 [1693–1765] and student Luo Ping 羅聘 [1733–99]) in writing upon objects.[14]

INKSTONES AND THE HISTORY OF WRITING

In a detailed preface to his collection of inscriptions on inkslabs, Jin Nong reflects on the history of writing, using the objecthood of an inkstone to assess the affordances of inscribed literature. He begins by reviewing canonical definitions of *ming* in both the *Explanation of Names* and *Zuo Tradition*:

> The forms of writing may vary, yet inscription is the oldest. The *Explanation of Names* states: "Inscription means to name, the act of recording meritorious deeds can be said to "make a name." Zang Wuzhong's discussion of inscription says its meaning lies in "manifesting virtue, tabulating achievements, and naming campaigns" so inscription is not only a matter of sincerity and reverence.

> 文章之體不一，而銘為最古。《釋名》云：『銘，名也，記其功使可稱名也。』臧武仲之論銘也，有令德紀功稱伐之義焉，則銘不專於誠儆矣。[15]

"As far as the ancients were concerned," Jin continues, "there was no category of thing that did not bear an inscription" 莫不有銘.[16] He then offers a list: "pans and basins, tables and mats, goblets and libation cups, dragon banners and sun-moon standards, buckthorn arrows, tilting vessels, the *chan* cauldron, the *jialiang* measure, the *jing* bell, the celestial body mirror, the water clock" 盤杅，几席，尊彝，旂常，楛矢，欹器，讒鼎，嘉量，景鐘，辰鑑，刻漏.[17] This assortment of artifacts encompasses generic models for inscription in early Chinese historiography: "pans and basins" refers to Cheng Tang 成湯 (ca. 1600s BCE), the first Shang king's "rule for daily renewal"; "tables and mats" served as shorthand for the King Wu admonitions; "buckthorn arrows" refers to a tribute presented by the Sushen 肅慎 tribe to King Wu after he defeated the Shang, tokens King Wu then inscribed to commemorate the good virtues of early kings; "the water clock" refers to one of the five *ming* preserved in *Selections of Refined Literature*. Jin finally claims that inkstones might also be included in this list by citing the legendary example of the Yellow Emperor's inkslab, an enigmatic object named "Sea of Ink" 墨海.¹⁸ While the Yellow Emperor's inkslab only became a topic of literary interest with the rise of connoisseurship manuals on writing tools in the Southern Tang and Northern Song, the detail nevertheless allows Jin to link the contemporary practice of inkstone inscription to the earliest examples of writing on things—or in the figure of the Yellow Emperor, to the very beginnings of Chinese civilization.¹⁹ The materiality and function of an inkstone, at the same time, invites Jin to pivot from literary thought to assess the imbrication of *ming* with the study of ancient stone monuments, with histories of calligraphic carving, and with techniques of artisanal knifework.

Jin Nong's own inkstone inscriptions draw from both admonitory and memorial inscriptive modes. Three out of ten, he claims, are intended to counsel or caution (*yugui zhe* 寓規者) in the manner of an "inscription placed to the right of my seat" (*zuoyouming* 座右銘); the other seven out of ten meanwhile "manifest beauty" (*zhangmei zhe* 彰美者) in the style of inscriptions to record virtuous merits on bronze vessels.²⁰ Jin similarly acknowledges the absence of rigid constraints in composing *ming*. Inscriptive rhetoric might by turns be "elegant" (*ya* 雅) or "vulgar" (*zheng* 鄭), "austere" (*zhuang* 庄) or "humorous" (*xie* 諧), "straightforward" (*zheng* 正) or "concealed" (*sou* 廋)—"stones cannot speak" 石不能言, Jin concedes, "they can only wait for one who possesses the Way to establish [their words]" 惟俟有道者定之耳.²¹

In line with his prefatory claim that an inkstone can variously serve as a "strict teacher" 嚴師 or "intimate friend" 執友, Jin's literary inscriptions waver between austerity, empathetic identification, and mocking self-deprecation. His "Inscription on a Round Inkstone" ("Tuanyan ming" 團硯銘), for instance, lambasts official greed by using a circular inkstone as a mirror with which to humiliate a fat scholar (or himself):

> It is not detestable for an inkstone to be round like this, but for a person's face it's vulgar. Runty-stunted scholars all stuffed on provisions, can the one who evaluates you today be truly without shame?

> 硯如此不惡，面如此便俗。侏儒侏儒多飽粟，今之相者兮果無怍。²²

EPILOGUE

Inkstone inscriptions for Jin Nong not only derive from sagely admonitions etched onto household tools and eulogies cast onto bronze ritual vessels but also embody a connection to histories of carved calligraphy on stone monuments: "an inkslab," he notes, "belongs to the category of stone" 硯正石類.[23] As such, writing on an inkstone, for Jin, provided a space within which to display his "obsession with epigraphy [or the writing on metal and stone]" 金石文字之癖.[24] Jin's inscription of inkstones draws upon and extends his scholarly inquiry into "stone writing" (*shiwen* 石文), from early epigraphic sources such as the Wufeng stone carvings 五鳳石刻 to the divergent "movements" (*liupai* 流派) of Han and Tang dynasty clerical-script calligraphy.[25] The literary act of composing an inkstone inscription for Jin at once entailed and became inextricably entwined with the calligraphic act of drafting that same composition in "*bafen* 八分 clerical script."[26] Jin's preoccupation with finding resilience in humble or outwardly disfigured things stimulated his inscription of damaged stones, anticipating the emergence of a broader mid-Qing investment in the refabrication of ruined fragments as inkslabs, as in his "Inscription on a Broken Corner Inkstone" ("Quejiao yan ming" 缺角硯銘): "A pointed head yet bald, don't worry about outward appearances, as long as you have ink in your belly, a gentleman takes you alone" 頭銳且禿，不修邊幅，腹中有墨，君所獨.[27]

A Duan inkstone bearing Jin's small self-portrait now held in the Tianjin Museum reveals his striking calligraphic innovations in writing on inkstones, in this case integrating the "square and angular scripts" carved onto stone stelae of the Northern Dynasties (especially the Northern Qi 北齊 [550–577]) with the woodcut typeface of printed Buddhist sutras from the Song, introducing clerical-script types into his regular script and vice versa.[28] Whereas there is no reliable evidence to ascertain whether late Ming writers like Zhang Dai were able to carve their own inscriptions on treasured slabs, eighteenth-century anecdotes relate Jin Nong's involvement in inkstone design. Jin allegedly collaborated with his retainer Zhu Long 朱龍 (n.d.) of Yongdong 甬東 in fashioning inkstones, personally carving inscriptions in *bafen* calligraphy onto Zhu's slabs. Other observers note that Jin made money on the side through his participation in the production and sale of lanterns and inkslabs.[29] A "Small Banana Palm Inkstone" in the Tianjin Museum meanwhile suggests Jin Nong's application of seal-carving techniques such as the "pushing cut" and "chopping knife" (*qiedao fa* 切刀法) method to the inscription of inkstones.[30]

Jin Nong's writings elucidate two tendencies that frame the conclusion to this book. On the one hand, inkstone inscription became for Jin a means with which to pursue and supplement research on the history of Chinese writing, from the development of what he called the "most ancient" literary genre (*ming*) and its association with other forms of classical poetry and prose, to the evolution of Chinese calligraphy from seal to clerical script, to the epigrapher's investigation of stone monuments and ruins. In this sense, an inscribed inkstone serves as a crucible within which the otherwise diffuse forms that Chinese writing might assume—whether poetry, calligraphy, or epigraphy—can be brought back together and considered as a whole.

On the other hand, Jin's inkstone inscriptions wryly exploit anachronism and inter-medial transposition to pioneer inventive forms of graphic art—combining ironic self-deprecation with austere admonition in free verse, mixing characters from Northern Dynasties' stelae with the woodcut typeface of Song dynasty printed sutras, repurposing techniques from seal carving for writing on inkslabs. In this second sense, inkstone inscription dwells on disjunctions between different sectors of the Chinese written landscape, seeking novelty through the juxtaposition of heterogenous graphic materials. These developments became inextricably entwined with the writer's firsthand involvement in the design and marketing of inkstones—a model of creativity attuned to the achievements of Ming entrepreneurs like He Zhen and Fang Yulu. Even as Qing inkstone inscriptions project chauvinistic faith in the longevity of Chinese written culture, they elicit critical reflection on the precarious supports and labor that sustain this vision. Jin's combinations at once register and creatively respond to widening rifts between the antiquarian's current predicament, his tools, and his ever more elusive objects of study.

THE REFABRICATION OF RUINS

The refabrication of old stones and earthenware tiles as ink-grinders elicited a shift in Qing approaches to literary inscription, from writing on unmarked objects to reinscribing excavated artifacts, or surfaces that already bear engraved words.[31] Zhu Yizun, a prolific collector of broken stones and a formative influence on Jin Nong, is a case in point. In some

EPILOGUE

instances, Zhu simply etched his name or the date of acquisition onto a slate: the Tianjin Museum, for instance, owns a circular Han dynasty roof-end tile (diameter 16.8 cm; height 2.6 cm) with the four-character auspicious phrase "Long Life Without Limit" (*changsheng wuji* 長生無極) and Zhu's mark "Zhucha" 竹垞.[32] Elsewhere, Zhu worked to reconstruct the biographies of rediscovered objects from their markings, as when he obtained a "city-wall" brick following the Qing conquest that bore an eight-character message in seal script, one he attributes to Wen Zhenmeng 文震孟 (1574–1636), a righteous protestor against the crimes of eunuch Wei Zhongxian 魏忠賢 (1568–1627).[33] Zhu presents his new inscription on the brick as a riff on Wen's carved message:

INSCRIPTION WITH PREFACE ON A CITY-WALL INKSTONE

This city-wall inkstone is a brick from an unknown city-wall, measuring around five foot by two foot. A sunken depression at the top of the brick forms a pool so that water is surrounded on four sides. Within the cavity there are two characters "city-wall inkstone" and along the side are eight characters "when the mind is correct, the brush is correct, when the mind is off-center, the brush is off-center" in seal script. The object was reportedly held in the Huiqing Temple in Pingjiang. Wen Zhenmeng, before he had taken the examinations, was studying at the temple where he encountered the stone and cherished it. A monk from the temple brought out a long sheet of paper for Wen to draft his calligraphy, which was then offered in exchange for the inkstone. After the wars of the *yiyou* year (1645), it passed into the mundane world, where it was eventually purchased by Wu Yuting of Xiuning, who later gave it to me. I have inscribed it thus:

When the mind is correct, the brush is correct,
Words set forth ensure stability.
Do not countenance perversity, this was the order of the sages.
Like meeting a great guest, this must be based in respect.

城硯銘并序

城硯不知何城之甄，修五尺，廣二尺，窪其頂以為池，水周四面。窪中有「城硯」二字，旁列「心正筆正，心邪筆邪」八字，皆篆書。相傳平江慧慶寺中物。大學士文文肅公未第日，讀書僧舍，見而心賞之。寺僧出長牋，請公書卷，以硯易焉。乙酉兵後，流轉人間，休寧吳于庭購得之，晚以贈予，乃作銘曰：

心正筆正，出辭安定。
勿納于邪，先民所命。
如見大賓，一主乎敬³⁴

Zhu's inscribed claims for self-correction, "stable" words, and respect for his forebears read as an appended commentary to the brick's initial eight-character engraving: his inscription constitutes a form of epigraphic exegesis, one that affirms an unbroken connection to the legacies of Ming loyalism while acknowledging the possibility of recovery in the early Qing—he adopts, for instance, the Shunzhi reign date.

Zhu Yizun's interest in the refabrication of ruined fragments as inkstones became entwined with his efforts to commemorate and work through the politics of the dynastic transition. His family, for instance, played a role in the restitution of a "broken-stele inkslab" (duanbei yan 斷碑硯), a stone bearing Su Shi's calligraphy that belonged to Ming martyr Huang Daozhou 黃道周 (1585–1646).³⁵ Zhu allegedly added a twelve-character inscription to the left-hand side of the object: "your body might be defiled, but your mind cannot be humiliated. Held for three years, your blood transformed to jade" 身可污，心不辱。藏三年，化碧玉.³⁶ The inscription invokes an allusion to the righteous official Chang Hong 萇弘 (582–492 BCE) whose blood, three years after his murder, turned into green jade: the damaged body and "pure" essence of the thing become material analogies for the Ming martyr's integrity (and Zhu Yizun's own implicit loyalism).³⁷ The idea of turning a broken segment of a lost stele into an inkstone bespeaks a search for "use" and a sense of "completion" within ruined fragments, evoking at once the longevity of writing on stone while documenting a material history of destruction and decay. And yet, the claim of continuity again rests on repeated acts of reinscription.

High Qing epigraphers in Weng Fanggang's circle started to repurpose fragments of ancient monuments, particularly bricks and tiles, as new inkstones.³⁸ As Ou Zhongrong and Hye-shim Yi have demonstrated, perhaps the most widely discussed mid-Qing example of this practice concerns a Western Han dynasty brick owned by Ruan Yuan 阮元 (1764–1849) and commemorated in poetry and prose by Weng.[39] Ruan adapted the brick as an inkstone, yet the object also served as material evidence for epigraphic research. Through a detailed analysis of the damaged second character *wu* 五 in the brick's inscription ("fifth year of the Wufeng reign [57–54 BCE]" 五鳳五年), a graph previously read as *san* 三, Weng not only provided a new dating for the antique but also discovered a rare, early example of Western Han clerical-script calligraphy, one that registers a formal move away from the conventions of seal script.[40] Weng also writes of another Han stone from the Wufeng reign, unearthed in 1191 as artisans in Qufu retrieved material from the Diaoyu Pond to renovate the Confucian Temple, this time inscribed: "second year of the Wufeng reign" (Wufeng er nian 五鳳二年). In his comments on this specimen, Weng playfully "mocks" in verse Zhu Yizun's erroneous assessment of the antique as a brick (*zhuan* 磚), claiming it was in fact a fragment of carved stone (*shi* 石)—the inscribed object becomes a platform for the scholarly efforts of a leading mid-Qing epigrapher to correct the mistakes of a leading early Qing epigrapher, a reprise of the contest staged around the Zhao family's rhinoceros horn cup. While stationed in Guangdong, Weng commissioned the calligraphy on this ancient object to be reproduced on a new Duan inkstone, a slab that later passed to fellow inkstone obsessive, Ji Yun 紀昀 (1724–1805).[41]

Approaches to inkstone inscription as a form of epigraphic commentary, a trend that emerges with early Qing collectors like Zhu Yizun before finding more sophisticated expression in the practice of Weng Fanggang, reaches its apotheosis with Ruan Yuan, a preeminent philologist in the first half of the nineteenth century. Ruan, who adopted the studio name "Study of Eight Bricks" (Bazhuan yinguan 八磚吟館) to commemorate his prized collection of ancient tiles (six of which he recarved as inkstones), patronized artists like Huang Yi 黃易 (1744–1802) in their efforts to fabricate inkstones from fragments of ruined monuments.[42] Huang, the excavator of the Wu Family Shrine in Shandong (ca. 147) in 1786 and a prominent Qing seal carver, repurposed a broken stone pillar from the site as a new inkstone—a specimen now held in the Tianjin Museum—engraving the slab: "A ruined stone pillar from a stone chamber in the Han dynasty Wu Family Shrines. In accordance with the material, I made an inkstone, carving the missing characters as a supplement, Huang Yi" 漢武氏石室碎石柱，因材為研補刻缺字，黃易.[43] This was not the only fragment from the Wu Family Shrines that Huang carved into an inkstone—Ruan Yuan owned another slab that Huang fashioned from a stone in the shrine's free-standing ceremonial gate tower (*que* 闕).⁴⁴

Ruan Yuan took the logic behind the refabrication of ancient fragments further, however, by transforming the body of a new inkstone into a pseudo-stele or independent epigraphic monument. Now preserved in the Yangzhou Museum, Ruan's "Supplemented Copy of the "Western Marchmount Huashan Temple Stele" Giant Duan Inkstone" (Ruan Yuan mubu "Xiyue Huashan miao bei" juxing Duan yan 阮元慕補《西嶽華山廟碑》巨型端硯), measuring 95 cm by 55.5 cm with a thickness of 4.5 cm, at first glance resembles a free-standing stele.⁴⁵ The titular "Western Marchmount Huashan Temple Stele" (Xiyue Huashan miao bei 西嶽華山廟碑) was erected in 165 CE (supposedly to replace earlier damaged monuments), rediscovered by Song antiquarians, and eventually destroyed by an earthquake in 1555. Ruan acquired a rubbing of the lost stele in 1808 and commissioned a replica stele to be produced the following year. In 1810, Ruan came across another rubbing that appeared to show the missing characters from the 1808 version. He commissioned a reproduction of these "missing characters" on the meter-long Duan inkstone, an object to be installed alongside his earlier replica Huashan stele.⁴⁶

Ruan's pseudo-stele evokes the power of a contemporary inscription to create a new monument, one that supplements, and thus potentially supersedes, past ruins. Inkstone inscription becomes a medium for both the production and preservation of epigraphic scholarship in stone, establishing a durable memorial to the work of "filling in" (*bu*) historical lacunae, an independent monument to the Qing antiquarian study and repair of ancient monuments. Ruan presents his "supplement" not as a standard replica stele but as an inkstone, as if placing faith in the object's putative function as a generative source of fresh ink.

A HISTORY OF INKSTONES

Rather than end with Ruan Yuan's imposing pseudo-stele, I wish to conclude by looking at another set of approaches to writing on inkstones in eighteenth-century China, turning instead to the quotidian practice of Jin Nong's associate—entrepreneurial inkstone maker, seal carver, and Shandong artist Gao Fenghan. Dorothy Ko has elsewhere introduced Gao's social position as what she terms an "artisan scholar."⁴⁷ In what follows,

EPILOGUE

I focus specifically on how Gao in his seminal *History of Inkstones*—a no longer extant collection of inkstone designs (approximately 168) transmitted by Wang Xiang 王相 (1789–1852) and later recarved on 120 wooden boards as models for the production of rubbings by Wang Yueshen 王曰申 (1788–1841) and Wu Xizai 吳熙載 (1799–1870)—responds to the conventions I have identified in the early- to mid-Qing resurgence of inkstone inscription.[48] Gao's attention as a collector ranges from the acquisition of relics associated with Ming loyalists to the refabrication of ancient bricks and tiles as epigraphic sources. He drew upon many of the models that I have discussed in preceding chapters, from Xu Wei to the seal carvers and ink makers of Huizhou—notably Fang Yulu. The final object preserved in Gao's *History of Inkstones* is based on an enigmatic seal bearing an inscription attributed to Zhou Lianggong (figure E.1). Nor was Gao's artistic practice limited to the design and production of inkstones: he also fashioned and inscribed wooden studio objects such as inkstone cases, branch and root sculptures, brush pots, and wrist-rests.[49] Gao mimics esteemed antiquarians such as Zhu Yizun in adapting antique scripts on old or broken slabs yet espouses a comparatively irreverent attitude toward the limitations of scholarship, casting his improvisatory approach to the craft of writing on inkstones as a form of "poetic" expression, one attuned like Jin

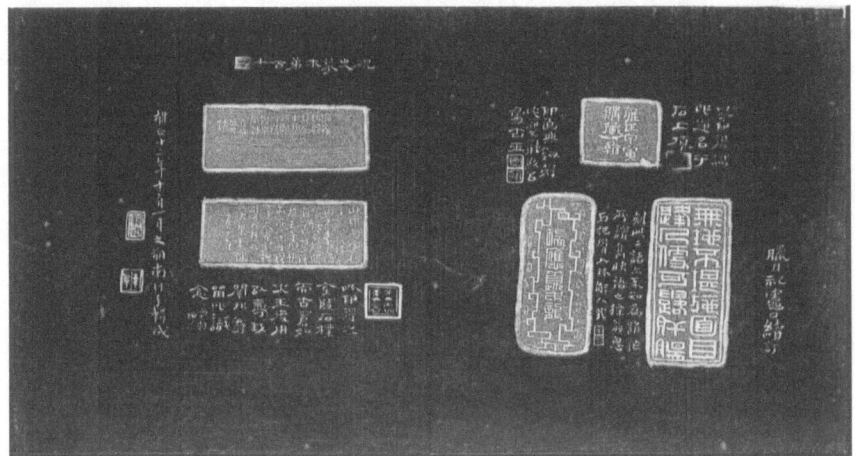

FIGURE E.1. Rubbing No. 112 from Gao Fenghan's (1683–1749) 高鳳翰 *History of Inkstones* 硯史. The design shows a seal that had been owned and inscribed by Zhou Lianggong. *Source:* Gao Fenghan, *Yanshi* 硯史, ed. Wang Xiang 王相 (1852), 112. Image courtesy of Harvard-Yenching Library.

Nong (who carved one of the inkstones in Gao's anthology) to fortuitous encounters in the urban marketplace.[50] Broken stones, for Gao, matter not primarily as epigraphic evidence or as prized relics that might bolster narratives of continuity but as a means with which to evoke and redress lived experiences of failure, destitution, and debility.

The first inkslab in Gao Fenghan's chronicle is an adapted eave-end tile from the Weiyang Palace (Weiyang gong 未央宮) of Han dynasty Chang'an and bearing the four characters "Lasting Joy Without End" (changle weiyang 長樂未央) (figure E.2).[51] Gao suggests that on the basis of its yellowy-purplish hue and robust calligraphy, this was not one of many later imitations of Han Palace tiles but an authentic specimen. His attached commentary, however, is less concerned with the antiquarian prestige of the tile than it is with the obsessive devotion of its owner, Wang Shi 王蓍 (1649–1737), a now poverty-stricken collector, Nanjing painter, and seal carver who despite having pawned most of his books held onto this object in the hope that he might present it before King Yama, one of the ten presiding judges in the courts of hell.[52] Gao begins his chronicle with the oldest inkslab he knows, yet what matters about the thing is the relationship it sustains with its current destitute custodian.

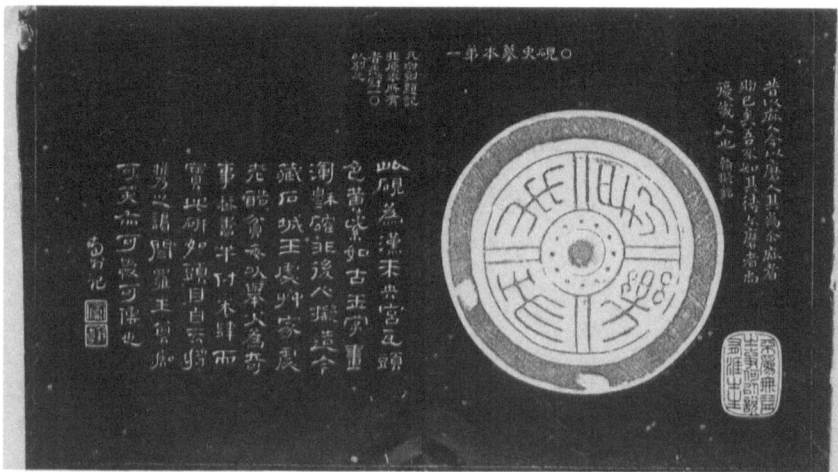

FIGURE E.2. Rubbing No. 1 from Gao Fenghan's *History of Inkstones*. This inkstone was created by repurposing an eave-end tile from the Weiyang Palace 未央宮 of Han dynasty Chang'an and bears the four characters "Lasting Joy Without End" 長樂未央. *Source:* Gao, *Yanshi*, 1.

EPILOGUE

Gao Fenghan's acts of refabrication often take the form of adding markings (*zhi* 識), an appended note (*xuti* 續題), or a new literary inscription (*ming*) to the surface of an inkstone that already bears engraved calligraphy. At a small bookstall, Gao encountered a slab in the shape of the character "wind" made from an old cut tile (*jian gu duanwa zhi* 剪古斷瓦製), a piece that had once belonged to eminent early Qing collector and poet Zhu Yizun (figure E.3).[53] The specimen bore Zhu's signature (Old Zhucha 竹垞翁) and inscription, an eight-character motto that plays on the object's former identity as a roof tile by invoking a correspondence between the movements of the "wind" and the loyal companionship of this newly commissioned inkstone: "Wind. I go in four directions and you follow me" 風。我行四方爾相從。[54] Gao inscribed the artifact with his own sixteen-character riff on Zhu's short message: "Blowing the ten-thousand pipes, briskly vigorous, you should be the earthen cave, not the tips of green duckweed" 鼓吹萬籟，活活潑潑，爾為土囊，勿為萍末。[55] Gao playfully tweaks a line from Song Yu's 宋玉 (fl. 298–263 BCE) "Wind Rhapsody" (Fengfu 風賦), "the wind is born from earth and springs up in the tips of the green duckweed" 夫風生於地，起於青苹之末, to address this "earthen" tile shorn

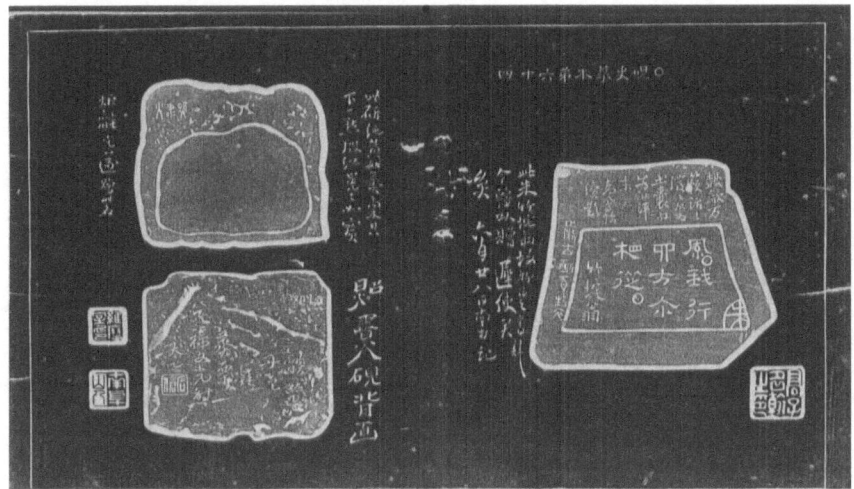

FIGURE E.3. Rubbing No. 64 from Gao Fenghan's *History of Inkstones*. This inkstone (right) in the shape of the character "wind" 風 was made from a cut roof tile. The object bears an inscription attributed to Zhu Yizun and an appended inscription by Gao Fenghan. Source: Gao, *Yanshi*, 64.

FIGURE E.4. Rubbing No. 4 from Gao Fenghan's *History of Inkstones*. The rubbing displays "before-and-after" ink-squeeze snapshots of an inkstone discovered under the wheel of a cart in Beijing and once owned by Southern Song poet Lu You 陸游 (1125–1209), later inscribed by Gao Fenghan. Source: Gao, *Yanshi*, 4.

of weeds.[56] An "earthen cave" possesses generative power, allowing wind to produce the "music of the earth" (*dilai* 地籟).

The fourth rubbing in Gao's collection dramatizes this step-by-step process of reinscription, presenting "before-and-after" ink-squeeze snapshots of an inkstone discovered under the wheel of a cart in Beijing, once owned by Southern Song poet Lu You 陸游 (1125–1209) (figure E.4). Gao made a rubbing of Lu's personal mark on the side of the slab (Lao xue'an zhushu di'er yan 老學庵著書第二硯), before making another rubbing after adding his new inscription: "From Jiannan, you came to the Yan Capital, before returning to my Western Pavilion" 出劍南，來燕市，歸我西亭.[57] While Lu You's engraving appears in an austere seal script reminiscent of Han stelae, Gao drafts his inscription in a running script with a "clerical manner": the interplay between the two styles of writing produces a dynamic contrast between a sense of stillness and movement, between weighty rectilinear graphs and curved, flowing lines—Gao's emendations, in other words, do not conform to the monumental aesthetic of the initial design but introduce a sense of instability through the play of opposing calligraphic styles.[58] Gao also includes an earlier copy of his "draft inscription" (*niming* 擬銘) as a caption to the inkstone, a record of the lines he had planned to inscribe

EPILOGUE

FIGURE E.5. Rubbing No. 61 from Gao Fenghan's *History of Inkstones*. Gao acquired this inkstone from an unsuspecting traveler in Zhejiang who did not understand that the scratchy signature "Student of the Heavenly Pool" 天池生 referred to late Ming calligrapher and poet Xu Wei 徐渭 (1521–1593). *Source*: Gao, *Yanshi*, 61.

before later changing his sobriquet from Nancun 南邨 to "Western Pavilion" 西亭.[59] Rather than fixing a single image of the inkstone in the form of a rubbing, Gao creates a palimpsest, documenting the career and evolving appearance of the object.

As responses to both Zhu Yizun's "wind" inkstone and Lu You's discarded stone suggest, Gao takes great pleasure in drawing attention to his uncanny ability to spot and obtain rare finds. The sixty-first rubbing, for instance, displays an inkstone Gao acquired from an unsuspecting traveler in Zhejiang who did not understand that the scratchy signature "Student of the Heavenly Pool" (Tianchi sheng 天池生) referred to late Ming calligrapher and poet Xu Wei (figure E.5).[60] Gao judges the authenticity of the inkstone, treasuring it as "truly [belonging to] my Green Vines [Xu Wei]" 當是我青藤, on the basis of the wording and calligraphy of its eight-character inscription: "I cherish your gritty demeanor, just like my untrammeled poor state" 愛爾磽確，象我落拓.[61] Gao rereads Xu's identification with the rough condition of the stone to prove his own identification with Xu.

Elsewhere in the collection, Gao similarly looks for personal meaning in his fortuitous encounters with disregarded antiques: he discovered one of his prized relics at an old residence in Huizhou, a circular stone inscribed and signed by Ming martyr Liu Zongzhou 劉宗周 (1578–1645).[62] Liu's engraving in seal script, dated to 1621 (Tianqi xinyou 天啓辛酉), runs around the circumference of the slab. Gao adapts a phrase from Liu's inscription—"ants climb the grindstone" (yixing moshang 蟻行磨上)—to coin a new studio name for himself: "Ant Mill Study" (Yimo zhai 蟻磨齋). This title alludes not only to Liu's relic but also to Gao's personal memory of his poetry teacher who had hung a placard with the three large characters "Ant Mill Study" in his classroom. Gao's relationship to the inkstone thus exceeds the object's historical significance as the material trace of a Ming loyalist; rather, its value derives from the way Liu's enigmatic inscription recalls Gao's own youthful experiences of becoming a poet.[63]

Gao Fenghan's concern with the refabrication of other objects as inkstones betrays the influence of Fang Yulu's creative recycling of epigraphic materials in *Master Fang's Ink Catalogue*. At least fifteen items in *History of Inkstones* are based on Fang's inkstick designs.[64] Gao's visual citations are not so much hidden clues for would-be connoisseurs; rather, he explicitly identifies his recourse to Fang Yulu's compendium in captions to images of his stones. Gao's copies of the Huizhou ink-maker's products dovetail with his records of retrieving rare inkstones in the markets of Huizhou or his formative years as an inkstone collector serving as an official in She County.[65] Gao treats Fang Yulu's catalogue not so much as an anthology of ink-cake designs but as a repository of epigraphic sources. The forty-ninth rubbing in *History of Inkstones*, for instance, displays a miniature inkslab, measuring just 5 cm by 7.5 cm and based on a Fang Yulu ink cake, which was itself based on a small square jade tablet with a pointed arrowhead. Fang's ink-cake design resembles an image of a jade artifact in the Song dynasty *Illustrated Catalogue of Ancient Jades* (*Guyu tupu* 古玉圖譜).[66] In an appended note, Gao invokes an analogy between the use of small jade tablets as girdle ornaments for officials and the use of his small inkstone as an "offering" to help officials manage affairs of "brush and ink."[67] By acknowledging the provenance of his design as a mass-produced ink cake while identifying the properties of the ancient jade implement Fang Yulu imitates, Gao Fenghan's inkstone playfully contests preconceptions of surface and substance, wavering between allusions to the materials of ink, stone, and paper—he had elsewhere, for instance, already adapted Fang's ink-cake designs for a tailormade set of stationery papers in 1737.[68] Despite being one of the smallest objects in his anthology, Gao's handheld

EPILOGUE

slab nevertheless registers a skeuomorphic impulse that shapes his collection as a whole, his search for endurance within the ephemeral. Just as Gao Fenghan repurposed Fang Yulu's inkcake designs, nineteenth-century potters also adapted Gao's inkstone designs to decorate purple-sand stoneware pots.[69]

Gao appears to have been particularly drawn to his small jade tablet inkstone, as he later carved another slab that was based on an ink cake that again approximates the shape of a square jade tablet with a pointed arrowhead from Fang Yulu's catalogue. In a short colophon, under the title "Following the *Ink Catalogue's* Old Design" 依墨譜舊式, Gao notes that he created this "Returned Pearl" (*huanzhu* 還珠) to compensate his own sense of loss after giving his earlier jade tablet inkstone away as a gift: he wryly asks himself "are you obsessed or not?" 痴否？痴否？[70] In the sixty-eighth rubbing of *History of Inkstones*, Gao pairs this later design with another inkstone that was based on illustrations from *Master Fang's Ink Catalogue*: an inkstone in the shape of two conjoined octagons displaying charts of the "eight tones" (*bayin* 八音) and "twelve musical pitches" (*shi'er lü* 十二律) (figure E.6).[71] In a scribbled commentary running around the circumference of the artifact, Gao reveals that this slab was crafted from leftover scraps of inkstone material.[72]

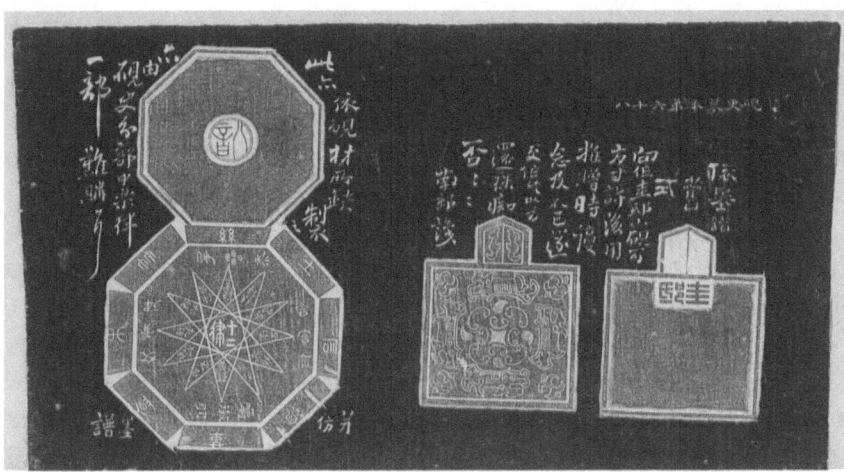

FIGURE E.6. Rubbing No. 68 from Gao Fenghan's *History of Inkstones*. Both inkstones are based on designs from Fang Yulu's *Master Fang's Ink Catalogue*. Source: Gao, *Yanshi*, 68.

Gao's resourceful tinkering with materials from *Master Fang's Ink Catalogue* extends to his creative appropriation of epigraphic sources. The ninety-fourth rubbing in the folio, for instance, displays an inkstone with the title "King Yu's Stele" and twelve characters from a copy of the stele inscription on a Fang Yulu inkstick: Gao again explicitly identifies the provenance of his source.[73] As if harkening back to his own earlier inkstones based on Fang's tablets, Gao cuts his "inkstone pool" (*yanchi*), the cavity for grinding and mixing ink with water, in the slender shape of an arrow-tip jade tablet.[74] His captions for this Chengni inkstone invoke a playful distinction between epigraphic knowledge and the mind-set of the poet: Gao admits that "when I was made this inkstone, I engraved the 'Ancient Yu Stele' upon it, even though I don't have the knack to properly read it" 余製此硯成，刻以古神禹碑，亦正讀之了不嫻耳.[75] Gao justifies his lack of knowledge by looking to poets, noting that Li Bai was ridiculed for not knowing how to read ancient script, professing instead to "again take Tao Yuanming as [my] teacher" 則淵明又為吾師矣.[76] Such comments represent a fulfillment of tendencies that emerge in Gao's focus on the obsessive collector, Wang Shi's relation to the Han eave-end tile, his riff on Zhu Yizun's wind inkstone inscription, or his memories of studying poetry in his acquisition of Liu Zongzhou's relic; namely, an interest in exploring forms of relation to things that cannot be reduced to, and delight in their capacity to exceed, scholarly approaches to antiques. If prominent Qing antiquarians like Weng Fanggang repurposed inkstones for epigraphic research and the construction of new monuments, Gao indulges in a wry misuse of epigraphic sources for explicitly poetic ends: he mis-transcribes characters he admits he cannot read and has no interest in deciphering; he notes he obtained these samples of script not from stelae or antiquarian catalogues but from published designs of ink cakes; he claims that his craft in carving inkstones is ultimately evidence of a poetic impulse to reimagine an object's meaning in terms of an irreducibly subjective experience or fortuitous encounter.

As Dorothy Ko has noted, Gao Fenghan took pride not simply in recycling humble materials but in repurposing other objects as inkstones.[77] In a memorable instance, he responds to a client's request to write a large sign that demanded three bushels of ink by "commandeering" his medicinal mortar (figures E.7 and E.8).[78] To commemorate this happenstance transformation of a mortar into inkstone in 1735, Gao inscribes the four sides

EPILOGUE

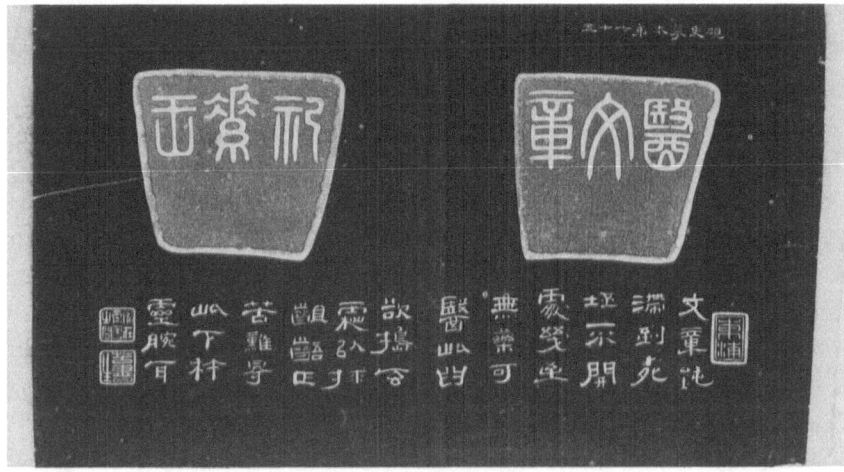

FIGURE E.7. Rubbing No. 74 from Gao Fenghan's *History of Inkstones*. Gao created this inkstone in 1735 by repurposing his medicinal mortar. Source: Gao, *Yanshi*, 75.

of the object: "Medicine of Writing" (Yi wenzhang 醫文章), "Worship the Plain King [Confucius]" (Si Suwang 祀素王), "Drug Mortar: Yongzheng *yimao* year [1735]" (yaojiu 藥臼; Yongzheng yimao 雍正乙卯), "Pound the Primal Frost" (Dao yuanshuang 搗元霜)—phrases that compare the

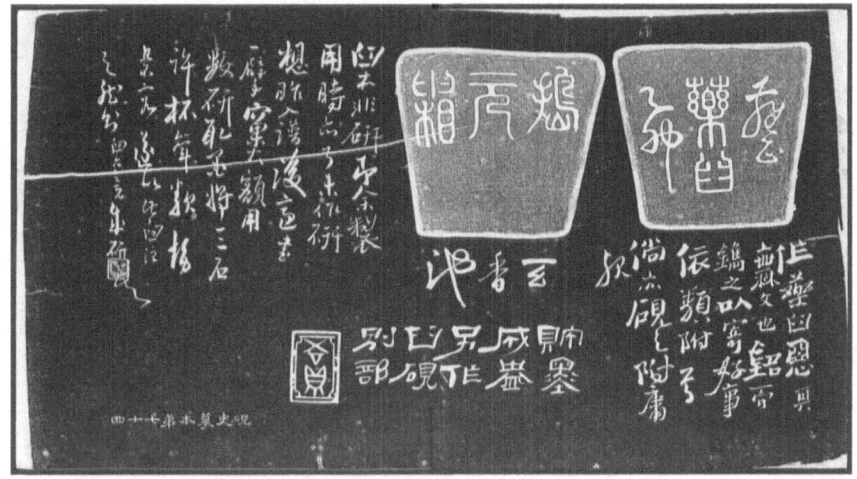

FIGURE E.8. Rubbing No. 74 from Gao Fenghan's *History of Inkstones*. Gao created this inkstone in 1735 by repurposing his medicinal mortar. Source: Gao, *Yanshi*, 75.

generative act of grinding ink to the restorative power of grinding medicinal herbs to cure an illness.⁷⁹ Despite the small size of the object (measuring 11.5 cm × 12.5 cm), Gao employs a "large character signage script" (*dazi bangshu* 大字榜書), a style of calligraphy typically associated with large signs or placards and thus an implicit reference to the occasion that prompted his discovery of the mortar's hidden virtues. Gao's engraved words exploit what we might call after Bill Brown the "misuse value" of his mortar, a term that designates "the efficacy and effects of some untoward deployment," one that captions the effectiveness of "broken routine (the interruption of habit) as an unanticipated mode of apprehending the object world anew."⁸⁰ Gao's act of inscription names this "new valuation emerging from the object's displacement from routine systems or networks of use."⁸¹

Gao's repurposed mortar encapsulates a thesis that I have traced across the course of this book; namely, that writing on things in early modern China was not so much a strident means of ensuring fixity and permanence in order to forestall the inevitability of decay but a way of apprehending and ultimately making do with conditions of impermanence, responding to precarity by celebrating improvisation, happy accidents, and inventive refabrication, embracing rather than working to negate processes of material transformation. His approach to the inkstone is not simply evidence of his social positioning as an "artisan scholar" but a reprise of themes I have traced across this book's four chapters, from the remnant subject's empathetic identification with discarded or damaged things (chapter 1), to the idiosyncratic reuse of epigraphic sources in Huizhou seal carving and inkstick design (chapters 2 and 3), to reflections on tensions between poetic sentiment and objective knowledge in the investigation of monuments (chapter 4). Building upon late Ming and early Qing approaches to the inscription of objects, Gao's practice shifts our attention from a sense of the durable as a quality inherent in cumbersome substrates to a sense of endurance as an everyday practice, one maintained through vigilant labor and care.

History of Inkstones anticipates increasingly inventive approaches to inscriptive art in the early nineteenth century, developments that ultimately lie beyond the purview of my book and yet nevertheless start to emerge in the work of artists who performed secretarial tasks as staff for leading antiquarians like Weng Fanggang. Huang Yi, a lead excavator of the Wu Liang Shrines, pioneered new forms of technical transfer between seal carving, epigraphy, and inscription, adapting the clerical calligraphy on

EPILOGUE

stelae for the designs and side markings of his seals while engraving scholarly accounts of his visits to stone monuments upon the surfaces of other desktop artifacts such as wooden wrist-rests.[82] Liuzhou 六舟 (the Buddhist monk Dashou 達受; 1791–1858), who amassed a collection of more than five hundred eave-end tiles and antique bricks, adapted the seal-carver's single-knife method to inscribe inkstones while also carving his calligraphy onto bamboo artifacts.[83] The monk at the same time experimented with rubbing techniques by incorporating refabricated bricks and self-carved inkstones into composite rubbing-paintings.[84] Chen Hongshou 陳鴻壽 (1768–1822), an associate of Huang Yi and fellow member of the "Eight Masters of the Xiling School," pioneered the entrepreneurial endorsement of "purple-sand" Yixing stoneware teapots (a brand of pottery already celebrated and inscribed by Zhang Dai), objects that were marketed as Man teapots (Man hu 曼壺).[85] Chen was personally involved in the production of Man teapots and appears to have inspired local potters to creatively imitate architectural monuments in their work—as with a Yixing water container that resembles the stone parapet of a Tang dynasty well in Liyang 溧陽.[86]

These artists each found in *ming* a means with which to transcend the boundaries between literature, calligraphy, epigraphy, seal carving, and craft, modeling a composite and multimedia art of writing. In each case, inscription no longer entails the forceful addition of words to a preformed artifact but rather the open-ended imbrication of thinking with making in craft practice—an acceptance of physical metamorphosis and chance.[87] Inscribed words emerge from embodied experiences of working with and responding to the mutability of things. Inscription does not circumscribe but partakes in this transformative manipulation of matter.[88]

BEYOND CLOSURE

Two years after inscribing his mortar, Gao Fenghan developed paralysis in his right arm and left official service to lodge in a Yangzhou temple. In 1741, Gao returned to his hometown in poverty and sickness after fourteen years in Jiangnan. Because of the severity of his illness and a string of natural disasters in Jiaozhou 膠州, Gao was forced to pawn prized inkstones and sell artifacts. The many difficulties Gao faced, from poverty to a short prison sentence and the paralysis of his right arm, fed into his own self-fashioning as he named himself an "Old Deformity" (Laobi 老痹) or

"Broken Man of the Dingsi Year" (Dingsi canren 丁巳殘人)—a move that extends to his identification with Sima Qian's castrated person in modeling *History of Inkstones* on the *Records of the Grand Historian*.[89]

History of Inkstones includes several inkstones that were carved or inscribed after the onset of Gao's right-arm paralysis in 1737, the second year of the Qianlong reign. The engraved calligraphy on these artifacts assumes a wildly cursive, broken, or almost trembling quality. Gao explicitly underscores that he carved these stones with his left hand, signing the slabs with variants of "inscribed by Fenghan with his left hand" (Fenghan zuoshou shu ming 鳳翰左手書銘), "inscribed by the left hand of the Nanfu Mountain Man" (Nanfu shanren zuoshou ming 南阜山人左手銘), "marked by the left hand of the Nanfu Mountain Man" (Nanfu shanren zuoshou zhi 南阜山人左手識), "signed in the Qianlong *dingsi* year by the Nanfu Mountain Man" (Qianlong dingsi Nanfu shanren zuoshou ti 乾隆丁巳南阜山人左手題). Gao similarly addresses his predicament in the short poems he engraved onto inkstones. The unstable flowing cursive of his inscription and signature on a "Half Moon Inkslab" (Banyue yan 半月硯) evokes the spontaneity and agitated improvisation of inky brushstrokes on paper, as if unencumbered by or at ease with the awkward material constraints of his substrate (figure E.9).[90] Gao's inscribed poem intones the

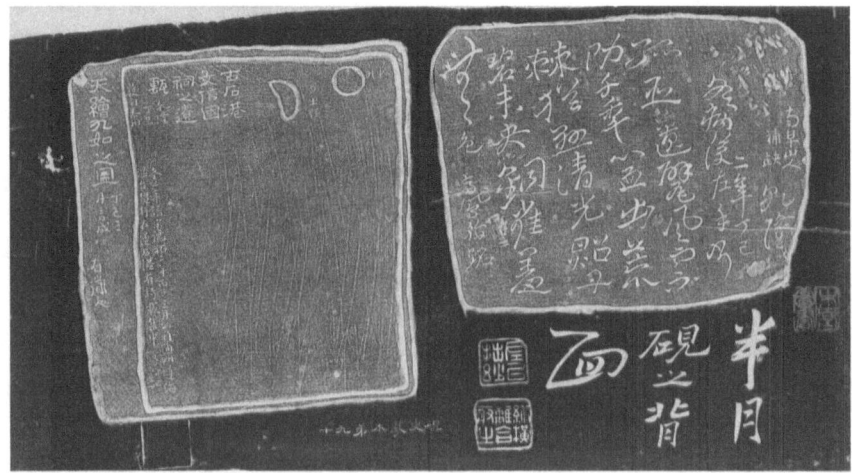

FIGURE E.9. Rubbing No. 90 from Gao Fenghan's *History of Inkstones*. Gao inscribed this "Half Moon Inkslab" 半月硯 after the onset of his paralysis in 1737. Source: Gao, *Yanshi*, 90.

resilience of this old Chengni clay brick found at a shrine to the Song loyalist Wen Tianxiang 文天祥 (1236–1283), the Duke of Xinguo 信國公, in Taizhou (Wen passed through Taizhou in 1276):

> The Nanfu Mountain Man mends deficiencies. I drafted this with my left hand following my illness in the winter of *dingsi*, the second year of the Qianlong reign.

> This leftover brick of a solitary minister is not broken by wind and rain,
> A thousand years of heart's blood seeps out of wild brambles,
> Hung in the clear light, it illuminates traces of red and green,
> Next to this a Weiyang or Bronze Finch tile would be ashamed by its lack of luster.
> Inscribed by Gao Fenghan.

> 南阜山人補缺。乾隆二年丁巳冬病後左手書。
> 孤臣遺甓風雨不汋，千年心血出荒棘 。
> 猶懸清光照丹碧，未央銅雀羞無色。
> 高鳳翰銘。[91]

Gao's fortuitous encounter with the brick occasions an implicit comparison between the torture of a loyalist martyr and the pain of his own recent hardships. His final signature "Inscribed by Gao Fenghan" is almost illegible, intimating the physical difficulties Gao now faced in grinding ink while constituting an inimitable claim of possession in an idiosyncratic calligraphic style.[92] The carved slab evokes a fragile sense of endurance within a scene of stark deprivation, an attempt to survive precarity through attachment to the tools that might yet render writing possible.

NOTES

Note: See the bibliography for abbreviations of multivolume Chinese compendia.

INTRODUCTION: THE MATTER OF INSCRIPTION

1. This line is drawn from *Fayan* 法言, 3.4; see Yang Xiong, *Exemplary Figures/Fayan*, trans. Michael Nylan (Seattle: University of Washington Press, 2013), 41.
2. David Knechtges, "From the Eastern Han Through the Western Jin (AD 25–317)," in *The Cambridge History of Chinese Literature, Vol 1: To 1375*, ed. Kang-I Sun Chang and Stephen Owen (Cambridge: Cambridge University Press, 2010), 138.
3. On temporal aporias, see Lynn A. Struve, "Introduction," in *Time, Temporality, and Imperial Transition: East Asia from Ming to Qing*, ed. Lynn A. Struve (Honolulu: Association for Asian Studies and University of Hawai'i Press, 2005), 3–30; Jonathan Hay, "The Suspension of Dynastic Time," in *Boundaries in China*, ed. John Hay (London: Reaktion, 1994), 172. For a discussion of changing approaches to ownership amid the breakup and dispersal of family collections, see Li Huiyi 李惠儀 [Wai-yee Li], "Shibian yu wanwu: lüelun Qing chu wenren de shenmei fengshang" 世變與玩物：略論清初文人的審美風尚, *Journal of the Institute of Literature and Philosophy* 中國文哲所研究集刊, Academica Sinica, no. 33 (September 2008): 1–40.
4. For a study of how these inscriptions participated in the symbolic construction and spatial organization of Wang Fuzhi's reclusive dwelling, see Wu Chengxue 吳承學 and Zhao Hongxiang 赵宏祥, "Wang Chuanshan guansheng ju tibi lian kaoshi" 王船山观生居题壁联考释, *Xueshu yanjiu* 学术研究 no. 4 (2014): 144–51. For a discussion and translation of the penultimate inscription in the sequence on a "South Facing Window" ("Nanchuang ming" 南窗銘), see Lynn A. Struve, *The Dreaming*

INTRODUCTION

Mind and the End of the Ming World (Honolulu: University of Hawai'i Press, 2019), 218–19. Wai-yee Li discusses and translates three other inscriptions (on an inkstick, inkstone cover, and tortoiseshell hairpin) from the sequence; see Wai-yee Li, *The Promise and Peril of Things: Literature and Material Culture* (New York: Columbia University Press, 2022), 226–28.

5. Lynn A. Struve, *The Southern Ming 1644–1662* (New Haven, CT: Yale University Press, 1984).
6. Wang addresses Yongli's fate explicitly in his inscription on a south-facing window; see Struve, *The Dreaming Mind and the End of the Ming World*, 218. On Wang's service for Yongli and experience of inter-dynastic war, see Zhang Hui 张晖, *Diguo de liuwang: Nan Ming shige yu zhanluan* 帝国的流亡：南明诗歌与战乱 (Beijing: Zhongguo shehui kexue chubanshe, 2014), 103–8.
7. Wang Fuzhi 王夫之, "Bi ming" 筆銘, in *Wang Chuanshan shiwen ji* 王船山詩文集 (Beijing: Zhonghua shuju, 2018), 9. 99.
8. The Palace Museum holds a famous "turtle-shaped" clay-fired inkslab dated to the Tang dynasty attesting to the antiquity of "turtle-shaped" (*guixing* 龜形) inkstone designs; see Wang Daiwen 王代文 and Cai Hongru 蔡鴻茹, eds., *Zhonghua guyan* 中華古硯 (Nanjing: Jiangsu guji chubanshe, 1999), 30. Turtle plastrons were the means through which the Shang and Zhou communicated with the dead.
9. Wang, "Yan ming" 硯銘, *Wang Chuanshan shiwen ji*, 9. 99. This narrative is recorded in a short preface that Wang Fuzhi composed for the inscription.
10. Wang, "Yan ming," 99.
11. Wang, "Mo ming" 墨銘, *Wang Chuanshan shiwen ji*, 9. 100; Wang, "Bige ming" 祕閣銘, *Wang Chuanshan shiwen ji*, 9. 100; Wang, "Yangai ming" 硯蓋銘, *Wang Chuanshan shiwen ji*, 9. 100.
12. For a classic survey of early Chinese approaches to inscription, see Tsuen-Hsuin Tsien, *Written on Bamboo and Silk: The Beginnings of Chinese Books and Inscriptions* (Chicago: University of Chicago Press, 2004).
13. See Bill Brown: "Often it is only some breakdown in your habitual interactions with the world that makes its materialities (and yours) suddenly meaningful." Bill Brown, "Materiality," in *Critical Terms for Media Studies*, ed. W. J. T. Mitchell and Mark B. N. Hansen (Chicago: University of Chicago Press, 2010), 60.
14. Benjamin Elman, *On Their Own Terms: Science in China, 1550–1900* (Cambridge, MA: Harvard University Press, 2005); Dagmar Schäfer, *The Crafting of the 10,000 Things: Knowledge and Technology in Seventeenth-Century China* (Chicago: University of Chicago Press, 2011).
15. Timothy Brook, *The Confusions of Pleasure: Commerce and Culture in Ming China* (Berkeley: University of California Press, 1998); Craig Clunas, *Superfluous Things: Material Culture and Social Status in Early Modern China* (Honolulu: University of Hawai'i Press, 2004); Rivi Handler-Spitz, *Symptoms of an Unruly Age: Li Zhi and Cultures of Early Modernity* (Seattle: University of Washington Press, 2017).
16. For a discussion of shifting attitudes toward literary immortality amid changes in publishing practices in early modern print culture, see Suyoung Son, *Writing for Print: Publishing and the Making of Textual Authority in Late Imperial China* (Cambridge, MA: Harvard University Asia Center, 2018). For an introduction to late imperial cultures of printing, see the essays in Cynthia J. Brokaw and Kai-wing Chow, eds., *Printing and Book Culture in Late Imperial China* (Berkeley: University

INTRODUCTION

of California Press, 2005). On the ascendancy of the imprint during the Ming, see Joseph McDermott, *A Social History of the Chinese Book: Books and Literati Culture in Late Imperial China* (Hong Kong: Hong Kong University Press, 2006).

17. On the prevalence of object markings in Ming China, see Craig Clunas, *Empire of Great Brightness: Visual and Material Cultures of Ming China, 1368–1644* (London: Reaktion, 2007), 196–97; Jonathan Hay, *Sensuous Surfaces: The Decorative Object in Early Modern China* (Honolulu: University of Hawai'i Press, 2010), 55–59; Dagmar Schäfer, "Inscribing the Artifact and Inspiring Trust: The Changing Role of Markings in the Ming Era," *East Asian Science, Technology and Society: An International Journal* 5 (2011): 239–65; Dagmar Schäfer, "Peripheral Matters: Selvage/Chef-de-piece Inscriptions on Chinese Silk Textiles," *UC Davis Law Review* 47, no. 2 (2013): 705–33.

18. Bonnie Honig raises a similar question in a comparative reading of Hannah Arendt and Donald Winnicott on durability: "For Winnicott, the capacity of objects to constitute a stable world derives not solely from their solidity, as Things, nor even from our fabrication of them. These are the suggestions of Arendt's phenomenology. The stability of Winnicott's transitional objects derives from their enchanted condensation of, and entry into, complicated sets of affective relations underwritten by certain affective, relational environments, and ultimately also by fantasy." Bonnie Honig, *Public Things: Democracy in Disrepair* (New York: Fordham University Press, 2017), 45–46.

19. Du Jun 杜濬, *Bianyatang quanji* 變雅堂全集, 5 vols. (China: s.n., 1853?; Harvard-Yenching Library Rare Book), 5. 17a–b.

20. Paul Kroll, *A Student's Dictionary of Classical and Medieval Chinese* (Leiden: Brill, 2017), 256.

21. In his "Inscription on a Mounded Tomb for Flowers" ("Huazhong ming" 花塚銘), Du similarly weighs the transformations writing engenders, imagining how the "souls" of interred stems, bundled together and buried in a tomb to the east of his thatched hut, might leave their skeletons behind to survive in literature: "You chrysanthemums, you plum blossoms, narcissus and osmanthus, desiccated lotus pods and fallen crabapple! With splendor comes the fall, without flourishing you would not fade away. Your bones are buried here, yet there is nowhere your soul might not go, perhaps transformed into sublime prose and true poetry?" 汝菊汝梅，汝水仙木樨，蓮房墜粉，海棠垂絲。有榮必落，無盛不衰。骨瘞於此，其魂氣無不之，其或化為至文與真詩乎。Du, *Bianyatang quanji*, 5. 18a–b.

22. While certain seventeenth-century inscriptions allude to or invoke Buddhist notions of "impermanence" (*wuchang* 無常), they dwell for the most part on what might be termed "worldly inconstancy," or material processes of ruination—and the ways in which such pressures modulate attachments to possessions and posthumous reputation—within the "mundane realm." The terms of my distinction, here, have been informed by Jie Shi, "'My Tomb Will Be Opened in Eight Hundred Years': A New Way of Seeing the Afterlife in Six Dynasties China," *Harvard Journal of Asiatic Studies* 72, no. 2 (2012): 244.

23. Historians of European literature—from Gotthold Ephraim Lessing (1729–1781) and Friedrich Schiller (1759–1805) to Geoffrey Hartman (1929–2016)—have found in the transition from inscriptions carved upon objects to detached or uninscribed inscriptions on paper evidence for the emergence of a modern poetic

INTRODUCTION

self-consciousness. For Lessing and Schiller, classical epigrams incorporated their monuments; the Romantic inscription on paper, by contrast, required a title to designate an external and absent substrate, creating an elegiac sense of self-division and estrangement from nature. Hartman builds upon these examples to read the modern lyric as a "monument to spontaneity," an inscribed poem that no longer coincides with a physical monument but with the "act and passion of its utterance." See Hartman's influential essay "Inscriptions and Romantic Nature Poetry" in Geoffrey Hartman, *The Unremarkable Wordsworth* (Minneapolis: University of Minnesota Press, 1987), 31–46. Hartman's arguments have been taken up by numerous other critics; see John Mackay, *Inscription and Modernity: From Wordsworth to Mandelstam* (Bloomington: Indiana University Press, 2006).

24. Here, for instance, we could also consider the Suzhou-based lens maker Sun Yunqiu 孫雲球 (ca. 1650–after 1681), who exploits the relationship between an inscribed message and its underlying substrate to probe the nuances of perception in his 1681 illustrated catalogue of optical devices, *A History of Lenses* (*Jingshi* 鏡史). The majority of the images in the catalogue are inscribed objects; see S. E. Kile and Kristina Kleutghen, "Seeing Through Pictures and Poetry: *A History of Lenses* (1681)," *Late Imperial China* 38, no. 1 (2017): 47–112.

25. Li Yu 李漁, "Meizi bei ming" 沒字碑銘, *Li Yu quanji* 李漁全集 (Hangzhou: Zhejiang guji chubanshe, 1991), 1: 2. 131. Li's "Inscription on a Stele with No Words" resembles designs in his landmark 1671 guide to everyday life, *Casual Expressions of Idle Feelings* (*Xianqing ouji* 閒情偶寄), bespoke devices that similarly perturb expectations of surface and solidity: whether a seal to make impressions in mounds of incense ash ("Liweng's incense seal" [Liweng xiangyin 笠翁香印]) or calligraphic placards fashioned from cheap wood and lacquer paint to imitate stone monuments.

26. Jonathan Hay makes the point that "inscriptional topographies" in the early modern decorative arts "are most commonly found in objects associated with the writing desk." Hay, *Sensuous Surfaces*, 205.

27. For an overview, see Pak-sheung Ng, "A Regional Cultural Tradition in Song China: 'The Four Treasures of the Study of the Southern Tang' ('Nan Tang wenfang sibao')," *Journal of Song-Yuan Studies* 46 (2016): 57–117. On inkstone inscription, see Lu Qingbin 盧慶濱 [Andrew Lo], "Su Shi yu yan wenhua" 蘇軾與硯文化, *Songdai wenxue yanjiu congkan* 宋代文學研究叢刊 8 (2002): 486. On ink, see Lu Qingbin, "Su Shi dui mo wenhua de gongxian" 蘇軾對墨文化的貢獻, *Songdai wenxue yanjiu congkan* 6 (December 2000): 409–29; Thomas Kelly, "The Death of an Artisan: Su Shi and Ink Making," *Harvard Journal of Asiatic Studies* 80, no. 2 (2020): 315–46.

28. For an introduction to late Ming transformations in seal carving, see Qianshen Bai, *Fu Shan's World: The Transformation of Chinese Calligraphy in the Seventeenth Century* (Cambridge, MA: Harvard University Asia Center, 2003).

29. For a discussion of this development as it pertains to inkstones, see Dorothy Ko, *The Social Life of Inkstones: Artisans and Scholars in Early Qing China* (Seattle: University of Washington Press, 2016), 190–91.

30. See Li, *The Promise and Peril of Things*; Sophie Volpp, *The Substance of Fiction: Literary Objects in China, 1550–1775* (New York: Columbia University Press, 2022).

31. Cao Xueqin, *The Story of the Stone: A Chinese Novel by Cao Xueqin in Five Volumes*, trans. David Hawkes (New York: Penguin, 1973), 1: 48. Recent scholarship on the novel's approach to materiality largely overlooks the significance of antiquarian

themes ("metal and stone"; object inscription) to focus instead on the book's relationship to the material culture of the Qing court. See Volpp, *The Substance of Fiction*, 109–68; Shang Wei, "Truth Becomes Fiction When Fiction Is True: The Story of the Stone and the Visual Culture of the Manchu Court," *Journal of Chinese Literature and Culture* 2, no. 1 (April 2015): 207–48. Shen Congwen 沈从文 (1902–1988) identified the significance of inscribed vessels in the novel in a pair of short articles from the 1960s, see Shen Congwen 沈从文, *Shen Congwen shuo wenwu: Qiwu pian* 沈从文说文物：器物篇 (Chongqing: Chongqing daxue chubanshe, 2014), 77–96.

32. For an overview of competing theories on the fate of the inkstone, see Wu Ligu 吴笠谷, *Mingyan bian* 名硯辨 (Beijing: Wenwu chubanshe, 2012), 83–117.

33. Roger Chartier, *Inscription and Erasure: Literature and Written Culture from the Eleventh to the Eighteenth Century*, trans. Arthur Goldhammer (Philadelphia: University of Pennsylvania Press, 2007), x.

34. Bill Brown, *Other Things* (Chicago: University of Chicago Press, 2015), 371.

35. The comments belong to Duan Yucai 段玉裁 (1735–1815); see Anthony Yu, "*Cratylus* and the *Xunzi* on Names," in *Comparative Journeys: Essays on Literature and Religion East and West*, ed. Anthony Yu (New York: Columbia University Press, 2009), 242.

36. Paul Goldin, "The Legacy of Bronzes and Bronze Inscriptions in Early Chinese Literature," in *A Sourcebook of Ancient Chinese Bronze Inscriptions*, ed. Paul Goldin and Constance A. Cook (Berkeley, CA: Society for the Study of Early China, 2016), lvi.

37. Wu Hung, "Practice and Discourse: Ritual Vessels in a Fourth-Century BCE Chinese Tomb," in *Vessels: The Object as Container*, ed. Claudia Brittenham (Oxford: Oxford University Press, 2019), 120, 138. On the self-referential principle of displaying aesthetic patterning "as an accomplishment *per se*," reflecting both the virtues of the ancestors eulogized and the donor's display of virtue in the expression of praise, see Martin Kern, "The Performance of Writing in Western Zhou China," in *The Poetics of Grammar and the Metaphysics of Sound and Sign*, ed. Sergio La Porta and D. Shulman (Leiden: Brill, 2010), 114.

38. Sun Xidan 孫希旦, ed., *Liji jijie* 禮記集解 (Beijing: Zhonghua shuju, 1989), 1250. For a discussion and translation of this passage from "Protocols of Sacrifice," see Goldin, "The Legacy of Bronzes and Bronze Inscriptions in Early Chinese Literature," lv–lxiv.

39. Timothy M. Davis, *Entombed Epigraphy and Commemorative Culture in Early Medieval China: A History of Early Muzhiming* (Leiden: Brill, 2015), 118.

40. See the definitions of the memorial and admonitory inscriptions in E. D. Edwards, "A Classified Guide to the Thirteen Classes of Chinese Prose," *Bulletin of the School of Oriental and African Studies* 12, no. 3–4 (1948): 781, 784. My introductory overview of *ming* as a literary genre is primarily intended to outline key features of the form as it was understood by late imperial writers. A full-length history of the genre lies beyond the scope of my study. See also James R. Hightower's cautionary comments: "Only confusion results from its [*ming*] use as the name of a literary genre." James R. Hightower, "The *Wen Hsüan* and Genre Theory," *Studies in Chinese Literature*, ed. John L. Bishop (Cambridge, MA: Harvard University Press, 1966), 153.

41. Davis, *Entombed Epigraphy and Commemorative Culture in Early Medieval China*, 92–93.

42. Martin Kern, "Early Chinese Literature, Beginnings Through Western Han," in Chang and Owen, *The Cambridge History of Chinese Literature*, 9.
43. Kern, "Early Chinese Literature, Beginnings Through Western Han," 11.
44. Kern, "Early Chinese Literature, Beginnings Through Western Han," 12; Edward L. Shaughnessy, *Sources of Western Zhou History: Inscribed Bronze Vessels* (Berkeley: University of California Press, 1991), 73–85.
45. Bruce Rusk, *Critics and Commentators: The Book of Poems as Classic and Literature* (Cambridge, MA: Harvard University Press, 2012), 82.
46. *Quan Hou Han wen* 全後漢文, in Yan Kejun 嚴可均, comp., *Quan shanggu sandai Qin Han sanguo liuchao wen* 全上古三代秦漢三國六朝文 (Beijing: Zhonghua shuju, 1958; repr. 1999), 74.5a.
47. Kenneth E. Brashier, "Text and Ritual in Early Chinese Stelae," in *Text and Ritual in Early China*, ed. Martin Kern (Seattle: University of Washington Press, 2005), 269. Cf. Davis, *Entombed Epigraphy and Commemorative Culture in Early Medieval China*, 104–5.
48. Mark Edward Lewis, *Honor and Shame in Early China* (Cambridge: Cambridge University Press, 2021), 173.
49. *Quan Hou Han wen*, 74.5a. Lu Ji 陸機 (261–303) similarly distinguishes the "stele" and "elegy" as memorial genres from the "inscription" and "needle" as monitory forms: "The stele unfurls ornament to match substance; the elegy swells with pent-up sorrow. / The inscription is broad and concise, gentle, and smooth; the needle represses, being clear and forceful." 碑披文以相質；誄纏綿而淒愴。銘博約而溫潤；箴頓挫而清壯. Lu Ji 陸機, *Lu Ji ji* 陸機集, ed. Jin Taosheng 金濤聲 (Beijing: Zhonghua shuju, 1982), 2. Stephen Owen, *Readings in Chinese Literary Thought* (Cambridge, MA: Harvard University Press, 1992), 132.
50. Liu Xie 劉勰 (ca. 465–ca. 520) in his seminal work, *Wenxin diaolong* 文心雕龍, for instance, moves his discussion of Western Zhou bronze inscription to his chapter on the "stele" (rather than his chapter on *ming*), noting: "The Zhou was a dynasty of great virtues, and inscriptions and elegies were written to commemorate them. . . . When in later times bronze artifacts became scarce, stelae were used instead as stone took the place of bronze; both are imperishable" 周世盛德，有銘誄之文 . . . 而庸器漸缺，故後代用碑，以石代金，同乎不朽. Liu Xie [Liu Hsieh], *The Literary Mind and the Carving of Dragons*, trans. Vincent Yu-chung Shih (Hong Kong: The Chinese University of Hong Kong Press, 2015), 85. Liu Xie 劉勰, *Wenxin diaolong jiaozhu shiyi* 文心雕龍校注拾遺, ed. Yang Mingzhao 楊明照 (Shanghai: Shanghai guji chubanshe, 1982), 100–101.
51. Martin Kern, *The Stele Inscriptions of Ch'in Shih-Huang: Text and Ritual in Early Chinese Imperial Representation* (New Haven, CT: American Oriental Society, 2000), 57.
52. Kern, *The Stele Inscriptions of Ch'in Shih-Huang*, 125.
53. For a study of *moya*, see Robert E. Harrist Jr., *The Landscape of Words: Stone Inscriptions from Early and Medieval China* (Seattle: University of Washington Press, 2008). On the relationship between mountain inscriptions and early stelae, see Davis, *Entombed Epigraphy and Commemorative Culture in Early Medieval China*, 105–11.
54. Knechtges, "From the Eastern Han Through the Western Jin," 138; Suh-jen Yang, "The Literary Merits of the Han (206 B.C.–A.D. 220) Stele Inscription" (PhD diss., University of Washington, 2007), 34–41.

INTRODUCTION

55. Mark Laurent Asselin, *A Significant Season: Cai Yong (ca. 133–192) and His Contemporaries* (New Haven, CT: American Oriental Society, 2010), 26–39. Cf. Davis, *Entombed Epigraphy and Commemorative Culture in Early Medieval China*, 111.
56. Asselin, *A Significant Season*, 282–84.
57. See, for instance, Harrist's discussion of the "virtual stele" on Mount Tie, in Harrist, *The Landscape of Words*, 215. Zhao Rong 趙榮 and Lothar Ledderose, eds., *Zhongguo fojiao shijing: Shaanxi sheng* 中國佛教石經：陝西省 (Wiesbaden: Harrassowitz Verlag; Hangzhou: China Academy of Art Press, 2020–).
58. Davis, *Entombed Epigraphy and Commemorative Culture in Early Medieval China*, 92. On the development of the form in the Tang, see Jessey J. C. Choo, *Inscribing Death: Burials, Representations, and Remembrance in Tang China* (Honolulu: University of Hawai'i Press, 2022).
59. Cao Cao 曹操, Cao Pi 曹丕, and Cao Zhi 曹植, *San Cao ji* 三曹集 (Changsha: Yuelu shushe, 1992), 178.
60. "As direct means to achieve posthumous immortality stone and metal had failed, but as enduring media on which to record words, they continued to prevail." Shi, "'My Tomb Will Be Opened in Eight Hundred Years,'" 241.
61. Rusk, *Critics and Commentators*, 77.
62. Boqun Zhou, "A Translation and Analysis of the Shanghai Museum Manuscript *Wu Wang Jian Zuo," *Monumenta Serica* 66, no. 1 (2018): 2.
63. "Wu Wang jianzuo" 武王踐阼, in *Da Dai liji huijiao jizhu* 大戴禮記彙校集注, ed. Huang Huaixin 黃懷信 (Xi'an: Sanqin chubanshe, 2005), 659. King Wu's inscriptions are preserved in a text entitled "King Wu Trod on the Eastern Stairs" ("Wu Wang jianzuo" 武王踐阼), transmitted in the Han compendium *Elder Dai's Record of Ritual* (*Da Dai liji* 大戴禮記), yet also survive on a bamboo manuscript from the Chu cultural area now held in the Shanghai Museum. See Zhou, "A Translation and Analysis of the Shanghai Museum Manuscript *Wu Wang Jian Zuo," 2.
64. "Wu Wang jianzuo," 659.
65. See also admonitory inscriptions preserved in epigraphic collections; Li Ling 李零, "Zhanguo niaoshu zhenming daigou kaoshi" 戰國鳥書箴銘帶鉤考釋, in *Li Ling zixuan ji* 李零自選集, ed. Li Ling (Guilin: Guangxi shifan daxue chubanshe, 1998), 273–77.
66. I have followed the transcription in Li Ling, "'Yuding bi' xinzheng: 'Shiliu jing' zhong de 'chiyou hai'" 魚鼎匕新證：〈十六經〉中的蚩尤醢, *Li Ling zixuan ji*, 76–83. This object has been discussed by a range of scholars; for an overview and introduction to the inscription, see Zang Kehe 臧克和, "'Yuding bi' mingwen youguan qiming xingzhi xinshi"《魚鼎匕》銘文有關器名性質新釋, *Kaogu yu wenwu* 考古與文物 5 (2004): 93–94; Zhan Yinxin 詹鄞鑫, "'Yuding bi' kaoshi"《魚鼎匕》考釋, *Zhongguo wenzi yanjiu* 中國文字研究 (2001): 175–79. For an image and rubbing of the spoon in Luo Zhenyu's 羅振玉 (1866–1940) collection, see Luo Zhenyu 羅振玉, *Zhensong tang jijin tu* 貞松堂吉金圖 (Dalian: Moyuan tang, 1935), 2: 42–43. A color image is included in *Zhongguo meishu quanji: Gongyi meishu bian: Qingtong qi* 中國美術全集：工藝美術編：青銅器, ed. Li Xueqin 李學勤 (Beijing: Wenwu chubanshe, 1985), 65. In 2010 another "fish cauldron ladle" bearing a similar inscription in the same format and calligraphic style was discovered in Shanxi, suggesting the spoon may have been serially produced from a mold. See Wu Zhenfeng 吳鎮烽, "'Yuding bi' xinshi" 魚鼎匕新釋, *Kaogu yu wenwu* 2 (2015): 54–57.

67. The increasingly tenuous associations of the literary inscription to rituals and sages became particularly apparent in the reception of the work of prolific Eastern Han writer Li You 李尤 (44–126), author of around 120 inscriptions for Emperor He 和帝 (88–106). Li is perhaps the only writer in the classical tradition whose posthumous fame derives primarily from his work in the *ming* form. Yu Guangrong 庾光蓉, "Li You shiji kaozheng" 李尤事迹考证, *Sichuan shifan daxue xuebao* 四川师范大学学报 24, no. 3 (1997): 124–27.
68. Mark Csikszentmihalyi, "Reimagining the Yellow Emperor's Four Faces," in *Text and Ritual in Early China*, 241.
69. Liu Xiang, *Garden of Eloquence/Shuoyuan* 說苑, trans. Eric Henry (Seattle: University of Washington Press, 2021), 612–13.
70. Late imperial anthologists grouped the "Metal Man Inscription" with a parodic companion piece, the "Anti-Metal Man Inscription" ("Fan Jinren ming" 反金人銘) attributed to the Western Jin writer Sun Chu 孫楚 (d. 293). If the metal man urges silence, Sun's "stone man" (*shiren* 石人), found in a Jin temple with a "large open mouth" 大張其口, and an inscription on his belly 而書其胸, vigorously promotes speech. Xu Shizeng 徐師曾, *Wenti mingbian* 文體明辨, in SKQSCMCS, jibu, vol. 312, 47. 116a.
71. Later writers treated the "Metal Man Inscription" as a template for inscriptions on the "mouth" itself, whether Fu Xuan 傅玄 (217–278) in his "Copying the Metal Man Inscription to Write a Mouth Inscription" ("Ni Jinren ming zuo kouming" 擬金人銘作口銘) or Xiao Ziliang 蕭子良 (460–494) in his "Mouth Inscription" ("Kou ming" 口銘). The admonition to be "cautious in speaking" pervades later approaches to inscription, yet it would become a guiding precept in a particular sub-genre named the "Inscription Placed to the Right of My Seat" (Zuoyouming 座右銘); see Li Nailong 李乃龙, "Cui Yuan 'Zuo you ming' rensheng guan de lilun dise—jian xi zuo you ming de wenti yiyi" 崔瑗《座右銘》人生觀的理論底色—兼析座右銘的文體意义, *Henan daxue xuebao (shehuikexue ban)* 河南大学学报（社会科学学报）46, no. 2 (2006): 79–81. On the development of this form in later periods, see Thomas J. Mazanec, "Of Admonition and Address: Right-Hand Inscriptions (*Zuoyouming*) from Cui Yuan to Guanxiu," *Tang Studies* 38, no. 1 (2020): 28–56.
72. Jesper Svenbro, *Phrasikleia: An Anthropology of Reading in Ancient Greece* (Ithaca, NY: Cornell University Press, 1993), 30.
73. In addition to Cui Yuan's 崔瑗 (77–142) *zuoyouming*, the other *ming* preserved in *Wenxuan* are inscriptions on cliffs, mountain passes, or architectonic structures such as Lu Chui's 陸倕 (470–526) piece on a "water clock" (*louke* 漏刻). Hightower, "The *Wen Hsüan* and Genre Theory," 153.
74. For an introduction to the sub-genre of mirror inscriptions as it developed in the late classical period, see Jie Shi, "Ornament, Text, and the Creation of *Sishen* Mirrors in Late Western Han and Xin China (ca. 50 BCE–23 CE)," *Monumenta Serica* 68, no. 1 (2020): 29–68.
75. Han Yu 韓愈, "Yi yan ming" 瘞硯銘, in *Han Changli wenji jiaozhu* 韓昌黎文集校注, ed. Ma Qichang 馬其昶 (Shanghai: Shanghai guji chubanshe, 2018), 8. 630.
76. Xiaofei Tian, "Cultural Politics of Old Things in Mid-Tang China," *Journal of the American Oriental Society* 140, no. 2 (2020): 333.
77. Lu, "Su Shi yu yan wenhua"; Lu Qingbin, "Sumen xueshi yanming chutan" 蘇門學士硯銘初探, in *Dierjie Songdai wenxue guoji yantaohui lunwenji* 第二屆宋代文學國

INTRODUCTION

際研討會論文集, ed. Mo Lifeng 莫礪鋒 (Nanjing: Jiangsu jiaoyu chubanshe, 2003), 739–68.

78. Extant slabs acquired by Qing emperors bearing Su's signature survive in the collections of the National Palace Museum; see Lu, "Su Shi yu yan wenhua," 489–90.
79. For a literary introduction to Ouyang Xiu's colophons, see Ronald Egan, *The Problem of Beauty: Aesthetic Thought and Pursuits in Northern Song Dynasty China* (Cambridge, MA: Harvard University Press, 2006), 7–59. For an introduction to rubbings, see Wu Hung, "On Rubbings: Their Materiality and Historicity," in *Writing and Materiality in China: Essays in Honor of Patrick Hanan*, ed. Judith T. Zeitlin and Lydia H. Liu (Cambridge, MA: Harvard University Asia Center, 2003), 29–72. For an overview of Song antiquarianism, see Ye Guoliang 葉國良, *Songdai jinshixue yanjiu* 宋代金石學研究 (Taipei: Taiwan shufang, 2011). For a study of Ouyang's place in the intellectual history of Northern Song epigraphy, see Jeffrey Moser, "Learning with Metal and Stone: On the Discursive Formation of Song Epigraphy," in *Powerful Arguments: Standards of Validity in Late Imperial China*, ed. Martin Hofmann, Joachim Kurtz, and Ari Daniel Levine (Leiden: Brill, 2020), 135–76. See also Yunchiahn C. Sena, *Bronze and Stone: The Cult of Antiquity in Song Dynasty China* (Seattle: University of Washington Press, 2019).
80. One case study that has been used to investigate possible intersections between *jinshixue* and the creation of *ming* on objects in this period (including inkstones) concerns the grave goods found in the recently excavated Northern Song Lü 呂 family cemetery. For introductions, see Hsu Ya-hwei 許雅惠, "Songdai shidafu de jinshi shoucang yu liyi shijian—yi Lantian Lüshi jiazu wei li" 宋代士大夫的金石收藏與禮儀實踐——以藍田呂氏家族為例, *Zhejiang daxue yishu yu kaogu yanjiu* 浙江大學藝術與考古研究 13 (2018): 131–64.
81. For an illuminating introduction to the relationship between epigraphy and the act of making new inscriptions in the High Qing, see Hye-shim Yi, "From Epigraphy to Inscribing Objects: Recarving Ancient Relics into Inkstones," *Orientations* 51, no. 6 (November/December 2020): 64–71.
82. Su Shi 蘇軾, "Kong Yifu longweiyan ming" 孔毅甫龍尾硯銘, in *Su Shi wenji jiaozhu* 蘇軾文集校注, in vols. 10–20 of *Su Shi quanji jiaozhu* 蘇軾全集校注, ed. Zhang Zhilie 張志烈, Ma Defu 馬德富, and Zhou Yukai 周裕鍇 (Shijiazhuang: Hebei renmin chubanshe, 2010), 12: 19. 2064.
83. Zhiyi Yang, "Dialectics of Spontaneity: Art, Nature, and Persona in the Life and Works of Su Shi (1037–1101)" (PhD diss., Princeton University, 2013), 185; Zhang Yuanqing 張元慶, *Gudai shiren yu yan zhi yanjiu* 古代士人與硯之研究 (Taibei: Wenjin chubanshe, 2005), 132.
84. Lu, "Su Shi yu yan wenhua," 486–87.
85. Su Shi, *Dongpo tiba jiaozhu* 東坡題跋校注, ed. Tu Youxiang 屠友祥 (Shanghai: Shanghai yuandong chubanshe, 2011), 305.
86. This strategy not only informs Su's personification of the Dragon Tail for Kong but also led to a full-length biography of the Dragon Tail as a political recluse, "The Biography of Luowen," and an extended prosopopoeia in his later poem, "The Song for the Dragon Tail."
87. Su, *Dongpo tiba jiaozhu*, 307, 313.
88. Igor Kopytoff, "The Cultural Biography of Things: Commoditization as Process," in *The Social Life of Things: Commodities in Cultural Perspective*, ed. Arjun Appadurai

(Cambridge: Cambridge University Press, 1986), 64 (italics mine). For engagements with Kopytoff's approach in the study of premodern Chinese literature, see Judith T. Zeitlin, "The Cultural Biography of a Musical Instrument: Little Hulei as Sounding Object, Antique, Prop, and Relic," *Harvard Journal of Asiatic Studies* 69 (2009): 395–441; Huijun Mai, "The Double Life of the Scallop: Anthropomorphic Biography, 'Pulu,' and the Northern Song Discourse on Things," *Journal of Song-Yuan Studies* 49 (2020): 149–205.

89. David Wengrow, "Introduction: Commodity Branding in Archaeological and Anthropological Perspectives," in *Cultures of Commodity Branding*, ed. Andrew Bevan and David Wengrow (London: Routledge, 2010), 15.
90. On elegance and vulgarity, see Wang Hung-tai 王鴻泰, "Ya su de bianzheng—Mingdai shangwan wenhua de liuxing yu shishang guanxi de jiaocuo" 雅俗的辯證—明代賞玩文化的流行與士商關係的交錯, *Xinshi xue* 新史學 17, no. 4 (2006): 73–143; Wai-yee Li, "The Collector, the Connoisseur, and Late-Ming Sensibility," *T'oung Pao* 81, no. 4 (1995): 269–302.
91. An inscription in this sense resembles what Bernhard Siegert terms a "cultural technique" (*Kulturtechnik*). "Essentially, cultural techniques are conceived of as operative chains that precede the media concepts they generate. . . . As a historically given micronetwork of technologies and techniques, cultural techniques are the 'exteriority/materiality of the signifier.'" Bernhard Siegert, *Cultural Techniques: Grids, Filters, Doors, and Other Articulations of the Real*, trans. Geoffrey Winthrop-Young (New York: Fordham University Press, 2015), 11. Also: "The study of cultural techniques, however, is not aimed at removing the anthropological differences between human animal and nonhuman animal . . . rather, it is concerned with decentering the distinction between human and nonhuman by insisting on the radical technicity of this distinction." Siegert, *Cultural Techniques*, 8.
92. In a short preface printed with this inscription, Xu explicitly identifies the cash value of the inkstone, noting that he bought this specimen at a local stall for a sum of 250 strings of cash, yet that his associate Wang Yin 王寅 (n.d.), a roving Huizhou scholar-merchant (and close associate of the figures I discuss in chapter 2), claimed he could sell it for 1,500 strings of cash. The gap between what Xu paid and the sum he is told he could potentially make measures the non-calculating "authenticity" of his attachment to the inkstone. Xu's performance of spontaneity is first contingent on recalling misguided navigation of the market. Xu Wei 徐渭, "Sheshi yanming bing xu" 歙石硯銘并序, in *Xu Wei ji* 徐渭集 (Beijing: Zhonghua shuju, 2017), 22. 590
93. Modern editions of Xu's poetry and prose parse the second line: "How can I guarantee that you eventually end up with [my person?]" 安保其終於吾人耶. Ming commentators, however, break the line after "me" 吾, underscoring the parallel between Xu's apostrophe to the rock ("Are you stone? Can you forget your feelings?" 石耶？能忘情耶？) and his final self-interrogation, which could also be construed as the rock's prosopopoeia to its interlocutor ("Are you human? Do you have feelings?" 人耶？能有情耶？). Lu Yunlong 陸雲龍, ed., *Huangming shiliu jia xiaopin* 皇明十六家小品 (Beijing: Beijing tushuguan chubanshe, 1997), 1: 387.
94. Xu, "Sheshi yanming bing xu," 590.
95. Xu, "Sheshi yanming bing xu," 590.

INTRODUCTION

96. Xu visited Hu Zongxian in Huizhou in 1562; see Xu Shuofang 徐朔方, ed., *Wan Ming qujia nianpu* 晚明曲家年譜 (Hangzhou: Zhejiang guji chubanshe, 1993), 109.
97. Bai Juyi 白居易, "Buneng wangqing yin" 不能忘情吟, in *Bai Juyi quanji* 白居易全集, ed. Ding Ruming 丁如明 and Nie Shimei 聶世美 (Shanghai: Shanghai guji chubanshe, 1999), 682. For a full translation, see Arthur Waley, *More Translations from the Chinese* (New York: Knopf, 1919), 93–95. The poem in turn alludes to a medieval anecdote, see Liu I-ch'ing, *Shih-shuo Hsin-yü: A New Account of Tales of the World*, trans. Richard B. Mather (Ann Arbor: University of Michigan Press, 2002), 347. I am grateful to Yan Weitian for sharing his thoughts on this inscription.
98. Bai, "Buneng wangqing yin," 682.
99. Bai, "Buneng wangqing yin," 682.
100. For this reading, see Zhu Liangzhi 朱良志, *Wanshi de fengliu* 頑石的风流 (Beijing: Zhonghua shuju, 2016), 74–75.
101. Ming commentators read this ending as an "indirect criticism" (*feng* 諷); see Lu, *Huangming shiliu jia xiaopin*, 1: 387.
102. Wang Gang 王鋼, *Xu Wei* 徐渭 (Taibei: Zhishufang chubanshe, 1993), 200.
103. The "She County Stone" was not the only inkslab Xu inscribed in jail. He also kept a small rock from the Duan Brook in Guangdong (a historical rival to the Dragon Tail of She County) with him upon which he wrote the following message: "If you follow me in expounding upon the *Changes* and working upon the *Documents*, then when among clear streams and verdant hills, I'd set you apart. It's like the saying if Xiaobai didn't forget the belt hook, then Zhong wouldn't have forgotten the caged prison cart" 演《易》治《書》，汝則從予；白水蒼山，我寧不汝俱。譬諸小白勿忘帶鉤，仲勿忘檻車. This inscription wryly alludes to Xu's imprisonment both in the image of the "caged prison cart" (in which Duke Huan retrieved Guan Zhong from the vanquished state of Lu) and in a reference to the *Changes*, an allusion to the *Yijing* 易經 and the term *yi* 易 with which Xu described his psychological malady. See Xu, "Duanxi yanming (xiansheng xieru yuzhong zhe)" 端溪硯銘（先生攜入獄中者）, in *Xu Wei ji*, 18. 990.
104. On this issue, see Ivan Drpic, *Epigram, Art, and Devotion in Later Byzantium* (Cambridge: Cambridge University Press, 2016), 7–9. On graffiti, see Juliet Fleming, *Graffiti and the Writing Arts of Early Modern England* (London: Reaktion, 2001).
105. See Hay's comments: "[Inscription] also introduced into decorative surface an aural dimension, for the Chinese reader often chanted out the text while reading, especially in the case of poetry." Hay, *Sensuous Surfaces*, 205.
106. Hay, *Sensuous Surfaces*, 207.
107. Hay, *Sensuous Surfaces*, 205–7. Unlike Hay, my book does not deal with inscriptional practices at the Qing court, a complex topic that merits a standalone study. For an introduction, see Nicole T. C. Chiang. *Emperor Qianlong's Hidden Treasures: Reconsidering the Collection of the Qing Imperial Household* (Hong Kong: Hong Kong University Press, 2019).
108. Ko, *Social Life of Inkstones*, 189–203.
109. For relevant sources on this case, see Deng Zhicheng 鄧之誠, "Ma Xianglan xiaoyin" 馬湘蘭小印, in *Zhongguo yinlun leibian: xiudingban* 中國印論類編：修訂版, ed. Huang Dun 黃惇 (Beijing: Rongbaozhai chubanshe, 2019), 254–55.
110. Christina Lupton, *Knowing Books: The Consciousness of Mediation in Eighteenth-Century Britain* (Philadelphia: University of Pennsylvania Press, 2012), 10.

111. Lisa Gitelman, *Scripts, Grooves, and Writing Machines: Representing Technology in the Edison Era* (Stanford, CA: Stanford University Press, 1999), 2. For Gitelman's claim that the "study of inscriptions" uniquely shows "the realm of writing and reading, of symbolic action and experience, in its proximity to objects and machines," see Gitelman, *Scripts*, 10–13.
112. Hongnam Kim, *The Life of a Patron: Zhou Lianggong (1612–1672) and the Painters of Seventeenth-Century China* (New York: China Institute in America, 1996); Zhu Tianshu 朱天曙 and Meng Han 孟晗, *Zhou Lianggong nianpu changbian* 周亮工年譜長編 (Shanghai: Shanghai shuhua chubanshe, 2021).
113. Zhongguo wenfang sibao quanji bianji weiyuanhui 中國文房四寶全集編輯委員會, ed., *Zhongguo wenfang sibao quanji 2: yan* 中國文房四寶全集2: 硯 (Beijing: Beijing chubanshe, 2007), 133.
114. Cai Hongru 蔡鴻茹, *Zhonghua guyan: 100 jiang* 中华古砚100讲 (Tianjin: Baihua wenyi chubanshe, 2007), 29–31. See also Tianjin bowuguan 天津市藝術博物館, ed., *Tianjin bowuguan cang yan* 天津市藝術博物館藏硯 (Beijing: Wenwu chubanshe, 2012), 67. This inkstone has also been discussed by Hyeshim Yi, "The Calligraphic Art of Chen Hongshou (1768–1822) and the Practice of Inscribing in the Middle Qing" (PhD diss., University of California Los Angeles, 2019), 106.
115. For a detailed analysis of the trend toward personally carved inscriptions on inkstones in the eighteenth century and the applicability of seal-carving techniques to inscriptions, see Yi, "The Calligraphic Art of Chen Hongshou," 95–114.
116. See Zhu Chuanrong 朱傳榮, ed., *Xiaoshan Zhushi cang yan xuan* 蕭山朱氏藏硯選 (Beijing: Sanlian chubanshe, 2012), 44–45. On the possibility that Zhou Lianggong carved his own seals, see Fang Quji 方去疾, *Ming Qing zhuanke liupai yinpu* 明清篆刻流派印譜 (Shanghai: Shanghai shuhua chubanshe, 1981), 56. The Anhui Provincial Museum also holds an inkstone bearing an inscription in seal script attributed to Zhou Lianggong; see Zhongguo wenfang sibao quanji bianji weiyuanhui, ed., *Zhongguo wenfang sibao quanji 2: yan*, 150.
117. Gao Fenghan was a follower of Zhang Zhen. Cai, *Zhonghua guyan*, 31.
118. Zhongguo wenfang sibao quanji bianji weiyuanhui, ed., *Zhongguo wenfang sibao quanji 1: mo* 中國文房四寶全集1: 墨 (Beijing: Beijing chubanshe, 2007), 90. On Zhou's handmade brushes, see Zhou Lianggong 周亮工, "Yu Ni'an gong" 與倪闇公, in *Laigu tang ji* 賴古堂集, ed. Li Hualei 李花蕾 (Shanghai: Huadong shifan daxue chubanshe, 2009), 20. 389–390. The word "inscription" (*ming*) had been used to describe labels stamped onto inksticks since at least the Northern Song period.
119. Zhou Shaoliang's supposition appears to be based on his comparison of the Palace Museum inkstick with a reference to another Zhou Lianggong ox-tongue inkstick in the Qing dynasty collector Xu Kang's 徐康 (n.d.) inventory *Yusou molu* 窳叟墨錄 that bears the markings: "A Prize Appraised by Master Liyuan" 櫟園先生珍賞 and "Made by the Laigu Studio" 賴古堂製. Zhou Shaoliang suggests this inkstick was likely made as a gift by another patron who sought to siphon Zhou Lianggong's fame as a collector and aficionado of ink. Zhou Shaoliang 周紹良, *Zhou Shaoliang xumo xiaoyan* 周紹良蓄墨小言, ed. Zhou Qiyu 周启瑜 (Beijing: Zijincheng chubanshe, 2009), 41.
120. Zhou Shaoliang, *Zhou Shaoliang xumo xiaoyan*, 39–40.

INTRODUCTION

121. Wu Weiye 吳偉業, "Zhou Liyuan you mopi, changxu mo wanzhong, suichu yi jiu jiao zhi, zuo jimo shi. Youren Wang Ziya hua qishi, manfu er lü" 周櫟園有墨癖，嘗蓄墨萬種，歲除以酒澆之，作祭墨詩. 友人王紫崖話其事，漫賦二律, in *Wu Meicun quanji* 吳梅村全集, ed. Li Xueying 李學穎 (Shanghai: Shanghai guji chubanshe, 1990), 6. 182.

122. Zhou Lianggong, "Dinghai chuxi dusu Shaowu cheng lou, yongye buchuang, chengshi sizhang" 丁亥除夕獨宿邵武城樓，永夜不寐，成詩四章, *Laigu tang ji*, 7. 152. The eminent collector Song Luo 宋犖 (1634–1714) treasured poems from Zhou's sacrifices as relics into old age: "Until now, my old things have all scattered away, yet of my left-over drafts I've still preserved my poems on the inkstick sacrifice" 即今舊物俱零落，遺草猶存祭墨篇. Zhou Shaoliang, *Zhou Shaoliang xumo xiaoyan*, 40.

123. Zhou Lianggong, "Shu Wu Zunsheng yinpu qian" 書吳尊生印譜前, in *Yinren zhuan* 印人傳, in *Zhou Lianggong quanji* 周亮工全集, ed. Zhu Tianshu (Nanjing: Fenghuang chubanshe, 2008), vol. 5, 3. 128. For discussions of Zhou's comments, see Kim, *The Life of a Patron*, 73; Bai, *Fu Shan's World*, 58. Zhou offers a variant of this claim (one that puns on his studio name Laigu 賴古) in another vignette: "I once said that the study of characters has become mired in confusion, only one thread has been preserved in seals that *rely on the ancients* (*laigu*)" 余嘗言字學迷謬耳，惟賴古印章存其一綫. Zhou, "Shu Shen Shimin yinzhang qian" 書沈石民印章前, *Yinren zhuan*, 2. 84.

124. Zhu Tianshu, *Ganjiu: Zhou Lianggong jiqi* Yinren zhuan *yanjiu* 感旧：周亮工及其《印人传》研究 (Beijing: Beijing daxue chubanshe, 2013); Thomas Kelly, "Impressions of Loss: Writing and Memory in *Biographies of Seal Carvers*," *Asia Major* 36, no. 1 (2023): 1–52.

125. On the book-burning episode, see Chen Shengyu 陈圣宇, "Zhou Lianggong wannian fenshu riqi quekao" 周亮工晚年焚书日期确考, *Gudian wenxian yanjiu* 古典文献研究 11 (2008): 541–544.

126. Zhou, "Yu Huang Jishu lun yinzhang shu" 與黃濟叔論印章書, *Laigu tang ji*, 19. 361.

127. Zhou, "Huang Jishu yu ren tong xingzi, xian ruolu yizai yu, jinri debai, fu ershi song qi huan li. Tong Zhilu, Yuanci fu" 黃濟叔與人同姓字，陷若盧一載余，今日得白，賦二詩送其還里。同芝麓園次賦, *Laigu tang ji*, 10. 221.

128. Zhou, "Huang Jishu yu ren tong xingzi," 221.

129. See, for instance, Thomas Ford's discussion of Freud's "Note on the 'Mystic Writing Pad'" (a wax "imprint receiving device" that retains layers of former traces yet can also be wiped clean): "But if memory is to speak to the present, its medium also needs to remain receptive to the new, and therefore to be capable of forgetting… the trace system of memory requires transience as much as permanence." Thomas H. Ford, *Wordsworth and the Poetics of Air* (Cambridge: Cambridge University Press, 2018), 85.

130. This carver's name was Xu Zhenmu 徐真木 (n.d.). Zhou, "Shu Xu Shibai yinzhang qian" 書徐士白印章前, *Yinren zhuan*, 2. 99.

131. Simon Leys, *The Hall of Uselessness: Collected Essays* (New York: New York Review of Books, 2013), 295.

132. Leys, *The Hall of Uselessness*, 298.

133. Leys, *The Hall of Uselessness*, 295.

INTRODUCTION

134. Cited in Leys, *The Hall of Uselessness*, 301.
135. Duncan Campbell, "Zhang Dai's Passionate Search for Orchid Pavilion," *Script and Print* 29, no. 1–4 (2005): 38. Shang Wei 商伟, *Tixie mingsheng: Cong Huanghe lou dao Fenghuang tai* 题写名胜：从黄鹤楼到凤凰台 (Beijing: Xinhua shudian, 2020), 178–81.
136. See Johanna Drucker: [materiality is composed of] "two major intertwined strands: that of a relational, insubstantial, and nontranscendent difference and that of a phenomenological, apprehendable, immanent substance." Johanna Drucker, *The Visible Word: Experimental Typography and Modern Art, 1909–1923* (Chicago: University of Chicago Press, 1994), 43. See also Matthew G. Kirschenbaum: "Materiality consists… in a sustainable dialectic between relational and contingent social values as they are expressed through various ideologies and economies of production on the one hand, and experiential, physiological, ultimately *bodily* encounters with incarnate phenomena on the other." Matthew G. Kirschenbaum, *Mechanisms: New Media and the Forensic Imagination* (Cambridge, MA: MIT Press, 2012), 10.

1. ON REMNANT THINGS

1. On Zhang Dai's biography, see Hu Yimin 胡益民, *Zhang Dai pingzhuan* 张岱评传 (Nanjing: Nanjing daxue chubanshe, 2009); She Deyu 佘德余, *Dushi wenren: Zhang Dai zhuan* 都市文人：張岱传 (Hangzhou: Zhejiang renmin chubanshe, 2021). For an English introduction to his life and work, see Jonathan D. Spence, *Return to Dragon Mountain: Memories of a Late Ming Man* (London: Penguin Books, 2008).
2. Ford, *Wordsworth and the Poetics of Air*, 90.
3. Zhang Dai 張岱, "Ershiba you ming bing xu" 二十八友銘并序, in *Zhang Dai shiwen ji (zengdingben)* 張岱詩文集（增訂本）, ed. Xia Xianchun 夏咸淳 (Shanghai: Shanghai chubanshe, 2014), 5. 403.
4. For Zhang's reflections on the temporal aporias of dynastic transition (the sense of living between two orders of time), see his essay on a utopian calendar, Zhang, "Taoyuan li xu" 桃源曆序, *Zhang Dai shiwen ji*, 1. 200.
5. While Zhang Dai's inscriptions are largely devoted to studio objects and desktop implements, he also inscribed local stelae. In his "dream reminiscences" on monuments for the "Dragon Spurt Pool" (Longpen chi 龍噴池) and "Yanghe Spring" (Yanghe quan 陽和泉) in Shaoxing, Zhang explicitly foregrounds tensions between claims to inscriptive permanence and ironic accounts of the extractive violence behind human efforts to possess water. His new inscription on the Yanghe Spring 陽和泉 (named after his great-grandfather's sobriquet) struggles to efface an earlier stone stele that accused the Zhang family of covertly seeking to appropriate this local mountain spring through inscription ([the prior stele read:] "this stone has been erected to name the site for fear [the Zhangs] might try to steal it" 立石署之，懼其奪也). Zhang Dai, "Longpen chi" 龍噴池, in *Tao'an mengyi; Xihu mengxun* 陶菴夢憶；西湖夢尋, ed. Lu Wei 路偉 and Zheng Lingfeng 鄭凌峰 (Hangzhou: Zhejiang guji chubanshe, 2018), 3. 43; "Yanghe quan" 陽和泉, *Tao'an mengyi*, 3. 40.

1. ON REMNANT THINGS

6. Zhang, "Shen Meigang" 沈梅岡, *Tao'an mengyi*, 2. 30. The vignette "Shen Meigang" in *Dream Reminiscences* largely copies Zhang Yuanbian's preface to his two inscriptions, see Zhang Yuanbian 張元忭, "Shen Jijian shouzhi wenju zongshan ming you xu" 沈給諫手製文具椶杉銘有序, in *Zhang Yuanbian ji* 張元忭集, ed. Qian Ming 錢明 (Shanghai: Shanghai guji chubanshe, 2015), 14. 356–57.
7. Zhang, "Shen Meigang," *Tao'an mengyi*, 2. 30.
8. For the full-length tomb inscription, see Zhang Yuanbian, "Nanjing youtong zheng qian like jishizhong Kuaiji Shen gong zhiming" 南京右通政前禮科給事中會稽沈公志銘, *Zhang Yuanbian ji*, 10. 262–65.
9. Zhang Yuanbian's epitaph, for instance, makes no mention of Shen Meigang's craftsmanship during incarceration.
10. On Zhang Dai's critique of "flattering epitaphs," see Zhang, "Zhou Wanwei muzhiming" 周宛委墓志銘, *Zhang Dai shiwen ji*, 5. 377. In lamenting the "lengthy tracts" carved onto contemporaneous gravestones, Zhang invoked the lessons of "the ancients," claiming that the "more concise" 愈簡 the inscription, "the more exquisite" 愈妙 it could be, concluding that "one phrase was enough to earn fame in the world" 一語名世. Zhang Dai, *Kuaiyuan daogu; Guanlang qiqiao lu* 快園道古；琯朗乞巧錄, ed. Lu Wei and Zheng Lingfeng (Hangzhou: Zhejiang guji chubanshe, 2019), 2. 38.
11. On Zhang Yuanbian's fame as a moralistic protestor, see Zhang, "Jiazhuan" 家傳, *Zhang Dai shiwen ji*, 4. 332–33.
12. The "gentleman" is Su Wu. A *maojie* 旄節, or staff ornamented with yaktail streamers, was carried by official emissaries. Shen Shu served as a supervising secretary (*jishizhong* 給事中) in the Office of Scrutiny for Rites (Li ke 禮科).
13. Zhang, "Shen Meigang," 30.
14. Su Wu was punished with starvation for refusing to submit to the Xiongnu, yet he survived by eating snow and bits of felt.
15. Zhang, "Shen Meigang," 30. For a partial translation and discussion of this essay, see Philip Kafalas, *In Limpid Dream: Nostalgia and Zhang Dai's Reminiscences of the Ming* (Manchester: Eastbridge Books, 2007), 72.
16. Zhang Yuanbian's epitaph discusses this issue in more detail: Zhang Yuanbian, "Nanjing youtong zheng qian like jishizhong Kuaiji Shen gong zhiming," 264. Zhang Dai records this anecdote in Zhang, *Kuaiyuan daogu*, 16. 231.
17. Zhang, *Kuaiyuan daogu*, 16. 231. For variant transcriptions of this anecdote see Zhang Dai, *Sanbuxiu tuzan* 三不朽圖贊, ed. Gong Huxia 公戶夏 (Hangzhou: Zhejiang guji chubanshe, 2017), 56.
18. Deng Zhicheng, *Gudong suoji* 古董瑣記 (Beijing: Renmin chubanshe, 2012), 7. 258.
19. Xu Wei, "Zhu bige ming" 竹祕閣銘, *Xu Wei ji*, 22. 593; Xu Wei, "Zhu bige ming" 竹秘閣銘, *Xu Wei ji*, 19. 992.
20. After helping secure Xu's release from prison in 1573, Yuanbian invited Xu to participate in the compilation of the *Kuaiji Gazetteer* (*Kuaiji xianzhi* 會稽縣志) in 1575. See Zhang Yuanbian, "Kuaiji xianzhi xu" 會稽縣志序, *Zhang Yuanbian ji*, 2. 36–37.
21. Zhang, *Sanbuxiu tuzan*, 56. This collection also includes portraits of Xu Wei and Zhang Yuanbian but not of the artisan Zhang Yingyao. For a study of the book, see Duncan Campbell, "Mortal Ancestors, Immortal Images: Zhang Dai's Biographical

1. ON REMNANT THINGS

Portraits," *PORTAL: Journal of Multidisciplinary International Studies* 9, no. 3 (November 2012): 1–26.

22. Extant artifacts attest to Zhang Yuanbian's fame as an author of inscriptions. See a surviving inkstone inscribed by Yuanbian owned by the Zhu family of Xiaoshan in Zhu Chuanrong, ed., *Xiaoshan Zhushi cang yan xuan*, 112–14.
23. Zhang, *Kuaiyuan daogu*, 2. 35.
24. Zhang, "Songhua shi" 松化石, *Tao'an mengyi*, 7. 113. I follow Lu Wei and Zheng Lingfeng's correction of *hua* 花 to *hua* 化. I also follow their suggestion that the reference to Xiaojiang 瀟江 in this vignette is a mis-transcription of Qingjiang 清江.
25. On "pine-turned-stone," see Lin Youlin 林有麟, *Suyuan shipu* 素園石譜 (Hangzhou: Zhejiang renmin meishu chubanshe, 2013), 1. 101–4.
26. Zhang Dai, *Yehang chuan* 夜航船, ed. Zheng Lingfeng (Hangzhou: Zhejiang guji chubanshe, 2020), 2. 93. Zhang, "Songjie yan ming" 松節研銘, *Zhang Dai shiwen ji*, 5. 392; Zhang, "Zhanghou zhu bige ming" 章侯竹臂閣銘, *Zhang Dai shiwen ji*, 5. 398.
27. Zhang, "Songhua shi," 113. My translation follows Kafalas with minor changes; see Kafalas, *In Limpid Dream*, 65.
28. For a translation and brief discussion of this essay, see Kafalas, *In Limpid Dream*, 65.
29. Zhuangzi, *Zhuangzi: The Complete Writings*, trans. Brook Ziporyn (Cambridge. MA: Hackett, 2020), 58–59. Guo Qingfan 郭慶藩, comp., *Zhuangzi jishi* 莊子集釋, annot. Wang Xiaoyu 王孝魚 (Beijing: Zhonghua shuju, 1961; reprinted 2010), 3. 264–6.
30. Zhuangzi, *Zhuangzi*, 58. Guo, comp., *Zhuangzi jishi*, 3. 266.
31. Kenneth Gross, *The Dream of the Moving Statue* (Ithaca, NY: Cornell University Press, 1992), 166.
32. The two intertwined pines with which Zhang Dai unfavorably compares Pine Fossil were owned by the family of Dong Qi 董玘 (1483–1546) in Kuaiji. These pines became entangled with a leftover stone once owned by Lu You 陸游 (1125–1210) that had managed to evade Zhu Mian's 朱勔 (1075–1126) notorious "Flower and Rock Flotilla" (Huashigang 花石綱). Zhang Dai's vignette "Leftover Stones from the Flower and Rock Flotilla" in *Dream Reminiscences* discusses the pines. The vignette is largely based on a transcription of Tao Wangling's 陶望齡 (1562–1609) inscription on a Dong family veranda named after the rock, see Zhang, "Huashigang yishi" 花石綱遺石, *Tao'an mengyi*, 2. 25. "Cloudy Grove's Secret Belvedere" is a double allusion to Ni Zan's 倪瓚 (1301–1374) Belvedere of Pure Intimacy (Qingbi 清閟) and studio name "Cloudy Grove" (Yunlin 雲林). Zhang, "Yunlin bige sanshou" 雲林閣閣三首, *Zhang Dai shiwen ji*, 4. 83. On the construction and naming of this study, see Zhang, "Meihua shuwu" 梅花書屋, *Tao'an mengyi*, 2. 28.
33. Zhang, "Cantong shuizhong cheng ming (Dafu suo yi)" 殘銅水中丞銘 (大父所遺), *Zhang Dai shiwen ji*, 5. 394.
34. Kong Yingda 孔穎達, *Shangshu zhengyi* 尚書正義, 10. 63, in *Shisanjing zhushu* 十三經注疏, ed. Ruan Yuan 阮元 (Beijing: Zhonghua shuju, 1980), 175.
35. Kong Yingda, *Zhouyi zhengyi* 周易正義, 90, in *Shisanjing zhushu*, 102.
36. Zhang, "Cantong shuizhong cheng ming (Dafu suo yi)," *Zhang Dai shiwen ji*, 5. 394.
37. For an introduction to the received and manuscript versions of this inscription, see Zhou, "A Translation and Analysis of the Shanghai Museum Manuscript *Wu Wang Jian Zuo*," 14.
38. Zhong Xing 鍾惺 and Tan Yuanchun 譚元春, eds., *Shi gui: 51 juan* 詩歸：五一卷, annot. Liu Xiao 劉斅 (China: 1621–1644?; Harvard-Yenching Library Rare Book), 1.8a.

1. ON REMNANT THINGS

39. Zhang, "Baoping yan ming" 寶瓶研銘, *Zhang Dai shiwen ji*, 5. 400.
40. Zhou, "Yu Lin Tieya" 與林鐵崖, *Laigu tang ji*, 20. 385.
41. Zhang refers to visiting Daozi, his "fifth brother," in the Shen Fucan 沈復燦 manuscripts; see Zhang Dai, "Ji shao zongbo Chen Mushu wen" 祭少宗伯陳木叔文, in *Shen Fucan chaoben: Langhuan wenji* 沈復燦鈔本：瑯嬛文集, ed. Lu Wei and Ma Tao (Hangzhou: Zhejiang guji chubanshe, 2015), 318.
42. Zhang, "Shanmin di muzhiming" 山民弟墓志銘, *Zhang Dai shiwen ji*, 5. 372.
43. Zhang, "Shanmin di muzhiming," 372.
44. Zhang elsewhere claims his great-grandfather Yuanbian lived a life of "simplicity and thrift," and it was only following the influence of Zhu Shimen 朱石門 (n.d.; Rulin's wife's relative)—mentor of Lianfang—that the family started collecting. Zhang, "Jiazhuan," 337. On Zhu Shimen, a figure whose influence on the Zhang family collectors lurks behind the "Twenty-Eight Friends," see Zhang, "Zhushi shoucang" 朱氏收藏, *Tao'an mengyi*, 6. 96.
45. Zhang, "Jin Tang xiaokai ming" 晉唐小楷銘, *Zhang Dai shiwen ji*, 5. 406; Zhang, "Baiding lu ming" 白定爐銘, *Zhang Dai shiwen ji*, 5. 404.
46. Zhang, "Lanhua xiao chang he ming" 蘭花小廠盒銘, *Zhang Dai shiwen ji*, 5. 403. On the Orchard Factory, see Liu Tong 劉侗 and Yu Yizheng 于奕正, *Dijing jingwu lüe* 帝京景物略, ed. Sun Xiaoli 孫小力 (Shanghai: Shanghai guji chubanshe, 2001), 240. Zhang discusses Ming lacquerware in Zhang, *Yehang chuan*, 12. 463. For an introduction to the reception of Ming lacquer in the late imperial period, see Zhenpeng Zhan, "Artisanal Luxury and Confucian Statecraft: The Afterlife of Ming Official Carved Lacquer at the Qianlong Court," *Late Imperial China* 42, no. 1 (June 2021): 45–91.
47. There is also a surviving commentary on this set of inscriptions by Wang Yuqian 王雨謙 (n.d.). A close friend of the author, Wang, also from Shanyin and a provincial graduate of 1633, composed both interlinear and eyebrow commentary for Zhang Dai's manuscript of *Langhuan wenji*; see Xia Xianchun, "Qianyan" 前言, in *Zhang Dai shiwen ji*, 28.
48. Anna Shields, *One Who Knows Me: Friendship and Literary Culture in Mid-Tang China* (Cambridge, MA: Harvard University Asia Center, 2015), 47.
49. In 1616, at the age of nineteen, he organized a society for studying the zither with six like-minded young friends and family members (including an inept Yanke), writing in a manifesto of a desire for the music of his *qin* to merge with the wind in the pines and the rushing waters, to form a triad of "standard Shaoxing sounds." Eventually, with a beloved teacher and the two most talented members of his society, Zhang Dai formed a quartet that held captivating performances, as if all four instruments "were played by a single hand" (*ru chu yi shou* 如出一手). Zhang, "Shaoxing qinpai" 紹興琴派, *Tao'an mengyi*, 2. 24. See also Zhang, "Sishe" 絲社, *Tao'an mengyi*, 3. 34.
50. Zhang, "Duanwen guqin ming" 斷紋古琴銘, *Zhang Dai shiwen ji*, 5. 406.
51. Confucius, *The Analects*, trans. Simon Leys (New York: Norton, 2014), 52. He Yan 何晏, *Lunyu zhushu* 論語注疏, 17. 68, in *Shisanjing zhushu*, 2524.
52. Confucius, *The Analects*, 52. With slight modifications. He Yan, *Lunyu zhushu*, 17. 68.
53. Confucius, *The Analects*, 52. He Yan, *Lunyu zhushu*, 17. 68.
54. Zhang returns to the symbolism of the *qin* in two of his most poignant sequences of poems written for deceased friends at the fall of the dynasty. See his ten poems for

his "zither friend" (*qinyou* 琴友), Zishen 資深 (n.d.), in which he compares himself to a dejected Boya 伯牙 (387–299 BCE), recounting their escape to the mountains: "Qinwang shizhang you xu" 琴亡十章有序, *Zhang Dai shiwen ji*, 1. 11–14; see also his ten poems that use the *qin* to explicitly commemorate the death of Chongzhen: "Ting Taichang tanqin he shi shishou you xu" 聽太常彈琴和詩十首有序, *Zhang Dai shiwen ji*, 4. 110.

55. Other mid-seventeenth-century writers inscribed objects with professions of intimacy to seek restitution amid the ruptures of the Ming-Qing transition: Chen Que 陳確 (1604–1677) carved a vow of friendship upon his "dragon staff" (*longzhang* 龍杖), a seven-foot crooked tree limb, twice stolen in the wars of 1646, yet a possession that eventually returned to him "floating on water": ". . . I swear to never leave you, and together we will reach the end of our days" 誓不遺子，終老盤桓. Chen Que 陳確, "Longzhang ming" 龍杖銘, in *Chen Que ji* 陳確集 (Beijing: Zhonghua shuju, 1979), 15. 354. Wai-yee Li translates and discusses the full inscription in more depth; see Wai-yee Li, *The Promise and Peril of Things*, 228.
56. Zhang, "Ershiba you ming bing xu," 403.
57. Ouyang Xiu, "Liuyi jushi zhuan" 六一居士傳, in *Ouyang Xiu shiwen ji jiaojian* 歐陽修詩文集校箋, ed. Hong Benjian 洪本健 (Shanghai: Shanghai guji chubanshe, 2009), 44. 1130–31.
58. He more explicitly affirmed his debts to Ouyang in later life by adopting the style name "Retired Scholar of Six Respites" (Liuxiu jushi 六休居士).
59. Gu Yuanqing 顧元慶 (1487–1565) in 1539 compiled a collection of encomia (*zan* 贊) on his "ten friends of a mountain study" (*shanfang shiyou* 山房十友), later republished with woodcut illustrations of the ten objects in the widely popular commercial print series *Compiled Tracts on Connoisseurship* (*Xinshang pian* 欣賞篇). On Ming prints of this title, see Craig Clunas, *Superfluous Things*, 34, 36.
60. See also Zhang's encomium (*zan*) for a portrait of Yang Weizhen with its reference to his lodging of "Seven Guests" (*qike* 七客) in Zhang, *Sanbuxiu tuzan*, 199. Zhang classed Yang, along with Xu Wei, as one of the "literary" (*wenxue* 文學) worthies of Yue.
61. Yang Weizhen 楊維楨, *Yang Weizhen shiji* 楊維楨詩集, ed. Zou Zhifang 鄒志方 (Hangzhou: Zhejiang guji chubanshe, 2010), 540–541.
62. Yang, *Yang Weizhen shiji*, 541.
63. For a brief and inconclusive consideration of whether the inscriptions were pseudo-epigraphic, see Zhang Haixin 張海新, *Shuiping shanniao: Zhang Dai jiqi shiwen yanjiu* 水萍山鳥：張岱及其詩文研究 (Shanghai: Zhongxi shuju, 2012), 320.
64. Other early Qing remnant subjects engaged in not dissimilar literary exercises. Wang Fuzhi in reclusion as a "recalcitrant rock" on Stone Boat Mountain, as Wai-yee Li has shown, composed encomia (*zan*) on sixteen miscellaneous objects (*zawu* 雜物), items that like Zhang's friends linger between presence and absence: "On rainy days I sit without purpose, pondering the scenes and things of ordinary life, some have already been destroyed, while others survive in the mundane world, yet I cannot attain them on this desolate mountain. For each thing I narrate its origins and appraise it" 雨坐無緒，念平生風物，或時已滅裂，或人間尚有，而荒山不得邂逅，各為敘其原委而贊之. Wang Fuzhi, "Za wu zan" 雜物贊, *Wang Chuanshan shiwen ji*, 9. 95. Chen Zhenhui 陳貞慧 (1604–1656) in his *Miscellaneous Accouterments for the Autumn Garden* (*Qiuyuan zapei* 秋園雜佩)

1. ON REMNANT THINGS

also used sixteen objects to limn a scene of ascetic reclusion, some of which he suggests had been lost due to the transition. Li, *The Promise and Peril of Things*, 228–32.
65. Zhang, "Yuhua shi ming" 雨花石銘, *Zhang Dai shiwen ji*, 5. 403.
66. Lin Youlin, *Suyuan shipu*, 4. 293-4.
67. Liu I-ch'ing, *Shih-shuo Hsin-yü*, 107.
68. Su Shi, "Hou guaishi gong" 後怪石供, *Su Shi wenji jiaozhu*, 64. 7144.
69. Zhu, *Wanshi de fengliu*, 75–79.
70. Clunas, *Superfluous Things*, 61, 66–67. Much of this work is based on the following essays: Zhang, "Wuzhong jueji" 吳中絕技, *Tao'an mengyi*, 1. 15; "Pu Zhongqian diaoke" 濮仲謙雕刻, *Tao'an mengyi*, 1. 16; "Zhu gong" 諸工, *Tao'an mengyi*, 5. 71; "Gan Wentai lu" 甘文臺爐, *Tao'an mengyi*, 6. 90. There is a significant degree of overlap between Zhang's list of top Ming craftsman (Lu Zigang, Fan Kunbai, Gan Wentai) and the artisanal markings that adorn his twenty-eight friends.
71. Zhang, "Xuantong xiangge lu ming" 宣銅象格爐銘, *Zhang Dai shiwen ji*, 5. 405; "Xuande tianqi he ming" 宣德填漆盒銘, *Zhang Dai shiwen ji*, 5. 407; "Xuantong fanfu lianhua shui yu ming" 宣銅反覆蓮花水盂銘, *Zhang Dai shiwen ji*, 5. 409. See Liu and Yu, *Dijing jingwu lüe*, 238–39, 242–45. For an introduction to the problem of authenticating late Ming bronze Xuande censers, see Lu Pengliang 陸鵬亮, "Xuanlu bianyi" 宣爐辨疑, *Wenwu* 文物, no. 7 (2008): 64–76. Zhang Dai's contemporary, the poet Mao Xiang 冒襄 (1611–1693), recast the Xuande bronze censer as a loyalist symbol of Ming culture, see Mao Xiang 冒襄, "Xuande gezhu" 宣德歌注, in *Mao Pijiang quanji* 冒辟疆全集, ed. Wan Jiufu 萬久富 and Ding Fusheng 丁富生 (Nanjing: Fenghuang chubanshe, 2014), 555–573.
72. Zhang, "Xuande tianqi he ming," 407.
73. Arthur Waley, trans., *The Book of Songs: The Ancient Chinese Classic of Poetry*, ed. Joseph R. Allen (New York: Grove Press, 1996), 276. Kong Yingda, *Maoshi zhengyi* 毛詩正義, 18-3. 300, in *Shisanjing zhushu*, 2524.
74. Zhang, "Lanhua xiao chang he ming," 403; "Yang Yao zhi sanxian zi ming" 楊繇之三弦子銘, *Zhang Dai shiwen ji*, 5. 408; "Dasheng er fen dang tonglu ming" 大繩耳分襠銅爐銘, *Zhang Dai shiwen ji*, 5. 410.
75. Zhang, "Gong Chun hu ming" 龔春壺銘, *Zhang Dai shiwen ji*, 5. 402. Gong Chun was a mid-sixteenth-century artisan, commonly praised as the first potter to make teapots from Yixing "purple sand" (*zisha*) stoneware; see Zhang, "Shaguan xizhu" 砂罐錫注, *Tao'an mengyi*, 2. 30; "Gong Chun hu wei Zhu Zhongshi zuo" 龔春壺為諸仲軾作, *Zhang Dai shiwen ji*, 2. 35. The phrase "autograph" (*kuan* 款) can refer, here, to both the signatures and seals on a painting and an artisanal mark on the surface of a decorative object. Zhang similarly invokes the Gong Chun "mark" (*kuan*) in another inscription for one of the "friends": "Li Jincheng Gong Chun tai ming" 李錦城龔春臺銘, *Zhang Dai shiwen ji*, 5. 408.
76. Wang Fuzhi, elsewhere, inscribed a tortoiseshell comb that he was given by a military commander of the Yongli court. Wang, "Shu ming" 梳銘, *Wang Chuanshan shiwen ji*, 9. 101.
77. Zhang, "Biyu zan ming" 碧玉簪銘, *Zhang Dai shiwen ji*, 5. 405.
78. Waley, *The Book of Songs*, 128. Kong Yingda, *Maoshi zhengyi*, 6-3. 102.
79. Hajime Nakatani, "Body, Sentiment, and Voice in Ming Self-Encomia (*Zizan*)," *Chinese Literature: Essays, Articles, Reviews* 32 (December 2010): 76.

1. ON REMNANT THINGS

80. For the inscription, see Zhang, "Mu you long ming" 木猶龍銘, *Zhang Dai shiwen ji*, 5. 389; for the essay, see Zhang, "Mu you long," *Tao'an mengyi*, 1. 13–14. Kafalas reads this piece as a "microcosm" of *Dream Reminiscences*; Kafalas, *In Limpid Dream*, 5–7, 14–17.
81. For Zhang's recently discovered letters to the Prince of Lu, see Zhang, *Shen Fucan chaoben*, 261–78.
82. On Zhang Dai's faith in the "cyclical progression of time," see Campbell, "Zhang Dai's Passionate Search for Orchid Pavilion," 39.
83. Wu Hung, *Monumentality in Early Chinese Art and Architecture* (Stanford, CA: Stanford University Press, 1995), 7. On dynastic portents in Ming thought, see Bruce Rusk, "Artifacts of Authentication: People Making Texts Making Things in Late Imperial China," in *Antiquarianism and Intellectual Life in Europe and China, 1500–1800*, ed. François Louis and Peter Miller (Ann Arbor: University of Michigan Press, 2012), 180–204. Zhang alludes to the nine cauldrons in his poem on the artifact, "Mu yu long you xu" 木寓龍有序, *Zhang Dai shiwen ji*, 3. 57.
84. Spence, *Return to Dragon Mountain*, 213.
85. Zhang, "Lu wang yan" 魯王宴, *Tao'an mengyi*, 136.
86. Zhang, "Mu you long," 13.
87. Zhang, "Mu you long," 13.
88. Zhang, "Mu you long," 13. Zhang also explores the difficulty of naming this wooden fragment in his poetry, composing different poems on the different names the object might possess, with a hepta-syllabic "old poem" on "Wood Residing Dragon" (Mu yu long 木寓龍) that matches the rhyme of Su Shi's poem on a "Wooden Artificial Mountain" (Mu jia shan 木假山) ("Mu yu long you xu," 57), and two poems on "Wood Like a Dragon": Zhang, "Mu you long ershou" 木猶龍二首, *Zhang Dai shiwen ji*, 4. 117.
89. Cao Shujuan 曹淑娟, *Qi Biaojia shizhuan: Yuanshan tang shici biannian jiaoshi* 祁彪佳詩傳：遠山堂詩詞編年校釋 (Xinbei: Lianjing chubanshe, 2020), 461.
90. Zhang, "Mu you long," 13.
91. Kafalas, *In Limpid Dream*, 16.
92. Qi Biaojia 祁彪佳, "Cong Zhang Zongzi zhai tou jian Mu you long Zhou Youxin xiansheng suo ti ye he sheyou fu zhi Zongzi yi you zuoyong da Su mujiashan shiyun yu duzhi er xi zhong qi he zuoge" 從張宗子齋頭見木猶龍周又新先生所題也合社友賦之宗子亦有作用大蘇木假山詩韻予讀之而喜躓其和作歌, in Zhao Suwen 趙素文, ed., *Qi Biaojia shici biannian jianjiao* 祁彪佳詩詞編年箋校 (Hangzhou: Zhejiang guji chubanshe, 2016), 9. 324. For a discussion, see Cao, *Qi Biaojia shizhuan*, 461.
93. The "mound-like protuberance" (*chimu* 尺木) is a lump in the shape of a *boshan* 博山 censer that appears on the top of a dragon's skull. Without this lump, the dragon cannot ascend to heaven.
94. A reference to Han official Zhang Qian's 張騫 (fl. 125 BCE) "soaring raft" (Qian cha 騫槎), a vessel that carried him from the Yellow River up into the Milky Way.
95. Zhang, "Mu you long," 14. My translation follows Kafalas with minor changes; see Kafalas, *In Limpid Dream*, 16.
96. Zhang, "Mu you long ming," 389.
97. Zhang, "Mu you long," 14.

1. ON REMNANT THINGS

98. Zhang, "Kuaiyuan shizhang you xu" 快園十章有序, *Zhang Dai shiwen ji*, 1. 1. Zhang offers a playful variant of this same apostrophe in his inscription on a Longquan "fish ear" censer: "call to [them] and [they] will emerge." Zhang, "Longquan yao yu'er lu ming" 龍泉窯魚耳爐銘, *Zhang Dai shiwen ji*, 5. 398.
99. Zhang, "Kuaiyuan shizhang you xu," 2.
100. Wai-yee Li, "Gardens and Illusions from Late Ming to Early Qing," *Harvard Journal of Asiatic Studies* 72, no. 2 (2012): 313, 329.
101. The terms of my reading here have also been inspired by Vilém Flusser's suggestive discussion of inscriptions: "[an inscription] digs holes of "spirit" into things too full of themselves so that these things no longer condition the subject… The digging aspect of writing is an informative gesture that seeks to break out of the prison of the conditional, that is, to dig escape tunnels into the imprisoning walls of the objective world… Writing, like digging, presses […] spirit into the object to inspire it, that is, to make it improbable." Vilém Flusser, *Does Writing Have a Future?*, trans. Nancy Ann Roth (Minneapolis: University of Minnesota Press, 2011), 12–13.
102. Zhang, "Ershiba you ming bing xu," 411.
103. Zhang, at various points in his *ming*, explicitly cites King Wu's inscriptions; see Zhang, "Baoping yan ming," 400; and Zhang, "Cantong shuizhong cheng ming," 394.
104. Alongside Wang Xinjian 王新建, Zhu Shimen, Xiang Yuanbian 項元忭, and Zhou Mingzhong 周銘仲, see Zhang, "Fuzhuan" 附傳, *Zhang Dai shiwen ji*, 4. 342. For a partial translation of excerpts from Zhang's "Family Biographies" and "Appended Biographies," see Duncan Campbell, "Flawed Jade: Zhang Dai's Family Biographies," *Ming Studies* 62 (2010): 22–55.
105. Zhang, "Fuzhuan," 343.
106. Zhang, "Fuzhuan," 344.
107. Usually read as the name of a type of green jade.
108. Zhang, "Zhongshu gudong" 仲叔古董, *Tao'an mengyi*, 6. 97.
109. Xiang Yuanbian.
110. Zhang, "Baiding lu ming," 404.
111. Li, *The Promise and Peril of Things*, 3–5. The "white ding ware censer" was acquired by Xiang Yuanbian from Dong Qichang 董其昌 (1555–1636) for a hundred and twenty *taels* and later passed to Donglin partisan Cheng Jibai, where it became the focus of a dispute with the eunuch Wei Zhongxian. Jiang Shaoshu 姜紹書, "Dingyao ding ji" 定窯鼎記, in *Yunshi zhai bitan* 韻石齋筆談, in *Zhibuzu zhai congshu* 知不足齋叢書, ed. Bao Tingbo 鮑廷博 (Beijing: Zhonghua shuju, 1999), vol. 1, 1. 255.
112. Li, *The Promise and Peril of Things*, 223–24.
113. Seventeenth-century commentators discuss how Xiang's collections were plundered during the violence of the transition. Jiang, "Xiang Molin shoucang" 項墨林收藏, *Yunshi zhai bitan*, 1. 268.
114. On *xun* and the death of palace ladies, see Huang Zhanyue 黃展岳, "Ming Qing huangshi de gongfei xunzang zhi" 明清皇室的宮妃殉葬制, *Gugong bowuyuan yuankan* 故宮博物院院刊, no. 1 (1988): 29–34. This resonates with a conversation that Zhang Dai records with one of Lianfang's concubines, where she claimed she wanted to be buried with him and "become a Zhang family ghost." Zhang, "Fuzhuan," 344.

115. Zhang, "Wu Yiren zhuan" 五異人傳, *Zhang Dai shiwen ji*, 4. 357; Zhang, "Ruicao xiting" 瑞草溪亭, *Tao'an mengyi*, 8. 132. For a discussion of Yanke's destructive whims in relation to Zhang Dai's descriptions of devastated landscapes, see Yingzhi Zhao, "What Remains of Mountains and Waters: Fragments, Mutilation, and Creation in Early Qing Literature and Culture," *Journal of Chinese Literature and Culture* 6, no. 1 (2019): 137–168.
116. Zhang, "Wu Yiren zhuan," 357; cf. Campbell, "Flawed Jade," 42; Li, "The Collector, the Connoisseur, and Late-Ming Sensibility," 295.
117. Zhang, "Wu Yiren zhuan," 357.
118. At the end of his biography of Yanke, Zhang Dai hints at how he was responsible for the loss of the "friends," in this case the second object in the collection of twenty-eight, a rock comparable to Mi Fu's inkstone mountain (and an anonymous antique bronze); Zhang, "Wu Yiren zhuan," 358. For Zhang Dai's inscription, see Zhang, "Yanshan ming" 研山銘, *Zhang Dai shiwen ji*, 5. 403.
119. He Yan, *Lunyu zhushu*, 6. 23. On the rhetorical uses of the line *gu bu gu* in Ming critiques of political corruption, see Kenneth J. Hammond, "The Decadent Chalice: A Critique of Late Ming Political Culture," *Ming Studies* 39 (2013): 32–49.
120. Zhang, "Xiao meiren gu ming" 小美人觚銘, *Zhang Dai shiwen ji*, 5. 404.
121. Zhang, *Yehang chuan*, 12. 462.
122. Zhang is circumspect in describing the provenance of the small beauty chalice, yet his attention to its tightened waist and three-foot height closely resembles the terms he uses to describe two bronze *zun* vessels stolen from the tomb of Count Jing of Qi, then sold to Zhang's father-in-law. Zhang uses both *zun* for displaying flowers, which was likely the function of the small beauty chalice in Lianfang's collection. Zhang, "Qi Jing gong mu huazun" 齊景公墓花罇, *Tao'an mengyi*, 6. 102.
123. Wai-yee Li, "Women as Emblems of Dynastic Fall from Late-Ming to Late-Qing," in *Dynastic Crisis and Cultural Innovation: From the Late Ming to the Late Qing and Beyond*, ed. David Der-wei Wang and Shang Wei (Cambridge, MA: Harvard University Asia Center, 2005), 93–150.
124. Zhang, "Fuzhuan," 344.
125. Zhang, "Zhongshu gudong," 97.
126. Whether as a result of Wang "Uncle Inkstone's" influence or not, Zhang Dai became a prolific author of inkstone inscriptions (his collected writings contain at least twenty-four *ming* for various slabs and ink grinders—two of which appear among his "Twenty-Eight Friends").
127. Zhang, "Tian yan" 天硯, *Tao'an mengyi*, 1. 14–55.
128. Zhang, "He yu congdi Jingyuan you xu" 和與從弟敬遠有序, *Zhang Dai shiwen ji*, 159; Zhang Dai, *He Tao ji; Tao'an duiou gushi* 和陶集；陶菴對偶故事, ed. Lu Wei and Zheng Lingfeng (Hangzhou: Zhejiang guji chubanshe, 2019), 104. In 2009, Zhang Haixin discovered a Qing dynasty manuscript in the Shanghai Library entitled *He Tao ji* 和陶集, a collection of forty-three poems by Zhang Dai matching the titles and rhyme schemes of poems by Tao Qian. Zhang Haixin dates the collection to Zhang Dai's adulthood under the Ming before the establishment of the Qing. See Zhang, *Shuiping shanniao*, 237–53.
129. Tao Qian 陶潛, "Guimao sui shier yue zhong zuo yu congdi Jingyuan" 癸卯歲十二月中作與從弟敬遠, in *Tao Yuanming ji jiaojian (xiudingben)* 陶淵明集校箋（修訂本）, ed. Gong Bin 龔斌 (Shanghai: Shanghai guji chubanshe, 2011), 194.

For a translation and reading of the poem, see Xiaofei Tian, *Tao Yuanming and Manuscript Culture: The Record of a Dusty Table* (Seattle: University of Washington Press, 2005), 171.

130. Lin Youlin, *Suyuan shipu*, 1. 60–2.
131. Zhang, *He Tao ji; Tao'an duiou gushi*, 104.
132. Zhang, *He Tao ji; Tao'an duiou gushi*, 104.
133. Barbara Herrnstein Smith, *Poetic Closure: A Study of How Poems End* (Chicago: University of Chicago Press, 1968), 196.
134. Zhang, "Pu Zhongqian diaoke," 16.
135. Zhang, "Jiuchai qigu ji xu" 鳩柴奇觚記序, *Zhang Dai shiwen ji*, 1. 223.
136. Zhang, "*Yinhui shupin* xu (dai Zhou Yuanliang)" 印彙書品序（代周元亮）, *Zhang Dai shiwen ji*, 1. 209.

2. WRITING WITH A KNIFE

1. See Peng Fei 彭飞, "Su Xuan de shengping, jiaoyou yu zhuanke wuti" 苏宣的生平，交游与篆刻五题, *Zhongguo shufa* 中国书法, no. 2 (2017): 126–30.
2. On this issue, see Yang Liang 杨亮, "Su Xuan yu guwen yinfeng de xingshuai" 苏宣与古文印风的兴衰, *Nanjing yishu xueyuan xuebao (Meishu yu sheji ban)* 南京艺术学院学报（美术与设计版）, no. 3 (2015): 22–25. Su likely based his use of variant graphs on inscriptions published in catalogues of epigraphic sources rather than on his firsthand inspection of excavated artifacts.
3. Many of Su Xuan's impressions are preserved in a 1617 printed seal catalogue, *Sushi yinlüe* 蘇氏印略. See Shu Wenyang 舒文扬, "Cong *Sushi yinlüe* kan Su Xuan de chuangzuo ji qita" 从《苏氏印略》看苏宣的创作及其他, in *Ming Qing Huizhou zhuanke xueshu yantaohui lunwen ji* 明清徽州篆刻学术研讨会论文集, ed. Xiling yinshe 西泠印社 (Hangzhou: Xiling yinshe chubanshe, 2008), 183–92.
4. Another Su Xuan seal was excavated in 1984 from a nearby Wuxi tomb belonging to Hua Shiyi 華師伊 (1566–1619). This seal, which bears the impression "Qingji ge" 清機閣, is also signed with Su's cognomen Yingzhi 應製. The calligraphy of the signature resembles the seal in Gu Lin's tomb. For a comparison, see Li Xingtao 李兴涛, "Cong Gu Lin mu yu Hua Shiyi mu chutu yinzhang kan Su Xuan zhuanke de yishu fengmao" 从顾林墓与华师伊墓出土印章看苏宣篆刻的艺术风貌, *Shufa shangping* 书法赏评, no. 5 (2017): 53–58.
5. For this seal, see Zhu Qi 朱琪, *Xinchu Mingdai wenren yinzhang jicun yu yanjiu* 新出明代文人印章辑存与研究 (Hangzhou: Xiling yinshe chubanshe, 2020), 51. For an overview of the seals preserved in Gu Lin's tomb, see Cai Weidong 蔡卫东, "Wuxi Gu Lin mu chutu Mingdai liupai yin shiwu kaoshu" 无锡顾林墓出土明代流派印实物考述, *Zhongguo shufa*, no. 6 (2016): 142–55.
6. For an overview of relevant sources, see Peng, "Su Xuan de shengping, jiaoyou yu zhuanke wuti," 126–27.
7. Li Yingzheng 李應徵, "Susheng Erxuan xiangchang renxia baochou, jianshan Qin Han zhuanke, jin cong Wumen guo yu shanzhong, zuo ge zengzhi" 蘇生爾宣向嘗任俠報仇，兼善秦漢篆刻，近從吳門過于山中，作歌贈之, in *Mingshi jishi* 明詩紀事, ed. Chen Tian 陳田, 38 vols. (China: Chenshi congshu tingshi zhai, 1899?; Harvard-Yenching Library Rare Book), 25. 1, 18b–19a.

8. Li, "Susheng Erxuan xiangchang renxia baochou."
9. Li, "Susheng Erxuan xiangchang renxia baochou."
10. Wang Hung-tai, "Wodao yu xiashi—Mingdai woluan chongji xia Jiangnan shiren de wuxia fengshang" 倭刀與俠士—明代倭亂衝擊下江南士人的武俠風尚, *Hanxue yanjiu* 漢學研究 30, no. 3 (2012): 63–97.
11. Zhang Jian 張健, *Huizhou hongru Wang Daokun yanjiu* 徽州鴻儒汪道昆研究 (Wuhu shi: Anhui shifan daxue chubanshe, 2014). A critical chronology of Wang's life can be found in Xu Shuofang, ed., *Wan Ming qujia nianpu*. Critical adjustments to Xu's chronology have been made by Wang Chaohong 汪超宏, *Ming Qing qujia kao* 明清曲家考 (Beijing: Zhongguo shehui kexue chubanshe, 2006), 128–237.
12. One of the longest surviving inscriptions on a late imperial inkstone is a two-hundred-character text attributed to Wang Daokun on a "Dragon Tail" rock now held in the collection of the Beijing Capital Museum. See Rong Dawei 榮大為, ed., *Shoudu bowuguan guancang mingyan* 首都博物館館藏名硯 (Beijing: Gongyi meishu chubanshe, 1997), 16.
13. On the symbiotic relationship between "go-betweens" and writing implements as "inconspicuous communication servers," see Markus Krajewski, *The Server: A Media History from the Present to the Baroque*, trans. Ilinca Iurascu (New Haven, CT: Yale University Press, 2018), 2.
14. For an early study of Wang's relationship to Qi, see Zhu Ze 朱澤, "Shijian zhi jiao—ji Wang Daokun, Qi Jiguang de youyi pianduan" 诗剑之交—记汪道昆、戚继光的友谊片断, *Anhui shixue* 安徽史学 5 (1984): 32–38. Several inaccuracies in this short piece have been corrected in Jiang Weitang 姜纬堂, "Qi Nantang yu Wang Taihan" 戚南塘与汪太函, in *Qi Jiguang yanjiu lunji* 戚继光研究论集, ed. Yan Chongnian 阎崇年 (Beijing: Zhishi chubanshe, 1990), 318–51.
15. A more detailed version of the pact is offered in Wang Daokun, "Ming gu tejin guanlu dafu shaobao jian taizi taibao zhongjun dudu fu zuo dudu Mengzhu Qi gong Jiguang muzhiming" 明故特進光祿大夫少保兼太子太保中軍都督府左都督孟諸戚公繼光墓志銘, in *Taihan ji* 太函集, ed. Hu Yimin 胡益民 and Yu Guoqing 余國慶 (Hefei: Huangshan shushe, 2004), 59. 1227. See Wang Daokun's later essay, "Cangzhou san hui ji" 滄洲三會記, *Taihan ji*, 76. 1552.
16. Wang, "Pingyuan tai legong ming" 平遠台勒功銘, *Taihan ji*, 78. 1594.
17. Wang, "Qi gong Jiguang muzhiming," 1231.
18. Wang, "Pingyuan tai legong ming," 1594. This large boulder, a fragment of which was excavated in 1983 and is now on display in the courtyard of a local shrine for Qi Jiguang, established Wang's public reputation as a prominent author of engraved memorials in Ming China.
19. Kern, *The Stele Inscriptions of Ch'in Shih-Huang*, 125.
20. This text was one of several works that Wang wrote during his service in Fujian: in 1561, after Qi's succession of nine victorious engagements against *wokou* in a single month on the Taizhou 台州 coast, Wang composed a "Biographical Record of the Pacification of the Barbarians in Taizhou" ("Taizhou ping yi zhuan" 台州平夷傳). In 1563, with the recovery of Pinghai and Xinghua, Wang authored a stele memorial on a "corpse mound" ("Jingguan bei" 京觀碑). In these compositions, we see Wang Daokun develop a self-consciously archaistic voice as a writer, modeling himself on the example of Sima Qian 司馬遷 (145–90 BCE), exploring the close relationship between inscriptional and biographical genres; see Wang, "Taizhou ping yi zhuan" 台

州平夷傳, *Taihan ji*, 27. 581. Wang commemorated Qi's victories in a series of poems; see Wang, "Qi Jiangjun ru Min pozei fu shi jueju" 戚將軍入閩破賊賦十絕句, *Taihan ji*, 120. 2754. Several commentators from the late Ming discussed Wang's close relationship to Qi; see, for instance, Shen Defu 沈德符, "Qi shuai junei" 戚帥懼內, in *Wanli yehuo bian buyi* 萬曆野獲編補遺, in *Mingdai biji xiaoshuo daguan* 明代筆記小說大觀, ed. Yang Wanli 楊萬里 (Shanghai: Shanghai guji chubanshe, 2005), 3: 2815.

21. For sources on this event, see Xu Shuofang, *Wan Ming qujia nianpu*, 3: 33–34.
22. Wang, "Qi jiangjun zhu liangjian er, ye yu ming zhi, tuo yijiu yao, sui fen qi yi. Shengshu huo, guwu xiwang, du shezhong er bao jian chu huozhong, lai de tuo. Guishi jiadi, xiang yu xing qi you ling, weizhi tanjia er ge, zuoshi sanshou" 戚將軍鑄良劍二, 謁予銘之, 託以久要,　遂分其一。省署火, 故物悉亡, 獨舍中兒抱劍出火中, 賴得脫。歸示家弟, 相與幸其有靈, 為之彈鋏而歌, 作詩三首, *Taihan ji*, 109. 2302.
23. Li Panlong 李攀龍, "Wang Zhongcheng tai huo jiuzhe du yi jian chu tanjia er ge he yi xiangdiao" 汪中丞臺火救者獨以劍出彈鋏而歌和以相吊, in *Cangming xiansheng ji* 滄溟先生集, ed. Bao Jingdi 包敬第 (Shanghai: Shanghai guji chubanshe, 2014), 10. 326.
24. Xu, *Wan Ming qujia nianpu*, 3: 37–38.
25. For a discussion of the meeting in 1568, see Tang Yuxing 汤宇星, *Yanshan zhi shi: Wang Shizhen yu Suzhou wentan de yishu jiaoyou* 弇山之石：王世贞与苏州文坛的艺术交游 (Hangzhou: Zhongguo meishu xueyuan chubanshe, 2015), 72–74. In his later poems, Wang downplays this event in favor of another meeting to discuss strategy between himself and Qi that he dates to the same year in the Tiger Forest 虎林 of Hangzhou.
26. Zhou Ying 周颖, *Wang Shizhen nianpu changbian* 王世贞年谱长编 (Shanghai: Shanghai sanlian shudian, 2016), 337.
27. John D. Langlois, "The Reversal of the Death Verdict Against Wang Shizhen's Father," *Ming Studies* 1 (2016): 72–98.
28. Wang, "Saishang shang zhengfu" 塞上上政府, *Taihan ji*, 98. 2003; Wang, "Jimen hui yue" 薊門會閱, *Taihan ji*, 113. 2500.
29. Wang, "Yanshan legong ming" 燕山勒功銘, *Taihan ji*, 78. 1596–1600.
30. On the pairing of the two monuments, see Liu Pengbing 刘彭冰, *Wang Daokun wenxue yu jiaoyou yanjiu* 汪道昆文学与交游研究 (Beijing: Zhongguo wenshi chubanshe, 2018), 28–31. The latter focuses closely on Tan Lun's 譚綸 (1519–1577) role in the border defense.
31. Wang Yan 王岩 ed., *Changcheng yiwen lu* 長城藝文錄 (Beijing: Beijing chubanshe, 2018), 176.
32. Zhang Yiqun 张艺群, "Laizi Jingcheng de kaogu baogao: 'Yanshan legong ming bei ke' kao" 來自京城的考古報告：《燕山勒功銘碑刻》考, *Minjian wenhua (renwen lüyou zazhi)* 民間文化（人文旅游杂志）10 (2009): 131. See also Beijing shi difangzhi bianyuan weiyuanhui 北京市地方志編纂委员会, ed., *Beijing zhi. Wenwu juan. Wenwu zhi* 北京志．文物卷．文物志 (Beijing: Beijing chubanshe, 2006), 492; Zheng Yunshan 郑云山, *Jingdong suibi* 京东随笔 (Beijing: Yanshan chubanshe, 1991), 85–88.
33. Xu, *Wan Ming qujia nianpu*, 3: 49. For drafts of the two poems that Wang likely engraved on the Wuling boulder, see Wang, "You Wuling shan shi wei zhi gongdao chang" 游霧靈山是為志公道場, *Taihan ji*, 113. 2503.

34. At the same time, however, Tan Lun and Qi's reformist agenda—their advocacy of an offensive war against Mongolian forces—was ultimately blocked by their same backer at court, Zhang Juzheng.
35. For a discussion of Qi's role in the Jizhou command, see Ray Huang, *1587 A Year of No Significance: The Ming Dynasty in Decline* (New Haven, CT: Yale University Press, 1981), 174–88. Qi Jiguang after his dismissal travelled to Wang Daokun's hometown in 1585 and participated in a gathering of his poetry society and Chan meditation group. Wang, "Dao zhong yu Shaobao jishi" 道中遇少保即事, *Taihan ji*, 117. 2636; Wang, "Tong Shaobao su Zhaolin" 同少保宿肇林, *Taihan ji*, 117. 2637.
36. Huang, *1587 A Year of No Significance*, 187–88.
37. Liu, *Wang Daokun wenxue yu jiaoyou yanjiu*, 8.
38. Wang, "Qi jiangjun zhu liangjian er," 2302.
39. Wang, "Xuyu ji" 徐于記, *Taihan ji*, 71. 1472. The final lines of Wang's essay on this studio also return to the sword: "Feeling idle, I strike the stone chime several times, or lean against the wood with my legs stretched out on the floor, or wash the head of my sword. Feeling indulgent, I then doze off in a deep slumber" 愈則擊磬什數聲，倚木箕踞，澤劍首，甚則齁齁睡矣. Wang, "Xuyu ji," 1472.
40. Wang, "Baojian pian" 寶劍篇, *Taihan ji*, 108. 2290.
41. Beijing tushuguan 北京圖書館 ed., *Beijing tushuguan cang Zhongguo lidai shike taben huibian* 北京圖書館藏中國歷代石刻拓本匯編 (Zhengzhou: Zhongzhou guji chubanshe, 1989), 57: 85. Cf. Xu, *Wan Ming qujia nianpu*, 3: 66. For the stele text, see Wang, "Dufu Liu gong ping man bei" 督府劉公平蠻碑, *Taihan ji*, 63. 1312–16.
42. For the Pu'an Temple, see Beijing tushuguan, ed., *Beijing tushuguan cang Zhongguo lidai shike taben huibian*, 57: 24. Cf. Xu, *Wan Ming qujia nianpu*, 3: 55. For the Changrun stupa, see Beijing tushuguan, ed., *Beijing tushuguan cang Zhongguo lidai shike taben huibian*, 57: 140. For a discussion of syncretistic themes in Wang's eulogy to Changrun, see Liu, *Wang Daokun wenxue yu jiaoyou yanjiu*, 13–14.
43. Fang Yulu 方于魯, *Fangshi mopu* 方氏墨譜, in SKQSCMCS, zibu, vol. 79, 296–297. Wang's preface for the 1588 edition of this ink catalogue was printed in an austere clerical script that invokes the monumental aesthetic of Han-dynasty stelae. For a discussion of this case, see Bai, *Fu Shan's World*, 188.
44. Wang worked with the Changzhou carver Shen Youwen 沈幼文 (n.d.) on the stele for Changrun. He appears to have also collaborated with Shen on an epitaph for Hu Yinglin's mother. For sources on Shen, see Cheng Zhangcan 程章燦, *Shike kegong yanjiu* 石刻刻工研究 (Shanghai: Shanghai guji chubanshe, 2008), 463.
45. The close association between Zhou and Wang Daokun's coterie can be seen in his 1580 ink painting "Orchids" (Molan tu 墨蘭圖) now held in the National Palace Museum in Taiwan, a scroll bearing colophons and seal impressions from Wang Daokun, Wang Daoguan, and numerous Huizhou merchants in their circle. For a study of the painting as a window onto exchanges between Suzhou artists and Huizhou entrepreneurs, see Zhang Changhong 张长虹, *Pinjian yu jingying: Mingmo Qingchu Huishang yishu zanzhu yanjiu* 品鉴与经营：明末清初徽商艺术赞助研究 (Beijing: Beijing daxue chubanshe, 2010), 54–58. Recent scholarship has attributed this painting to Fang Yongbin. For poetic sources on Wang and Zhou's relationship, see Xu Chengyao 許承堯, "Zhou Gongxia ceng ru Baiyu she" 周公瑕曾入白榆社, in *Sheshi xiantan* 歙事閑譚, ed. Li Minghui 李明回 (Hefei: Huangshan shushe, 2001), 175–6.

46. Beijing tushuguan, ed., *Beijing tushuguan cang Zhongguo lidai shike taben huibian*, 57: 140.
47. Chen Zhichao 陳智超, ed., *Meiguo Hafo daxue Hafo Yanjing tushuguan cang Mingdai Huizhou Fangshi qinyou shouzha qibai tong kaoshi* 美國哈佛大學燕京圖書館藏明代徽州方氏親友手札七百通考釋 (Hefei: Anhui daxue chubanshe, 2001), 495.
48. Fang, *Fangshi mopu*, 323-331.
49. For evidence of his role in the connoisseurship and sale of inkstones, see Wang Daoguan (Metal 148) in Chen, *Fangshi qinyou shouzha*, 714. On Daoguan's role as an ink dealer, see Fang, *Fangshi mopu*, 309.
50. For Wang Daokun's reprimand of Wang Daoguan (and Daohui), see Wang, "Xianfu jun zhuang" 先府君狀, *Taihan ji*, 44. 938. See also Wang, "Shedi kun zhusheng, gu you shijiu fangyan, wanwu zhi pi, zuoshi fengzhi" 舍弟困諸生，顧有嗜酒放言，萬物之癖，作詩諷之, *Taihan ji*, 109. 2339-2340. On Wang Daoguan's activities as an art collector see Xu Chengyao, "Wang Boyu suocang hua" 汪伯玉所藏畫, *Sheshi xiantan*, 1093-1094. For a letter from Wang Daokun to a client explaining Daohui's role as a go-between, see Wang, "Chen Yushu" 陳玉叔, *Taihan ji*, 104. 2171. For the final inscriptions, see Wang, "Chen Yushu de Wu shi liu ze jie shenqi zhuzuozhe zanzhi yu wei ming er le zhi shi" 陳玉叔得吳石六則皆神奇諸作者贊之余為銘而勒之石, *Taihan ji*, 78. 1609.
51. The collector Wan Shouqi 萬壽祺 (1603-1652) owned an inkstick attributed to the Two Zhongs, see Wan Shouqi, *Mobiao* 墨表, in *Sheyuan mocui* 涉園墨萃, ed. Tao Xiang 陶湘 (Beijing: Wujin taoshi, 1929), vol. 8, 6b.
52. See, for instance, a letter to Qi Jiguang that asks for the general to procure a travel permit for talented Huizhou carvers 徽人善鐫者 to help engrave his inscription on the Yiwulü Mountain, rather than leave the task to less talented local carvers. Wang, "Qi Changgong" 戚長公, *Taihan ji*, 98. 2020. For Wang's reflections on the creation of the inscription, see Wang, "Yiwulü shan legong ming ba" 醫無閭山勒功銘跋, *Taihan ji*, 86. 1789-90.
53. Zhou, "Shu He Zhuchen zhang" 書何主臣章, *Yinren zhuan*, 1. 27.
54. James C. Y. Watt, "The Literati Environment," in *The Chinese Scholar's Studio: Artistic Life in the Late Ming Period*, ed. Chu-tsing Li and James C. Y. Watt (New York: Asia Society Galleries, 1987), 12. Zhai Tunjian 翟屯建, *Huipai zhuanke* 徽派篆刻 (Hefei: Anhui renmin chubanshe, 2005), 119.
55. For a detailed discussion of military themes in Fang Yulu's ink cake designs and their association with Wang Daokun's military service, see Liu Jingjing 劉晶晶, "Daxuan zhenmi: *Fangshi mopu* tuxiang kaobian" 大玄珍秘：《方氏墨譜》圖像考辨 (PhD diss., China Academy of Art, 2017), 78-80.
56. Zhou, "Shu Xu Shibai yinzhang qian," 99.
57. Joseph P. McDermott, *The Making of a New Rural Order in South China: I. Village, Land, and Lineage in Huizhou 900-1600* (Cambridge: Cambridge University Press, 2013).
58. For an overview of these developments, see Wang Zhenzhong 王振忠, *Cong Huizhou dao Jiangnan: Ming Qing Huishang yu quyu shehui yanjiu* 从徽州到江南：明清徽商与区域社会研究 (Shanghai: Shanghai renmin chubanshe, 2018).
59. Wu Qizhen 吳其貞, *Shuhua ji* 書畫記 (Shanghai: Renmin meishu chubanshe, 1963), 160-61. For a brief introduction to art-collecting practices in sixteenth- and

seventeenth-century Huizhou, see Jason Chi-sheng Kuo, "Hui-chou Merchants as Art Patrons in the Late Sixteenth and Early Seventeenth Centuries" in *Artists and Patrons: Some Social and Economic Aspects of Chinese Painting*, ed. Chu-tsing Li (Lawrence, KS: Kress Foundation Dept. of Art History in association with University of Washington Press, 1989), 177–88. On Wang's advocacy for Huizhou merchants, see Qitao Guo, *Ritual Opera and Mercantile Lineage: The Confucian Transformation of Popular Culture in Late Imperial Huizhou* (Stanford, CA: Stanford University Press, 2005), 60.

60. Liu Xinru 劉心如 [Liu Hsin-ju], "Xin'an juyan: Zhan Jingfeng yu wan Ming jianshang jia de diyu jingzheng" 新安具眼：詹景鳳與晚明鑑賞家的地域競爭, *Mingdai yanjiu* 明代研究 18, no. 6 (2012): 83–104.

61. For sources on this event, see Xu Chengyao, "Wang Yanzhou zhuren you She" 王弇州諸人游歙, *Sheshi xiantan*, 413.

62. The "Xin'an eyes" slogan can be traced to a meeting between Zhan Jingfeng and Wang Shizhen at the Waguan Temple in Nanjing: on this occasion, Zhan had correctly dated a rubbing of a stone engraving to the Five Dynasties solely on stylistic grounds, an attribution that was later confirmed by a reign mark, causing a mutual acquaintance to remark, "although in the past the men of Wu were commended for 'possessing eyes,' now it seems as if those 'with the eyes' are the men of my home, Xin'an?" 曩者昔但稱吳人具眼，今具眼非吾新安人耶—and Wang Shizhen is left standing, again, in silence 弇山公默然. Zhan Jingfeng 詹景鳳, *Zhanshi xuanlan bian* 詹氏玄覽編 (Taibei: Guoli zhongyang tushuguan chubanshe, 1970), 246.

63. For Zhan's version of this anecdote, see Zhan Jingfeng, *Zhanshi xingli xiaobian* 詹氏性理小辨, in SKQSCMCS, zibu, vol. 112, 38. 12b.

64. Zhan, *Zhanshi xuanlan bian*, 308.

65. Zhu Wanshu 朱万曙, *Huishang yu Ming Qing wenxue* 徽商与明清文学 (Beijing: Renmin chubanshe, 2014), 153.

66. Wen Zhengming 文徵明, "Zhi Zhang Jianfu" 至章簡甫, in *Wen Zhengming ji (zengdingben)* 文徵明集 （增訂本）, ed. Zhou Daozhen 周道振 (Shanghai: Shanghai guji chubanshe, 2019), 27. 1432.

67. Cheng Zhangcan, *Shike kegong yanjiu*, 146–62. See also the discussion in Jiang Hui 蔣晖, *Mingdai dali shiping kao* 明代大理石屏考 (Jinan: Shandong huabao chubanshe, 2018), 146–47.

68. Wang, "Ming gu chushi Xiyang Wu Changgong muzhiming" 明故處士谿陽吳長公墓誌銘, *Taihan ji*, 54. 1142.

69. Wang, "Haiyang chushi Jin Zhongweng pei Daishi hezang muzhiming" 海陽處士金仲翁配戴氏合葬墓誌銘, *Taihan ji*, 52. 1099. My translation follows Qitao Guo with slight modifications.

70. See Qitao Guo, *Huizhou: Local Identity and Mercantile Lineage Culture in Ming China* (Oakland: University of California Press, 2022), 108.

71. On spirit tablets, see Wang, "Chushi Wang Yinweng pei Yuanshi hezang muzhiming" 處士汪隱翁配袁氏合葬墓誌銘, *Taihan ji*, 53. 1116–19; on the reclamation of ritual lands from local strongmen, see Wang, "Ming chushi Xiuning Wang Changgong mubiao" 明處士休寧程長公墓表, *Taihan ji*, 61. 1265–68.

72. Geng Chuanyou 耿传友, "Lun Ming Qing Huishang zhuanji de lishi jiazhi yu wenxue jiazhi" 论明清徽商传记的历史价值与文学价值, *Nanjing shida xuebao*

(shehui kexue ban) 南京师大学报（社会科学版）2 (2012): 130. See, for instance, Wang, "Ming gu taixuesheng Jiuzhou Wang gong xingzhuang" 明故太學生九州汪公行狀, *Taihan ji*, 41. 889; Wang, "Xian bofu Wang Cigong xingzhuang" 先伯父汪次公行狀, *Taihan ji*, 43. 924; Wang, "Ming gu tongyi dafu Nanjing hubu you shilang Cheng gong xingzhuang" 明故通議大夫南京戶部右侍郎程公行狀, *Taihan ji*, 43. 915.

73. Wang, "Ming gu biaoqi jiangjun dudu qianshi zhenshou Guizhou defang zongbing guan Qi Cigong ji pei zeng shuren Li shi hezang muzhiming" 明故驃騎將軍都督僉事鎮守貴州地方總兵官戚次公暨配贈淑人李氏合葬墓誌銘, *Taihan ji*, 54. 1136; Wang, "Ming gu jiexiao Humu Wangshi muzhiming" 明故節孝胡母汪氏墓誌銘, *Taihan ji*, 49. 1041; Wang, "Hu Shaoqing muzhiming" 胡少卿墓誌銘, *Taihan ji*, 56. 1170; Wang, "Wu Taigong ji Taimu hezang muzhiming" 吳太公暨太母合葬墓誌銘, *Taihan ji*, 57. 1194.
74. Zhu Wanshu, *Huishang yu Ming Qing wenxue*, 153.
75. Chen, *Fangshi qinyou shouzha*, 848.
76. Chen, *Fangshi qinyou shouzha*, 849.
77. Lien Chi-Yuan 連啟元, "Ruxia zhi bian: Wang Daokun dui Huizhou renwu 'ruxia' xingxiang de lunshu yu xingsu" 儒俠之辨：汪道昆對徽州人物「儒俠」形象論述與型塑, *Mingdai yanjiu* 明代研究 19 (2012): 121–40. Fang was an affinal relation of Wang Daokun's younger brother Wang Daoguan and appears to have sustained close links, recorded in poetry, with the author of his biography. Wang, "Ruxia zhuan" 儒俠傳, *Taihan ji*, 40. 856–60.
78. Sima Qian 司馬遷, *Shiji* 史記, annot. Pei Yin 裴駰, Sima Zhen 司馬貞, and Zhang Shoujie 張守節 (Beijing: Zhonghua shuju, 1975), vol. 4, 67. 2191.
79. As a literary character, Fang Jingzhen's deft ability to generate profit is predicated on public recognition of his "right-mindedness" or Confucian propriety (*yi* 義): in a representative example, he opens a tea business in Jingzhou, yet his start-up capital consists of donations—up to "two thousand strings of cash" received in a single day—from admiring local supporters. Wang, "Ruxia zhuan," 858.
80. Wang, "Ruxia zhuan," 859. On iterations of similar themes in late imperial literature, see Ariel Fox, "Playing Against Type: The Moral Merchant on the Early Qing Stage," *Journal of Chinese Literature and Culture* 6.2 (November 2019): 383–411.
81. Central to Wang's thesis is the Warring States thinker Han Feizi's 韓非子 (d. 233 BCE) two-fold critique of the *ru* and the *xia* in his "Five Vermin" ("Wudu" 五蠹) chapter; namely, that both groups represent threats to the stability of the state. Lien, "Ruxia zhi bian," 124.
82. Wang, "Ruxia zhuan," 860.
83. Wang, "Ruxia zhuan," 857.
84. For the letter, see Chen, *Fangshi qinyou shouzha*, 486–95. As a child, Fang Jingzhen studied the *Classic of Poetry* and six scripts, yet at the age of fifteen turned to the salt trade with his uncle to support his family as his father fell ill. Fang's mercantile activities and scholarly aspirations are, in Wang's biographical account, mutually constitutive: he travels to Linqing 臨清 in Shandong, for instance, to profit from the prospects of the local economy (Linqing was an important tax station on the Grand Canal, responsible for the collection of almost a quarter of Jiajing fiscal revenue—a sum close to 80 million *taels*), but also to study under the tutelage of the renowned classicist Wu Chong 吳寵 (n.d.).

85. Wang, "Wang Yuanli bishou ming" 汪元釐匕首銘, *Taihan ji*, 28. 1610. The text was later anthologized in He Fuzheng 賀復徵, *Wenzhang bianti huixuan* 文章辨體匯選, in WYGSKQS, jibu, vol. 1407, 557.
86. Li Weizhen 李維楨, "Wang Yuanli jiazhuan" 汪元釐家傳, *Dami shanfang ji* 大泌山房集, in SKQSCMCS, jibu, vol. 153: 71. 226.
87. Zhan, *Zhanshi xingli xiaobian*, 42. 5–6.
88. Joseph McDermott, *The Making of a New Rural Order in South China II. Merchants, Markets, Lineages* (Cambridge: Cambridge University Press, 2020), 145–46.
89. As McDermott shows, Wang Daokun makes this very point, see McDermott, *The Making of a New Rural Order in South China II*, 146.
90. Wang, "Zha Bashi pipa ming" 查八十琵琶銘, *Taihan ji*, 78. 1610.
91. Sun, *Liji jijie*, 303.
92. Yao Lü 姚旅, *Lushu* 露書, in SKQSCMCS, zibu, vol. 111, 683. An anecdote recorded in *Kezuo zhuiyu* 客座贅語 tells of Zha visiting a brothel in Nanjing and meeting an old blind lady, his true *zhiyin*: Zha boasts that if he plays a courtesan's *pipa* he will destroy its strings in one stroke, and when he starts to play the lady recognizes at once that this "official's *pipa* is out of the ordinary" 此官人琵琶與尋常不同, ordering the courtesan offering accompaniment on clappers to cease. The title of this episode, "Zha Bashi's *pipa*," can refer either to a distinctive object or his virtuosic style of playing, and the old blind lady seems to suggest that the two are mutually constitutive. Gu Qiyuan 顧起元, *Kezuo zhuiyu* 客座贅語, ed. Kong Yi 孔一 (Shanghai: Shanghai guji chubanshe, 2012), 93.
93. For other biographies of *pipa* artists from the late Ming, see Eric C. Lai, "Pipa Artists and Their Music in Late Ming China," *Ming Studies* 43 (2008): 43–71; on the place of the *pipa* in Ming musical culture more broadly, see Joseph Lam, "Ming Music and Music History," *Ming Studies* 38 (1997): 21–62.
94. Wang, "Zha Bashi zhuan" 查八十傳, *Taihan ji*, 28. 601. Wang's biography for Zha was widely disseminated. The text was included in a range of late imperial anthologies of classical prose and compendia: Liu Shilin 劉士鏻, *Gujin wenzhi* 古今文致, in SKQSCMCS, jibu, vol. 373. 557–58; Huang Zongxi 黃宗羲, *Ming wenhai* 明文海, in WYGSKQS, jibu, vol. 1458, 55–56; He, *Wenzhang bianti huixuan*, 570–71.
95. Wang, "Zha Bashi zhuan," 601.
96. See, for instance, Qitao Guo's remarks: "When Wang Daokun wrote about Huizhou merchants, he was reflecting not just merchants as individuals, but also local mercantile lineage culture as a whole." Guo, *Huizhou*, 99.
97. Wang later composed another inscription on a vertical "endblown flute" (*xiao* 簫) for aspiring Huizhou flutist (and ink maker), Wu Tingyu 吳廷羽 (Zuogan 左干). Wang, "Zuogan xiao ming" 左干簫銘, *Taihan ji*, 78. 1610. On Wu's career as a painter, see Cai Xinquan 蔡鑫泉, "Ming Huizhou zhuming huajia Wu Tingyu Zuogan shilüe" 明徽州著名畫家吳廷羽左干事略, *Huizhou shehui kexue* 徽州社会科学 5 (2011): 44–48.
98. On Wang Daokun's plays, see Wang, *Ming Qing qujia*, 143–53.
99. Wang, "Zha Bashi" 查八十, *Taihan ji*, 97. 1986.
100. For an introduction to these seals, see Zhu, *Xinchu Mingdai wenren yinzhang jicun yu yanjiu*, 6–9, 47–50. See also Sheng Shilan 盛詩瀾, "He Zhen baiwen yin de xingshi tezheng—cong Wuxi bowuyuan cang He Zhen yin shuo qi" 何震白文印的形式特征—从无锡博物院藏何震印说起, *Zhongguo shufa* 2 (2017): 118–25.

101. Zhu, *Xinchu Mingdai wenren yinzhang jicun yu yanjiu*, 140.
102. While these developments can be said to originate in the work of He Zhen, Su Xuan, Zhan Lian, and others, they came to maturity in the work of later eighteenth-century seal carvers such as Ding Jing 丁敬 (1695–1765) and his follower Huang Yi 黃易 (1744–1801) in the Zhe School 浙派. On the seal carvers of the Zhe School and their influence on mid-Qing practices of inscribing objects, see Yi, "The Calligraphic Art of Chen Hongshou," 81–90.
103. Cai, "Wuxi Gu Lin mu chutu Mingdai liupai yin shiwu kaoshu," 144.
104. Cai, "Wuxi Gu Lin mu chutu Mingdai liupai yin shiwu kaoshu."
105. We can observe this same tendency with Zhan Lian's seals.
106. On seals and material intimacy, see Verity Platt, "Making an Impression: Replication and the Ontology of the Graeco-Roman Seal Stone," *Art History* 29, no. 2 (2006): 241.
107. Cai Yaoqing 蔡耀慶 [Tsai Yao-ching], *Mingdai yinxue fazhan yinsu yu biaoxian zhi yanjiu* 明代印學發展因素與表現之研究 (Taibei: Guoli lishi bowuguan, 2007), 103–11.
108. Catalogues that copy *Yinsou* include Zhang Xueli's 張學禮 *Kaogu zhengwen yinsou* 考古正文印藪 (1589), Gan Yang's 甘暘 *Jigu yinpu* 集古印譜 (1596), Wu Yuanman's 吳元滿 *Jigu yinxuan* 集古印選, Fan Dache's 范大澈 (1524–?) *Jigu yinpu* 集古印譜 (1600), Zhu Xiuneng's 朱修能 (d. 1624) *Yinpin* 印品 (1601), Fang Yongguang's 方用光 *Gujin yinxuan* 古今印選 (1604), and Pan Yunjie's 潘雲杰 *Qin Han yintong* 秦漢印統 (1607).
109. On the charge of stagnation, see Wang Zhideng 王穉登, "*Jin Yifu yinpu* xu" 《金一甫印譜》序, in *Lidai yinxue lunwen xuan* 历代印学论文选, ed. Han Tianheng 韩天衡 (Hangzhou: Xiling yinshe, 1985), 459; on "loss of spirit," see Zhu Shilu 祝世祿, "*Liang Qianqiu Yinjun* xu" 《梁千秋印雋》序, *Lidai yinxue lunwen xuan*, 447. Dong Qichang offers a comparatively favorable assessment of how He Zhen diligently studied *Yinsou* and thus was able to "touch the feet" of Wen Peng; see Dong Qichang, "Xu *Wu Yibu yinyin*" 序《吳亦步印印》, *Lidai yinxue lunwen xuan*, 481. References to the publication of *Yinsou* as a watershed moment in the development of Ming seal carving proliferate in prefaces to late Ming seal catalogues. Wang Zhideng's comments on *Yinsou*, for instance, constitute a repeatable formula that he recycles in assessments of different catalogues; compare his preface for Jin Yifu with Wang Zhideng, "*Sushi yinlüe* ba" 《蘇氏印略》跋, *Lidai yinxue lunwen xuan*, 474; and Wang, "*Gujin yinze* ba" 《古今印則》跋, *Lidai yinxue lunwen xuan*, 440.
110. Zhou Lianggong's anthology inspired late imperial connoisseurs to compile collections of "seal carver biographies" (*yinren zhuan*), a trend that extends from Wang Qishu's 汪啟淑 (1728–1800) *Feihong tang yinren zhuan* 飛鴻堂印人傳 (later reprinted as *Xu yinren zhuan* 續印人傳) in the Qianlong era and Feng Chenghui's 馮承輝 (1786–1840) *Lichao yinshi* 歷朝印識 (1829–1837) in the Daoguang era, to Ye Weiming's 葉為銘 (or Ye Ming 葉銘; 1867–1948) *Zaixu yinren zhuan* 再續印人傳 and *Guang yinren zhuan* 廣印人傳 in the Republican period.
111. Platt, "Making an Impression," 234.
112. Feng Mengzhen 馮夢禎, "Ti He Zhuchen fuzhang ce" 題何主臣符章册, *Kuaixue tang ji* 快雪堂集, in SKQSCMCS, jibu, vol. 164, 446.
113. For Feng's diary records of this trip to Huizhou, see Feng Mengzhen, *Kuaixue tang riji* 快雪堂日記, ed. Ding Xiaoming 丁小明 (Nanjing: Fenghuang chubanshe,

2010), 221–225. Feng Mengzhen also records a number of visits that He Zhen had made to his residence alongside Wang Daohui (Wang Daokun's cousin) who came to sell inkstones. Feng, *Kuaixue tang riji*, 108-9.
114. Kelly, "Impressions of Loss," 1–52.
115. On He Zhen's reputation as a drinker, see Wang, "Song He Zhuchen zhi Chu shi jueju" 送何主臣之楚十絕句, *Taihan ji*, 120. 2781.
116. Wang, "He Changqing guzhuan yinzhang" 何長卿古篆印章, *Taihan ji*, 116. 2594.
117. Wang makes a similar claim for He's diligence as a student of epigraphy in his poem "He Changqing guzhuan yinzhang," "Carving your designs [you] directly copy the nine tripods" 刻畫直須摹九鼎, *Taihan ji*, 116. 2594.
118. The reference to the stone drums appears in a poem sending He Zhen north; see Wang, "Song He Zhuchen beiyou si jueju" 送何主臣北游四絕句, *Taihan ji*, 120. 2771. For other poems on He Zhen's travels, see Wang, "Jingkou song He Zhuchen huan Haiyang wei mu Chen Ru ren qishi shou" 京口送何主臣還海陽為母陳孺人七十壽, *Taihan ji*, 117. 2663; Wang, "Song He Zhuchen zhi Chu shi jueju," 2781.
119. Li Weizhen, "Ji He Zhuchen yinba" 集何主臣印跋, in *Zhongguo yinlun leibian*, 665.
120. Zhou Yingyuan 周应愿, *Yinshuo* 印说, ed. Zhu Tianshu (Beijing: Beijing daxue chubanshe, 2014), 38.
121. Zhou, *Yinshuo*, 42.
122. Zhou, *Yinshuo*, 46.
123. Zhou, *Yinshuo*, 46. The notion that soft stone removes any material constraints on the refined calligrapher (notably Wen Peng) so that he might wield the knife as if it were a brush resurfaces in other prefaces to seal catalogues. See Wu Mingshi 吳名世, "*Hanyuan yinlin* xu" 《翰苑印林》序, *Lidai yinxue lunwen xuan*, 504.
124. Ming commentators start to reflect upon this irony; see Dong, "Xu *Wu Yibu yinyin*," 481.
125. Zhou, *Yinshuo*, 67.
126. Watt, "The Literati Environment," 11; Zhou, "Shu Wen Guobo yinzhang qian" 書文國博印章前, *Yinren zhuan*, 1. 23–26.
127. The story of Wen Peng's discovery builds upon and came to epitomize efforts to distinguish a scholar's seal (*wenren zhi yin* 文人之印) from the artisan's seal (*gongren zhi yin* 工人之印). Zhu Jian 朱簡, "Yinzhang yaolun" 印章要論, *Lidai yinxue lunwen xuan*, 141.
128. Other Ming poets commemorated Wang Daokun's ability to inspect seals as a connoisseur; see Wu Guolun 吳國倫, "Hu Tong houzi qinian shandiao yu yinzhang, wei yu you Wang Boyu, Fang Zhongmei suoshang, yin jizeng yi shi" 胡通侯子祈年善雕玉印章, 為予友汪伯玉, 方仲美所賞, 因寄贈一詩, in *Zhongguo yinlun leibian*, 226.
129. Zhou, "Shu Wen Guobo yinzhang qian," 1. 19.
130. Zhou, "Shu He Zhuchen zhang" 1. 27.
131. The earliest date Wang could have been posted to the Southern Capital was the fifth month of 1572 by which point Wen was already in Beijing. For a study of Wen Peng's time in Beijing and Nanjing in his later years, see Liu Dongqin 劉東芹, "Wen Peng wannian shufa zhuanke huodong ji liangjing xingji kaoshu" 文彭晚年書法篆刻活動及兩京行跡考述, *Shuhua yishu xuekan* 書畫藝術學刊 3 (2007): 431–47.
132. To the best of my knowledge, the earliest literary source to refer to He Zhen as Wen Peng's student was a colophon by Hu Yinglin 胡應麟 (1551–1602) on an ink

painting of bamboo produced by the two men in collaboration, see Hu Yinglin, "Ti He Changqing Wen Shoucheng mozhu tu" 題何長卿文壽承墨竹圖, in *Zhongguo yinlun leibian*, 235.

133. Zhan Jingfeng, "Yinzhang" 印章, in *Zhongguo yinlun leibian*, 233-34.
134. Zhou, "Yu Huang Jishu lun yinzhang shu," 361.
135. Zhou, "Yu Huang Jishu lun yinzhang shu," 361.
136. Wu Xiang 無相, "Lun Wen Peng zai zhuanke shi shang de diwei he gongxian" 論文彭在篆刻史上的地位和貢獻, *Shufa yanjiu* 書法研究 122 (2005): 78-96. For a recent discussion of evidence for Wen's use of soft stone, see Xue Longchun 薛龙春, "Ming zhong hou qi Wumen wenren zhuanke kaolun" 明中后期吴门文人篆刻考论, *Wenyi yanjiu* 文艺研究 9 (2017): 130-38.
137. For studies of this book, see Zhai Tunjian, "He Zhen de shengping yu zhuanke yishu" 何震的生平与篆刻艺术, *Ming Qing Huizhou zhuanke xueshu yantaohui lunwen ji*, 65-68.
138. For an introduction to Liang Zhi's work, see Qiao Zhongshi 乔中石, "Liang Qianqiu zhuanke chutan" 梁千秋篆刻初探, *Ming Qing Huizhou zhuanke xueshu yantaohui lunwen ji*, 82-92.
139. Li Weizhen, "*Yinjun xu*" 印雋序, in *Zhongguo yinlun leibian*, 666-67.
140. Zhou, "Shu Liang Qianqiu pu qian" 書梁千秋譜前, *Yinren zhuan*, 1. 32. Zhou reiterates his claim that "Strive to Eat" and "Sipping Wine, Reading Lyrics" became widely imitated impressions in a letter to Huang Jishu, see Zhou, "Yu Huang Jishu lun yinzhang shu," 361.
141. Zhai, "He Zhen de shengping yu zhuanke yishu," 89.
142. Zhu Shilu, "*Liang Qianqiu Yinjun* xu," 447.
143. Sheng, "He Zhen baiwen yin de xingshi tezheng," 122-23. For a reproduction of the seal, see Tong Yanfang 童衍方, *Jinshi qishou: jinshijia shuhua mingke tezhan tulu* 金石齊壽：金石家書畫銘刻特展圖錄 (Shanghai: Shanghai sanlian shudian chubanshe, 2016), 2: 8.
144. Zhang Hao 張灝, *Chengqing guan yinpu* 承清館印譜 (1617; Kyoto University Library), xuji: 5b.
145. Zhou Lianggong, *Laigu tang yinpu* 賴古堂印譜, in *Zhou Lianggong quanji*, vol. 17, 103.
146. Zhou, "Shu Liang Qianqiu pu qian," 1. 32. Some scholars read *shiyu* 世語 as a reference to *Shishuo xinyu*, yet such a narrow allusion overlooks the logic of Zhou's three-fold comparison of Wen Peng, He Zhen, and Liang Zhi.
147. Zhou, "Shu Liang Qianqiu pu qian," 1. 32.
148. Zhou, "Shu Diange nüzi tuzhang qian" 書細閣女子圖章前, *Yinren zhuan*, 1. 49-52. On the biography of Han Yuesu, see Cai Mengchen 蔡孟宸, "Xiri penglan bo ruanqu, jinchao fu'an nong jinshi: Lun nü zhuanke jia Han Yuesu" 昔日凭栏拨阮曲，今朝伏案弄金石—论女篆刻家韓約素, *Ming Qing Huizhou zhuanke xueshu yantaohui lunwen ji*, 93-108.
149. If Liang Zhi represents cheap imitation and the deceptions of ghostwriting, Liang Danian 梁大年 (n.d.) represents the firsthand adjudication of epigraphic materials, whether bronze vessels ("he was able to discern ancient vessel inscriptions" 君又能辨別古器款識) or excavated ancient jade seals (he "scrubbed it down, judged its inscription and recognized that it was a small imperial seal with six characters from the Qin" 後為浣洗，辨其文，秦六字小璽也). Zhou, "Shu Liang Danian yinpu

qian" 書梁大年印譜前, *Yinren zhuan*, 1. 36. For a discussion, see Kelly, "Impressions of Loss," 36–39.

150. Zhu Qi, *Zhenshui wuxiang: Jiang Ren yu Qingdai Zhepai zhuanke yanjiu* 真水无香：蒋仁与清代浙派篆刻研究 (Hangzhou: Zhejiang renmin meishu chubanshe, 2018), 43–44.

151. See Bedos-Rezak: "[. . .] the moment of contact between die and impression, between seal and owner was, however undoubtedly historical, only transient. That which remained, visible and tangible, was the consistency, the identity between successive imprints produced from a single die." Brigitte Miriam Bedos-Rezak, *When Ego Was Imago: Signs of Identity in the Middle Ages* (Leiden: Brill, 2011), 204–5.

152. Zhou, "Shu Liang Danian yinpu qian," 1. 36.

153. Zhou, "Shu Fang Zhizhi yi yin qian" 書方直之一印前, *Yinren zhuan*, 1. 38–39.

154. Perhaps the closest work to a "seal carver's autobiography" we find is a self-preface attributed to Su Xuan; see Su, "*Yinlüe* zixu" 《印略》自序, *Lidai yinxue lunwen xuan*, 470–1.

155. The Harvard papers were discovered and have been annotated by Chen Zhichao.

156. For an introduction to the Leiden cache, see Shi Ye 施曄, "Cong xinjian Ming ceye kan Jia Wan nianjian Huizhou shishang jiaoyou" 从新见明册页看嘉万年间徽州士商交游, *Jianghuai luntan* 江淮论坛 4 (2013): 138–47.

157. On the Harvard cache, see Shum Chun, "The Chinese Rare Books: An Overview," trans. Sarah M. Allen, in *Treasures of the Yenching: Seventy-Fifth Anniversary of the Harvard-Yenching Library Exhibition Catalogue*, ed. Patrick Hanan (Cambridge, MA: Harvard University Press, 2003), 16; Thomas Kelly, "Paper Trails: Fang Yongbin and the Material Culture of Calligraphy," *Journal of Chinese History* 3, no. 2 (2019): 325–62; Lin Li-yueh 林麗月, "Wanming 'Rushang' yu diyu shehui: *Mingdai Huizhou Fangshi qinyou shouzha* de kaocha" 晚明「儒商」地域社會：《明代徽州方氏親友手札》的考察, in *Jinshi Zhongguo de shehui yu wenhua (860–1800)* 近世中國的社會與文化 (Taibei: Shida lishi, 2007), 467–507; Wang Shiqing 汪世清, "Huizhou xue yanjiu de zhongda gongxian: *Mingdai Huizhou Fangshi qinyou shouzha qibai tong kaoshi* du houji" 徽州学研究的重大贡献《明代徽州方氏亲友手札七百通考释》读后记, *Hefei xueyuan xuebao* 合肥学院学报 21, no. 1 (2004): 12–20; Zhu Wanshu, *Huishang yu Ming Qing wenxue*, 50–59; Xu Min 许敏, "Shixi Mingdai houqi Jiangnan shanggu jiqi zidi de wenrenhua xianxiang—cong Fang Yongbin tanqi" 试析明代后期江南商贾及其子弟的文人化现象—从方用彬谈起, *Zhongguo shi yanjiu* 中国史研究 3 (2005): 157–72.

158. Gillian Russell, *The Ephemeral Eighteenth Century: Print, Sociability, and the Cultures of Collecting* (Cambridge: Cambridge University Press, 2020), 15.

159. Russell, *The Ephemeral Eighteenth Century*, 16.

160. Chen, *Fangshi qinyou shouzha*, 142–45. Cf. Zhu, *Huishang yu Ming Qing wenxue*, 55.

161. Fang's poem for Ma, entitled "To a Beauty Painting Orchids" (Fude meiren hualan 賦得美人畫蘭), is appended to a letter from Yu Ce 俞策 (Moon 110) in Chen, *Fangshi qinyou shouzha*, 470–71.

162. On Fang's practice in the late Ming art market, see Zhang, *Pinjian yu jingying*, 73–95.

163. For evidence of Fang sending bullies to extract debt payments, see Wu Shouhuai 吳守淮 (Fire 28) in Chen, *Fangshi qinyou shouzha*, 898. Incidentally, Wu was the author of the largest number of letters in the cache and had been a member (along

with Fang Yongbin) of Wang Daokun's poetry society. On the request for peacock feathers see Wang Daohui (Metal 75) in Chen, *Fangshi qinyou shouzha*, 612.

164. For examples of Fang giving ink and paper in his requests for paintings, see Liu Jue 劉爵 (Water 23) in Chen, *Fangshi qinyou shouzha*, 825–6; Liu Zhijie 劉之節 (Wood 66) in Chen, *Fangshi qinyou shouzha*, 798.

165. Wang Daohui (Metal 75) in Chen, *Fangshi qinyou shouzha*, 612. On the catalogue of hats, see Wang Daoguan et al., (Metal 6) in Chen, *Fangshi qinyou shouzha*, 497–8. For further evidence of Fang Yongbin's skill as a designer and maker of hats, see Wang Yin (Water 62) in Chen, *Fangshi qinyou shouzha*, 871. On Fang Yongbin's work as a paper-marker, see Qiao Zuoqing 鄔佐卿 (Moon 33) in Chen, *Fangshi qinyou shouzha*, 349–50; Jiang Hongxu 姜鴻緒 (Moon 82) in Chen, *Fangshi qinyou shouzha*, 415; Zhu Duozheng 朱多炡 (Moon 30) in Chen, *Fangshi qinyou shouzha*, 341. I discuss evidence of his work as an ink maker in chapter 3.

166. An inkstick entitled "Golden Terrace" (Huangjin tai 黃金臺) bearing an image of two horses survives in the Palace Museum and appears to have been designed as a commemorative souvenir for Yongbin's journey to Beijing to sit for the civil service examinations. Wang "Huangjin tai wei Fang Yuansu fu" 黃金臺為方元素賦, *Taihan ji*, 100. 2349.

167. On the reference to He Zhen, see the letter titled Zun 遵 (Metal 52) in Chen, *Fangshi qinyou shouzha*, 571. Some notes appear to have been preserved by Fang as samples of work from talented local seal carvers, as if he were compiling his own private seal catalogue. Take, for instance, one of the more ornate letters in the cache, a green sheet with gold flecks from the bronze cutter Wu Liangzhi 吳良止. See the letter from Wu Liangzhi (Metal 94) in Chen, *Fangshi qinyou shouzha*, 633. Wu Liangzhi became famous for his skill in working with bronze and, through his collaboration with Zhang Xueli 張學禮 of Yangzhou, produced copies of three thousand seals for an influential anthology of ancient impressions, primarily from the Qin and Han, *Kaogu zhengwen yinsou* 攷古正文印藪, published in 1589.

168. See the letter from Zhan Jingfeng (Metal 100) in Chen, *Fangshi qinyou shouzha*, 641.

169. On Fang's calligraphy, see Bai Qianshen 白謙慎 and Xue Longchun, "Chenshi de shiji" 尘世的史跡, *Dushu* 读书1 (2007): 55. A letter from Sheng Shitai 盛時泰 (1529–1578) to Fang Yongbin from the eighth month of 1575 records an invitation to meet with Li Minbiao in Beijing (Water 6); see Chen, *Fangshi qinyou shouzha*, 810.

170. See the letter from Huang Xueceng 黃學曾 (Earth 17) in Chen, *Fangshi qinyou shouzha*, 1036.

171. See the letter from Wang Jun 汪濬 (Metal 45) in Chen, *Fangshi qinyou shouzha*, 563.

172. See the letter from Fang Maoxue 方懋學 (Metal 48) in Chen, *Fangshi qinyou shouzha*, 567.

173. See the letter from Pan Wei 潘緯 (Wood 8) in Chen, *Fangshi qinyou shouzha*, 753.

174. Jin Shaofang 金紹坊, "Kezhu xiaoyan" 刻竹小言, in *Zhuke yishu* 竹刻藝術, ed. Jin Shaofang and Wang Shixiang 王世襄 (Beijing: Renmin meishu chubanshe, 1980), 28.

175. Chen, *Fangshi qinyou shouzha*, 801. On requests for tea, see the letter from Wu Liangqi 吳良琦 (Metal 93) in Chen, *Fangshi qinyou shouzha*, 632.

176. Adding a certificatory seal to print adverts (in order to guarantee their authenticity) is a well-attested practice in sources from the Qing; see Zhai Tunjian, "Huizhou sanjian yinshua pin yanjiu" 徽州散件印刷品研究, in *Huizhou: Shuye yu diyu*

wenhua 徽州：书业与地域文化, ed. Michaela Bussotti and Zhu Wanshu (Beijing: Zhonghua shuju, 2010), 394.

177. The use of multicolored ink in late Ming Huizhou is usually traced to a red-and-black edition of Lü Kun's 呂坤 (1536–1618) *Ten Volumes of Prescriptions for the Inner Chamber* (*Guifan shiji* 閨范十集) and the five-colored prints in Cheng Junfang's 程君房 (1541–1610) *Master Cheng's Garden of Inks* (*Chengshi moyuan* 程氏墨苑). Zhai Tunjian, "Huizhou sanjian yinshua pin yanjiu," 399–401.
178. Reprinted in Chen, *Fangshi qinyou shouzha*, 12–13.
179. Wang Daokun's circle was instrumental in the promotion of Pine Lichen tea; see Wang, "Songluo shi xincha" 松蘿試新茶, *Taihan ji*, 111. 2428; Wang wrote various other poems on his trips to Mount Pine Lichen: Wang, "Songluo daozhong" 松蘿道中, *Taihan ji*, 111. 2428; Wang, "Su Songluo Wu Tian zhu junzi zai jiu jianfang" 宿松蘿吳田諸君子載酒見訪, *Taihan ji*, 111. 2429. Wang also composed another poem on testing free tea yet does not refer to a particular site—the imagery of this poem closely resembles his poem on Songluo; see Wang, "Shi xincha" 試新茶, *Taihan ji*, 109. 2295.

3. THE INK-MAKER'S MARK

1. Zhang Zigao's 張子高 (1886–1976) ink cakes were included in the joint publication of the *Record of Four Ink Collectors* (*Sijia cangmo tulu* 四家藏墨圖錄), a lithographic printed copy of eighty-four rubbings of prized ink cakes from the Ming and Qing, alongside pieces from the collections of Ye Gongchuo 葉恭綽 (1881–1968), Yin Runsheng 尹潤生 (1908–1982), and Zhang Jiongbo 張絅伯 (1885–1969). The catalogue was reprinted in 2006; see Ye Gongchuo, Zhang Jiongbo, Zhang Zigao, and Yin Runsheng, eds., *Sijia cangmo tulu* 四家藏墨圖錄 (Shanghai: Shanghai shudian chubanshe, 2006). For an introduction, see Wang Yi 王毅 and Cai Xinquan 蔡鑫泉, *Zhongguo mo wenhua wenxue* 中國墨文化問學 (Shanghai: Shanghai yuandong chubanshe, 2014), 171–96.
2. See Jonathan Hay: "The historical passage from an inscriptional topography created over time in an antique object to a similar topography created with a decorative purpose as part of the production of a modern object . . . may, in fact, underpin the historical emergence of inscriptional topography as a surface-scape resource." Hay, *Sensuous Surfaces*, 209.
3. Compare, for instance, with Dorothy Ko on the collector's inscription: "most patrons would not have composed an inscription when the [object] was still in the hands of the artisan." Ko, *The Social Life of Inkstones*, 97.
4. Schäfer, "Inscribing the Artifact and Inspiring Trust," 260–63.
5. David Wengrow, "Prehistories of Commodity Branding," *Current Anthropology* 49 (2008): 7–34.
6. David Wengrow, "Introduction: Commodity Branding in Archaeological and Anthropological Perspectives," 29.
7. Li-chiang Lin, "The Proliferation of Images: The Ink-stick Designs and the Printing of the *Fang-shih mo-p'u* and the *Ch'eng-shih mo yuan*" (PhD diss., Princeton University, 1998); Lin Li-chiang 林麗江, "Wanming Huizhou moshang Cheng Junfang yu

Fang Yulu moye de zhankai yu jingzheng" 晚明徽州墨商程君房與方于魯墨業的開展與競爭, in *Huizhou: Shuye yu diyu wenhua*, 121–97.

8. Adrian Johns, "Ink," in *Materials and Expertise in Early Modern Europe: Between Market and Laboratory*, ed. Ursula Klein and E. C. Spary (Chicago: University of Chicago Press, 2010), 120–21.
9. Johns, "Ink," 121.
10. Historians of material culture assume that the evidence for branding in early modern China consists of reign titles, place names, and the names of artisans or workshops.
11. On the later history of ink marketing, see Lin Huan's 林欢 study of the Hu Kaiwen 胡開文 business; Lin Huan 林欢, *Huimo Hu Kaiwen yanjiu* 徽墨胡开文研究 (Beijing: Gugong chubanshe, 2016), esp. 101–58 on markings.
12. Adrian Johns writes, "what is being passed over is a substance without which not a single character of a single line of a single page of a single book could ever have existed." It is as though, he reflects, one were to "write about the industrial revolution without mentioning coal or iron." Johns, "Ink," 105.
13. For an introduction to the history of ink making in China, see Herbert Franke, *Kulturgeschichtliches über die chinesische Tusche* (Munich: Verlag der Bayerischen Akademie der Wissenschaften, 1962); Tsuen-hsuin Tsien, *Science and Civilization in China*, vol. 5, *Chemistry and Chemical Technology*, bk 1: *Paper and Printing* (Cambridge: Cambridge University Press, 1985), 233–53.
14. Tsien, *Written on Bamboo and Silk*, 186.
15. This partial list is adapted from Tsien, *Paper and Printing*, 242–43.
16. Tsien, *Paper and Printing*, 247.
17. Tsien, *Paper and Printing*, 247.
18. On the snake-pit scandal, see Pan Dexi 潘德熙, *Wenfang sibao* 文房四宝 (Shanghai: Shanghai guji chubanshe, 1991), 77–78.
19. Ma Sanheng 麻三衡, *Mozhi* 墨志, in *Shewen zijiu* 涉聞梓舊, ed. Jiang Guangxu 蔣光煦 (Shanghai: Hanfen lou, 1924), vol. 15, 20a.
20. See Yuan Fuzhi 袁福徵 (Moon 55) in Chen, *Fangshi qinyou shouzha*, 294; Wang Wuze 汪無擇 (Metal 74) in Chen, *Fangshi qinyou shouzha*, 607.
21. Bai, *Fu Shan's World*, 5.
22. Xie Bi 謝陛 (Fire 56) in Chen, *Fangshi qinyou shouzha*, 934. On Fang Yulu's name, see Tu Long's 屠隆 (1543–1605) biography: "Fang Yulu, courtesy name: Jianyuan, was from Xindu [Huizhou]. His first name was Da'ao and his courtesy name was Yulu. Later when the Emperor heard of the inscription 'Yulu's Ink' and praised 'Yulu,' Fang changed his proper name to Fang Yulu and took Jianyuan as his courtesy name." 方于魯，字建元，新都人。初名大澂，字于魯，後以于魯墨銘聞于今上，今上亟稱之為魯，遂更以為名，字建元。Fang, *Fangshi mopu*, 301.
23. Wang "Huangjin tai wei Fang Yuansu fu," 2349.
24. Tian Yiheng 田藝蘅 (Wood 51) in Chen, *Fangshi qinyou shouzha*, 778. For other letters involving requests for Fang Yulu's ink, see Yang Yizhou 楊一洲 (Moon 19) in Chen, *Fangshi qinyou shouzha*, 313; Zhang Zhengmeng 張正蒙 (Moon 35) in Chen, *Fangshi qinyou shouzha*, 353; Wu Wanchun 吳萬春 (Metal 64) in Chen, *Fangshi qinyou shouzha*, 597.
25. Bai, *Fu Shan's World*, 5.

3. THE INK-MAKER'S MARK

26. Li Weizhen, "Fang Waishi muzhiming" 方外史墓誌銘, *Dami shanfang ji*, 150. 87. The editors of the *Imperial Catalogue of the Complete Library in Four Branches of Literature* (*Siku quanshu zongmu tiyao* 四庫全書總目提要) note that Fang's studio, the "Pavilion of Halcyon Days" (Jiari lou 佳日樓), burned down destroying all of his calligraphy and paintings with only his fourteen-volume collection of poetry, *Fang Jianyuan ji* 方建元集, and his illustrated catalogue of ink-cake designs surviving.
27. For a comprehensive introduction to these publications, see Lin, "The Proliferation of Images." Cai Meifen 蔡玫芬 [Ts'ai Mei-fen], "Mingdai de moshu" 明代的墨書, in *Zhonghua Minguo jianguo bashi nian Zhongguo yishu wenwu taolunhui lunwenji* 中華民國建國八十年中國藝術文物討論會論文集/*International Colloquium on Chinese Art History, 1991, Proceedings*, vol. 4: *Qiwu* 器物/*Antiquities*, part 2 (Taibei: Guoli gugong bowuyuan, 1992), 681–726.
28. Cheng Dayue 程大約 ed., *Li Madou ti baoxiang tu* 利瑪竇題寶像圖, in *Sheyuan mocui* 涉園墨萃, ed. Tao Xiang 陶湘 (Beijing: Wujin taoshi, 1929), vol. 2. The first two prints were designed by Maarten de Vos (1532–1603) and engraved by Antonie Wierix II (1555–1603), and the third print was executed by Crispijn van de Passe I (ca. 1565–1637). The fourth print (likely a gift from Matteo Ricci himself) was based on a Japanese version of a print likely produced by Jesuit Jean Nicolao. The scholarship on these prints is voluminous; see Paul Pelliot, "La Peinture et La Gravure Européennes en Chine au Temps de Mathieu Ricci," *T'oung Pao* 20, no. 1 (1920): 1–18; Carmen Guarino, "The Interpretation of Images in Matteo Ricci's Pictures for 'Cheng shi mo yuan,'" *Ming Qing yanjiu* 6, no. 1 (1997): 21–44.
29. For a comprehensive study of the Sanskrit texts on these eighteen designs, see Liao Yang 廖旸, "Mingdai Handi liuchuan de shangle, xi jingang xi yu jingangjie fanzi lun—yi *Fangshi mopu Chengshi moyuan* suo kan wei zhongxin" 明代汉地流传的上乐、喜金刚系与金刚界梵字轮—以《方氏墨谱》、《程氏墨苑》所刊为中心, in *Hanzang foxue yanjiu: Wenben, renwu, tuxiang he lishi* 汉藏佛学研究：文本，人物，图像和历史, ed. Shen Weirong 沈卫荣 (Beijing: Zhongguo zangxue chubanshe, 2013), 483–520. Liao suggests that the akṣaracakra diagrams seem to be primarily related to tantric meditations for Hevajra (Xijin gang 喜金刚), Cakrasamvara (Shangle 上樂), and Vajradhatu (Jingang jie 金剛界).
30. Lin, "Proliferation of Images," 93–94.
31. Cai, "Mingdai de moshu," 285.
32. Cai, "Mingdai de moshu," 285. For a rare example of a named mold carver, see Zhongguo wenfang sibao quanji bianji weiyuanhui, ed., *Zhongguo wenfang sibao quanji 1: mo*, 73.
33. For a recent discussion of the place of philosophical syncretism in the visual system of *Master Fang's Ink Catalogue*, see Liu, "Daxuan zhenmi," 42–55. For an illuminating discussion of Wang Daokun's interest in Buddhism, see Yuhang Li's recent study of his identification with Guanyin, his organization of Water Land (*shuilu* 水陸) rites at Jiaoshan 焦山, and his devotion to the Buddhist courtesan dancer Xu Jinghong 徐鶯鴻, also named Xu Pianpian 徐翩翩 (for whom he composed a pseudo-Buddhist scripture, "A Chapter on the Heavenly Being Huiyue" [*Huiyue tianren pin* 彗月天人品]). Yuhang Li, *Becoming Guanyin: Artistic Devotion of Buddhist Women in Late Imperial China* (New York: Columbia University Press, 2020), 51–58. On Wang Daokun's patronage of Daoist pilgrimage sites and Ming Daoist

3. THE INK-MAKER'S MARK

communities, see Richard G. Wang, "Qiyunshan as a Replica of Wudangshan," *Journal of Chinese Religions* 42, no. 1 (2014): 33.

34. Liu, "Daxuan zhenmi," 126–59.
35. For Wang Daokun's own theorization of this organizational logic, see Wang, "Fang Yulu mobiao" 方于魯墨表, *Taihan ji*, 85. 1769–70.
36. Ban Gu 班固, *Hanshu* 漢書 (Beijing: Zhonghua shuju, 1962), 21. 964; Liu Xu 劉昫 (887–947) uses this line to support his reading of Laozi's principle: "the Dao generates one, one generates two, two generates three, three generates ten-thousand things" 道生一，一生二，二生三，三生萬物; see Liu Xu, *Jiu Tang shu* 舊唐書 (Beijing: Zhonghua shuju, 1975), 22. 858.
37. Hu Yinglin (a sponsor of Fang's ink business and a member of Wang Daokun's coterie) had, as Peter Bol demonstrates, started to query the Neo-Confucian presumption that scholarship "return" to a fundamental "unity and coherence." Peter K. Bol, "Looking to Wang Shizhen: Hu Yinglin (1551–1602) and Late Ming Alternatives to Neo-Confucian Learning," *Ming Studies* 1 (2006): 126.
38. Both the reprinted *Xuanhe bogu tu* and *Master Fang's Ink Catalogue* were published in 1588, and both were carved by the typecutter Huang Shouyan 黃守言 (n.d.). On the publication history of *Xuanhe bogu tu*, see François Louis, "The Hejiacun Rhyton and the Chinese Wine Horn (Gong): Intoxicating Rarities and Their Antiquarian History," *Artibus Asiae* 67, no. 2 (2007): 233.
39. For a recent discussion of these tendencies, see Liu, "Daxuan zhenmi," 27–34.
40. Liao Kebin 廖可斌, *Mingdai wenxue fugu yundong yanjiu* 明代文學復古運動研究 (Beijing: Shangwu yinshuguan, 2008), 348–62.
41. For a brief overview of the fate of the Qin seal in the sixteenth century, see Rusk, "Artifacts of Authentication," 181–87.
42. Wang Fu 王黼, ed., *Boruzhai chongxiu Xuanhe bogutu* 泊如齋重修宣和博古圖錄, ed. Wu Gonghong 吳公弘 (Dongshutang 1603; Harvard-Yenching Library Rare Book), 22. 17a.
43. Liu, "Daxuan zhenmi," 350–51.
44. On the symbolism of mirrors and their significance in Huizong's collections of antiquities, see Patricia Ebrey, *Accumulating Culture: The Collections of Emperor Huizong* (Seattle: University of Washington Press, 2008), 198.
45. Three of the first ink cake designs published in *Master Fang's Ink Catalogue* similarly adapt impressions from Qin-Han "imperial seals" (*xi* 璽) printed at the beginning of *Gushi jigu yinpu*, suggesting that the editors of the ink catalogue loosely modeled the ink-book's structure upon the organizational scheme of antiquarian Qin-Han seal folios that open with markers of imperial authority. Fang, *Fangshi mopu*, 333.
46. Tsien, *Paper and Printing*, 248–49.
47. See Stephen Houston: "Most skeuomorphs appear in more resistant materials. . . . The durability of the skeuomorph, motivated by conditions of heavy use and environmental onslaught, must have had semantic freight, too. If not a direct or primary form, it would soon become so; the salient form was the one that lasted." Stephen Houston, *The Life Within: Classic Maya and the Matter of Permanence* (New Haven, CT: Yale University Press, 2014), 60–61.
48. On the influence of *Master Fang's Ink Catalogue* on other illustrated books, see Anne Burkus-Chasson, *Through a Forest of Chancellors: Fugitive Histories in Liu*

Yuan's *Lingyan ge, an Illustrated Book from Seventeenth-Century Suzhou* (Cambridge, MA: Harvard Asia Center, 2010), 25–26, 195, 203, 216–21.

49. Later Qing ink makers still continued to print illustrated catalogues, see for instance the Huizhou collector and seal connoisseur Wang Qishu's *Feihong tang mopu* 飛鴻堂墨譜 (Wang was also the author of a sequel to Zhou Lianggong's *Biographies of Seal Carvers*), a single-volume edition of which survives in Peking University Library. The catalogue contains a copy of an inkstick with the title "One with Clear Heaven" and a section of Wang Daokun's inscription for the brand. Wang Qishu ed., *Feihong tang yanpu mopu pingpu dinglu pu: liu juan* 飛鴻堂硯譜墨譜瓶譜鼎鑪譜：六卷 (Beijing: Guojia tushuguan chubanshe, 2013), vol. 4, 50a. The most lavishly illustrated Qing inkstick catalogue is Wang Junwei's 汪君蔚 multi-color edition of his grandfather, Huizhou ink maker Wang Jinsheng's 汪近聖 (fl. 18th century) designs, a project explicitly presented as a tribute to the Qianlong and Jiaqing courts, see Wang Junwei et al., *Jiangu zhai mosou* 鑑古齋墨藪, in *Sheyuan mocui*, vols., 9–11.

50. Zhou Shaoliang, *Qingdai mingmo tancong* 清代名墨談叢 (Beijing: Wenwu chubanshe, 1982), 4.

51. The interconnections between Wang's promotion of Fang Yulu's ink and his broader engagement with the inscription of objects for Huizhou artists can be observed in his relations with two of the leading illustrators for Fang's catalogue: Ding Yunpeng and Wu Tingyu. Wang Daokun composed inscriptions on signature objects belonging to both of these Huizhou artists: an inkstone for Ding and an end-blown flute for Wu. See Wang, "Jieyuan yan ming you xu" 結緣硯銘有序, *Taihan ji*, 78. 1611; Wang, "Zuogan xiao ming," *Taihan ji*, 78. 1610. For an introduction to Ding Yunpeng's career as a painter, see Sewall Oertling II, "Ting Yun-P'eng: A Chinese Artist of the Late Ming Dynasty" (PhD diss., University of Michigan, 1980). Wang Daokun was related to Ding's mother, a fellow Wang 汪 of Xiuning. On Wu's career as a painter, see Cai, "Ming Huizhou zhuming huajia Wu Tingyu Zuogan shilüe," 44–48.

52. "Er zhi" 二芝 bears an inscription for Long Ying 龍膺(1560–1622) from Wang Daokun, see Fang, *Fangshi mopu*, 372. For the inscription, see Wang, "Er zhi mo ming" 二芝墨銘, *Taihan ji*, 78. 1612.

53. See, for instance, the design "Daqian chun" 大千春, bearing the date 1584, originally a gift for Wang Daokun's birthday in Fang, *Fangshi mopu*, 387. Fang's "Xian Li pan gen" 僊李蟠根, also dated 1584, was dedicated to Li Weizhen, see Fang, *Fangshi mopu*, 371.

54. If we look, for instance, at a colophon that Wang wrote to commemorate the acquisition of a decorated inkstone attributed to the eminent Yuan dynasty painter Zhao Mengfu 趙孟頫 (1254–1322) bearing images of the "True Forms of the Five Peaks" (*wu yue zhenxing tu* 五嶽真形圖), we learn that he also obtained copies of two famous sets of pictures: "Images of the Five Planets" (*wuxing tu* 五星圖) and "Images of the Twenty-Eight Lunar Mansions" (*ershiba xiu tu*). Wang's colophon suggests he displayed the Zhao Mengfu inkstone alongside a prized scroll bearing both the Five Planets and Twenty-Eight Lunar Mansions owned by the famous art collector and calligrapher Mo Shilong 莫是龍 (1537–1587) and that the Suzhou scholars Wang Shizhen and his brother Wang Shimao wrote appreciative comments for this scroll. Wang, "Zhao Wenmin yuanyan tu ba" 趙文敏圓研圖跋, *Taihan ji*,

86. 1779. For Wang Shizhen's comments on Mo Shilong's scroll with the Five Planets and Twenty-Eight Lunar Mansions, see "Wuxing ershiba xiu moben" 五星二十八宿摹本 and "You wei Mo Tinghan ti wuxing ershiba xiu wuyue zhenxing tu" 又為莫廷韓題五星二十八宿五嶽真形圖 in Wang Shizhen 王世貞, *Yanzhou shanren tiba* 弇州山人題跋, ed. Tang Zhibo 湯志波 (Zhejiang: Renmin meishu chubanshe, 2012), 601–3.
55. On the popularity of astral themes and the "gathering of five planets" in ink-cake design, see Huang Taiyang 黃台陽, *Moxiang shijia* 墨香世家 (Haikou: Hainan chubanshe, 2017), 145–47. For an overview of the iconography of astral designs in *Master Fang's Ink Catalogue*, see Liu, "Daxuan zhenmi," 429–70.
56. The Wolf and Porcupine are animal spirits for the Walls and Legs Mansions, respectively.
57. Wang, "Wuxing ju kuibi mo ming" 五星聚奎壁墨銘, *Taihan ji*, 78. 1613.
58. For a poem by Wang Daokun celebrating this occasion and listing the White Elm members who attended the event, see Wang, "Jiashen sanyue yiwei Zaigong jiang yi kaoji xing Sun Mishu, Ding Mingfu, Guo Cifu, Pan Jingsheng ji buning ersan xiongdi jianzhi hubi xingying qu Baiyu she chajin shi ri wuxing ju yu kuibi shi Zaigong lankui zhi chen wenqi nian chunqiu ershi you wu xiang yu deng ge wei shou shu yu xianming" 甲申三月乙未宰公將以考績行孫秘書丁明府郭次父潘景升及不佞二三兄弟餞之扈蹕行營去白榆社差近是日五星聚於奎壁適宰公攬揆之辰問其年春秋二十有五相與登歌為壽屬余先鳴, *Taihan ji*, 116. 2612.
59. For sources on the Fenggan Society, founded in 1567, see Wang, "Fenggan she ji" 豐干社記, *Taihan ji*, 72. 1481–82; "Ji Fenggan she zhu junzi" 寄豐干社諸君子, *Taihan ji*, 109. 2332; "Beiyou bie she zhong zhuzi" 北游別社中諸子, *Taihan ji*, 109. 2332–33; "Ji Fenggan she zhuzi" 寄豐干社諸子, *Taihan ji*, 113. 2495. The members were: Wang Daokun, Wang Daoguan, Wang Daohui, Chen Quan 陳筌 (1535–1576), Fang Ce 方策, Fang Jian 方簡 (1542–1584), Fang Yu 方宇 (1546–1610), Fang Yongbin, Wu Shouhuai, Cheng Benzhong 程本中 (1547–1584), Xie Bi 謝陛 (1547–1615), and Fang Yulu.
60. In addition to Wang Daokun, Daoguan, and Daohui, the main members of the White Elm Society were: Long Ying 龍膺 (1560–1622), Guo Di 郭第, Pan Zhiheng 潘之恆 (1556–1622), She Xiang 佘翔, Chen Rubi 陳汝壁, Ding Yingtai 丁應泰, Li Weizhen, Zhu Duozheng, Shen Mingchen 沈明臣 (1518–1595), Zhang Jiazhen 章嘉禎, Zhou Tianqiu 周天球 (1514–1595), Tu Long, Xu Gui 徐桂, Yu Ce 俞策 (1550–1627), Lü Yinchang 呂胤昌 (1560–?), Wu Jiadeng 吳稼㵥, Hu Yinglin and Zhang Yigui 張一桂 (1540–1592). Geng Chuanyou, "Baiyu she shulüe" 白榆社述略, *Huangshan xueyuan xuebao* 黃山學院學報 1 (2007): 29–33.
61. There are, for instance, no prefatory materials by the ink maker included in the book.
62. Mei Nafang 梅娜芳, *Mo de yishu*: Fangshi mopu *he* Chengshi moyuan 墨的艺术:《方氏墨谱》和《程氏墨苑》(Haining: Guangxi meishu chubanshe, 2011), 68.
63. Fang, *Fangshi mopu*, 296.
64. This label, in the left-hand box of the design, accompanies a leisure seal that is based on a motto or a literary allusion that compliments Fang Yulu's ink business.
65. Burkus-Chasson, *Through a Forest of Chancellors*, 134.
66. For a brief overview of the background to this inscription, see Bruce Rusk, "The Rogue Classicist: Feng Fang (1493–1566) and His Forgeries" (PhD diss., University of California, Los Angeles, 2004), 184–85, 193–94.

3. THE INK-MAKER'S MARK

67. The source was printed in Zhu Yun's 朱雲 *Expanded Rhyming Epigraphic Dictionary* (*Guang jinshi yunfu* 廣金石韻府) published in 1530.
68. Waley, *The Book of Songs*, 314. Kong Yingda, *Maoshi zhengyi*, 20-2. 346.
69. A combination of two allusions from the *Classic of Poetry*: "Within the sea-boundaries of the land, All are the king's servants" 率土之濱，莫非王臣 and "The country was all reduced to order; Its [chiefs] appeared before the king" 四方既平，徐方來庭. Kong Yingda, *Maoshi zhengyi*, 13-1. 195; 18-5. 309.
70. Fang, *Fangshi mopu*, 306.
71. Zhu's poem was incorporated onto other inkstick designs. The Suzhou Museum holds an inkstick that pairs the poem with another design from *Master Fang's Catalogue* that displays an image of a "one-legged dragon" *zun* 夔龍尊 bronze vessel (an image, in turn, taken from the *Xuanhe Hall*). Liu, "Daxuan zhenmi," 96-7. This inkstick, bearing the mark "Paint the One Ink" 畫一墨, a brand released in 1596, shows how different designs within *Master Fang's Catalogue* could be adapted and recombined to produce new inksticks.
72. Cheng-hua Wang, "Material Culture and Emperorship: The Shaping of Imperial Roles at the Court of Xuanzong (r. 1426-35)" (PhD diss., Yale University, 1998), 288-307.
73. Hay, *Sensuous Surfaces*, 58. Zhang, "Biyu zan ming," 405.
74. Clunas, *Superfluous Things*, 61-2.
75. For examples of the Xuande reign mark on extant Ming ink cakes, see Zhongguo wenfang sibao quanji bianji weiyuanhui, ed., *Zhongguo wenfang sibao quanji 1: mo*, 6 (plate 9), 7 (plate 10).
76. On the Ming connoisseurship of Chai ware, see Clunas, *Superfluous Things*, 102, 104, 111. On Li Tinggui's ink, see Cai Meifen, "Moyunshi li de Li Tinggui mo" 墨雲室裡的李廷珪墨, *Gugong wenwu yuekan* 故宮文物月刊 92 (1990): 109-110.
77. Fang, *Fangshi mopu*, 301.
78. Liu and Yu, *Dijing jingwu lüe*, 238-39.
79. Liu and Yu, *Dijing jingwu lüe*, 242.
80. Yin Runsheng provides an introduction to *mopin* 墨品 in his brief chapter on the subject in Yin Runsheng 尹潤生, *Molin shihua* 墨林史話 (Beijing: Zijincheng chubanshe, 1986), 27-30.
81. Yin, *Molin shihua*, 28.
82. Xie Zhaozhi 谢肇制, *Wu za zu* 五杂组, ed. Fu Cheng 傅成 (Shanghai: Shanghai guji chubanshe, 2012), 238.
83. Ink-cake designs could then be manufactured from these different batches of ink. The Palace Museum, for instance, holds a number of ink cakes that copy designs in Fang's 1588 catalogue yet are marked with the grade title "Paint the One Ink" released in 1596 to counteract the widespread counterfeiting of his earlier labels. An ink maker could, in other words, continue to use the same ink-cake designs while refining or simply renaming a new and improved ink recipe.
84. Wang, "Fang Yulu mobiao," 1770.
85. Fang, *Fangshi mopu*, 316.
86. The letter was authored by Wang Daokun's brother, Wang Daoguan; see Fang, *Fangshi mopu*, 316.
87. Fang, *Fangshi mopu*, 316.

88. John Frow, "Signature and Brand," in *High-Pop: Making Culture into Popular Entertainment*, ed. Jim Collins (Oxford: Blackwell, 2002), 67.
89. Roland Barthes, "The Advertising Message," in *The Semiotic Challenge*, trans. Richard Howard (Berkeley: University of California Press, 1994), 177.
90. See also the discussion of *xuande* in Wang and Cai, *Zhongguo mo wenhua wenxue*, 4–5.
91. Fabrizio Pregadio, *Great Clarity: Daoism and Alchemy in Early Medieval China* (Stanford, CA: Stanford University Press, 2006), 8–10.
92. Yin, *Molin shihua*, 27–30.
93. Sima Qian, *Shiji*, vol. 2, 27. 1339.
94. Su Shi, "Shu Huaimin suo yi mo" 書懷民所遺墨, *Su Shi wenji*, 70. 7961.
95. Gordon Teskey, *Delirious Milton: The Fate of the Poet in Modernity* (Cambridge, MA: Harvard University Press, 2006), 127.
96. Jacques Derrida, *Signéponge–Signsponge*, trans. Richard Rand (New York: Columbia University Press, 1984), 118.
97. "Auspicious clouds" are "ethers (*qi*) of joy" 卿雲見，喜氣也; later taken to be synonymous with *qingyun* 慶雲, a five-colored auspicious cloud (*wuse xiangyun* 五色祥雲). Sima Qian, *Shiji*, vol. 2, 27. 1339.
98. Wang Daokun, "Feiyan mo ming" 非煙墨銘, *Taihan ji*, 78. 1613.
99. Fang, *Fangshi mopu*, 415.
100. Su Shi, "Sun Xinlao ji mo sishou" 孫莘老寄墨, *Su Shi shiji jiaozhu* 蘇軾詩集校注, vols. 1–8, in *Su Shi quanji jiaozhu*, 4: 25. 2754.
101. Fang, *Fangshi mopu*, 415. Ankeney Weitz, trans., *Zhou Mi's Record of Clouds and Mist Passing Before One's Eyes: An Annotated Translation* (Leiden: Brill, 2002), 180.
102. Liu Yuejin 劉躍進, *Wenxuan jiuzhu jicun* 文選舊註輯存, ed. Xu Hua 徐華 (Nanjing: Fenghuang chubanshe, 2017), vol. 8, 25. 4730.
103. Wendy Hui Kyong Chun, "The Enduring Ephemeral, or the Future Is a Memory," in *Media Archaeology: Approaches, Applications, and Implications*, ed. Erkki Huhtamo and Jussi Parikka (Berkeley: University of California Press, 2011), 199.
104. Fang, *Fangshi mopu*, 305.
105. Shen Defu, *Wanli yehuo bian* 萬曆野獲編 (Beijing: Zhonghua shuju, 1997), 3: 663.
106. Jiang Shaoshu 姜紹書, "Mokao" 墨考, *Yunshi zhai bitan*, 1. 271.
107. Cheng Junfang, *Chengshi moyuan*, in SKQSCMCS, zibu, vol. 79, 77.
108. Xu, "Cheng Junfang: Baomo zhai ji" 程君房《寶墨齋記》, in *Sheshi xiantan*, 932.
109. See Huang Taiyang, *Moxiang shijia*, 57. Song Luo, for instance, lists a product marked with Cheng's name and the brand "Not Soot." Song Luo 宋犖, *Mantang xu mopin* 漫堂續墨品, in *Shiliu jia moshuo* 十六家墨說, ed. Wu Changshou 吳昌綬 (Hang xian: Renhe Wushi shuangzhao lou, 1922), 51a. Ye Gongchuo contributed a rubbing of an inkstick bearing Cheng's mark and the stamp "Not Soot" to the "Illustrated Catalogue of Four Ink Collections." Ye et al., *Sijia cangmo tulu*, 42.
110. Zhang Renxi, *Xuetang Mopin* 雪堂墨品, in *Shiliu jia moshuo*, 36a; see also Sun Jiong 孫炯, *Yanshan zhai mopu* 硯山齋墨譜, in *Shiliu jia moshuo*, 55b.
111. Cao Shengchen 曹聖臣, *Caoshi molin* 曹氏墨林, in SKQSCMCS, zibu, vol. 79, 475. Collector Yin Runsheng owned a Cao Sugong inkstick bearing the brand "Not Soot" in embossed seal script with blue highlights and an image of a *ding* cauldron

dated to 1688. The other side of the rectangular inkstick, weighing around 19 grams, bears a fourteen-character marking in running script: "Manufactured by Cao Sugong of Old She County Following the Yishui Method in the Wuchen year of the Kangxi reign (1688)" (Kangxi wuchen gu She Cao Sugong fang Yishui fa zhi 康熙戊辰古歙曹素功仿易水法制). Yin Runsheng, *Yin Runsheng moyuan jiancang lu* 尹润生墨苑鉴藏录 (Beijing: Zijincheng chubanshe, 2008), 196–197.

112. "Composed by an Emei He of Jinling" 晉陵峨眉禾題. Cao, *Caoshi molin*, 475.
113. Yin, *Yin Runsheng moyuan jiancang lu*, 196–97.
114. Lin Li-chiang, "Riben Gumeiyuan xiangguan moshu zhi yanjiu: Shiba shiji Zhongri yishu wenhua jiaoliu zhi yi duan" 日本古梅園相關墨書之研究—十八世紀中日藝術文化交流之一端, *Hanxue yanjiu* 漢學研究 28.2 (2011): 127–68.
115. Zhuangzi, *Zhuangzi: The Complete Writings*, 61; Guo, comp., *Zhuangzi jishi*, 3. 275.
116. Wang, "Fang Yulu Liaotian yi mo ming" 方于魯寥天一墨銘, *Taihan ji*, 78. 1612; Fang, *Fangshi mopu*, 397.
117. Waley, *The Book of Songs*, 40; Kong Yingda, *Maoshi zhengyi*, 3-1. 46.
118. Kong Yingda, *Shangshu zhengyi*, 18. 125.
119. On musk in ink, see Tsien, *Paper and Printing*, 246–47.
120. Zhuangzi, *Zhuangzi: The Complete Writings*, 71. See also therein Ziporyn's note on *chong* 沖: "The word means to flush something out with a surge of water, but is also used to denote the apparently derivative meanings of both 'emptiness' (open space) and 'harmony.' One may combine these ideas into the image of a cleansing flush of water that empties, and that restores harmony by washing away all one-sided cloggings, that blends all the elements by allowing fluid interconnections between them" (71n19). Guo, comp., *Zhuangzi jishi*, 3. 302.
121. Kroll, *A Student's Dictionary*, 313.
122. Fang, *Fangshi mopu*, 324.
123. "Hongzhong" refers to an estate on the Yellow Mountains to the northwest of Shexian. The name initially designated Jiang Luan's 蔣鑾 (n.d.) estate. Wang married a woman from the Jiang family. Later Wang appears to have adopted the name as a cognomen. Wang, "Hongzhong ji" 䍐中記, *Taihan ji*, 72. 1484–1486. Zhou Lianggong, as shown in chapter 2, referred to Wang Daokun as Hongzhong in his biographical sketches of Wen Peng and He Zhen.
124. "One with Clear Heaven" appears as Fang Yulu's leading label, prioritized over "Not Soot," in a range of publications including Gao Lian's 高濂 (1573–1620) *Eight Disquisitions on Nurturing Life* (*Zunsheng bajian* 遵生八箋; 1591).
125. Xing Tong 邢侗, "Mo tan" 墨談, in *Xing Tong ji* 邢侗集, ed. Gong Xiaowei 宮曉衛 and Xiu Guangli 修廣利 (Jinan: Qi Lu shushe, 2017), 21. 566. Xing returns to his critique of Fang (and "Not Soot" and "One with Clear Heaven") in a further essay on ink, see Xing, "Mo ji" 墨紀, *Xing Tong ji*, 712–713.
126. Cheng Dayue 程大約, *Chengshi moyuan*, in XXSKQS, zibu, vol. 1114, 309.
127. Zhan Jingfeng, *Mingbian leihan* 明辨類函 (1632 edition; Gest Library, Princeton University), 43. 6a.
128. Yin, *Yin Runsheng moyuan jiancang lu*, 16. Fang Ruisheng reprints both the first section of Wang Daokun's inscription for "One with Clear Heaven" in Zhou Tianqiu's calligraphy (a design he explicitly marks as "Made by Fang Yulu" 方于魯製), and yet on the opposing page adapted the "One with Clear Heaven" inscription from Cheng Junfang (beneath a reprint of "Dark Origin of Numinous Vitality"), as

129. if he were trying to have it both ways, allowing Fang and Cheng to share the recipe. Fang Ruisheng, *Mohai*, in *Sheyuan mocui*, vol. 6, 4. 25b–26a.
129. Zhang, *Xuetang mopin*, 33a. Zhang also comments on Fang Yulu's version of "One with Clear Heaven" and cites Xing Tong's evaluation, see Zhang, *Xuetang mopin*, 34b–35a.
130. A contemporary Taiwanese collector possesses a perhaps improbable 30-gram artifact (8.7 cm × 2.7 cm × 1.0 cm) that pairs a copy of Cheng Junfang's inscription for "One with Clear Heaven" with the maker's mark of Wang Daokun's relative Wang Daohui: "Made by Wang Zhongjia of She County in Accordance with the Methods of Yishui" (She Wang Zhongjia an Yishui fa zao 歙汪仲嘉按易水法造). Huang Taiyang, *Moxiang shijia*, 59.
131. The inkstick, weighing around 30 grams, is rectangular with a lacquer coating bearing the three characters "First Grade Jewel" (yipin zhu 一品珠) in seal script and a three-character circular studio-name seal Shangpu zhai 尚樸齋 on one side and illustrated patterns of clouds, water, and a suspended pearl on the other. The "One with Clear Heaven" mark appears on the top edge of the inkstick in embossed regular script. A four-character mark "Made by Jin Xuanfu" appears in embossed regular script along the side-edge of the inkstick. Little is now known about Jin Xuanfu, but his name was adapted on inksticks in the Kangxi era as Jin Yuanfu 金元甫 (*xuan* was altered to *yuan* in line with the proscription on using characters in the Kangxi emperor's personal name Xuanye 玄燁). For Yin Runsheng's comments on Jin Xuanfu's "One with Clear Heaven," see Yin, *Yin Runsheng moyuan jiancang lu*, 35.
132. Yin Runsheng's collection also contained a square ink cake as part of a luxury set, weighing 59 grams, attributed to Pan Jiake. The piece bears an image of a dancing phoenix and an eight-character label in embossed running script: "Pan Jiake of She County's One with Clear Heaven Ink" (She Pan Jiake Liaotian yi mo 歙潘嘉客寥天一墨). The label is accompanied by two seals: Jiake 嘉客 and Pan's studio name Huiye zhai 慧業齋. The ink cake is dated to 1622 (Tianqi renxu nianzhi 天啓壬戌年制). Pan Yiju 潘一駒 was a native of Shexian and yet served as an assistant prefect in Guangdong. Yiju was the younger brother of drama critic Pan Zhiheng, a close confidant of both Wang Daokun and Fang Yulu, original member of the Fenggan Society, and relative of the more famous late Ming ink maker Pan Yingzhi. Given the family connection, it is possible Pan studied the "One with Clear Heaven" recipe with Fang Yulu. Yin, *Yin Runsheng moyuan jiancang lu*, 25. Yin owned five inksticks attributed to Pan, one of which (also dated to 1622) appropriates Fang Yulu's "Nine Mysteries and Three Absolutes" brand; see Yin, *Yin Runsheng moyuan jiancang lu*, 24.
133. Xu, "Mingmo bulu" 明墨補錄, *Sheshi xiantan*, 688; Zhang, *Xuetang mopin*, 34b–35a; Sun, *Yanshan zhai mopu*, 54a; Li, "Fang Waishi muzhiming," 87.
134. The first stick, dated to 1624, is attributed to Wu Wenbo 吳文伯 and bears a literary inscription attributed to Dong Qichang; see Yin, *Yin Runsheng moyuan jiancang lu*, 28. A second set of two cylindrical sticks is attributed to Ye Xuanqing 葉玄卿, a native of Xiuning in Anhui; see Yin, *Yin Runsheng moyuan jiancang lu*, 30. A third stick, dated to 1610, is attributed to Wang Hongjian 汪鴻漸; see Yin, *Yin Runsheng moyuan jiancang lu*, 33. All three pieces are painted with golden flecks. Yin also owned a further three sets of inksticks bearing the brand from the Qing and a set of

3. THE INK-MAKER'S MARK

two pieces in the shape of an ox tongue attributed to Cao Sugong dated to 1667; see Yin, *Yin Runsheng moyuan jiancang lu*, 188. A further set of eight inksticks is also dated to 1667 and attributed to Cao Sugong, and an identical batch of eight inksticks is dated to 1667 but attributed to Zhan Fanghuan 詹方環; see Yin, *Yin Runsheng moyuan jiancang lu*, 195.

135. Ko, *The Social Life of Inkstones*, 103.
136. Cai Xinquan, "Liangding Gugong cang mopin shang" 两锭故宫藏墨品赏, *Shoucang* 收藏 6 (2013): 120–24.
137. Cai, "Liangding Gugong cang mopin shang," 120–22. Adaptations of Wang Daokun's inscription also circulated on inksticks attributed to Fang Yulu bearing the "One with Clear Heaven" mark. Song Luo records an inkstick that also switched the two characters qing 清 and qing 輕. Song Luo, *Mantang xu mopin*, 48.
138. Wang Liyan 王儷閻 and Su Qiang 苏强, *Ming Qing Huimo yanjiu* 明清徽墨研究 (Shanghai: Shanghai guji chubanshe, 2007), 163.
139. Zhongguo wenfang sibao quanji bianji weiyuanhui, ed.,*Zhongguo wenfang sibao quanji 1: mo*, 138 (plate 140).
140. Ma, *Mozhi*, 4b–6b; Xu, "Mingmo bulu," 688.
141. Xu, "Mingmo bulu," 688.
142. Wan Shouqi, *Mobiao*, in *Sheyuan mocui*, vol. 8.
143. Jiang, *Yunshi zhai bitan*, 270–272.
144. Wan was also an acclaimed seal carver; see Zhou, "Shu Shamen Huishou yinpu qian" 書沙門慧壽印譜前, *Yinren zhuan*, 1. 40–44.

4. ANTIQUARIAN POETRY

1. For more on the significance of the Zhang Juzheng case and the politics of *duoqing* more generally, see Norman Kutcher, *Mourning in Late Imperial China: Filial Piety and the State* (Cambridge: Cambridge University Press, 1999), 25–26, 61–72.
2. Zhang Tingyu 張廷玉 et al., *Ming shi* 明史 (Beijing: Zhonghua shuju, 1974), 5647.
3. See Tang Xianzu's 湯顯祖 (1550-1616) response in Xu Shuofang, ed., *Tang Xianzu shiwen ji* 湯顯祖詩文集 (Shanghai: Shanghai guji chubanshe, 1982), 179.
4. Zhang et al., *Ming shi*, 6000.
5. Zhang et al., *Ming shi*, 6000.
6. As an early example of how these acts of protest were sanctified by the families and supporters of those involved, a story started to circulate that during the beating, a "palm-sized heap of pulverized flesh" was carved from Zou's body and that his wife dutifully preserved it as an example to his descendants. See Liu Jianming 刘建明, *Zhang Juzheng bingzheng yu wan Ming wenxue zouxiang* 张居正秉政与晚明文学走向 (Shanghai: Fudan daxue chubanshe, 2013), 22–34.
7. On *zhongxiao* ethics in the late Ming, see Ying Zhang, *Confucian Image Politics: Masculine Morality in Seventeenth-Century China* (Seattle: University of Washington Press, 2016), 19–22, 168–69.
8. Among the other officials, Ai Mu 艾穆 (*juren* 1558) and Shen Sixiao 沈思孝 (1542-1611, *jinshi* 1568) from the Ministry of Justice 刑部 were banished after receiving eighty blows.

4. ANTIQUARIAN POETRY

9. Xu Guo 許國, *Xu Wenmu gong quanji* 許文穆公全集 (National Central Library: 1625 edition), 10. 23. The inscriptions were removed from the Wanli edition; see reprint in SKJHSCK, jibu, vol. 40.
10. Kong Yingda, *Liji zhengyi* 禮記正義, 30. 292, in *Shisanjing zhushu*, 1520. Xu's engraved words recall classical correspondences between "a person possessing a special capacity or useful function" and the properties of a "vessel" (*qi* 器): Confucius described his disciple Zigong 子貢 as a "vessel wrought from fine jade" (*hulian* 瑚璉); the phrases "great vessel" (*daqi* 大器) or a "superlative vessel" (*lingqi* 令器) served to compliment a "talented man"; Wang Bao 王襃 (fl. first century BCE) wrote of "worthy men" as "vessels and tools of the state" 夫賢者國家之器用也. For a discussion of these analogies, see Tian, "Cultural Politics of Old Things in Mid-Tang China," 324.
11. The description of a "single-horned ram" became synonymous with the *xiezhi*, a mythical one-horned ram that was able to detect and attack evil or immoral figures.
12. An allusion to Bi Gan 比干, a prominent historical figure of the Shang dynasty. Bi was the son of King Wen Ding 文丁 and an uncle of the last king of the Shang, Di Xin 帝辛. Di Xin, famed for his corruption, was angered by Bi Gan's advice to rectify his behavior and so ordered his execution through the extraction of the heart (Bi Gan pouxin 比干剖心). Bi Gan became a model loyal minister.
13. Xu Guo, *Xu Wenmu gong quanji*, 10. 23.
14. Partisans of the Donglin faction, for instance, commissioned copies of Zhao Nanxing's 趙南星 (1550–1628) legendary "iron *ruyi* scepter" (*tie ruyi* 鐵如意), a material metaphor or inscribed mascot for his outspoken integrity and perceived incorruptibility: "Its hook has no barb; it is upright without giving injury. With it, sing and dance; If it disapproves it will break, this is truly a gentleman's implement." Deng, *Gudong suoji*, 675; Xu Chengyao, *Sheshi xiantan*, 74; Watt, "The Literati Environment," 179–80.
15. Zhang Dai, in his *Shishuo*-style manuscript collection of anecdotes on Ming history, transcribes the first line of the inscription as: "The single horn of a patterned rhinoceros horn" (*wenxi yijiao* 文犀一角) instead of "The single patterned horn of a mystic ram" (*shenyang yijiao* 神羊一角) Zhang, *Kuaiyuan daogu*, 2. 32.
16. Zou Yuanbiao, who had been savagely beaten in 1577, returned in early 1583 and began to memorialize against the Wanli Emperor's personal conduct.
17. Zhang Zaogong 章藻功, "Cang jiantao Zhao gong sigong ji" 藏檢討趙公兕觥記, *Siqi tang wenji* 思綺堂文集, in QDSWJHB, vol. 198, 7. 54.
18. Zhang, "Cang jiantao Zhao gong sigong ji," 54.
19. For an introduction to the sources on craftsmen from the late Ming and early Qing, see Ji Ruoxin 嵇若昕, *Jiangxin yu xiangong: Ming Qing diaoke zhan xiangya xijiao pian* 匠心與仙工：明清雕刻展 象牙犀角篇 (Taibei: Guoli gugong bowuyuan, 2009), 100–103. For an overview of the relations between the development of maritime trade in the sixteenth century and ivory and rhinoceros horn carving, see Cai Meifen, "Gangbu de gongyi: Guanyu Ming mo Qing chu Zhangzhou gongyi pin er san shi" 港埠的工藝：關於明末清初漳州工藝品二三事, in *Zhongguo Haiyang fazhan shi lunwen ji* 中國海洋發展史論文集, ed. Liu Xufeng 劉序楓 (Taibei: Zhongyang yanjiu yuan renwen shehui kexue yanjiu zhongxin zhuanshu, 2008), 29–87.

20. This cup was paired with an inscribed rhinoceros horn cup carved in the shape of a lotus; see Wang, "Heye xibei ming" 荷葉犀杯銘, *Taihan ji*, 78. 1615. As Cai Meifen notes, lotus and hibiscus were popular themes for cups made from jade. Lu Dian 陸佃 (1042–1102) wrote of contemporary vessels with "mouths" fashioned to resemble both lotus and hibiscus blossoms suggesting precedence for pairing cups based on these two petals. See Cai Meifen, "Xi huajie zuo bei: jijian shiqi shiji de lianzuo huabei" 犀花解作杯—幾件十七世紀的連座花杯, *Gugong wenwu yuekan* 故宮文物月刊 270 (September 2005): 76–85.
21. The address to a guest, here, draws from a well-known passage in a memorial presented to the emperor by Cao Zhi 曹植 (192–232) in which he compares himself to the mallow and bean as plants that lean toward the sun even if the sun does not always return its light to them.
22. Wang, "Xi kui bei ming" 犀葵杯銘, *Taihan ji*, 78. 1615.
23. On a surviving cup of questionable provenance bearing Wang Daokun's "Mallow Flower" engraving, the characters are incised on the lips of the vessel, evoking a symbolic relationship between the inscription and ingestion.
24. Cai, "Xi huajie zuo bei," 76–85.
25. Dennis Gillman, "A Source of Rhinoceros Horn Cups in the Late Ming Dynasty," *Orientations* 12 (1984): 10–17.
26. Included in the 1656 catalogue *Musaeum Tradescantianum* along with "unicorn and albado horns," this cup, together with the rest of the contents of the cabinet, eventually served as the foundation of the collection of the Ashmolean Museum in Oxford. For more, see Arthur Macgregor, ed., *Tradescant's Rarities: Essays on the Foundation of the Ashmolean Museum, 1683, with a Catalogue of the Surviving Early Collection* (Oxford: Clarendon Press, 1983), 180–81.
27. Paleontological evidence suggests that the *si* referred to in pre-Qin texts was a now extinct wild buffalo. See Jean Lefeuvre, "Rhinoceros and Wild Buffalo North of the Yellow River at the End of the Shang Dynasty," *Monumenta Serica* 39 (1990–1991): 131–57.
28. It is likely, as François Louis suggests, that Nie Chongyi 聶崇義 (fl. 948–964) was exposed to images of horn-shaped drinking vessels with animal-head protomes from the Tang dynasty and that he mistook (unintentionally or intentionally it is unclear) what were actually luxury cups in a Hellenistic style that had been imported along the Silk Road to be artifacts of high antiquity. Louis, "The Hejiacun Rhyton and the Chinese Wine Horn," 201–42.
29. Louis, "The Hejiacun Rhyton and the Chinese Wine Horn," 233.
30. The most radical attempts to identify the ancient *gong* were taken by Ruan Yuan (1764–1849), a prominent collector who owned a bronze vessel that resembled an oversized classical bronze *jue* with three legs inscribed "Xie's *sigong*," and Wang Guowei 王國維 (1877–1927), who in his influential 1915 essay "Shuo gong" 說觥 (Explaining the *gong*), suggested the object was originally a lidded pouring vessel wrought from bronze.
31. Zhang Cizhong 張次仲, *Daixuan shiji* 待軒詩記, in WYGSKQS, jingbu, vol. 82, 49.
32. Yao Bing 姚炳, *Shishi mingjie* 詩識名解, in WYGSKQS, jingbu, vol. 80, 372–73.
33. Dong Qichang, *Rongtai ji* 容臺集, in SKQSCMCS, jibu, vol. 171, 483.
34. The preface for the inscription reads: "Wang Guishu, Aide to the Left, showed me a picture of a rhinoceros horn: its patterning and form were extraordinary. It could

4. ANTIQUARIAN POETRY

be a fantastic geography, a drinking vessel, or an "as you wish" scepter: a single thing with three merits. And so, I composed an inscription for it" 王左丞圭叔际余犀角圖, 色理形質甚奇, 可為山經, 可為酒器, 可為如意, 一物而三善具焉. 遂為之銘. Li, *Dami shanfang ji*, 153, 511.

35. Yao Zhiyin 姚之駰, *Yuan Ming shilei chao* 元明事類鈔, in WYGSKQS, zibu, vol. 884, 435–36.
36. The entry stands out within the section on "miscellaneous treasure" for the way Li Weizhen's words refer not to an artifact but to a representation of an object. The title of the entry, similarly, is conspicuous for the way it cites not a description of a given object or the name of the object itself (as in every other entry) but the title of Li's inscription.
37. Li, "Shibian yu wanwu," 37–42.
38. Wai-yee Li, "Introduction," in *Trauma and Transcendence in Early Qing Literature*, ed. Wilt L. Idema, Wai-yee Li, and Ellen Widmer (Cambridge, MA: Harvard University Asia Center, 2003), 19.
39. Bai, *Fu Shan's World*, 162.
40. Zhang Zongyou 張宗友, *Zhu Yizun nianpu* 朱彝尊年譜 (Nanjing: Fenghuang chubanshe, 2014), 181–82, 186, 201, 211, 215, 218.
41. According to *Xijing zaji* 西京雜記, the "fragrant conch flagon" (*xiangluo zhi* 香螺卮) comes from the Southern Ocean.
42. Zhu refers to Wanli as Dingling, the name of the Wanli Emperor's mausoleum.
43. "A Phoenix singing at the morning sun" (*fengming zhaoyang* 鳳鳴朝陽) is an allusion from the poem "A Bend in the Hillside" (Juan'a 卷阿) from the Major Odes in the *Book of Songs*. It is usually taken to refer to a talented person finding an opportunity to use his or her talent. Zhu's use of the phrase alludes to its association with remonstrators of the past: *Supplement to the Tang History* (*Tangshi bu* 唐史補) recalls how the phrase was used to celebrate Li Shan'gan 李善感, the first censor since the death of Chu Suiliang 褚遂良 (596–658) who dared to remonstrate with the emperor. Sun Chengze 孫承澤 (1592–1676) notes that the Wu Gate was popularly referred to as the Tower of Five Phoenixes (Wufeng lou 五鳳樓).
44. "Breaking the balustrade" (*zhekan* 折檻) refers to the biography of Han official Zhu Yun 朱雲, who submitted a memorial to Emperor Cheng 成 (r. 32–37 BCE) in which he asked to behead the imperial favorite Zhang Yu 張禹. The emperor, in a rage, ordered for Zhu to be executed, but Zhu clung so strongly to the palace balustrade that the guards broke the balustrade when they pulled him away. The emperor rescinded the sentence and preserved the broken balustrade as a memorial to Zhu's integrity.
45. "The inverted scale" (*nilin* 逆鱗) is a reference from *Han Feizi* to the "inverted scale" on a dragon's throat, which when touched provokes the dragon to instantly kill. The *Han Feizi* uses this image to warn a persuader against "brushing the bristling scales" of a ruler.
46. "South-facing beds" (*nanchuang* 南床) came to refer to the official position of the "assistant to the imperial oversight advisor" (*shiyushi* 侍御史). These advisors were not allowed to sit in the palace. After several months of service, they were moved to the Department of State Affairs (Shangshu sheng 尚書省 or Nansheng 南省).
47. The *baishou zun* is a reference to an anecdote from *Sanguo zhi* 三國志 concerning the way Cao Cao placed a wine vessel with a lid decorated with a white tiger in the

center of a hall during festivities. Those who offered direct advice were asked to drink from the vessel.
48. Zhu Yizun 朱彝尊, "Sigong ge, gong wei Xu Wenmu gongjian Zhao Taishi Dingyu wu. Wei He Shaoqing fu" 兕觥歌觥為許文穆公餞趙太史定宇物。為何少卿賦, in *Pushu ting quanji* 曝書亭全集, ed. Wang Limin 王利民 et al. (Changchun: Jilin wenshi chubanshe, 2009), 154.
49. Stephen Owen, *The Making of Early Chinese Classical Poetry* (Cambridge, MA: Harvard Asia Center, 2006), 196.
50. Zhang Zaogong, "Cang jiantao Zhao gong sigong ji," 57.
51. Zhang Zaogong, "Cang jiantao Zhao gong sigong ji," 57.
52. Zhang Zaogong, "Cang jiantao Zhao gong sigong ji," 57.
53. Zhang Zaogong, "Cang jiantao Zhao gong sigong ji," 57.
54. According to Weng Fanggang's later study, Zhang Zaogong may have given the cup to the Sichuan official Fu Zuoji 傅作楫 (1656–1721). There is no explanation as to why Zhang gave the cup to Fu or what Fu did with it.
55. Michele Matteini, "The Aesthetics of Scholarship: Weng Fanggang and the Cult of Su Shi in Late-Eighteenth-Century Beijing," *Archives of Asian Art* 69, no. 1 (2019): 103–20.
56. Matteini, "The Aesthetics of Scholarship," 103–4.
57. Weng curated several similar projects intended to commemorate famous antiques throughout his career. In 1790 he acquired the Yanshan rock—one of the most prized antiques in the late imperial period, originally owned by the Southern Tang ruler Li Yu 李煜 (r. 961–975) and an object that had also once belonged to Xu Guo—and set about producing a scroll with painted renditions of the specimen from different angles, alongside rubbings taken from the textured surface of the object. For a full study of this scroll, see Michele Matteini, "The Story of a Stone: Mi Fu's Ink-Grinding Stone and Its Eighteenth-Century Replications," *Arts Asiatiques* 72, no. 1 (2017): 81–96.
58. Weng Fanggang, *Fuchu zhai wenji*, in XXSKQS, jibu, vol. 1455, 366.
59. Weng Fanggang, *Fuchu zhai shiji*, in XXSKQS, jibu, vol. 1454, 503; Weng Fanggang, *Fuchu zhai wenji*, 493.
60. Weng, *Fuchu zhai wenji*, 493. His comments on this rubbing ignore altogether the visual or physical properties of the horn cup (he makes no reference to the size, shape, or surface of the object).
61. Weng, *Fuchu zhai shiji*, 503.
62. Wing-Ming Chan, "The Qianlong Emperor's New Strategy in 1775 to Commend Late-Ming Loyalists," *Asia Major* 13, no. 1 (2000): 109–37.
63. Chan, "The Qianlong Emperor's New Strategy," 124.
64. R. Kent Guy, *Emperor's Four Treasuries: Scholars and the State in the Late Ch'ien-lung Era* (Cambridge, MA: Harvard University Press, 1987), 157–200.
65. Weng's circle also wrote on other relics associated with Ming martyrs, such as an inkstone inscribed by the loyalist Kuang Lu 鄺露 (1604–1650) and acquired by Weng's acquaintance Wang Chang 王昶 (1725–1806). This example suggests the subversive potential of writing on leftover Ming things in that discussions of the inkstone allowed poets to address the legacy of Jin Bao 金堡 (1614–1680), whose work was censored under Qianlong. For a detailed study of this case, see Yip Cheuk-wai 葉倬瑋, "Yijian Nanming lieshi yiwu de liuzhuan" 一件南明烈士遺物的流轉, *Zhongguo wenhua* 中國文化 49 (2019): 152–65.

66. Weng, *Fuchu zhai wenji*, 366.
67. Compare, for instance, with the description of this event in Weng's preface for Yan Hengzhai; see Weng, *Fuchu zhai wenji*, 366.
68. Weng Fanggang, *Weng Fanggang tiba shouzha jilu* 翁方綱題跋手札集錄, ed. Shen Jin 沈津 (Guilin: Guangxi shifan daxue chubanshe, 2002), 460.
69. Weng, *Fuchu zhai shiji*, 675.
70. For a description and pictures of this vessel, see Ma Peilin 馬培林, *Xintai wenshi ziliao xuan* 新泰文史資料選輯 2 (1987): 81–84.
71. For an overview of the carvings, see Changshu shi beike bowuguan 常熟市碑刻博物館 ed., *Changshu beike ji* 常熟碑刻集 (Shanghai: Shanghai cishu chubanshe, 2007), 106–11.
72. Craig Clunas, *Chinese Carving* (London: Victoria and Albert Museum, 1996), 30.
73. On Alois Riegl's distinction, see Robert S. Nelson and Margaret Olin, "Introduction," in *Monuments and Memory, Made and Unmade*, ed. Robert S. Nelson and Margaret Olin (Chicago: University of Chicago Press, 2003), 2. For a translation of the original essay, see Kurt W. Forster and Diane Ghirado, trans., "The Modern Cult of Monuments: Its Character and Its Origin," *Oppositions* 25 (1982): 21–51.
74. Smaller commemorative souvenirs were manufactured to supplement this monument: Xu Kang's 徐康 1897 catalogue contains a record of a limited-edition "Sigong Returns to Zhao" ink cake, displaying an image of the vessel and the mark "made in Qianlong mou nian" 乾隆某年製, a piece allegedly owned by Zhao Cihou 趙次侯, a resident of the Old Mountain Pavilion (Jiushan lou 舊山樓) in Changshu. Weng continued to provide literary services for the Zhao family and even composed a stele inscription for Zheting's tomb that again thematizes the story of the *sigong*; see Weng, *Fuchu zhai wenji*, 488.
75. Deng Changfeng 邓长风, "Zhou Ang de shengping jiqi 'Sigong ji' chuanqi de benshi" 周昂的生平及其《兕觥记》传奇的本事, in *Ming Qing xiqujia kaolüe quanbian* 明清戏曲家考略全编, ed. Deng Changfeng (Shanghai: Shanghai guji chubanshe, 2009), 462.
76. For a study of the circumstances surrounding the production of this drama, see Deng, "Zhou Ang de shengping jiqi 'Sigong ji' chuanqi de benshi," 454–67.
77. Lu Tingshu 陸廷樞, "*Fuchu zhai shiji* xu" 復初齋詩集序, in Weng Fanggang, *Fuchu zhai shiji*, 361.
78. Wei Shang, "The Literati Era and Its Demise (1723–1840)," in *The Cambridge History of Chinese Literature*, vol. 2, 262. On *jili*, see Yip Cheuk-wai, *Weng Fanggang shixue yanjiu* 翁方纲诗学研究 (Beijing: Zhongguo shehui kexue chubanshe, 2013), 130–47; Tang Yunyun 唐芸芸, *Weng Fanggang shixue yanjiu* 翁方纲诗学研究 (Beijing: Zhonghua shuju, 2018), 30–42.
79. Shang, "The Literati Era and Its Demise (1723–1840)," 262. Yuan Mei is typically cast as Weng's nemesis and staunchest critic, yet he also composed numerous poems on epigraphic topics; see Yip Cheuk-wai, "Lun Yuan Mei ji xingling pai de kaodingshi chuangzuo—jiantan kaodingshi dui bixing chuantong de fanbo" 論袁枚及性靈派的考訂詩創作—兼談考訂詩對比興傳統的反撥, *Taibei daxue zhongwen xuebao* 臺北大學中文學報 30 (2021): 635–88.
80. Weng, "Yishu ji xu" 蛾朮集序, *Fuchu zhai wenji*, 4. 386.
81. Jin Zhengxi 金正喜 [Kim Chŏnghŭi], "Yu Shen Weitang guan hao" 與申威堂觀浩, *Ruan tang xiansheng quanji* 阮堂先生全集 (Sŏul: Sinsŏng Munhwasa, 1972), 2.

35–38. On Kim's relationship with Weng, see Matteini, "The Aesthetics of Scholarship," 115.

82. Yip Cheuk-wai, "Wenwu zhi guangxia de huayu jiangou yu buxiu zhuiqiu—lun Weng Fanggang de jinshi shi" 文物之光下的話語建構與不朽追求—論翁方綱的金石詩, *Zhengda zhongwen xuebao* 政大中文學報 28 (2017): 103–39.

83. Yip, "Wenwu zhi guangxia," 110–22.

84. For an overview of these definitions, see Yip, "Wenwu zhi guangxia," 120

85. Stephen Owen, *The Late Tang: Chinese Poetry of the Mid-Ninth Century (827–860)* (Cambridge, MA: Harvard Asia Center, 2006), 459. See also Paula Varsano, "Disappearing Objects/Elusive Subjects: Writing Mirrors in Early and Medieval China," *Representations* 124, no. 1 (2013): 96.

86. Weng, "Ti Yusan zhi zi Putian jianji xiao xihu huashan" 題雨三侄自蒲田見寄小西湖畫扇, *Fuchu zhai shiji*, 1. 367–68. For a detailed analysis of this poem and its relationship to the structure of contemporary examination poems, see Tang, *Weng Fanggang shixue yanjiu*, 222–25.

87. Tang, *Weng Fanggang shixue yanjiu*, 230–32.

88. For a translation and discussion of Han Yu's "Song of the Stone Drums," see Stephen Owen, *The Poetry of Meng Chiao and Han Yü* (New Haven, CT: Yale University Press, 1975), 248–51.

89. For a discussion of the influence of Han Yu's "Song of the Stone Drums" on Weng's poetics of "direct display" 正面鋪寫, see Tang, *Weng Fanggang shixue yanjiu*, 116–21.

90. Li, *The Promise and Peril of Things*, 251–54.

91. We might also compare, for instance, Wu Weiye and Weng Fanggang's poems on "Palace Fans" 宮扇. Wu eulogizes a token of imperial favor that he received while lecturing before the Chongzhen Emperor in 1637, punning on the word *shan* 扇 to evoke experience of dispersal and loss *san* 散. Weng's "Song on a Palace Fan," by contrast, focuses squarely on the dimensions of a Ming antique, avoiding any mention of either the fan's personal significance or its status as an allegory of dynastic fall.

92. Weng, "Wufeng ernian shike jiuben wei Yi Moqing fu" 五鳳二年石刻舊本為伊墨卿賦, *Fuchu zhai shiji*, 49; Weng, "Wufeng wunian zhuan ge" 五鳳五年磚歌, *Fuchu zhai shiji*, 52.

93. Shang, "The Literati Era and Its Demise (1723–1840)," 262; Tang, *Weng Fanggang shixue yanjiu*, 202–21.

94. Mei Zengliang 梅曾亮, "Jinshi huixuan xu" 金石彙選序, in Mei, *Baijian shanfang quanji* 柏梘山房全集, in XXSKQS, jibu, vol. 1513, 649.

95. Mei, "Jinshi huixuan xu," 649.

96. This work established a model for his later well-known book on Han dynasty epigraphy, *Liang Han jinshi ji* 兩漢金石記, in 22 *juan*, printed in 1789.

97. Weng later decorated the gate to his Su Mi Studio (Su Mi zhai 蘇米齋) in the Southern City of Beijing with two characters transferred from rock inscriptions by Su Shi and Mi Fu in Guangdong. Matteini, "The Aesthetics of Scholarship," 108.

98. Weng's associate, Huang Wenyang 黃文暘 (b. 1736), in the preface to a poem appended to a rubbing of a Han dynasty bronze ruler, for instance, succinctly makes this point when he notes how: "I have attached poems to this study, to serve as credible proof" 而系以詩，俾有所徵信焉. Yip compares such claims to the tendency

in works of drama and fiction to preface cited passages of verse with the line: "there is a poem as proof" 有詩為證. Yip Cheuk-wai, "Jianchu tongchi de kaoding yu shiqing: Qian-Jia kaoding jia de wuyuan yu shiqing" 建初銅尺的考訂與詩情：乾嘉考訂家的物緣與詩情, *Zhongguo wenhua* 中國文化 52 (2020): 345.

99. Weng's second poem in his study of the Jiuyao carvings, for instance, is a matching response to engraved poems on local cliffs by both the Song poet Xu Yanxian 許彥先 (fl. 1079) and the Kangxi-era poet Zhang Mingxian 張明先 (1652–ca.1728). For an illuminating discussion of this same tendency in Qing antiquarian poetry on antique seals, see Yip Cheuk-wai, "Yi shi wei wu: lun Qian-Jia yinxue yu yinge" 以詩為物：論乾嘉印學與印歌, *Malaixiya hanxue kan* 馬來西亞漢學刊 4 (2020): 58.
100. Yip, "Jianchu tongchi de kaoding yu shiqing."
101. On Weng's repeated references to the Jianchu ruler in other poems on antiques, see Tang, *Weng Fanggang shixue yanjiu*, 258–59.
102. My formulation, here, is inspired by the discussion in Rachel Eisendrath, *Poetry in a World of Things: Aesthetics and Empiricism in Renaissance Ekphrasis* (Chicago: University of Chicago Press, 2018), 150.

EPILOGUE: BROKEN STONES

1. Yan Zhixiong 嚴志雄, "Tiwu, jiyi, yu yimin qingjing: Qu Dajun yiliu wujiu nian yongmei shi tanjiu" 體物，記憶與遺民情境—屈大均一六五九年詠梅詩探究, *Zhongguo wenzhe yanjiu jikan* 中國文哲研究集刊 21 (2002): 43–87. For an introduction to Qu's relationship with Duan inkstones, see Guo Daxiang 郭达祥, "Qu Dajun yu duanyan" 屈大均与端砚, *Zhaoqing xueyuan xuebao* 肇庆学院学报 40, no. 3 (2019): 17–21; Wu Ligu, *Mingyan bian*, 164–65.
2. Qu Dajun 屈大均, "Duanzhou ganhuai" 端州感懷, in *Qu Dajun shici biannian jiaojian* 屈大均詩詞編年校箋, ed. Chen Yongzheng 陳永正 (Shanghai: Shanghai guji chubanshe, 2017), 5. 562; Qu, "Duanzhou diaogu" 端州弔古, *Qu Dajun shici biannian jiaojian*, 9. 1055; Qu, "Banzhu" 斑竹, *Qu Dajun shici biannian jiaojian*, 9. 1053; Qu, "Deng Yuejiang lou yougan ershou" 登閱江樓有感二首, *Qu Dajun shici biannian jiaojian*, 9. 1054. This second set of poems commemorates a gathering with the poet Wang Shizhen 王士禛 (1634–1711).
3. Qu Dajun, "Chongzhu yan ming" 蟲蛀硯銘, in *Qu Dajun quanji* 屈大均全集, ed. Wang Guichen 王貴忱 (Beijing: Renmin wenxue chubanshe, 1996), 3: 11. 197.
4. Qu, "Feng zi banyan ming you xu" 風字半硯銘有序, *Qu Dajun quanji*, 11. 202.
5. Qu, "Zeng Qi Qi Yiyi shuiyan yan" 贈祁七奕儀水巖硯, *Qu Dajun shici biannian jiaojian*, 9. 1002.
6. Qu, "Duan shi" 端石, in *Guangdong xinyu* 廣東新語, in *Qu Dajun quanji*, 5. 170.
7. Zhong Yufa 钟玉发, "Qingchu duanyan minglun 'Duanshi kao' zhuzhe kao" 清初端砚名论《端石考》著者考, *Zhaoqing xueyuan xuebao* 41, no. 3 (2020): 12–16.
8. Loyalist concerns inflect Qu's collaboration with fellow scholars on these research projects: Gao Zhao 高兆, in his "Study of the Inkstones from Duan Brook" (Duanxi yanshi kao 端溪硯史考), for instance, continues to use the reign titles of Yongle, Xuande, and Chongzhen, yet refuses to mention the Qing emperors Shunzhi or Kangxi when recording such important dates as 1647, the year that imperial controls on quarrying were lifted and private prospecting flourished.

9. Qu, "Duan shi," 5. 170. The emphasis Qu places on his personal acquisition of such stones registers the fact that he was present in the Duan area as the Qing state "reopened" prospecting at the Old Pit in the early 1680s. While the relaxing of imperial control stimulated private mining in the late seventeenth century, access to the best quarries still demanded complex negotiations with magistrates. See Qu's poem to Zhaoqing magistrate and Qing official Wang Xiaozong 王效宗, a piece that led to his acquisition of a "Great Unhewn Inkstone" (Dapu yan 大璞硯) from the Underwater Lode; Qu, "Qiyan xing" 乞硯行, *Qu Dajun shici biannian jiaojian*, 9. 1076. This specimen (one whose properties resemble the "Water Fat Inkstone") became one of Qu's most celebrated inkstones, an object he commemorated through inscription; see Qu, "Dapu yan ming" 大璞硯銘, *Qu Dajun quanji*, 11. 193.
10. Zhu, "Bu Changong: Duanxi guan cai yan" 步蟾宮—端溪觀採硯, *Pushu ting quanji*, 28. 338.
11. For extant inkstones inscribe by Zhu, see Tianjin bowuguan, ed., *Tianjin bowuguan cangyan*, 69–70; Zhongguo wenfang sibao quanji bianji weiyuanhui, ed., *Zhongguo wenfang sibao quanji 2: yan*, 108–9; Bai Lifan 白黎瑤, "Zhu Yizun jiqi mingyan kaolüe" 朱彝尊及其銘硯考略, in *Tianjin bowuguan luncong* 天津博物館论丛, ed. Tianjin bowuguan 天津博物馆 (Tianjin: Tianjin renmin chubanshe, 2011), 200–205.
12. Zhu Qi, *Penglai songfeng: Huang Yi yu Qian-Jia jinshixue* 蓬莱松风：黄易与乾嘉金石学 (Shanghai: Shanghai guji chubanshe, 2020), 313–15.
13. Ko, *The Social Life of Inkstones*, 245.
14. Liang Shaoren 梁绍壬, "Ming" 铭, in *Liangban qiuyu'an suibi* 两般秋雨盦随笔, ed. Zhuang Wei 庄葳 (Shanghai: Shanghai guji chubanshe, 2012), 188–89.
15. Jin Nong 金農, "Dongxin zhai yanming" 冬心齋研銘, in *Jin Nong ji* 金農集, ed. Yong Qi 雍琦 (Hangzhou: Zhejiang renmin meishu chubanshe, 2016), 228.
16. Jin, "Dongxin zhai yanming," 228.
17. Jin, "Dongxin zhai yanming," 228.
18. Jin, "Dongxin zhai yanming," 228.
19. Ko, *The Social Life of Inkstones*, 272.
20. Jin, "Dongxin zhai yanming," 229.
21. Jin, "Dongxin zhai yanming," 229.
22. Jin, "Tuanyan ming" 團硯銘, *Jin Nong ji*, 232.
23. Jin, "Dongxin zhai yanming," 229.
24. Jin, "Dongxin zhai yanming," 229.
25. Jin, "Dongxin zhai yanming," 229.
26. Jin, "Dongxin zhai yanming," 229.
27. Jin, "Quejiao yan ming" 缺角研銘, *Jin Nong ji*, 231. A rubbing of Jin's "Inscription on a Broken Corner Inkstone" survives in a folio in the Palace Museum. The rubbing reveals a damaged stone measuring 12 cm in width and 19.5 cm in length with two other sets of markings: "The Fifth Inkstone of Dongxin Studio" 冬心齋第五研 carved in regular script on the lip of the ink pool and "Obtained by Master Dongxin in the Wangwu Mountains" 冬心先生得于王屋山中 carved in an iron-wire seal script along the side of the slab by Huang Yi's father, Huang Shugu 黃樹穀 (1701–1751). For a detailed study of the album, see Zhu, *Penglai songfeng*, 303–20.
28. Cai, *Zhonghua guyan: 100 jiang*, 105–7. On Jin Nong's calligraphic innovations, see Marshall Pei-sheng Wu, "Chin Nung: An Artist with a Wintry Heart" (PhD diss.,

University of Michigan, 1989), 118–89; Jonathan Hay, "Culture, Ethnicity, and Empire in the Work of Two Eighteenth-Century 'Eccentric' Artists," *RES* 35 (1999): 204.

29. Ginger Cheng-chi Hsü, *Bushel of Pearls: Painting for Sale in Eighteenth-Century Yangchow* (Stanford, CA: Stanford University Press, 2001), 175.

30. Cai, *Zhonghua guyan: 100 jiang*, 108–9; He Lianhai 何连海, "Lianwu yu ganhuai: Jin Nong yanming shufa kaolüe" 恋物与感怀：金农砚铭书法考略, *Zhongguo shufa* 13 (2016): 140. See also Tianjin bowuguan, ed., *Tianjin bowuguan cang yan* 天津博物館藏硯 (Beijing: Wenwu chubanshe, 2012), 94–95. On the banana palm as a central motif in Jin's painting, see Zhu Liangzhi, *Yizhi shougu xie kongshan: Jin Nong hua de jinshi qi* 一枝瘦骨写空山：金农画的金石气 (Hangzhou: Zhejiang renmin meishu chubanshe, 2020), 41–48. Jin, "Dongxin xiansheng huafo tiji" 冬心先生畫佛題記, *Jin Nong ji*, 286.

31. The early Qing fashion for using ruined fragments as inkstones draws upon the literary legend of the "Bronze Finch Inkstone" (Tongque yan 銅雀硯), or the history of inscribing crumbled segments from Cao Cao's 曹操 (155–220) Bronze Finch Terrace in the Eastern Wei capital of Ye 鄴. The tiles of the Wei Terrace, allegedly first fired from clay filtered through fine linen and mixed with walnut oil, became popular commodities in the Song, eliciting poems and literary inscriptions from Ouyang Xiu, Su Shi, and Huang Tingjian 黃庭堅 (1045–1105) among others. A "Bronze Finch Inkstone" at once presented the historical imagination of a lost city as a tangible souvenir to be bought and sold while converting a ruined fragment into a newly useful instrument for writing and the transmission of literary culture. The act of inscribing an old brick was by the early Qing no longer simply a response to an established poetic topic but an activity that intersects with antiquarian research into newly excavated fragments.

32. Bai, "Zhu Yizun jiqi mingyan kaolüe," 204.

33. Zhu, "Chengyan ming bing xu" 城硯銘并序, *Pushu ting quanji*, 61. 609.

34. Zhu, "Chengyan ming bing xu," 609.

35. Huang Daozhou 黃道周, *Huang Zhangpu wenxuan* 黃漳浦文選 (Taibei: Datong shuju, 1987), 386. For detailed studies see Wu Ligu, *Yanyan kao* 贋硯考 (Beijing: Wenwu chubanshe, 2010), 195–220; Chen Liangwu 陈良武, "Huang Daozhou duanbeiyan kaolun" 黄道周断碑砚考论, *Shenzhen daxue xuebao (renwen shehui kexueban)* 深圳大学学报（人文社会科学版）30, no. 1 (2013): 53–57. Huang Daozhou's broken-stele inkslab was not the first fragment of Su Shi's "Poem on the Pavilion of Ink Marvels" engraving to have been repurposed as an inkstone: Ming philosopher Wang Yangming 王陽明 (1472–1529) also owned a slab supposedly taken from Sun Jue's pavilion, a piece that was likewise recovered and commemorated by Qing scholars in poetry and painting; see Wu, *Yanyan kao*, 187–200. Rival collectors in twentieth-century China have laid claim to competing copies of the Huang Daozhou broken-stele inkslab. On the five different rubbings, see Wu, *Yanyan kao*, 206–10.

36. Liang, "Huang Shizhai duanbeiyan" 黃石斋断碑砚, *Liangban qiuyu'an suibi*, 3. 108. Wu Ligu doubts the authenticity of the attribution to Zhu Yizun; see Wu, *Yanyan kao*, 214–15.

37. On Huang Daozhou's performance of writing in blood, see Zhang, *Confucian Image Politics*, 123–28.

38. Cai Hongru, "Gu zhuanwa yan" 古甎瓦硯, *Shupu* 書譜 84 (1988): 76–78.

39. For a detailed analysis of this case, see Ou Zhongrong 欧忠荣, *Sanlao yanshi kao* 三老砚事考 (Beijing: Wenhua yishu chubanshe, 2014), 364–65; Yi, "From Epigraphy to Inscribing Objects," 65–66.
40. Ou, *Sanlao yanshi kao*, 364–65; Yi, "From Epigraphy to Inscribing Objects," 65–66.
41. For a detailed study of Ji Yun's inkstone inscriptions, see Ou, *Sanlao yanshi kao*, 209–346.
42. Ruan's contemporary (and fellow collector of ancient tiles and bricks) Zhang Tingji 張廷濟 (1769–1848) named his studio "Studio of Eight Bricks" (Bazhuan jingshe 八磚精舍). Ou, *Sanlao yanshi kao*, 269. For Zhang's adaptation of a Jin dynasty brick as an inkstone, see Tong, *Jinshi qishou*, 2: 108–9.
43. Cai, *Zhonghua guyan: 100 jiang*, 80–83; Ou, *Sanlao yanshi kao*, 368; Yi, "From Epigraphy to Inscribing Objects," 69.
44. Ou, *Sanlao yanshi kao*, 368.
45. Ou, *Sanlao yanshi kao*, 385–88. See Wang and Cai, eds., *Zhonghua guyan*, 108–9.
46. Zhou Changyuan 周长源, "Ruan Yuan moke 'Xiyue huashan miao bei' he mobu bei zhong quezi de juyan" 阮元摹刻《西岳华山庙碑》和摹補碑中缺字的巨砚, *Wenwu* 文物 8 (1992): 86–89.
47. Ko, *The Social Life of Inkstones*, 193–98.
48. Zang Huayun 臧华云, "Mantan Gao Fenghan *Yanshi*" 漫谈高凤翰砚史, *Wenwu* 9 (1962): 48–53; Liu Yunhe 刘云鹤, "Gao Fenghan *Yanshi* yanjiu" 高凤翰《砚史》研究, in *Liu Yunhe xueshu wenji* 刘云鹤学术文集 (Hangzhou: Xiling yinshe, 2007), 5–22. The collection has been reprinted in Gao Fenghan, *Gao Fenghan quanji* 高鳳翰全集, ed. Liu Caidong 劉才棟, Zheng Wenguang 鄭文光, and Gao Shifu 高石副 (Beijing: Beijing daxue chubanshe, 2014), vol. 5. The collection also contains two inkstone cases and one seal in addition to an inkstone made to resemble a seal, so there are only 164 actual inkstones in current editions of *History of Inkstones*. See also Gao Fenghan, *Yanshi jianshi* 硯史箋釋, ed. Tian Tao 田濤 and Cui Shichi 崔士篪 (Beijing: Beijing shenghuo dushu xinzhi sanlian shudian, 2011).
49. Gao, "Muying pingzuo ming" 木癭瓶座銘, *Gao Fenghan quanji*, 2: 194; Gao, "Muying zhen ming" 木癭枕銘, *Gao Fenghan quanji*, 2: 194; Gao, "Zhuzhi bige ming" 竹制筆閣銘, *Gao Fenghan quanji*, 2: 194; Gao, "Limu yanxia ming" 梨木硯匣銘, *Gao Fenghan quanji*, 2: 198.
50. Gao, "*Yanshi* moben di jiushiba" 《硯史》摹本第九十八, *Gao Fenghan quanji*, 5: 251.
51. Gao, "*Yanshi* moben di yi" 《硯史》摹本第一, *Gao Fenghan quanji*, 5: 10–11. An earlier version of this inscription dated to 1735 appears in Gao's calligraphic folio *Yanming wenjuan* 硯銘文卷.
52. Gao, "*Yanshi* moben di yi," 11.
53. Gao, "*Yanshi* moben di liushisi" 《硯史》摹本第六十四, *Gao Fenghan quanji*, 5: 183.
54. Gao, "*Yanshi* moben di liushisi," 183.
55. Gao, "*Yanshi* moben di liushisi," 183.
56. Burton Watson, trans., *Chinese Rhyme-Prose* (New York: Columbia University Press, 1971), 26.
57. Gao, "*Yanshi* moben di si" 《硯史》摹本第四, *Gao Fenghan quanji*, 5: 21.
58. Li Gang 李刚, "'Yan pi' Gao Fenghan" 「硯癖」高凤翰, *Zhongguo shufa* 7 (2016): 134.

59. Gao, "*Yanshi* moben di si," 20.
60. Gao, "*Yanshi* moben di liushiyi" 《硯史》摹本第六十一, *Gao Fenghan quanji*, 5: 176–77.
61. Gao, "*Yanshi* moben di liushiyi," 176.
62. Gao, "*Yanshi* moben di liu" 《硯史》摹本第六, *Gao Fenghan quanji*, 5: 26–7.
63. Gao, "*Yanshi* moben di liu," 26.
64. See the following instones: 66, 67, 74, 76, 93, 94, 97, 105, 119, 133, 134, 145, 135, 154, 157.
65. See his comments: "I obtained this inkstone in the markets of Xin'an" 此硯得之新安市上. Gao, "*Yanshi* moben di shiliu" 《硯史》摹本第十六, *Gao Fenghan quanji*, 5: 56.
66. Gao, "*Yanshi* moben di sishijiu" 《硯史》摹本第四十九, *Gao Fenghan quanji*, 5: 148.
67. Gao, "*Yanshi* moben di sishijiu," 148.
68. For a preliminary study of these papers, see Hsin-Chen Chien 簡欣晨, "Yan wei xinsheng: Gao Fenghan (1683–1749) *Yanshi* yanjiu" 硯為心聲：高鳳翰 (1683–1749)《硯史》研究 (MA Thesis., National Taiwan University, 2017), 120–122.
69. Chien, "Yan wei xinsheng," 220–224; Chengyang yishu wenhua jijin huibian 成陽藝術文化基金會編, ed., *Guhu zhi mei* 古壺之美 (Taibei: Chengyang yishu wenhua jijinhui, 2013), 86–89.
70. Gao, "*Yanshi* moben di liushiba" 《硯史》摹本第六十八, *Gao Fenghan quanji*, 5: 191.
71. Gao, "*Yanshi* moben di sishijiu," 190.
72. See his comments: "This was also fabricated from scraps of leftover inkstone material" 此亦依硯材所缺製之. Gao, "*Yanshi* moben di sishijiu," 190.
73. Gao, "*Yanshi* moben di jiushisi" 《硯史》摹本第九十四, *Gao Fenghan quanji*, 5: 243.
74. This detail echoes the previous design in the catalogue, a stone that also bears graphs taken from copies of "King Yu's Stele." Gao, "*Yanshi* moben di jiushisan" 《硯史》摹本第九十三, *Gao Fenghan quanji*, 5: 241.
75. Gao, "*Yanshi* moben di jiushisi," 243.
76. Gao, "*Yanshi* moben di jiushisi," 243.
77. Ko, *The Social Life of Inkstones*, 197.
78. Gao, "*Yanshi* moben di qishiwu" 《硯史》摹本第七十五, *Gao Fenghan quanji*, 5: 202–205.
79. Gao, "*Yanshi* moben di qishiwu."
80. Brown, *Other Things*, 373.
81. Brown, *Other Things*, 373.
82. On Huang Yi's wrist-rest, see Tong, *Jinshi qishou*, 2: 144. On Huang Yi's practice as an epigrapher, see Xue Longchun, *Guhuan: Huang Yi yu Qian-Jia jinshi shishang* 古欢：黄易与乾嘉金石时尚 (Beijing: Sanlian shudian, 2019); Zhu, *Penglai songfeng*.
83. Wang Yifeng 王屹峰, *Guzhuan huagong: Liu Zhou yu 19 shiji de xueshu he yishu* 古磚花供：六舟與19世紀的學術和藝術 (Hangzhou: Zhejiang renmin meishu chubanshe, 2018), 122–25. On his bamboo carvings, see Wang, *Guzhuan huagong*, 53–55. For Liuzhou's carved wrist-rest, see Tong, *Jinshi qishou*, 2: 145.
84. Wang, *Guzhuan huagong*, 272–74.
85. Lai Suk-Yee 黎淑儀, ed., *The Art of Chen Hongshou: Painting, Calligraphy, Seal-carving and Teapot-design* 書畫印壺：陳鴻壽的藝術 (Hong Kong: Shanghai

Museum, Nanjing Museum and Art Museum, The Chinese University of Hong Kong, 2005); Yi, "The Calligraphic Art of Chen Hongshou."
86. On this container, see Lai, The Art of Chen Hongshou, 198; Yi, "The Calligraphic Art of Chen Hongshou," 151.
87. Richard Sennett, *The Craftsman* (New Haven, CT: Yale University Press, 2008), 119; Catherine Stuer, "To Have Temperature: Material and Metamorphosis in Nineteenth-Century China," in *The Allure of Matter: Materiality Across Chinese Art*, ed. Orianna Cacchione and Wei-Cheng Lin (Chicago: Smart Museum of Art, 2021), 117.
88. Stuer, "To Have Temperature," 117.
89. Gao structured his catalogue upon the organizational system of *Shiji*.
90. Gao, "*Yanshi* moben di jiushi" 《硯史》摹本第九十, *Gao Fenghan quanji*, 5: 234–35.
91. Gao, "*Yanshi* moben di jiushi," 235.
92. While Gao made the inkstone before the onset of his paralysis, he "inscribed" it afterwards. It could have been carved by another artisan on Gao's behalf. The inkstone may later have been acquired by Gao's brother Gao Shuzeng 高淑曾.

BIBLIOGRAPHY

ABBREVIATIONS

CSJCCB: *Congshu jicheng chubian* 叢書集成初編, 4,000 vols. Shanghai: Shangwu yinshu guan, 1935.
QDSWJHB: *Qingdai shiwen ji huibian* 清代詩文集彙編, 801 vols. Shanghai: Shanghai guji chubanshe, 2009–2011.
SKJHSCK: *Siku jinhui shu congkan* 四庫禁燬書叢刊, 311 vols. Beijing: Beijing chubanshe, 1997.
SKQSCMCS: *Siku quanshu cunmu congshu* 四庫全書存目叢書, 1,200 vols. Jinan: Qilu shushe, 1997.
WYGSKQS: *Wenyuan ge Siku quanshu* 文淵閣四庫全書, 1,500 vols. Facsimile reprint. Taibei: Taiwan shangwu yinshuguan, 1983–1986.
XXSKQS: *Xuxiu Siku quanshu* 續修四庫全書, 1,800 vols. Shanghai: Shanghai guji chubanshe, 1995–2002.

SOURCES

Appadurai, Arjun, ed. *The Social Life of Things: Commodities in Cultural Perspective*. New York: Cambridge University Press, 1988.
Asselin, Mark Laurent. *A Significant Season: Cai Yong (ca. 133–192) and His Contemporaries*. New Haven, CT: American Oriental Society, 2010.
Bai Lifan 白黎璠. "Zhu Yizun jiqi yanming kaolüe" 朱彝尊及其硯銘考略. In *Tianjin bowuguan luncong* 天津博物館論叢, 200–205. Tianjin: Tianjin renmin chubanshe, 2012.
Bai Qianshen. *Fu Shan's World: The Transformation of Chinese Calligraphy in the Seventeenth Century*. Cambridge, MA: Harvard University Asia Center, 2003.

BIBLIOGRAPHY

Bai Qianshen 白谦慎 and Xue Longchun 薛龙春. "Chenshi de shiji" 尘世的史跡. *Dushu* 读书 1 (2007): 51–58.
Ban Gu 班固. *Hanshu* 漢書. Beijing: Zhonghua shuju, 1962.
Barthes, Roland. "The Advertising Message." In *The Semiotic Challenge*, trans. Richard Howard. Berkeley: University of California Press, 1994.
Bedos-Rezak, Brigitte Miriam. *When Ego Was Imago: Signs of Identity in the Middle Ages*. Leiden: Brill, 2011.
Beijing shi difangzhi bianyuan weiyuanhui 北京市地方志编纂委员会, ed. *Beijing zhi. Wenwu juan. Wenwu zhi* 北京志。文物卷。文物志. Beijing: Beijing chubanshe, 2006.
Beijing tushuguan 北京圖書館, ed. *Beijing tushuguan cang Zhongguo lidai shike taben huibian* 北京圖書館藏中國歷代石刻拓本匯編. Zhengzhou: Zhongzhou guji chubanshe, 1989.
Bol, Peter K. "Looking to Wang Shizhen: Hu Yinglin (1551–1602) and Late-Ming Alternatives to Neo-Confucian Learning." *Ming Studies* 1 (2006): 99–137.
Brashier, Kenneth E. "Text and Ritual in Early Chinese Stelae." In *Text and Ritual in Early China*, ed. Martin Kern, 249–84. Seattle: University of Washington Press, 2005.
Brittenham, Claudia, ed. *Vessels: The Object as Container*. Oxford: Oxford University Press, 2019.
Brokaw, Cynthia J., and Kai-wing Chow, eds. *Printing and Book Culture in Late Imperial China*. Berkeley: University of California Press, 2005.
Brook, Timothy. *The Confusions of Pleasure: Commerce and Culture in Ming China*. Berkeley: University of California Press, 1998.
Brown, Bill. *Other Things*. Chicago: University of Chicago Press, 2015.
Burkus-Chasson, Anne. *Through a Forest of Chancellors: Fugitive Histories in Liu Yuan's* Lingyan ge: *An Illustrated Book from Seventeenth-Century Suzhou*. Cambridge, MA: Harvard University Asia Center, 2010.
Bussotti, Michela [Migaila 米盖拉], and Zhu Wanshu 朱萬曙, eds. *Huizhou: Shuye yu diyu wenhua* 徽州：書業與地域文化. Faguo Hanxue vol. 13. Beijing: Zhonghua shuju, 2010.
Cai Hongru 蔡鴻茹. "Gu zhuanwa yan" 古甎瓦硯. *Shupu* 書譜 84 (1988): 76–78.
———. *Zhonghua guyan: 100 jiang* 中华古砚 100 讲. Tianjin: Baihua wenyi chubanshe, 2007.
Cai Meifen [Ts'ai Meifen] 蔡玫芬. "Gangbu de gongyi: Guanyu Ming mo Qing chu Zhangzhou gongyi pin er san shi" 港埠的工藝：關於明末清初漳州工藝品二三事. In *Zhongguo Haiyang fazhan shi lunwen ji* 中國海洋發展史論文集, ed. Liu Xufeng 劉序楓, 29–87. Taibei: Zhongyang yanjiu yuan renwen shehui kexue yanjiu zhongxin zhuanshu, 2008.
———. "Mingdai de moshu" 明代的墨書. In *International Colloquium on Chinese Art History, 1991: Proceedings: Antiquities, Part 2*, 681–726. Taibei: National Palace Museum, 1992.
———. "Xi huajie zuo bei: jijian shiqi shiji de lianzuo huabei" 犀花解作杯—幾件十七世紀的連座花杯. *Gugong wenwu yuekan* 故宮文物月刊 270 (2005): 76–85.
Cai Weidong 蔡卫东. "Wuxi Gu Lin mu chutu Mingdai liupai yin shiwu kaoshu" 无锡顾林墓出土明代流派印实物考述. *Zhongguo shufa*, no. 6 (2016): 142–55.
Cai Xinquan 蔡鑫泉. "Liangding Gugong cang mopin shang" 两锭故宮藏墨品赏. *Shoucang* 收藏 6 (2013): 120–24.

———. "Ming Huizhou zhuming huajia Wu Tingyu Zuogan shilüe" 明徽州著名畫家吳廷羽左干事略. *Huizhou shehui kexue* 徽州社會科學 5 (2011): 44–48.
Cai Yaoqing 蔡耀慶 [Tsai Yao-ching]. *Mingdai yinxue fazhan yinsu yu biaoxian zhi yanjiu* 明代印學發展因素與表現之研究. Taibei: Guoli lishi bowuguan, 2007.
Campbell, Duncan. "Flawed Jade: Zhang Dai's Family Biographies." *Ming Studies* 62 (2010): 25–55.
———. "Mortal Ancestors, Immortal Images: Zhang Dai's Biographical Portraits." *PORTAL: Journal of Multidisciplinary International Studies* 9, no. 3 (November 2012): 1–26.
———. "Zhang Dai's Passionate Search for Orchid Pavilion." *Script and Print* 29, no. 1–4 (2005): 30–44.
Cao Cao 曹操, Cao Pi 曹丕, and Cao Zhi 曹植. *San Cao ji* 三曹集. Changsha: Yuelu shushe, 1992.
Cao Shengchen 曹聖臣. *Caoshi molin* 曹氏墨林. Facsimile reprint of 1688 edition in SKQSCMCS, zibu, vol. 79.
Cao Shujuan 曹淑娟. "Cong Yushan dao Ninggu ta: Qi Bansun de kongjian tiren yu yimin xinshi" 從寓山到寧古塔—祁班孫的空間體認與遺民心事. In *Kongjian yu wenhua changyu: Kongjian yidong zhi wenhua quanshi* 空間與文化場域：空間移動之文化詮釋, ed. Wang Ailing 王愛玲. Taibei: Guojia tushuguan, 2009.
———. *Qi Biaojia shizhuan: Yuanshan tang shici biannian jiaoshi* 祁彪佳詩傳：遠山堂詩詞編年校釋. Xinbei: Lianjing chubanshe, 2020.
———. *Wan Ming xingling xiaopin yanjiu* 晚明性靈小品研究. Taibei: Wenjin chubanshe, 1988.
Cao Xueqin. *The Story of the Stone: A Chinese Novel by Cao Xueqin in Five Volumes*, vol. 1. Trans. David Hawkes. New York: Penguin, 1973.
Chan, Wing-Ming. "The Qianlong Emperor's New Strategy in 1775 to Commend Late-Ming Loyalists." *Asia Major* 13, no. 1 (2000): 109–37.
Chartier, Roger. *Inscription and Erasure: Literature and Written Culture from the Eleventh to the Eighteenth Century*. Trans. Arthur Goldhammer. Philadelphia: University of Pennsylvania Press, 2007.
Chen Liangwu 陈良武. "Huang Daozhou duanbeiyan kaolun" 黄道周断碑砚考论. *Shenzhen daxue xuebao (renwen shehui kexueban)* 深圳大学学报（人文社会科学版）30, no. 1 (2013): 53–57.
Chen Que 陳確. *Chen Que ji* 陳確集. 2 vols. Beijing: Zhonghua shuju, 1979.
Chen Shengyu 陈圣宇. "Zhou Lianggong wannian fenshu riqi quekao" 周亮工晚年焚书日期确考. *Gudian wenxian yanjiu* 古典文献研究 11 (2008): 541–544.
Chen Zhichao 陳智超. *Meiguo Hafo daxue Hafo Yanjing tushuguan cang Ming dai Huizhou Fangshi qinyou shouzha qibai tong kaoshi* 美國哈佛大學燕京圖書館藏明代徽州方氏親友手札七百通考釋. Hefei: Anhui daxue chubanshe, 2001.
Cheng Dayue 程大約. *Chengshi moyuan* 程氏墨苑. Facsimile reprint of Wanli edition in SKQSCMCS, zibu, vol. 79.
———. *Chengshi moyuan*. In XXSKQS, zibu, vol. 1114.
Cheng Zhangcan 程章灿. *Shike kegong yanjiu* 石刻刻工研究. Shanghai: Shanghai guji chubanshe, 2008.
Chiang, Nicole T. C. *Emperor Qianlong's Hidden Treasures: Reconsidering the Collection of the Qing Imperial Household*. Hong Kong: Hong Kong University Press, 2019.

Choo, Jessey J. C. *Inscribing Death: Burials, Representations, and Remembrance in Tang China.* Honolulu: University of Hawai'i Press, 2022.

Chun, Wendy Hui Kyong. "The Enduring Ephemeral, or the Future Is a Memory." In *Media Archaeology: Approaches, Applications, and Implications,* ed. Erkki Huhtamo and Jussi Parikka, 184–206. Berkeley: University of California Press, 2011.

Clunas, Craig. *Chinese Carving.* London: Victoria and Albert Museum, 1996.

——. *Empire of Great Brightness: Visual and Material Cultures of Ming China, 1368–1644.* London: Reaktion, 2007.

——. *Superfluous Things: Material Culture and Social Status in Early Modern China.* Honolulu: University of Hawai'i Press, 2004.

Confucius. *The Analects.* Trans. Simon Leys. New York: Norton, 2014.

Csikszentmihalyi, Mark. "Reimagining the Yellow Emperor's Four Faces." In *Text and Ritual in Early China,* ed. Martin Kern, 226–48. Seattle: University of Washington Press, 2005.

Davis, Timothy M. *Entombed Epigraphy and Commemorative Culture in Early Medieval China: A History of Early Muzhiming.* Leiden: Brill, 2015.

Deng Changfeng 邓长风. "Zhou Ang de shengping jiqi 'Sigong ji' chuanqi de benshi" 周昂的生平及其《兕觥记》传奇的本事. In *Ming Qing xiqujia kaolüe quanbian* 明清戏曲家考略全编, ed. Deng Changfeng, 454–67. Shanghai: Shanghai guji chubanshe, 2009).

Deng Zhicheng 鄧之誠. *Gudong suoji* 古董瑣記. 2 vols. Beijing: Renmin chubanshe, 2012.

Derrida, Jacques. *Signéponge-Signsponge.* Trans. Richard Rand. New York: Columbia University Press, 1984.

Dong Qichang 董其昌. *Rongtai wenji* 容臺文集. Facsimile reprint of 1630 edition in SKQSCMCS, jibu, vol. 171.

Drpic, Ivan. *Epigram, Art, and Devotion in Later Byzantium.* Cambridge: Cambridge University Press, 2016.

Drucker, Johanna. *The Visible Word: Experimental Typography and Modern Art, 1909–1923*. Chicago: University of Chicago Press, 1994.

Du Jun 杜濬. *Bianyatang quanji* 變雅堂全集. 5 vols. China: s.n., 1853?; Harvard-Yenching Library Rare Book.

Dung Chau Hung 董就雄. "Qu Dajun shilun yu Qingchu jijia shilun zhi bijiao" 屈大均詩論與清初幾家主要詩論之比較. *Journal of Oriental Studies* 40, no. 1/2 (2009): 169–201.

Durrant, Stephen, Wai-yee Li, and David Schaberg, trans and annot. *Zuo Tradition / Zuozhuan: Commentary on the "Spring and Autumn Annals,"* 3 vols. Seattle: University of Washington Press, 2016.

Ebrey, Patricia. *Accumulating Culture: The Collections of Emperor Huizong.* Seattle: University of Washington Press, 2008.

Edwards, E. D. "A Classified Guide to the Thirteen Classes of Chinese Prose." Oriental and African Studies Presented to Lionel David Barnett by His Colleagues, Past and Present. *Bulletin of the School of Oriental and African Studies* 12, no. 3–4 (1948): 770–88.

Egan, Ronald. *The Problem of Beauty: Aesthetic Thought and Pursuits in Northern Song Dynasty China.* Cambridge, MA: Harvard University Press, 2006.

Eisendrath, Rachel. *Poetry in a World of Things: Aesthetics and Empiricism in Renaissance Ekphrasis.* Chicago: University of Chicago Press, 2018.

BIBLIOGRAPHY

Elman, Benjamin A. *From Philosophy to Philology: Intellectual and Social Aspects of Change in Late Imperial China.* Los Angeles: University of California Press, 2001.

———. *On Their Own Terms: Science in China, 1550–1900.* Cambridge, MA: Harvard University Press, 2005.

Fang Quji 方去疾. *Ming Qing zhuanke liupai yinpu* 明清篆刻流派印譜. Shanghai: Shanghai shuhua chubanshe, 1981.

Fang Yulu 方于魯. *Fang Jianyuan ji* 方建元集. Nanjing Library: Wanli edition.

———. *Fangshi mopu* 方氏墨譜. Facsimile reprint of Wanli edition in SKQSCMCS, zibu, vol. 79.

Feng Mengzhen 馮夢禎. *Kuaixue tang ji* 快雪堂集. Facsimile reprint of 1616 edition in SKQSCMCS, jibu, vol. 164.

———. *Kuaixue tang riji* 快雪堂日記. Ed. Ding Xiaoming 丁小明. Nanjing: Fenghuang chubanshe, 2010.

Fleming, Juliet. *Graffiti and the Writing Arts of Early Modern England.* London: Reaktion, 2001.

Flusser, Vilém. *Does Writing Have a Future?* Trans. Nancy Ann Roth. Minneapolis: University of Minnesota Press, 2011.

Ford, Thomas H. *Wordsworth and the Poetics of Air.* Cambridge: Cambridge University Press, 2018.

Forster Kurt W. and Diane Ghirado, trans. "The Modern Cult of Monuments: Its Character and Its Origin." *Oppositions* 25 (1982): 21–51.

Fox, Ariel. "Playing Against Type: The Moral Merchant on the Early Qing Stage." *Journal of Chinese Literature and Culture* 6.2 (November 2019): 383–411.

Franke, Herbert. *Kulturgeschichtliches über die chinesische Tusche.* Munich: Verlag der Bayerischen Akademie der Wissenschaften, 1962.

Frow, John. "Signature and Brand." In *High-Pop: Making Culture into Popular Entertainment*, ed. Jim Collins, 56–74. Oxford: Blackwell, 2002.

Gao Fenghan 高鳳翰. *Gao Fenghan quanji* 高鳳翰全集. Ed. Liu Caidong 劉才棟, Zheng Wenguang 鄭文光, and Gao Shifu 高石副. Beijing: Beijing daxue chubanshe, 2014.

———. *Yanshi jianshi* 硯史箋釋. Ed. Tian Tao 田濤 and Cui Shichi 崔士箎. Beijing: Beijing shenghuo dushu xinzhi sanlian shudian, 2011.

Geng Chuanyou 耿傳友. "Baiyu she shulüe" 白榆社述略. *Huangshan xueyuan xuebao* 黃山學院學報 1 (2007): 29–33.

———. "Lun Ming Qing Huishang zhuanji de lishi jiazhi yu wenxue jiazhi" 论明清徽商传记的历史价值与文学价值. *Nanjing shida xuebao (shehui kexue ban)* 南京师大学报（社会科学版） 2 (2012): 130.

Gillman, Dennis. "A Source of Rhinoceros Horn Cups in the Late Ming Dynasty." *Orientations* 12 (1984): 10–17.

Gitelman, Lisa. *Scripts, Grooves, and Writing Machines: Representing Technology in the Edison Era.* Stanford, CA: Stanford University Press, 1999.

Goldin, Paul. "The Legacy of Bronzes and Bronze Inscriptions in Early Chinese Literature." In *A Sourcebook of Ancient Chinese Bronze Inscriptions*, ed. Paul Goldin and Constance A. Cook, lv–lxiv. Berkeley, CA: Society for the Study of Early China, 2016.

Gross, Kenneth. *The Dream of the Moving Statue.* Ithaca, NY: Cornell University Press, 1992.

Gu Qiyuan 顧起元. *Kezuo zhuiyu* 客座贅語. Ed. Kong Yi 孔一. Shanghai: Shanghai guji chubanshe, 2012.

Guarino, Carmen. "The Interpretation of Images in Matteo Ricci's Pictures for 'Cheng shi mo yuan,'" *Ming Qing yanjiu* 6, no. 1 (1997): 21–44.

Guo Daxiang 郭达祥. "Qu Dajun yu duanyan" 屈大均与端砚. *Zhaoqing xueyuan xuebao* 肇庆学院学报 40, no. 3 (2019): 17–21.

Guo Qingfan 郭慶藩, comp. *Zhuangzi jishi* 莊子集釋. Annot. Wang Xiaoyu 王孝魚. Beijing: Zhonghua shuju, 1961; reprinted 2010.

Guo, Qitao. *Huizhou: Local Identity and Mercantile Lineage Culture in Ming China*. Oakland: University of California Press, 2022.

———. *Ritual Opera and Mercantile Lineage: The Confucian Transformation of Popular Culture in Late Imperial Huizhou*. Stanford, CA: Stanford University Press, 2005.

Guy, R. Kent. *Emperor's Four Treasuries: Scholars and the State in the Late Ch'ien-lung Era*. Cambridge, MA: Harvard University Press, 1987.

Hammond, Kenneth J. "The Decadent Chalice: A Critique of Late Ming Political Culture." *Ming Studies* 39 (2013): 32–49.

Han Tianheng 韩天衡, ed. *Lidai yinxue lunwen xuan* 历代印学论文选. 2 vols. Hangzhou: Xiling yinshe, 1985.

Han Yu 韓愈. *Han Changli wenji jiaozhu* 韓昌黎文集校注. Ed. Ma Qichang 馬其昶. Shanghai: Shanghai chubanshe, 2018.

Handler-Spitz, Rivi. *Symptoms of an Unruly Age: Li Zhi and Cultures of Early Modernity*. Seattle: University of Washington Press, 2017.

Harrist Jr., Robert E. *The Landscape of Words: Stone Inscriptions from Early and Medieval China*. Seattle: University of Washington Press, 2008.

Hartman, Geoffrey. *The Unremarkable Wordsworth*. Minneapolis: University of Minnesota Press, 1987.

Hay, Jonathan. "Culture, Ethnicity, and Empire in the Work of Two Eighteenth-Century 'Eccentric' Artists." *RES* 35 (1999): 201–23.

———. "Guo Zhongshu's Archaeology of Writing." *Journal of Chinese History* 3, no. 2 (2019): 233–324.

———. *Sensuous Surfaces: The Decorative Object in Early Modern China*. Honolulu: University of Hawai'i Press, 2010.

———. "The Suspension of Dynastic Time." In *Boundaries in China*, ed. John Hay. London: Reaktion, 1994.

He Fuzheng 賀復徵. *Wenzhang bianti huixuan* 文章辨體匯選. In WYGSKQS, jibu, vol. 1407; 1408.

Hightower, James R. "The *Wen Hsüan* and Genre Theory." In *Studies in Chinese Literature*, ed. John L. Bishop. Cambridge, MA: Harvard University Press, 1966.

Honig, Bonnie. *Public Things: Democracy in Disrepair*. New York: Fordham University Press, 2017.

Houston, Stephen. *The Life Within: Classic Maya and the Matter of Permanence*. New Haven, CT: Yale University Press, 2014.

Hsü, Ginger Cheng-chi. *Bushel of Pearls: Painting for Sale in Eighteenth-Century Yangchow*. Stanford: Stanford University Press, 2001.

Hsu Ya-hwei 許雅惠, "Songdai shidafu de jinshi shoucang yu liyi shijian—yi Lantian Lüshi jiazu wei li" 宋代士大夫的金石收藏與禮儀實踐—以藍田呂氏家族為例. *Zhejiang daxue yishu yu kaogu yanjiu* 浙江大學藝術與考古研究 13 (2018): 131–64.

Hu Yimin 胡益民. *Zhang Dai pingzhuan* 张岱评传. Nanjing: Nanjing daxue chubanshe, 2002.
———. *Zhang Dai yanjiu* 張岱研究. Hefei: Anhui jiaoyu chubanshe, 2002.
Hu Yinglin 胡應麟. *Shaoshi shanfang ji* 少室山房集. In WYGSKQS, vol. 1290.
Huang Daozhou 黃道周. *Huang Zhangpu wenxuan* 黃漳浦文選. Taibei: Datong shuju, 1987.
Huang Dun 黃惇. "Mingdai chu, zhongqi wenren yinzhang yishu gouchen" 明代初, 中期文人印章藝術鉤沉. In *Xiling yinshe guoji yinxue yantao hui lunwen ji* 西泠印社國際印學研討會論文集, ed. Xiling yinshe. Hangzhou: Xiling yinshe chubanshe, 1998.
———. *Zhongguo gudai yinlun shi* 中國古代印論史. Shanghai: Shanghai shuhua chubanshe, 1994.
———, ed. *Zhongguo yinlun leibian: xiudingban* 中國印論類編：修訂版. Beijing: Rongbaozhai chubanshe, 2019.
Huang Huaixin 黃懷信. *Da Dai liji huijiao jizhu* 大戴禮記彙校集注. Xi'an: Sanqin chubanshe, 2005.
Huang, Ray. *1587 A Year of No Significance: The Ming Dynasty in Decline*. New Haven, CT: Yale University Press, 1981.
Huang Taiyang 黃台阳. *Moxiang shijia* 墨香世家. Haikou: Hainan chubanshe, 2017.
Huang Zhanyue 黃展岳. "Ming Qing huangshi de gongfei xunzang zhi" 明清皇室的宮妃殉葬制. *Gugong bowuyuan yuankan* 故宮博物院院刊, no. 1 (1988): 29–34.
Huang Zongxi 黃宗羲. *Jinshi yaoli* 金石要例. In WYGSKQS, jibu, vol. 1483.
———. *Ming wenhai* 明文海. In WYGSKQS, jibu, vol. 1458.
Inoue Mitsuyuki 井上充幸. "Jiang Shaoshu yu Wang Yueshi: *Yunshi zhai bitan* suojian Ming mo Qing chu yishu shichang yu Huizhou shangren de huodong" 姜紹書與王越石——《韻石齋筆談》所見明末清初藝術市場與徽州商人的活動. Trans. Wan Shuang 萬爽 and Lu Peirong 陸蓓容. In *History of Art and History of Ideas: Meishushi yu guannian shi* 美術史與觀念史, ed. Fan Jingzhong 范景中 and Cao Yiqiang 曹意強, 383–411. Nanjing: Nanjing shifan daxue chubanshe, 2004.
Ji Ruoxin [Chi Jo-hsin] 嵇若昕. *Jiangxin yu xiangong: Ming Qing diaoke zhan: xiangya xijiao pian* 匠心與仙工：明清雕刻展：象牙犀角篇. Taibei: Guoli gugong bowuyuan, 2009.
———. *Ming Qing zhuke yishu* 明清竹刻藝術. Taibei: Guoli gugong bowuyuan, 1999.
Ji Yun 紀昀. *Yuewei caotang yanpu* 閱微草堂硯譜. Beijing: Zhongguo wenlian chuban gongsi, 1990.
Jiang Guangxu 蔣光煦 ed. *Shewen zijiu* 涉聞梓舊. Shanghai: Hanfen lou, 1924.
Jiang Hui 蔣暉. *Mingdai dali shiping kao* 明代大理石屏考. Jinan: Shandong huabao chubanshe, 2018.
Jiang Shaoshu 姜紹書. *Yunshi zhai bitan* 韻石齋筆談. In *Zhibuzu zhai congshu* 知不足齋叢書, ed. Bao Tingbo 鮑廷博, vol. 1, 247–272. Beijing: Zhonghua shuju, 1999.
Jiang Weitang 姜緯堂. "Qi Nantang yu Wang Taihan" 戚南塘與汪太函. In *Qi Jiguang yanjiu lunji* 戚繼光研究論集, ed. Yan Chongnian 閻崇年, 318–51. Beijing: Zhishi chubanshe, 1990.
Jin Nong 金農. *Jin Nong ji* 金農集. Ed. Yong Qi 雍琦. Hangzhou: Zhejiang renmin meishu chubanshe, 2016.
Jin Shaofang 金紹坊 and Wang Shixiang 王世襄, ed. *Zhuke yishu* 竹刻藝術. Beijing: Renmin meishu chubanshe, 1980.

Jin Zhengxi 金正喜 [Kim Chŏnghŭi]. *Ruan tang xiansheng quanji* 阮堂先生全集. Sŏul: Sinsŏng Munhwasa, 1972.
Johns, Adrian. "Ink." In *Materials and Expertise in Early Modern Europe: Between Market and Laboratory*, ed. Ursula Klein and E. C. Spary. Chicago: University of Chicago Press, 2010.
Kafalas, Philip A. *In Limpid Dream: Nostalgia and Zhang Dai's Reminiscences of the Ming*. Norwalk, CT: Eastbridge, 2007.
Kelly, Thomas. "Impressions of Loss: Writing and Memory in Biographies of Seal Carvers." *Asia Major* 36, no. 1 (2023): 1–52.
———. "Paper Trails: Fang Yongbin and the Material Culture of Calligraphy." *Journal of Chinese History* 3, no. 2 (2019): 325–62.
———. "The Death of an Artisan: Su Shi and Ink Making." *Harvard Journal of Asiatic Studies* 80, no. 2 (2020): 315–46.
———. "The Inscription of Remnant Things: Zhang Dai's 'Twenty-Eight Friends.'" *Late Imperial China* 42, no. 1 (2021): 1–43.
Kern, Martin. "Early Chinese Literature, Beginnings Through Western Han." In *The Cambridge History of Chinese Literature, Vol 1: To 1375*, ed. Kang-I Sun Chang and Stephen Owen. Cambridge: Cambridge University Press, 2010.
———. "The Performance of Writing in Western Zhou China." In *The Poetics of Grammar and the Metaphysics of Sound and Sign*, ed. Sergio La Porta and D. Shulman, 109–76. Leiden: Brill, 2010.
———. *The Stele Inscriptions of Ch'in Shih-Huang: Text and Ritual in Early Chinese Imperial Representation*. New Haven, CT: American Oriental Society, 2000.
Kile, S. E., and Kristina Kleutghen, "Seeing Through Pictures and Poetry: A History of Lenses (1681)." *Late Imperial China* 38, no. 1 (2017): 47–112.
Kim, Hongnam. *The Life of a Patron: Zhou Lianggong (1612–1672) and the Painters of Seventeenth-Century China*. New York: China Institute in America, 1996.
Kirschenbaum, Matthew G. *Mechanisms: New Media and the Forensic Imagination*. Cambridge, MA: MIT Press, 2012.
Knechtges, David. "From the Eastern Han Through the Western Jin (AD 25–317)." In *The Cambridge History of Chinese Literature, Vol 1: To 1375*, ed. Kang-I Sun Chang and Stephen Owen, 116–98. Cambridge: Cambridge University Press, 2010.
———. *Wenxuan, or Selections of Refined Literature*. Princeton, NJ: Princeton University Press, 1996.
Knechtges, David, and Taiping Chang. *Ancient and Early Medieval Chinese Literature: A Reference Guide. Part One*. Leiden: Brill, 2010.
Ko, Dorothy. *The Social Life of Inkstones: Artisans and Scholars in Early Qing China*. Seattle: University of Washington Press, 2017.
Kopytoff, Igor. "The Cultural Biography of Things: Commoditization as Process." In *The Social Life of Things: Commodities in Cultural Perspective*, ed. Arjun Appadurai. Cambridge: Cambridge University Press, 1986.
Krajewski, Markus. *The Server: A Media History from the Present to the Baroque*. Trans. Ilinca Iurascu. New Haven, CT: Yale University Press, 2018.
Kroll, Paul. *A Student's Dictionary of Classical and Medieval Chinese*. Leiden: Brill, 2017.
Kuai Songlin 鄶松鄰, ed. *Shiliu jia moshuo* 十六家墨說. Beijing: Zhongguo shudian, 1993.
Kuo, Jason Chi-sheng. "Hui-chou Merchants as Art Patrons in the Late Sixteenth and Early Seventeenth Centuries." In *Artists and Patrons: Some Social and Economic*

Aspects of Chinese Painting, ed. Chu-tsing Li, 177–88. Lawrence, KS: Kress Foundation Dept. of Art History in association with University of Washington Press, 1989.

———. *Word as Image: The Art of Chinese Seal Engraving*. New York: Chinese House Gallery, 1992.

Kuo, Jason C., and Peter C. Sturman, eds. *Double Beauty: Qing Dynasty Couplets from the Lechangzai Xuan Collection*. Hong Kong: Art Museum, The Chinese University of Hong Kong, 2003.

Kutcher, Norman. *Mourning in Late Imperial China: Filial Piety and the State*. Cambridge: Cambridge University Press, 1999.

Lai, Eric C. "Pipa Artists and Their Music in Late Ming China." *Ming Studies* 43 (2008): 43–71.

Lai Suk-Yee 黎淑儀, ed. *The Art of Chen Hongshou: Painting, Calligraphy, Seal-carving and Teapot-design* 書畫印壺：陳鴻壽的藝術. Hong Kong: Shanghai Museum, Nanjing Museum and Art Museum, The Chinese University of Hong Kong, 2005.

Lam, Joseph. "Ming Music and Music History." *Ming Studies* 38 (1997): 21–62.

Langlois, John D. "The Reversal of the Death Verdict Against Wang Shizhen's Father." *Ming Studies* 1 (2016): 72–98.

Lefeuvre, Jean. "Rhinoceros and Wild Buffalo North of the Yellow River at the End of the Shang Dynasty." *Monumenta Serica* 39 (1990–1991): 131–57.

Lewis, Mark Edward. *Honor and Shame in Early China*. Cambridge: Cambridge University Press, 2021.

Leys, Simon. *The Hall of Uselessness: Collected Essays*. New York: New York Review of Books, 2013.

Li Ling 李零, ed. *Li Ling zixuan ji* 李零自選集. Guilin: Guangxi shifan daxue chubanshe, 1998.

Li Nailong 李乃龍. "Cui Yuan 'Zuo you ming' rensheng guan de lilun dise—jian xi zuo you ming de wenti yiyi" 崔瑗《座右銘》人生觀的理論底色－兼析座右銘的文體意義. *Henan daxue xuebao* 河南大學學報 46, no. 2 (2006): 79–81.

Li Panlong 李攀龍. *Cangming xiansheng ji* 滄溟先生集. Ed. Bao Jingdi 包敬第. Shanghai: Shanghai guji chubanshe, 2014.

Li Rihua 李日華. *Liuyan zhai biji* 六研齋筆記. Ed. Yu Zhenhong 郁震宏 and Li Baoyang 李保陽. Nanjing: Fenghuang chubanshe, 2010.

———. *Weishui xuan riji* 味水軒日記. Ed. Tu Youxiang 屠友祥. Shanghai: Shanghai Yuandong chubanshe, 1996.

———. *Zitao xuan zazhui* 紫桃軒雜綴. Ed. Xue Weiyuan 薛維源. Nanjing: Fenghuang chubanshe, 2010.

Li Tiemin 李鐵民. *Yandiao yishu yu zhizuo* 硯雕藝術與製作. Shanghai: Shanghai shudian chubanshe, 2004.

Li, Wai-yee. "The Collector, the Connoisseur, and Late-Ming Sensibility." *T'oung Pao* 81, no. 4 (1995): 269–302.

———. "Gardens and Illusions from Late Ming to Early Qing." *Harvard Journal of Asiatic Studies* 72, no. 2 (2012): 295–336.

———. "History and Memory in Wu Weiye's Poetry." In *Trauma and Transcendence in Early Qing Literature*, ed. Wilt L. Idema, Wai-yee Li, and Ellen Widmer, 99–148. Cambridge, MA: Harvard University Asia Center, 2006.

———. "Shibian yu wanwu: lüelun Qing chu wenren de shenmei fengshang" 世變與玩物：略論清初文人的審美風尚. *Journal of the Institute of Literature and Philosophy* 《中國文哲研究集刊》, Academica Sinica, no. 33 (2008): 1–40.

———. *The Promise and Peril of Things: Literature and Material Culture*. New York: Columbia University Press, 2022.

———. *Women and National Trauma in Late Imperial Chinese Literature*. Cambridge, MA: Harvard University Asia Center, 2014.

———. "Women as Emblems of Dynastic Fall from Late-Ming to Late-Qing." In *Dynastic Crisis and Cultural Innovation: From the Late Ming to the Late Qing and Beyond*, ed. David Der-wei Wang and Shang Wei, 93–150. Cambridge, MA: Harvard University Asia Center, 2005.

Li Weizhen 李維禎. *Dami shanfang ji* 大泌山房集. Facsimile reprint of 1611 edition in SKQSCMCS, jibu, vols. 150–53.

Li Xingtao 李兴涛. "Cong Gu Lin mu yu Hua Shiyi mu chutu yinzhang kan Su Xuan zhuanke de yishu fengmao" 从顾林墓与华师伊墓出土印章看苏宣篆刻的艺术风貌. *Shufa shangping* 书法赏评, no. 5 (2017): 53–58.

Li Xueqin 李學勤, ed. *Zhongguo meishu quanji: Gongyi meishu bian: Qingtong qi* 中國美術全集：工藝美術編：青銅器. Beijing: Wenwu chubanshe, 1985.

Li Yu 李漁. *Li Yu quanji* 李漁全集. 20 vols. Hangzhou: Zhejiang guji chubanshe, 1991.

Li Yuhang. *Becoming Guanyin: Artistic Devotion of Buddhist Women in Late Imperial China*. New York: Columbia University Press, 2020.

Liang Shaoren 梁绍壬. *Liangban qiuyu'an suibi* 兩般秋雨盦随笔. Ed. Zhuang Wei 庄葳. Shanghai: Shanghai guji chubanshe, 2012.

Liao Kebin 廖可斌. *Fugu pai yu Mingdai wenxue sichao* 復古派與明代文學思潮. Taibei: Wenjin chubanshe, 1994.

———. *Mingdai wenxue fugu yundong yanjiu* 明代文学复古运动研究. Beijing: Shangwu yinshuguan, 2008.

Liao Yang 廖暘. "Mingdai Handi liuchuan de shangle, xi jingang xi yu jingangjie fanzi lun—yi *Fangshi mopu Chengshi moyuan* suo kan wei zhongxin" 明代汉地流传的上乐、喜金刚系与金刚界梵字轮—以《方氏墨谱》、《程氏墨苑》所刊为中心. In *Hanzang foxue yanjiu: Wenben, renwu, tuxiang he lishi* 汉藏佛学研究：文本，人物，图像和历史, ed. Shen Weirong 沈卫荣, 483–520. Beijing: Zhongguo zangxue chubanshe, 2013.

Lien, Chi-Yuan 連啟元. "Ruxia zhi bian: Wang Daokun dui Huizhou renwu 'ruxia' xingxiang de lunshu yu xingsu" 儒俠之辨：汪道昆對徽州人物「儒俠」形象論述與型塑. *Mingdai yanjiu* 明代研究 19 (2012): 121–40.

Lin Huan 林欢. *Huimo Hu Kaiwen yanjiu* 徽墨胡开文研究. Beijing: Gugong chubanshe, 2016.

Lin Li-chiang. "The Proliferation of Images: The Ink-Stick Designs and the Printing of the *Fang-Shih Mo-P'u* and the *Ch'eng-Shih Mo-Yuan*." PhD diss., Princeton University, 1998.

———. "Riben Gumeiyuan xiangguan moshu zhi yanjiu: Shiba shiji Zhongri yishu wenhua jiaoliu zhi yi duan" 日本古梅園相關墨書之研究—十八世紀中日藝術文化交流之一端. *Hanxue yanjiu* 漢學研究 28.2 (2011): 127–68.

———. "Wanming Huizhou moshang Cheng Junfang yu Fang Yulu moye de zhankai yu jingzheng" 晚明徽州墨商程君房與方于魯墨業的開展與競爭. In *Huizhou: Shuye yu diyu wenhua*, 121–97.

Lin Li-yueh 林麗月. "Wanming 'Rushang' yu diyu shehui: *Mingdai Huizhou Fangshi qinyou shouzha* de kaocha" 晚明「儒商」地域社會:《明代徽州方氏親友手札》的考察. In *Jinshi Zhongguo de shehui yu wenhua (860–1800)* 近世中國的社會與文化, 467–507. Taibei: Shida lishi, 2007.

Lin Youlin 林有麟. *Suyuan shipu* 素園石譜. Hangzhou: Zhejiang renmin meishu chubanshe, 2013.

Liu Dongqin 劉東芹. "Wen Peng wannian shufa zhuanke huodong ji liangjing xingji kaoshu" 文彭晚年書法篆刻活動及兩京行跡考述. *Shuhua yishu xuekan* 書畫藝術學刊 3 (2007): 431–47.

Liu Jianming 劉建明. *Zhang Juzheng bingzheng yu wan Ming wenxue zouxiang* 張居正秉政與晚明文學走向. Shanghai: Fudan daxue chubanshe, 2013.

Liu Jingjing 劉晶晶. "Daxuan zhenmi: *Fangshi mopu* tuxiang kaobian" 大玄珍秘:《方氏墨譜》圖像考辨. PhD diss., China Academy of Art, 2017.

Liu Pengbing 刘彭冰. *Wang Daokun wenxue yu jiaoyou yanjiu* 汪道昆文学与交游研究. Beijing: Zhongguo wenshi chubanshe, 2018.

Liu Shilin 劉士鏻. *Gujin wenzhi* 古今文致. Facsimile reprint of Tianqi edition in SKQSCMCS, jibu, vol. 373.

Liu Tong 劉侗 and Yu Yizheng 于弈正. *Dijing jingwu lüe* 帝京景物略. Ed. Sun Xiaoli 孫小力. Shanghai: Shanghai guji chubanshe, 2001.

Liu Xiang. *Garden of Eloquence/Shuoyuan* 說苑. Trans. Eric Henry. Seattle: University of Washington Press, 2021.

Liu Xie [Liu Hsieh]. *The Literary Mind and the Carving of Dragons*. Trans. Vincent Yu-chung Shih. Hong Kong: The Chinese University of Hong Kong Press, 2015.

Liu Xie 劉勰. *Wenxin diaolong jiaozhu shiyi* 文心雕龍校注拾遺. Ed. Yang Mingzhao 楊明照. Shanghai: Shanghai guji chubanshe, 1982.

Liu Xinru [Liu Hsin-ju] 劉心如. "Xin'an juyan: Zhan Jingfeng yu wan Ming jianshang jia de diyu jingzheng" 新安具眼:詹景鳳與晚明鑑賞家的地域競爭. *Mingdai yanjiu* 明代研究 18, no. 6 (2012): 83–104.

Liu Xu 劉昫. *Jiu Tang shu* 舊唐書. Beijing: Zhonghua shuju, 1975.

Liu Yuejin 劉躍進. *Wenxuan jiuzhu jicun* 文選舊註輯存. Ed. Xu Hua 徐華. Nanjing: Fenghuang chubanshe, 2017.

Liu Yunhe 刘云鹤. "Gao Fenghan *Yanshi* yanjiu" 高凤翰《硯史》研究. In *Liu Yunhe xueshu wenji* 刘云鹤学术文集. Hangzhou: Xiling yinshe, 2007.

Louis, François. *Design by the Book: Chinese Ritual Objects and the Sanli tu*. Chicago: University of Chicago Press, 2017.

———. "The Hejiacun Rhyton and the Chinese Wine Horn: Intoxicating Rarities and Their Antiquarian History." *Artibus Asiae* 67, no. 2 (2007): 201–42.

Lu Ji 陸機. *Lu Ji ji* 陸機集. Ed. Jin Taosheng 金濤聲. Beijing: Zhonghua shuju, 1982.

Lu Pengliang 陸鵬亮. "Xuan lu bianyi" 宣爐辯疑. *Wenwu* 文物 7 (2008): 64–76.

Lu Qingbin 盧慶濱 [Andrew Lo]. "Su Shi dui mo wenhua de gongxian" 蘇軾對墨文化的貢獻. *Songdai wenxue yanjiu congkan* 宋代文學研究叢刊 6 (December 2000): 409–22.

———. "Su Shi yu yan wenhua" 蘇軾與硯文化. *Songdai wenxue yanjiu congkan* 宋代文學研究叢刊 8 (2002): 471–93.

———. "Sumen xueshi yanming chutan" 蘇門學士硯銘初探. In *Dierjie Songdai wenxue guoji yantaohui lunwenji* 第二屆宋代文學國際研討會論文集, ed. Mo Lifeng 莫礪鋒, 739–68. Nanjing: Jiangsu jiaoyu chubanshe, 2003.

Lu Yunlong 陸雲龍. *Huangming shiliu jia xiaopin* 皇明十六家小品. 2 vols. Beijing: Beijing tushuguan chubanshe, 1997.

Luo Zhenyu 羅振玉. *Zhensong tang jijin tu* 貞松堂吉金圖. Dalian: Moyuan tang, 1935.

Lupton, Christina. *Knowing Books: The Consciousness of Mediation in Eighteenth-Century Britain*. Philadelphia: University of Pennsylvania Press, 2012.

Macgregor, Arthur, ed. *Tradescant's Rarities: Essays on the Foundation of the Ashmolean Museum, 1683, with a Catalogue of the Surviving Early Collection*. Oxford: Clarendon Press, 1983.

Mackay, John Kenneth. *Inscription and Modernity: From Wordsworth to Mandelstam*. Bloomington: Indiana University Press, 2006.

Mai Huijun. "The Double Life of the Scallop: Anthropomorphic Biography, 'Pulu,' and the Northern Song Discourse on Things." *Journal of Song-Yuan Studies* 49 (2020): 149–205.

Mao Xiang 冒襄. *Mao Pijiang quanji* 冒辟疆全集. Ed. Wan Jiufu 萬久富 and Ding Fusheng 丁富生. 2 vols. Nanjing: Fenghuang chubanshe, 2014.

Matteini, Michele. "The Aesthetics of Scholarship: Weng Fanggang and the Cult of Su Shi in Late-Eighteenth-Century Beijing." *Archives of Asian Art* 69, no. 1 (2019): 103–20.

——. "The Story of a Stone: Mi Fu's Ink-Grinding Stone and Its Eighteenth-Century Replications." *Arts Asiatiques* 72, no. 1 (2017): 81–96.

Mazanec, Thomas J. "Of Admonition and Address: Right-Hand Inscriptions (*Zuoyouming*) from Cui Yuan to Guanxiu." *Tang Studies* 38, no. 1 (2020): 28–56.

McDermott, Joseph. *A Social History of the Chinese Book: Books and Literati Culture in Late Imperial China*. Hong Kong: Hong Kong University Press, 2006.

——. *The Making of a New Rural Order in South China: I. Village, Land, and Lineage in Huizhou 900–1600*. Cambridge: Cambridge University Press, 2013.

——. *The Making of a New Rural Order in South China II. Merchants, Markets, Lineages*. Cambridge: Cambridge University Press, 2020.

McNair, Amy. "Engraved Calligraphy in China: Recension and Reception." *Art Bulletin* 77, no. 1 (March 1995): 106–14.

Mei Nafang 梅娜芳. *Mo de yishu:* Fangshi mopu he Chengshi moyuan 墨的艺术：《方氏墨谱》和《程氏墨苑》. Haining: Guangxi meishu chubanshe, 2011.

Mei Zengliang 梅曾亮. *Baijian shanfang quanji* 柏梘山房全集. In XXSKQS, jibu, vol. 1513.

Mitchell, W.J.T., and Mark B.N. Hansen, eds. *Critical Terms for Media Studies*. Chicago: University of Chicago Press, 2010.

Moser, Jeffrey. "Learning with Metal and Stone: On the Discursive Formation of Song Epigraphy." In *Powerful Arguments: Standards of Validity in Late Imperial China*, ed. Martin Hofmann, Joachim Kurtz, and Ari Daniel Levine, 135–76. Leiden: Brill, 2020.

Nakatani, Hajime. "Body, Sentiment, and Voice in Ming Self-Encomia (*Zizan*)." *Chinese Literature: Essays, Articles, Reviews (CLEAR)* 32 (December 2010): 73–94.

Nelson Robert S. and Margaret Olin. "Introduction." In *Monuments and Memory, Made and Unmade*, ed. Robert S. Nelson and Margaret Olin, 1–10. Chicago: University of Chicago Press, 2003.

Ng, Pak-sheung. "A Regional Cultural Tradition in Song China: 'The Four Treasures of the Study of the Southern Tang' ('Nan Tang wenfang sibao')." *Journal of Song-Yuan Studies* 46 (2016): 57–117.

Oertling II, Sewall. "Ting Yun-P'eng: A Chinese Artist of the Late Ming Dynasty." PhD diss., University of Michigan, 1980.

BIBLIOGRAPHY

Ou Zhongrong 欧忠荣. *Sanlao yanshi kao* 三老砚事考. Beijing: Wenhua yishu chubanshe, 2014.
Ouyang Xiu 歐陽修. *Ouyang Xiu shiwen ji jiaojian* 歐陽修詩文集校箋. Ed. Hong Benjian 洪本健. Shanghai: Shanghai guji chubanshe, 2009.
Owen, Stephen. *Readings in Chinese Literary Thought*. Cambridge, MA: Harvard University Press, 1992.
———. *The Late Tang: Chinese Poetry of the Mid-Ninth Century (827-860)*. Cambridge, MA: Harvard Asia Center, 2006.
———. *The Making of Early Chinese Classical Poetry*. Cambridge, MA: Harvard Asia Center, 2006.
———. *The Poetry of Meng Chiao and Han Yü*. New Haven, CT: Yale University Press, 1975.
Pan Dexi 潘德熙. *Wenfang sibao* 文房四寶. Shanghai: Shanghai guji chubanshe, 1991.
Pelliot, Paul. "La Peinture et La Gravure Européennes en Chine au Temps de Mathieu Ricci." *T'oung Pao* 20, no. 1 (1920): 1-18.
Peng Fei 彭飛. "Su Xuan de shengping, jiaoyou yu zhuanke wuti" 蘇宣的生平，交遊與篆刻五題. *Zhongguo shufa* 中國書法, no. 2 (2017): 126-30.
Petrucci, Armando. *Public Lettering: Script, Power, and Culture*. Chicago: University of Chicago Press, 1993.
Pines, Yuri. "Confucian Irony? King Wu's Enthronement Reconsidered." In *At Home in Many Worlds Reading, Writing and Translating from Chinese and Jewish Cultures: Essays in Honour of Irene Eber*, ed. Raoul D. Findeisen et al., 55-68. Wiesbaden: Harrassowtiz, 2009.
Platt, Verity. "Making an Impression: Replication and the Ontology of the Graeco-Roman Seal Stone." *Art History* 29, no. 2 (2006): 233-257.
Pregadio, Fabrizio. *Great Clarity: Daoism and Alchemy in Early Medieval China*. Stanford, CA: Stanford University Press, 2006.
Qi Biaojia 祁彪佳. *Qi Biaojia shici biannian jianjiao* 祁彪佳詩詞編年箋校. Ed. Zhao Suwen 趙素文. Hangzhou: Zhejiang guji chubanshe, 2016.
Qi Jiguang 戚繼光. *Zhizhi tang ji* 止止堂集. Beijing: Zhonghua shuju, 2001.
Qu Dajun 屈大均. *Qu Dajun quanji* 屈大均全集. Ed. Wang Guichen 王貴忱, 8 vols. Beijing: Renmin wenxue chubanshe, 1996.
———. *Qu Dajun shici biannian jiaojian* 屈大均詩詞編年校箋. Ed. Chen Yongzheng 陳永正, 5 vols. Shanghai: Shanghai guji chubanshe, 2017.
Rong Dawei 榮大為, ed. *Shoudu bowuguan guancang mingyan* 首都博物館館藏名硯. Beijing: Gongyi meishu chubanshe, 1997.
Ruan Yuan 阮元, ed. *Shisanjing zhushu* 十三經注疏. Beijing: Zhonghua shuju, 1980.
———. *Yanjing shi ji* 揅經室集. Ed. Deng Jingyuan 鄧經元. Beijing: Zhonghua shuju, 1993.
Rusk, Bruce. "Artifacts of Authentication: People Making Texts Making Things in Late Imperial China." In *Antiquarianism and Intellectual Life in Europe and China, 1500-1800*, ed. François Louis and Peter Miller, 180-204. Ann Arbor: University of Michigan Press, 2012.
———. *Critics and Commentators: The Book of Poems as Classic and Literature*. Cambridge, MA: Harvard University Press, 2012.
———. "The Rogue Classicist: Feng Fang (1493-1566) and His Forgeries." PhD diss., University of California, Los Angeles, 2004.

Russell, Gillian. *The Ephemeral Eighteenth Century: Print, Sociability, and the Cultures of Collecting*. Cambridge: Cambridge University Press, 2020.

Sang Xingzhi桑行之, ed. *Shuo mo* 說墨. Shanghai: Shanghai keji jiaoyu chubanshe, 1994.

Schäfer, Dagmar. "Inscribing the Artifact and Inspiring Trust: The Changing Role of Markings in the Ming Era." *East Asian Science, Technology and Society: An International Journal* 5 (2011): 239–65.

———. "Peripheral Matters: Selvage/Chef-de-piece Inscriptions on Chinese Silk Textiles." *UC Davis Law Review* 47, no. 2 (2013): 705–33.

———. *The Crafting of the 10,000 Things: Knowledge and Technology in Seventeenth-Century China*. Chicago: University of Chicago Press, 2011.

Sena, Yunchiahn C. *Bronze and Stone: The Cult of Antiquity in Song Dynasty China*. Seattle: University of Washington Press, 2019.

Sennett, Richard. *The Craftsman*. New Haven, CT: Yale University Press, 2008.

Shang Wei 商伟. *Tixie mingsheng: Cong Huanghe lou dao Fenghuang tai* 题写名胜：从黄鹤楼到凤凰台. Beijing: Xinhua shudian, 2020.

———. "Truth Becomes Fiction When Fiction Is True: *The Story of the Stone* and the Visual Culture of the Manchu Court." *Journal of Chinese Literature and Culture* 2, no. 1 (April 2015): 207–48.

Shao Xiping 邵喜平. "Shu Shi zhuan kao" 蜀師磚考. *Yinxue yanjiu* 印學研究 12 (2018): 102–6.

Shaughnessy, Edward L. *Sources of Western Zhou History: Inscribed Bronze Vessels*. Berkeley: University of California Press, 1991.

She Deyu 佘德余. *Dushi wenren: Zhang Dai zhuan* 都市文人：張岱传. Hangzhou: Zhejiang renmin chubanshe, 2021.

Shen Congwen 沈从文. *Shen Congwen shuo wenwu: Qiwu pian* 沈从文说文物：器物篇. Chongqing: Chongqing daxue chubanshe, 2014.

Shen Defu 沈德符. *Wanli yehuo bian* 萬曆野獲編. 3 vols. Beijing: Zhonghua shuju, 1997.

Sheng Shilan 盛诗澜. "He Zhen baiwen yin de xingshi tezheng—cong Wuxi bowuyuan cang He Zhen yin shuo qi" 何震白文印的形式特征—从无锡博物院藏何震印说起. *Zhongguo shufa* 2 (2017): 118–25.

Shi, Jie. "'My Tomb Will Be Opened in Eight Hundred Years': A New Way of Seeing the Afterlife in Six Dynasties China." *Harvard Journal of Asiatic Studies* 72, no. 2 (2012): 217–57.

———. "Ornament, Text, and the Creation of *Sishen* Mirrors in Late Western Han and Xin China (ca. 50 BCE–23 CE)." *Monumenta Serica* 68, no. 1 (2020): 29–68.

Shi Ye 施曄. "Cong xinjian Ming ceye kan Jia Wan nianjian Huizhou shishang jiaoyou" 从新见明册页看嘉万年间徽州士商交游. *Jianghuai luntan* 江淮论坛 4 (2013): 138–47.

Shields, Anna. *One Who Knows Me: Friendship and Literary Culture in Mid-Tang China*. Cambridge, MA: Harvard University Asia Center, 2015.

Shum Chun. "The Chinese Rare Books: An Overview," trans. Sarah M. Allen. In *Treasures of the Yenching: Seventy-Fifth Anniversary of the Harvard-Yenching Library Exhibition Catalogue*, ed. Patrick Hanan. Cambridge, MA: Harvard University Press, 2003.

Siegert, Bernhard. *Cultural Techniques: Grids, Filters, Doors, and Other Articulations of the Real*. Trans. Geoffrey Winthrop-Young. New York: Fordham University Press, 2015.

BIBLIOGRAPHY

Sima Qian 司馬遷. *Shiji* 史記. Annot. Pei Yin 裴駰, Sima Zhen 司馬貞, and Zhang Shoujie 張守節. 10 vols. Beijing: Zhonghua shuju, 1975.
Smith, Barbara Herrnstein. *Poetic Closure: A Study of How Poems End*. Chicago: University of Chicago Press, 1968.
Son, Suyoung. *Writing for Print: Publishing and the Making of Textual Authority in Late Imperial China*. Cambridge, MA: Harvard University Asia Center, 2018.
Song Luo 宋犖. *Mantang mopin* 漫堂墨品. Facsimile reprint of 1695 edition in SKQSC-MCS, zibu, vol. 79.
Spence, Jonathan D. *Return to Dragon Mountain: Memories of a Late Ming Man*. London: Penguin, 2007.
Struve, Lynn A. "Introduction." In *Time, Temporality, and Imperial Transition: East Asia from Ming to Qing*, ed. Lynn A. Struve, 3–30. Honolulu: Association for Asian Studies and University of Hawai'i Press, 2005.
———. *The Dreaming Mind and the End of the Ming World*. Honolulu: University of Hawai'i Press, 2019.
———. *The Southern Ming 1644–1662*. New Haven, CT: Yale University Press, 1984.
Stuer, Catherine. "To Have Temperature: Material and Metamorphosis in Nineteenth-Century China." In *The Allure of Matter: Materiality Across Chinese Art*, ed. Orianna Cacchione and Wei-Cheng Lin, 114–45. Chicago: Smart Museum of Art, 2021.
Su Shi 蘇軾. *Dongpo tiba jiaozhu* 东坡题跋校注. Ed. Tu Youxiang 屠友祥. Shanghai: Shanghai yuandong chubanshe, 2011.
———. *Su Shi quanji jiao zhu* 蘇軾全集校注. Ed. Zhang Zhilie 張志烈, Ma Defu 馬德富, and Zhou Yukai 周裕鍇, 20 vols. Shijiazhuang: Hebei renmin chubanshe, 2010.
Sun Xidan 孫希旦, ed. *Liji jijie* 禮記集解. Beijing: Zhonghua shuju, 1989.
Svenbro, Jesper. *Phrasikleia: An Anthropology of Reading in Ancient Greece*. Ithaca, NY: Cornell University Press, 1993.
Tang Yunyun 唐芸芸. *Weng Fanggang shixue yanjiu* 翁方纲诗学研究. Beijing: Zhonghua shuju, 2018.
Tang Yuxing 湯宇星. *Yanshan zhi shi: Wang Shizhen yu Suzhou wentan de yishu jiaoyou* 弇山之石：王世貞與蘇州文壇的藝術交遊. Hangzhou: Zhongguo meishu xueyuan chubanshe, 2015.
Tao Qian 陶潛. *Tao Yuanming ji jiaojian (xiudingben)* 陶淵明集校箋（修訂本）. Ed. Gong Bin 龔斌. Shanghai: Shanghai guji chubanshe, 2011.
Tao Xiang 陶湘, ed. *Sheyuan mocui* 涉園墨萃. Beijing: Wujin taoshi, 1929.
Teskey, Gordon. *Delirious Milton: The Fate of the Poet in Modernity*. Cambridge, MA: Harvard University Press, 2006.
Tian, Xiaofei. "Cultural Politics of Old Things in Mid-Tang China." *Journal of American Oriental Studies* 140, no. 2 (2020): 317–43.
———. *Tao Yuanming and Manuscript Culture: The Record of a Dusty Table*. Seattle: University of Washington Press, 2005.
Tianjin bowuguan 天津博物館, ed. *Tianjin bowuguan cang yan* 天津博物館藏硯. Beijing: Wenwu chubanshe, 2012.
Tianjin shi yishu bowuguan 天津市藝術博物館, ed. *Tianjin shi yishu bowuguan cang yan* 天津市藝術博物館藏硯. Beijing: Wenwu chubanshe, 1979.
Tong Yanfang 童衍方. *Jinshi qishou: jinshijia shuhua mingke tezhan tulu* 金石齊壽：金石家書畫銘刻特展圖錄. Shanghai: Shanghai sanlian shudian chubanshe, 2016.

Tsien, Tsuen-Hsuin. *Collected Writings on Chinese Culture.* Hong Kong: Chinese University Press, 2011.

———. *Science and Civilization in China*, vol. 5, *Chemistry and Chemical Technology*, bk 1: *Paper and Printing*, 233–53. Cambridge: Cambridge University Press, 1985.

———. *Written on Bamboo and Silk: The Beginnings of Chinese Books and Inscriptions.* Chicago: University of Chicago Press, 2004.

Tu Long 屠隆. *Kaopan yushi* 考槃餘事. Facsimile reprint of Wanli edition in SKQSCMCS, zibu, vol. 118.

Varsano, Paula. "Disappearing Objects/Elusive Subjects: Writing Mirrors in Early and Medieval China." *Representations* 124, no. 1 (2013): 96–124.

Vedal, Nathan. *The Culture of Language in Ming China: Sound, Script, and the Redefinition of Knowledge.* New York: Columbia University Press, 2022.

Volpp, Sophie. *The Substance of Fiction: Literary Objects in China, 1550–1775.* New York: Columbia University Press, 2022.

Von Falkenhausen, Lothar. *Suspended Music: Chime Bells in the Culture of Bronze Age China.* Berkeley: University of California Press, 1993.

Waley, Arthur. *More Translations from the Chinese.* New York: Knopf, 1919.

———. *The Book of Songs: The Ancient Chinese Classic of Poetry.* Ed. Joseph R. Allen. New York: Grove Press, 1996.

Wan Muchun 萬木春. *Weishui xuan li de xianju zhe: Wanli monian Jiaxing de shuhua shijie* 味水軒里的閑居者：萬曆末年嘉興的書畫世界. Hangzhou: Zhongguo meishu xueyuan chubanshe, 2008.

Wang Chaohong 汪超宏. *Ming Qing qujia kao* 明清曲家考. Beijing: Zhongguo shehui kexue chubanshe, 2006.

Wang Daiwen 王代文 and Cai Hongru 蔡鴻茹, eds. *Zhonghua guyan* 中華古硯. Nanjing: Jiangsu guji chubanshe, 1999.

Wang Daokun 汪道昆. *Fu mo* 副墨. Facsimile reprint of 1574 edition in SKQSCMCS, jibu, vol. 119.

———. *Taihan ji* 太函集. Facsimile reprint of Wanli edition in SKQSCMCS, jibu, vols. 117–18.

———. *Taihan ji.* Ed. Hu Yimin 胡益民 and Yu Guoqing 余國慶, 4 vols. Hefei: Huangshan shushe, 2004.

Wang Fuzhi 王夫之. *Wang Chuanshan shiwen ji* 王船山詩文集. 2 vols. Beijing: Zhonghua shuju, 2018.

Wang Gang 王鋼. *Xu Wei* 徐渭. Taibei: Zhishufang chubanshe, 1993.

Wang Hung-tai 王鴻泰. "Wodao yu xiashi—Mingdai woluan chongji xia Jiangnan shiren de wuxia fengshang" 倭刀與俠士－明代倭亂衝擊下江南士人的武俠風尚. *Hanxue yanjiu* 漢學研究 30, no. 3 (2012): 63–97.

———. "Ya su de bianzheng—Mingdai shangwan wenhua de liuxing yu shishang guanxi de jiaocuo" 雅俗的辯證－明代賞玩文化的流行與士商關係的交錯. *Xinshi xue* 新史學 17, no. 4 (2006): 73–143.

Wang Liyan 王儷閻, and Su Qiang 蘇強. *Ming Qing Huimo yanjiu* 明清徽墨研究. Shanghai: Shanghai guji chubanshe, 2007.

Wang Qishu 汪啟淑, ed. *Feihong tang yanpu mopu pingpu dinglu pu: liu juan* 飛鴻堂硯譜墨譜瓶譜鼎鑪譜：六卷. Beijing: Guojia tushuguan chubanshe, 2013.

Wang, Richard G. "Qiyunshan as a Replica of Wudangshan." *Journal of Chinese Religions* 42, no. 1 (2014): 28–66.

Wang Shiqing 汪世清. "Huizhou xue yanjiu de zhongda gongxian: *Mingdai Huizhou Fangshi qinyou shouzha qibai tong kaoshi* du houji" 徽州学研究的重大贡献《明代徽州方氏亲友手札七百通考释》读后记. *Hefei xueyuan xuebao* 合肥学院学报 21, no. 1 (2004): 12–20.

Wang Shizhen 王世貞. *Gu bu gu lu* 觚不觚錄. In CSJCCB, vol. 2811.

———. *Yanzhou shanren tiba* 弇州山人題跋. Ed. Tang Zhibo 湯志波. Zhejiang: Renmin meishu chubanshe, 2012.

Wang Yan 王岩, ed. *Changcheng yiwen lu* 長城藝文錄. Beijing: Beijing chubanshe, 2018.

Wang Yi 王毅. "'Wenren zizhi mo' chengwei de juxiangxing jiqi duice" 文人自制墨稱謂的局限性及其對策. *Huizhou Shehui kexue* 徽州社會科學 8 (2012).

Wang Yi and Cai Xinquan, eds. *Zhongguo mo wenhua wenxue* 中國墨文化問學. Shanghai: Shanghai yuandong chubanshe, 2014.

Wang Yifeng 王屹峰. *Guzhuan huagong: Liu Zhou yu 19 shiji de xueshu he yishu* 古磚花供：六舟與19世紀的學術和藝術. Hangzhou: Zhejiang renmin meishu chubanshe, 2018.

Wang Zhenghua [Wang Cheng-hua]. "Material Culture and Emperorship: The Shaping of Imperial Roles at the Court of Xuanzong (r. 1426–35)." PhD diss., Yale University, 1998.

Wang Zhenzhong 王振忠. *Cong Huizhou dao Jiangnan: Ming Qing Huishang yu quyu shehui yanjiu* 从徽州到江南：明清徽商与区域社会研究. Shanghai: Shanghai renmin chubanshe, 2018.

Watt, James C. Y. "The Literati Environment." In *The Chinese Scholar's Studio: Artistic Life in the Late Ming Period*, ed. Chu-tsing Li and James C. Y. Watt. New York: Asia Society Galleries, 1987.

Weitz, Ankeney, trans. *Zhou Mi's Record of Clouds and Mist Passing Before One's Eyes: An Annotated Translation*. Leiden: Brill, 2002.

Wen Zhengming 文徵明. *Wen Zhengming ji (zengdingben)* 文徵明集（增訂本）. Ed. Zhou Daozhen 周道振. Shanghai: Shanghai guji chubanshe, 2019.

Weng Fanggang 翁方綱. *Fuchu zhai shiji* 復初齋詩集. Reprint in XXSKQS, jibu, vols. 1454–55.

———. *Fuchu zhai wenji* 復初齋文集. Reprint in XXSKQS, jibu, vol. 1455.

———. *Weng Fanggang tiba shouzha jilu* 翁方綱題跋手札集錄. Ed. Shen Jin 沈津. Guilin: Guangxi shifan daxue chubanshe, 2002.

Wengrow, David. "Introduction: Commodity Branding in Archaeological and Anthropological Perspectives." In *Cultures of Commodity Branding*, ed. Andrew Bevan and David Wengrow. London: Routledge, 2010.

———. "Prehistories of Commodity Branding." *Current Anthropology* 49 (2008): 7–34.

Wilkinson, John. *Lyric in Its Times: Temporalities in Verse, Breath and Stone*. London: Bloomsbury Academic, 2015.

Wu Changshou 吳昌綬, ed. *Shiliu jia moshuo* 十六家墨說. Hang xian: Renhe Wushi shuangzhao lou, 1922.

Wu Chengxue 吳承学 and Zhao Hongxiang 赵宏祥. "Wang Chuanshan guansheng ju tibi lian kaoshi" 王船山观生居题壁联考释. *Xueshu yanjiu* 学术研究 no. 4 (2014): 144–51.

Wu Hung. "From Temple to Tomb: Ancient Chinese Art and Religion in Transition." *Early China* 13 (1988): 78–115.

———. *Monumentality in Early Chinese Art and Architecture*. Stanford, CA: Stanford University Press, 1995.

———. "On Rubbings: Their Materiality and Historicity." In *Writing and Materiality in China: Essays in Honor of Patrick Hanan*, ed. Judith T. Zeitlin and Lydia H. Liu, 29–72. Cambridge, MA: Harvard University Asia Center, 2003.

———. "Practice and Discourse: Ritual Vessels in a Fourth-Century BCE Chinese Tomb." In *Vessels: The Object as Container*, ed. Claudia Brittenham, 120–72. Oxford: Oxford University Press, 2019.

———, ed. *Reinventing the Past: Archaism and Antiquarianism in Chinese Art and Visual Culture*. Chicago: Center for the Art of East Asia, University of Chicago, 2010.

Wu Ligu 吳笠谷. *Mingyan bian* 名硯辨. Beijing: Wenwu chubanshe, 2012.

———. *Yanyan kao* 贋硯考. Beijing: Wenwu chubanshe, 2010.

Wu Na 吳訥. *Wenzhang bianti* 文章辨體. Facsimile reprint of 1464 edition in SKQSCMCS, jibu, vol. 291.

Wu Qingshi 鄔庆时. *Qu Dajun nianpu* 屈大均年谱. Guangzhou: Guangdong renmin chubanshe, 2006.

Wu Qizhen 吳其貞. *Shuhua ji* 書畫記. Shanghai: Renmin meishu chubanshe, 1963.

Wu Renshu 巫仁恕 [Wu Jen-shu]. "From Viewing to Reading: The Evolution of Visual Advertising in Late Imperial China." In *Visualising China, 1845–1965: Moving and Still Images in Historical Narratives*, ed. Christian Henriot and Wen-Hsin Yeh, 231–66. Leiden: Brill, 2013.

———. *Pinwei shehua: Wan Ming de xiaofei shehui yu shidafu* 品味奢華：晚明的消費社會與士大夫. Taibei: Zhongyang yanjiu yuan, Lianjing chubanshe, 2007.

Wu Weiye 吳偉業. *Wu Meicun quanji* 吳梅村全集. Ed. Li Xueying 李學穎. Shanghai: Shanghai guji chubanshe, 1990.

Wu Xiang 無相. "Lun Wen Peng zai zhuanke shi shang de diwei he gongxian" 論文彭在篆刻史上的地位和貢獻. *Shufa yanjiu* 書法研究 122 (2005): 78–96.

Wu Yulian. *Luxurious Networks: Salt Merchants, Status, and Statecraft in Eighteenth-Century China*. Stanford, CA: Stanford University Press, 2017.

Wu Zhengfeng 吳鎮烽. "'Yuding bi' xinshi" 《魚鼎匕》新釋. *Kaogu yu wenwu* 考古與文物 2 (2015): 54–57.

Xie Zhaozhi 谢肇制. *Wu za zu* 五杂组. Ed. Fu Cheng 傅成. Shanghai: Shanghai guji chubanshe, 2012.

Xiling yinshe 西泠印社, ed. *Ming Qing Huizhou zhuanke xueshu yantaohui lunwenji* 明清徽州篆刻學術研討會論文集. Hangzhou: Xiling yinshe chubanshe, 2008.

Xing Tong 邢侗. *Xing Tong ji* 邢侗集. Ed. Gong Xiaowei 宮曉衛 and Xiu Guangli 修廣利. Jinan: Qi Lu shushe, 2017.

Xu Chengyao 許承堯. *Sheshi xiantan* 歙事閑譚. Ed. Li Minghui 李明回. Hefei: Huangshan shushe, 2001.

Xu Guo 許國. *Xu Wenmu gongji* 許文穆公集. Facsimile reprint of Wanli edition in SKJHSCK, jibu, vol. 40.

———. *Xu Wenmu gong quanji* 許文穆公全集. Taiwan National Central Library: 1625 edition.

Xu Min 許敏. "Shixi Mingdai houqi Jiangnan shanggu jiqi zidi de wenrenhua xianxiang—cong Fang Yongbin tanqi" 試析明代後期江南商賈及其子弟的文人化現象－從方用彬談起. *Zhongguo shi yanjiu* 中國史研究 3 (2005): 157–72.

Xu Shizeng 徐師曾. *Wenti mingbian* 文體明辨. Facsimile reprint of Wanli edition in SKQSCMCS, jibu, vols. 310–12.

Xu Shuofang 徐朔方, ed. *Tang Xianzu shiwen ji* 湯顯祖詩文集. Shanghai: Shanghai guji chubanshe, 1982.

———. *Wan Ming qujia nianpu* 晚明曲家年譜. 3 vols. Hangzhou: Zhejiang guji chubanshe, 1993.
Xu Wei 徐渭. *Xu Wei ji* 徐渭集. 4 vols. Beijing: Zhonghua shuju, 2017.
Xue Longchun 薛龙春. *Guhuan: Huang Yi yu Qian-Jia jinshi shishang*. 古欢：黄易与乾嘉金石时尚. Beijing: Sanlian shudian, 2019.
———. "Ming zhong hou qi Wumen wenren zhuanke kaolun" 明中后期吴门文人篆刻考论. *Wenyi yanjiu* 文艺研究 9 (2017): 130–38.
Yan Kejun 嚴可均, comp. *Quan Hou Han wen* 全後漢文. In *Quan shanggu sandai Qin Han sanguo liuchao wen* 全上古三代秦漢三國六朝文. Beijing: Zhonghua shuju, 1958; repr. 1999.
Yan Zhixiong 嚴志雄. "Tiwu, jiyi, yu yimin qingjing: Qu Dajun yiliu wujiu nian yongmei shi tanjiu" 體物，記憶與遺民情境—屈大均一六五九年詠梅詩探究. *Zhongguo wenzhe yanjiu jikan* 中國文哲研究集刊 21 (2002): 43–87.
Yang Liang 杨亮. "Su Xuan yu guwen yinfeng de xingshuai" 苏宣与古文印风的兴衰. *Nanjing yishu xueyuan xuebao (Meishu yu sheji ban)* 南京艺术学院学报（美术与设计版）, no. 3 (2015): 22–25.
Yang, Suh-jen. "The Literary Merits of the Han (206 B.C.–A.D. 220) Stele Inscription." PhD diss., University of Washington, 2007.
Yang Wanli 楊萬里, ed. *Mingdai biji xiaoshuo daguan* 明代筆記小說大觀. Shanghai: Shanghai guji chubanshe, 2005.
Yang Weizhen 楊維楨. *Yang Weizhen shiji* 楊維楨詩集. Ed. Zou Zhifang 鄒志方. Hangzhou: Zhejiang guji chubanshe, 2010.
Yang Xiong. *Exemplary Figures/Fayan*. Trans. Michael Nylan. Seattle: University of Washington Press, 2013.
Yao Bing 姚炳. *Shishi mingjie* 詩識名解. In WYGSKQS, jingbu, vol. 80.
Yao Lü 姚旅. *Lushu* 露書. Facsimile reprint of Tianqi edition in SKQSCMCS, zibu, vol. 111.
Yao Zhiyin 姚之駰. *Yuan Ming shilei chao* 元明事類鈔. In WYGSKQS, zibu, vol. 884.
Ye Gongchuo 葉恭綽, Zhang Jiongbo 張絅伯, Zhang Zigao 張子高, and Yin Runsheng 尹潤生, eds. *Sijia cangmo tulu* 四家藏墨圖錄. Shanghai: Shanghai shudian chubanshe, 2006.
Ye Guoliang 葉國良. *Songdai jinshixue yanjiu* 宋代金石學研究. Taipei: Taiwan shufang, 2011.
Yi, Hye-shim. "From Epigraphy to Inscribing Objects: Recarving Ancient Relics into Inkstones." *Orientations* 51, no. 6 (November/December 2020): 64–71.
———. "The Calligraphic Art of Chen Hongshou (1768–1822) and the Practice of Inscribing in the Middle Qing." PhD diss., University of California Los Angeles, 2019.
Yin Runsheng 尹潤生. *Molin shihua* 墨林史話. Beijing: Zijincheng chubanshe, 1986.
———. *Yin Runsheng moyuan jiancang lu* 尹润生墨苑鉴藏录. Beijing: Zijincheng chubanshe, 2008.
Ying Zhang. *Confucian Image Politics: Masculine Morality in Seventeenth-Century China*. Seattle: University of Washington Press, 2016.
Yip Cheuk-wai 葉倬瑋. "Jianchu tongchi de kaoding yu shiqing: Qian-Jia kaoding jia de wuyuan yu shiqing" 建初銅尺的考訂與詩情：乾嘉考訂家的物緣與詩情. *Zhongguo wenhua* 中國文化 52 (2020): 340–349.
———. "Lun Yuan Mei ji xingling pai de kaodingshi chuangzuo—jiantan kaodingshi dui bixing chuantong de fanbo" 論袁枚及性靈派的考訂詩創作—兼談考訂詩對比興傳統的反撥. *Taibei daxue zhongwen xuebao* 臺北大學中文學報 30 (2021): 635–88.

———. *Weng Fanggang shixue yanjiu* 翁方纲诗学研究. Beijing: Zhongguo shehui kexue chubanshe, 2013.

———. "Wenwu zhi guangxia de huayu jiangou yu buxiu zhuiqiu—lun Weng Fanggang de jinshi shi" 文物之光下的話語建構與不朽追求—論翁方綱的金石詩. *Zhengda zhongwen xuebao* 政大中文學報 28 (2017): 103–39.

———. "Yijian Nanming lieshi yiwu de liuzhuan" 一件南明烈士遺物的流轉. *Zhongguo wenhua* 中國文化 49 (2019): 152–65.

———. "Yi shi wei wu: lun Qian-Jia yinxue yu yinge" 以詩為物：論乾嘉印學與印歌. *Malaixiya hanxue kan* 馬來西亞漢學刊 4 (2020): 51–76.

Yu, Anthony C. "*Cratylus* and the *Xunzi* on Names." In *Comparative Journeys: Essays on Literature and Religion East and West*, ed. Anthony Yu. New York: Columbia University Press, 2009.

Yu Guangrong 庾光蓉. "Li You shiji kaozheng" 李尤事迹考证. *Sichuan shifan daxue xuebao* 四川师范大学学报 24, no. 3 (1997): 124–27.

Yu Yingshi 余英時. *Zhongguo jinshi zongjiao lunli yu shangren jingshen* 中國近時宗教倫理與商人精神. Taibei: Lianjing chuban shiye gongsi, 1987.

Zang Huayun 臧华云. "Mantan Gao Fenghan *Yanshi*" 漫谈高凤翰砚史. *Wenwu* 9 (1962): 48–53.

Zang Kehe 臧克和. "'Yuding bi' mingwen youguan qiming xingzhi xinshi" 《魚鼎匕》銘文有關器名性質新釋. *Kaogu yu wenwu* 考古與文物 5 (2004): 93–94.

Zeitlin, Judith T. "Disappearing Verses: Writing on Walls and the Anxiety of Loss." In *Writing and Materiality in China: Essays in Honor of Patrick Hanan*, ed. Judith T. Zeitlin and Lydia H. Liu, 73–132. Cambridge, MA: Harvard University Press, 2003.

———. "The Cultural Biography of a Musical Instrument: Little Hulei as Sounding Object, Antique, Prop, and Relic." *Harvard Journal of Asiatic Studies* 69 (2009): 395–441.

Zhai Tunjian 翟屯建. *Huipai zhuanke* 徽派篆刻. Hefei: Anhui renmin chubanshe, 2005.

Zhan Jingfeng 詹景鳳. *Mingbian leihan* 明辨類函. Gest Library, Princeton University, 1632 edition.

———. *Zhanshi xingli xiaobian* 詹氏性理小辨. Facsimile reprint of Wanli edition in SKQSCMCS, zibu, vol. 112.

———. *Zhanshi xuanlan bian* 詹氏玄覽編. Taibei: Guoli zhongyang tushuguan chubanshe, 1970.

Zhan Yinxin 詹鄞鑫. "'Yuding bi' kaoshi" 《魚鼎匕》考釋. *Zhongguo wenzi yanjiu* 中國文字研究 (2001): 175–79.

Zhan, Zhenpeng. "Artisanal Luxury and Confucian Statecraft: The Afterlife of Ming Official Carved Lacquer at the Qianlong Court." *Late Imperial China* 42, no. 1 (June 2021): 45–91.

Zhang Changhong 张长虹. *Pinjian yu jingying: Mingmo Qingchu Huishang yishu zanzhu yanjiu* 品鉴与经营：明末清初徽商艺术赞助研究. Beijing: Beijing daxue chubanshe, 2010.

Zhang Cizhong 張次仲. *Daixuan shiji* 待軒詩記. In WYGSKQS, jingbu, vol. 82.

Zhang Dai 張岱. *Gujin yilie zhuan* 古今義烈傳. Ed. Ding Hong 丁紅. Hangzhou: Zhejiang guji chubanshe, 2018.

———. *He Tao ji; Tao'an duiou gushi* 和陶集；陶菴對偶故事. Ed. Lu Wei 路偉 and Zheng Lingfeng 鄭凌峰. Hangzhou: Zhejiang guji chubanshe, 2019.

———. *Kuaiyuan daogu; Guanlang qiqiao lu* 快園道古；琯朗乞巧錄. Ed. Lu Wei and Zheng Lingfeng. Hangzhou: Zhejiang guji chubanshe, 2019.

———. *Langhuan wenji* 瑯嬛文集. Ed. Luan Baoqun 欒保群. Beijing: Gugong chubanshe, 2012.

———. *Sanbuxiu tuzan* 三不朽圖贊. Ed. Gong Huxia 公戶夏. Hangzhou: Zhejiang guji chubanshe, 2017.

———. *Shen Fucan chaoben Langhuan wenji* 沈復燦鈔本瑯嬛文集. Ed. Lu Wei and Ma Tao 馬濤. Hangzhou: Zhejiang guji chubanshe, 2015.

———. *Tao'an mengyi; Xihu mengxun* 陶菴夢憶；西湖夢尋. Ed. Lu Wei and Zheng Lingfeng. Hangzhou: Zhejiang guji chubanshe, 2018.

———. *Yehang chuan* 夜航船. Ed. Zheng Lingfeng. Hangzhou: Zhejiang guji chubanshe, 2020.

———. *Zhang Dai shiwen ji* 張岱詩文集. Ed. Xia Xianchun 夏咸淳. Shanghai: Shanghai guji chubanshe, 2014.

Zhang Fangtong 章放童. *Sheyan wengu* 歙硯溫故. Beijing: Renmin meishu chubanshe, 2007.

Zhang Haixin 張海新. *Shuiping shanniao: Zhang Dai jiqi shiwen yanjiu* 水萍山鳥：張岱及其詩文研究. Shanghai: Zhongxi shuju, 2012.

Zhang Hui 張暉. *Diguo de liuwang: Nan Ming shige yu zhanluan* 帝国的流亡：南明詩歌与战乱. Beijing: Zhongguo shehui kexue chubanshe, 2014.

Zhang Jian 張健. *Huizhou hongru Wang Daokun yanjiu* 徽州鴻儒汪道昆研究. Wuhu shi: Anhui shifan daxue chubanshe, 2014.

Zhang Tingyu 張廷玉 et al. *Ming shi* 明史. Beijing: Zhonghua shuju, 1974.

Zhang Ying. *Confucian Image Politics: Masculine Morality in Seventeenth-Century China*. Seattle: University of Washington Press, 2017.

Zhang Yingjie 張應杰. *Tangdai mingwen gailun* 唐代銘文概論. Beijing: Zhongguo shuji chubanshe, 2012.

Zhang Yiqun 张艺群. "Laizi Jingcheng de kaogu baogao: 'Yanshan legong ming bei ke' kao" 來自京城的考古報告：《燕山勒功銘碑刻》考. *Minjian wenhua (renwen lüyou zazhi)* 民间文化（人文旅游杂志） 10 (2009): 131.

Zhang Yuanbian 張元忭. *Zhang Yuanbian ji* 張元忭集. Ed. Qian Ming 錢明. Shanghai: Shanghai guji chubanshe, 2015.

Zhang Yuanqing 張元慶. *Gudai shiren yu yan zhi yanjiu* 古代士人與硯之研究. Taibei: Wenjin chubanshe, 2005.

Zhang Zaogong 章藻功. *Siqi tang wenji* 思綺堂文集. Facsimile reprint in QDSWJHB, vol. 198.

Zhang Zongyou 張宗友. *Zhu Yizun nianpu* 朱彝尊年譜. Nanjing: Fenghuang chubanshe, 2014.

Zhao Rong 趙榮 and Lothar Ledderose, eds. *Zhongguo fojiao shijing: Shaanxi sheng* 中國佛教石經：陝西省. Wiesbaden: Harrassowitz Verlag; Hangzhou: China Academy of Art Press, 2020–.

Zhao Yingzhi. "What Remains of Mountains and Waters: Fragments, Mutilation, and Creation in Early Qing Literature and Culture." *Journal of Chinese Literature and Culture* 6, no. 1 (2019): 137–168.

Zheng Yunshan 郑云山. *Jingdong suibi* 京东随笔. Beijing: Yanshan chubanshe, 1991.

Zhong Yufa 钟玉发. "Qingchu duanyan minglun 'Duanshi kao' zhuzhe kao" 清初端硯名论《端石考》著者考. *Zhaoqing xueyuan xuebao* 41, no. 3 (2020): 12–16.

Zhongguo wenfang sibao quanji bianji weiyuanhui 中國文房四寶全集編輯委員會, ed. *Zhongguo wenfang sibao quanji 1: Mo* 中國文房四寶全集1: 墨. Beijing: Beijing chubanshe, 2007.

——. *Zhongguo wenfang sibao quanji 2: Yan* 中國文房四寶全集2: 硯. Beijing: Beijing chubanshe, 2007.

Zhou, Boqun. "A Translation and Analysis of the Shanghai Museum Manuscript *Wu Wang Jian Zuo*." *Monumenta Serica* 66, no. 1 (2018): 1–31.

Zhou Changyuan 周长源. "Ruan Yuan moke 'Xiyue huashan miao bei' he mobu bei zhong quezi de juyan" 阮元摹刻《西岳华山庙碑》和摹補碑中缺字的巨硯. *Wenwu* 文物 8 (1992): 86–89.

Zhou Lianggong 周亮工. *Laigu tang ji* 賴古堂集. Ed. Li Hualei 李花蕾. Shanghai: Huadong shifan daxue chubanshe, 2009.

——. *Zhou Lianggong quanji* 周亮工全集. Ed. Zhu Tianshu 朱天曙, 18 vols. Reprint, Nanjing: Fenghuang chubanshe, 2008.

Zhou Shaoliang 周紹良. *Qingdai mingmo tancong* 清代名墨談叢. Beijing: Wenwu chubanshe, 1982.

——. *Zhou Shaoliang xumo xiaoyan* 周紹良蓄墨小言. Ed. Zhou Qiyu 周启瑜. Beijing: Zijincheng chubanshe, 2009.

Zhou Ying 周颖. *Wang Shizhen nianpu changbian* 王世贞年谱长编. Shanghai: Shanghai sanlian shudian, 2016.

Zhou Yingyuan 周應願. *Yinshuo* 印說. Ed. Zhu Tianshu. Beijing: Beijing daxue chubanshe, 2014.

Zhu Chuanrong 朱傳榮, ed. *Xiaoshan Zhushi cang yan xuan* 蕭山朱氏藏硯選. Beijing: Sanlian chubanshe, 2012.

Zhu Dong 朱棟. *Yan xiaoshi* 硯小史. Shanghai: Shanghai guji shudian, 1979.

Zhu Liangzhi 朱良志. *Wanshi de fengliu* 頑石的風流. Beijing: Zhonghua shuju, 2016.

——. *Yizhi shougu xie kongshan: Jin Nong hua de jinshi qi* 一枝瘦骨写空山：金农画的金石气. Hangzhou: Zhejiang renmin meishu chubanshe, 2020.

Zhu Qi 朱琪. *Penglai songfeng: Huang Yi yu Qian-Jia jinshixue* 蓬莱松风：黄易与乾嘉金石学. Shanghai: Shanghai guji chubanshe, 2020.

——. *Xinchu Mingdai wenren yinzhang jicun yu yanjiu* 新出明代文人印章輯存與研究. Hangzhou: Xiling yinshe chubanshe, 2020.

——. *Zhenshui wuxiang: Jiang Ren yu Qingdai Zhepai zhuanke yanjiu* 真水无香：蒋仁与清代浙派篆刻研究. Hangzhou: Zhejiang renmin meishu chubanshe, 2018.

Zhu Tianshu 朱天曙. *Ganjiu: Zhou Lianggong jiqi* Yinren zhuan *yanjiu* 感舊：周亮工及其《印人傳》研究. Beijing: Beijing daxue chubanshe, 2013.

——. and Meng Han 孟晗. *Zhou Lianggong nianpu changbian* 周亮工年譜長編. Shanghai: Shanghai shuhua chubanshe, 2021.

Zhu Wanshu 朱萬曙. *Huishang yu Ming Qing wenxue* 徽商與明清文學. Beijing: Renmin chubanshe, 2014.

Zhu Yizun 朱彝尊. *Pushu ting ji* 曝書亭集. Facsimile reprint in QDSWJHB, vol. 116.

——. *Pushu ting quanji* 曝書亭全集. Ed. Wang Limin 王利民 et al. Changchun: Jilin wenshi chubanshe, 2009.

Zhu Ze 朱澤. "Shijian zhi jiao—ji Wang Daokun, Qi Jiguang de youyi pianduan" 詩劍之交—記汪道昆，戚繼光的友誼片斷. *Anhui shixue* 安徽史學 5 (1984): 32–38.

Zhuangzi. *Zhuangzi: The Complete Writings*. Trans. Brook Ziporyn. Cambridge: Hackett, 2020.

INDEX

"Add and Subtract" poem (*lihe shi* 離合詩), 158
admonitory inscription, 14–16, 64, 240
alchemy, 139, 165, 228
anachronism, embracing, 195–98
Anhui Provincial Museum, 186, 272n116
"Ant Mill Study" (Yimo zhai 蟻磨齋), 252. *See also* Gao Fenghan
antiquarianism: 17, 26, 31–34; inscription politics, 192–94; introduction to, 188–91; monumental vessels, 214–24; poetry on metal and stone, 224–30; recovery of lost things, 199–205; returning gifts, 205–10; reunion, 210–14; strange antiques, 195–98
Arranged Anecdotes of the Yuan and the Ming (*Yuan Ming shilei chao* 元明事類鈔), 198
artisanal brands, study of, 38, 160
artisans, 5, 8, 22, 26, 33, 42, 55–59, 76–77, 84, 97, 118, 120, 127, 137, 140, 142, 155, 160, 183–89, 235, 240, 245–46
"Autumn Tides and Summer Clouds" (*qiutao xiayun* 秋濤夏雲) (Zhang), 37, 62–63

Bai Juyi 白居易, 20
bamboo, 42, 44, 76, 83, 128, 257
Ban Gu 班固, 12, 82, 88
Barthes, Roland, 164
"Best Crafts in Suzhou, The" ("Wuzhong jueji" 吳中絕技) (*Dream Reminiscences*), 38
Bian He 卞和, 192
"Biographies of Confucius's Disciples" ("Zhongni dizi liezhuan" 仲尼弟子列傳) (Sima), 100
Biographies of Seal Carvers (*Yinren zhuan* 印人傳) (Zhou), 28, 116, 124, 273n123, 291n110, 294n149
"Biography of a Worthy Knight Errant" (*Yixia zhuan* 義俠傳) (Fang Yongbin), 125–26
Bodhidharma, 141–42
Book of Ceremony and Ritual (*Yili* 儀禮), 10
brands, ink makers, 160–71, 186–87
Broken Bronze Water Dipper, 46–47
"Broken Man of the Dingsi Year" (Dingsi canren 丁巳殘人). *See* Gao Fenghan
broken stones, inscribing on: alternate approaches to writing on inkstones,

broken stones (*continued*)
246–57; history of writing, 239–42; introduction, 233–35; post-paralysis inscriptions, 257–59; remnant inkslabs, 235–39; ruin refabrication, 242–46. *See also* Gao Fenghan

bronze vessels, 7, 10–11, 14, 17, 26, 31, 46–47, 51, 66, 68–70, 116, 147–49, 191, 195, 197, 229, 240–41, 266n50, 308n30

Brown, Bill, 256, 262n13

Buddhism, 3, 13, 56, 84, 90, 143–144, 194, 200, 241, 257, 263n22, 298n33

burial-plot purchase contracts (*maidiquan* 買地券), 13

Burst Pattern Antique Zither, inscription on, 52–53

Cai Xinquan, 184

Cai Yong 蔡邕, 11–12

calligraphy: 26, 33, 91–93, 120, 130, 241–45, 148–49; *bafen* 八分, 241; boundaries, 117; carved, 33, 85, 241; clerical-script, 241, 245; engraved, 249, 258; entombed epigraphy and, 97; forgery of, 112; "large character signage script" (*dazi bangshu* 大字榜書), 256; primitivist, 156–57; seal-script, 7, 93, 118, 133

"Calligraphy and Painting Boat" (*shuhua chuan* 書畫船), 213

Cao Pi 曹丕, 13

Cao Sugong 曹素功, 150, 171

Cao Xueqin 曹雪芹, 8

carver, 76–77; biographies of, 82–83, 114; common sayings and, 123; Huizhou carvers, 94, 106, 132, 234, 287n52; as literary protagonist, 106–14; publishing formats and, 120–24; refabricating scraps of material, 127–28; and remnant things (*yiwu* 遺物), 76–77; soft stones and, 114–20. *See also* seal carvers

catalogue, as publishing format, 120–24. *See also* ink books (*moshu* 墨書)

"Celestial Inkstone" ("Tian yan" 天硯) (*Dream Reminiscences*), 38, 55, 71–76, 234–35

censer, inscription on, 67–68

chalice, inscription on, 49, 65–66, 68–71

Chang Hong 萇弘, 244

Chang Yuchun 常遇春, 59

Changrun 常潤, 90

Changshu 常熟, 210

Changshu City Museum of Stelae Carvings, 216

Chen Hongshou 陳洪綬, 44, 60

Chen Hongshou 陳鴻壽, 257

Chen Qianfu 陳潛夫, 194, 202, 204

Chen Que 陳確, 278n55

Cheng Junfang 程君房, 142, 162–63, 165–71, 176–77

Cheng Tang 成湯, 239

Cheng'en Temple 承恩寺, 114

Chengqing guan yinpu 承清館印譜, 122

chi 螭, 221

China: early modern marketplace in, 19–21; literature in, 10–21; writing/materiality in, 21–22; writing tools in, 22–31. *See also* Ming China, landscape of

Chinese literature: admonitory inscription, 14–16; commodity production and, 18–19; epigraphy-literary inscription interplay, 17; materiality and, 149, 174, 191, 224–29; memorial inscriptions, 12–13; objects in early modern marketplace, 19–21; overview of, 10–11; Su Shi inkstones, 16–19. *See also* Ming China, landscape of

chong 沖, 304n120

Chongzhen 崇禎, 2

Chun, Wendy Hui Kyong, 168

circular stone, inscription on, 251–52

Classic of Changes (*Yijing* 易經), 47

Classic of Documents (*Shujing* 書經), 11, 173–74

Classic of Poetry (*Shijing* 詩經), 11–12, 57–58, 158, 173, 196–97

classicist (*ru* 儒), 98

clerical script (*lishu* 隸書), 26–27, 108–9, 127, 207, 216, 226, 229, 241–42, 245, 286n43

Cloudy Grove's Secret Belvedere (Yunlin bige 雲林閟閣), 46

INDEX

Clunas, Craig, 161
coffin lid (*guo* 槨), epitaph on, 156–57
Collected Writings of Langhuan (*Langhuan wenji* 瑯嬛文集) (Zhang), 38, 46, 59, 72
collectors, 7, 23, 26, 65–66, 78, 116, 119, 127, 133, 141, 151, 203, 248–49, 252, 254; devotion of, 68; epigraphic commentary and, 245; ethics of historical transmission and, 214; false inksticks and, 176; Gao Fenghan as, 247; Huizhou merchants as, 96–97; impressions/seals owned by, 113; inksticks and, 26; inscription of, 16–19; inventorying, 51; recording markings, 144; remnant inkslabs and, 238; self-censored *ming* and, 238–39; sense of self of, 53–54; sly inkstick reproduction and, 186
"Colophon for the *Sigong*, A" 跋叺觥 (Weng), 210–11
colophons, 8, 28, 32, 116, 119, 210, 217, 222, 226, 253
Colophons on Collected Records of the Past (*Jigulu bawei* 集古錄跋尾) (Ouyang), 17
Colophons to Bronze and Stone Artifacts from the Pushu Pavilion (*Pushuting jinshi bawei* 曝書亭金石跋尾) (Zhu), 200
"Companion of Her Lord till Death" ("*Junzi xielao*" 君子偕老), 173
Complete Library in Four Sections (*Siku quanshu* 四庫全書), 205–6
Confucian Knight-Errant (*ruxia* 儒俠), 33, 100–102, 104, 106, 112, 116–17, 124–25, 132–33
Confucius, 15, 52, 69, 100–101, 104, 146, 205, 255
consciousness of mediation, 23
Continuation of Learning from Antiquity, A (*Xuxue gubian* 續學古編) (He), 121
counterfeit, 68, 120, 176, 184–85, 204
courtesans, 9, 22, 104–5, 123, 298n33
Cui Yuan 崔瑗, 268
cultural biography of things. *See* Kopytoff, Igor

cultural technique, 270n91
"Cup That 'Reflects Events of the World'" (*zhaoshi bei* 照世杯), 198
"Cyan Jade Hairpin" ("Twenty-Eight Friends"), 58–59

Daoism, 144, 151, 164–65, 174, 198n33
"Darkness" (*xuan* 玄), branding, 164–65
Dehua 德化, 196
Delgerkhangai Mountains, 12
Diaoyu Pond, 245
Ding Yunpeng 丁雲鵬, 133, 168, 300n51
"Disquisition on Inscription" ("Ming lun" 銘論) (Cai), 11–12
Dodo, prince, 194
Dong Qichang 董其昌, 96, 140, 198, 291n109
Donglin 東林, 189
Dou Xian 竇憲, 12
dragon mushroom (*longzhi* 龍芝), 151
Dragon Tail inkstone, inscription on, 17–19
Dream Reminiscences of Tao'an (*Tao'an mengyi* 陶庵夢憶), 37–39, 66; "Best Crafts in Suzhou, The," 38; "Celestial Inkstone," 38, 55, 71–76, 234–35; "Gan Wentai's Censers," 38; and "Inscriptions on Twenty-Eight Friends," 38–39, 48–55, 64–65, 71, 162, 187, 199; "Leftover Stones from the Flower and Rock Flotilla," 38; "Pine Fossil," 38, 43–46, 48, 54, 70–71, 276n32; "Pu Zhongqian's Carving," 38, 76–77; "Second Uncle's Antiques," 38, 66–67, 69; "Shen Meigang," 38, 40–43, 46, 48, 51, 54, 71, 76, 193; "Wood Like a Dragon," 38, 59–64, 70–72, 76, 199, 210, 237
Du Jun 杜濬, 6, 23
Duan 端, emperor, 236
Duan Brook 端溪, 3, 236–37, 271n103
"Duan Brook Inkstones" (Duanxi yanshi 端溪硯石) (Qu), 237
Duan inkstone, 23–25, 97, 235–37, 241, 245–46
"Duan Rock" (Duan shi 端石) (Qu), 237
Duke of Teng 滕公, 156

duoqing 奪情, 188, 194, 202, 231, 306n1
durability, significance of, 34–36
dwarf pirates (*wokou* 倭寇), 85

Eastern Zhou, 10
Eighteen Arhats, 141
elegance (*ya* 雅), 19, 38
emperors: Han, 41, 200; Jiajing, 41; Kangxi, 200; Qin, 5, 12, 105; Qing, 187, 189, 200, 203, 236–37, 269n78; Shunzhi, 200; Wanli, 141, 188, 307n16, 309n42; Xuande, 160; Yellow Emperor (Huangdi 黃帝), 12, 15, 240; Yongli, 3, 236
encomia (*zan* 贊), 42, 150, 278n59
Encomia on Portraits of the Ming Dynasty Imperishable Worthies of Yue, 42
ephemera: enduring, 184–86; inscription and, 128–33
epigraphy (*jinshixue* 金石學), 17, 23; entombed, 97–99; epigraphic sources, 13, 40, 85, 97, 99; epigraphic style (bei feng 碑風), 26–28; research, 120, 200, 229, 245, 254; scholarship, 28, 225, 227–28, 235, 238, 265; soft-stone seal carving and, 112; sources, 48, 114, 147, 241, 247, 252, 254, 256
epitaphs, "entombed accounts with inscriptions" (*muzhiming* 墓誌銘), 13, 16, 39–40, 48, 76, 84–85, 90, 97–99, 106, 125, 132, 156–57, 275n10,
eulogies (*song* 頌), 12
European engravings, 142–43, 298n28
"Evaluation of Fang Yulu's Ink, An" (Fang Yulu moping 方于魯墨評), 158
Evaluation of Ink (*Moping* 墨評) (Pan), 150
examination poems (*shitie shi* 試帖詩), 227–28
Explanation of Names (*Shiming* 釋名), 239

Fang Ruisheng 方瑞生, 142, 150, 165, 171, 304n128
Fang Yangeng 方嚴耕, 100, 102, 133
Fang Yongbin 方用彬, 83, 99, 102, 124–33, 140–41, 155, 193

"Fang Yongbin's Inscription for Pine Lichen Splendor" ("Fang Yongbin Songluo lingxiu ming" 方用彬松蘿靈秀銘), 128–33
Fang Yulu 方于魯, 41, 93, 95, 133, 156–57, 165–71, 174–75, 242, 247
"Fang Yulu's Ink" (Fang Yulu mo 方于魯墨), 158–60
fans, 41–42, 118, 127, 225
Feng Mengzhen 馮夢禎, 114, 116, 119, 124
Fenggan Society (Fenggan she 豐干社), 154–55
filling in (*bu* 補), 246
First Qin Emperor (Qin Shi Huang 秦始皇), 12, 54, 94, 105
"Fish Cauldron Ladle" (Yuding bi 魚鼎匕), 14, 267n66
"Five Planets Gathering Between the Legs and Wall Mansions, The," ink cake, 151, 153–55
Flusser, Vilém, 281n101
"Folio of Poems on the Return of the *Sigong* to Zhao, A" (*Sigong* gui Zhao shice 兕觥歸趙詩冊), 216
fragments, refabricating, 242–46
friends, collection, 48–52
funerary banners (*mingjing* 明旌), 10. *See also* inscription

Gan Wentai 甘文臺, 57
"Gan Wentai's Censers" ("Gan Wentai lu" 甘文臺爐) (*Dream Reminiscences*), 38
Gao Fenghan 高鳳翰, 26, 246–55, 257–59
Gao Jianli 高漸離, 104
ghostwriter, 123
Gillman, Dennis, 196
Gitelman, Lisa, 23, 272n111
Gonggong 龔工, 73
"Goulou Mountain" ("Goulou shan" 岣嶁山) (Han Yu), 226
grades, ink, 162–65, 186–87
Grand Canal, 100, 290n84
Gu Congde 顧從德, 113
Gu Lin 顧林, 78, 106–13
Gu Yuanqing 顧元慶, 278n59

INDEX

Guangdong Provincial Museum, 238
guardian ram (*shenyang* 神羊). *See* rhinoceros horn cup, inscription on
Guilin 桂林, 3, 90
Gulik, Robert Van, 124–25
Gushi jigu yinpu 顧氏集古印譜, 113

Haicheng 海澄, 196
hair. *See* "Cyan Jade Hairpin"
hairpin, inscription on, 58–59
"Halcyon Days" (*jiari* 佳日), 156–57
half inkstone, inscription on, 236–38
Han Yu 韓愈, 16, 226
Han Yuesu 韓約素, 22, 123
"Han's Third Studio Seal" (Hansan shi yin 函三室印), 175
Hartman, Geoffrey, 263–64n23
Harvard-Yenching Library, 99, 125
Hay, Jonathan, 22
He Yuanying 何元英, 199–203, 207, 209
He Zhen 何震 (Zhuchen 主臣), 106–20, 133, 140–41, 242
High Qing, 194, 213–14, 224, 244
History of Inkstones (Gao), 247–57, 252–53, 256–57, 258
History of the Ming, 188
Hu Zongxian 胡宗憲, 20
Huang Duanbo 黃端伯, 194, 202, 204, 207, 210–11
Huang Yi 黃易, 245, 256–57, 291n102
Huizhou 徽州: 19, 33, 76–77; collectors, 96–97, 154–55, 189, 247, 252; competition with Suzhou, 96–96, 117–20; entrepreneurs, 82–84, 102–6, 124–33, 138, 140–42, 154–55; merchant lineages, 96, 99–102; seal carving, 93–94, 106–24

Illustrated Antiquities of Xuanhe Hall (*Xuanhe bogu tu* 宣和博古圖), 147–49, 197
Illustrated Catalogue of Ancient Jades (*Guyu tupu* 古玉圖譜), 252
Illustrated Investigations of Antiquity (*Kaogu tu* 考古圖), 147
Illustrations to the Three Classics on Ritual (*San li tu* 三禮圖), 197

ink, fundamentality of, 139–42
ink books (*moshu* 墨書), 142–49
ink cake: comparing with inkstone, 16; designs, 34, 138, 143, 149–51, 155, 252; "Double Ganoderma" ink cake, 151; enlarging idea of, 149; "Enveloping the Three as One" (Hansan wei yi 函三為一), 144–45; family-owned antique Yulu ink cake, 141–42; of Fang Yulu, 141, 151; "Five Planets Gathering Between the Legs and Wall Mansions, The" (Wuxing ju kui bi 五星聚奎壁), 151, 153–55; "Four Character Seal" (sizi xi 四字璽), 148; "Images of the Twenty- Eight Lunar Mansions" (Ershiba xiu tu 二十八宿圖), 151; pictures, 149–50; round ink cake, 143, 148; writing on, 137–39
"Ink for Transcribing Sutras in the Laigu Studio" 賴古堂寫經墨, 26. *See* Zhou Lianggong
ink makers: advertising language of, 164; brands of, 160–71, 186–87; comprehensive table of merchandise (*mobiao* 墨表), 156; counterfeiting and, 171–83; enduring ephemeral, 184–86; four major ink makers, 165; grades and, 162–65, 186; ink books and, 142–49; inscriptional designs, 156–60; introduction to, 134–37; Ming ink, 139–42; poetics, 149–55; writing on ink cake, 137–39
ink obsessions (*mo pi* 墨癖). *See* Zhou Lianggong
inkslab: "broken-stele inkslab" (duanbei yan 斷碑硯), 244; inscription on, 19–21; remnant inkslabs, 235–39; She County stone inkslab, 19–21, 175. *See also* broken stones, inscribing on; inkstones
inksticks, 31, 33, 36, 84, 141, 157; "Black Unicorn Marrow" (Qinglin sui 青麟髓), 183; design of, 26, 84, 90, 93–94, 135, 137–38, 233–35, 252, 256, 302n71; as disposable product, 139, 150, 169; documenting dimensions of, 187;

INDEX

inksticks (*continued*)
ephemera and, 130; of Fang Yulu, 252, 254; finishing up, 134; grades, 162–64; grinding, 72, 75; "Hongzhong qicao" 餱中起草 inkstick, 93; limited edition, 26, 127, 186; lure of scent of, 173–74, 177; Ming inksticks, 137, 140–42, 144, 161, 187; molded inscription on, 31; mortar inkstone, 254–57; "Not Soot Inscription" inkstick, 167, 169, 171; "One with Clear Heaven" inkstick, 135–36, 156, 172, 177–82, 234; "ox-tongue" (*niushe* 牛舌) inkstick, 26–27; Palace Museum inkstick, 134, 184, 272n119; production of, 94, 132, 234; recommending suicide, 3–4; "sacrificial offerings for inksticks" (*jimo zhi hui* 祭墨之會), 26; shape of, 140, 149; stele publishing and, 94; of Sun Ruiqing, 136, 171, 185, 252; as writing tool, 26

inkstone: alternative approaches to writing on, 246–57; broken corner inkstone, 241; "Bronze Finch Inkstone" (Tongque yan 銅雀硯), 315n31; cash value of, 270n92; Celestial Inkstone, 71–75; city-wall inkstone, 243–44; Dragon Tail inkstone, 17–19; Duan inkstone, 23–26; Duan inkstones, 23–25, 97, 235–37, 241, 245–46; epigraphic commentary and, 244–46; "fitting inkstone" inscription, 238; freestanding ceremonial gate tower (*que* 闕) and, 245–46; history of writing and, 239–42; "inkstone pool" (*yanchi* 硯池), 254; inscription on, 3–5; inscriptions on, 233–59; inscriptive modes and, 240–41; *Materia Medica* inkstone, 238; mortar, 254–57; Phoenix Beak inkstone (Fengzhou yan 鳳咮硯), 18; refabricating stones/tiles as, 242–46; remnant inkslabs, 235–39; round inkstone inscription, 240–41; searching for "use," 244; Small Banana Palm Inkstone, 241–42; of Su Shi, 16–19; Water Fat Inkstone, 237–38

inscription (*ming* 銘), 97; admonitory, 14–16; affordances of, 37–77; antiquarians and, 188–231; on banners, 10; on Broken Bronze Water Dipper, 46–47; on broken corner inkstone, 241; "bronze-inscription seal-script" (*kuanzhi zhuan* 款識篆), 121; on Burst Pattern Antique Zither, 52–53; on censer, 67–68; on chalice, 49, 65–66, 68–71; chapters focusing on, 31–34; Chinese literature and, 10–21; on circular stone, 252–52; draft inscription (*niming* 擬銘), 250–51; entombed account with inscription (*muzhiming* 墓誌銘), 13, *see also* epitaphs; ephemera and, 128–33; epigraphy (*jinshixue* 金石學) and, 17; four perfections and, 42; on half inkstone, 236–38; and He Zhen seal, 115–20; history of writing and, 239–42; ink cake, 151, 153–55; ink makers and, 134–87; on inkstones, 233–59; inscriptional designs, 156–60; interpretation/transmission of, 188–231; introduction to, 1; jade cup, 192–93; on jade hairpin, 58–59; *locus classicus* for, 10; on *Materia Medica* inkstone, 238; memorial, 12–13; "Metal Man Inscription," 268n70, 268n71; metamorphosis and, 59–64; Ming-era inscriptive projects, 90–95; modern poetic self-consciousness of, 263–64n23; modes for composing, 240; modes of writing, 10–12; on "Not Soot" (label), 166–71; on objects, 5–9; on "One with Clear Heaven," 171–83; on "Pine Lichen Splendor," 128–33; on *pipa*, 104–6; politics of, 192–94; on pyxis, 57–58; on rain-flower pebbles, 54–57; rhinoceros horn cup, 193–94; rhinoceros horn mallow cup, 195–98; on round inkstone, 240–41; scenes of, 39–46; significance of durability, 34–36; spoon-head dagger, 103–4; on Treasure Vase Inkstone, 47–48; virtual, 54–59; on writing brush, 2–3; writing with knife, 78–133

INDEX

"Inscription for a Buried Inkstone" ("Yi yan ming" 瘞硯銘) (Han Yu), 16

"Inscription for a *Sigong*" ("Sigong ming" 兕觥銘), 222

"Inscription on a Broken Corner Inkstone" ("Quejiao yan ming" 缺角硯銘) (Jin), 241

"Inscription on a Fitting Inkstone" ("Heyan ming" 合硯銘) (Jin), 238

"Inscription on a Round Inkstone" ("Tuanyan ming" 團硯銘) (Jin), 240–41

"Inscription on a She County stone inkslab" (Xu), 19–21

"Inscription on an Armrest" ("Ji ming" 几銘), 47

"Inscription on an Inkstone for Copying *Materia Medica*" ("Chao *Bencao* yan ming" 抄本草硯銘) (Jin), 238

"Inscription on Kong Yifu's Dragon Tail Inkstone" ("Kong Yifu longwei yan ming" 孔毅甫龍尾硯銘) (Su), 17–19

"Inscription on Rain Flower Stones" ("Yuhua shi ming" 雨花石銘) (Zhang), 55–57

"Inscription on the Ceremonial Mounding of Mount Yanran" ("Feng Yanran shan ming" 封燕然山銘) (Ban Gu), 12, 81–82, 86, 88

inscriptional designs, 156–60

"Inscriptions on Twenty-Eight Friends" ("Ershiba you ming" 二十八友銘) (Zhang), 38–39, 48–55, 64–65, 71, 162, 187, 199; "Cyan Jade Hairpin," 58–59; preface of, 53–54; "Rain Flower Stones," 49, 55–57; "Small Beauty Chalice," 49, 65–66, 68–71; "White Ding Ware Censer," 67–68; "Xuande Filled-In Lacquer Pyxis," 49, 57–58, 64, 71

instability, writing about, 6–7

intentional monument, 222–24. *See also* rhinoceros horn cup

inter-dynastic war, 4, 6, 21, 33–34, 124, 195, 199, 203, 227, 233

"Investigation of Duan Stone, An" (Duanshi kao 端石考) (Qu), 237–38

ivory, 76, 118, 128, 132

jade, 18, 24, 51, 58–59, 76, 133, 188, 120, 123, 144, 160, 168, 214, 244, 252

jade cup, inscription on, 192–93

Jenyns, Soame, 196

Ji Yun 紀昀, 245

Jiang Shaoshu 姜紹書, 68, 169, 187. *See Notes from the Resonant Rock Studio*

Jiaozhou 膠州, 257

Jin Nong 金農, 238–42, 243

Jin Xuanfu 金玄甫, 179, 180–81, 184–86

jinshi shi 金石詩. *See* metal and stone, poetry on

jinshixue 金石學, 17, 269n80. *See* epigraphy

Jiulong River 九龍江, 196

Jiuyao 九曜, 228

Kafalas, Philip, 59

Kangxi 康熙, 200

"Kerchief Table Methods" ("Jinji fa" 巾機法), 12

Kim Chŏnghŭi 金正喜, 225

King Mu of Zhou 周穆王, 11

King Wu of Zhou 周武王, 14, 47, 64, 239; "King Wu Trod on the Eastern Stairs" ("Wu Wang jianzuo" 武王踐阼), 14–15, 267n63

knifework: chopping knife (*qiedao fa* 切刀法) method, 241–42; double-knife method (*shuangdao fa* 雙刀法), 108; entombed epigraphy and, 97–99; Huizhou merchants as collectors, 96–97; introduction to, 78–80; in Ming marketplace, 80–84; Ming-era inscriptive projects, 90–95; seal carver as literary protagonist, 106–24; seal catalogue as publishing format, 120–24; shopkeeper and, 124–33; single-knife method (*dandao fa* 單刀法), 79; sword poetic career and, 84–90

knight-errant (*xia* 俠), 82, 95, 100–114. *See also* Confucian Knight-Errant

Ko, Dorothy, 22, 184, 235, 238, 246, 254

Kobaien Bokufu 古梅園墨譜, 171
Kopytoff, Igor, 18–19
Kuaiyuan daogu 快園道古 (Zhang), 194

labels: "Dark Origin of Numinous Vitality" (Xuanyuan lingqi 玄元靈氣) (Cheng), 162–63; "Nine Mysteries and Three Absolutes" (Jiuxuan sanji 九玄三極) (Fang), 162–63
lacquer, 51, 57, 64, 71, 76, 139, 160–61
Legs Lunar Mansion (kuixiu 奎宿), 151–52
Leiden Institute of Sinology, 125
leiwen 雷紋, 221
Lessing, Gotthold Ephraim, 263–64n23
letters, 41, 99, 105–6, 125–28, 140–41, 164, 198
Li Minbiao 黎民表, 127
Li Shan 李善, 168
Li Shiying 李石英, 118
Li, Wai-yee, 68
Li Weizhen 李維禎, 198
Li You 李尤, 268n67
Li Yu 李漁, 7, 23, 36, 310n57
Liang Shaoren 梁紹壬, 238
Liang Tongshu 梁同書, 215
Liang Zhi 梁衷, 122–23, 124, 133
liemin 烈愍, 210
life-mandate, 13
Lin Xiangru 藺相如, 192
lishu 隸書. See clerical script
Liu Bang 劉邦, 120
Liu Xijun 劉細君, 104
Liu Xie 劉勰, 266n50
Liu Yan 劉龑, 228
Liu Zongzhou 劉宗周, 252
Liulichang 琉璃廠, 206
Liuzhou 六舟 (Dashou 達受), 257
lost things, recovery of, 199–205
"Loyal Remonstrators" ("Zhongjian" 忠諫), 2
Lu You 陸游, 250
Lu Yun 陸雲, 168
Luo Ping 羅聘, 239
Lupton, Christina, 23
lute. See *pipa*, inscription on

Ma Sanheng 麻三衡, 186–87
Ma Xianglan 馬湘蘭, 22, 126
mallow (*kui* 葵). See rhinoceros horn cup: mallow cup inscription
manuscripts, 9, 99, 124–27, 194, 208
Mao Xiang 冒襄, 226–27, 279n71
marketplace: inscribed objects in, 19–21; Ming marketplace, 32, 58, 78, 80, 82, 90, 101, 112, 124, 130–31, 155, 234; writing with knife in, 80–84
"Markets of the City God Temple" (Chenghuangmiao shi 城隍廟市), 161
markings (*kuanzhi* 款識), 26, 57, 76, 144, 161–62, 249
Master Cao's Ink Forest (*Caoshi molin* 曹氏墨林) (Cao), 150, 171
Master Cheng's Ink Garden (*Chengshi moyuan* 程氏墨園), 142–43
Master Fang's Ink Catalogue (*Fangshi mopu* 方氏墨譜), 142, 155, 161, 163–64, 179, 184; comments in, 169; dragons in, 168; ink poetics and, 149–51; inkstone designs in, 90–94 "Investigating Antiquity" (Bogu 博古), 144–46; "Investigating Things" (Bowu 博物), 144–45; recycling epigraphic materials from, 252–54
Master Liyuan 櫟園先生, 26. See Zhou Lianggong
materiality, early modern China, 21–22
Matsui Gentai 松井元泰, 171
Matteini, Michele, 206
McDermott, Joseph, 96, 103
media: media history, 23, 28, 125–26, 235; intermediality, 23, 130, 147–49, 190–91, 195–96, 242, 257; remediation, 190–91, 199
Memorial Folio for Fang Yuansu's Glorious Return, A, 125
memorial inscription, 12–13
merchants, 78–133
metal and stone, poetry on, 224–30
"Metal Man" (*jinren* 金人), inscription on, 14–16, 268n70
metamorphosis, inscriptions and, 59–64
Mi Fu 米芾, 45–46, 74, 213, 228

INDEX

ming 銘, 1, 10, 12, 17, 63, 97, 101, 141, 150, 165, 242, 249. *See also* inscription

Ming China, landscape of: affordances of handwriting, 125; collectors, 96–97; Confucian Knight-Errant, 100–101; entombed epigraphy, 97–99; ink, 139–42; ink cakes, 137–39; inscriptive projects, 90–95; introduction to, 84–85; merchant weapons, 102–6; poetic career of sword, 84–90

Miscellaneous Records of the Western Capital (*Xijing zaji* 西京雜記), 157

misuse value, 256

mortar inkstone, 254–57

moshu 墨書. *See* ink books

Mote, Frederick W., 35–36

Mu Dazhan 穆大展, 215

musculature (*jili* 肌理), 224

music of the earth (*dilai* 地籟), 250

National Academy (Guozijian 國子監), 114

New Account of Tales of the World, A (*Shishuo xinyu* 世說新語), 56

New Words from Guangdong (*Guangdong xinyu* 廣東新語), 237

niu 牛. *See* ox; ox-tongue (*niushe* 牛舌) inkstick

Northern Dynasties, 241–42

"Not Soot" (Feiyan 非煙) (label), inscription on, 166–71

Notes from Select Luminaries of the Ming, 125

Notes from the Resonant Rock Studio (*Yunshi zhai bitan* 韻石齋筆談), 68; "Study of Ink" (Mokao 墨考), 187. *See* Jiang Shaoshu

objects of the former dynasty (*qianchao yiwu* 前朝遺物). *See* antiquarianism

objects, inscriptions on, 43, 48, 76, 265n31; art objects, 126, 206; banners, 10; in early modern marketplace, 19–21; inkstone, 3–5; inscribed objects, 5, 15, 19, 22, 37, 39, 51, 191, 278n55; overview of, 5–9; solid objects, 5, 7, 28, 79, 83; studio objects, 9, 17, 19, 90–95, 99, 247, 274n5; writing brush, 2–3

"Old Deformity" (Laobi 老痹). *See* Gao Fenghan

"Old Han's Inscription" (Hanweng ming 函翁銘), 156–57

"On a Painted Fan Showing Little West Lake Sent to Me from Putian by Yusan's Nephew" (題雨三侄自蒲田見寄小西湖畫扇) (Weng), 225

"One with Clear Heaven" (Liaotian yi 寥天一): enduring ephemeral and, 184–86; inscription on, 171–83; label, 134–39

Orchard Factory (Guoyuanchang 果園廠), 51

Ou Zhongrong, 244

"Outlines and Details of the Ming History," 208

Ouyang Xiu 歐陽修, 17, 53–54

ox (*niu* 牛), 196–97

ox-tongue (*niushe* 牛舌) inkstick, 26–27

Palace Museum, 134–35, 171, 177–78, 184

Pan Fangkai 潘方凱, 180

Pan Yingzhi 潘膺祉, 150, 165, 177–78

pawnbroker, 99, 101, 124–26, 141, 155

Peng Haogu 彭好古, 175–76

perishability, 6

philological poetry (*kaoding shi* 考訂詩). *See* metal and stone, poetry on

Phoenix Beak inkstone (Fengzhou yan 鳳咮硯), 18

"Pine Fossil" ("Songhuashi" 松花石) (*Dream Reminiscences*), 43–46

pine, inscription on, 128–33

Pingyuan 平遠, monument at, 85–86

pipa 琵琶, inscription on, 104–6

poetry, 137, 231, 258; "Add and Subtract" poem (*lihe shi* 離合詩), 158; antiquarian, 188–231; celebrating Su Xuan, 80–83; classical, 203, 242; dismembering, 158–60; examination poems (*shitie shi* 試帖詩), 227–28; form and tone (*gediao* 格調), 224; ink poetics, 149–55; inscribed poems, 258–59, 264n23; manuscript poems,

poetry (*continued*)
124–25; matching with inscriptions, 74; "pacing the void" poems (*buxu ci* 步虛詞), 144–45; poems in praise of pictures of the *sigong*'s return to Zhao, 217–20; poetry on metal and stone (*jinshi shi* 金石詩), 224–30; prose-poetry, 22–23, 39; proto-poems, 14; spirit resonance (*shenyun* 神韻), 224; sword poetic life, 85–90; "Weng Fanggang poem," 213; *yongwu* poetry, 225–26

Poetry Return (*Shigui* 詩歸), 47
Prince Chang of Kaiping 常開平王, 59
print, 5–7, 126–27; print culture, 5; technical advances in wood-block printing, 112–14, 128–31, 142–44
prose preface (*xu* 序), 97
protagonists, early modern object culture, 33; antiquarian, 188–231; artisan, 134–87; merchant, 78–133
protest, 41–42, 188–89, 194, 199, 202, 243
protobank, 96
"Protocols of Sacrifice" ("Jitong" 祭統), 10
Pu Cheng 濮澄, 112
"Pu Zhongqian's Carving" ("Pu Zhongqian diaoke" 濮仲謙雕刻) (*Dream Reminiscences*), 38
Pu'an Temple 普安寺, 90
publishing format, seal catalogue as, 120–24
purple-sand stoneware (*zisha* 紫砂), 51, 253, 257
pyxis, inscription on, 57–58

Qi Biaojia 祁彪佳, 62, 237
Qi Jiguang 戚繼光, 78, 85, 87, 89, 94–95, 126, 151
Qianlong 乾隆, 209, 216, 224, 229, 258–59
Qingtian 青田, 78–79, 107–8, 110, 118, 120
Qu Dajun 屈大均, 236–38

rain-flower pebbles (*yuhua shi* 雨花石), inscription on, 55–57
"Record of Censor Zhao's *Sigong*, A" ("Cang jiantao Zhao gong sigong ji" 藏檢討趙公兕觥記), 203–5. See also rhinoceros horn cup
Record of Clouds and Mist Passing Before My Eyes (*Yunyan guoyan lu* 雲煙過眼錄), 168
Record of Rites (*Liji* 禮記), 192
"Record of The Studio of Ink Treasure" (*Baomo zhai ji* 寶墨齋記) (Cheng), 170
Records of All Subjects Who Died Out of Loyalty to the Fallen Dynasty Authorized by the Emperor (*Qinding shengchao xunjie zhuchen lu* 欽定勝朝殉節諸臣錄), 209
Records of the Grand Historian (*Shiji* 史記) (Sima), 100, 168; "Astronomer's Treatise" ("Tianguan shu" 天官書), 166
refabrication, fragments, 242–46
reign marks, 51, 160–61
remnant subject (*yimin* 遺民), 4, 58, 64, 68, 235–37, 256, 278n64
remnant things (*yiwu* 遺物): carver and, 76–77; friendship with, 46–54; introduction to, 37–39; judgment of things and, 64–70; metamorphosis and, 59–64; scenes of inscription, 39–46; virtual inscription, 54–59
"Return of the Jade Disc to Zhao" (*wanbi gui Zhao* 完璧歸趙), 214
rhinoceros horn cup (*xibei* 犀杯), 59, 189, 202, 226, 229–30, 245; "Disquisition on the *Sigong*, A" ("Sigong bian" 兕觥辨), 209; inscription on, 190–94; image of, 221; as intentional monument, 222–24; mallow cup inscription, 195–98; removing from "Han palaces," 203; return of, 205–10; and role of things in collective life, 199; as unintentional monument, 222–24; and *xiezhi* 獬豸, 193, 307n11
Ricci, Matteo, 140, 142, 298n28
"Rouge Inkstone" (Zhiyan 脂硯), 9
round inkstone, inscription on, 240–41
Ruan Xiu 阮修, 56
Ruan Yuan 阮元, 244–46
rubbing: collection of, 53, 200; from Gao Fenghan's *History of Inkstones*, 247–53,

255, 258; ink-squeeze, 17, 25, 32, 134, 144, 190, 194, 199, 206, 227, 234; mounted, 210, 213; of stone carving, 190, 215–16, 221, 223; technique experiments, 257. *See also History of Inkstones*
ruins. *See* fragments, refabricating
Rujia 儒家, 10
Rusk, Bruce, 14
Ryckmans, Pierre, 35–36

"Sacrificial-Animal-Head Cup of the Han" (Han xishou bei 漢犧首杯), 197
Sanskrit, 137, 143, 298n29
Schiller, Friedrich, 263–64n23
Sea of Ink (*Mohai* 墨海), 142
Sea of Ink 墨海, object, 240
seal carver (*yinren* 印人), 8, 22, 24–25, 94–95, 130, 138; biographies of, 123–24; first seal carver, 133; inkstones and, 246–48; as literary protagonist, 106–14; "scholar seal-carver's" repertoire, 127–28; shopkeeper knife and, 124–25; soft stones and, 114, 116, 119–20; "Wang Daokun epitaphs," 99; writing with knife in Ming marketplace, 80–84
seal-script calligraphy (*zhuan* 篆), 7–8, 28, 93, 117, 121, 125, 229, 245
seals (*yin* 印): 8; carver as literary protagonist, 106–14; carving, 78, 81–82, 94, 101–2, 106, 117, 123, 132; catalogue as publishing format, 120–24; catalogue of seal designs (*yingao* 印稿), 127; catalogues collecting ancient seals (*jigu yinpu* 集古印譜), 114; common sayings (*shiyu* 世語), 123; general's seal (*da jiangjun yinzhang* 大將軍印章), 94–95; inscription on, 115–20; leisure seals (*xianzhang* 閑章), 112; seal catalogues (*yinpu* 印譜), 93, 112; personal name seals (*mingzi zhang* 名字章), 123; refabricating scraps of material, 127–28; seal-script calligraphy (*zhuan*), 93; side markings (*biankuan* 邊款), 79, 112–13, 257; soft stones and, 112–20, 122, 127, 130, 147; as writing tool, 26–31

"Select Craftsmen" ("Zhu gong" 諸工) (*Dream Reminiscences*), 38
Selections of Refined Literature (*Wenxuan* 文選), 240, 268n73
Shashi 沙市, 100
Shaolin Temple 少林寺, 90
She 歙 County, stone inkslab from, 19–21, 175. *See* Huizhou
Shen Deqian 沈德潛, 224
"Shen Meigang" 沈梅岡 (*Dream Reminiscences*), 40–43, 193
shitie shi 試帖詩. *See* examination poems
shopkeeper, knife of, 124–33
Shunzhi 順治, 200
signatures, 25, 31, 42, 76, 78, 108, 112, 131, 249, 251, 258–59
sigong 兕觥, 227, 229–30; as label, 196–98; as monumental vessel; 214–16; poems about, 217–20; preserving, 214–24; reunion with, 210–14. *See also* rhinoceros horn cup
Sima Qian 司馬遷, 100, 166, 258
"Six Ones" (Liuyi 六一), 53. *See* Ouyang Xiu
Sketch of Sites and Objects in the Imperial Capital, A (*Dijing jingwu lüe* 帝京景物略), 161–62
"Small Beauty Chalice" ("Twenty-Eight Friends"), 49, 65–66, 68–71
Snow Hall Ink (*Xuetang Mopin* 雪堂墨品), 171
soft stones: carving, 117–20; discovering, 114–20; gelid rock (*dongshi* 凍石), 118; seals, 112, 117, 119–20, 122, 127, 130, 147
"Song for the Return of the *Sigong* to Zhao, A" ("*Sigong* gui Zhao ge" 兕觥歸趙歌) (Weng), 211–20, 226, 231
"Song for the *Sigong*" ("Sigong ge" 兕觥歌) (Zhu), 200–203. *See also* rhinoceros horn cup
"Song of the Stone Drums, The" ("Shigu ge" 石鼓歌) (Han Yu), 226
Song Yu 宋玉, 249–50
Speaking of the Past at Flower Village (*Huacun tan wang* 花村談往), 68
spoon-head dagger, inscription on, 103–4

stele, stelae (*bei* 碑), 7, 11–13, 15, 31, 33, 83–85, 90–95, 97, 100, 108, 130–32, 135, 216, 227, 241, 244, 246, 250, 254, 257
Stone Boat Mountain, 2, 278n64
stone, outlasting, 6. *See also* broken stones, inscribing on; circular stone, inscription on; inkstone; soft stones
"Stoneware Jar, Pewter Carafe" ("Shaguan xizhu" 砂罐錫注) (*Dream Reminiscences*), 38
Story of the Stone (*Shitouji* 石頭記), 8–9
"Studio for Contemplating Life" (Guansheng ju 觀生居), 2–5; inkstone inscription, 3–5; writing brush inscription, 2–3. *See* Wang Fuzhi
"Study of Eight Bricks" (Bazhuan yinguan 八磚吟館), 245
Su Shi 蘇軾, 16–19, 55–56, 61, 168, 206, 244
Su Wu 蘇武, 41
Su Xuan 蘇宣, 78, 125, 133
Sun Chu 孫楚, 268
Sun Ruiqing 孫瑞卿, 135–37, 184–86
sword, poetic life of, 85–90. *See also* Wang Daokun 汪道昆

Table of Ink (*Mobiao* 墨表), 187
Tale of the Sigong (*Sigong ji* 兕觥記), 224
Tan Yuanchun 譚元春, 28, 47
Tao'an mengyi 陶庵夢憶. *See Dream Reminiscences of Tao'an*
Tao'an 陶庵, 53. *See* Zhang Dai
Tao Qian 陶潛, 74–75
taste, 19, 38, 70, 162
tea, 6, 100, 128–32, 134
Tian, Xiaofei, 16
"Tian yan" 天硯. *See* "Celestial Inkstone"
Tianjin Museum, 23–24, 241, 243, 245
tomb inventories (*qiance* 遣策), 13
tomb-stabilizing writs (*zhenmuwen* 鎮墓文), 13
Treasure Store (Baodian 寶店), 126–27
Treasure Vase Inkstone, inscription on, 47–48
Treatise on Ink (*Mozhi* 墨志), 186
Two Zhongs 二仲. *See* Wang Daoguan 汪道貫; Wang Daohui 汪道會

"Uncle Inkstone," 72, 76–77, 112
un-inscribed inscriptions, 7
unintentional monument, 222–24. *See also* rhinoceros horn cup

virtual inscription, 54–59
"Vista of Green Pines and White Clouds" ("Qingsong baiyun chu" 青松白雲處), 122–23
vulgarity (*su* 俗), 19

Wall Lunar Mansion (bixiu 壁宿), 151, 153
Wan Shouqi 萬壽祺, 187
Wang Benhu 汪本湖, 102–4, 133
Wang Chang 王常, 113
Wang Daoguan 汪道貫, 92–94, 133
Wang Daohui 汪道會, 94, 133
Wang Daokun 汪道昆, 78, 94, 96, 98, 134, 161–63, 172, 175–76, 193, 196; "Biography of a Confucian Knight-Errant" ("Ruxia zhuan" 儒俠傳), 100; borrowing sword from, 78–80; collaborations of, 90–95; Confucian Knight-Errant and, 100–101; cultural entrepreneurs in circle of, 133; defining career of sword of, 85–90; enduring ephemeral and, 184–86; inscriptional designs and, 156–57; inscriptions of, 84–85; "Inscription to Commemorate Accomplishments at Yanshan" ("Pingyuan tai legong ming" 平遠台勒功銘), 85–86, 88; ink poetics and, 149–55; literary celebrity of, 84–85; meditation group of, 144–45; on product labels, 161, 163, 166–71; "Record on a Stupa for Chan Master Changrun" ("Changrun chanshi ta ji" 常潤禪師塔記), 92; leading "returning to the ancients" movement, 147; "Stele on the Pacification of the Man-Barbarians" ("Ping Man bei" 平蠻碑), 90; "Studio of the Enveloped Three" (Hansan shi 函三室), 147, 174; third sword of, 87–88; Wang Daokun epitaphs, 97–99

Wang Fuzhi 王夫之, 2, 235–36; inkstone inscription, 3–5; writing brush inscription, 2–3
Wang Jinsheng 汪近聖, 186
Wang Shi 王蓍, 248
Wang Shimao 王世懋, 51, 158
Wang Shiqi 王士琦, 198
Wang Shizhen 王世貞, 28, 87–88, 96–97, 126, 147, 155
Wang Shizhen 王士禎, 224
Wang Wenzhi 王文治, 215
Wang Xiang 王相, 247
Wang Yan 王衍, 56
Wang Yueshen 王曰申, 247
Wang Yuqian 王雨謙, 277n47
Wang Zhideng 王穉登, 9
Water Fat Inkstone (Shuifang yan 水肪硯), 237–38
Wei Zhongxian 魏忠賢, 243
Weiyang Palace, inkslab from, 248
wen 文, 4, 22, 235
Wen Jia 文嘉, 116
Wen Peng 文彭, 117–23, 133
Wen Tianxiang 文天祥, 259
Wen Zhengming 文徵明, 96–97
Wen Zhenmeng 文震孟, 243
Weng Fanggang 翁方綱, 194, 205–6, 209, 222–24, 224–26, 256
Western Marchmount Huashan Temple Stele (Xiyue Huashan miao bei 西嶽華山廟碑), 246
"White Cloud Bridge" (Baiyun qiao 白雲橋), 100
"White Ding Ware Censer" ("Twenty-Eight Friends"), 65–68, 71
White Elm Society (Baiyu she 白榆社), 151–56, 301n60
wind 風, inkstone in shape of character for, 236–38, 249. See also half inkstone, inscription on
wind inkstone, 236, 249–51, 254
"Wind Rhapsody" (Fengfu 風賦) (Song), 249–50
"Wood Like a Dragon" (Dream Reminiscences), 38, 59–64, 70–72, 76, 199, 210, 237

writing: early modern China, 21–22; history of, 239–42; inscription on writing brush, 2–3; tools for, 26–31. See also Chinese literature
"Written After a Rubbing of the Sigong Inscription by Xu Guo of the Ming," 206–10, 231. See also Weng Fanggang
Wu Chengqi 吳成器, 21
Wu Liang Shrines 武梁祠, 206, 245, 256
Wu Shuda 吳叔大, 171, 179, 182, 184–86
Wu Tingyu 吳廷羽, 133
Wu Wanyou 吳萬有, 9
Wu Weiye 吳偉業, 226
Wu Xizai 吳熙載, 247
Wu Zhongxing 吳中行, 189, 192–93

Xiang Yuanbian 項元忭, 51, 67–68
xiao 孝, 189
Xiaohou Ying 夏侯嬰, 156–57
xibei 犀杯. See rhinoceros horn cup
Xie Zhaozhi 謝肇淛, 162
xiezhi 獬豸, mythical animal, 193, 307n11
Xing Tong 邢侗, 175–76
Xiongnu 匈奴, 12, 41
Xiushui 秀水, 199
Xu Chu 許初, 116
Xu Guangqi 徐光啓, 140
Xu Guo 許國, 189–91, 194, 195, 197, 208, 222–24
Xu Wei 徐渭, 19–21, 42, 251
Xuande 宣德, 56; reign mark of, 160–61
Xuande bronze censer, 50, 56–57, 68, 160–61, 226, 279n71
"Xuande Filled-In Lacquer Pyxis" ("Twenty-Eight Friends"), 49, 57–58, 64, 71
Xue Susu 薛素素, 9

Yan Hengzhai 顏衡齋, 206
Yan Maolun 顏懋倫, 222
Yan Song 嚴嵩, 40–43
Yan 顏 family of Qufu, 205
Yang Jie 楊傑, 74
Yang Jisheng 楊繼盛, 41
Yang Weizhen 楊維楨, 53–54
Yangzhou Museum, 246
Yanke 燕客. See Zhang E

Yanshan 燕山, monument at, 87–88
Yansi Market Town 巖寺鎮, 125
Yao Bing 姚炳, 197
Yao Li 要離, 81
Yaozhou 藥洲, 228
Yellow Emperor (Huangdi 黃帝), 12, 15, 240
Yi, Hye-shim, 24, 244
yimin 遺民. *See* remnant subject
Yin Runsheng 尹潤生, 184
Yinjun 印雋, 121–22
yinren 印人. *See* seal carver
Yinshuo 印說, 117–18
Yip, Cheuk-wai, 225, 228
yiwu 遺物. *See* remnant things
Yiwulü Mountain 醫無閭山, 94
Yongdong 甬東, 241
Yongli 永曆, 2
yongwu 詠物, 225, 229
Yu 禹, 60
Yuan Mei 袁枚, 224
Yuan Rang 原壤, 104
Yuedong jinshi lüe 粵東金石略 (Weng), 228

Zha Bashi 查八十 (or Zha Nai 查鼐), 104–6, 133
Zhan Jingfeng 詹景鳳, 96, 119, 127, 176
Zhan Lian 詹濂, 106–10
Zhang Cizhong 張次仲, 197
Zhang Dai 張岱, 32–33, 84, 160–62, 193–94, 241, 257, 277n49; crystallizing experiences of, 59–64; and emergence of carver as literary protagonist, 111–12; friendship with remnant things, 46–54; inscriptions of, 37–46; judgment of, 64–70; virtual inscriptions, 54–59. *See also* "Celestial Inkstone" ("Tian yan" 天硯); "Inscriptions on Twenty-Eight Friends" ("Ershiba you ming" 二十八友銘); remnant things (*yiwu* 遺物); "Uncle Inkstone"; "Wood Like a Dragon"
Zhang E 張萼 (Yanke 燕客), 48, 65–76
Zhang Juzheng 張居正, 89, 188–89, 194
Zhang Lianfang 張聯芳, 48, 65–70
Zhang Min 張岷 (Shanmin 山民), 48

Zhang Renxi 張仁熙, 171, 176–77
Zhang Rulin 張汝霖, 43–46
Zhang Wen 章文, 97
Zhang Yaofang 張耀芳, 51
Zhang Yefang 張燁芳, 48
Zhang, Ying, 189
Zhang Yingyao 張應堯, 42
Zhang Yuanbian 張元忭, 40–43
Zhang Zaogong 章藻功, 204–5, 209
Zhang Zhen 張貞, 24–26
Zhang Zigao 張子高, 134
Zhangzhou 漳州, 196
Zhao Liangbi 趙良璧, 161
Zhao Mengfu 趙孟頫, 168, 210, 220, 231
Zhao Wanghuai 趙王槐, 210, 220, 231
Zhao Yongxian 趙用賢, 189–99, 201–5, 207, 210–11, 223, 231
Zhaolin Society (Zhaolin she 肇林社), 144–45
Zhaoqing 肇慶, 236
Zheng Xie 鄭燮, 239
Zheng Xuan 鄭玄, 196
Zhong Xing 鍾惺, 28, 47
zhong 忠, 189
zhongjie 忠節, 210
zhongxiao 忠孝, 189, 199
Zhou Ang 周昂, 224
Zhou Lianggong 周亮工 (Liyuan 櫟園), 23, 26–31, 48, 95, 120, 121, 122–23, 187, 247
Zhou Shaoliang 周紹良, 26
Zhou Tianqiu 周天球, 91–93, 175, 286n45
Zhu Duozheng 朱多炡, 155, 158
Zhu Long 朱龍, 241
Zhu Shouyong 朱壽鏞, 59
Zhu Yihai 朱以海, 60
Zhu Yizun 朱彝尊, 194, 199–201, 202, 204–5, 222–24, 226, 242–43, 247, 249
Zhu Youlang 朱由榔, 2
zhuan 篆. *See* seal-script calligraphy
Zhuangzi 莊子, 45, 172, 174, 304n120
Zilu 子路, 100
Zixia 子夏, 101
Ziyou 子游, 101
Zou Yuanbiao 鄒元標, 189
zun 尊 vessel, 282n122, 302n71, 309n47
Zuo Tradition (*Zuozhuan* 左傳), 239
zuoyouming 座右銘, 240, 268n73

GPSR Authorized Representative: Easy Access System Europe, Mustamäe tee 50, 10621 Tallinn, Estonia, gpsr.requests@easproject.com